MACARTHUR'S COALITION

MACARTHUR'S COALITION

US and Australian Operations in the Southwest Pacific Area, 1942–1945

Peter J. Dean

University Press of Kansas

Published by the University Press of Kansas (Lawrence, Kansas
66045), which was organized by the Kansas Board of Regents and
is operated and funded by Emporia State University, Fort Hays State
University, Kansas State University, Pittsburg State University, the
University of Kansas, and Wichita State University.

Library of Congress Cataloging-in-Publication Data

Names: Dean, Peter J. (Peter John), 1974– author.
Title: MacArthur's coalition : US and Australian operations in the
Southwest Pacific area, 1942–1945 / Peter J. Dean.
Description: Lawrence : University Press of Kansas, 2018. | Includes
bibliographical references and index.
Identifiers: LCCN 2017054865 | ISBN 9780700626045 (hardback) |
ISBN 9780700626052 (ebook)
Subjects: LCSH: Allied Forces. South West Pacific Area. | United
States—Military relations—Australia. | Australia—Military
relations—United States. | MacArthur, Douglas, 1880–1964. | World War,
1939–1945—Pacific Area. | World War, 1939–1945—Australia. | World War,
1939–1945—United States. | World War, 1939–1945—Campaigns—Philippines. |
World War, 1939–1945—Campaigns—Pacific Area. | Theater of war.
| BISAC: HISTORY / Military / World War II. | HISTORY / Australia &
New Zealand. | HISTORY / United States / 20th Century.
Classification: LCC D767.95 .D43 2018 | DDC 940.54/265—dc23.
LC record available at https://lccn.loc.gov/2017054865.

British Library Cataloguing-in-Publication Data is available.

Printed in the United States of America

10 9 8 7 6 5 4 3 2 1

For Madeline
Forever our little sweetie pie

CONTENTS

Contents

ILLUSTRATIONS

ACKNOWLEDGMENTS

THIS BOOK HAS HAD A RATHER LONG JOURNEY. Its genesis was in my biography of Lt. Gen. Sir Frank Horton Berryman. Berryman spent more time working with the US military in the Southwest Pacific Area (SWPA) than any other senior Australian officer. While completing his biography, I marveled at the wealth of material available on the US-Australian relationship in the SWPA and wondered why there was no specific book on this topic. From here I realized that I might as well combine this material with my long and ongoing interest in the US-Australian alliance and my passion for the Pacific War.

I started this project while working at the University of Notre Dame Australia. The university generously provided me with a research sabbatical in the second half of 2011 to travel to the archives in the United States. This trip was generously funded by a grant from the United States Studies Centre at Sydney University. While on this trip, I was offered a position at the Strategic and Defence Studies Centre (SDSC) at the Australian National University (ANU). I returned from my sabbatical early to move to Canberra, and with a much more generous research allocation in the new job, I planned to complete this project in twelve to twenty-four months. Alas, that was not to be. The journey to the completion of this book took a number of related but parallel paths. In between then and now, I have edited five books: three on Australia and the Pacific War, one on Australian defense policy, and another on the US-Australian alliance, among a number of other projects.

While each of these projects pulled me away from writing this book, they were enormously helpful in forming my ideas and developing my knowledge and skills. Most significant, they were instrumental in forming new research partnerships and friends. The utility of the Pacific War books is well demonstrated by their liberal use in the footnotes for this work, and I am grateful to all of the authors who were part of these projects and the great work that they did, in particular David Horner, Garth Pratten, Karl James, Ian Pfenningwerth, Mark Johnston, Horoyuki Shindo, and Kevin Holzimmer. In addition to other research tasks, in the intervening five and a half years I have also been a program convener, a director of studies, an associate dean (twice), and a head of department. During this time, my "MacArthur book," as it was colloquially known, became a somewhat mystical beast, hovering over me. I'm exceptionally pleased that I got there in the end.

Any good historical work must be grounded in deep archival research, and this book would not have been possible without the help of the staff at a number of Australian and overseas archives, libraries, and institutions. Sir Frank Berryman's son Richard and daughter Ann allowed me continued access to their father's personal papers. The staff at the Australian War Memorial, the National Archives of Australia, the US National Archives, and the US Army and US Navy archives, as well as the Douglas MacArthur Memorial Archives in Norfolk, Virginia, were all exceptionally helpful. A special thanks goes to John Moremon.

A special note must be made of the support of Roger Lee and the Australian Army History Unit (AHU). Like the USSC, the AHU and the ANU provided financial assistance to support the research of the book, making an exceptionally valuable contribution to this project. Tristian Moss did a wonderful job searching archives and collection records on the operations in New Guinea in 1943, and Jay Vlazlovski did a great job of reviewing the manuscript and preparing it for the publisher. Kay Dancey, Jenny Sheehan, and Karina Pelling at the College of Asia and the Pacific Cartography unit once again did a fabulous job with the maps. I would also like to offer thanks to Joyce Harrison, Mike Kehoe, Kelly Chrisman Jacques, Don McKeon, and the team at the University Press of Kansas (UPK). UPK showed great enthusiasm, patience, and support for this work.

My thanks also extend to my colleagues at the SDSC. They have created a most collegial atmosphere built on a spirit of cooperation, mutual respect, hard work, and dedication. In particular I owe a great debt to Brendan Taylor—boss, mentor, and most important a great friend. A special note goes to Rhys Crawley and Joan Beaumont, who were particularly supportive of my family and me over the last year and a half. David Horner, as always, was generous with his time, thoughts, and insights. Karl James was always keen to swap insights on the Papua and New Guinea campaigns and, along with the rest of the YMMHA, was always available for a beer. Thanks go to Richard Frank, Jonathan Fennel, Peter Williams, and an anonymous reviewer who read the manuscript and made important comments and corrections.

I would not have been able to complete this project without the encouragement, patience, guidance, and humor of my family, especially my wife, Sarah, and my three children, Flynn, Jessica, and Maddie. You continue to provide me with wonderful care, love, and comfort. My most special thanks go to my immediate family: my sister, Sharon, whose love and support I can always rely on; my parents, John and Ann; and Victoria and John and all the Warmsleys for their wonderful support. They have all provided me with unconditional love and support, and I am deeply grateful.

ABBREVIATIONS

AAF	Allied Air Forces
ABDA	American, British, Dutch, and Australian Command
ACNB	Australian Commonwealth Naval Board
Adv GHQ	Advanced General Headquarters
Adv LHQ	Advanced Headquarters, Allied Land Forces
Adv NGF	Advanced New Guinea Force
AHU	Army History Unit
AIF	Australian Imperial Force
ALF	Allied Land Forces
AMF	Australian Military Forces
ANF	Allied Naval Forces, Southwest Pacific Area
ANU	Australian National University
ANZAB	Australia, New Zealand, America, and Britain
ANZAC	Australian and New Zealand Army Corps
APA	amphibious attack transport
ATC	Amphibious Training Center
ATG	Amphibious Training Group
AWM	Australian War Memorial
BGS	brigadier, general staff
BFP	Berryman Family Papers
CANFSWPA	commander, Allied Naval Forces, Southwest Pacific Area
CAS	chief of the Air Staff
CAS	close air support
CCS	Combined Chiefs of Staff
CGS	chief of the General Staff (Australian Army)
C-in-C	commander in chief
CMF	Citizen Military Forces
CNO	chief of naval operations
CNS	chief of the Naval Staff
CO	commanding officer
COMANZAC	commander, ANZAC Naval Area
CoS	chief of staff
CPA	Central Pacific Area
CRA	commander, Royal Artillery

CTS	combined training school
DA&QMG	deputy adjutant and quartermaster general
DCGS	deputy chief of the General Staff (Australian Army)
DMMA	Douglas MacArthur Memorial Archives
EATS	Empire Air Training Scheme
ESB	engineering special (amphibious) brigade
Forland	Forward Echelon of Blamey's Advance LHQ based at GHQ
FRUMEL	Fleet Radio Unit, Melbourne
FTP	fleet training publication (US Navy doctrine)
G-1	personnel staff
G-2	intelligence staff
G-3	operations staff
G-4	logistics staff
GHQ	General Headquarters, SWPA
GOC	general officer commanding
HQ	headquarters
IC	independent company
IGHQ	Imperial (Japanese) General Headquarters
IJA	Imperial Japanese Army
IJN	Imperial Japanese Navy
JCS	Joint Chiefs of Staff (US)
JOOTS	Joint Overseas Operational Training School
LCI	landing craft, infantry
LCM	landing craft, mechanized
LCT	landing craft, tank
LCVP	landing craft vehicle, personnel
LHQ	Land Headquarters
LSI	landing ship, infantry
LST	landing ship, tank
LVT	landing vehicle, tracked
MGGS	major general, general staff
MP	military policeman
NAA	National Archives of Australia
NARA	National Archives and Records Administration (US)
NCO	noncommissioned officer
NEI	Netherlands East Indies
NGF	New Guinea Force
NLA	National Library of Australia
NOIC	naval officer in charge

NPA	North Pacific Area
NSW	New South Wales
NT	Northern Territory
PIB	Papuan Infantry Battalion
PIR	parachute infantry regiment
POA	Pacific Ocean Areas
POW	prisoner of war
PX	post exchange
RAA	Royal Australian Artillery
RAAF	Royal Australian Air Force
RAF	Royal Air Force
RAN	Royal Australian Navy
SDSC	Strategic and Defence Studies Centre
VII Phib	Seventh Amphibious Force
SLV	State Library of Victoria
SOP	standard operating procedure
SOPAC	South Pacific Area (Pacific Ocean Command, Admiral Nimitz)
SSF	South Seas Force
SWPA	Southwest Pacific Area
SWPSF	Southwest Pacific Sea Frontiers
TAF	tactical air force
USAAF	US Army Air Forces
USAFIA	US Army Forces in Australia
USAHEC	US Army Heritage and Education Center
USARPAC	US Army Pacific
USASOS	US Army Services of Supply
USMC	US Marine Corps
USN	US Navy
WRANS	Women's Royal Australian Naval Service
WVM	Wisconsin Veterans Museum

MACARTHUR'S COALITION

Introduction

FROM 1942 TO 1945, the war in the Pacific was divided into two major theaters: the Pacific Ocean Areas (POA), under the command of Adm. Chester Nimitz (US Navy [USN]), and the Southwest Pacific Area (SWPA), under the command of Gen. Douglas MacArthur (US Army). The POA was fundamentally an all-US command, while at the heart of the SWPA lay a coalition of allies: the United States, Australia, and the Netherlands. With the Dutch under Nazi occupation and their forces in the Far East largely destroyed in the first months of the Pacific War, they were able to play only a very minor role in the SWPA. MacArthur's coalition was, therefore, principally a bilateral one between the United States and Australia.

Given the disparity in size, power, and status on the international stage, this was not an even partnership. The coalition that was formed in the SWPA in early 1942 was to be heavily influenced by the vast inequalities that existed between these two nations, especially in economic and military power. Power, however, is relative. In the early phases of the war, Australia was able to concentrate the vast majority of its resources in the theater, while MacArthur had to constantly haggle, harangue, beg, and plead for resources from the US Joint Chiefs of Staff (JSC). The JCS set the means and ends of the war against Japan; MacArthur merely controlled the ways in which the war would be fought in the SWPA. With the JCS running a two-front war across multiple theaters of conflict, in which the defeat of Japan had been relegated to a second-tier priority, MacArthur faced an uphill battle to achieve *his* objectives of liberating the Philippines and commanding the Allied forces in the defeat of Japan.

Complicating MacArthur's mission was the fact that within the Pacific War the JCS saw Nimitz's POA as the main theater of conflict. With the SWPA far down the JCS's strategic priority list, MacArthur was forced in 1942 and 1943 to rely heavily on his Australian partners. In particular during this period, MacArthur's ground forces were overwhelmingly Australian, as were considerable elements of his air and naval capabilities. Therefore, the coalition between MacArthur and the Australians was central to the operations of the SWPA and of significant importance to the Allied victory against Japan in the Pacific, especially during the period of 1942–1943.

This book is about the military partnership that developed between the United States and Australia at this time. In light of the competing national interests and strategic priorities that drive all coalitions, it looks to explore this relationship through a number of key questions: Why did Allied strategy lead to the creation of the SWPA? How was this military theater organized? How did the coalition in the SWPA operate on the battlefield? What where the stresses, strains, and areas of success for this coalition? These questions need to be addressed if we are to construct an understanding of how the SWPA functioned as a military command and to understand its role in the defeat of the Japanese.

For over sixty-five years, there has been a formal military alliance between the United States and Australia. During this period, Australian and US interests in the Asia-Pacific region (and globally) have been tied to each other by geography, intelligence, and security cooperation, economics, the support of liberal democracy, and a rules-based global order. Over time this relationship has been one of the closest alliance relationships in the modern era, ranging from the five-eyes intelligence cooperation (the United States, United Kingdom, Canada, Australia, and New Zealand) to combined military operations in Korea, South Vietnam, the Persian Gulf, Iraq, and Afghanistan. Today thousands of US and Australian personnel serve on operations, on exchange, and in liaison and staff positions in each other's militaries, including an Australian Army major general who currently serves as deputy commander, US Army Pacific (USARPAC).

To many, the US-Australian "alliance" was forged in the dark days of the Pacific War, and it has continued ever since. This "special" relationship is founded on a mutual understanding of two roughly similar societies. Both countries, once British colonies, aligned by a similar frontier foundation myth, and possessing complimentary values and culture, were driven together by the assault of imperialist Japan. This notion has become a part of the alliance mythology. The starting point of this relationship is seen by many to be 27 December 1941, when the Australian prime minister, John Curtin, noted, "Without any inhibitions of any kind, I make it quite clear that Australia looks to America, free of any pangs as to our traditional links or kinship with the United Kingdom."[1] Ever since Curtin wrote these immortal words, Australian prime ministers and US presidents have spoken of the long and enduring friendship between Australia and the United States and the development of this relationship through war.[2]

Given the strength of this alliance, its longevity, and its foundations in war, it is surprising that there has not been a comprehensive study of the

US and Australian military partnership in the SWPA. To be sure, there have been compelling histories of Australia and the United States in the Pacific War, including studies of the US-Australian relationship and its impact on social relations and at the foreign policy level,[3] as well as a multitude of biographies of MacArthur and Curtin and other wartime military and civilian leaders.[4] Professor David Horner has produced authoritative studies on Australian strategy,[5] and there have been a significant number of works on individual battles and campaigns.[6]

Horner's masterful studies on Australian strategy have focused on policymaking and military strategy while providing fascinating glimpses into "battlefield cooperation." However, no one has attempted to focus a work on the US-Australian military relationship in the theater. The aim of this work is to build on Horner's studies and fill in the next layers of this relationship by focusing on the military-to-military partnership at the operational level and an analysis of the key tactical actions and relationships.

In doing so, what is stripped bare is the reality of the US-Australian relationship at this time. In the period up to World War II, there was no significant military contact between these two nations. Despite the oratory of contemporary political leaders, it is important to remember that there was no "alliance" in 1942. There was no mutual defense planning, no joint exercises, and little work on interoperability. When the SWPA command was set up in 1942, it was not an alliance but rather a coalition, that being a "temporary ad hoc arrangement, united against a specified enemy."[7] The alliance that the Australian public and politicians on both sides of the Pacific like to recall did not form until the signing of a formal treaty in 1951, and even then it was to be years before it matured into an important strategic partnership for both countries.[8]

In order to explore and understand this military coalition, the book is organized around key themes and areas of study. These themes include Allied strategy, military organization in the SWPA, command, and the conduct of operations. Within these themes the focus is on key areas, such as the asymmetrical nature of the coalition and the relative balance of forces in the SWPA, command culture and doctrine, the personalities and performance of key commanders, the nature of the operating environment, operational planning, the conducting of operations, and the phases of operations and the stages of the war against Japan. These themes and areas of study are reflected in the structure and approach of the book and are woven through the fabric of the text. In approaching this topic, the book applies an analytical narrative. While themes and case studies can allude to key areas of cooperation or failure, only by thinking through time and exploring the evolution of this relationship can we extrapolate the key principles that guided, drove, and influenced the nature and character of this coalition.[9]

In outlining the approach and scope of this work, it is important to note what the book is and is not. Cognizant of the depth of material that has already been produced on various aspects of both the SWPA and the US-Australian relationship, there are a number of key areas that the work will *not* focus on. First, intelligence: This topic has received detailed coverage in a number of works, and thus the exceptionally close and integrated US-Australian intelligence relationship in the SWPA will not be explored.[10] Second, strategy: While strategy is discussed in detail, the book is not a study of Allied, Australian, or US strategy in the Pacific War. Rather, strategy is used as a context setter in order to explore how the coalition in the SWPA worked and to understand the development of operations. Third, logistics: While logistics are important at the strategic, operational, and tactical levels of war, this is not a major focus of the book. Instead, logistics are referred to, like strategy, as a contextual element for the conduct of operations and an important framework to understand the coalition. There is simply not the space in this work to cover logistics in the detail that it warrants and deserves.[11] Finally, operations: This work is focused on the US and Australian military operations, and as such it confines itself to those battles, operations, and campaigns where there was a significant crossover in capabilities and commitment of resources, especially land forces. It does not attempt to provide comprehensive coverage of all the campaigns and battles of the SWPA.

This work *is* focused on the military-to-military relationship that developed in the SWPA between US and Australian military forces at the operational level from 1942 to 1945. It explores this topic through the work's key themes and areas of focus while investigating the conduct of combined military campaigns and operations. In order to bring balance to a potentially detailed and broad topic, it narrows its focus in a number of ways. While triservice in nature, the book is more heavily focused on the interaction of the US and Australian armies. This is a product not of service bias but of the nature of the coalition, the interaction of the different services, the more platform-centric nature of air and maritime forces, the types of operations undertaken, the organization and command structure of the theater, and the relative balance and weight of the coalition.

This work is also focused in time. There is a definite and deliberate focus on the early to middle part of the war against Japan, covering the period 1942 to early 1944. This is done in order to outline the strategic rationale for the establishment of the SWPA, to analyze its organization and structure, and to focus on the period of time in the relationship when the coalition was more symmetrical and strategic interests and objectives were more mutually aligned. In doing so, the book aims to provide an up-to-date analytical narrative of the campaigns in the SWPA through an assessment of the strategic and operational levels of war in the SWPA in the period 1942–1943. In the period 1944–1945, it concentrates on the strategic interplay between MacArthur and his Australian coalition partner.

What emerges from this investigation is a coalition that is fundamentally ad hoc, profoundly asymmetrical, and deeply dominated by its US Army commander in chief (C-in-C), General MacArthur. The dominance of MacArthur is reflected in the title of the book. MacArthur has been deliberately chosen as the lead in the title not just because of his infamous persona and name recognition but also mainly because he was *the* dominating force and personality in the theater. As will be revealed, it was *his* coalition; it was forged and evolved under his leadership, and it ultimately operated on his terms.[12] This is also reflective of the United States being mentioned first in the subtitle. As a global power, the United States set the parameters of the relationship, and Australia, as a minor power, struggled to influence Allied strategy and the thoughts, ideas, and preferences of its new great and powerful friend.

In pursuing this topic, I have endeavored to draw as much as possible from sources from both sides of the coalition. Conscious of my own nationality, I have attempted to balance my assessment, and if there is a natural bias toward the Australians in the book, I hope it is seen as a product of the asymmetrical nature of the relationship. Traditionally there is greater emphasis on the smaller power to manage a coalition in order to exert its authority and influence on the dominant partner. As the great international affairs scholar Coral Bell wrote in her treatise on the US-Australian alliance, *Dependent Ally*, "the patron is high on the client's horizon: the client (except in special circumstances) is low on the patron's horizon."[13] As such, the Australian government and military were heavily focused on managing the coalition with the United States. MacArthur, however, could afford a much more narrow view concentrated on US national priorities, especially from late 1943, when US forces in the theater became predominant. This relative balance is also a reflection of the source material from each country's archives, in particular the relative focus of US archival material on the balance of the US war effort in the SWPA.

From these boundaries flow the organization and layout of the book. Part 1 begins by tracing the evolution of Australian and US strategy in the Asia-Pacific region from the end of World War I to the beginning of the Pacific War. Chapter 1 outlines just how disjointed the two countries were from one another and how little they initially figured in each other's strategic approach to the region. Chapter 2 explains the reasons that Australia came to prominence in US strategic calculations in the war against Japan in the period after Pearl Harbor, the failure of American, British, Dutch, and Australian Command (ABDA), and the decision to establish the SWPA in early 1942. Chapter 3 explores MacArthur's military command: his arrival in Australia, the SWPA's initial organization, the dominance of the US Army and MacArthur's general headquarters, and an assessment of his three combatant commands.

Part 2 of the book moves from the strategic and organizational realms into the operational and tactical relationship during the campaigns of 1942. Chapter 4 assesses the initial development of the relationship between senior US and Australian officers and details the cultural, doctrinal, and philosophical differences that came to dominate the relationship. Chapter 5 outlines Japanese plans and intentions toward the South Pacific in 1942 and the Allied response in the SWPA in Australia and Papua. It ends with a discussion of the relationship between the two militaries in Australia during 1942, culminating in the Battle of Brisbane in November. Chapters 6 and 7 detail the battles at Gona, Buna, and Sanananda, especially the injection of the 32nd US Infantry Division into operations and the collaboration between the US and Australian forces in Advanced New Guinea Force in the period from October 1942 to January 1943.

Part 3 of the book returns to the strategic and organizational levels. It investigates the changes made to the command and organization of the SWPA as a result of the campaigns of 1942 and lays out the strategy for the theater in 1943. Chapter 8 details the strategy and plan for Operation Cartwheel—the reduction of Rabaul—and the establishment of aerial superiority by the Allies in this section of the theater with the Battle of the Bismarck Sea. Chapter 9 assesses the command, organization, and doctrinal developments in amphibious warfare in the SWPA. This was a key element in the development of MacArthur's strategic approach in the theater and an essential military capability for the development of offensive operations from 1943. It forms the area where the closest military-to-military cooperation occurred between the United States and Australia.

Part 4 returns to the operational and tactical levels for the campaign in New Guinea in 1943. Chapter 10 outlines the difficulties of coalition collaboration in the successful battle for Salamaua. Chapter 11 investigates the details of coalition planning for Operation Postern at the theater, task force, corps, and division levels. Chapter 12 details the operations for the assault on Lae and Finschhafen, the liberation of the Huon Peninsula, the landing at Saidor, and the capture of Madang. It includes an assessment of the key turning points in the relationship in late 1943 and early 1944 when US power become preponderant and the underlying nature of the coalition changed and was subsequently reconceived by MacArthur and his headquarters.

Part 5 concludes the work. With the change in the asymmetry of the coalition in early 1944 and the exhaustion of the Australian war effort, the changes to the coalition's arrangements were profound. Chapter 13 details the search and struggle by Australia to find a role in the SWPA in 1944, the split between the theater C-in-C, General MacArthur, and the Australian C-in-C, Gen. Thomas Blamey, and the exclusion of the Australians from the operations in the Philippines. It finishes with the final combined operations in the theater (and the Pacific War) in Borneo and a discussion of the controversies surrounding the Australian war effort in the SWPA in 1944 and 1945 and MacArthur's role in these events. The conclusion provides an assessment of the nature and character of "MacArthur's coalition" in relation to the themes and key areas of investigation.

As a whole, the chapters in the book trace the evolution of the US-Australian coalition in the SWPA, with a focus on the military-to-military relationship. This relationship starts from a low base and is immediately inflicted with doctrinal, cultural, and personality problems. The key themes and areas of focus form the basis of investigating how this coalition formed and worked.

With major differences on issues of command, control, and doctrine underpinned by the fact that this relationship was a temporary, ad hoc coalition, moves toward integration and interoperability were minimal. The focus on overcoming issues of cooperation became centered on the personalities and capabilities of senior officers and commanders. This individual initiative and a focus on operational and tactical problems were the key to enabling mutually supportive and effective means of collaboration. Such a system lacked a systemic organizational approach and was thus heavily dependent on individuals from both nations.

In understanding the coalition in the SWPA, the personalities of commanders and senior staff officers are critically important. The very top of the command structure in the SWPA was dominated by the challenging relationship between MacArthur and Blamey, an association that would break down in 1944 under diverging priorities and MacArthur's megalomaniac and narcissistic personality. Underneath these two officers, the detailed components of the coalition partnership were worked out by a group of exceptionally talented senior commanders and staff officers. These men rose above (eventually) a lot of the petty squabbling to get things done. It is here, and at the front lines, that systems and approaches to cooperation were established and worked out. This, however, was an approach that was thwarted with difficulties, not least the fact that it was very challenging to systematize such an approach. As the book details, changes in formations, units, staff officers, and commanders—for good or ill—had a major impact on the operation of the coalition.

As the book highlights, in the period of greater equity in the relationship between the two countries, when strategic interests and objectives were mutually aligned, an exceptionally high degree of cooperation, especially at the operational and tactical levels, was achieved (despite a number of issues). It was only after the true asymmetry of the relationship became apparent and strategic interests started to diverge that the relationship became strategically and operationally dysfunctional.

Ultimately, however, this was a successful coalition. Despite its ad hoc nature, it defeated the Japanese in the theater, and this is highlighted by the triumphs in battle that the Allies had. It is hoped that this work explains and explores the success in the SWPA and the US-Australian cooperation, as much as it details the more theatrical areas of sharp disagreement and discord. In the end, despite all of its issues and problems, the coalition was critical to the defeat of the Japanese in the Pacific War.

Part 1

The Southwest Pacific Area, 1942

I

War Plans and Preparations
US-Australian Relations in the Interwar Period

THE END OF THE WAR IN 1918 brought about a major change to Australia's strategic situation. Despite raising an expeditionary force of over six divisions during the war for service in Europe and the Middle East,[1] in the postwar period the orientation of Australian defense policy moved squarely to the Pacific, with Japan emerging as the only major threat to Australian security. This was also a part of a broader acknowledgment that the Pacific Ocean would probably provide "the arena for the next world conflict."[2]

Japan had been expanding its power base since the latter half of the nineteenth century, and in 1919 it used its support for the Allied powers during World War I to successfully push for control of the German Pacific colonies in the Mariana, Caroline, and Marshall Islands at the Paris Peace Conference. This in effect cemented Japanese "domination of the central and western Pacific."[3] In 1921, a League of Nations mandate granted administration of German New Guinea to Australia, which included the excellent harbor at Rabaul on New Britain. This effectively made Australia and Japan uncomfortable neighbors in the Southwest Pacific. The result of these moves was a radically altered strategic position for both Australia and the United States.

During World War I, Australian security against Japan had been provided by the Anglo-Japanese Naval Agreement (1902). This alliance had seen Imperial Japanese Navy (IJN) warships escort the convoys carrying the Australian Imperial Force (AIF) through the Indian Ocean to the Middle East during the war. The continuation of this pact in the years immediately after the war, in addition to the advent of the League of Nations and a general push toward disarmament, seemed to guarantee Australian security in the Pacific. As Craig Wilcox reminds us, war had "lost its glory in the mud of France and Belgium sometime between 1914 and 1918." It was "now not something to be prepared for."[4] However, Japan's emergence from World War I as a major military power coupled

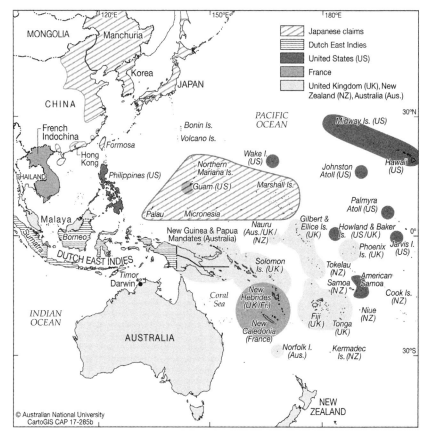

Figure 1.1 Japanese, Australian, British, and American Colonial Possessions,
Interwar Period

with its gains made at the Paris Peace Conference meant that any further
territorial expansion into the South or Southwest Pacific would bring it
into direct conflict with the United States and/or Australia and the British
Empire.[5]

The first significant event of the postwar period in Asia-Pacific security
occurred at the Washington Naval Conference of 1922. This conference
was to have major ramifications for Australian security. It was hoped
that the Washington Naval Treaty, which created a fixed ratio of capital
ships between the powers and placed limitations on the building and
tonnage of new warships, would avoid a repeat of the naval arms race
that was seen as one of the principal causes of World War I. Its other
major outcome was, at the urging of the United States, the end of the

Anglo-Japanese Naval Agreement, something that both Australia and New Zealand fought hard to retain.[6]

Despite this setback, the Australian government, ever reliant on Britain for protection and specifically the Royal Navy, was initially not overly perturbed by this development and publicly welcomed the outcome of the Washington Naval Conference. With a country weary of war and with a prevailing belief in disarmament, the Australian parliament saw "few votes in defence."[7] To the government, the Washington Conference seemed to go some way to actually solving Australia's strategic dilemma over Japan. This stance was, however, a "misguided perception" that was to have "catastrophic [results] for Australian defence."[8]

The Australian government's faith in peace and disarmament was soon undermined. In the year after the Washington Naval Conference, Britain and the empire became embroiled in the Chanak Crisis when British and French troops in the neutral channel zone of the Dardanelles came under threat, and it appeared that Britain was on the brink of war with Turkey. Australia instantly threw its support behind the "Mother Country." Luckily the crisis quickly passed, but it served to remind the Australian government of the potential for international conflict and that this had "in no way lessened as a result of the Great War."[9]

After Chanak there was a growing recognition that the Washington Naval Conference provided little real security for Australia. So when Australian prime minister Stanley Bruce went to the 1923 Imperial Conference, he was resolved to confirm the proposal to provide a British base in the Pacific.[10] The outcome of this conference was the Singapore Strategy and Australia's continued commitment to imperial defense.[11] Imperial defense was, in essence, the "joint defence of United Kingdom possessions and interests by a combination of United Kingdom, Dominion and Colonial Forces."[12] It rested on the notion that the Royal Navy would provide the first line of defense through command of the seas and that the colonies would provide for their own defense against local attacks and would also contribute to any common empire cause in the event of a major international crisis or war.[13] Australian participation dated back to the Sudan conflict of 1885, and under this strategy the British colonies in Australia committed forces to the Boer War and the Boxer Rebellion. Only thirteen years after establishment of the Federation of Australia, the new nation committed forces to World War I.

At the end of the 1923 Imperial Conference, it was agreed that while each part of the empire was responsible for its own local defense, in the Pacific a naval base would be built at Singapore to service the British battle fleet, thereby providing a deterrent to Japanese aggression.[14] Australia was responsible for the protection of maritime trade in the Australian region, and financial support was pledged for the construction of the Singapore base. At the time, it was viewed by the British chiefs of staff as one of the "keystones on which the survival of the British Commonwealth of Nations would depend,"[15] and this strategy formed the foundation of Australian defense policy throughout the interwar period.[16] This policy was, however, to have serious repercussions for the security of Australia.

One of the other major effects of the Singapore Strategy was the division that it created between the Australian Army, which was vehemently opposed to the strategy, and the navy, the air force, the Department of Defence, and the government, which remained steadfastly rusted onto it. As a consequence of this naval strategy, the Royal Australian Navy (RAN) would receive the bulk of the defense vote, and the army and the Royal Australian Air Force (RAAF) had to battle it out for the remainder. For the army it was not just a failed strategy but also one that dramatically curtailed its strategic relevance, as it meant that it was effectively reduced to planning only to defeat "raids" on the Australian mainland.[17]

Despite the maritime nature of the strategy, it was never intended for Australia to maintain a fleet for the defense of the continent, but rather the RAN would augment the Royal Navy based at Singapore. This was despite the fact that it was never adequately revealed how the base in Singapore, some 3,900 miles (by air) from Sydney, would provide protection for the eastern seaboard of Australia from Japanese naval aggression or how the British were going to be able to actually provide a fleet to Singapore for its protection. A more realistic appraisal of the Singapore Strategy based on recognition of strategic geography meant that this naval enclave on the edge of Asia looked more like a base to bottle up the Japanese in the Pacific and deny their fleet access to the Indian Ocean, rather than a base to project waning British power into the Southwest Pacific. Compounding these problems were the constant delays in the construction of the base. From 1919, there were also questions as to the ability of the British to provide a fleet to man it, a problem that became acute after the onset of the Great Depression in 1929. Yet, despite all of these issues, the Singapore Strategy's position as the basis of Australian defense policy became an "article of faith that was not to be questioned."[18]

A lack of clear, critical strategic thinking on the Singapore Strategy was amply demonstrated as early as 1923. At the imperial conference held in London that year, Prime Minister Bruce commented that "while I am not quite clear as to how the protection of Singapore is to be assured, I am quite clear on this point, that apparently it can be done."[19] During the 1920s and 1930s, this faith in the strategy was, to a large degree, built on the passionate support that it received from the Department of Defence and in particular from Frederick Shedden, the departmental secretary from 1937. Shedden had been at the forefront of setting Australian defense policy since 1929, and ably supported by the respective chiefs of the RAN and the RAAF (a considerable number of whom in the interwar period were senior British officers), he was able to effectively advocate for Australia's rock-solid commitment to the Singapore Strategy. His position was further bolstered in the lead-up to World War II by the 1934 defense review undertaken by Sir Maurice Hankey, secretary of the Committee of Imperial Defence, which, unsurprisingly, gave the Singapore Strategy its full support.[20]

Despite the weight of support from the RAN, the RAAF, and the Department of Defence, the Australian Army continued its opposition into the 1930s. This stance became more aggressive when Maj. Gen. John Lavarack became chief of the General Staff in 1935. While the army had consistently pointed out the inherent weaknesses of the Singapore Strategy, the criticism became more aggressive under Lavarack. He was particularly critical in the years leading up to the start of World War II in regard to the growing importance of airpower, the weakness of British sea power, and the fact that the "British government was very unlikely to send the Fleet to the Far East if war broke out in Europe."[21]

Still, the army's most senior officers were fighting a losing battle that led to an inevitable dispute with both the Department of Defence and the government. Relations between Lavarack, Shedden, and Minister for Defence Sir Archdale Parkhill soured, helped along by Lavarack's poor temperament.[22] He "made it plain . . . how little he was prepared to suffer fools, even when they were his political or military superiors."[23] In August 1936, Parkhill rebuked Lavarack in a Council of Defence meeting for his criticism of defense policy, and in November relations between the government and the army broke down over the controversy surrounding the dismissal from army headquarters (HQ) of one of Lavarack's close friends and supporters, Lt. Col. H. D. Wynter. Wynter had been accused of leaking sensitive defense reports to the leader of the opposition, John Curtin.[24]

Parkhill directed the Military Board to investigate, and it was discovered that Wynter had been responsible for the wording of the specific section of the report that Curtin used in Parliament.[25] Parkhill demanded disciplinary action, while Wynter countercharged by demanding a formal court-martial, arguing that he had in fact broken no regulations.[26] In what has been described as a "petty" move,[27] Parkhill pushed the Military Board into moving Wynter to the First Military District in Queensland, a demotion in responsibility and a reduction in rank, and on Shedden's advice he also withdrew his recommendation for Lavarack to be made a Companion of the Bath.[28]

Arguments persisted over defense policy among the chiefs of staff, the government, and Shedden until the outbreak of war, and while, as Eric Andrews argues, the "Army leaders might have been motivated by their own special interests . . . their arguments, pointing to the threat of Japan were logical."[29] A few years later, the army's arguments were proved to be not just logical but also unnervingly correct.

The major question, then, is why did the Australian government persist with the Singapore Strategy despite its obvious flaws and some strong opposition from within the military? Consecutive Australian governments, from both sides of politics, remained firmly committed to the strategy during the interwar period for five major reasons: the cost of defense; reliance on its great, powerful protector—Britain; Australia's perception of its place as the jewel in the crown of the British Empire (which in reality was India and the Middle East); Australian nationalism and its attachment to Britain; and the economic reliance of Australia upon the empire.[30]

Dependence on Britain economically, along with imperial loyalty, drove the Australian government's adherence to the Singapore Strategy. This gave it a rationale for a reduction in spending on defense far below levels that its military advisers thought wise. Instead of seeing the Singapore Strategy as requiring Australia to invest in defense capability, especially as imperial defense was centered on self-reliance in a constituent country's immediate region, it saw it as a way to outsource Australia's defense and place it in the hands of the Royal Navy. This led to the endorsement of massive cutbacks in defense spending after the signing of the Washington Naval Treaty in 1922.[31] Such cutbacks were further entrenched after the onset of the Great Depression in 1929.

For the Australian government to admit that its defense policy was bunk would have meant that the Australian taxpayer would have had to front the bill for home defense and Australian security policy would have had to have been drastically recast. Furthermore, even if by the mid- to late 1930s this policy approach was changed, Australia did not have the capacity to produce modern military equipment, especially cutting-edge aircraft and mechanized land forces—equipment that would prove so decisive in Europe during the period 1939–1941. By the mid- to late 1930s, rearmament in Europe and also the United States placed enormous pressure on the international arms market and restricted Australia's ability to procure arms from overseas.[32]

Consecutive Australian governments had also come to the conclusion that it was more likely that other dominions within the empire would be in the front lines in the next war, obviating the need for a heightened security posture. At the same time, the poor state of Australia's defenses meant that if the continent were threatened, it would have to rely upon Britain anyway. Furthermore, there was widespread community and political support for Britain. Most Australians still thought of themselves as independent Briton Australians, and it was argued that Australia owed its allegiance to the British.[33]

This fundamental attachment to Britain, in addition to the White Australia Policy, led to an underdeveloped sense of Australian national identity.[34] This was reflected in Australia's total reliance on Britain for foreign intelligence and diplomacy. It has been argued that this meant that the British just told Australians what they wanted to hear in international relations, especially as they had no independent sources to verify the information. To be fair to the British, however, the Australians did not really want to hear the strategic reality.

This diplomatic subservience also spilled over into an almost total economic reliance of Australia upon Britain. As late as the 1930s during rearmament, Australia rejected American products and a direct air link to the United States on the sole basis of supporting British industry. In the end, blind faith, economic underdevelopment, and dependence, along with imperial loyalty, led to an acceptance of the Singapore Strategy. As Albert Palazzo has noted, this meant that during the interwar period,

> the [Australian] Government's security policy supported a navalist strategy that in turn rested on great power acquiescence. It was up to the Royal Navy to prevent an enemy from approaching Australia's shores and the policy downplayed the need for land and air forces. In addition, in doing so, it emphasised the defence of territory at the expense of interests, while still insisting on the security of Australia's interests within the imperial network. This was an incompatibility that the Government chose not to reconcile, because to do so would have prevented it from achieving the second objective of its security policy: a desire to transfer the greatest possible share of defence responsibility onto the shoulders—and finances—of a great power.[35]

WAR PLAN ORANGE

In contrast to the Singapore Strategy, which rested on highly optimistic assumptions bordering on an outright delusion of strategic reality, the United States war-gamed and devised a strategy for war in the Pacific that would be enacted with great success. It was, in the judgment of one American historian, "history's most successful war plan."[36]

After the Spanish-American War of 1898, the United States gained control of some seven thousand islands, including the Philippine archipelago, Guam, and the Wake, Johnston, and Midway atolls. Most significant, the war spurred the annexation in 1898 of Hawaii, the future home of the US Pacific Fleet.[37] As noted, a little over two decades later at the end of World War I, the strategic situation in the Pacific changed following the acquisition of ex-German territories in the Pacific by the Japanese. This led to the United States having to place more emphasis on the need to devise a plan to defend its new possessions. The 1921–1922 Washington Naval Conference had attempted to limit aggression and a naval arms race in the region by prescribing a 10:10:6 ratio of capital ships between the United States, Britain, and Japan. However, this measure did not provide for a security guarantee.

As noted, the Washington Naval Conference had also led to the end of the Anglo-Japanese Naval Agreement. This removed the threat to the United States of a war in the Pacific against both Japan and Britain. But under Article XIX of the Five-Power Naval Treaty, the United States was not able to fortify its bases in Manila and Guam.[38] This meant that US defense planners had to work on the provision that their nearest major fleet base in the Pacific for the defense of the Philippines would be Honolulu.[39]

After the Washington Naval Conference, Assistant Secretary of the Navy Theodore Roosevelt had detailed defense planners to work on a strategy for war in the Pacific.[40] While the US military did not have much of an insight into how the Japanese would approach the war, abductive reasoning led them to a number of conclusions:

- US superiority in both population and economic capacity meant that Japan would have to strike quickly against US assets in the Pacific.
- This would cut off the possibility of the US Pacific Fleet from operating in the Western Pacific in the initial stages of the war.
- The Japanese would then form a defensive barrier to try to withstand an attrition phase against the United States.

On the basis of these assumptions, US planners believed that the war would unfold in three distinct phases:

Phase 1: the Japanese occupation of US possessions in the Western Pacific, mainly Guam, Wake Island, and the Philippines
Phase 2: the return of the US force to the area
Phase 3: the blockade of Japan[41]

Significantly this meant that American planners were thinking in terms of a possible war against Japan as a series of campaigns rather than a single climatic battle. This planning was part of a broader series of inter-war plans and scenarios that the US military set out to undertake using designated color code names for each country that was a potential opponent. Germany was "Black," England "Red," Russia "Purple," and Japan "Orange." From here a number of "Rainbow" plans were devised that would pit different combinations of alliances, coalition partnerships, and enemy combatants against the United States.

Orange is by far and away the most famous of these plans, and for good reason. As Henry G. Cole notes,

war with Japan was a concern, even an obsession, for the US Navy beginning in 1907. From 1919 to 1940 Orange was regularly revised in Washington by army and navy war planners in their respective services and in the Joint Army and Navy Board and Joint Planning Committee. It was also the centerpiece of the curriculum at the Naval War College . . . [where] year after year faculty and students planned and "fought" the war with Japan.[42]

Based on their assumptions, War Plan Orange was set around a primarily offensive naval war. This was to be conducted by a blockade of the Japanese home islands, occupation of their outlying territories, and an air war against Japanese territory.[43] The planners developed two basic scenarios for war in the Pacific. The "thrusters" advocated an immediate movement of the fleet and reserves to secure the base at Manila in the Philippines, followed by a "lunge" into the heart of the Japanese Empire. This was primarily an attempt to stop the loss of the US possessions predicted in the Japanese offensive during phase 1. Meanwhile, the "cautionaries" advocated for the virtual abandonment of the Philippines and a more deliberate island-hopping advance across the Pacific.[44]

By 1933, the Naval War College projected that a rapid "dash" across the Pacific to take on the Japanese battle fleet would have major repercussions for the USN. Instead, it recommended a containment of Japanese offensive action early in the war, followed by a buildup of American forces for a deliberate advance across the Pacific, something they argued would take four to five years. Despite this view, debate continued right up until the surprise attack on the US Pacific Fleet on 7 December 1941, which ultimately removed any possibility of a rapid advance toward Japan as advocated by the thrusters.[45]

War Plan Orange was fundamentally an operational contingency plan, and thus it was not restricted by existing force structures. While in many senses this was problematic, especially as the USN throughout the 1920s and 1930s did not possess the capacity to implement most variants of the plan, it did serve to act as a means of predicting the requirements for war against Japan.[46] Besides a naval rearmament plan, the other major factor was how the US military would seize territory in the Pacific to develop naval and air bases for the fleet. This was the mission to which the US Marine Corps (USMC) devoted itself in the interwar period, turning itself from a counterinsurgency force into a full-fledged amphibious assault force.[47]

Based on the work of one of the USMC's legendary figures, Maj. Pete Ellis, the Corps studied the problem of launching assaults across defended beaches. Ellis had developed *Advance Base Operations in Micronesia*,[48] and "soon after the Joint Army-Navy Board approved the amphibious assault mission for the Marine Corps."[49] The USMC then undertook studies into how it was going to achieve its mission, including overcoming the difficulties of landing troops ashore, naval gunfire support, logistics, and air support. This would result in the development of the *Tentative Landings Operations Manual* in 1934, which was accepted as USN doctrine in 1938 under the title Fleet Training Publication (FTP) 167.[50]

US plans in the interwar period suffered from the same limitation that plagued other Western militaries at this time—namely, a lack of funds. This was coupled with a return to "isolationism" that severely restricted the development of the US armed services. In the 1930s, the Great Depression, public opposition to involvement in European politics, and the continued commitment to isolationism by elements of Congress hampered the development of the forces needed to implement the US military's interwar plans. Such moves were also complicated by the corresponding internal divisions within the military over the role of the armed forces, debates over the future of war, and the likely scenarios for the use of force and the development of doctrine, in particular the USMC's amphibious assault doctrine and the role of the USN's aircraft carriers.[51]

In the end, War Plan Orange accurately predicted the phases that the war in the Pacific would undertake. The plan evolved over the course of the interwar period with the original notion of the quick thrust into the Western Pacific to undertake a glamorized Mahanian-style fleet engagement against the Japanese, giving way in the 1930s to a more deliberate option of a steady advance. This plan virtually wrote off the possibility of holding the Philippines and worked toward an island-hopping campaign across the Central Pacific. The planning process to reach this outcome was, as Miller points out, "competitive and untidy," but it produced a plan that had widespread understanding among the senior military staff. This was solidified through its war-gaming by these officers while students at the Naval War College. While War Plan Orange may not have been followed to the letter to achieve victory in the Pacific War, it certainly laid out a series of contingency plans that were the foundation of US Pacific strategy during the war and laid the platform for the development of the USMC's amphibious mission and the rearmament of the US fleet.[52]

AUSTRALIA AND US WAR PLANNING

Most of the US military war planning in the interwar period was premised on the United States fighting alone against the Japanese. As a result of this and a number of other factors, plans for the US advance across the Pacific had primarily focused on the central and northern part of the ocean. The first planned use of Australia came with discussion of Rainbow Two in 1939, which assumed an alliance between the United States, Britain, France, and the Netherlands. This contingency plan called for US support in the defense of Indochina, Borneo, and Malaya and envisaged the US Pacific Fleet moving from Hawaii to Fiji, Rabaul, Darwin, and Java, and then on to Singapore before driving north for operations in the South China Sea. Besides the stopover of US fleet units in Darwin, on Australia's far northern coastline, Australia was also envisaged to be one of a series of transit airfields to deliver aircraft from Hawaii to Borneo and then Singapore, bypassing the Japanese mandated territories in the Central Pacific.

This was a plan that the USN chiefs were not happy with, and by 1940 it was "out of touch with reality."[53] The only other major planning contingency linked to the support of Singapore was the idea of an "Asiatic Reinforcement" group made up of an aircraft carrier, four heavy cruisers, and supporting craft that would make its way to Manila by way of Darwin, but the idea lasted only two months. In the end, Australia was never envisaged as being anything more than a staging post to pass through on the way to fighting the Japanese elsewhere.

Of greater concern, and possible use, to US planners were the Australian territories in the South Pacific. During the 1920s and 1930s, this region had often been suggested by planning groups as an avenue of advance against the Japanese mandated territories, but after detailed discussions it "had always been rejected."[54] After the start of the war in Europe, US planners began to toy with different strategic concepts involving Britain and other European powers in the Pacific. In the spring of 1940, Rainbow Two had contemplated an advance from the Australian mandated territory of Rabaul, in New Britain, to establish a fleet base in the Palaus, but by the summer of 1940 these ideas had been rejected.

In the same summer, US planners considered the use in Rainbow Three of Rabaul, which would serve as a major base for an advance toward Borneo. Nevertheless, this idea was rejected by Adm. Husband E. Kimmel, commander of the US Pacific Fleet. The other major alternative was discussed in 1941 (Rainbow Five), which restricted US naval operations to only escorting and hunting for raiders in the Pacific as far south as Australia and New Zealand so as to free the navies of these two countries to participate in the defense of Singapore. In the end, Australia received no assistance in the defense of Rabaul and the SWPA in the interwar period, although by October 1941 the United States had conceded to providing mines, antiaircraft defenses, and patrol boats for its defense. The problem was that by the time they were ready for deployment, the base had already fallen to the Japanese.[55]

US AND AUSTRALIAN MILITARY COOPERATION TO 1942

The United States' most influential effect on Australia in its earliest of years was as a model for the Australian Parliament decided upon at Federation in 1901. While this was exceptionally important, it did not mean that the United States and Australia enjoyed close relations or cooperation. Ten years after Federation, New South Wales appointed a commercial agent in San Francisco, but it was not until after World War I that a British Commonwealth representative arrived in the United States as a trade representative based in New York City.[56]

The first major instance of military engagement came through the arrival in 1908 of the USN's Great White Fleet. In 1906, President Theodore

Roosevelt had decided to send a portion of the US fleet to the Pacific on permanent station, and in 1907 it was decided to send the Atlantic Fleet to San Francisco. With tensions rising between the United States and Japan, the president thought that this would "send a useful diplomatic message."[57] This move was soon supplemented by a decision to send the fleet on a round-the-world cruise, and the Australian prime minster, Alfred Deakin, through the British Colonial Office, extended an invitation for the fleet to visit Australia. This was enthusiastically received in the United States, where Secretary of State Elihu Root noted that "sending the fleet to Australia will be good business. . . . The time will surely come, although probably after our day, when it will be important for the United States to have all ports friendly and all causes of sympathy alive in the Pacific."[58]

The visit of the fleet struck an enthusiastic response from Australians, and half a million Sydneysiders lined the harbor when the US ships arrived. Much of this interest was inspired by the rise of Japanese power, which had been demonstrated to the world by Japan's victory over the Russian fleet in 1905. Interestingly, the existence of the Anglo-Japanese Naval Agreement meant the US Navy had a plan for a US-Japanese war in the Pacific that included the possibility of British involvement on Japan's side due to Britain's alliance commitments. This meant that US naval officers spent some time on their visit collecting intelligence on Australian defenses.[59]

Overall, though, the visit was highly successful, and it was to be duplicated in 1925 when the US Pacific Fleet visited Sydney and Melbourne. Fifty-six vessels visited Australia on this occasion, including the twelve battleships and one escort that went to Sydney and the forty-three cruisers and destroyers that went to Melbourne. Like the 1908 visit, this event was, socially, highly successful. The political outcomes of these visits, however, were less certain.[60]

The 1908 visit had undertones of a possible security alliance or pact with the United States. Such a move was met with mixed reactions in Australia as well as in the United States and Britain. Deakin was pushing for an extension of the US Monroe Doctrine (hegemony) into the Pacific that drew on an enhanced base of nations that included Britain, the Netherlands, France, China, and the United States.[61] Deakin's hopes were quashed by the Anglo-Japanese Naval Agreement and the Root-Takahira Agreement (1908), which was an arrangement to maintain the status quo in the Pacific.[62]

Importantly, while US fleet visits did involve "attempts to forge new friendships in the Pacific through symbolic visits by the American navy, as well as calls for a regional security agreement with Washington[, they] . . . did not undermine [Australia's] affection for Britain and the Empire."[63] Military relations between the United States and Australia during World War I can be recounted by the small number of interactions between Australian and American forces on the western front, the most notable being the limited US participation in the attack of the Australian Corps at the Battle of Hamel on 4 July 1918 and the participation of the 27th and 30th US Infantry Divisions in the Australian assault on the Hindenburg Line in 1918.[64] These promising interactions were, however, overshadowed in the immediate postwar period, where US-Australian relations were set by the clashes that occurred between President Woodrow Wilson and Prime Minister Billy Hughes at the Paris Peace Conference. Their differences of opinion over a number of issues were both "public and colourful."[65]

Wilson and Hughes's jousting derived from their different views of the world, while Australia's continued commitment to the empire and the United States' rejection of the Treaty of Versailles, followed by its adoption of "isolationism," did nothing to foster relations in the 1920s. Despite the success of the two US Navy fleet visits to Australia, for the majority of the 1920s and 1930s "Australian strategic culture had little to do with the United States."[66]

The early period of the 1930s did not improve US-Australian relations. The Great Depression had a negative impact on trade between the two countries. The 1932 Imperial Conference in Ottawa led to a series of trade agreements between empire countries. This was reinforced by the 1936 Trade Diversion Policy, which restricted Japanese and American goods from coming into Australia and led to a downgrading of Australia's most-favored-nation status in the United States.[67] These measures reinforced the maxim that Australia, rightly or wrongly, looked to Britain not just for its defense but also for its economic prosperity.[68]

Notwithstanding these setbacks, Prime Minister Joseph Lyon visited Washington in 1935, the outcome of which was increased diplomatic representation between the two countries. This glacial move toward greater cooperation was being driven by Japanese aggression in the Pacific. Japan's invasion of Manchuria in 1931, followed by its attack on China six years later, dramatically raised tensions in the region. Pressure started to rise in Australian-British relations as differences emerged regarding the countries' approaches to Asia, and it became clear that a truly imperial policy in the Asia-Pacific region could not be achieved. This resulted in

Australia deploying its own representatives to Asia, the first of whom was Keith Officer, posted to Washington in 1937.[69] In 1938, the decision was made to exchange ministers, and in 1940 R. G. Casey took up the position as Australian minister in Washington, and Clarence E. Gauss arrived in Australia as the first US minister to Australia.

Nevertheless, Australia was still intricately linked to Britain. This is evident through the fact that the Australian minister in Washington was there only as a part of a British delegation and therefore unable to exert any real influence. As David Day has noted, Casey and the British ambassador, Lord Lothian, "would often visit the state department or [President Franklin D.] Roosevelt in tandem, as if there was no distinction between the interests they were representing."[70]

Australia had attempted in the mid-1930s to undertake some international initiatives to promote its regional security interests independent of Britain but without success. Lyon had raised with Roosevelt in 1935 the idea of a Pacific pact between the two countries, and this was expanded at the 1937 Imperial Conference into a broader Pacific conference of nations. Lyon got a "polite reaction" at the conference, but British support was eventually forthcoming. The reaction from Pacific nations, however, was very mixed. The Chinese were enthusiastic, the Soviets interested, the United States cautious, and the Japanese dead opposed. London soon went cold on the idea, and it was eventually killed off by the Japanese invasion of China in July.[71]

In the end, as the 1930s drew to a close, both the United States and Australia had been slow to abandon their interwar policies in order to meet the changing strategic circumstances in the Pacific.[72] In 1939, after the outbreak of World War II in Europe, Australia had made the decision to send a large number of its troops, naval forces, and aircrews to the Middle East and Europe. It was believed that Australian security in the Pacific would continue to be guaranteed by Singapore. It was only slowly that Australia accepted the reality of British weakness in the Pacific.

In September 1940, Australian officials became aware that British planners had made overtures to the United States to undertake joint planning in the Pacific. The Americans soon came to realize that the British were relying on the United States in the Pacific as they were unable to provide an adequate fleet to the region in the event of war with Japan, information that the British had not shared with Australia.[73] While the Americans were cautious of these moves, the Australian chiefs of staff were enthusiastic and immediately set about plans to send a delegation to Washington. Australia was allowed to send a naval representative, Cdr. H. M. Burrell, for "private talks," while a USN officer was sent to observe at the imperial conference held in Singapore in October 1940. At this conference a discussion was held on the possibility of British, Australian, New Zealand, and Dutch forces serving under US command in the event of war with Japan, a proposition that had Australian War Cabinet support.[74]

Commander Burrell became an important link for Australia in the coming months. His communiqués with the Australian chiefs of staff and government in February 1941 revealed British discussions with the Americans of a policy of "Europe first" in the event of war with Japan. Casey revealed in the same month that the Americans had no intention of sending US warships to defend Singapore and that they believed its loss would not have a decisive effect on the outcome of the war. Talks in Singapore and Washington in the following months between the British and the Americans reaffirmed the Europe first policy, the US view of Singapore's defense, and the adoption of a defensive posture of the Pacific theater in the event of war.[75]

The war in Europe took a bad turn in June 1941 with the German attack on the Soviet Union. As a result, the Japanese considered their options and, with the Soviets no longer a threat, Japan decided to strike south, a decision quickly known to the British and Americans as a result of the United States' ability to read Japanese diplomatic codes. American planning, however, oscillated in relation to Australia and the Southwest Pacific. In September, the Australian naval attaché in Washington reported that the USN did not intend on operating ships in the Southwest Pacific. However, in October it made a firm commitment to support the defense of Rabaul.[76]

This commitment was off the back of a proposal from the US government on 20 August 1941, over three months before the start of the Pacific War, to "establish a chain of landing grounds suitable for heavy bombers between Honolulu and New Zealand; Australia, Malaya and the Philippines."[77] The plan, which the Australian government readily agreed to, included the establishment of air bases in Darwin, Port Moresby, Townsville, Rabaul, and Noumea. In late November, three US Army Air Forces (USAAF) officers, headed by Maj. Gen. Lewis Brereton, commander of the US Far East Air Force based in the Philippines, made a secret visit to Australia, and over a three-day conference in Melbourne the details were thrashed out.

The plan soon evolved beyond a ferry service to basing options, which included locating 450 US Army officers and men in northern Australia, along with over £3.3 million worth of infrastructure development to accommodate three US heavy bomber squadrons and four fighter squadrons at Darwin, Charters Towers, and Cloncurry in Australia and in Rabaul.[78] The Australians were further buoyed by British prime minister Winston Churchill's announcement of Force Z in Singapore, consisting of the battleship *Prince of Wales* and the battlecruiser *Repulse*, to be followed by more battleships later on. By November, Australia was also fully aware that Japanese preparations for war were almost complete.[79]

During the second half of 1941, Australia could not ignore Japanese moves, and despite its reinforcement of Malaya and New Britain and a heightening of home defenses, it continued to provide the majority of its support for the British military effort in the Mediterranean and Europe. Australia attempted to coordinate defense planning with the US, British, and Dutch forces in the Pacific, but as David Stevens has argued, "firmly tied to the imperial view of the world, the Australians had little previous experience to call upon and for the most part remained only concerned observers."[80] Australia's inability to direct a role in Pacific defense was coupled with the US refusal to give Australia, Britain, or the Netherlands an explicit commitment of military assistance against Japan in the Pacific until the outbreak of war on 7 December 1941.[81]

LITTLE HEADWAY

Australia and the United States had never formed a close relationship between the wars. Australia had turned to Britain for defense and economic protection, and it had resisted measures such as radio-telegraph links and landing rights for Pan American Airways. Australia had not figured as a major part of US planning for the war against Japan. At best, its possessions in the South Pacific might have provided for a base for part of the US Pacific Fleet, or Darwin might have provided a transit stop for US ships or aircraft. However, these plans were not infallible, and they could not predict the future with any certainty (nor were they meant to do so).

What eventually transpired was that the first US troops sent to Australia had originally been intended for the Philippines. They arrived in Brisbane after being diverted there as a result of the imminent collapse of the US forces at Corregidor. Darwin also served its purpose of a staging ground, but rather than being where US forces passed through to fight the Japanese farther north, it would serve as the front lines of Australia in resisting the Japanese advance in early 1942. US aircraft and ships were to play a significant role in the defense of this area in 1942. Meanwhile,

MacArthur arrived in Melbourne to assume command of the SWPA, after President Franklin Roosevelt ordered him to withdraw from Bataan. His initial task, set by the US Joint Chiefs of Staff (JCS), was the recapture of Rabaul in New Britain as a precursor to a thrust toward the Philippines and Borneo.

MacArthur's task was considerably complicated by the lack of US-Australian military cooperation in the interwar period, even when it became obvious that war in the Pacific was inevitable. As naval historian Tom Frame has noted,

> contact between the RAN and the USN at all levels and in every aspect was piecemeal between 1919 and 1938 despite the need for a closer relationship between the two navies. Even though the USN would provide the bulk of the defence for Australia's immediate region in the event that Britain was occupied with Germany and Europe, there was no plan for cooperation in naval defence and no agreed strategy for joint operations.[82]

Frame's observation regarding the lack of cooperation between the two navies was reflective of US-Australian interwar military interaction in general. There had been no prewar exchanges of personnel at the operational level, strategic-level talks had only started in 1940 and were very limited, and there was no joint planning, no war-gaming of possible military scenarios, and no common military doctrine or functions for cooperation. It was a poor foundation from which to derive a relationship in the turmoil of war.

2

MacArthur's Retreat and Resurrection

The Establishment and High Command of the Southwest Pacific Area

ON 17 MARCH 1942, GEN. DOUGLAS MACARTHUR stepped defeated but triumphant from a USAAF B-17 onto Batchelor Airfield, forty miles south of Darwin in northern Australia. While he had been forced to retreat from the Philippines, he now stood ready to seek redemption by leading the US charge to victory in the Pacific.

In true MacArthur style, he awarded each member of the plane's crew a Silver Star Medal, inspected a ragtag honor guard that had been hastily organized, and then inquired about the "powerful" American army that he believed had been organized in Australia for his "return to the Philippines." After making his way to South Australia, MacArthur addressed a knot of reporters who had gathered to greet him, stating, "The President of the United States ordered me to break through the Japanese lines and proceed from Corregidor to Australia for the purpose, as I understand it, of organizing the American offensive against Japan, a primary objective of which is the relief of the Philippines. I came through and I shall return."[1] This statement is fascinating in what it reveals about MacArthur's intentions. It makes no mention of Australia, other than the fact that the president had ordered him there, it pays no heed to the security or defense of the nation in which he found himself standing, and he spoke only of the "American offensive" rather than an Allied one for victory against Japan.

Despite this initial bravado, MacArthur's confidence had already been sapped as the realization of the magnitude of his defeat in the Philippines sank in. On arrival in Adelaide, MacArthur had been met by his deputy chief of staff, Brig. Gen. Richard Marshall. Marshall revealed that there was no US army in Australia awaiting the great general. Rather, there were only some twenty-five thousand US troops in country at that time, and most of them were USAAF personnel. There was not a single rifleman among them.[2]

At this time, the US Army in Australia had no tanks and no heavy artillery, and most of its combat aircraft were obsolescent and in poor condition. There was also little likelihood that large numbers of US combat units would be forthcoming any time soon. To compound his problems, MacArthur soon discovered that Australia, his newfound coalition partner, had lost one of its few highly trained infantry divisions in Singapore and the islands to Australia's north. The remainder of its elite all-volunteer army formations, the 2nd Australian Imperial Force (2nd AIF), along with a considerable number of its air force squadrons and naval units, were either staying in the Middle East or only just making their way to the Pacific. At home, Australia's defenses were manned by a poorly trained and ill-equipped conscripted militia. It was also clear that the US troops at Bataan and Corregidor in the Philippines were doomed: "MacArthur was dumbfounded. The color drained from his face. His knees shook. His lips twitched. For a long time he was unable to speak. When he finally regained control of his body and his emotions, all he could do was whisper hoarsely, 'God have mercy on us!'"[3]

ABDA AND THE INITIAL MOVES IN THE PACIFIC

After the start of the Pacific War, disaster after disaster befell the Allies. The heavy damage to the US Pacific Fleet at Pearl Harbor on 7 December 1941 was followed on the tenth by the sinking of the British battleship *Prince of Wales* and the battlecruiser *Repulse* off Malaya. These two naval defeats meant that the Japanese would be able to exert sea control over the majority of the Pacific Ocean for the rest of 1941 and the first six months of 1942. This was a major advantage to the Japanese as they launched their amphibious assaults on Malaya, the Philippines, Guam, Wake Island, the Netherlands East Indies (NEI), the Bismarck Sea, and the South Pacific to secure the southern resources area and establish their "Greater East Asia Co-Prosperity Sphere."[4]

In the wake of these disasters and with the need to coordinate the forces of a number of different countries across the Pacific region, the Allies moved quickly to establish a command and organizational structure. One of the first moves was to establish a combined HQ for the control of the Allied forces in the Philippines, Malaya, the NEI, Australia, and New Zealand. From December 18 to the twentieth, a conference was held in Singapore between the Allies, out of which developed a proposal by Col. Francis Brink (US Army) for a combined headquarters to coordinate the

Allied forces in this region. Brink suggested that it should be based in Java. The idea was soon picked up by senior commanders and policymakers in Washington in the period just before the First Washington Conference (code-named Arcadia) between the British prime minister, Winston Churchill, and the US president, Franklin Roosevelt.[5]

During the Arcadia discussions (22 December 1941–1 January 1942), both Hong Kong and Manila fell to the Japanese as they continued their unrelenting advance through the Pacific. One of the key decisions of this conference was the creation of the American and British Combined Chiefs of Staff (CCS) to set the overall direction of the Allied war effort. At the conference, the CCS produced a resolution on "interim guidance for the various commands," and this was adopted "as Allied strategy." For the Pacific, this resolution stated that Allied strategy was:

(a) To *hold* the Malay Barrier . . . as the basic defensive position in that Far East theatre, and to operate sea, land, and air forces in as great depth as possible forward of the Barrier in order to oppose the Japanese southward advance.

(b) To *hold* Burma and Australia as essential supporting positions for the theatre and Burma as essential to the support of China, and to the defense of India.

(c) To *re-establish* communications through the Dutch East Indies with Luzon and to *support* the Philippines' Garrison.

(d) To *maintain* essential communications within the theatre.[6]

One of the major features of this statement was that while it committed to "holding" Malaya, Burma, and Australia, the CCS was only willing to "support" MacArthur in the Philippines. So, while the US JCS and especially the US Army were to support MacArthur as much as possible, they were conceding that the likely success of ongoing resistance in the Philippines was low.

In order to enact the Arcadia conference resolutions, the CCS established ABDA to direct operations of all Allied forces in the general area of Burma, Malaya, the NEI, the Philippines, western New Guinea, and northwestern Australia.[7] While this was the first iteration of an Allied combined headquarters, and as such as it was in many ways innovative and farsighted, "ABDA's existence was painful and short-lived." It was to be an "unsuccessful band of brothers."[8]

ABDA was under the command of Sir Archibald Wavell, a third-generation British Army general officer who had most recently been the British commander in the Middle East before being moved to the position of C-in-C India. Now fifty-eight years old, Wavell was "known to his soldiers as Archie, and to his officers as Guinea-a-Word Wavell," a nickname given to him "because he spoke so little."[9] He is often referred to as one of Britain's finest generals, but no matter how intelligent or capable an officer he was, ABDA would prove to be beyond the scope of any commander. Wavell's first major issue was that his command scope was limited. Although he was the C-in-C, ABDA was more about unity of effort than joint command, with each national component being able to exert considerable control over its own forces. It was also a command in which the full weight of divergent national priorities would take precedence over any common goal.[10]

Coalition politics in relation to command and representation would also be a key feature of ABDA. Sensibilities over positions within the command structure caused immediate problems with Cdr. V. E. Kennedy, a RAN staff officer in the ABDA HQ, observing that after the initial composition of the HQ was announced, there was "considerable and rather unfavorable criticism by the local press" regarding the lack of Dutch military officers in either high command or positions on Wavell's staff. In addition, while Wavell's staff and the ABDA air and naval staffs were colocated in the one building in Lembang for ease of coordination, the C-in-C of the NEI Army was "situated in Bandoeng, about 10 miles" away.[11]

Wavell's initial deputy was Lt. Gen. George H. Brett (USAAF), who was also to play an influential role in relation to the establishment of the US Army in Australia during 1942. Adm. Thomas C. Hart (USN), "a weather-beaten energetic seaman, who is said to have—when roused by inefficiency—a seaman's gift of profanity,"[12] had been US Asiatic Fleet commander in the Philippines. Despite having reached retirement age, he was named naval commander at the request of the US president. The Dutch officer Lt. Gen. H. Ter Poorten was the land forces commander, and Air Marshal Sir Richard Peirse (RAF) the air commander. Wavell formally assumed command on 15 January.[13]

Wavell's ABDA command would last less than two months. This period was to see continued setbacks in the Allied effort to slow or stop the relentless Japanese advance. The Japanese had invaded the NEI via Borneo on 11 January 1942, four days before Wavell took formal command of ABDA. Soon after, Wavell concluded that there was no hope of supporting MacArthur in the Philippines, that he was hopefully to hold Singapore, and that Burma should hold out but that Borneo and the

Celebes were lost and the Japanese would attempt to cut the supply line between Australia and the NEI.[14]

The Japanese were superbly positioned. They had sea control and air superiority throughout most of the area, and they had gained and maintained the initiative. ABDA responded to the moves against Borneo and the Celebes with air and naval forces that saw two naval surface actions in mid- to late January with some success, but they were unable to stop the Japanese invasion. Wavell's chances of holding Java were, however, boosted on 26 January when Lt. Gen. John Lavarack, the general officer commanding (GOC) I Australian Corps, and his brigadier general staff (BGS), Brig. Frank Berryman, arrived in country with a small advance party.[15] Lavarack's position included that of senior Australian officer in the ABDA. Unfortunately for Lavarack and his headquarters staff, by the time they arrived in Batavia on 26 January the details of this post had not been resolved by the Australian government.[16]

Lavarack and Berryman were also dismayed at the briefings that they received from Wavell and Ter Poorten about the general situation in ABDA and in particular the role that their corps was given in holding the "southern end of Sumatra and the middle belt of Java."[17] By this time, conditions in ABDA had started to deteriorate rapidly, but not everyone understood the gravity of the situation. As one Australian officer noted, for many officers in ABDA's HQ an "Alice in Wonderland [view of the] situation" prevailed.[18]

Lavarack and Berryman, like all the national contingents, had one eye on the events unfolding in ABDA and the other on the potential repercussions to their own nation's security. A few days after their arrival, the corps intelligence staff, under Berryman's direction, produced an appreciation that stated the bulk of the I Australian Corps troops "cannot arrive and establish themselves . . . *in time* to hold and save [Sumatra and Java] . . . from capture by the Japanese. That if a portion arrives before the enemy attack, this portion will be lost . . . and bearing in mind the time factor, the defence and safety of Australia itself is being jeopardised."[19] This report and its findings would have a major impact on the role and destination of I Australian Corps, which would eventually end up in Australia rather than Java, subsequently allowing it to play a critical role in the Papua campaign in the SWPA in the second half of 1942, rather than going into captivity.

On 31 January 1942, the British and Australian forces abandoned the Malayan Peninsula and withdrew to Singapore Island, which meant that the collapse of ABDA was almost inevitable. Singapore fell on

15 February 1942, and the "Malaya barrier" started to disintegrate. The Japanese invaded Bali on 18 February, and the following day they bombed Darwin in order to cover their occupation of Timor on 20 February. Despite being vastly outnumbered at sea and in the air, ABDA naval forces had attempted to intercept the Java invasion force, which led to the Battle of the Java Sea on 27 February 1942. The Dutch lost two cruisers, *De Ruyter* and *Java*, and the surviving ships, which included the light cruiser HMAS *Perth* and the heavy cruiser USS *Houston*, pulled back to Batavia but were lost the following evening in the Sunda Strait.[20]

Meanwhile, events for I Australian Corps on Java had become complicated. The fall of Singapore and the pending invasion of the rest of the NEI before the bulk of the Australia troops could arrive meant that the imminent landing of the corps in Sumatra and Java was out of the question.[21] This led Lavarack to recommend to the Australian government that the convoys carrying his troops be sent straight to Australia. However, an advance element of the corps had arrived in Java aboard the fast transport *Orcades*, and despite the fact that Wavell had cabled London on 16 February that the loss of Java "would not be fatal" and that the AIF should be diverted to Burma, he insisted that the *Orcades* troops should be disembarked and used in the defense of the island.[22]

I Australia Corps HQ was bitterly opposed to Wavell's order. However, once Wavell had these troops off the ship, Lavarack lacked the authority to order them to reembark, and he referred the decision to the Australian government. Meanwhile, Berryman noted in his diary that "ROME BURNS WHILE NERO FIDDLES."[23] The *Orcades* issue was considered by the War Cabinet in Australia on 16, 18, and 19 February, while in the meantime the troops disembarked, and the 2,920 men ashore were named "Blackforce."

When ABDA was dissolved a few days later, on 22 February, Lavarack had departed by air for Australia and Berryman had boarded *Orcades* with the majority of the I Australian Corps staff to rejoin the convoy carrying the Australian troops home, while Blackforce was ordered by the British CCS to stay and fight on. The vast majority of these troops surrendered to the Japanese on 12 March 1942 and became prisoners of war (POWs). Lavarack saw the loss of Blackforce as a "flagrant betrayal" of the troops and a consequence of the indecision of the Australian government.[24] The senior Australian staff officer on Wavell's HQ, Maj. Gen. Charles "Gaffer" Lloyd, believed that Wavell's decision to disembark Blackforce in Java, despite the hopeless situation, was a clear case of "political influence on military dispositions."[25]

Despite some hard fighting on the part of the Allies and some very heavy Allied losses, ABDA had not been much more than a speed bump in the path of the unrelenting Japanese advance. General Wavell noted that it was a gallant effort by the ABDA forces and that he "deeply regret[ted the] failure to hold [the] Abda Area," but "it was a race against time and the enemy was too quick for us."[26] Historian Samuel Eliot Morison noted that the end came with the loss of *Perth* and *Houston*, which meant that the US Asiatic Fleet, and by extension ABDA, "seldom tasted victory. . . . [Rather] it drank from the cup of defeat to the bitter dregs."[27] In the end, ABDA was a command that was beset with problems. It faced a vastly superior military force with a scratch coalition of disparate forces from nations with few resources and poor communication. These coalition forces lacked a common doctrine, culture, and set of operational procedures. All of these factors combined meant that it was, in reality, a forlorn hope.

THE ANZAC AREA AND THE ATTEMPTS TO REINFORCE THE PHILIPPINES

While the Australians had committed troops to both the defense of Malaya and Singapore and ground-force elements and naval assets to ABDA, Australian forces were also engaged in the islands to Australia's north and northeast. Only two-thirds of the 8th Australian Division had deployed to Malaya and Singapore, and the rest of the division had been split up to occupy Rabaul, Ambon, and Timor. Ambon was garrisoned by a battalion group known as Gull Force, which, along with twenty-six hundred Dutch troops, would fight a rear-guard action over four days against a Japanese invasion force between 31 January and 3 February 1942. Timor was invaded on 20 February 1942, with the Japanese looking to secure an airfield within fighter range of Darwin. Fourteen hundred Australians of Sparrow Force fought the Japanese for three days in some fierce actions that included Japanese paratroopers. But against overwhelming odds and faced with annihilation, the bulk of the Australian force surrendered.[28]

The 2/2nd Independent (Commando) Company would fight a guerrilla campaign against the Japanese on Timor until it was reinforced with the 2/4th Independent Company in September 1942. The Japanese then reinforced their presence on the island to twelve thousand troops, and from December 1942 the Australians started to wind down their presence, with the bulk of the troops withdrawn in December 1942 and January

1943 and the last Australian servicemen withdrawn by the USN sub-marine *Gudgeon* on 10 February 1943, a year after the initial Japanese occupation.[29]

Rabaul was the most significant of these island redoubts. Located on the northern end of New Britain, it was a critical port and airfield situated in the gateway to Australia through the Southwest Pacific. As noted in chapter 1, Rabaul had been part of the US war plan Rainbow Three. In addition, a US-Australia Joint Defence Board (which included discussions with New Zealand) had been working on areas of mutual interest in the Pacific from 1940, a matter that had been speculated on in the American press in late 1940 and leaked to the press in New York and Japan in February 1941. However, the Australian government was unwilling to confirm these reports, as it wished to ensure that "America . . . continue to act on the assumption that American defence policy . . . [was] based on American interests."[30]

In October 1941, an agreement had been reached for US reinforcements to go to Rabaul, but these had not arrived by the time the Japanese were ready to strike. Instead, the Japanese arrived off Rabaul on 23 January 1942 with a five-thousand-man invasion force made up of Maj. Gen. Tomitaro Horii's South Seas Force, backed up by heavy IJN support. Rabaul had been under air attack since 4 January 1942, which had all but "wiped out" No. 24 Squadron RAAF, and by the time of the invasion it had only a couple of obsolescent Wirraway training aircraft and one Hudson bomber left.[31] The Australian ground forces consisted of only one battalion group of fourteen hundred men under Col. J. J. Scanlan, and without air or naval support they quickly succumbed to the Japanese invasion force. The majority of the Australians went into captivity or escaped into the interior of New Britain. One hundred and sixty POWs were murdered by the Japanese at Tol Plantation, while four hundred men were rescued from the island in late March and early April.[32] The Japanese set about turning Rabaul and its excellent harbor into a major base. Rabaul was soon to become Japan's unsinkable aircraft carrier from which they could project power into the South Pacific. The recapture (later isolation) of Rabaul would occupy the Allied war effort in the region for the next two years.

According to the US official history, "the fall of Rabaul had alarmed the Australians like nothing else."[33] These concerns arose from the fact that, at the time of its fall, the organization for ABDA was still incomplete. Australia and New Zealand had been excluded from the first ABDA proposal, but eventually, on 24 January, ABDA was extended to include

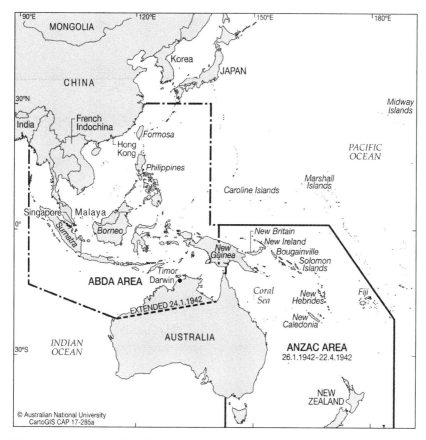

Figure 2.1 ABDA and ANZAC Areas, 1941–1942

Darwin and areas of northern Australia.[34] This gave Australia more of a measure of protection from the northwest, but the "Northeast was now virtually unprotected."[35]

In response, the Australian government protested over the exclusion of Australian waters from the US naval zone in the Pacific. The inclusion of Australia in this area was pushed by both the governments of Australia and Britain and accepted by the USN's C-in-C and chief of naval operations (CNO), Adm. Ernest King. As a consequence, a naval force under the C-in-C USN was directed to operate in what was known as the ANZAC Naval Area.[36] This area included the bulk of the Australian continent, New Zealand, New Guinea, New Britain, Bougainville, the Solomon Islands, Nauru, New Caledonia, and Fiji.

This force, under the command of Vice Adm. Herbert F. Leary (USN), was to initially consist of one British aircraft carrier, two USN cruisers and destroyers, two New Zealand cruisers and one New Zealand armed merchant ship, and, from the RAN, two heavy cruisers, one light cruiser, three armed merchant ships, two destroyers, and a number of antisubmarine vessels. The rest of the RAN vessels (two cruisers and five destroyers) were allocated to ABDA. Rear Adm. John Crace (RN), commanding the Australian Squadron, was to command the ANZAC squadron afloat.[37]

The ANZAC naval forces took a while to form. The promised British carrier never arrived, and the Australian squadron on formation consisted of only the heavy cruiser HMAS *Australia*. Another heavy cruiser, USS *Chicago*, two New Zealand light cruisers, HMNZ *Achilles* and *Leander*, and two US destroyers soon reinforced *Australia*. During February and March, Leary was to receive major reinforcements in the form of the aircraft carrier USS *Lexington*; four US heavy cruisers, *Minneapolis*, *Indianapolis*, *Pensacola*, and *San Francisco*; and ten destroyers.[38] What was especially significant about the creation of the ANZAC Naval Area in relation to the future role of Australia in US strategy in the Pacific was the view of USN C-in-C Admiral King. The Australian minister to the United States, Richard Casey, reported that King

> tends to be very interested and conscientious regarding areas for which he is definitely responsible . . . [and] he makes little or no distinction in his mind between his responsibility for the Pacific area as a whole (exercised through his subordinate commanders at Honolulu) and his responsibility for A.N.Z.A.C. area (through Leary). Under present conditions northern and eastern boundaries of the A.N.Z.A.C. area mean very little to him, and if A.N.Z.A.C. area command remains as it is he is likely to operate considerable United States naval forces (drawn from Honolulu) in or close to A.N.Z.A.C. area (as he has done lately) in addition to forces officially designated to A.N.Z.A.C. area.[39]

Other moves were also afoot in relation to Australia and its relevance to US Pacific strategy. For the US military, the bulk of its commitment to the broader Pacific region during this period, other than its extensive naval operations in ABDA and now the ANZAC Naval Area, came from the continuing resistance of MacArthur's forces in the Philippines.

Wavell and ABDA had direct responsibility for the Philippines, and he saw MacArthur's task as hopeless. To ABDA, the most significant role that MacArthur's forces could play was to delay the Japanese offensive across the Pacific and tie up a large Japanese force for as long as possible. In the United States, though, there was some glimmer of hope, and the urge to try to support MacArthur, the one US commander in contact with the enemy, was overwhelming in some quarters.

MacArthur had been praised as a war hero in the American press, and he had demanded relief for his besieged army. In addition, President Roosevelt had publicly proclaimed his support for MacArthur and the Philippines. He also made this clear to Richard Casey. Roosevelt told Casey on 17 December that he "regarded the defence of the Philippines as one of the real key points in the Far Eastern situation and said that [the US military was] doing everything possible to get air reinforcements to the Philippines by all available methods. He said that he regarded, and they hoped to use, Australia as a bridge-head and base."[40] Roosevelt wrote to Secretary of War Henry Stimson on 30 December 1941 that he wished to explore "every possible means of relieving the Philippines."[41] The US Army had also changed its position in mid-1941. Rather than conceding the Philippines, it now started to plan to hold out against a Japanese invasion for an extended period.

As Roosevelt had noted to Casey, Australia was the key to US plans to reinforce the Philippines. With the Japanese in control of their mandated territories in the Central Pacific since 1919, Australia was the logical location for an American advanced base through which these reinforcements could stage. The same day that Roosevelt had spoken to Casey, Marshall had approved Brig. Gen. Dwight D. Eisenhower's plans for the establishment of this base.

The first stage would be the establishment of an air line of communication, so a senior USAAF officer, General Brett, was placed in command (he would also soon become the deputy C-in-C in ABDA). While the forces under Brett's command would be a part of MacArthur's USAAF in the Far East, it was, as the US official history noted, evident that the establishment of Brett's command "implied a more comprehensive [US] strategy in the Southwest Pacific."[42] It was a decision wholeheartedly supported by the Australian government. As early as 23 December 1941, the Australian prime minister made it clear to his representative in Washington that with three infantry divisions serving in the Middle East and airmen fighting in Britain and the Middle East (as well as training in Canada), and after Australia had "sent great quantities supplies to Britain, Middle East and India [its] resources here are very limited. . . . [With] reinforcements earmarked by United Kingdom Government for despatch seem[ing] to us to be utterly inadequate [Australia would] gladly accept a United States commander in Pacific area."[43]

This decision also led to a conclusion as to the destination of the Pensacola convoy. This convoy (named after the cruiser escorting the force), carrying reinforcements for the US Army in the Philippines via the South Pacific route, had been ordered to put in at Suva, Fiji, on 8 December 1941. The convoy had been part of the reinforcements pledged to the defense of the Philippines as part of the US Army's decision in mid-1941 to try to hold the islands in the event of a Japanese attack. After 7 December, debate raged in Washington as to the convoy's destination. Should it attempt to break through to Manila, return to the United States, or be rerouted elsewhere? The original decision had sent the convoy back toward Hawaii. However, on 10 December, the US Joint Services Board decided that the convoy should head for Brisbane and wait there until the means could be found to send it forward to the Philippines.[44]

The Pensacola convoy thus carried the first US troops to Australia. It docked in Brisbane on 22 December 1941, and there it would stay. Soon after its arrival, the USN told MacArthur that it was not possible to send the troops forward to reinforce the Philippines, and Admiral King urged that the troops be used to support the defense of the NEI, Australia, and, in particular, Darwin. Under Eisenhower's plan, the troops from the convoy became the first designated units of the United States Army Forces in Australia (USAFIA), essentially an air and supply command. Brett, who was then in Chungking, would take command with Col. Stephen J. Chamberlin, who was later to become the highly influential operations officer at MacArthur's SWPA HQ, as his chief of staff.

With the dissolution of ABDA, Brett moved to Australia, and while the ANZAC naval force was still in the process of forming, the Australians were concerned about the overall direction of the defense of the area. On 26 February 1942, the Australian and New Zealand chiefs of staff and General Brett, as the commanding general USAFIA, reviewed the situation in the Pacific. Brett advised the Australian prime minister that the Allies (or "United Nations," as he referred to them) "are not just defending Australia. They are fighting Japan. The primary objective in defending Australia and New Zealand is to provide bases for offensive action against Japan. They should formulate a strategical plan, develop the production of their material requirements and organise their resources so that they will be able to deal an effective blow against the enemy."[45] The Australian and New Zealand chiefs of staff emphasized that their countries were in danger of attack but also agreed with Brett that there was a need to plan for offensive action with Australia and New Zealand as bases.[46] This reiterated the Australian War Cabinet's view of 18 February that noted the "importance of building Australia as the main base in the South West Pacific for development of counter-offensive action against Japan with American assistance."[47] The chiefs of staff appreciation also suggested that the best way to achieve this was to replace the ANZAC Naval Area with a joint-service ANZAC Area with an American as the supreme commander.

Just over a week later, the Australian War Cabinet decided that it would welcome General Brett as the supreme commander of this proposed ANZAC Area.[48] The Australian government went so far as to draft a formal communiqué outlining the supreme commander's roles and responsibilities, and sent it off to the secretary of state for Dominion affairs in London and to the New Zealand prime minister. In the document, the Australian government proposed a coalition of ANZAB nations (Australia, New Zealand, America, and Britain) to contribute to the ANZAC Area and followed both Brett's and the Australian chiefs' suggestions as to the basic strategy and responsibilities.[49]

While the Australian government was maneuvering to solidify US cooperation in the defense of the region, Task Force 6184 under Brig. Gen. Alexander Patch (US Army) arrived in Melbourne. It included some four thousand USAAF and service troops for Australia; however, the bulk of his forces—some fifteen thousand troops from elements of the 26th and 33rd US Infantry Divisions—were shipped out to secure New Caledonia on 6 March 1942.[50] This force was part of a broader US commitment to station troops along the Hawaii-Australia axis, and New Caledonia was deemed important because it was "the logical target of [any] Japanese attempt to gain control of the northern and eastern approaches to Australia and New Zealand because it was large enough to be strongly held and contained important nickel mines."[51] Small US garrisons were also sent to Bora Bora, Christmas Island, Canton Island, and Fiji.

In addition to the dissolution of ABDA and the debate over an ANZAC Area, February 1942 saw two major defining events for Australia and the war in the SWPA. The first of these was the debate over the destination of I Australian Corps. After it was agreed that its deployment to the NEI was not viable, a vigorous debate ensued between British prime minister Winston Churchill and Australian prime minister John Curtin over its destination. Churchill had ordered the convoy carrying the Australian troops to divert to Burma and then informed the Australian government of his decision. Curtin, however, was adamant that the troops should return to Australia in order to defend the continent and the island chain to the northeast of Australia from the Japanese.[52]

Churchill's unilateral move to reroute the convoy without reference to the Australian government was highly presumptuous, arrogant, and disrespectful of Australian sovereignty. It was also militarily unsound, as the proposed location for disembarking the troops, Rangoon, was directly in the path of the advancing Japanese troops who were rampaging through Burma. The landing of I Australian Corps at Rangoon would have been a repeat of the *Orcades* incident all over again, but this time an entire army corps, as opposed to a small brigade, was proposed to be unceremoniously dumped, unsupported, in front of the Japanese, putting it at grave risk of being cut off and forced into captivity. Curtin's steadfast opposition to Churchill saved the corps from almost certain captivity and meant that it would play a critical role in the fighting in Papua from mid-1942.

The other significant event at this time was the bombing of Darwin. This was the first-ever attack on Australian soil by a foreign power and a defining moment for the Australian War Cabinet, convincing them that I Australian Corps must be returned home—a course of action that Churchill acceded to only after a series of increasingly curt cablegrams.[53]

COMMAND AND STRATEGY IN THE PACIFIC

With the dissolution of ABDA, the bombing of Darwin, and the return of I Australian Corps to Australia, it was imperative that a new command structure be set up to ensure the protection and security of Australia and the surrounding region. President Roosevelt mused that Australia must be defended at all cost, and with the British Empire on its knees it was clear that the United States must bear this burden. At Arcadia, the vast Indo-Pacific theater of war in which the Allies were fighting the Japanese was split between the western section—the Indian Ocean and Southeast Asia, under British command—and the eastern section—the broader Pacific Ocean, including Oceania and Australasia, under US command. Even with this division, the Pacific was an enormous theater of war covering over sixty million square miles.

The first task for the US president and his senior commanders would be to organize a US command structure in the Pacific. To many, the obvious choice for a C-in-C for the entire Pacific theater was MacArthur, but Admiral King, the USN C-in-C, was bitterly opposed to such a move, and there was no compromise candidate acceptable to both the US Army and USN to take joint command of the Pacific. In particular, the admirals saw the Pacific as "their" theater of war.[54] They had spent the interwar decades preparing plans and developing capabilities for the defeat of Japan, and as the topography would dictate a maritime strategy, they were loath to entrust their aircraft carriers, battleships, and Marines to an army commander. The USN's problem was that its top commander in the region, the new C-in-C of the Pacific Fleet, Adm. Chester Nimitz, was very junior in rank to MacArthur.[55]

The solution to this problem was compromise. King suggested that the ANZAC Area be expanded to include the portions of ABDA still in Allied hands and that a new theater be created. Meanwhile, the Australian suggestion for a new ANZAC theater had made it, via the Dominion Office, to the CCS, which simply passed it on to the US JCS, which had been delegated command of the Pacific. At this point it seemed both Marshall and King were set on carving out two theaters in the Pacific, so the real battle became one over the boundaries of these new theaters. This resolution would mean a split in the command of the US Pacific War into the POA under Admiral Nimitz and the SWPA under General MacArthur.[56] The lack of a unified command structure would plague the development of operations in the broader Pacific for the remainder of the war. Here interservice rivalry and personal egos triumphed over sound military practice.

Admiral Nimitz served as overall commander of the US Pacific Fleet and the POA. The POA was then subdivided into three commands: the North Pacific Area (NPA), the Central Pacific Area (CPA), and the South Pacific Area (SOPAC). The most important of these areas in the early part of the Pacific War would be SOPAC, which was situated alongside Mac-Arthur's SWPA. SOPAC would initially be commanded by Vice Adm. Robert L. Ghormley and, from October 1942, Vice Adm. William Halsey. The SOPAC commander would report to Nimitz, whose own chain of command was to the JCS through the chief of the navy and chief of naval operations, Admiral King. MacArthur, theater strategic commander in the SWPA and Nimitz's army equivalent, would, meanwhile, report to the JCS through the chief of staff of the US Army, Gen. George C. Marshall.[57]

This division would also mean a constant battle over strategy in the Pacific. The USN favored the direct route to the Japanese homelands through the Central Pacific that it had war-gamed in War Plan Orange. This would give the navy plenty of room to maneuver its fast carrier groups and to force the Japanese into a Mahanian-style climatic naval battle to decide the war. The US Army favored going through MacArthur's SWPA. While this was a more indirect route, the army argued that this would allow the Allies to exploit the resources, manpower, and secure base of Australia and the larger land forms on this route, including New Guinea—the second largest island in the world. The large islands of the Philippines archipelago would also allow them enough room to deploy large-scale formations of the US and Australian armies, cut the Japanese supply line to the NEI, and reclaim the Philippines, and with it US honor.

The decision to divide the command and violate the principle of unity of effort and concentration of force in the Pacific was the "price to preserve inter-service harmony."[58] There were, however, benefits to this strategy. In particular, it kept the Japanese off balance as to where the next blow would fall and which of the arms of this dual drive was the main Allied effort. However, it also meant that there was no single commander to coordinate the efforts of these two drives against Japan. Rather, there would be coordination and cooperation rather than unity of command.

This meant that the JCS was in fact the command authority for the Pacific War. As the JCS was not an operational headquarters with a full staff but rather a committee, major decisions could only be made after lengthy debate, discussion, and negotiation, which ultimately led to command by compromise. If this committee was deadlocked—which it frequently was—the sole command responsibility belonged to the US president.[59] Williamson Murray has noted that such a command structure is typical of military organizations that generally "reach decisions by corporate agreement." He notes, however, that "there are few institutions in human life more dysfunctional in reaching clear, distinct, purposeful direction than committees. If true for life in general, the terrible challenges of war multiply the fundamental flaws inherent in human nature and character."[60] The other major consequence for this haphazard and inefficient command organization was that it prompted competition for scarce resources. As Ronald Spector argues, this competition was based on "the traditional elements of careerism and doctrinal differences within the armed forces [that] combined to produce a monstrosity."[61]

MACARTHUR, CURTIN, AND THE ESTABLISHMENT OF THE SWPA

The exact details of MacArthur's role and authority would take some time to evolve. President Roosevelt had ordered MacArthur out of the Philippines on 26 February 1942, and, after some delay, he arrived in

Australia on 17 March. His appointment as supreme commander of the SWPA was to be requested by the Australian government, though prompted from Marshall via Brett. On 17 March, Prime Minister Curtin cabled the Australian minister to the United States that

> General Douglas MacArthur having arrived in Australia the Commonwealth Government desire to nominate him as Supreme Commander of the Allied forces in this theatre. His heroic defence in the Philippine Islands has evoked the admiration of the world and has been an example of the stubborn resistance with which the advance of the enemy should be opposed. The Australian Government feels that his leadership of the Allied forces in this theatre will be an inspiration to the Australian people and all the forces who will be privileged to serve under his command.[62]

MacArthur's arrival was, according to one of his biographers, Geoffrey Perret, "like a promise written in flame across the azure antipodean sky."[63] While a little ornate in his prose, Perret was correct in noting that MacArthur's arrival had an immediate and positive impact on Australian morale, both in the government and among the people.

On arrival, MacArthur was hailed in the Australian press as the "Napoleon of Luzon"[64] who had commanded the "heroic resistance on the Bataan Peninsula"[65] and as an officer whose "knowledge of military history is so profound and his memory so prodigious that he almost overawes subordinates."[66] Gen. Gordon Bennett, who like MacArthur had escaped from his command to avoid captivity at the hands of the Japanese but without a direct order to do so, noted on his arrival that "MacArthur's stand in the Philippines has stamped him as a man with the fighting spirit which is so much needed at the moment, and which will be extremely welcome to the people of Australia particularly."[67] The positive sentiments of his appointment were also shared by the populace of the United States, with the Melbourne newspaper *Argus* reporting that "news of the appointment was announced in big headlines in papers throughout USA, and the welcome tidings were taken up by news commentators over the radio, all of whom joined in the chorus of acclamation."[68]

The praise was widespread in Australia. The Sydney newspaper the *Sun* argued that "no war leader has made a more decisive impact upon the imagination of the English-speaking world than General Douglas MacArthur."[69] Such high praise went way over the top, and it drove senior American officials to consider how much this rapturous welcome was actually a reflection of anxiety in Australia over its wartime management. Earle R. Dickover, the American consul general in Melbourne, noted to the American minister in Canberra, Nelson T. Johnson, that MacArthur's arrival "evoked such enthusiasm among the press and public of this district to imply a serious lack of confidence on the part of the Australian people on the ability of their own British and Australian military leaders."[70] They were also concerned that the arrival of MacArthur and US troops would mean that the Australian population would feel overly secure and that, as a consequence, it would slacken in its war efforts. In his memoirs, MacArthur recalled that upon arrival he sprang into action: "As quickly as possible I arranged a conference with . . . the Australian Prime Minister John Curtin. . . . I put my arm about his strong shoulder [and said] 'Mr Prime Minister . . . we two, you and I, will see this thing through together. We can do it and we will do it. You take care of the rear and I will handle the front.'"[71]

MacArthur's recollection is indicative of his personality and reputation as one of the more colorful officers in US history. Lt. Col. Gerald Wilkinson, the British liaison officer in the SWPA, described him as "shrewd, proud, remote, highly strung and vastly vain. He has imagination, self-confidence, physical courage and charm, but no humor about himself, no regard to truth, and is unaware of these defects. He mistakes emotions and ambitions for principles. With moral depth he would be a great man; as it is he is a near miss which may be worse than a mile."[72] MacArthur's air force commander, General Brett, would describe him as a "brilliant, temperamental egotist; a handsome man, who can be as charming as anyone who ever lived, or harshly indifferent to the needs and desires of those around him. His religion is deeply part of his nature. . . . Everything about MacArthur is on a grand scale; his virtues and triumphs and shortcomings."[73]

MacArthur was the son of the well-known US Army general Arthur MacArthur and was a West Point graduate (class of 1903). He served in the Philippines as a junior officer and had accompanied his father on a tour of Asia. In 1914, he played a prominent role in the occupation of Veracruz. He served on the western front in 1918 as chief of staff, and later commander of the 42nd Infantry Division, earning the Distinguished Service Cross (twice), the Distinguished Service Medal, and the Silver Star Medal (seven times). In the interwar period, he was chief of staff of the US Army and created the modern Purple Heart Medal (awarding himself the first one).[74] In 1935, MacArthur became military adviser to the Commonwealth of the Philippines and retired from the US Army in 1937, becoming a field marshal in the Philippine Army.[75] During this time, he continually overstated the preparedness of the Philippine military while spending a good portion of his time cultivating close relations with President Manuel Quezon.

Roosevelt federalized the Philippine armed forces on 26 July 1941 and returned MacArthur to active service. His performance in the campaign against the Japanese that followed was less than exemplary. He failed to act decisively on the announcement of the attack on Pearl Harbor. He refused to allow his air force commander, Maj. Gen. Lewis H. Brereton, to launch strikes on Japanese bases on Formosa, which subsequently meant that his own air force units were caught on the ground and suffered serious losses.[76] After the Japanese landing on Luzon, his forces soon fell back to the Bataan Peninsula, where MacArthur unsuccessfully attempted to slow the Japanese advance. On Christmas Eve, he retreated to Corregidor. Here, his soldiers would refer to him as "Dugout Doug," and in one of his more venal moves, on New Year's Day 1942, he accepted a half-million-dollar payment from President Quezon, while a number of his staff also received secret payments.[77]

After MacArthur's escape to Australia, seventy-six thousand of his troops surrendered at Bataan on 9 April 1942 and the remainder at Corregidor on 6 May. It was one of the largest defeats in US military history, and for his inconspicuous command performance MacArthur was awarded the Medal of Honor "to offset any propaganda by the enemy directed at his leaving his command."[78] The awarding of the medal was proposed by Marshall and supported by a number of Republican congressmen, but Marshall convinced Secretary of War Stimson that it would be best if the medal came from the president, who agreed and awarded it to MacArthur on 25 March 1942. Unsurprisingly, given his actual inaction, the medal had more to do with "popular approval" than his actual command performance.[79]

MacArthur and the Australian prime minister, John Curtin, were to form an exceptionally close and mutually supportive relationship over the coming years. Curtin, a Labor Party leader and former trade union official, had little experience in military affairs. He had spent time during World War I as an anticonscription campaigner, became a member of Parliament in 1928 with a focus on "extensive grassroots [political] experience," and it was said that he was "better intellectually prepared than most members who have entered Australian parliament." He lost his seat in Parliament in 1931 but returned in 1934, becoming leader of his party the following year with a pledge to abstain from alcohol, which had plagued him for much of his life.

Curtin came close to an outright victory in the 1940 elections and became prime minister and minister for defense coordination on 7 October 1941, when the coalition government disintegrated.[80] Curtin, while often portrayed by some as having a "wimpish" side, displayed ingenuity, dexterity, and resourcefulness as prime minister.[81] Many laud him, in particular his own party, as the greatest prime minister that Australia has produced. The great irony of the MacArthur-Curtin relationship was that it was between a left-wing, almost socialist Australian prime minister and a conservative, Republican American general—unlikely collaborators in the best of times.

Recollections of the Curtin-MacArthur relationship note a number of important characteristics.[82] Curtin is often represented as a leader heavily pressured by the burden of his wartime role. This has been reinforced by the fact that, like President Roosevelt, he died in office in 1945 just before the war ended. Curtin is often portrayed as an admirable man who worked judiciously to achieve the best outcome for his country while the nation was on the back foot, but it is a representation that, as Peter Edwards has noted, is one of "Australian weakness and incompetence and American strength."[83]

HIGH COMMAND IN THE SOUTHWEST PACIFIC AREA

MacArthur's arrival in Melbourne heralded a major change in the dynamics of Australian strategy and strategic policy. The Australian command structure was completely revised, and where previously the Australian chiefs of staff had been the principal advisers to the Australian government on strategy, they "were now replaced by a foreign general." Their role was now "more administrative than strategy."[84] MacArthur soon took over operational control of all Australian forces in the SWPA and was directly responsible for the defense of the Australian continent. Most significantly, Curtin, supported by his secretary of defense, Fredrick Shedden, "looked to MacArthur as the main source of [strategic] advice."[85] As David Horner has noted, "in placing the Australian forces under MacArthur, the [Australian] Federal government surrendered a large measure of sovereignty, but, considering Australia's limited strength and the magnitude of the Japanese threat, there was no real alternative."[86]

Prior to the arrival of MacArthur, the Australian government had valiantly pressed its case to be involved in the highest levels of authority for the setting of strategy and the conduct of the Pacific War. But as a "very minor power, dependent, anxious and insecure, Australia could not influence high policy."[87] This meant that, as Geoffrey Serle has noted, "it is futile to deplore the loss of Australian sovereignty and the subservience involved" in placing MacArthur in command of Australia's forces and appointing a US officer as the principle military adviser to the Australian government.[88]

In particular, the command arrangements and the relationship between Curtin and MacArthur developed in the manner in which they did as a result of Australia's desire to influence strategic decision making in the Pacific War. Australian representation had been excluded from the CCS and there was no Australian representative on the US JCS. Thus, the Australian government had to find a way to try to influence Allied grand strategy.

Some input was possible for Australia via its representative on the Pacific War Council. The original idea was for this body to sit in London with the committee having access to the British Chiefs of Staff and then through them to the CCS in Washington. But from London it was unclear how this committee could affect the decisions of the JCS or the CCS sitting in Washington. In addition, it was never made clear as to what would happen if the views of the Australians, or any other member of the council, disagreed with the British or the CCS. Thus, the Australian government was rightfully skeptical of this approach from the start.[89]

Australian skepticism over Australia's role in influencing Allied strategy in the Pacific in early 1942 was only reinforced by Churchill's actions during the debate between London and Canberra over the fate of I Australian Corps in February. In particular, Churchill's desire to prioritize Burma over the approaches to Australia and his willingness to order Australian troops around as he saw fit, and only then inform the Australian government of his decision, cemented his bellicose and indifferent views of Australia's strategic interests. These actions made it clear that Churchill had no desire to include Australia, let alone any other country, in the direction of grand strategy.[90]

The final form of the Pacific War Council was established at the end of March 1942 after the Pacific had been divided into British and US commands.[91] The purpose of the council was to give countries such as Australia a voice in the development of strategy in the Pacific, although it never would. The Australians had been hopeful that the council would set strategic policy in the Pacific theater advised by the JCS, but instead the reverse happened. The Pacific War Council did provide Australia, New Zealand, and the Netherlands with a voice on Pacific strategy, but it could only make recommendations to the JCS, and there was no guarantee that its voice would be heard.[92] The British foreign secretary Lord Halifax thought the council was "merely a façade," and Christopher Thorne has noted that the JCS did not attend the meetings, that the council had "no bearing on decision-making," and that "long before the end of the war, the Council's meetings were regarded by most of those taking part as a waste of time."[93]

As a result of the Pacific War Council being only advisory to the JCS, Secretary of Defense Shedden believed that the only way Australia would be able to influence Allied strategy in the Pacific was to use MacArthur's access to the JCS through General Marshall. This path would be highly dependent on the relationship that developed between MacArthur and Curtin. It was fortuitous, then, that from the time of MacArthur's arrival in Melbourne in March 1942, MacArthur had "won the trust and confidence of the government."[94] MacArthur would call Curtin the "heart and soul of Australia" and recalled in his memoirs that he developed with the prime minister "a sense of mutual trust, cooperation and regard that was never once breached by word, thought or deed."[95] Curtin would be one of MacArthur's staunchest political allies, and together they would campaign earnestly, using all channels available, to garner resources for the SWPA.

Under this arrangement, the entire strategic decision-making structure in Australia was recast. As noted, MacArthur became the principal adviser on strategy to the prime minister, and, in turn, he ensured that Curtin would deal with the armed forces in the SWPA only through him. At the Prime Minister's War Conference on 8 April 1942 (after his appointment as C-in-C SWPA but before he took full command of Australia's forces), MacArthur made it clear that he "desired that the Prime Minister should have contact only with the Supreme Commander . . . [and] at the request of the Supreme Commander the reference to a contact between the Commanders of Allied Naval, Army and Air Forces, in paragraph 1 of the Agendum [outlining MacArthur's authority], was deleted."[96] In the same meeting, the Australian Chiefs of Staff were removed from "functioning under the Supreme commander in the operational sphere as this was a matter for the supreme commander." Through this process, MacArthur set himself up as the "de facto field marshal of the Australian armed forces."[97] The one exception to this arrangement was Gen. Sir

Thomas Blamey, who, in his capacity as C-in-C of the Australian Military Forces (AMF) (but not in his concurrent role of commander of Allied Land Forces, SWPA), could deal directly with the prime minister.[98]

The body established to coordinate this strategic decision-making structure was the Prime Minister's War Conference, originally named the "Allied War Council" but changed once power had been consolidated into the hands of MacArthur and Curtin. This body would consist of the prime minister and MacArthur "and such Ministers and Officers as the Prime Minster might summon to attend."[99] This decision cemented MacArthur's position as the main, and virtually the sole, military adviser to the head of the Australian government. The Prime Minister's War Conference would be "the mainspring of the machinery for the higher direction of the war," and beside MacArthur and Curtin the only other person to attend all of the meetings was Secretary Shedden. Even the Australian C-in-C, General Blamey, was excluded, most likely at the behest of Shedden, who saw his absence as a way to "strengthen his own position."[100] This triumvirate of Curtin, MacArthur, and Shedden represented the consolidation of power for strategic policymaking in the SWPA in 1942 and 1943 and cemented MacArthur's hold over Australian strategic policymaking for the rest of the Pacific War.

It was a considerably unique situation. As Shedden noted to MacArthur after the war, the three men found themselves in a situation during 1942 that led Shedden to recall "Disraeli's comment to Lord Derby in 1866 about British Troops in Canada [being] 'an army maintained in a country which does not permit us even to govern it! What an anomaly!' For the South West Pacific Area I would substitute for 'what an anomaly!,' 'what co-operation!' The coincidence of two personalities such as yourself and Mr Curtin was providential."[101]

It is clear from this letter, and a good deal more, that Shedden was an unabashed MacArthur admirer and had fallen under MacArthur's spell during the war. Unfortunately for the long-term direction of Australian war strategy, Shedden despised the C-in-C of the AMF, Blamey, as much as he venerated MacArthur. It was also clear that Curtin, as well as a good many other Australian politicians, would remain admirers of MacArthur even after Australia's strategic interests had departed from the personal crusade of the C-in-C SWPA.

Curtin, Shedden, and a good number of other Australian politicians remained convinced of MacArthur's genuine affection for Australia and remained convinced that he had played a critical role the defense of the nation in 1942. Arthur Calwell, minister of information during the war,

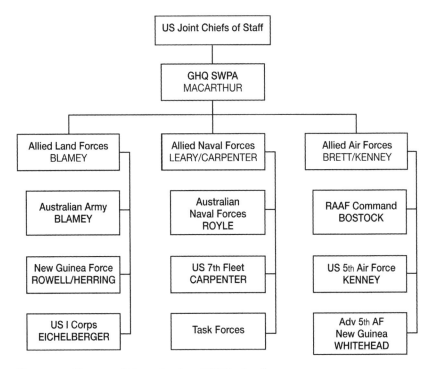

Figure 2.2 Command Organization, SWPA, April 1942

noted that MacArthur "belongs forever in the hearts and history of the Australian people. In the words of the poet, this country, as does his own, owes him 'the debt of immense and endless gratitude.'"[102]

There were, however, to be limits to this new coalition. Despite the rhetoric of Curtin's now infamous article on 27 December 1941, in which he stated that "without any inhibitions of any kind, I make it quite clear that Australia looks to America, free of any pangs as to our traditional links or kinship with the United Kingdom," as well as the decision in March 1942 to appoint MacArthur as his principal military adviser, the country's deep connection to the British Empire remained omnipresent.

As James Curran has revealed, Curtin's rhetoric of moving toward the United States and away from the empire was not matched by either his short- or long-term actions. In fact, he spent considerable time directly after his 27 December article backing away from his "turn" to America. The reality of Curtin's policy was "looking to America . . . anchored in Empire." This was clearly demonstrated in 1943 by his call for a "new approach to Empire."[103] As Clem Lloyd and Richard Hall have noted,

"Curtin may have looked to America without inhibition, but there is no evidence . . . that he did so with enthusiasm."[104] Rather, it was an "expedient call for help at a time when Australia was facing the prospect of a Japanese invasion . . . [and] it was entirely consistent with the orthodox Australian foreign policy of searching for security in the Pacific."[105]

There was also recognition of Curtin's approach by MacArthur and a clear set of limitations to this new coalition from the United States. The supreme commander of the SWPA made it very clear that he saw Australia's turn to America as only temporary and specifically related to the defeat of Japan. At the Prime Minister's War Conference on 1 June 1942, the day after the Japanese midget submarine raid on Sydney Harbor, MacArthur made the following statement to Curtin and Shedden:

> The Commander-in-Chief desired to point out the distinctions between the United States and the United Kingdom in their relations and responsibilities to Australia. Australia was part of the British Empire and it was related to Britain and the other Dominions by ties of blood, sentiment and allegiance to the Crown. *The United States was an ally whose aim was to win the war, and it had no sovereign interest in the integrity of Australia.* . . . The Commander-in-Chief added that, though the American people were animated by a warm friendship for Australia, their purpose in building up forces in the Commonwealth *was not so much from an interest in Australia but rather from its utility as a base from which to hit Japan.* In view of the strategical importance of Australia in a war with Japan, *this course of military action would probably be followed irrespective of the American relationship to the people who might be occupying Australia.*[106]

The limitations of the relationship would remain present during the course of the war, and while Australia's and MacArthur's strategic interests coincided (in 1942 and 1943), the system developed around the Prime Minister's War Conference would work exceptionally effectively. However, cracks would appear at the end of 1943 as the relative weight of the forces of the two countries in the theater changed and MacArthur's plans and Australia's interests started to diverge. Despite these changes, there would be no move to alter the setup for the higher direction of the war in the SWPA, even though, as the war moved farther away from Australia's shores, the Prime Minister's War Conference would meet a lot less frequently, and MacArthur's concern for Australia's perspective on strategy in the SWPA would rapidly diminish.

3

Command and Organization in the Southwest Pacific Area, 1942

It took the US JCS until 30 March to formally establish both of the Pacific commands and even longer for the final arrangements to be clarified. In particular, it took some negotiation and time before MacArthur's power in relation to the Australian forces under his command was clarified. In fact, it was not until midnight on Saturday, 18 April 1942, that all Australian combat units in theater were assigned to MacArthur's command.[1]

During the period of February to April 1942, the command arrangements between the US and Australian forces in the SWPA would be shaken out and the roles and responsibilities set. But directives and structures could only go so far. With the establishment of the SWPA, there had to be a long-term means of coordinating US and Australian military forces in the theater. Militaries that had never worked together before, systems that were not necessarily compatible, and commanders and staffs who did not know each other were driven together by the circumstances of the time—a time when the enemy was on Australia's doorstep and seemingly unstoppable.

MACARTHUR'S COMMAND

MacArthur's directive from the JCS outlined his command and responsibilities. The JCS made him "Supreme Commander" (or "C-in-C," as MacArthur preferred to be called) of all Allied forces in the area irrespective of nationality, although it did note that he was not "eligible to command directly any national force."[2]

He was ordered to hold Australia "as a base for future operations," to "check the Japanese conquest of the Southwest Pacific Area," to secure the lines of communication with Australia by the destruction of the "enemy in Eastern Malaysia and the New Guinea–Bismarck–Solomon Islands Region . . . and prepare to take the offensive."[3] It was a daunting undertaking and, according to one Adelaide newspaper, the most "complex organisational task . . . [that any] United States officer [had] faced . . . in American military history."[4]

To carry out this mission, MacArthur set up General Headquarters (GHQ) to command and exercise authority in the SWPA theater. Despite orders to the contrary, all of the senior staff officers appointed to GHQ were American, and all but three had been with MacArthur in the Philippines. Maj. Gen. Richard Sutherland was chief of staff, with Brig. Gen. Richard Marshall as his deputy. Col. Charles Stivers was the G-1 (personnel), Col. Charles Willoughby G-2 (intelligence), Brig. Gen. Stephen Chamberlin G-3 (operations), Col. Lester J. Whitlock G-4 (logistics), Brig. Gen. Spencer Akin the chief signals officer, Brig. Gen. Hugh Casey the chief engineer, Brig. Gen. William Marquat the antiaircraft officer, and Col. Burdette Fitch the adjutant general.[5] Only Chamberlin, who had been Brett's chief of staff, and Whitlock and Fitch, who had served in the USAFIA, had not been with MacArthur at Corregidor.[6]

MacArthur's refusal to appoint any Australian officers was in direct violation of the directive issued to him for the establishment of the SWPA, which stated that "your staff *will* include officers assigned by the respective governments concerned, based upon requests made directly to the national commanders of the various forces in your Area."[7] It was also in opposition to the chief of the US Army, George Marshall, who repeatedly urged MacArthur to appoint Australian and Dutch officers to his staff. MacArthur, however, refused to budge, and this meant that his HQ would stand in stark contrast to the approach Eisenhower would take when he established Supreme Headquarters Allied Expeditionary Force to command the European Theater of Operations. To the RAAF, RAN, and AMF, it was an inauspicious start to their relationship with the C-in-C SWPA.

Underneath GHQ, MacArthur had three senior commanders: commander of Allied Naval Forces (ANF), commander of Allied Air Forces (AAF), and commander of Allied Land Forces (ALF). The first two commands were placed under US officers Vice Adm. Herbert F. Leary, who had commanded the ANZAC Force from 27 January 1942, which was now absorbed into the SWPA command, and Lt. Gen. George Brett, who had commanded the USAFIA. The land forces command would go the Australian general Sir Thomas Blamey, whom the Australian government had recently ordered back from the Middle East and made C-in-C of the AMF. All national contingents would come under the command of these three service commanders.[8] The USAFIA now became an administrative

and supply organization under Maj. Gen. Julian Barnes and was soon renamed the US Army Services of Supply (USASOS). The final area of command belonged to Maj. Gen. Jonathan Wainwright, who commanded the
ill-fated US Army forces in the Philippines, which would surrender just
over two weeks after the SWPA was created.

ALLIED NAVAL FORCES

Admiral Leary's ascension to command of the ANF was relatively straightforward, given his command of the ANZAC Naval Force. This organization, which absorbed both the forces of the RAN and those of the Royal
Netherlands Navy, transitioned relatively smoothly to ANF SWPA. This
move was helped along by the fact that the Australian Commonwealth
Naval Board (ACNB) had been used to placing its ships under the command of the British Admiralty.[9] Despite this close relationship with RN,
it did not inhibit the RAN from "taking a practical approach to tactical
communications with the USN."[10]

During the time of ABDA, the ACNB had maintained control of the
units operating in Australian waters. This control was passed to Admiral
Leary. With the creation of the ANZAC Naval Area during February 1942
and now with the establishment of the SWPA, Leary became known as
commander, Allied Naval Forces, Southwest Pacific Area (CANFSWPA).
Thereafter, the ACNB was "responsible for support and naval facilities,"
while CANFSWPA was responsible for operations including those of
coastal convoys, although this task was delegated by Leary back to the
ACNB.[11]

To say that there were reservations on both sides of this "alliance"
at its start would be an understatement. In American eyes, exaggerated
suspicions of "the British" were extended to the Australians, with whose
character and capabilities they were totally unfamiliar. For their part, the
Australians, with justifiable pride in their achievements in over two years
of furious warfare against the best that Europe could offer, had reservations about the effectiveness and battle-readiness of the USN.[12]

While the new coalition partners had eyed each other with some degree
of suspicion, the combined operations between the two navies in ABDA
and the ANZAC Naval Area command had gone some way toward
smoothing over some of the rough edges. This meant that of the three
services in early 1942, the Allied navies were best positioned to forge an
effective working relationship.

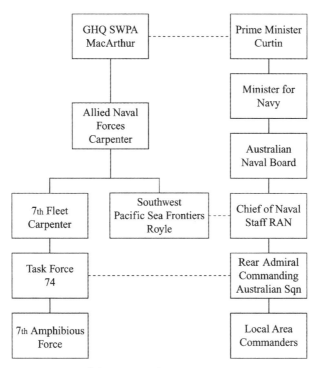

Figure 3.1 Organization of the ANF in the SWPA, 1942

In terms of organization, Leary reported to MacArthur but also had a line of communication open with Nimitz and King. In 1942, his major combatant command was the ANZAC Squadron, soon redesignated as Task Force 44, comprising the heavy cruisers HMAS *Australia* (flagship), *Canberra*, and USS *Chicago*, the light cruiser HMAS *Hobart*, and the destroyer USS *Perkins*, with the Australian-born RN officer Rear Adm. John Crace in command.[13] Leary would remain ashore, close to GHQ in Melbourne, while Crace would command the seagoing element of the ANF. Two USN submarine squadrons, one each at Brisbane and Fremantle, would also be established in Australia but only nominally under CANFSWPA, as their operational control effectively remained with the US submarine commander based at Pearl Harbor.[14]

In addition to Task Force 44, Leary also inherited the Special Intelligence Bureau, which operated three direction-finding stations as part of the British Pacific Naval Intelligence Organization, tracking and intercepting Japanese naval movements. This organization would combine with other RAN intelligence sources and the USN signals intelligence unit that had been based in the Philippines to form the Fleet Radio Unit, Melbourne (FRUMEL), commanded by a USN officer but with a high number of RAN and Women's Royal Australian Naval Service (WRANS) personnel. FRUMEL would play a critical role in the Battle of the Coral Sea and in deciphering the Japanese plans for operations in the SWPA and the South Pacific in 1942. General cooperation in naval communications was also high, with Australian stations filling in the gaps for the USN created by the loss of its stations in Guam and the Philippines. The final piece of the intelligence collection apparatus in the ANF was the RAN's Coastwatchers Organization. The Coastwatchers, established in 1928, had watching posts throughout the South and Southwest Pacific and would provide vital information during the campaigns of 1942 and 1943.[15]

On a practical level, there were a number of factors that helped to ensure relatively smooth cooperation. These included the fact that the organization of the RAN was similar enough to the USN's that it "caused no concern to the Americans."[16] The RAN adapted to the USN's "General Signal Book" in only forty-eight hours, a feat greatly facilitated by the transfer of several USN signalers from the USS *Chicago* to HMAS *Australia*. Most significantly, and in what was to become a key theme across all three services in the SWPA, good personal relations between senior operational commanders were critical in the establishment of smoothing cooperation between the two navies. Crace developed a strong rapport with Capt. Howard Bode of the *Chicago*, and the feeling was reciprocated. This was no easy feat, as Bode had a strong reputation in the USN for being a difficult officer to deal with.[17] Crace was also well received by the other USN commanders in his squadron. The USN's historian, Samuel Eliot Morison, described him as an "energetic warrior" and noted that he was "characterized by his American destroyer screen commander as an 'excellent seaman' and 'gallant gentleman who accepted the United States ships into his command with warmth, affection and admiration for their efficiency.'"[18]

At the high-command level, the ANF did not cause anywhere near the same number of problems as did command and organizational arrangements in the AAF and ALF. The RAN had a long history and tradition of operating as part of the RN, and this organizational culture, plus the experience with the ANZAC Naval Area and in ABDA, had helped facilitate cooperation. Lacking major capital ships such as aircraft carriers or battleships, it was also inevitable that the RAN would play a subordinate role to the USN in any major task force or organization. This was only reinforced by the dominance of the naval effort against Japan being undertaken by the USN in the POA. The RAN was also too small for MacArthur to have considered the idea of a joint command or of offering the position of CANFSPWPA to the senior RAN officer, especially as the RAN chief of the Naval Staff (CNS), Adm. Sir Guy Royle, was actually an RN officer.[19]

It is important to note, though, that in 1942 the RAN provided for the largest effective naval force to oppose the IJN in the SWPA. The RAN had a proud battle history in the Mediterranean and European theaters from 1939 to 1941. This meant that the USN was inheriting a highly effective, battle-proven, and professional organization in 1942, despite its limited size and lack of capital ships. As James Goldrick has noted, "the material advantages were not wholly on the American side," and "the performance of the major units [of the RAN] in operations with the Americans was good and became progressively better. Ship for ship, the RAN cruisers and destroyers felt that they were more than a match in fighting power for the Americans."[20]

The biggest problem for the ANF in the SWPA was its relationship with MacArthur and GHQ. Both Leary and Royle came under immediate suspicion from GHQ because of the color of their uniforms. MacArthur had a stormy relationship with his USN commander in the Philippines, Adm. Thomas C. Hart, and his impression of the navy had not improved in the bitter dispute over the division of the Pacific into two commands, especially as the navy refused to work under MacArthur or any other army officer.

MacArthur was also particularly obsessed with the notion of loyalty from his subordinates, and he was especially displeased that the Australian CNS continued to correspond with the British Admiralty after the SWPA was established. Royle criticized MacArthur in his cables to the Admiralty, referring to him as an "exhibitionist." Unsurprisingly, MacArthur was disappointed at not being consulted in 1943 on the extension of Royle's post as CNS, stating that if he had been consulted he would have preferred the promotion of an RAN officer, namely Capt. John Collins, to be CNS.[21]

MacArthur's original CANFSWPA, Admiral Leary, was not only smeared with the navy brush but also on the wrong end of a personal beef with the C-in-C. When MacArthur was ordered out of the Philippines in early 1942, General Brett was told to arrange for a number of B-17 aircraft to fly in and retrieve him, his family, and his staff. With few resources on hand, Brett had approached Leary as C-in-C ANZAC Naval Area to borrow some B-17s under his command to do the job, but Leary had refused. The one aircraft that Brett could scrounge up was sent back by MacArthur as "dangerously decrepit," and he cabled Washington his extreme displeasure. Brett went back to Leary, and this time he relented, but MacArthur would not forgive either Brett or Leary for the snub. This event would feed his already voracious appetite for negative views of senior USAAF and USN commanders.[22]

Soon after taking command in the SWPA, MacArthur noted that he was "disappointed" in Leary's performance and that their relationship became "tense."[23] Like with Royle's communications with the British Admiralty, MacArthur was continually irritated by Leary's direct correspondence with Admiral King, and he protested that this contact made a "mockery" of his command structure in the SWPA. Underneath, MacArthur remained bitter about the central role of the USN in the war against Japan. He even went so far as to write to General Marshall in June 1942 to argue that the navy was completely power-hungry, noting that he had uncovered a "plot" when he was chief of staff (CoS) in the late 1930s that the navy was planning to take over the "entire national defense system and reduce the Army to a training and supply organization."[24]

MacArthur's bitterness against the navy ran deep, and by mid-1942 Leary was fast becoming the focus of his hostility. As the Papua campaign developed in July and August 1942, Leary and MacArthur would clash again over the CANFSWPA's refusal to operate his ships in the uncharted, reef-strewn coastal areas of Papua in support of the ALF. This time MacArthur would push for Leary's replacement, and on 11 September 1942 Vice Adm. Arthur S. Carpenter arrived to take command of the ANF. Unfortunately for MacArthur, Carpenter's approach to the Papua operations would remain consistent with his predecessor's.[25] MacArthur would continue to have a tense relationship with his naval commander, but Carpenter would remain in his position for another fourteen months before being replaced. In November 1943, Vice Adm. Thomas Kincaid arrived to become commander of the Seventh Fleet (as CANFSWPA had become in 1943), and in him MacArthur finally found an admiral with whom he could develop a decent rapport.

MacArthur's command disputes with both the US and Australian navies meant that they were to receive little recognition from the C-in-C for their efforts. MacArthur's sole reference to the RAN in his *Reminiscences* is the remark that it lacked battleships and aircraft carriers; the fact that the US Asiatic Fleet in the Philippines also lacked these units was not lost on him either. During 1942, MacArthur spent most of his time scolding the navy, arguing over command of the Pacific War, and making unrealistic requests for aircraft carriers and amphibious support for his theater. Other than this, he expended little effort on understanding the details of naval matters.[26] His GHQ remained set in its army ways, meaning that as the war progressed, he "never fully comprehended the principles of modern naval warfare, especially the complexities of operating fast carrier groups."[27] Despite these deficiencies, MacArthur and his commanders would in time learn to exploit the power of his naval assets, especially his amphibious forces. In 1942, however, the SWPA's lack of naval resources and the character of the war in the SWPA would mean that he would fight for prolonged periods of time under contested sea control in forward operating areas.

The first major action of the ANF in the SWPA would be in the now famous Battle of the Coral Sea. Lacking aircraft carriers, Crace's Task Force 44 would play only a supporting role in the battle, the first of its kind where the opposing naval forces would not directly sight each other, but rather where the conduct of the battle would be via carrier-based aviation. As noted, FRUMEL and the code breakers in Hawaii had been instrumental in deciphering the Japanese plan to invade Port Moresby on the southern coast of Papua, and with the involvement of two IJN aircraft carriers, Admiral King decided to risk two of his own carriers as part of the core of the Allied response. Task Force 44 (renamed TF 17.3 for the battle) operated in support and under the command of the carrier Task Force 17 from the Central Pacific under Rear Adm. Frank Fletcher. Fletcher's plan called for Crace's squadron, without air cover, to wait off the Jomard Passage and block any moves by the Japanese invasion force out of the Solomon Sea while Fletcher maneuvered his carriers in the Coral Sea in an attempt to find and join the battle with the IJN carrier force.[28]

While Fletcher engaged in a fierce carrier battle that resulted in the loss of one large US carrier and one small IJN carrier, Crace and his squadron operated under close observation from Japanese aircraft that resulted in two major aerial attacks from the enemy and one from US units of the AAF in the SWPA that had misidentified his ships as Japanese. Crace's skillful handling of his ships, the Japanese belief that his forces consisted of at least one battleship, and the loss of the invasion force's support carrier led the Japanese commander to abandon the operation. The result was a tactical loss for the Allies in terms of ships and tonnage sunk in the battle but a major strategic victory in that the invasion of Port Moresby was thwarted. While the Coral Sea was a major defeat for the Japanese, they would not abandon their plans for the conquest of Port Moresby. Rather, they turned the task over to the IJA, which would make an overland assault on the town via the Kokoda Trail. As James Goldrick has noted, the Japanese defeat meant that "the course of the future campaign for the island [Papua] was thus resolved, [and it was] one absolutely determined by seaborne logistics."[29]

Task Force 44's role in the battle is, more often than not, overlooked, but Crace had achieved his mission and maintained his force in the face of a fierce Japanese attack. As Morison would note in his history, a feature of the battle was the close cooperation between the RAN and the USN and the effectiveness of Task Force 44 despite its difficult role:

> Crace's chase [of the Japanese invasion fleet after it turned away] may have served no useful purpose but it was far from inglorious. It proved, as the ABDA Command never did, that ships of two nations could be made into an excellent tactical unit. And, as the Japanese attack was of the same type and strength [of air attack] as the one that sank H.M.S. Prince of Wales and Repulse, on 10 December 1941, the escape of the Support Group without a single hit is a tribute to its training, and to the high tactical competence of its commander.[30]

Overall, the Battle of the Coral Sea was a major turning point in the war in the SWPA and, although overshadowed by the much larger USN victory at Midway a month later, it deserves to be seen as one of the turning points in the Pacific War as a whole.

The ANF was also kept busy on the Australian station during 1942. A Japanese midget submarine raid on the night of 31 May–1 June resulted in the sinking of only one Sydney Harbor ferry that was being used as a RAN accommodation ship (the torpedo missed the real target, USS *Chicago*), while destroying all three of the Japanese midget submarines. This raid marked the start of a short but concerted Japanese submarine campaign on the eastern coast of Australia.[31] The role of the ANF in this campaign, the building up of forces in Australia, and the ability of the SWPA to conduct operations were critical. The protection of inbound convoys from the United States and outbound convoys to forward operating areas such as Papua, as well as the conduct of local trade, was essential to maintaining the war effort in the SWPA.

During the period from May to August 1942, seven ships would be lost and another eight attacked by IJN submarines operating out of Truk and Rabaul. The limited number of RAN and USN escorts available in the SWPA were hard-pressed to provide a decent level of protection to the local convoys.[32] But one of the major weapons that the ANF possessed was code breaking, which played a major role in the rerouting of convoys and in planning to defeat the Japanese attacks. In addition, the RAN and the USN were helped by the fact that the IJN submarine fleet had been designed not to undertake a commercial shipping war but rather to supplement the Japanese battle fleet and attack USN vessels.

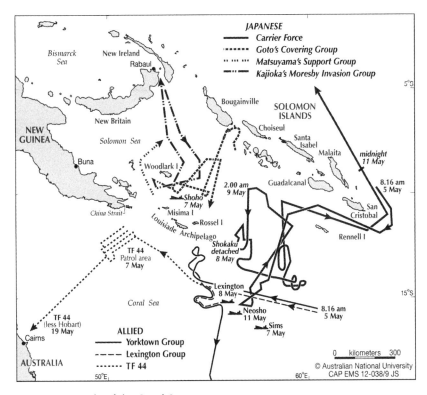

Figure 3.2 Battle of the Coral Sea, 1942

These factors, in combination with the IJN not maintaining a sustained offensive in this area, meant that the ANF was able to maintain trade and convoy protection. There were also some small successes, the most significant being the destroyer HMAS *Arunta* sinking the Japanese submarine *RO-33* off Port Moresby in August, which heralded the end of the first phase of the IJN submarine actions off Australia. The IJN would return in January 1943, undertaking a campaign through to June 1943, torpedoing another fourteen ships. The major impact of its initial offensive was to convince the CANFSWPA to create a new organization, Southwest Pacific Sea Frontiers (SWPSF), under the RAN CNS to run the convoy network.[33]

The other major operation for the ANF was the reinforcement and sustainment of the Australian guerrilla activities on the island of Timor, which had fallen to the Japanese in February 1942. A significant Australian force would be maintained on the island until the end of the year, but under Japanese air superiority it was a costly enterprise. A major relief effort in September led to the loss of the destroyer HMAS *Voyager*, while the corvette HMAS *Armidale* was lost in the logistics service to Timor, Operation Hamburger, on 1 December 1942.[34] The ANF would continue to play a critical role in the operations to come, not only in Papua but also in SOPAC, as naval vessels would demonstrate their flexibility by crossing theater boundaries and moving across the vast expanses of the Pacific much more easily than ground and air units.

ALLIED AIR FORCES IN THE SWPA

Like its sister branches of service, in early 1942 the AAF in the SWPA faced major personnel, logistics, and technical problems. In addition to shortages of aircraft and maintenance facilities, one of the most crippling shortages was the lack of air bases in Australia and the islands to the northeast.[35] Within this milieu of challenges, three problems would stand out above the rest in the six months after the establishment of the SWPA theater. These were major challenges that would doom its commander and its original organizational structure. Two of these would be solved by the end of 1942, while the third would fester until the end of the war.

In many respects, the creation of the AAF organization was relatively easy. Brett had been in Australia since the early part of the year, as his command had principally been built around the establishment of bases for the USAAF. As a result, there was already a good deal of cooperation between the USAAF and the RAAF, and the bulk of the RAAF had been placed under Brett's command in April. In addition, the basic organization of the units and formations of the two air forces were very similar, with only one major difference in the nomenclature and structure:

USAAF	RAAF
Wing	Group
Group	Wing
Squadron	Squadron[36]

Brett's presence in Australia and his role as commander of the US Army in Australia before MacArthur's appointment meant that he had been able to develop a plan with the RAAF for a combined command before the announcement of the creation of the AAF.[37] Brett had been given command of all USAAF and RAAF operational units, except for RAAF training and administration.[38] Given the tasks that he faced in the defense of Australia, with a shortage of units, personnel, equipment, infrastructure, and in particular US officers in his command, he opted for a system of organization that was almost totally integrated. It was a decision largely predicated on "an unavoidable dependence upon the RAAF for communications and administrative facilitates."[39]

Brett's integration of the USAAF and RAAF started with his HQ and spread downward throughout the organization. On 2 May, he announced a completely integrated HQ staff that included the following appointments:

Chief of Staff: Air Vice Marshal William D. Bostock, RAAF
Deputy Chief of Staff: Colonel Edwin S. Perrin, USAAF
Senior Air Staff Officer: Brigadier General Ralph Royce, USAAF
Director of Plans: Colonel Eugene L. Eubank, USAAF
Director of Operations: Colonel Ross G. Hoyt, USAAF
Director of Intelligence: Air Commodore Joseph C. Hewitt, RAAF
Director of Defense: Group Captain F. R. W. Scherger, RAAF
Director of Communications: Group Captain Cam S. Wiggins, RAAF[40]

Brett assured MacArthur that the selection of officers in the HQ and further down through the command chain would be done by merit rather than nationality, but as the Australian official history records, "the system of almost mechanical alternation of American and Australian staff officers right down the lines of command, was applied at Allied Headquarters and in the North-Eastern Area."[41]

While this structure seemed to diffuse responsibility and command between the two national services, in reality it concentrated control in favor of the RAAF. As a result of the dependence of the USAAF on RAAF facilities and air bases in Australia, Brett exercised command through the five main military areas into which Australia was divided. Each of these areas was under the command of an RAAF officer. This meant that US air units were under RAAF command and an Australian officer commanded "every airfield at which American air units were stationed."[42] This raised the immediate question, why were US officers not given command of some of these military districts?

While Brett's rationale for the establishment of a combined organization was that the USAAF lacked experienced personnel in Australia, it seems incredible that he could not find one senior USAAF officer who could have been appointed to one of the two key commands in Australia, in particular the North-East Area, where the majority of his US bombers would be concentrated to operate against Rabaul and in support of Allied forces in the Coral Sea, Papua, and the South Pacific. If there was not a suitable officer in Australia, then surely Brett could have cabled for one to be sent to the SWPA by the US War Department.

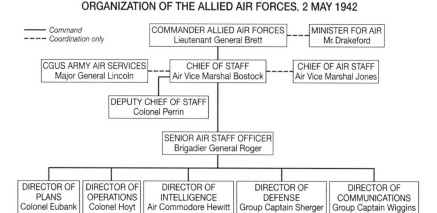

Figure 3.3 Organization of Allied Air Forces HQ, SWPA, May 1942

There were, of course, plenty of benefits to Brett's integrated command structure. It threw the two nationalities together in a way that they would not have otherwise done, which meant that they were forced to learn how to work with each other and become familiar with each other's military culture, organization, operational procedures, and doctrine. Overwhelmingly, accounts of this period at the unit level reaffirm the close relationship that developed between the USAAF and the RAAF. The Australian official history notes that there was "considerable goodwill" between the two services and that in the North-East Area "the atmosphere was happy and the staff extremely cooperative."[43] Brett noted in a report to the US War Department that cooperation was "excellent."[44] Air Comdr. Joseph Hewitt, the director of intelligence at Brett's HQ, recalled that during this time he made "some of the happiest and most lasting of all associations and American friendships I made during the war."[45]

There were other positive benefits of this system. In 1942, the RAAF had a surplus of aircrews and the USAAF a surplus of aircraft, and thus an integrated system could make the best use of both issues. In addition, many RAAF leaders had considerably more combat experience than their USAAF counterparts, and lessons could be more readily spread across both services with an integrated system. This was particularly evident in the bomber force. As many US bomber units arrived in the SWPA incomplete in terms of training and personnel, RAAF aircrews were integrated into individual crews throughout 1942. The RAAF had originally not been in favor of this arrangement, but Brett, with MacArthur's backing, had pushed the issue with success.[46]

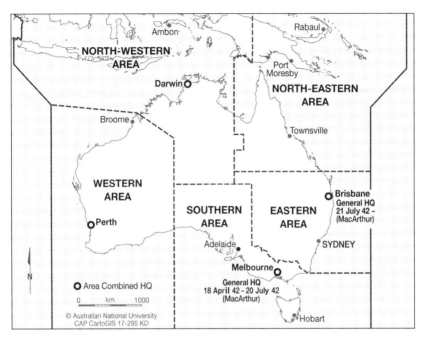

Figure 3.4 Air Commands in Australia, 1942

At the unit level this seemed to operate smoothly and effectively in 1942, and relations between the two countries were deemed to be excellent. However, this supposedly "smoothly-operating organization" did not work out that way. Brett was concerned that he did not have full command due to Australian political interference, and he was worried about the dependence he had on RAAF infrastructure and RAAF commanders due to USAAF deficiencies in Australia. Furthermore, there were difficulties in "coordination of effort and control of operations."[47]

The integration of crews and aircraft on missions and the RAAF dominance of the North-West and North-East Air Areas were not welcome developments at GHQ, nor were they well received throughout the USAAF in Australia. Maj. Gen. Robert C. Richardson, who was sent out to the SWPA by the US Army CoS to investigate conditions in the theater, reported in a letter to MacArthur on 4 July 1942 that "the present organization of the American Air Forces, under which our pilots receive their combat missions from Australians, is resented throughout the entire command from top to bottom." He also highlighted differences in tactical approaches in Port Moresby, problems with the administrative integration of the two air forces, and questions over the messing of RAAF non-commissioned officer (NCO) pilots with USAAF commissioned officer pilots and crew. The other most persistent problem that he identified was the mixing of aircrews. He noted to MacArthur:

> The Australian officers in command of the air fields are assigning individual officer pilots and non-commissioned co-pilots to certain Americans squadrons as replacements. The commander of one of the bomber groups informed me that these men are not good pilots and should not be entrusted with our equipment. Besides, there are other difficulties such as our personnel being unable to understand the Australians over the inter-plane phone, which presents serious and dangerous complications.[48]

What Richardson was overlooking was the dependence of the USAAF on the RAAF in 1942 due to its deficiencies in airfields, logistics, personnel, and equipment. Moreover, Brett was being hamstrung by the USAAF command back in the United States, which was restricting the appointment of staff officers and senior commanders to the SWPA until adequate numbers could be provided to other theaters with a higher priority in the national war effort.[49] That said, Richardson had touched on a few nerves, and given the asymmetrical differences in the RAAF and USAAF efforts in the SWPA, it was inevitable that Brett's system would have evolved over time and that the role and influence of the RAAF would eventually decline.

GEORGE KENNY TAKES COMMAND

General Brett suffered from a number of issues in his time in command. As the presumptive nominee as C-in-C SWPA in early 1942, Brett was seen by MacArthur as a rival and a potential replacement should he falter in command. In addition, all of MacArthur's prejudices about the USAAF from the Philippines were carried over to Brett and his command in the SWPA. Thus, from the outset, MacArthur did everything he could to freeze Brett out and make his life as difficult as possible. Probably the final nail in Brett's coffin occurred in June 1942 when MacArthur rebuked Brett for talking to the media. In terms of MacArthur's warped sense of loyalty and his authoritarian approach to his command, and especially his total control of the media, this was a major sin, committed as it was by a potential rival.

Brett was also hamstrung by the fact that he had not stamped his authority on his command, the AAF was underperforming, and he lacked the political skills to overcome the issues he faced, not least his relationship with MacArthur and Sutherland. According to the Australian chief of the Air Staff (CAS), Air Vice Marshal George Jones, one of Brett's major problems was that he was "too gentlemanly."[50] Brett had been so ineffective in his dealings with GHQ that he was unable to secure time with MacArthur to try to build some trust; thus, his replacement was inevitable. On 26 June, MacArthur cabled the War Department, making it clear that he was unimpressed with Brett and that he was seeking his relief. Brett lacked support back in Washington, and many in the USAAF questioned his suitability to command. In his report to Marshall, MacArthur questioned Brett's authority, his staff work, his relationships, and his judgment. It was the death knell for his career.[51] On 6 July 1942, Marshall offered MacArthur a replacement, and on 12 July the commander of the USAAF and a member of the JCS, Gen. Henry H. "Hap" Arnold, offered the position to Maj. Gen. George Kenney.[52]

The appointment of Kenney overcame the first of the three major issues facing the AAF in the SWPA: command and leadership. By the end of the war, Kenney had established himself as one of the greatest air force commanders of World War II. From his briefings in Washington and his first discussions with Sutherland and Brett on arrival in Australia, Kenney knew that forging a relationship with MacArthur was the key to his success, and in this endeavor he was highly effective.[53] In the process of demanding and receiving direct access to the C-in-C, Kenney also emasculated Sutherland, removing the heavy centralized control over the AAF in the SWPA from GHQ. Kenney brought energy, vision, and vigor to his new command; he was a new broom who within a short space of time swept away many of the issues that had hamstrung the effectiveness of the air forces in the theater.

In almost every respect Kenney was completely different from Brett. Beryl Daley, private secretary to both Brett and Kenney, noted that whereas Brett was "tall . . . imposing . . . beautifully mannered, everything right and proper," Kenney was "an ugly little man." The differences for Daley went beyond the physical. Having worked side by side with both men, she regarded that the office under Kenney "became much more effective" and that there was "far less time wasted." This she put down to her belief that he was of "quick brain" with a "brilliant mind" and much more of a "maverick" than Brett.[54]

Kenney, for his part, formed a close bond with MacArthur and was able to work with GHQ and outmaneuver many of its best political officers. In the SWPA, Kenney's relationship and sense of trust with MacArthur were to be among his greatest assets. Within a very short time, he became one of MacArthur's most trusted confidants.[55] In addition, he got along with most of the Australians and held a high opinion of the majority of Australian commanders.[56] He also did his best within MacArthur's cooperative command setup by working closely with his army and navy counterparts.

Kenney, however, did not see eye to eye with everyone, especially given his "tough guy" persona. Like many in the SWPA, he despised Sutherland, believing him to be ill-informed, opinionated, and arrogant—a feeling that seemed mutual.[57] The Australian CAS, Air Vice Marshal Jones, never developed a rapport with Kenney. He did not admire Kenney but rather found him "a very difficult man to deal with." He saw him as always "hostile, or 'tough'—in the American vernacular," and Jones tolerated Kenney's manner only because he did not want to create a scenario that would lead to conflict between Curtin and MacArthur.[58] Nevertheless, Sutherland's and Jones's opinions were the decided minority, and Kenney quickly gained a strong reputation throughout the SWPA.

The appointment of Kenney also led to a change to the second major problem with the AAF in the SWPA: its organizational structure. On arrival in the SWPA, Kenney met with MacArthur and then toured his command, inspecting bases and units and talking to senior officers as well as aircrews. At the end of the tour, he assessed that "no matter what I accomplished, it would be an improvement."[59] Kenney disliked the organizational structure and the command system, and when shown an organizational diagram explaining the relationships between the USAAF and the RAAF and between administration, training, maintenance, and operations, he described it as being like "a can of worms as you look at it."[60] Furthermore, he was highly critical of the caliber of USAAF leadership in the SWPA, as well as its training and the maintenance of his USAAF squadrons.[61]

Kenney moved quickly to fix these problems. He was ruthless in weeding out incompetent officers and would later boast that, soon after arriving in the SWPA, he got rid of forty colonels and lieutenant colonels and one captain.[62] Next, he moved to reorganize his command. Kenney had been made aware of the concerns GHQ had with Brett's integrated command structure before he even arrived in theater, and MacArthur pushed him on this matter in their first meeting. As Air Commodore Hewitt, director of intelligence at AAF, noted, the combined command approach did not find any favor at GHQ. Hewitt noted that, as 1942 progressed, this was being exacerbated steadily by the "the inflow of American forces [which] necessitated more and more staff work by their own officers. . . . Combined staffs were unpopular with MacArthur and the subject of diatribes by Sutherland, who had no time for Australians," which meant that it was almost inevitable that the USAAF would establish "their own command system at all levels."[63]

In early September 1942, MacArthur announced the creation of two commands within the AAF: the Fifth US Air Force and the RAAF Command.[64] Air Vice Marshal Bostock, formerly chief of staff to Brett, was given the RAAF Command, while Kenney retained direct control of the Fifth Air Force and appointed two recently arrived USAAF officers, Brig. Gen. Ennis Whitehead and Brig. Gen. Ken Walker, to senior commands in the Fifth Air Force. Kenney divided his command by tasking the Fifth Air Force as the forward offensive operational command responsible for operations in New Guinea, while the RAAF was responsible for the air defense of Australia, including antisubmarine warfare and bombing missions from northern Australia. Kenney was thus able to allocate capabilities and assets from both national air forces to these commands to suit their respective missions.

In addition, in order to improve command in the forward area, Whitehead would soon take over Advance Echelon, Fifth Air Force, in New Guinea to command all operations there. This was the most important air command in the SWPA, and it was critical that the senior officer could work well with the Australians and GHQ. In Whitehead, Kenney could not have picked a more able subordinate. Like Kenney, he developed a close relationship with MacArthur and proved to be a popular commander among both the Americans and the Australians.[65] Whitehead would have a considerable number of RAAF assets, principally No. 9 Operational Group, the only Australian unit not under Bostock's RAAF Command. Among the Australians he was well respected by the likes of Air Commodore Hewitt and the CAS, Air Vice Marshal Jones.[66] Air Commodore Hewitt, who would move from his role as director of intelligence at AAF to command No. 9 Operational Group under Whitehead, noted that he was "of medium height and build with a wiry physique. His rugged face topped by sandy hair beamed with intelligence and determination, and inspired confidence. . . . We had seen eye to eye at once and I could not have wished to serve with a better man. He became a trusted friend and a sagacious advisor."[67]

With Whitehead and Bostock responsible for operations, Kenney was able to concentrate on relations with GHQ, his operational plans, providing MacArthur strategic advice, and fixing the myriad of problems with the infrastructure, maintenance, and training of his command, as well as the procurement of aircraft, personnel, and equipment from the United States.[68]

The logic behind Kenney's reorganization was not lost on the Australians. Air Vice Marshal Richard Williams, the RAAF representative to the CCS in Washington, noted that "this was a logical decision. Kenney was setting up an organization that should have been established when the decision was made to place the operational units of the RAAF under United States command."[69] However, the RAAF CAS Jones was not so enamored. He argued strongly against the change on the grounds that the original organization had split the RAAF's combat and logistics arrangements and that the new organizational structure had not solved this problem. Jones wanted the RAAF organized into one structure with one officer in command.[70] This was at the nub of the third major challenge for the AAF in the SWPA: the command and organization of the RAAF. This, however, was a problem that no one was able to solve. It would have disastrous repercussions for the effectiveness of the RAAF during the Pacific War that would help sideline the force as the war progressed.

The RAAF's problems stemmed from expiration of Air Chief Marshal Sir Charles Burnett's term as the CAS (Australia). Burnett was an elderly RAF officer, and there was a strong desire that an Australian take command. The Australian government had given a considerable amount of thought to his replacement, and Air Vice Marshal Peter Drummond was offered the position but, according to the Australian official history, declined because of the split between the AAF HQ and RAAF HQ responsibilities. As a result, debate abounded between the senior command in the RAAF, the USAAF, GHQ, and the Australian government over Burnett's replacement, unity of command with the United States, and the command organization within the RAAF.[71]

When the Prime Minister's War Conference discussed the issue of Burnett's replacement on 30 April 1942, its attendees were in some ways hamstrung by Brett's integrated organization, as he had selected Air Vice Marshal Bostock, the most senior member of the RAAF and frontrunner for CAS, as his chief of staff. Furthermore, for political reasons, the minister for air, Arthur Drakeford, opposed Bostock's appointment as CAS, as well as that of a potential senior British officer. With an impasse reached, the War Cabinet deliberated organizational structures but deferred a decision until Curtin spoke with Brett and MacArthur.[72]

Curtin wrote to Brett the same day stating that all operational elements of the RAAF were assigned to the AAF but that the RAAF's CAS was responsible for "personnel, provision and maintenance of aircraft, supply and equipment, works and buildings." Curtin also asked that Air Cmdr. George Jones, the head of training command who had been on Brett's list of requested staff officers, be retained by the RAAF outside of the AAF.[73] After a series of discussions, the War Cabinet stunned the RAAF by naming Jones, a substantive wing commander, the CAS.

An unassuming, diligent, but uninspiring officer, Jones had not been mentioned by the Australian Air Board as a contender and admitted that he was shocked by the appointment. In fact, it was so out of left field that RAAF historian Alan Stephens has suggested Jones may have been appointed by mistake.[74] This was down to an unofficial organizational chart that the War Cabinet had access to in the meeting. This chart showed Brett in command, Bostock as his deputy, and then a USAAF officer in the diagram, followed thereafter by George Jones. Stephens argues that the War Cabinet, on advice to appoint the next most senior RAAF officer, confused an organizational chart for a command diagram and appointed Jones! However, the advice about appointing the "next on the list" referred to the *Air Force List*, an annual publication that cataloged every RAAF officer in order of seniority.[75]

The appointment of Jones was a genuine shock to many. He was appointed as an air vice marshal (a two-star rank), which made him junior to his RAN and Australian Army equivalents and gave him rank parity only with Bostock, who, under Kenney's reorganization of the AAF, took command of the operational component of the RAAF. The RAAF now effectively had two heads: one for operations and another for administration and training.

With a divided command imposed on the RAAF by a weak and indecisive War Cabinet and a strong and effective AAF head in Kenney, it was essential that the two senior RAAF officers work in tandem. This, however, was never going to happen. Jones and Bostock had a relatively poor past relationship, and this now became toxic. Bostock, who expected to become CAS, was bitter by the decision and never got over it, while Jones proved to be obstinate and stubborn in the face of his elevation.[76]

This command structure was to have a devastating impact on the RAAF's war. In 1999, the RAAF's Air Power Centre published a major two-volume study on the higher command of the force during World War II, titled *How Not to Run an Air Force*.[77] Stephens noted in his history of the RAAF that "at the highest level, the command of the RAAF during World War II was a disgrace. Because of political weakness and personal selfishness, a divisive rivalry between the services' two most senior officers . . . was allowed to continue unresolved for three and a half years.

There is no doubt that their corrosive relationship . . . diminished the Air Force."[78] Interestingly this arrangement might well have suited Kenney. As historian and retired air commodore Mark Lax has noted, Kenney preferred to have Jones and Bostock in the positions that they held and never complained to MacArthur about the arrangement. If he was suitably unimpressed about it, he could have gone to MacArthur and asked him to see Curtin about resolving the issue. Instead it remained as it was, which allowed Kenney to "exploit control of the RAAF as he saw fit, and it appears he did just that."[79]

ALLIED LAND FORCES

MacArthur had originally planned to take command of the ground forces himself, but it was made clear to him that the directive establishing him as supreme commander of the SWPA also excluded him from any national command. As such, he proposed Maj. Gen. Julian Barnes be given the position. The chief of staff of the US Army, George C. Marshall, "strongly opposed the suggestion,"[80] given the fact that the vast bulk of the ground forces in MacArthur's command were Australian, a situation that would remain in the SWPA until late 1943. The appointment of an Australian would also be, as Marshall stated to MacArthur, in "accordance with the policy developed for combined commands."[81]

As a result, MacArthur was forced to appoint the Australian general Sir Thomas Blamey as his commander of the ALF. Blamey's persistent problem thereafter was that his boss wanted his job. MacArthur continued to resent the requirement to accommodate a land forces commander, especially a foreigner. He chose to express this frustration by inserting himself into the running of the ALF throughout 1942, much to Blamey's displeasure. After the conclusion of the Papua campaign in 1942, MacArthur would deliberately undermine Blamey's position and ensure that he had few US Army units under his command. This had nothing to do with Blamey's competence but rather everything to do with his nationality and MacArthur's desire to control the US Army elements of his command directly.

Blamey had been the senior Australian Army officer since the beginning of the war. A regular officer, he had completed the British Staff College course in Quetta, India, in 1913 before seeing extensive service in World War I. He landed at Gallipoli in 1915 as a senior staff officer in the 1st Australian Division and served on the western front as its chief of staff until June 1918, when he was then promoted to temporary brigadier general and made chief of staff of the Australian Corps under Lt. Gen.

Sir John Monash. In the interwar period, he held a number of senior staff positions in Australia and Britain until 1925, when he decided to leave the army to become the commissioner of police in his home state, Victoria. After a scandal involving his police badge being found in a raid on a well-known Melbourne brothel, and with a change of government, Blamey was forced to "resign for issuing an untrue statement in an attempt to protect the reputation of one of his senior police officers."[82]

During the interwar period, Blamey had remained an active member of the Citizen Military Forces (CMF), an organization that dominated the interwar Australian Army, but in 1937 he was forced to give up his command of the 3rd Division, and his career seemed over. However, in the following year, the government made him chairman of the Manpower Committee and controller general of recruiting, which brought him back into the defense organization. At the outbreak of war he was made GOC of the 6th Australian Division, the first formation in the newly raised Second AIF.[83] Blamey would take command of I Australian Corps at its creation in 1940 and would be commander of the 2nd AIF when it moved to the Middle East. His performance in this theater was seen as "uneven." He commanded the Australian Corps, later the ANZAC Corps, in Greece, and on 23 April 1941, he was appointed deputy commander in chief of British forces in the Middle East. In September 1941, he was promoted to general.

Small in stature and quite rotund by 1942, Blamey had mixed relations with the other senior Australian officers in the AIF. During his period of command in the Middle East, he had also had rather strained relations with the senior British command, who often failed to appreciate or understand his position as a national commander. Furthermore, he never managed to develop a rapport with the troops under his command, although popularity with troops seemed to be the least of his concerns or worries in his military career. While enjoying a mixed reputation in Australian military history, he is widely acknowledged for his strategic and political skills and would perform admirably during the Pacific War, with some moments of operational brilliance and political naivety in equal measure.[84]

Blamey would also enjoy a mixed reputation with the Americans. Most significantly, he never really developed a strong rapport with MacArthur, and their relationship would deteriorate during the course of the Papua campaign in 1942. The low point would come in late 1942, but the relationship would be put back on somewhat of an even keel in 1943, although there was to be little trust between the two men from the time of the operations along the Kokoda Trail. As Australian combat power declined and US power in the theater accelerated, MacArthur would become more dismissive of Blamey, and their relationship would fall apart in 1944 over the future of Australia's role in the region. Ultimately MacArthur would take the extraordinary position of actively lobbying the Australian prime minister to replace him as C-in-C of the AMF.

Among the senior US commanders and the officers of GHQ, Blamey was treated with the highest degree of professionalism, but views of his abilities and performance were mixed. He got along well with the generals Brett and Kenney.[85] Willoughby called him a "fourteen-carat politician,"[86] while Faubion Bowers, who worked for the Allied Translator and Intelligence Service from 1943 to 1945 in the SWPA before serving as MacArthur's military secretary in Japan during the occupation, described Blamey as a "drunken old fool."[87] Brig. Gen. Robert Van Volkenburgh, the antiaircraft commander in the SWPA, saw Blamey as more of a "rough and ready Irish policeman" than a military commander, although he did note that he also "had pretty good qualities."[88]

At the time of Blamey's appointment as commander of the ALF, the armies of the two countries were the least integrated of the three services in the SWPA. Blamey's appointment had come at a critical time but also after some tense maneuvering in the Australian Army. On 23 February, Lt. Gen. John Lavarack, commander of I Australian Corps, recently of ABDA command, had returned to Australia and was made acting C-in-C of the AMF. Lavarack was Blamey's most bitter rival and a former chief of staff of the Australian Army in the lead-up to World War II. Although it seems that Lavarack was never under serious consideration for the position permanently, not long after his appointment Maj. Gen. Gordon Bennett, the senior CMF officer before the war, a fierce Blamey critic, and a controversial commander in Malaya, returned from Singapore after his "escape" and met with the War Cabinet on 2 March.

Not knowing that the prime minister had ordered Blamey to return from the Middle East on 20 February 1942 to become the C-in-C,[89] on 11 March 1942 the major generals Edmund Herring (GOC 6th Division) and George Vasey (chief of staff of Home Forces) and Brig. Clive Steele (chief Administration Officer Southern Command), believing Lavarack or Bennett might well be named C-in-C, proposed to the minister of the army, Frank Forde, that Maj. Gen. Horace Robertson be named C-in-C and that all officers over the age of fifty be retired. The plan, dubbed the "revolt of the generals," never got off the ground.[90] Forde remained uncommitted, knowing full well that Blamey was expected back in Australia soon. However, it created a tense atmosphere for Blamey on his appointment, and it meant that he would need to reconcile his own senior officer corps in addition to building relations with MacArthur, his staff, and the US formations that would soon come under his command.

Blamey's arrival back in Australia and confirmation as C-in-C AMF led to a major reorganization of the Australian Army. In early 1942, the 7th Australian Division (AIF) and part of the 6th Australian Division (AIF) (the remainder had temporarily gone to support the British in Ceylon) from I Australian Corps had returned to Australia after Curtin had won his bitter dispute with Churchill over their ultimate destination. This meant the army in Australia soon had the strength of some eight infantry divisions, two motorized divisions, and one armored division. In addition, two American infantry divisions, the 32nd and 41st National Guard formations, had begun to arrive in Australia.

With concern over the possibility of direct attacks on the mainland and with insufficient naval or air forces in the SWPA to support large land forces forward-deployed in Papua, New Guinea, and other islands to Australia's northeast, most of the land forces were initially deployed in southern Australia, where the Australian units had been raised and trained and where there was sufficient training and accommodation facilities to house the newly arrived US formations.[91]

These forces were arranged into the main force, the First Australian Army under Lavarack in New South Wales (NSW) and Queensland, with responsibility for the defense of eastern Australia. The Second Australian Army, under Lt. Gen. Iven Mackay (formerly GOC of the 6th Division in North Africa and later C-in-C of the Home Forces), was responsible for the defense of southern Australia. The First Army would provide for the defense of eastern Australia. This encompassed Queensland, including the Torres Strait Islands and NSW. Under command of the First Army was Maj. Gen. Sydney Rowell's I Corps (3rd Militia Division and 7th Division AIF) in Queensland, II Australian Corps (1st, 2nd, and 10th Militia Divisions) in the Newcastle–Sydney–Port Kembla area, the 5th Militia Division in Queensland, and the 1st Motor Division in NSW.[92]

Blamey also commanded III Australian Corps (Maj. Gen. Gordon Bennett), whose task was to defend Western Australia, and the 8th Military District (Maj. Gen. Basil Morris), which was responsible for the defense of Papua and New Guinea.[93] General Herring, formerly GOC of the 6th Division AIF, was appointed to command Northern Territory (NT) Force.[94] Given the direct threat to this region by continual Japanese air bombardment and concerns over a possible Japanese invasion of Darwin, Herring was given the powers of a C-in-C with "full operational and

Level	Description	Unit/formation
A	Efficient and experienced for mobile operations	7th Division AIF
B	Efficient for mobile offensive operations, but not yet experienced	2/7th Cavalry Rgt ↓ AIF
C	Efficient for mobile offensive operations. Higher training not complete	—
D	Efficient in a static role. Additional brigade and higher training required	32nd US Division ↓ 7th Militia Brigade
E	Units have completed training. A considerable amount of brigade and high training is required	14th Militia Brigade ↓
F	Unit training is not yet complete	30th Militia Brigade

Figure 3.5 Army Brigade Combat Efficiency Ratings, 1942

administrative responsibilities" over all forces in his area of responsibility.[95] During most of 1942, only Herring and Morris would exercise command in actual operations, with NT Force's RAAF and USAAF assets repelling Japanese air raids, while Morris would have to contend with a full-scale Japanese invasion over the Kokoda Trail from July 1942 until he was replaced with Lt. Gen. Sydney Rowell in August.

While these forces appear formidable on paper, most were a long way from achieving any degree of combat efficiency, and only the AIF formations and units had combat experience. In July 1942, the Australian Army rated its brigades and the two US divisions under its command on the basis of an *A*-to-*F* scale for efficiency (*A* being the highest). Of the thirty-two brigades and two US divisions on paper, only the four AIF brigades from the 6th and 7th Divisions were rated *A*. No brigade was rated a *B*, four were rated *C*, six rated *D*, nine rated an *E*, and eight rated an *F*! The 32nd US Infantry Division was rated *C* and the 41st Infantry Division an *F*. Only the AIF formations and the troops transferred to Papua in 1942 were complete in their establishment of vehicles, and most other units, other than the 41st US Division, were lacking in equipment; the average brigade equipment standard across the ALF was only 77 percent.[96]

Upon taking command, Blamey made a number of major changes to the administration and operation of the Australian Army and the ALF. He utilized the Australian Army's Land Headquarters (LHQ) in Melbourne to work alongside MacArthur's GHQ, and when MacArthur moved his HQ forward to Brisbane, Blamey established Advanced LHQ (Adv LHQ) to control the operations of the ALF. LHQ would remain in Melbourne as an Australian Army HQ under the Australian chief of the General Staff

(CGS), who was responsible for administration and lines of communication. In line with the Australian use of the British staff system at division, corps, army, and senior HQ levels, Blamey appointed two senior staff officers, one covering operational planning and the other administration and logistics, who reported to the commander. This was substantially different from the US Army system used at GHQ and senior US Army and USAAF formations, which utilized a chief of staff and department heads. Significantly, Adv LHQ, like GHQ, was strictly organized along national lines, with all senior positions being taken up by Australian Army officers.

For LHQ and then Adv LHQ, Blamey used the Australian deputy chief of the General Staff (DCGS) as his senior operations officer and the Australian deputy adjutant and quartermaster general (DA&QMG) as his other senior staff officer, with responsibility for staff appointments, administration, and quartermaster sections. Traditionally the operations officer was the senior of the two officers and would act as the de facto chief of staff, commanding the headquarters in the commander's absence. Thus, the DCGS was the most important operational staff position within the Australian Army and the ALF.

The DCGS's roles and responsibilities at Adv LHQ were immense. Beside coordination with the various operational units under Blamey and Adv LHQ's direct command, he was responsible for liaison with Mac-Arthur's GHQ on all operational matters, and more often than not he had the task of representing the C-in-C at daily conferences. This in itself was a major undertaking, particularly given the exceptionally tense situation at GHQ during the latter half of 1942. At the time of the creation of Adv LHQ, Blamey appointed a senior Australian regular army officer, Maj. Gen. George Vasey, as DCGS, but after a few months it became clear that Vasey's temperament and relatively poor relationship with GHQ meant that he was more suited to command. He was therefore transferred to be GOC of the 6th Australian Division, while another senior regular army officer, Maj. Gen. Frank Berryman, who had been major general, general staff (MGGS)—the senior staff officer at the First Australian Army—was brought in to replace him. Except for a few months in command of a corps, Berryman would remain Blamey's senior operations officer/CoS for the rest of the war.

Blamey's role in the early part of 1942 was defense of the Australian continent, Papua, and New Guinea. Given the lack of air and naval forces and the desperate situation in terms of equipment, supplies, and trained formations, Blamey kept only a few poorly trained militia brigades forward-deployed in Papua, wisely keeping the bulk of his trained and equipped land force on the continent. During this period, there was the ongoing air battle over Port Moresby and the climactic naval battle in the Coral Sea, which forestalled the Japanese attempt to take Port Moresby, the Papuan capital. The Australians had advanced positions in New Guinea at Lae and Salamaua, but on 8 March 1942, when the Japanese landed there, the Australian forces pulled back to Wau in the highlands. Here they were formed as Kanga Force and were maintained by transport aircraft operating out of Port Moresby from the 21st US Troop Carrier Squadron and the Australian National Airways. This force conducted a major raid on Salamaua on 28–29 June 1942, in which as many as 113 Japanese soldiers were killed, with only three Australians slightly wounded.[97]

After the twin victories of Coral Sea in May and Midway in June, the US JCS issued a directive to SOPAC and the SWPA that called for an offensive to seize the New Britain–New Ireland–New Guinea area. As a result, the ALF and the Australian Army started to prepare for the offensive, and Blamey called all of his senior commanders and staff officers down to a conference in Melbourne on 6–7 July. Here it was decided that as part of these offensive plans, the US 41st and 32nd Infantry Divisions, which had been in southern Australia since May, were to be moved to Queensland and come under the command of the First Army. II Australian Corps was to move to Rockhampton in Queensland, and the Second Australian Army was to take over the defense of all of NSW. Both MacArthur's GHQ and Blamey's Adv LHQ were to move forward to Brisbane by the end of the month.[98]

Preparations for the Allied offensive in Papua were forestalled on 21 July when the Japanese landed at Buna. On 30 July, Col. Ken Wills, the senior intelligence officer for the First Australian Army in Toowoomba, who had predicted the Japanese landing at Buna, now wrote an appreciation stating that he was convinced that the Japanese planned to send a large-scale land force to capture Port Moresby via an overland attack. On 30 July, Wills took his appreciation to the MGGS of the First Army (Berryman), who in turn took it down to MacArthur's CoS, General Sutherland, on the same day. Sutherland and MacArthur's chief of intelligence, Brig. Gen. Charles Willoughby, dismissed the report out of hand and managed to persuade Berryman to accept their assessment.[99] Despite GHQ's denials, the Japanese did launch an overland assault, and in response, on 1 August, Blamey ordered Rowell's I Australian Corps and the 7th Division AIF from Queensland to Port Moresby. The stage was now set for the first major campaign in the SWPA.

Part 2

The Papua Campaign, 1942

4

The US-Australian Military Relationship in 1942

MacArthur recalled in his memoirs that on arrival in Australia he

> replaced the pessimism of failure with the inspiration of success. What the Australians needed was a strategy that held out the promise of victory. . . . The Australian chiefs of staff . . . had been thinking and planning only defensively . . . behind this so-called Brisbane line . . . [a] concept [that] was purely of passive defense and I felt it would result only in eventual defeat. . . . I decided to abandon the plan completely, to move the thousand miles forward into eastern Papua and to stop the Japanese on the rough mountains of the Owen Stanley Range of New Guinea—to make the fight for Australia beyond its own borders. . . . The decision gave the Australians an exhilarating lift.[1]

This recollection contains nothing more than a small kernel of truth hidden behind a fabricated reality. Like much if not all of MacArthur's writings, press statements, and announcements, it was part of a carefully orchestrated propaganda campaign aimed at unabashed self-promotion. The Australian chiefs of staff, General Brett, and the Australian government based their appreciations of the strategic situation in the Pacific in February and March 1942 on the premise of the development of Australia as a base for offensive operations against Japan. As David Horner and a number of other writers have demonstrated comprehensively, there was no "Brisbane Line," and efforts had been under way *before* MacArthur arrived to prepare Papua for defense against the Japanese.[2] In fact, shortly after his arrival, MacArthur accepted the overwhelming majority of Brett's and the Australian chiefs' of staff appreciations. The major difference between MacArthur's assessments and the Australians' was that GHQ believed that the Japanese would soon attack Darwin with three divisions, while the Australians correctly assessed that they would focus their attack on Papua and Port Moresby.

MacArthur's position on this matter was made clear to the Australian government. As Prime Minister Curtin noted in a cablegram to his minister for external affairs, H. V. Evatt, who was then in Washington, MacArthur was

> in entire agreement with the . . . observations that were submitted [by] . . . the Australian Chiefs of Staff [, who] have indicated that the defence of Australia as a base for offensive operations can be secured by adequate naval and air forces; otherwise extensive land forces are necessary . . . [to] . . . hold the key military regions of Australia as bases for future offensive action against Japan, and strive to check Japanese aggression in the south-west Pacific area.[3]

In addition, MacArthur was hardly pushing the offensive when he first arrived in Australia or throughout March and April 1942. In April he told the prime minister that the "meager assistance promised for the Southwest Pacific Area for the performance of the tasks imposed on him by the [JCS] directive . . . [meant] that the only item of this directive with which he can comply, either now or in the immediate future, is to route shipping in the Southwest Pacific Area." Curtin also noted that MacArthur considered as "highly dangerous the many references which have been or are being made to offensive action against Japan from Australia as a base."[4] Compounding this assessment is the fact that a number of his biographers note that after his arrival in Australia, MacArthur seemed to withdraw into a "funk" or type of melancholy that may well have been a sign of the onset of depression. This is hardly the image of an offensive-minded, hard-driving commander that he portrayed himself as in his memoir.

Ignoring self-serving postwar accounts and assessing the strategic situation on its merits in March and April 1942, it is easy to understand MacArthur's actual apprehension. The difficulties facing the SWPA command for both the development of the defense of Australia and preparations for offensive operations were immense. Brig. Gen. Hugh Casey (USA), the chief engineer in the SWPA and one of MacArthur's closest confidants, outlined the sheer scale of the problem in 1942:

> When it is realized that Australia is as large as the United States with little more than five percent of this population, [with] relatively underdeveloped communication facilities, with railroads of changing gauges, limited port facilities and with a future operations area through undeveloped country in New Guinea and the Solomon Is-

lands, coupled with heavy demands for large Air Force operations requiring many airdromes with their pertinent accessories of docks, access roads, etc. it can well be appreciated that engineer construction and operations requirements are heavy. In the face of these extensive requirements, industrial, construction and transport facilities [in Australia] are most limited. Since this headquarters was established in March of this year, large increments of additional Air Forces have been assigned to this theatre. During that same time period, not a single engineer construction unit has been revived.[5]

Casey went on in this letter to outline his lack of units and the poor qualifications and training of his personnel. The inventory lacking in his command included everything from large-scale machinery to communications equipment and topographical maps of operational areas. In addition, he outlined his almost total reliance on the Australian government for materials, support, and construction crews. To Casey and many other officers in GHQ, the tasks before them in 1942 must have seemed to be almost insurmountable.[6]

FIGHTING PHILOSOPHY AND COMMAND CULTURE

Beyond the physical, material, and organizational requirements, one of the most important factors in the SWPA in 1942 was the need to establish a firm working relationship at the military level between the two new coalition partners. As noted at the creation of the SWPA, there was not much of a shared knowledge or history between the two countries to build upon. In addition to this lack of strong foundations, a number of doctrinal and philosophical approaches to warfare would soon become evident.

With the division of the Pacific into two theaters along service lines and MacArthur constituting his GHQ with US Army personnel only, it was clear that there would be no joint (all three services) or combined (US, Australian, and Dutch) senior headquarters in the theater. Rather, GHQ would remain exclusively American and wholly dominated by the US Army. MacArthur's aim from the outset was to firmly establish centralized control over operations in his theater that reinforced the dominance of the United States over Australia and the supremacy of the US Army over the other services. The major point of intersection in this approach at the military level would develop through GHQ's relationship with its service commands and with the Australians through the relationship with the senior Australian Army commander, Thomas Blamey, and his Australian staff. Critical to the relationship between MacArthur and Blamey, and between GHQ and Adv LHQ, was the differing US and Australian doctrinal approaches to operations and the rapport (or lack thereof) among the high command.

On a practical level, one of the greatest impediments to cooperation was that the US and Australian/British armies placed a different emphasis on their style of command. MacArthur's view was very much influenced by US Army interwar doctrine on command as well as by his personality.[7] While for both armies the focus in relation to the commander was their ability "to make decisions," for the Americans this meant that the commander would hold singular authority for the operations and functions under his command.[8] As part of this construct, the US Army placed much more emphasis on a centralized approach to operations. US Army field manual *FM 100-5: Tentative Field Service Regulations; Operations, 1939* stipulated that "so long as a commander can exercise effective control he does not decentralize."[9] This was the guiding principle for command in the US Army, an approach that also fitted well with MacArthur's personal approach. From the time of his arrival in the SWPA, he sought to impose his "omnipotent notions of generalship, and his assertion of total top-down control from the summit," and he "exerted influence in a way that probably no other individual, with the possible exception of [US Army CoS] General George C. Marshall, could have done."[10]

MacArthur's approach was reflective of broad ideas about command in US doctrine. Devolving command authority downward was "not . . . part of the fabric of the American leadership philosophy."[11] US Army field manual *FM 100-5: Field Service Regulations; Operations, 1944* noted that "the subordinate unit is a part of the tactical team employed by the higher commander to accomplish a certain mission, and *any* independence on the part must conform to the general plan."[12] In addition, the US Army approach had a "command culture that prioritized effective processes and procedures over the human and moral elements of command such as intuition and individual judgement."[13]

The US emphasis on centralized control is critical. Independent actions were deemed to be rare, although it was also emphasized that subordinates should act under the guiding principles of an operation if they were left without clear orders while concurrently attempting to reestablish contact with the senior commander. In addition, the 1941 version of *FM 100-5* noted that "personal conferences between the higher commander and his subordinates who are to execute his orders may at times be advisable, that the latter may arrive at a correct understanding of the plans and intentions of their superior. Commanders do not justify their decisions to subordinates, nor do they seek the approval of subordinates for their actions."[14] This makes it clear that conferences were not forums for discussion and planning but rather an orders group under centralized control.

This top-down hierarchical system of command was at odds with the decentralized British Commonwealth Army method that was used by the Australians and that placed responsibility, faith, and confidence in subordinate commanders to plan and run operations. *British Field Service Regulations, Volume III: Higher Operations* noted: "In dealing with his subordinates, a commander will allot them definite tasks, clearly explaining his intentions, and will then allow them liberty of action in arranging the methods by which they will carry out these tasks. Undue centralisation and interference with subordinates is harmful, since they are apt either to chafe at excessive control or to become afraid of taking responsibility."[15]

This system evolved out of the British experience in World War I, whereby in 1917 and 1918 there was considerable devolution of responsibilities and planning to more junior commanders and their staff. This is not to argue that the British system was completely different in its approach to command. The historian David French regards that despite this emphasis in doctrine to decentralize, in practice the British approach often "remained committed to an autocratic command and control system that inhibited subordinate commanders from exercising initiative."[16] However, in British doctrine there was also a much greater degree of flexibility in command at the divisional level and above, where commanders were allowed to "interpret doctrine as they saw fit,"[17] although this could also cause problems in relation to developing a "common understanding of the meaning . . . of doctrine throughout the Army."[18]

The great advantage for the Australians in World War II and their approach to command was that the commander of the AIF from the time of its creation in 1939, General Blamey, set the tone and approach for senior command. He was then able to exert even more influence when from 1942 he was made C-in-C of the AMF, a position he held until the end of the war. This meant that not only was he able to heavily influence the Australian Army's approach to command, staff work, planning, and doctrine, but also that he was able to hand select the officers he believed would carry out his methods. Experience would show that Blamey preferred the process outlined in *British Field Service Regulations, Volume III*, although he was also equally capable of reinterpreting this approach by allocating different levels of planning and coordination to different head-quarters based on the personality and capabilities of his subordinate com-manders and their staff.[19]

Beyond differences over command, there was also no system of plan-ning, control, and coordination shared by the two armies.[20] In US Army formations, the head of the commander's control apparatus was his HQ CoS. However, this officer was first and foremost a supervisor of the HQ's staff procedures, as opposed to the British system where the senior staff officers were a "point of primary interaction with subordinates over the issue of orders and instructions."[21]

The US system was based on the French general staff system, repre-sented by the classification and organization of the staff into branches—G-1, personnel; G-2, intelligence; G-3, operations; and G-4, logistics. This system was, as Eitan Shamir has noted, an "expression of the mana-gerial approach" to command and control evident in the US Army at the time. This was particularly important as the branches in this system were coequal; thus it required a strong manager to oversee the process. Hence, the role of the CoS. This was an approach that had been built on industrial management ideas in the United States that placed an emphasis on a centralized control process to create efficiencies. The managerial ap-proach was also heavily emphasized in the curriculum in the interwar US Army staff colleges.[22]

The British/Australian staff system was fundamentally different. Ac-cording to British doctrine, the commander was primarily responsible for making decisions, while "the staff convert[ed his] ideas . . . into orders and by working out all details related to their execution [to] free his mind to deal with other, more important, matters."[23] The staff consisted of two senior staff officers rather than a US-style CoS. The senior general staff officer was responsible for operations, intelligence, and training, while a senior administrative staff officer was responsible for personnel and lo-gistics. Each of these senior officers had his own staff, and coordination across the whole staff was carried out by the senior general staff officer when necessary. The senior general staff officer also had the power to act with the commander's authority in his absence.[24] The advantage of this system was the integration of intelligence and training under the senior general staff officer, who could also be regarded as the de facto CoS if required.

Maj. Gen. Frank Berryman, who was Blamey's DCGS and thus the senior general staff officer in the Australian Army throughout most of

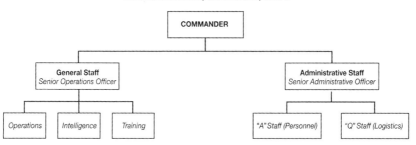

Figure 4.1 US and Australian Staff Systems

the Pacific War, noted that the primary duties of the staff in this system were assisting the "commander in execution of his function of command and assisting the fighting troops in execution of those tasks." This
was essential, he noted, as the Australian "decentralised command [ap-
proach required] careful co-ordination of effort [in order to] . . . produce
max[iumum] results." Underneath this overarching task, he laid out four
key areas for the staff to work on:

A. Collection of info[rmation] and dissemination so that action
can be taken intelligently on orders transmitted,

B. Transmitting of the cdr's [commander's] orders and instructions,

C. Exercise of forethought to ensure timely anticipation of difficulties and of material required,

D. Arrangements to remove anticipated difficulties and facilitate
[the] cdr's plan.[25]

This British Commonwealth system was more heavily influenced by the German model of staff organization, which gave prominence to the operations staff above administration. Historian Martin van Creveld summed up the philosophical differences between these systems, noting that the German/British staffs asked, "What is the core of the problem? The American trained staff . . . asked what are the problem's component parts?"[26]

The different philosophical approaches were also reflected in the differences in the planning process between GHQ and Adv LHQ. GHQ, under MacArthur and his CoS Sutherland, would write the plans, and only *after* they were written would the three service commands—Air, Naval, and Land HQs—be involved. This meant they had little influence on shaping the original plans produced by GHQ. In addition, per US doctrine, conferences with the subordinate formations were about the commander delivering his orders and not about seeking approval or generating debate.

In contrast, Adv LHQ would develop a plan seeking some input from the component commanders and then present this plan at a planning conference or series of conferences. At these meetings, subordinate commanders were free to raise questions, propose different ideas, and request support for various aspects of the plan. If this was the final or only conference before an operation, the subordinate commanders would leave with verbal orders for their own planning and preparations, with confirmatory orders being sent down afterward by the senior HQ incorporating the changes agreed upon on the conference.[27] The other major difference was that, in the British system, staff officers often were given a liaison role to transmit orders of the commander to subordinate units, while in the US Army this role was reserved for the commander alone.[28]

In the end this meant that in the SWPA, GHQ would fundamentally adopt a highly centralized, top-down approach to planning and that its staff procedures would be based on US doctrine. The Australian preference was to decentralize the "working process to subordinate formations, then progressively coordinate on the way up."[29] Both systems had their own advantages. The US system, in particular, produced officers who were very proficient at mobilization, logistics, and the deployment of forces,[30] and this approach would produce great dividends for MacArthur in 1943 and 1944. The Australian system had more built-in flexibility, which allowed it to be more effective at combat command and at times more able to adapt quickly to changing operational and tactical circumstances in the face of the enemy. As Van Creveld notes, "all other things being equal, a command system that allows for initiative on the lowest level, and for intelligent cooperation between subordinate commanders, is likely to be superior to one that does not."[31] However, what should not be overlooked is the role of individual commanders and staff officers in this process. The individual commanders' personalities could overcome the constraints of their doctrinal approach, or conversely they could just as easily squander its relative advantages or reinforce its most constraining elements.

Overall, the fact remains that there were major differences in organization, philosophical approaches to command, planning, and coordination of operations between GHQ and Adv LHQ. There was to be no systematic or structural solution to these problems during the course of the Pacific War. It would mean that the two systems would have to find ways of working together, and principally this would come down to the willingness and ability of senior commanders and their staffs to overcome problems and find practical solutions. The different systems would create tension in the relationship in 1942 and some very heated debates in 1943.

MACARTHUR AS A "JOINT" COMMANDER

Under US doctrine, MacArthur's role as the theater strategic commander in the SWPA was to "organize his forces and area so as to permit the necessary unity of command for both combat and administration."[32] In addition, it was within his "responsibilities that operational plans [were developed to] provide for [the] coordination of . . . land, sea, and air forces at his disposal and that such plans are energetically and effectively executed."[33]

MacArthur's view of his role as a theater commander, however, went well beyond the bounds of US doctrine. He stated at the end of the war that a "theatre commander is not merely limited to the handling of his troops; he commands the whole area, politically, economically, and militarily. At that stage of the game when politics fails and the military takes over, you must trust the military."[34]

This exceptionally wide remit meant that, for all intents and purposes, MacArthur saw himself as "co-equal" to the Prime Minister Curtin and, in relation to "his" return to the Philippines, preeminent. This would mean that MacArthur would operate concurrently at all four levels of warfare: political, strategic, operational, and tactical. In addition, as he did not indulge the notion of combined HQs or the idea of delegation of joint command to subordinates, he was the supreme power in the SWPA. He would also see it as within his prerogative to take on a much broader role in the direction of Allied strategy in the Pacific than his position allowed.

As well as imposing his will upward, he also used his omnipotent ideas of command to impose himself on his subordinates in complete indifference to his own chain of command. In order to run his theater in this manner, he also saw it as an imperative that GHQ be given a constant running commentary on operations. This amounted to a desire for an almost play-by-play description of actions on the battlefront as they took place.

MacArthur did not foster the idea of subordinate joint commands but instead insisted on keeping a firm control of *his* air, land, and naval assets. This theoretically made him the "joint commander" in the SWPA, although he never really acted as one. This was further complicated by his preference of allocating single-service task forces to undertake operations. It was then up to his subordinate commanders to "'bury inter service' and inter army rivalry and plan, integrate and execute the operation."[35] As Kevin Holzimmer has noted, "for all practical purposes [operations therefore] fell under the challenging principle of cooperation rather than unity of command."[36]

Yet MacArthur did not see "cooperation" as an impediment to the development and execution of military operations. He believed that, under his guidance and leadership, his senior officers were beyond interservice or interarmy rivalry. This, however, was a view shared by neither his subordinates nor by the approach of his HQ. As the VII Amphibious Force (VII Phib) commander, Vice Adm. Daniel Barbey, noted on his arrival in theater in late 1942, "I was to learn his team was not functioning as smoothly as he [MacArthur] indicated."[37]

US doctrine, combined with MacArthur's single-service emphasis and "cooperative" approach to operations, would also mean that only in "the most remote sense" was the planning process in the SWPA integrated. General Brett, the AAF commander, would note in mid-1942 to his replacement, Lt. Gen. George Kenney, about MacArthur's command arrangements and the running of GHQ, that

> MacArthur is prone to make all his decisions himself, depending only upon his immediate staff. One of the prerequisites of command, the coordination of the three services in a combined effort, is absolutely neglected. Commanders are not conferred with prior to either

major or minor decisions. Lack of command and staff meetings results in directives impossible to interpret and orders issued without the help of those who must carry them out and who should presumably have the most specialized knowledge of the subject. As far as I am concerned, it has been extremely difficult tying in orders which have been issued. I get the same reflection from Admiral Leary and from General Blamey, although I believe they have consulted more often with General MacArthur than I have.[38]

While Brett's position may well have been influenced by his replacement with Kenney and his poor relationship with MacArthur and Sutherland, his observations of GHQ in 1942 can be seen as accurate. Furthermore, this high degree of centralization under MacArthur would blur the lines of command arrangements. This approach would work reasonably well in practice during 1942, when operations were largely confined to small areas of Papua, but as MacArthur's responsibilities expanded at all levels of command, his inability to delegate would cause delays and friction and would impede success at the operational and tactical levels.

US-AUSTRALIAN RELATIONS IN 1942

With the differences in command and staff systems in the SWPA, personalities and individual relationships were critically important. This is particularly the case in regard to the senior headquarters, as "the higher the administrative level, the greater the emphasis on interpersonal skill."[39] This fact was amplified in the SWPA under MacArthur's leadership style, with its emphasis on cooperation rather than unity of command.[40] Cooperation would mean that the coordination of operations would rely heavily on good personal relationships at the highest echelon between the different branches of the military services and the different national forces in the region. Unfortunately, from almost the very first day after the creation of the SWPA, relations between senior Australian and American officers and headquarters largely got off on the wrong foot.

At the time of MacArthur's arrival in Australia in March 1942, his new headquarters, GHQ, prepared a holistic appraisal of Australia and the strategic situation for the new C-in-C. This document did not present a flattering assessment. GHQ saw the Australian people and government exhibiting sentiments of "deep-rooted complacency . . . a lack of realism and . . . some tendency to panic when suddenly faced by reality." These factors were compounded by a lack of "self-reliance" in the country, both individual and collective, and this meant that the Australians "appear[ed] to be willing to lay the burden of responsibility on someone else and, lacking prospects of effectual direction and support from England, they [we]re turning to the United States to assume that responsibility."[41]

If GHQ's assessment of the direction of Australia's war effort was not flattering, it was just as skeptical as to the capabilities of its military forces. The report argued that "England has probably humoured [the Australian military] and praised them excessively, particularly in regard to AIF activities, in order to offset a touchy inferiority complex on their part."[42] While this document was confidential for MacArthur only, it goes a long way to illustrating the attitude of GHQ and the senior US officers during early 1942. This was reflective of what would become an ongoing debate during the year as to the abilities and experience of the US and Australian military forces in the SWPA, and it was to be carried out at all ranks and levels of command—most significantly, at the very top echelons of the SWPA.

While the focus on US-Australian relations is central to understanding the complexities of this relationship, it is also critical to understand the personalities and internal tensions that dominated MacArthur's headquarters. As Maj. Gen. Richard Marshall, GHQ's deputy CoS, noted, there were not just disagreements with the Australians but just as strong feelings against the navy and the air force and almost as strong feelings within GHQ, which itself was fractured into several groups that were set "by the way of personality."[43]

MacArthur's GHQ was well known for the dominance of the so-called Bataan Gang, a group of officers inside the HQ who had served with MacArthur in the Philippines and who resented the intrusion of outsiders. As one senior staff officer noted, they formed "an exclusive little coterie."[44] This group of senior staff officers was led by GHQ's CoS, the highly irritable Richard Sutherland. Sutherland was the son of a US senator from West Virginia and graduated from Yale University in 1916 before joining the army and fighting in World War I. After the war he chose to stay in the army, making steady progress up through the ranks and graduating from both the Command and General Staff School and the War College. He worked for MacArthur during his time as US Army CoS, and he took over as MacArthur's CoS in the Philippines in 1939, replacing Dwight D. Eisenhower.[45]

Along with being very capable and intelligent, Sutherland was "arrogant, opinionated and very ambitious,"[46] which made him "universally disliked."[47] Sutherland has been described by his US Army contemporaries as emotionless, mean-spirited, untrustworthy, and coldhearted—unsurprisingly, he made lots of enemies.[48] Blamey's senior staff officer, Frank Berryman, saw him as nothing much more than an "armchair editor."[49] Gen. Walter Krueger, MacArthur's first US Army commander in the SWPA, would state upon learning of Sutherland's death in 1966 that "it was a good thing for mankind."[50] Brett, who had an exceptionally hostile relationship with Sutherland (not a hard thing to achieve), described him as an "egoist . . . arbitrary in his attitude and [who] often renders decisions in the name of the C-in-C which it is felt the C-in-C has never had an opportunity to discuss." Brett also saw him as a "bully, who should he lose his ability to say 'by order of General MacArthur' would be practically a nobody."[51] Brett's engagement with Sutherland is reflective of the latter's vitriol, which in 1942 was focused most clearly on anyone outside the mainstream of the US Army, be they Australians, USAAF officers like Brett, or the USN. But as MacArthur's CoS, he was highly influential, and he was at the height of his powers from 1942 to 1944.

The next most controversial figure at GHQ was Brig. Gen. Charles Willoughby, the head of the G-2 section. Willoughby was equally as prickly as Sutherland, and his abrasive personality, temper tantrums, and German heritage earned him the nickname "Baron von Willoughby."[52] He was emotional, moody, explosive, and physically intimidating. At six feet three inches and 220 pounds, he "struck terror into field-grade officers."[53] While these traits made him just as unpopular as Sutherland with the staff and senior commanders, where Sutherland was capable and efficient Willoughby demonstrated high levels of mediocrity. His intelligence estimates in 1942 and 1943, before the widespread availability of signals intelligence acquired through the code-breaking operation Ultra, were at times highly questionable, and the Australian intelligence staff at Adv LHQ consistently proved more apt at analyzing Japanese strengths and intentions. His performance has suggested that he may well have been one of the poorest, if not the worst, senior Allied intelligence officers of the war. He was, however, exceptionally loyal to MacArthur, to the point of being a total sycophant. MacArthur's loyalty in return is most likely the only thing that saved him from being sacked on a number of occasions. He was the only staff officer to serve MacArthur continually from 1941 to 1951.

Sutherland and Willoughby's personalities meant that they were "often at odds" with one another, and despite Willoughby's own unpopularity, he was still able to generate some sympathy among the staff as no one was despised more than Sutherland.[54] Willoughby's and Sutherland's abrasive personalities were somewhat offset by the other two key staff officers in the HQ, who would prove not only to be exceptionally capable but also had personalities that were much more amenable.

Behind Sutherland in GHQ's hierarchy was Brig. Gen. Richard Marshall, who was the deputy CoS and the senior logistics officer at GHQ. Like Willoughby and Sutherland, he had served in the Philippines disaster with MacArthur, but unlike the aforementioned officers he was one of the few members of the Bataan Gang who was well liked and respected among both the US officers in GHQ and the senior Australian high command. He lacked the "dash and brilliance" of Sutherland and was seen as an officer who remained in the background at GHQ. Compared to the C-in-C and the CoS, he was seen as "quiet and amiable." Geoffrey Perret noted that Marshall was a "valuable counter weight to Sutherland" and the "kind of officer MacArthur was always looking for but not always able to get assigned to him."[55] His greatest assets were his ability to expertly navigate the US Army logistics system, "his ability to harmonize staff relations," and that he was willing to delegate and empower subordinates to get things done.[56]

The other key senior staff officer at GHQ was the head of the G-3 section, Brig. Gen. Stephen Chamberlin. Chamberlin had not served with MacArthur during the Philippines disaster and thus was not one of the Bataan Gang. In fact, he was one of only a couple of "outsiders" among the senior staff at GHQ. Chamberlin had served on the staff of General Brett, and MacArthur selected him because of his excellent work as CoS of the USAFIA and his dedication in organizing supplies to get from Australia to support MacArthur in the Philippines. Thereafter, he managed to convince MacArthur of his loyalty. While Chamberlin was seen as an "unprepossessing gnome who was physically distinguished by his big beautiful nose," he was also regarded as intelligent, talented, and "a clever tactician."[57] In GHQ and across the SWPA, he was a widely respected officer,[58] one who had the ability to translate MacArthur's broad directives into clear operational plans.[59] General Brett, who had no time for almost all of GHQ's staff, noted that his criticisms of GHQ did not extend to Chamberlin, who "is a good man working under strenuous handicaps [and] he has accomplished a great deal."[60]

Chamberlin was widely recognized as a "superb planner," and while he "did not suffer fools,"[61] he had a much more affable personality in comparison to Sutherland and Willoughby. In addition, he carefully "guarded his domain" within GHQ and "resented unsolicited recommendations" from other officers in the headquarters. Once MacArthur had decided on a course of action, it was Chamberlin who turned his "ethereal concepts into reality"[62] and then worked with senior commanders to implement the plan and work out the details. D. Clayton James, the author of the most authoritative and balanced account of MacArthur, called him "probably the most competent of [the] GHQ section chiefs."[63]

Chamberlin and Marshall, who ran the logistics command at GHQ, were two of the key officers who were instrumental in developing a smooth working relationship with the Australians. During the course of 1942–1945, Chamberlin would develop a close rapport with his Australian counterparts, such as General Berryman, who would note that "without you I cannot visualise how [General] Headquarters would have worked as you were the linch-pin that held it together and also the motive power in the implementation of General MacArthur's plans." Chamberlin was thus "one of the most popular senior Americans with the Australians."[64]

In addition to these senior officers, there were fifteen other staff officers at GHQ who had also come out of the Philippines with MacArthur and owed their rank and positions at GHQ to him. These included Brig. Gen. Spencer Akin, the chief signals officer; Col. Charles Stivers, the G-1; Col. L. G. Whitlock, the G-4; MacArthur's personal aides; and his public relations officer, Lt. Col. Le Grande Diller. They were all important officers in terms of the operation of GHQ, but the senior staff, especially Sutherland, Willoughby, Marshall, and Chamberlin, had the key relationships with the Australians that had to be fostered in order to make the coalition function. At least, the latter two of these officers had the ability, professionalism, and temperament to try to make the new relationship work.

It is easy to overprescribe to the role, power, and influence of the Bataan Gang members inside GHQ. While they were key elements in the running of the SWPA, the staff at GHQ did not command MacArthur's combat forces. In order to achieve cooperation on the battlefield, it was essential that solid relationships were built between these commanders. It must not be overlooked that General Brett and his replacement, General Kenney, both developed very strong relationships with not only the RAAF but also with Blamey and his staff. The same can be said of the commander of the ANF, Admiral Leary, and his replacement, Admiral Carpenter. Admiral Barbey (VII Phib) would develop a very close relationship with his Australian counterparts and would include Australians on his planning staff throughout the war.

These commanders are the key officers who at the operational level worked so closely and effectively with the Australians. Furthermore,

Blamey was able to circumvent Sutherland via his position as C-in-C of the AMF and commander of the ALF, which gave him direct access to MacArthur. Meanwhile, his senior operations officer from September 1942, Berryman, dealt largely with the more affable Chamberlin, and his senior logistics officer, Maj. Gen. John Chapman, dealt with Marshall. All of these highly proficient officers developed excellent relationships with their Australian subordinates. It was in these series of relationships that much of Sutherland's and the Bataan Gang's power and influence could be dissipated. In addition, while the often obstructionist officers at GHQ could not be avoided, at the operational and tactical levels GHQ had much less power and influence. The Bataan Gang's power, and especially Sutherland's influence, would also steadily decline as the war progressed.

There is no doubting that there was a tense atmosphere inside Mac-Arthur's HQs in 1942; this was also mirrored among the US military's different branches of service. Admiral Barbey noted that "nowhere in the military world was the inter-service bickering so bitter in the early days of World War II as around Allied Headquarters [GHQ] in Brisbane Australia."[65] Both of the USAAF commanders noted in 1942 that Mac-Arthur and his staff had a hostile attitude to the air force.[66] The USN, meanwhile, was widely despised by MacArthur and his staff. This was hardly a satisfactory state of affairs, given that MacArthur's modus operandi called for coordination between services on operations rather than through joint command.

MacArthur and GHQ's attitude toward the senior Australian command would also become evident through the course of 1942. He told commander of I US Corps, Lt. Gen. Robert L. Eichelberger, that he should "pay my respects to the Australians and then have nothing further to do with them."[67] General Brett, MacArthur's USAAF commander, remarked that GHQ gave "little consideration to the Australians" and noted that "there is every indication that the Australians are being side stepped altogether and certainly very little effort has been made to incorporate them in the general scheme."[68] Brett's replacement, Kenney, noted that Sutherland "thought the Australians were about as undisciplined, untrained, over advertised, and generally useless as the Air Force."[69] The British Army liaison officer at GHQ, Maj. Gen. R. H. Dewing, wrote later in the war that MacArthur and GHQ were "working steadily to exclude the Australians from any effective hand in control of land or air operations or credit them, except as a minor element in a US show."[70]

However, the denigration of the Australians by the US military was not only restricted to GHQ. The most extreme of the US criticisms came from Maj. Gen. Robert C. Richardson. In July 1942, Richardson was sent by the US Army CoS, Gen. George C. Marshall, out to Australia on an inspection tour to assess the situation in the SWPA. Marshall and MacArthur also had in mind the possible appointment of Richardson as the first US corps commander in the theater. Richardson's report to Marshall is filled with culturally imperialistic and xenophobic comments that were the staple of the petty barbs being thrown from officers of *both* armies at this time. However, Richardson took it to a whole new level of contempt. He noted: "The fact that American troops were commanded by Australians [under ALF] is deeply resented by officers and men and the consciousness of being placed under a group of *colonial officers*, most of whom were *non-professional* officers, had a chilling and depressing effect upon the commanders of our divisions and upon the commanders of subordinate units which have been attached to Australian commands."[71] Richardson argued "the present organisation [under Blamey] was an affront to national pride and to the dignity of the American army." In regard to the AAF and General Brett's integrated organizational structure with the RAAF, he noted that "no American Commander should be placed in the position of being dependent on foreigners." The report goes on to refer to the Australian Army as a "pretentious organisation" with "grandiose ideas of expansion," which he believes was entirely based on elevating Australian officers above their US counterparts.[72]

Privately, Richardson also referred to Blamey as nothing more than the former police chief of Melbourne and argued that the Australian and American commands should be kept entirely separate. Richardson initially refused the corps command as it would still be under Blamey, whom he regarded as a "non-professional Australian drunk."[73] MacArthur, however, was still happy to have him, but George Marshall vetoed the idea, arguing that the "difficulties inherent in any allied command organization and your especially difficult problems as commander-in-chief in a country not your own, combined with Richardson's intense feelings regarding service under Australian command, made his assignment unwise."[74]

It is hard to say to what extent the Richardson report represented majority opinion among US officers who served in the SWPA in 1942. What is clear is that it is based on Richardson's philosophy of the need for a unified American command structure and on the views of several US officers in Australia whom he interviewed. It is also clear that the view among the US command—that Australians were mainly an "amateur" army made of up "part-time soldiers"—was well entrenched, so much so that it persisted far beyond the war years. A number of senior US officers also concurred with Richardson that the Australian C-in-C was little more than one of these "part-time soldiers."[75]

This perception of Australian officers as part-time amateurs was a poor example of entrenched cultural imperialism that had no basis in fact. During 1942, the US Army in Australia was dealing with a largely professional Australian military command that had seen extensive service in World War I and in the Mediterranean in World War II. As a whole, most of these Australian officers—including the regular army generals Blamey, Berryman, George Vasey, Sydney Rowell, Vernon Sturdee, John Northcott, Lavarack, and Horace Robertson—were much more experienced and qualified than their American counterparts, who had little or no experience of operations before their arrival in the SWPA. The same could be said of most senior Australian militia officers who served in operations with the Americans,[76] especially so of the three key militia generals, Arthur Allen, Stan Savige, and Leslie Morshead, who would serve in New Guinea in 1942 and 1943.

MacArthur recognized this fact when Blamey requested the transfer of several senior US Army officers to ALF HQ in order to create a combined US-Australian staff. Sutherland was hostile to Blamey's move to create an Allied staff, and MacArthur was not enthusiastic.[77] Blamey was to later claim that "my requests for American officers to establish a joint staff were met with face saving acceptance that was completely ineffective."[78] GHQ was opposed on the basis of its open opposition to combined staffs, as well as MacArthur's recognition that "senior Australian staff officers had vastly more experience than their American counterparts" and that the "dispatch to Australia of poor officers would result in a 'black eye for [the] US men placed with experienced and capable Australian officers.'"[79]

Despite this recognition from MacArthur, it was clear that in 1942, US officers held a clear sense that they possessed military superiority over their Australian counterparts. Tensions, however, always work both ways, and the Australians were not above going out of their way to cause trouble with their new "Allies." The CGS in Australia, Lt. Gen. Vernon Sturdee, commented that he believed US officers to be very academic in their outlook but with a lack of practical experience in warfare. The DCGS, Maj. Gen. George Vasey, Blamey's senior general staff officer in mid-1942, noted that GHQ was "like a bloody barometer in a cyclone . . . up and down every two minutes." Vasey claimed that the Americans "will never make good soldiers" because they had "defects . . . [in] . . . their civilization." He saw them as "sex crazed" and with an "obsession that they would die as soon as they got into action."[80] Vasey's view was, however, a minority opinion among the Australian senior command, although Maj. Dudley McCarthy (later an author in the Australian official histories) was not far off the mark in 1942 when he noted that "our people *want* to find fault with things US. They are secretly pleased when things go wrong with them."[81]

It is undeniable that relations in 1942, at all levels, were tested. What is important to note is that MacArthur's senior operations officer, Chamberlin, and his senior commanders, Brett and Kenney in AAF, admirals Leary, Carpenter, and Barbey in the navy, and Eichelberger, the I US Corps commander who would serve in the Papuan campaign, were not part of the Bataan Gang. The one exception to this was his senior logistics officer at GHQ, Richard Marshall, who proved he was exceptionally competent and without the same hang-ups or personality defects shared by Sutherland and Willoughby.

The relationship between senior American and Australian officers, in particular between GHQ and Adv LHQ during 1942, was tied heavily to preconceived ideas and cultural ignorance on both sides, as well as professional misunderstandings and different command and staff systems. It would take a considerable period of time to overcome these issues, and under the pressure of combat relations they would get much worse before they would improve. These differences would inhibit the Allies' ability to conduct operations, but it was simply another point of what German military theorist Carl von Clausewitz called the "friction of war." Overall, while it certainly caused problems, it would not prove to be a fatal impediment to achieving victory in the SWPA.

In the end, due to the different systems and MacArthur's preference for cooperative command, the key to the coalition being made to work (or not) in the SWPA would be the personal relations and personalities of the senior officers. The ability of formation and unit commanders and their senior staff officers, from both nations, to develop strong personal relationships to overcome many of these differences and to get the job done was paramount. This approach, as the Papua campaign would prove, was much more easily accomplished the farther US and Australian officers were away from GHQ and the closer they got to the front lines.

5

The Battles for Kokoda and Milne Bay

MACARTHUR'S POSITION IN EARLY 1942 and the assessments of his HQ were reflected in the lack of US war planning in the interwar period in relation to Australia. In addition, moves to coordinate defenses between the two countries had been slow despite the evident threat from Japan.[1] Once the war started, the importance of Australia to the Pacific War was, however, self-evident.

As early as the afternoon of 8 December 1941, an amended US war plan was sent to the remnants of the US Pacific Fleet in Pearl Harbor. This plan included, as a priority, the protection of the sea lines of communication to Australia.[2] To the commander of the USN, Admiral King,

> the entire Allied strategy in the Pacific depended on two cardinal points: Hawaii must not fall, and Australia must not fall. To those ends King ordered the new Pacific Fleet chief, Admiral Nimitz, to secure the seaways between Midway, Hawaii and the North American mainland. That was to be his first priority. His second priority, in only a "small degree less important," was to protect the lifeline between North American and Australia. . . . Every other concern was to be ruthlessly subordinated to what King call those "two vital Pacific tasks."[3]

This focus on the security of the sea lines of communication with Australia would bring US and Japanese plans in the Pacific into conflict. The defense of Midway and Hawaii was secured with Japanese defeat at the Battle of Midway in June 1942, while the forward defenses of the SWPA in Papua were secured with the Allied victory in the Coral Sea in May 1942. MacArthur told Curtin at the Prime Minister's War Conference on 11 June that the victories at Coral Sea and Midway "had resulted in a transformation of the position in the southwest Pacific area, and the security of Australia had now been assured."[4]

The Coral Sea victory meant that MacArthur and the Australians could focus their attention on the security of Papua and consideration

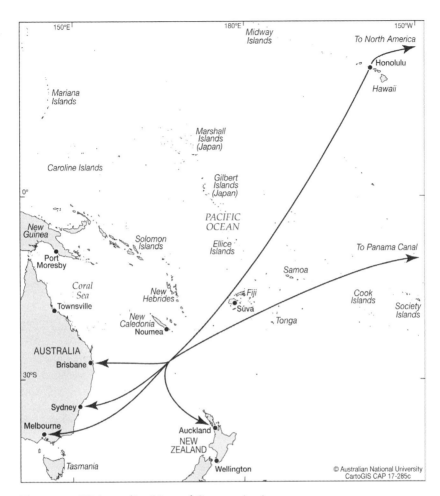

Figure 5.1 US-Australian Lines of Communication, 1942

of offensive action toward the Japanese base at Rabaul. The victory at Midway allowed Admiral King to start planning to move over to the offensive. As a result, King decided that the first point of counterattack would be the island of Guadalcanal in the South Pacific to put in place the final link of his initial strategy to secure the lines of communication to Australia.[5]

MacArthur's moves to secure Papua as a springboard to assault Rabaul and King's move to push for an immediate counterattack in the South Pacific to secure the sea lines of communication with Australia would mean that large-scale operations in the Pacific War would became centered during the latter half of 1942 and most of 1943 in the USN's SOPAC and MacArthur's SWPA. This focus would be manifested through the two major campaigns in the Pacific during the second half of 1942: the Papuan campaign, within SWPA's purview, and the Solomons campaign (centered on Guadalcanal), within SOPAC's.

The focus of the Pacific War on the South and Southwest Pacific areas was also a direct result of Japanese plans and movements in the first half of 1942. The rapid success of Japanese forces across the Pacific in the initial stages of the war had meant that they were able to secure their first-stage operations much more quickly than they anticipated. First-stage operations included the occupation of most of Southeast Asia, the NEI, the Gilbert Islands, the Admiralty Islands, and parts of northern New Guinea. This area would secure them the resources they required to continue the prosecution of the war in China, to protect their East Asia conquests, and to develop their Greater East Asia Co-Prosperity Sphere.[6]

The rapid success in their first-stage operations led the Japanese to focus on plans for the second-stage operations in early 1942. The debate over Japanese strategic policy split the Army and Navy General Staffs at Imperial General Headquarters (IGHQ) and the IJN's Combined Fleet. The lack of a supreme commander or a unified command organization meant that the army and navy developed plans separately, which severely hampered Japan's decision making and its development of strategy. On the navy side of the ledger, this was further complicated by the growing power of the Combined Fleet, and especially its C-in-C, Adm. Isoroku Yamamoto.[7]

In prewar planning, the navy, which had primary responsibility for the Pacific War, had not identified Australia as a strategic objective, although it had recognized the need to "raid and destroy" forward Allied bases in the second stage of operations. These operations were primarily designed to secure the "defensive line through the central Pacific, Rabaul, the Solomon Islands, New Guinea, Java, Malaya and Burma."[8] However, their rapid success early in the war meant that the IJN began to reconsider its second-stage operations in early 1942.

As part of these discussions, IGHQ committed at the end of January to an invasion of Port Moresby in Papua by the army's South Seas Force (SSF), which had earlier captured Rabaul. This part of the second-stage operations represented an expansion of the war by the IJN. To the IJN, Port Moresby was important as a result of the threat that it posed to Rabaul, which had been occupied as part of stage-one operations to protect the main IJN Central Pacific naval base at Truk.[9] The SSF investigated the

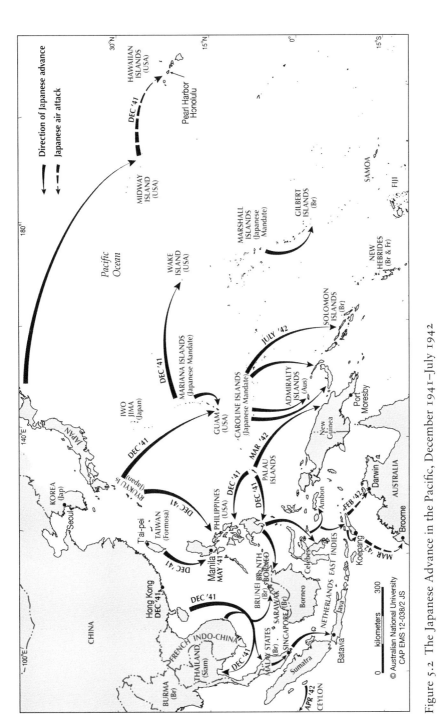

Figure 5.2 The Japanese Advance in the Pacific, December 1941–July 1942

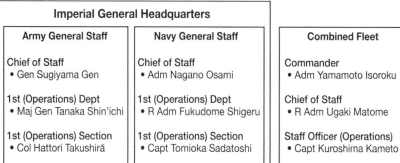

Figure 5.3 Japanese Command Organization, Imperial General Headquarters, 1942

possibility of an overland route from the northern coast of Papua, while the navy considered the sea route.[10] The major problem with the sea route was that it would bring any Japanese naval force into the Coral Sea and require it to operate beyond the range of Japanese aircraft in Rabaul and Lae while at the same time placing it well within range of Allied aircraft based in both Papua and northern Australia. The numbers of passages around the eastern end of Papua were limited, and this would channel the Japanese force into a relatively small area, making operational surprise difficult. In the face of these obstacles, and with IGHQ stating that the operation should be undertaken only "if at all possible," the invasion of Port Moresby, or Operation Mo as it was known, was not acted upon immediately.[11]

Discussion also turned to the fate of Australia. The Navy General Staff believed that Australia had to be neutralized, while some officers even advocated the invasion of northern Australia. For the Imperial Japanese Army (IJA), the expansion of the war in the Pacific and proposals for any invasion of Australia were not welcome developments. It remained focused on the war in China, which would occupy the vast bulk of the IJA well into 1944. An invasion of Australia would require up to twelve divisions, and the army argued that the expansion of the war in this direction would be "very dangerous and [would] go beyond what should be Japan's culminating point in the offensive."[12] As the army was adamantly refusing to endorse an invasion of Australia, the IJN turned toward plans for its neutralization, code-named Operation FS.

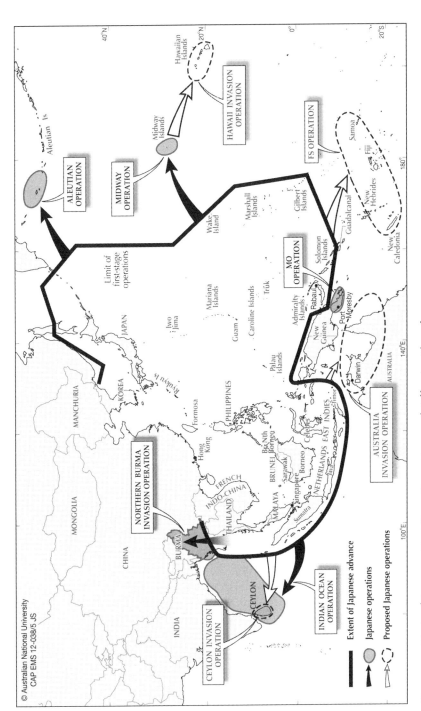

Figure 5.4 Limit of Japanese First-Stage Operations and Offensive Plans for 1942

© Australian National University
CAP EMS 12-038/5 JS

Extent of Japanese advance
Japanese operations
Proposed Japanese operations

ALEUTIAN OPERATION
MIDWAY OPERATION
HAWAII INVASION OPERATION
FS OPERATION
MO OPERATION
AUSTRALIA INVASION OPERATION
INDIAN OCEAN OPERATION
CEYLON INVASION OPERATION
NORTHERN BURMA INVASION OPERATION

Limit of first-stage operations

Hawaiian Islands
Aleutian Is
Midway Islands
Wake Island
Marshall Islands
Gilbert Islands
Samoa
Fiji
New Hebrides
New Caledonia
Guadalcanal
Solomon Islands
Admiralty Islands
Rabaul
Port Moresby
New Guinea
Mariana Islands
Caroline Islands
Truk
Guam
Iwo Jima
Palau Islands
Darwin
AUSTRALIA
Timor
Celebes
NETHERLANDS EAST INDIES
Borneo
Brunei
Br Nth Borneo
Sarawak
Sumatra
Singapore
MALAYA
THAILAND
FRENCH INDO-CHINA
Hong Kong
PHILIPPINES
Formosa
Ryukyu Is
JAPAN
KOREA
MANCHURIA
MONGOLIA
CHINA
BURMA
CEYLON
INDIA

40°N
20°N
0°
20°S
100°E
140°E
180°

Operation FS involved the occupation of the Fiji Islands, Samoa, and New Caledonia. The IJA was happy to agree to this proposal, as it would involve only those soldiers who had already been allocated to the Pacific War, so it represented no new troop commitments on its part. The agreement between the IJA and the IJN for Operation FS was concluded in February and planned for March.[13] Yamamoto, meanwhile, had his Combined Fleet staff preparing plans to attack Hawaii and strike a blow designed to defeat the remnants of the US Pacific Fleet, as well as another series of offensive operations in the west to attack Ceylon and the British fleet in the Indian Ocean. These operations were opposed by the navy and army staffs, which had already agreed on Operation FS.[14]

The interjection of the Combined Fleet and the disagreements between the army and navy staffs meant that debate dragged on into March 1942. The final agreement on 7 March of the "outline of war leadership to be hereafter adopted," presented and adopted by the prime minster and the emperor on 12 March, ended any consideration of the invasion of Australia.[15] The debate that did follow was focused on the IJN's offensive action, and by early April Yamamoto had won over the IJN staff with his plan to strike the US Pacific Fleet. In the interim, based on the agreement of 12 March, the Combined Fleet carried out Operation C, a raid into the Indian Ocean that included strikes against Ceylon on 5 and 9 April 1942. After returning from the Indian Ocean, the Combined Fleet reorganized, and two fleet carriers were allocated to conduct Operation Mo, which led to the Japanese defeat at the Battle of the Coral Sea, while the rest of the Combined Fleet prepared for the Hawaii operations, which led to their defeat at the Battle of Midway in June.[16]

The Battle of the Coral Sea had ended for Japan what John Lundstrom and Richard Frank have called the "First South Pacific Campaign." Yet, despite these losses, the Japanese initially remained committed to their operations in the South Pacific. On 18 May, the IJA activated the Seventeenth Army HQ for the purpose of commanding Operation Mo (via an overland assault on Port Moresby) and Operation FS.

The defeat at Midway caused Operation FS to be delayed, and in early July the operation was finally canceled. Despite its cancellation, the Japanese were still pushing forward with their plans for what would become their Second South Pacific Campaign. This would include an overland assault from the northern coast of Papua to take Port Moresby and complete Operation Mo. In addition, Vice Adm. Shigeyoshi Inoue, the commander of the Fourth (or South Seas) Fleet, believed that the defense of Rabaul required not only the completion of Operation Mo but also the establishment of a number of fortified air bases in the Solomon Islands region. This push led to Japanese forces landing on the island of Tulagi in the southern Solomons on 3 May.[17] The Japanese soon occupied the nearby island of Guadalcanal after recognizing its utility as an advance air base.

OPERATIONS OF THE AAF IN THE DEFENSE OF AUSTRALIA, 1942

While the Japanese debated strategy, they embarked on an air campaign to pound Allied bases in northern Australia. Initially the defense of Darwin was undertaken by only a few understrength squadrons from the RAAF with no frontline fighter aircraft to speak of. The Japanese first arrived on 19 February 1942 when IJN aircraft from the same task force that had struck Pearl Harbor hit Darwin's port and airfield. Some 188 naval aircraft struck Darwin, followed up eighty minutes later by 54 IJA land-based bombers.[18] Eight ships were sunk, major damage was done to the airfield and town, and 243 people were killed. As Mark Johnston has noted, this was the nadir of the RAAF's history, as it offered "no airborne resistance to the first raid" on Australian soil because it had not a single fighter squadron in the country at this time.[19]

Resistance to the Japanese raid on Darwin came in the form of ten USAAF P-40 Kittyhawk aircraft that were in Darwin on their way to Java. Maj. Floyd Pell shot down two Japanese dive-bombers, but two other pilots were killed and two others forced down. Thereafter, the Japanese launched a number of raids on northern Australia, including a major one on Broome that killed eighty-eight people. Darwin, the major military port in northwestern Australia, was hit again a number of times, but it would take three weeks before a fighter force was provided to defend the town. This force was provided by the USAAF's 49th Fighter Group under Lt. Col. Paul Wurtsmith.[20] Wurtsmith would operate under the regional commander, RAAF Air Cmdr. Frank Bladin, in a relationship that worked exceptionally well.[21] The 49th Fighter Group would stay in Darwin for five months and was accredited with shooting down sixty-four Japanese aircraft. However, "surprisingly, few Australians know anything of this commitment by the USAAF to the direct defence of Australia . . . [and] the contribution of Paul Wurtsmith and his 49th Fighter Group has not been properly acknowledged."[22]

While the 49th Fighter Group provided for the defense of Darwin, in mid-March three RAAF fighter squadrons (also P-40 aircraft) were formed in Australia and deployed to Port Moresby, Milne Bay, and Pearce

in western Australia. Soon thereafter, the RAAF squadrons in Papua were
reinforced by the USAAF's 8th Fighter Group, flying P-39 Airacobras.[23]
These forces were supplemented by RAAF and USAAF reconnaissance
aircraft, light and medium bombers operating in Papua and from Australia, and heavy bombers operated by the USAAF out of northern Australia. By the time of Kenney's arrival and his reforms, the situation had
improved dramatically for both the air defense of Australia and in regard
to operations in Papua and against Rabaul. However, developing and
projecting combat airpower in the SWPA still had an exceptionally long
way to go in order for the Allies to gain and maintain air control, let alone
air supremacy, over the main battlefields. By this time, however, Kenney
and the Fifth Air Force's dominance over the RAAF was starting to show.
Air Commodore Hewitt noted to his wife in August 1942:

> Our allied air forces would not be sweeping through the Japs until
> the USAAF had a much larger air force in our theatre. In the R.A.A.F
> we were now beginning to feel the impact of the U.S. equipment and
> personnel—the personalities of their generals and the quality of their
> leadership. Our officers were well trained and knew their work well
> but minor details seemed to absorb their energies, while the Ameri-
> cans, with their masses of equipment, speeded up the essential field
> work.[24]

Hewitt had hit on what would become the key issue for the relationship
between the two air forces—the already evident, and growing, disparity
between the two countries in the air war. He astutely noted, "I felt there
was a growing need for us to match the American effort proportionally
from our own resources, and not be left behind them but to be in front
beside them, as we were in the beginning. I told Kenney, Bostock and
Jones that and kept on repeating it."[25]

MACARTHUR'S STRATEGY, MARCH–AUGUST 1942

While MacArthur had initially been very cautious about the possibilities
of offensive action when he became C-in-C SWPA, after the Japanese
defeats at the Coral Sea and Midway he recovered his morale and once
again started to put faith in his "destiny." The first major obstacle that
stood in his way to redemption in the Philippines was the large Japanese
base at Rabaul on the eastern tip of New Britain. The first campaigns

of the SWPA in Papua and the POA command at Guadalcanal in the South Pacific were a direct response to the Japanese decision to develop Rabaul as a major base. There the Japanese had built runways and developed extensive defensive positions, including 367 antiaircraft weapons, forty-three coastal guns, and 6,543 machine guns, mortars, howitzers, and grenade launchers for ground defense, all of which were manned by just under one hundred thousand men.[26]

In response, the JCS had ordered MacArthur and Nimitz to retake Rabaul. Recovering from his "funk" soon after the victory at Midway, MacArthur had demanded two aircraft carriers from the USN for his theater and an additional division, trained in amphibious operations, to supplement the 32nd and 41st US Infantry Divisions. With this force, he intended to retake Rabaul in only fourteen days. Soon after this pronouncement, the realization of the impossibility of this task led MacArthur to revise his schedule and replace his Tulsa operational plan with Tulsa II. This revised plan took into account the difficulties of his task and the friction of war by adding a total of *four* days to his schedule for the advance.

MacArthur forwarded Tulsa II to Washington despite not having the backing of his operations chief, Stephen Chamberlin, or taking into consideration logistics requirements or the response of the enemy. Unsurprisingly, it was not adopted.[27] What these initial plans revealed was a troubled commander still coming to terms with his defeat in the Philippines and trying to get a grip on his new command, the broader Allied strategy, and the limitations of the Allied forces in mid-1942. It is also indicative that MacArthur's plans were built largely around US forces; no Australian units were mentioned.

On 2 July, MacArthur and Nimitz were provided with the JCS directive that outlined the three tasks for the capture of Rabaul. Task 1—the Guadalcanal operation—was allocated to the SOPAC area under the USN. In order to accommodate this operation, the boundary of the SWPA and SOPAC was moved westward from 160 degrees to 159 degrees east longitude. MacArthur was allocated task 2—the capture of Salamaua and Lae in New Guinea—and task 3—the capture of Rabaul. For the final task, the forces of SOPAC would come under MacArthur's "strategic direction" while remaining under Nimitz's command.

In response, GHQ SWPA revised Tulsa II with a focus on the establishment of an airfield at Buna on the northern coast of Papua to support operations against Salamaua and Lae. This was to become Operation Providence, and the order for its implementation was issued on 12 July

1942.[28] Under the command of Brig. Gen. Robert H. Van Volkenburgh, a task force consisting of four Australian infantry companies would march overland from Port Moresby to Buna, via Kokoda, to secure the area (serial 1, D–1). US antiaircraft troops, an advance engineering detachment and port detachment, and an RAAF radar and communications detachment (serial 2, D-day) would follow on and arrive by sea.

On D+1, serial 3 would arrive, consisting of an Australian infantry brigade HQ, more US and Australian engineers, more RAAF troops, and two pursuit (fighter) squadrons. The remaining ground and air elements (serial 4) would be in place by D+14. The first troops were set down to be in place 10–12 August and the last by the end of the month. The total force was set at some 2,272 troops. As part of MacArthur's broader offensive plans, especially task 2, which he still believed could be undertaken in a "matter of weeks,"[29] the 41st and 32nd US Infantry Divisions were to be moved to Queensland for final training and would come under the command of the First Australian Army before moving forward into combat.

In terms of command organization for Operation Providence, Van Volkenburgh, as task force commander, had "joint" command of the force and any enabling forces he needed to move his troops and to support them tactically if required. He was also responsible directly to MacArthur for "coordinating all details of the operation" until the force was in place, whereupon the garrison duties and protection of the airfield would be handed over to the Australian brigade commander. This was an early indication of MacArthur's wish to cut Blamey and the Australians out of the control of major operations in the SWPA and also to have the Australians garrison the rear areas once the front lines moved on.[30]

GHQ's plan brought MacArthur and the Japanese directly into each other's path, as the latter attempted to put in motion their plan for an overland assault on Port Moresby to complete Operation Mo. The delay in MacArthur's plans, however, brought Operation Providence into question. On 13 July, intelligence revealed a large enemy convoy departing Rabaul with its destination assessed as Buna.[31] Despite a large but ineffective effort by the AAF, the Japanese convoy managed to land Maj. Gen. Tomitarō Horii's SSF against no ground opposition on 21 July 1942. Three days later, MacArthur rescinded the orders for Providence.[32] MacArthur's delay, allowing the Japanese to seize the initiative, would prove to be exceptionally costly in both time and lives. It would take MacArthur six months and over three thousand Australian and American lives before the Japanese were pushed out of Papua.

Prior to the Battle of the Coral Sea, the Australians had wisely kept limited forces in Port Moresby. Without air superiority or sea control, the forces there risked falling to the Japanese in exactly the same way those in Java, Timor, and New Britain had. However, with the strategic victory in the Coral Sea, Blamey realized that the chances of holding the last Allied bastion on the island of New Guinea had somewhat improved. As a result, within a few days of the naval victory he had sent GHQ a request for reinforcements, which included two antiaircraft batteries and an infantry brigade.[33] This force would supplement the 30th Militia Brigade that had been there since January. Yet these moves did not mean that the threat to Port Moresby from an amphibious assault was removed. In fact, GHQ and LHQ considered another Japanese attempt to be well within both their capabilities and intent.[34]

Following on from the decision to increase the garrison at Port Moresby was the decision, in early June, to develop an airfield on the southeastern tip of Papua at Milne Bay. This airfield would protect against a further Japanese amphibious attempt on Port Moresby and would also provide a route for Allied aircraft to attack Rabaul and the surrounding region without having to cross the Owen Stanley Range.[35] This force, which was built around the 7th Australian Militia Brigade and US Army engineers, left Townsville on 9 July and arrived at Milne Bay on 11 July 1942.[36] In addition, in order to strengthen his left flank, MacArthur also authorized the construction of an airfield with a small garrison force at Merauke on the southern coast of Dutch New Guinea.[37]

The Japanese landing at Buna had, however, driven a new urgency into Allied preparations for the defense of Papua. At the end of the month, Blamey meet with MacArthur at GHQ in Brisbane. Here, as with Operation Providence, MacArthur again tried to direct operations from GHQ, dealing out the Australians. He proposed to Blamey that the US 32nd Division be sent to Papua under GHQ's direct command. Blamey, however, managed to convince MacArthur that a more appropriate course of action would be to send the 7th Australian Division to Papua, along with the HQ of I Australian Corps, to take over New Guinea Force (NGF).

The following day, Lt. Gen. Sydney Rowell, commanding I Australian Corps, met with Blamey, and it was agreed that he would go to Port Moresby to command NGF. Maj. Gen. Cyril Clowes (GOC 1st Australian Division) was ordered to fly out and take command of Milne Force, which Blamey would reinforce with the 18th Brigade AIF from the 7th Division. Maj. Gen. Arthur "Tubby" Allen (GOC 7th Division) was ordered to take his HQ and the 21st Brigade AIF to Port Moresby. On arrival, he would also take under command the 14th and 30th Militia Brigades. This redistribution of forces would commence on 5 August and be complete by the twelfth. In addition, Blamey had completed the move of his Adv LHQ to Brisbane by 1 August to be alongside GHQ.[38]

While these plans were being put in place, the 30th Brigade had already established contact with the Japanese on the Kokoda Trail. A small force from the 39th Militia Battalion had set out from Port Moresby to walk to Buna on 8 July 1942 under the code name "Maroubra Force." The 39th would meet up with elements of the Papuan Infantry Battalion (PIB) that had been in Buna-Gona area and made the first contact with the Japanese. Maroubra Force's role was to defend Kokoda and "patrol towards Gona and Ioma."[39] However, it was soon reinforced by the 53rd Militia Battalion, then later by the 21st Brigade AIF, as it was forced to retreat back along the Kokoda Trail.

THE KOKODA TRAIL AND THE "GAP"

Papua, and more specifically the Kokoda Trail, was a formidable environment in which to conduct military operations. The overland route from Buna to Kokoda is one of the most challenging trails in the world, and as the GHQ terrain report of 17 June 1942 noted, it was an almost ten-day trek from Port Moresby to Buna, crossing "extremely rugged country" that included a thirteen-thousand-foot central range (the highest part of the actual trail was seven thousand feet), dense jungle, and "numerous streams which impeded the passage."[40] Lt. Col. Frank Norris, the 7th Division's chief medical officer, described the terrain as such: "Imagine an area 100 miles long—crumple and fold this into a series of ridges, each rising higher . . . cover this thickly with jungle, short trees and tall trees tangled with great . . . savage vines. [Through this] cut a little native track 2–3 feet wide, up the ridges, over the spurs, around gorges and down swiftly flowing mountain streams."[41] Add to this stifling heat during the day, very cold temperatures at night, constant heavy tropical rain, malaria, and other tropical diseases, and you have what journalist Osmar White, who trekked the trail with the troops during the campaign, referred to as the "green armour" of Papua.[42]

The terrain was not only a constant factor for any operation on the ground (and in the air) in Papua but also a significant factor in the relationship between MacArthur, GHQ, and NGF during the campaign. In addition, as all the ground forces were Australian, operations became

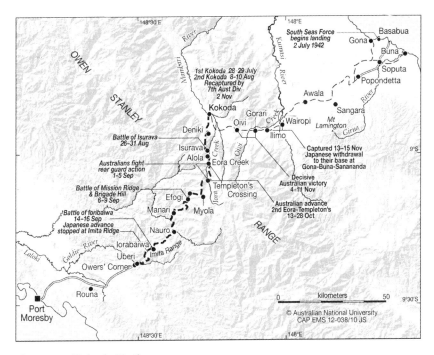

Figure 5.5 Kokoda Trail, 1942

increasingly seen as a tussle between the American theater HQ and the Australian operational and tactical commanders and their troops. The biggest issue for the Australians fighting along the trail in their relationship with GHQ was MacArthur's and his staff's lack of appreciation for the difficulty of the terrain, exacerbated by the fact that no one from GHQ made a visit to the front lines or attempted to walk the trail. MacArthur would eventually come forward to visit the troops (on 3 October 1942) but only traveled as far as Owers Corner, not far from Port Moresby, where the jeep track finished and the trail proper started.

However, the constant criticism in the Australian literature of Mac-Arthur not visiting the trail is overblown. Because MacArthur was theater commander, it was not his business to be on the front lines visiting the troops other than for morale reasons, and such a task was fulfilled with his visit to Owers Corner. In the chain of command, MacArthur was far removed from the front lines, with Blamey, I Australian Corps (Rowell), and the 7th Australian Division (Allen) all reporting up the command chain before it got to the SWPA's C-in-C. As Peter Williams has noted, "taking a 10-day round trip half way up the track, with uncertain communications with the outside, was the worst place to be to exercise the wide command responsibilities of a theatre commander."[43]

Too often it is forgotten that Papua was just one of MacArthur's many responsibilities. What MacArthur should have been doing was relying on his operational and tactical commanders to provide a picture of the front lines and pass on sound advice, while he and GHQ concentrated on equipping the ALF with the tools, resources, and coordination it needed to prosecute the campaign. However, with MacArthur's approach to command and the culture fostered in GHQ, this was never going to happen. Interference at the operational and tactical levels was de rigueur for MacArthur and GHQ.

One of the many problems caused by MacArthur's and GHQ's unreserved propensity to interfere in the tactical handling of operations at Kokoda and Milne Bay was that they consistently demonstrated that they had little understanding of the conditions on the ground. This is somewhat surprising, given the fact that MacArthur and the Bataan Gang at GHQ had recent operational experience in jungle-covered mountainous regions in the Philippines campaign. However, they constantly underestimated the logistics challenges on the Kokoda Trail and misread the terrain. The clearest example of this is their belief in the mythical Kokoda Trail "Gap."

On 13 August, the day after Rowell took command, and three days after Kokoda Village fell (for the second time) to the Japanese, Sutherland cabled Rowell directly that the "pass" through the mountains should be "blocked by demolition."[44] Sutherland's reference to a pass related to the often discussed (at GHQ) "gap" in the Owen Stanley Range, where the valley of Eora Creek cut into the Yodda Valley just south of Kokoda.[45] GHQ completely misunderstood the nature of the gap, which related to a lowering of the mountains for aircraft to pass through the towering peaks. On the ground, no such gap existed, as the feature was some four and a half miles wide.[46] However, the mythical gap remained at the forefront of the thinking of many of the officers at GHQ throughout much of the battle and was exacerbated by reports from the front lines, such as those of MacArthur's air force commander, George Kenney, who, after returning from a tour of the frontline air force units in Papua, told MacArthur on 3 September that he had no faith in the Australians "holding the Kokoda Gap."[47]

GHQ's misreading of the unfolding events on the Kokoda Trail was also exacerbated by poor intelligence. The First Australian Army's intelligence estimate had argued that the Japanese would attempt an overland assault from Buna on Port Moresby via the Kokoda Trail to complete Operation Mo.[48] This report had been dismissed by Sutherland and GHQ. Willoughby, GHQ's prickly G-2, had convinced MacArthur that the Japanese at Buna would be content to garrison the airfield there.[49] Three days after the landing at Buna, Willoughby dismissed the "relatively swift advance" of the Japanese forces toward Kokoda as an attempt to establish an outpost line rather than a general advance and did not consider it indicative of a "further overland advance."[50] As late as 17 August, MacArthur told the Australian prime minister "that the Japanese could not attack Port Moresby with any strength of land forces over the mountain range,"[51] while on the following day he told Curtin the Japanese in Papua were a "minor tactical affair."[52] Blamey, meanwhile, was exceptionally confident that NGF—now under command of Rowell and reinforced by the 7th Division—would be able to withstand any Japanese advance.[53]

NANKAI SHITAI

The Japanese had landed at Buna with every intention of advancing overland to capture Port Moresby. The Japanese force that landed at Buna in late July was the Nankai Shitai, a light infantry division under the command of Maj. Gen. Tomitarō Horii. At the core of this force stood six Japanese infantry battalions from the 144th and 41st Infantry Regiments. Both were veteran regiments, the 144th having served at the invasion of Guam and Rabaul and the 41st Regiment having fought in the Malaya campaign. While having one less infantry regiment than a standard Japanese division, the Nankai Shitai was strong in combat engineers and labor and medical units. During the course of the campaign, the division would reach around 16,700 personnel. However, the fighting core of the division stood more at around 7,300.[54]

The numbers of Japanese engaged in the battles along the Kokoda Trail are important, as this was one area of firm disagreement between MacArthur and the Australians, the former insisting either that the Australian and Japanese numbers were equal or that the Australians outnumbered the Japanese. Meanwhile, the commanders on the front lines, especially Brig. Arnold Potts, commander of the 21st Brigade and the Maroubra Force during much of the withdrawal, and General Allen, GOC 7th Division, insisted that they were vastly outnumbered by the Japanese. The idea of the Australians being vastly outnumbered has grown even more in the subsequent Australian historiography of the campaign. As Peter

William's excellent work *Kokoda Campaign 1942: Myth and Reality* states, an assessment of Japanese sources on their strength largely disproves these assertions. It is a myth perpetuated by the focus of the majority of Australian histories on the tactical level of war at the expense of the operational and strategic levels and the neglect of senior officers such as Blamey and MacArthur, whom they paint as out of touch.

But, as Williams goes onto explain, there was a disparity between the two forces on the Kokoda Trail. However, it was not one of numbers—they were generally evenly matched in most of the early battles as the Australians withdrew—but rather firepower. The Japanese, with their mountain artillery, mortars, and medium machine guns, completely overmatched the Australians in the early battles, who could bring into action nothing heavier than a Bren light machine gun. Throughout the defensive battles, as the Australians withdrew, this disparity in firepower was the key to the Japanese success.

The Japanese advantage in artillery was "the single most important element explaining the outcome of the Australian defensive battles."[55] Thus, in the case of intelligence regarding numbers, MacArthur was not out of touch with conditions at the front. Rather, his intelligence estimates were much more accurate than those emanating out of the Australian units and formations fighting in Papua. Nevertheless, the disputes over the differences in the assessment of Japanese strength on the Kokoda Trail were yet another factor in the ongoing arguments between the Australians and GHQ, and this fed into the general, and growing, distrust on both sides of the fragile Allied coalition.

One of the key factors in the Papua campaign was airpower and sea control. The key reason that Horri's forces were able to land at Buna and be constantly supplied and reinforced from Rabaul was that the Allies lacked air and sea control north of the Owen Stanley Range. In particular, the AAF had not only failed to prevent the Japanese from landing at Buna but also failed to inflict any significant damage on them. MacArthur was bitterly disappointed and explained to Prime Minister Curtin that this was why General Brett, Maj. Gen. Ralph Royce, and Brig. Gen. Mike Scanlan from the USAAF had been returned to the United States.[56]

After landing, Horri's regiments quickly pushed inland against the limited resistance that could be offered by the 39th Militia Battalion. Horri's advance force captured Kokoda on 29 July but was pushed out again in early August, forcing him to deploy more troops. After recapturing the village and its airfield on 10 August, he pushed south along the trail. The key phase of the Japanese advance began on 26 August with Horri's attack on the Australian defensive position at Isurava, which coincided with a Japanese landing at Milne Bay to capture the airfield that had been recently completed by General Clowes's Milne Force. The assault on Milne Bay was a prelude to a second amphibious assault on Port Moresby (the first being defeated at the Battle of the Coral Sea) that would be combined with Horri's final push from the mountains.

The Japanese landing at Milne Bay had "an electrifying effect" on MacArthur and GHQ, and immediately after it occurred Sutherland ordered Blamey's Adv LHQ to take action. While Blamey remained reassured that Milne Force, which had superior numbers and direct close air support from the Australian Kittyhawk squadrons based at Milne Bay, would be successful, MacArthur was rather worked up.[57] Adding to the anxiety at GHQ, Blamey left Brisbane that day to be with his wife, as his father-in-law had passed away. As David Horner has stated, Blamey had misread MacArthur's mood, and it was clear that MacArthur was feeling "extreme" pressure from Washington and that he was liable to blame any reverse in Papua on the Australians.[58] The Japanese offensive and the withdrawal of the Australians at Isurava, despite the arrival of the 21st Brigade AIF on the Kokoda Trail, would set off a series of events back in Australia that would culminate in Blamey being ordered to Port Moresby, in Rowell, Allen, and Potts all being relieved of their commands, and in some major changes at Adv LHQ.

US–AUSTRALIAN RELATIONS AND THE WITHDRAWAL ON THE KOKODA TRAIL

Coordination between GHQ and its component combatant commanders was undertaken at noon in the AAF war room in Brisbane. Here each day, as air force commander George Kenney explained, "the commanders and top staff officers of the Air Force, the Navy and the Australian Land Forces, together with a few representatives of GHQ gathered." Here they

> were given the latest information from the combat zone, an analysis of enemy land, sea and air strengths, locations of units and movements, with an estimate of probable hostile intentions. The briefing was done by reference to a huge map, about twenty square feet, of the whole Pacific theatre from China to Hawaii on which coloured markers and miniature airplanes and ships were correctly spotted to represent our own and enemy forces. The map was laid on the

floor in front and a few feet below a raised platform on which we sat. . . . A valuable feature was that each day the heads and top staff officers of the three services saw each other and had a chance for brief discussion of the common problem: What were we all going to do about defeating the Japs?[59]

The Australians and the ALF were represented by Blamey, who was accompanied by his senior staff officer at Adv LHQ, the DCGS. When Blamey was unable to make the meetings, the DCGS attended in his stead. Here, once again, the relationship between GHQ and the Australians was heavily influenced by the personalities of the senior coalition officers involved. Of all the senior officers in the Australian Army, probably the one most likely to quarrel with the staff of GHQ, especially Sutherland and Willoughby, was Blamey's DCGS at the beginning of the Papuan campaign, Maj. Gen. George Vasey.

Vasey was known in the army as "Bloody George" due to his colorful use of language, hard drinking, and reputation as a hard-driving commander. He was a regular army officer whose class at the Royal Military College (RMC) Duntroon had been graduated a year early in 1915 as a result of the outbreak of World War I. Vasey was commissioned, along with classmate Frank Berryman (MGGS, First Australian Army) and 1914 RMC graduate Cyril Clowes (GOC Milne Force), into the artillery and saw extensive service on the Western Front, earning a Distinguished Service Order (DSO) and two Mentions in Dispatches. After the war, he graduated from the British Indian Army Staff College at Quetta and served in a number of staff positions in senior HQ in Australia.[60]

At the outbreak of World War II, he was made the senior logistics officer in the 6th Australian Division and served at Bardia and Tobruk. Soon after Tobruk, he was promoted to GSo1 (senior operations officer) of the division, replacing Berryman, who was moved across to the 7th Australian Division as a brigadier. In March 1941, he was promoted brigadier and took command of the 19th Brigade AIF, which he took into action in Greece. He was one of the few senior officers to enhance his reputation during this ill-fated campaign and was awarded a bar to his DSO and made a commander of the Order of the British Empire.

Vasey returned to Australia at the outbreak of the Pacific War and was promoted to major general and made chief of staff of Home Forces. Soon after Blamey returned to become C-in-C AMF, he made Vasey DCGS at LHQ and then Adv LHQ when Blamey moved his HQ forward to Brisbane. His blunt, forthright, and aggressive manner, as well as his drinking, meant that his relationships with his fellow senior officers were mixed, although his abilities were universally respected. George Kenney, the new AAF commander, described him as "like the Australian that we generally visualize, tall, thin, keen-eyed, almost hawk-faced."[61] He was also moody and introspective,[62] and the Australian official historian described him as "highly strung, thrustful, [and] hard working."[63]

As DCGS, Vasey had the next most important position in dealing with GHQ after Blamey. Significantly, Vasey held this position in what was fast becoming one of the most testing periods in this embryonic relationship. Unfortunately, it would not be a happy partnership. Vasey was both a "glass half empty" type of personality and prone to complaining about *all* the officers that he worked with. Added to this was his deeply ingrained suspicion of his new coalition partners. Thus, his relationship with GHQ in the period from mid-1942 through to the early part of the Papua campaign was strained. He argued constantly with Sutherland and his staff and claimed that they were difficult to work with—a feeling, however, that was very mutual.[64] In the end, Vasey was not a natural staff officer, preferring command to staff work.

As the pressure at the front mounted, especially at Milne Bay, so did the tension in Brisbane. News of the imminent withdrawal of the Australian troops from Isurava on Kokoda and the withdrawal of the 2/10th Battalion AIF at Milne Bay now convinced "MacArthur that the Australians were not doing all that they might."[65] With Blamey absent, Vasey was bearing the brunt of the pressure from GHQ.

What frustrated Sutherland and GHQ was their belief that the information flow from Clowes and Rowell was poor. The lack of information predisposed a lack of activity and action to GHQ. In addition, without information from NGF, GHQ was collecting information from the American-run AAF in New Guinea that, as Vasey stated to Rowell, "generally indicates a lack of activity on the part of our troops in the area." In response to the constant requests for information, Rowell had replied that he was not going to give "a ball by ball description," and, while agreeing in principle, Vasey urged Rowell to do more to keep both Blamey and MacArthur informed.[66]

The interference of GHQ in the tactical operations in Papua again raised the question of "who is commanding this Army—MacA[rthur] or TAB [Blamey] and it seems the sooner that is settled the better." As 27 August passed to the twenty-eighth, Vasey wrote to Rowell and explained that he was now awaiting the results of "Cyril's [Clowes's] activities yesterday. I'm dying to go to those b——s [GHQ] and say I told you so—we've killed the b—y lot." Vasey also had a suggestion to placate GHQ; Rowell's "sitreps [should] be worded in the most offensive (not to us or GHQ!) manner. For example rather than . . . [saying Milne Force] . . . 'recaptured' the mission: Why recapture? Why not say 'our troops stormed and captured the mission killing—Japs.'"[67]

To Vasey, GHQ were prone to "panic," and he stated to Rowell, who at NGF in Port Moresby was on the receiving end of a lot of GHQ's outbursts and direct orders, that "for GHQ this is their first battle and they are therefore, like many others, nervous and dwelling on the receipt of frequent messages." At the end of this letter, he noted that "by the tone of this morning's conversation with Sutherland, I feel that a wrong impression of our troops has already been created in the minds of the great, and it is important for the future that that impression be corrected at the earliest possible moment."[68]

What Vasey had identified was both the tension and pressure on MacArthur and GHQ and the fundamental differences in relation to Australian and US (MacArthur's) approaches to command culture. While recognizing the problem, with Blamey largely absent for much of this time, Vasey lacked the tact and the authority to respond in a manner that would placate GHQ. In his defense, he obviously felt the need to protect both the Australian Army in general, and his friend and colleague Sydney Rowell in particular, from GHQ's barbs.

While Vasey was bearing the brunt of the pressure and trying to placate both Rowell and GHQ, the commander of NGF was becoming increasingly irate at what he saw as GHQ's interference in his operations. In reply to Vasey, he noted that "it is perilously easy to criticise a commander [Clowes] for his actions at a distance of 250 miles" and that "I'm sorry that GHQ take a poor view of Australians. . . . I wish Chamberlin [G-3, GHQ] and Co could visit the jungle and see what the conditions are, instead of sitting back and criticising." He added, "I'm personally very bitter over the criticism from a distance and I think it damned unfair to pillory any commander without any knowledge of the conditions. It has rained for ten days at Milne Bay and it keeps on raining. I suppose there will be heresy hunts and bowler hats [sackings] soon. I hate to think what would have happened with our Allies in charge up here."[69]

On 30 August, at the height of the fighting for Milne Bay, MacArthur told the CoS of the US Army, George C. Marshall, that he "was not yet convinced of the efficiency of the Australian units." When word arrived of the success of Milne Force in defeating the Japanese landing, MacArthur reported to the War Department that "the enemy's defeat at Milne

Bay must not be accepted as a measure of relative fighting capacity of the troops involved [i.e., the Australians]. The decisive factor was the complete surprise obtained over him by our preliminary concentration of superior forces."[70] MacArthur's point was that the victory was *his*, in deciding to send the troops to Milne Bay in the first place (although this suggestion had actually come from NGF, Blamey's headquarters, and the AAF), and not the performance of the Australian troops stationed there. Thus, his victory was in spite of the Australian efforts. So, he publicly claimed the victory in one of his infamous communiqués while at the same time attacking Clowes's performance as commander of Milne Force.

Blamey had returned to Brisbane on 29 August, and after the situation at Milne Bay became clear, he cabled Rowell on 1 September to congratulate him but also took the opportunity to criticize Clowes's tactics. He also reiterated Vasey's point of a few days earlier about the need for more information to keep Adv LHQ and GHQ informed of developments.[71] The victory at Milne Bay had improved the situation with GHQ but only marginally, and it was to last only a few days. However, the distrust between GHQ and the Australian Army had only been exacerbated by their actions during the Milne Bay operation.

In the immediate aftermath of the victory, Vasey noted that Blamey had returned from a visit to GHQ, where he said of GHQ's attitude that it was like they "thought they had just won the battle of Waterloo."[72] However, the euphoric feeling soon soured as attention turned to the Kokoda Trail, where the Australians had been forced to retreat from Isurava. To Rowell, the key problem was one of supply and the maintenance of the troops over the precarious track, especially with a lack of native carriers and transport aircraft. To MacArthur, the withdrawal was further evidence of the poor performance and unreliability of the Australians. He cabled Marshall in Washington that the Australians had "proven themselves unable to match the enemy in jungle fighting. Aggressive leadership is lacking."[73]

In September, Lt. Gen. Hap Arnold, chief of the USAAF, visited Australia and recorded in his notes after a meeting with MacArthur that Australian troops "are not even a good militia." Both Sutherland and Kenney, who had recently returned from trips to New Guinea, influenced MacArthur's view. Kenney had stated to MacArthur on his return from Port Moresby that vigorous leadership from the Australians was lacking and that Rowell was not up to the task.[74]

The situation continued to deteriorate along the Kokoda Trail in early September, with the Australians withdrawing to Myola on the fifth. On

7 September, MacArthur sent Chamberlin to see Vasey with the message that the Australians were superior in numbers to the Japanese and not demonstrating sound leadership in Papua. Chamberlin indicated that if an American divisional commander had been fighting on the Kokoda Trail, he would have been relieved.[75]

The first of the sackings, however, was already in train. The next day Rowell decided to relieve Potts. Rowell's decision was based on the defeat at Isurava, the 2/27th Battalion AIF having become scattered and cut off from the main Australian forces, and his belief that Potts had mishandled his brigade in the battle. As Karl James notes, Potts was "aggressive but ultimately [an] overwhelmed leader."[76] Rowell sent Brig. Selwyn Porter, commander of the 30th Brigade, back up the trail to take command of Maroubra Force. The next day, the 25th Brigade AIF, under the command of Brig. Ken Eather, arrived at Port Moresby to bolster NGF. Blamey also alerted the 16th Brigade AIF for a move to Papua in the near future. Port Moresby now had four infantry brigades on hand: the 14th and 30th Militia Brigades and the 21st and 25th Brigades AIF. Maroubra Force on the Kokoda Trail consisted of 21st Brigade and elements of the 39th and 53rd Battalions from 30th Brigade.

On 9 September, Blamey visited Rowell at Port Moresby in an endeavor to get a firsthand view of the situation and put in place a number of changes to respond to MacArthur and GHQ's claims. Rowell had wanted an additional senior officer at NGF to take command of the immediate defense of Port Moresby so as to release Allen and his HQ to concentrate on the operations along the Kokoda Trail. Blamey returned to Brisbane on 11 September, met with MacArthur to inform him of the outcome of his visit, and then announced two major changes. Vasey was to be moved from DCGS to command the 6th Australian Division, and he was to take his HQ to Port Moresby as Rowell's additional senior officer. Meanwhile, Maj. Gen. Frank Berryman, MGGS First Australian Army, would replace Vasey as DCGS. After meeting with Blamey and being informed of Berryman's promotion to DCGS, the First Army commander, Lt. Gen. John Lavarack, noted in his diary that "Vasey's staff work [has been] found out, as I expected. T. A. B. [Blamey] proposed [to] give him a command."[77]

Soon after, on 17 September, Rowell decided to replace his BGS, Brig. Henry Rourke, with Brig. Ronald Hopkins due to Rourke's "deteriorating physical and mental condition."[78] He reported to Adv LHQ in Brisbane on 22 September, and Berryman noted in his diary after meeting with him that "he [had] cracked up under the strain of PM [Port

Moresby]. [Rourke] was very pessimistic—does not see how we can hold Moresby."[79]

Blamey's moves were a recognition of a number of key factors. The first was that Vasey was not a natural staff officer and that he was much more suited to command. Second, by moving him to Papua, Blamey would inject vigorous leadership into NGF as well as provide another senior officer in which the C-in-C had confidence and who had a depth of knowledge regarding the broader strategic situation, as well as an understanding of the relationship between GHQ, Adv LHQ, and NGF. Finally, the replacement of Vasey with Berryman as DCGS would allow this new senior officer to develop a better relationship with MacArthur's staff at GHQ and also improve the operational performance and organization of Adv LHQ.

Berryman was to prove to be an inspired choice as DCGS. He was one of the most proficient staff officers in the Australian Army, and his particular talents in inter-Allied cooperation enhanced his importance within the army high command. One of the most beneficial skills that he possessed, which assisted both Blamey and the army, was that Berryman would develop an intimate, personnel, and professional relationship with the Americans. He entered the role during a period fueled by competing political and military objectives and cultural misunderstandings, and the situation between GHQ and Adv LHQ would initially get worse before it improved. Nevertheless, as John Hetherington pointed out during his time as DCGS and CoS to Blamey,[80] "Berryman understood the Americans and they understood him; he had a knack of avoiding friction without sacrificing Australian dignity or interests. His achievements in keeping the peace were of no mean order in light of America's preponderant contribution to the overall forces under MacArthur's command. It was a time when a careless word or a thoughtless gesture could have upset the delicate balance of the Australian-American partnership."[81]

However, this assessment was a long-term prospect, and in the first few weeks of Berryman's appointment he saw only a marginal improvement in relationships. After taking up his position as DCGS, Berryman noted that "Sutherland and Kenney [were] worried saying [that the] Australians can't and won't fight"[82] and that GHQ were "very pessimistic" about the outcome of the fighting on the Kokoda Trail.[83] To make matters worse, Berryman did not get off on the right foot. On the very day that Berryman took over as DCGS, the 25th Brigade (Brig. Ken Eather) had arrived on Ioribaiwa Ridge to confront the Japanese. Berryman had every confidence in Eather, whom he regarded as one of the finest young

commanders in the Australian Army. Berryman had taken a personal interest in his career and had gone out of his way to provide patronage to
Eather, just as many senior officers had done for him in the past.[84] As
a result, at his first midday conference at GHQ, Berryman gave a solid
endorsement of Eather's qualities to Sutherland and the other officers at
GHQ. Eather then promptly assessed the situation on the ground and ordered a withdrawal to Imita Ridge, twenty-five miles closer to Moresby.[85]

After Berryman's confident endorsement, this caused grave fears among
the Americans, and Kenney told Berryman that if the Japanese reached
the Goldie River just over the Imita Ridge, he would then withdraw all his
aircraft from New Guinea.[86] GHQ considered the "situation disturbing"
and noted that the "enemy drive is assuming threatening proportions."
They also considered the threat from a Japanese amphibious assault or
parachute assault on Port Moresby could not be discounted.[87]

For Berryman, this was a tense period. He was trying his best to develop good relations with GHQ, and while he was certainly much better than Vasey at forging relationships with some officers, he would not
"sit in a conference and let any adverse criticism [of Australians] pass
without some comment."[88] His private assessments of GHQ were also
sometimes damning. After a week of daily conferences at GHQ, Berryman noted on 20 September that he "saw Sutherland who gave the usual
type of lecture one would except from an armchair editor." Berryman
was, however, starting to develop some positive relations with the other
officers at GHQ, notably Kenney and the chief operations officer, Brig.
Gen. Stephen Chamberlin. Unbeknownst to Berryman, Blamey, Adv
LHQ, or GHQ, Eather's withdrawal was to be the last by the Australians
on the Kokoda Trail, and by 21 September he would have moved over
to the offensive.

In the meantime, Eather's withdrawal had wider repercussions. While
in the long run the period of 12–16 September would prove to be the
turning point on the Kokoda Trail, the Australians' ability to regain the
initiative was not immediately apparent, and MacArthur remained convinced as to their poor performance. He also persuaded Curtin of this
point of view as well. While Blamey, who returned to Port Moresby on
12 September, remained confident and gave a national radio address to
this effect on 15 September, the mood in the Advisory War Council that
Blamey attended on 17 September was anything but. Later that night,
MacArthur spoke to Curtin and suggested that Blamey be sent to Papua
to take direct command. The decision was supported by members of the

government, with supply minister Jack Beasley noting that "Moresby is going to fall. Send Blamey up there and let him fall with it."[89]

Blamey, meanwhile, thought that "Canberra's lost it." Curtin would later confess that "in my ignorance (of military matters) I thought that the Commander-in-Chief should be in New Guinea."[90] Berryman believed that when Blamey flew north to Papua, he was fighting for his military life and that MacArthur had asked Curtin to send Blamey to Port Moresby because the C-in-C SWPA wanted the "biggest scapegoat" possible there in case the Japanese succeeded. Blamey, quite rightly, saw his correct place to be in Brisbane, near MacArthur's headquarters, where he could exercise proper command.[91]

Blamey's arrival in Port Moresby on 23 September was even more uncomfortable for Rowell. Despite Blamey's assurances that it was not a reflection of his performance, Rowell's relationship with Blamey quickly deteriorated. Rowell was not able to recognize the political maneuvering behind the decision to send the Australian C-in-C north, nor did he fully grasp the pressure that Blamey was coming under from MacArthur and the government. The problem was that Rowell believed that the C-in-C should have shown more moral fiber and told the prime minister that his presence in New Guinea was not necessary.

Four days after Blamey's arrival, Maj. Gen. Samuel Roy Burston (commander of the Australian Army's medical services) told Berryman that "Rowell took a poor view of the C-in-C's arrival and that relations were strained and unless [he] changed his attitude he would probably be relieved."[92] Rowell lasted only two days after Burston's comments. The antagonism between Blamey and Rowell was further complicated by the resentment that Rowell harbored against Blamey since the two had clashed in the Greece campaign of 1941. But if Blamey had wanted to sack Rowell, his attitude toward the C-in-C had made it especially easy. As Brigadier Hopkins, the new BGS NGF, noted, "Rowell had [effectively] sacked himself."[93]

On 1 October, Lt. Gen. Edmund Herring arrived to replace Rowell, although there was never any doubt that Blamey was now in charge of operations in New Guinea. By now, the tide had turned for the Australians on the Kokoda Trail, and with further reinforcements for Papua, including the first regiment of the 32nd US Infantry Division in Port Moresby, plans had turned to a systematic advance on the Japanese positions at Buna, Gona, and Sanananda. GHQ, however, remained heavily critical of the Australians' performance.

By late October, MacArthur had signaled Blamey that he was "perturbed by the slow progress." In particular, he signaled Blamey on 17 October that he needed to "press General Allen's advance. . . . His extremely light casualties indicate no serious effort yet made to displace enemy. . . . It is essential that Kokoda airfield be taken."[94] It was an offensive signal to send, and it showed how little regard for the troops or recognition of the character of the fighting along the trail MacArthur had. In fact, at Templeton's Crossing, the Japanese had skillfully established an in-depth defensive position to cover their withdrawal, and it took fifty Australians killed and another 133 wounded to clear them out. While these casualties may seem small, it is important to note that the terrain meant that normally only a single infantry company could be maintained at the forward point of contact with the enemy. A little later at the next major Japanese defensive position, Eroa Creek, the fresh 16th Brigade AIF took three hundred casualties in just nine days.[95]

MacArthur, however, was not to be satisfied. He followed up the signal of 17 October with another three days later that included a long diatribe to Blamey on the strategic situation in the Pacific and the logistics situation in the SWPA, including a further denouncement of the slow progress of Allen's advance and criticism of the tactics used by the Australians. To rub salt into the wounds, four days later MacArthur cabled Blamey in regard to the report General Clowes had submitted on the victory at Milne Bay, demanding the addition of the signals for vigorous action from GHQ be included and again heavily criticizing Clowes's tactics. He was, however, correct in one thing: the Australians did have the superiority of forces on the trail.[96]

To Blamey, the major cause of the Australians problems, both during the retreat from Kokoda and now in the counterattack along the Kokoda Trail, was not the tactics or the lack of casualties but rather the difficulty in providing for adequate supplies.[97] The maintenance of supply, especially the lack of transport aircraft and native carriers, was the very reason for the "slow" (according to GHQ) progress in the counteroffensive to retake Kokoda.[98] He made this clear to GHQ on a number of occasions and expressed confidence in the troops and their commanders. Operations, he stated, "were proceeding as speedily as the limitations imposed by the conditions of terrain and facilities for movement and supply will permit."[99] However, on both the sixteenth and eighteenth, Blamey did have to admit that the 7th Division was making "slow progress." This, however, was due to the "determined and well organised enemy opposition in the Templeton's Crossing" area, and he indicated to MacArthur that he had impressed upon Allen the necessity of increasing the tempo of operations.[100]

Nevertheless, the pressure was again mounting. From MacArthur's perspective, it is easy to understand what prompted his outbursts on 17 and 20 October. This was directly attributable to the pressure he was feeling from Washington: The US JCS had signaled MacArthur on 16 October, reminding him that they regarded the situation in Papua as "critical." Heightening MacArthur's own sense of vulnerability was the fact that, between his signals to Blamey on 17 October and 20 October, Vice Adm. Robert Ghormley, C-in-C of SOPAC (who commanded the forces fighting on and around Guadalcanal), was sacked.[101]

To MacArthur, speed was of the essence, not only to retain his position as C-in-C in the SWPA but also to secure Papua. By this stage, it was clear that the major offensive in the region, from both the Allied and Japanese perspectives, was Guadalcanal. MacArthur's operations in Papua were clearly of secondary importance. It was this factor that had led the Japanese command at Rabaul to order Horri's withdrawal from the Kokoda Trail to defensive positions on the northern coast of Papua. This, however, also meant that MacArthur's position in Papua was heavily dependent on the outcome of the US operations at Guadalcanal. If they were to fail, and Ghormley's sacking was a clear indication of troubles in SOPAC, then MacArthur had to establish the strongest possible defensive positions in Papua as quickly as possible in order to shore up the Allied position in the SWPA. This pressure then flowed down the command chain, meaning that the next in line for a "bowler hat" was the division commander on the trail, Maj. Gen. "Tubby" Allen.

As he was "in command" at Port Moresby, Blamey was now at the forefront of MacArthur signals (like Rowell previously), while back in Brisbane Berryman was feeling the heat at the daily GHQ conferences. Berryman considered MacArthur's constant stream of messages demanding attacks against the enemy with "all possible speed" and at "each point of resistance" as "silly." Allen's replies, however, he deemed as "strong and solid."[102] However, since arriving in Papua with the 7th Division in August, Rowell, Vasey, Blamey, and Berryman had all been called on to defend Allen to MacArthur and GHQ. But now, just as at GHQ in Brisbane, internal personality factors started to compound matters for the Australians in Papua. While Rowell, Allen, and Vasey all had close personal and professional relationships, Rowell's replacement at NGF, Edmund Herring, had deeply ingrained feelings of animosity toward Allen. These feelings were also reciprocated on the part of Allen.

Allen believed that the choice of Herring as Rowell's replacement was a personal snub. Having been anointed as the proposed successor to the I Australian Corps command in Java in early 1942 and with experience of fighting the Japanese in New Guinea, Allen believed that he was more qualified for the command than Herring. Adding to this volatile mix was the deep personal animosity between the two men, which was still unresolved from their clashes in Cyrenaica in 1940 and 1941.[103] Allen's bitterness over Herring's appointment also started to affect his relationship with Blamey. The inevitable result of these developments, plus the pressure from MacArthur over the performance of the 7th Division, led to Allen's replacement on 29 October.

An even greater tragedy for Allen was that his relief took place just a few days before his tactics on the Kokoda Trail were about to be fully vindicated. Berryman noted in his diary a few days after Allen's relief that "our troops took Kokoda yesterday. . . . The plan was worked out by Tubby Allen [and] his appreciation was correct—he said there would be no resistance after he [had] crushed [the] enemy at Eora Creek."[104] Berryman followed up his diary entry with a telegram to Allen from LHQ in Melbourne: "Successful results of your sustained hard work in the mountains at Eora Creek now manifest and I congratulate you heartily and personally."[105] Despite Allen's achievement, Herring was to ensure that Allen was never to command troops in action again.[106] It was a bitter end to a highly successful military career.

General Vasey now took command of 7th Division in time for the triumphant entry in Kokoda. He followed up this victory by smashing the remainder of Horii's force at the Battle of Oivi-Gorari (4–11 November), which was one of the tactical masterpieces of the campaign. With the fall of Kokoda, attention now turned to the concentration of the 7th Australian Division and the newly arrived US 32nd Division around the last remaining Japanese positions in Papua at Gona, Sanananda, and Buna.[107] Meanwhile, back in Brisbane, events on the domestic front between the Australians and Americans would reveal the extent of the fragility of the coalition between the countries' two military forces in the SWPA.

THE LOW POINT: THE BATTLE OF BRISBANE,
NOVEMBER 1942

The criticisms by GHQ of the Australians in Papua were not confined to the offices and corridors of the Lennon Hotel in Brisbane. Nor did the responses from Adv LHQ remain confined to the grounds of the University of Queensland at St. Lucia. The disparaging comments being made by both sets of officers were patronizing, and each side was influenced by its own beliefs in the superiority of its methods, background, and experience. American comments about Australian troops were, however, much more critical and more widely reported at this stage.

US criticisms of Australian troops circulated throughout the country in August and September of 1942, leading to bad feelings and poor relations between senior US and Australian officers. For instance, Lt. Gen. Richard Eichelberger, who took on the command of I US Corps after Richardson rejected it, noted after the war that a "very high ranking Australian officer serving under me in those days [probably Berryman, who was also acting BGS at Adv NGF HQ under Eichelberger at the end of the beachhead battles] made the following statement:

> Sir, there is one thing you do not understand about conditions. American officers with their Australian girlfriends around the Lennon Hotel [in Brisbane] have noted that MacArthur has been making joking remarks about the surrender at Singapore and the Australian retreat over the Kokoda Trail to Port Moresby. This has been contrasted with the great fighting ability of the Americans at Bataan. The Australian girls have repeated these jokes and they spread all over Australia. A number of our highest-ranking officers were included.[108]

While Eichelberger would eventually forge a very close professional relationship with the Australians in the months ahead, in late October 1942 he was very much acculturated to the mind-set of US military superiority that was entrenched at GHQ. After his first visit to Papua to advise MacArthur on the use of US troops in the campaign, he indicated a lack of faith and trust in the Australian high command. In contrast, he noted that his "I Corps staff is a very efficient one and there is not another staff that compares to it, with the exception of the GHQ staff." It was therefore "preferable to have American troops under American command."[109]

The incidence of poor relations between senior US and Australian military officers became so frequent and serious that, in November 1942, Secretary of Defence Fredrick Shedden felt obliged to write to John Curtin to apprise him of these events and of his concerns about the poor nature of the relationship. November was to be the touchstone month that highlighted the tension that now existed in the relationship. Relations would reach their lowest point during the supposed "battle for Brisbane" between Australian and US soldiers in the same month.

Relations among the two nations' servicemen had been in steady decline since the dizzying heights of the arrival of the first US troops in Brisbane in early 1942. As time passed, the threat to Australia diminished, the presence of the US troops became routine, and divisions started to open up over pay, conditions, fighting prowess, food, transport, women, and just about any other point of cultural or military difference that could be found. It was noted that the otherwise good relationship was being marred by a series of "street brawls, stabbings and actual fights between small groups . . . principally in Townsville, Brisbane and Melbourne."[110]

From September to November 1942, the number of incidents increased until there were "almost daily" occurrences in Queensland, where the overwhelming majority of US and Australian troops were based. Numbers were also a telling figure, with Brisbane's wartime population rising by 90,000 Americans off a base of only 325,000 locals. However, according to Col. William H. Donaldson Jr., commander of the US Army Base Section No. 3 in Brisbane, the problems were almost wholly caused by the Australians.[111]

Tensions reached their peak in late November 1942 when a riot broke out in Brisbane. On 26 November, after a dispute between a drunken US Army soldier and an American military policeman (MP), about one hundred Australians "besieged" the US Army post exchange (PX) on the corner of Creek and Adelaide Streets. Throwing rocks and bottles, the crowd began to grow, and several fights broke out in the city. By 8:00 p.m., the disturbance had grown to some five thousand people. At the PX, the MPs armed themselves, which only further inflamed the situation. A scuffle broke out, a shotgun was discharged three times, and an Australian soldier was killed, while another five Australian soldiers and two civilians were wounded. By 10:00 p.m., the crowd had dispersed, leaving much of the PX in ruins. The following night, another crowd gathered, and numerous scuffles between Australians and Americans broke out, with eight US MPs and four US officers hospitalized.[112]

In the report into the incidents that followed, Colonel Donaldson continued to blame the Australian military. While Australian soldiers were undoubtedly the ringleaders, the US MPs had flamed the fire and made little to no attempt to calm the situation. Donaldson, however, stated that the "Australian military police had failed to perform their functions of maintaining order." In his assessment he was supported by Maj. Gen. James Durrant, the Australian officer commanding the Queensland Lines of Communication Area, who believed that "the whole incident was caused by Australian soldiers" and went on to state that "while we cannot expect that the personnel of the American forces are always innocent and pure, nevertheless, in this particular instance it would appear that they were." Donaldson claimed, "The unfortunate part is that I see no solution to such difficulties until discipline is instilled in our Ally's army. This is not to be expected at an early date."[113]

From the Australians' point of view, they admitted that the violence was often a result of a "lack of discipline, especially self-discipline, on the part of some Australian troops." However, they also noted that a major part of the problem was a series of cultural misunderstandings, most notably

> the complete failure of the men of each nation to understand the attitude towards violence and the normal police methods of the other. The carrying of arms, especially fire-arms, is provocative to most Australians and is apt to be regarded as a direct challenge which should be taken up as soon as possible. On the other hand Americans are quite unable to comprehend that attitude of the Australian military and Civil Police and consider that their normal methods of handling a difficult situation are "namby-pamby" and the result of spineless fear or culpable weakness.[114]

The irony of the whole incident is that it started when some Australian soldiers involved themselves in an issue between a US Army private and a US Army MP. The Australians believed that the MP was being heavy-handed, a reputation US MPs had among the Australians, when he tried to use his baton on the young US soldier. It was only after the death and injury of the Australian soldiers that the tenor of the incident took on an anti-US flavor.[115] In reality, for the Australian soldiers, the original cause of the riot was an anti-MP one rather than an anti-US one.[116] Still, the incident sparked a deep set of feelings between the US and Australian military at the time. In the Australian Army report on the incident, it was noted that the Australians soldiers had "a general hostility towards the Americans . . . [that] is partly caused by the attitude of superiority frequently affected by US soldiers themselves. Constant boastings of what the Americans Forces have done and will do in this war is resented."[117]

Thus, it seems that this attitude was widespread, encompassing the entire length of the military hierarchy. The response of GHQ to the "battle for Brisbane" is also reflective of this sense of superiority and of its attitude toward its coalition partner at this time. Episodic disturbances would continue to occur in Australian cities and towns thereafter, but they were generally few and only on very small scale. In particular, it should be noted that relations between Australian and US service person-nel were overwhelmingly "harmonious." They shared similar outlooks on life and shared similar burdens and discomforts.[118] This was particu-larly apparent the closer one got to the front lines. As General Blamey noted in response to the battle for Brisbane, "strangely enough as always, the nearer one gets to the actual war the better the feeling and we have nothing here [in Papua] to indicate the curious outlook that has grown up in Queensland."[119] Blamey's view was insightful. However, the movement of elements of GHQ to Port Moresby would bring into focus the relation-ship of the higher command and drive the more conducive battlefront relationship farther north, over the Owen Stanley Range.

US–AUSTRALIAN RELATIONS IN THE PAPUA CAMPAIGN

There were a number of factors that contributed to the tense relation-ship between the Australians and the US commanders and troops during the early stage of the Papua campaign. First, this was a period of great tension. The pressures from the Allied high command and especially the US JCS were heavily focused on GHQ. MacArthur was still reeling from his defeat in the Philippines, and he knew that another setback in Papua would most likely end his career.

Second, the relationship between the US and Australian forces was new. Ground operations during this period in Papua were almost exclusively an all-Australian affair, and the personalities and capabilities of com-manders and troops were largely unknown to MacArthur and the Ameri-cans. Third, MacArthur and GHQ had to rely on the Australians to both fight the battle and provide information on their progress. Here we see a clash of command culture between the two military services, exacerbated by the political pressure from Washington and Canberra. The final sig-nificant contextual factor was the sense of cultural superiority evident in GHQ and the US Army in Australia at this time. This is most poignantly demonstrated by the Richardson Report in July 1942. The attitude of GHQ and senior US officers at this time toward the Australian Army in particular is summed up by US Army colonel Harry Knight, who noted that "opinions were freely expressed by officers of all ranks . . . that the only reason 32nd US Infantry Div was not ordered to advance earlier in

NG was because GHQ was afraid to turn the Americans loose at Buna because it would be a blow to the prestige of the Australians."[120]

Such an attitude was evident in a number of the key personalities at GHQ. Sutherland was a highly negative influence on the US-Australian relationship and also on MacArthur, whose views of his coalition partner Sutherland helped shape. A number of senior officers at GHQ noted that Sutherland had a low opinion of everyone at this time but especially the air forces and the Australians. He was also the officer at GHQ who was most intimate with MacArthur, and his attitude undoubtedly rubbed off on the C-in-C. George Kenney, who quickly developed a rapport with MacArthur after he arrived at the end of July, also initially put forward highly negative reports of the Australians in New Guinea. Both Sutherland and Kenney were also some of the few senior US officers who had visited Port Moresby during this period, so their opinions carried even more weight in MacArthur's mind.

On the Australian side, this was not helped by Blamey's frequent absences from Brisbane to deal with personal issues and his responsibilities beyond being C-in-C ALF, specifically his position as C-in-C AMF. This meant that of the forty-two days Vasey was DCGS in Brisbane, Blamey was absent for twenty-one of them.[121] Vasey's temperament and attitude toward the Americans often had the effect of antagonizing the already volatile Sutherland. Because of the lack of information from NGF and Adv LHQ, GHQ filled the perceived information void with communications from the USAAF stationed in New Guinea, which itself was largely ignorant of the conditions on the ground. This information source clearly reinforced the negative attitudes toward the Australians to which GHQ was already predisposed.

Compounding these issues was the scant recognition of the Australian efforts in Papua by GHQ in the press. MacArthur was vain, egotistical, and a cultural imperialist. This led him to describe his command in relation to MacArthur's forces, MacArthur's army, MacArthur's navy, and so on. It must, however, be noted that it was not just the Australians who missed out on public or official recognition from MacArthur—the US units and their commanders in the SWPA barely received a mention either. Recognition for the Australian efforts at Milne Bay and Kokoda would eventually be forthcoming from MacArthur, but it would not take place until toward the end of the war. In March 1945, he would publicly acknowledge that the Australian success in Papua had "turned the tide" in the SWPA and that it had been the basis for "all future success" in the theater. But for many this was a case of too little and too late.[122]

In relation to his comments about Australian forces under his command to his US superiors, especially the JCS strategic, the strategic context and MacArthur's intent for his command are critically important factors that cannot be overlooked. While vain, MacArthur was also intelligent, farsighted, and strategically aware, as well as focused on his personal mission to liberate the Philippines. Australia, Papua, New Guinea, and the Japanese at Rabaul were all just stepping-stones to the Philippines, and MacArthur knew that to get there he would require substantial US reinforcements.

The question to ask, then, is what would MacArthur have to gain in praising the Australian troops under his command to the US JCS vis-à-vis his objective of securing more US troops, aircraft, ships, and supplies for the SWPA? Most likely it would, in fact, have had exactly the opposite effect. This is not to deny that MacArthur was horribly insensitive, egotistical, and more often than not unfair in his criticism, but recognition of MacArthur's broader strategic ambition is essential in understanding his motivations and actions. MacArthur was a commander with a strategic vision—a vision that meant that the Australian forces under his command were simply a convenient means to achieve his operational objectives in 1942 and 1943. They also provided a convenient excuse if his tactical operations were less than successful and could be easily used to rebuff any criticism of his command and to shore up his position as C-in-C in the SWPA.

Operationally, MacArthur performed poorly during this period. He misread Japanese strategic intentions, he was slow to realize the limitations of his new command (e.g., the Tulsa operational plans), and he was slow to exploit its relative strengths. About the only thing he got right was the balance of forces on the Kokoda Trail, but this was offset by the fact that he constantly underestimated the impact of the terrain on operations and remained ignorant of the disparity in firepower between the two forces. However, he was correct in his assessment of the broader strategic picture, especially the importance of Guadalcanal to his plans and the necessity of clearing the Japanese out of Papua quickly in order to provide for its security. It cannot be overlooked that if SOPAC had failed in task 1 of the JCS directive, MacArthur's plan and directives for task 2 stood little chance of success. However, these failings have to be offset by the fact that while he was vain, interfering, over-the-top, and egotistical, each time that MacArthur proved himself completely insufferable he would also demonstrate a capacity for strategic analysis and forethought. He was also particularly apt at ensuring that the SWPA remained at the forefront of the minds of the JCS and the American people, despite its lowly position in terms of Allied global strategic priorities.

In terms of his coalition command, MacArthur's intentions were clear early on. From the very start he attempted to command ground forces directly from his HQ. He made clear his plan to use Australian forces to garrison areas reconquered in the preliminary operations before US forces forged ahead toward Rabaul and later the Philippines. In addition to his commitment to running SWPA operations through task force commands, direct responsibility to himself (through GHQ) was evident from GHQ's assessment of "Defensive and Offensive Possibilities" in March and the Richardson Report in July 1942. His actions in signaling NGF directly, thus bypassing Adv LHQ, and then ensuring that Blamey was sent to Papua to take direct command in order for him to be in place as a potential scapegoat are further evidence of his approach to command in the SWPA.

In the end, the US military were always going to be the main driver for MacArthur to achieve the ends of *his* strategy, and he knew full well that when the United States was fully mobilized those forces would vastly outnumber the Australians. However, at the end of the Kokoda and Milne Bay operations, US ground forces were still small, and MacArthur knew that his ability to secure Papua was still heavily dependent on the Australians. The injection of the US 32nd Division into NGF for the operations to clear Papua would, however, give him a chance to show the Australians how the US Army could fight and prove that they could outperform the sluggish Australians.

6

The Battle for the Beachheads, November 1942

Strategy and Stalemate

The American soldiers of the 3rd Battalion, 128th Infantry Regiment, 32nd Infantry Division, were lucky, or so they thought. Rather than walking over the hellish tracks that covered the Owen Stanley Range like the Australians and one of their sister battalions in the 126th Regiment had, they were airlifted onto the northern plains of Papua. But after the landing on the small grass airstrip near Wanigela, the men had to walk through the jungle and swamps to Cape Nelson. Inadequate logistics meant doing this in the blistering heat with fifty-five pounds on their back and only one C ration meal and a little rice per day. Still, they thought, this was better than a trek over the mountains.

However, the swollen Musa River soon stopped the battalion in its tracks, and here its luck ran out. The battalion was forced to camp at Guri Guri while searching for a new route to continue the advance. Guri Guri was hardly resort country; in fact, it was not fit enough to even march through, let alone camp in. As the commanding officer, Lt. Col. Kelsie E. Miller would note,[1] Guri Guri was "the most filthy, swampy, mosquito infested area that he had seen in New Guinea."[2] With the river impassable, the battalion trekked to Gobe, where it consolidated its position before finally moving to Embogo, where it met up with regimental HQ. By now, however, the damage had been done. Malaria had infected most of the men, and the battalion was now physically exhausted by its ordeal. But the worst was yet to come, for a few days later it would encounter something much more harrowing than the jungle and mosquitos of New Guinea—well dug-in and expertly camouflaged Japanese veteran infantry who were hell-bent on stopping the American march to the sea.[3]

For Sgt. James F. Kincaid from Beloit, Wisconsin, and the rest of L Company in Miller's battalion, the exhausting experience of the march from Wanigela was temporarily overcome by the adrenaline he felt as his company closed in on the enemy. As the battalion moved along the Simemi Trail toward the Japanese airstrip at Buna, the already poor terrain was supplemented by the rain that came down in buckets, removing any chance of promised air support being available. Kincaid and his light machine-gun squad advanced along the narrow trail, flanked by deep swamps that gave them and their battalion little room for maneuver. As the point element of their company crossed the bridge over Simemi Creek, machine-gun fire echoed through the swamps. The Japanese, waiting in their hidden, heavily fortified dugouts, opened fire at point-blank range. Then sniper fire from the treetops slashed the pinned-down US infantrymen, and mortar fire and grenades soon added to the carnage. Kincaid, who was still on the near side of the bridge, quickly deployed his machine gun and provided covering fire as the advance guard tried to withdraw.[4]

Kincaid's weapons squad then pulled back to allow the rest of L Company to withdraw. Once in cover, the company commander came past and called for volunteers to retrieve the wounded. Kincaid and a number of others moved back toward the bridge. Unable to make their way over in the face of withering Japanese fire, Kincaid and his fellow volunteers took out their .45-caliber pistols and waded into the neck-deep water to cross the creek. Crawling up the bank, they found some of their wounded comrades but also "discovered that every time you moved the kunai grass it brought a burst of machine gun fire in your direction." Kincaid saw a buddy whom he had gone to school with in Wisconsin shot through the ankle, his foot "dangling by a little flesh and skin." Ignoring the calls of his childhood friend to shoot him and leave him behind, Kincaid dragged him to the riverbank, slipped him onto his shoulders and swam back through the sniper fire to an aid station.[5]

Lacking air and artillery support and without mortars of its own, Colonel Miller's battalion was pinned down and going nowhere. Unable to attack or to dig in due to the terrain and falling gravely short of ammunition, the men prayed that the Japanese would not counterattack. On Miller's flank, the attack of the 1st Battalion, 128th Regiment (1/128th), had also been stopped cold, and the next day, while Miller and his battalion held on, the 1st Battalion tried again, only to meet the same fate. As more supplies arrived on the third day, both battalions, supported by the 2/6th Australian Independent (Commando) Company and a battalion from the 126th Regiment, would move forward with heavy air support.[6]

But on the morning of 21 November, plans were not yet complete, and Miller and his battalion had not even received their orders to attack when

A-20 and B-25 medium bombers from the USAAF arrived to pound the Japanese lines. As the aircraft screamed into the attack, Sergeant Kincaid looked up "at the underside of [one of] our own plane[s] with the bomb bay doors open and watch[ed] a 500lb bomb exit the plane and get larger and larger as it fell and wonder[ed]" if it "would land right on top of me." Luckily for Kincaid and his squad, it sailed overhead, which meant it was not so lucky for the next platoon, where it killed four men and wounded two others. Rather than coming in and bombing across their front, the aircraft had bombed directly down the length of the trail, and some of the ordnance had fallen among L Company. As Kincaid noted, "the only thing that saved more people from being hurt or killed" was that most of the bombs "landed to one side of the trail in the swamp and most of the force went upward."[7]

At 8:40 a.m., Miller received an order to attack at 8:00 a.m. Despite the failure of this first attempt, the commanding general of the 32nd Division, Maj. Gen. Edwin Harding, was determined to launch an attack that day, so he arranged for the air force to return at 12:45 p.m., with a ground assault to follow close on its heels. Fearing that it would not make it on time, the air force never showed up. The bombing run and the attack were rescheduled a second time, for 4:00 p.m. On this occasion, the aircraft arrived in strength and on time, but most missed the target area, while one B-25 cut its run short and dropped its bombs on B and C Companies of Lt. Col. Robert McCoy's 1st Battalion, "killing six, wounding twelve and almost burying seventy others."[8]

At the end of the airstrike, with no artillery fire and only twenty rounds of unobserved 60 mm mortar fire in direct support, Miller's men advanced at 4:28 p.m. into intense Japanese fire. They closed in on the clearing around the bridge but were unable to cross it. After the loss of forty-two men killed, wounded, or missing, the attack was called off. Colonel McCoy's 1/128th fared no better. Not only were the attacks a failure, but also the stiff resistance was a massive shock to the US troops. It stripped bare both the shortcomings of their training and the poor leadership in the rifle battalions.

Maj. W. B. Parker, an engineering officer present in Colonel McCoy's 1st Battalion area to observe the attack and report back to I US Corps HQ, noted that

> the first opposition from the enemy here [at Buna] was a surprise and shock to our green troops. . . . The enemy positions were amazingly well camouflaged, and seemed to have excellent fields of fire. . . . They

had been sited to take advantage of any natural alleyways throu
the jungle. Snipers were everywhere. . . . It was dangerous to sh
even a finger from behind one's cover, as it would immediately dra...
a burst of fire. It was impossible to see where the enemy fire was coming from; . . . it was impossible to cover advance of squads by fire, as
the enemy positions could not be located.

Our tactics were initially bad. . . . Our troops [*sic*] first attempt
to advance in mass formation, utilizing cover, with disastrous results. . . . It was obvious that our troops were poorly trained in almost every aspect of jungle warfare . . . and because of the inferior
junior leadership, resiliency was greatly reduced. . . . Our defensive
outposts were very poor. . . . Our patrol activity was sporadic and
generally not up to good standard. . . . Our own night activity was
deplorably limited to defensive outposting. No aggressive, offensive
or preparatory combat measures were taken during the hours of
darkness. The reason attributed for this was that the troops had
had no previous training in night combat. . . . Supporting weapons
(MG's, mortars, arty) were not effectively employed by our troops
because of a lack of observation. . . . There was no liaison between
the ground forces and the air forces.

In addition, there was a great deficiency in the psychological con-
ditioning of our troops and our junior leaders. Some of the shock
of first encountering stiff resistance might have been ameliorated by
previous advice and by warning. . . . Our junior leadership in this
operation was poor, the most striking and depressing effect gleaned
from our whole observation. It was clear in many instances to rifle-
men in the line that their leaders were frightened and reluctant to
lead the men into fire. The men themselves, of course, were often
reluctant and frequently had to be individually pressed forward by
their junior leaders. . . . The 2/6 Aust Ind Company [serving side
by side with the Americans] . . . appeared much better prepared
for jungle combat, as far as training and psychological condition-
ing were concerned, than our troops. . . . More than one man [in
the 32nd Division] was heard to remark that he wished his officers
were more like the Australian officers, who were believed to lead
their men into the enemy fire. . . . This lack of confidence in their
leaders caused our troops to have no resiliency, no desire to get back
into the fight and win it; instead of being angered by enemy resistance, the casualties mostly appeared glad to get out of the combat
area.[9]

The same conditions occurred on the 2/126th's and 1/128th's front outside of Buna Village. Thus concluded the opening phase of the operations of the 32nd Division at Buna, the first action of this division in the Pacific War and the first action of US ground forces in the SWPA.

The resulting stalemate on the 32nd Division's front at Buna would lead to massive recriminations. Harding would soon lose his job, and MacArthur would tell his replacement to take Buna "or not come back alive." Many other senior US officers would lose their commands, while a number of Australians, including Blamey, would use this initial poor performance to rub salt into MacArthur wounds and claim that US troops were not up to the job.

Many populist Australian historians would subsequently use this failure as a chance to push a rather nationalist approach to Australian military history. It is claimed (often indirectly) that the poor initial performance of the 32nd Division proved the superiority of the Australian fighting soldier over his bigger Alliance partner, reinforcing the ANZAC legend.[10] On the other side, one American historian would view the outcome of these operations as evidence of the incompatibility of the US and Australian military systems.[11]

Blinded by the tactical problems on the battlefield and the rawness of the US troops, most of these accounts of the Battle of the Beachheads overlook the broader strategic context and the operational restrictions on these battles, especially logistics.[12] Instead, these histories concentrate their narratives on small tactical actions demonstrating the heroism of the Australian troops and the supposed incompetence of senior US and Australian officers. They highlight the callousness of MacArthur in declaring victory well before it was actually won and for largely ignoring the valor and sacrifice of the units that secured this, the first, major campaign victory in the SWPA.

STRATEGIC CONTEXT

By the time of the fall of Kokoda on 2 November 1942, General Blamey's plan for the elimination of the Japanese in Papua was well advanced.[13] With his right flank at Milne Bay secured in August, the 7th Australian Division on the advance back over the Owen Stanley Range, and elements of the US 32nd Division available from late September, Blamey had decided on a plan to close in on the Japanese along three lines of approach. The 7th Division would emerge out of the mountains and advance to

Gona and Sanananda, while the 126th and 128th Infantry Regiments of Maj. Gen. Edwin Harding's 32nd Division would close in on Buna via two combined air, sea, and land routes to the south.

Initially, on orders from MacArthur and NGF, the 32nd Division had sent the 2/126th Regiment and supporting troops over the Owen Stanley Range via the Kapa Kapa Trail, to the south of Kokoda, to outflank the Japanese. This effort was a disaster. With the trail being largely unusable, the 2/126th took some forty-two days to reach its assigned destination at Soputa and in the process was wrecked as a fighting unit: the commanding officer (CO) had a heart attack, and most of the men caught malaria or some other tropical disease. The only thing that they could take away from their experience, besides exhaustion, malnourishment, and disease was their new nickname, the "Ghost Mountain Boys," after Mount Suwemalla, the nine-thousand-foot peak that they had crossed during their ordeal.[14]

As a result, the Kapa Kapa Trail was abandoned as a line of advance, and with improving air superiority over the battlefield, coupled with the increasing availability of transport aircraft in the SWPA in early October, NGF moved the 1/126th Regiment directly from Port Moresby to Abel's airfield. From there, it was then able to march to Embogo. In addition, as noted above, two battalions of the 128th Regiment and the 2/6th Australian Independent Company were flown to Wanigela and then moved overland or by sea to Pongani and then to Embogo, while the final battalion of the 128th moved by air directly from Port Moresby to Pongani. With the 7th Australian Division advancing across the Kumusi River and through Wairopi, the Japanese at the beachheads were now hemmed in on three sides with their backs to the sea.[15]

At this point, the Allied high command in the SWPA was gripped with a mixture of anxiety and impending triumph. GHQ and Adv LHQ recognized that their ongoing success in Papua was largely dependent on the positive outcome of the SOPAC forces fighting in the southern Solomon Islands. Since the landing at Guadalcanal, this had become the main effort for both the Japanese and Allied forces in the Pacific, while Papua remained an important but secondary theater. The Japanese focus on Guadalcanal had led to Maj. Gen. Tomitarō Horii being ordered to abandon his overland assault on Port Moresby until the situation at Guadalcanal could be resolved in Japan's favor. For MacArthur, all of his plans hinged on Guadalcanal. As MacArthur's operations chief, General Chamberlin, noted in late October, "the key to our plan of action lies in the success or failure of the South Pacific in holding Guadalcanal. None

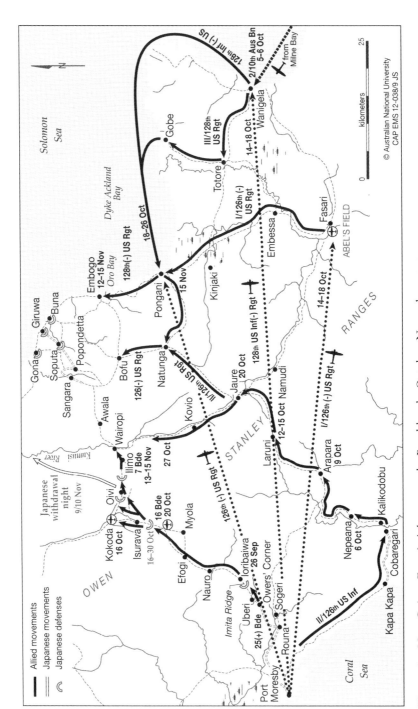

Figure 6.1 New Guinea Force's Advance on the Beachheads, October–November 1942

of [our] ... plans ... has a reasonable chance of success if Guadalcanal falls. Their failure will adversely affect the success of our basic and fundamental mission. If Guadalcanal holds, the success of [our] plan is assured."[16] The effect on operations in Papua was clear, and Blamey had noted to MacArthur only three days earlier that "the security of Port Moresby remains a prime consideration until the result of the Guadalcanal fighting is concluded."[17]

Victory at Guadalcanal was an essential element to MacArthur's plans. Defeat there would unravel everything and allow the Japanese to reorient their air and sea power to Papua, which would then facilitate a massive reinforcement of the Japanese position at the beachheads. While the main Japanese land offensive to retake Henderson Field was defeated by the US Marines on 29 October, the fate of Guadalcanal ultimately hinged on which side could exert sea control and air superiority around the island, and this battle remained in doubt until mid-January 1943.[18] Up until the second week of January 1943, the United States feared that the heavy Japanese naval activity around the island was a precursor to a renewed offensive operation rather than the actual withdrawal of Japanese ground forces from the island that was occurring.[19]

Prudence therefore required GHQ to plan for the worst-case scenario. The day after Chamberlin detailed the importance of Guadalcanal to the operations in Papua, his staff completed the "Petersburg Plan" for the "Redistribution of Allied Forces in the SWPA in the event of a Japanese success in the Solomon Islands." This plan outlined a wholesale withdrawal of Allied forces from the northern and southeastern coasts of Papua, including Milne Bay, the reversal to a defensive position on the Kokoda Trail based around only one brigade, and a large number of troops and aircraft withdrawing from Port Moresby back to the Australian mainland.[20]

The SWPA's problems did not stop there. Although Guadalcanal was at the forefront of MacArthur and Blamey's concerns, a second source of strategic pressure would soon begin to play on their minds. While Japan's power in the South Pacific emanated out of its base at Rabaul, confronting the SWPA both head-on and on its eastern flank, growing Japanese power to the west in Southeast Asia, and in particular in the Arafura Sea and around Java and East Timor, was becoming an increasing concern through November and December 1942. Darwin continued to come under air attack, with raids on 25–27 October and again on 23, 26, and 27 November 1942. In mid-December, GHQ was closely monitoring the expansion of the Sixteenth Japanese Army through its occupation of the

Tanimbar Islands, the Kai Islands, and the Aroe Islands and the building of an airfield in eastern Timor.[21] MacArthur was to become so concerned about the force posture of the Japanese Army in East Timor and the surrounding islands that on 23 December he ordered Blamey to place garrison forces in the Cape York Peninsula and send reinforcements to the small Allied outpost at Merauke on the southeastern coast of Dutch New Guinea.[22] Two days later, on Christmas Day, he was urging his commanders onward at the beachheads, as "I feel convinced that our time is strictly limited and that if results are not achieved shortly the whole picture [strategic situation] may radically change."[23]

The anxieties over Guadalcanal and Japanese operations to Papua's west were initially allayed by the expectation of a quick and easy victory at the beachheads. This assessment was based on a flawed calculation of Japanese strength and intentions in Papua at the end of 1942. Both the US and Australian high commands falsely believed that the main Japanese force in Papua had been defeated on the Kokoda Trail and that fewer than four thousand Japanese troops occupied the beachheads area. In addition, they believed that those troops left in Papua consisted only of "two depleted regiments, one battalion of mountain artillery and normal reinforcing and service elements."[24]

Blamey wrote to MacArthur in early October and stated that "evidence is accumulating that the morale of the enemy troops at Buna is not of the highest and unless reinforced we should be able to deal with him."[25] At the same time, GHQ intelligence speculated that the lack of Japanese interest in repairing the aerodrome at Buna, coupled with a supply line effective only as far as the Kumusi River, meant that they may well have "withdrawn completely" from the "vulnerable [and] unprofitable" Buna sector.[26] A few days later, they regarded that the most likely Japanese course of action would be to pull back what troops they had at Buna to Lae, which they considered to be the main Japanese defensive locality in New Guinea.[27]

This underestimation of the Japanese and their intentions lasted through October and November. However, at the end of October, the G-2 section at GHQ had started to slowly revise its assessments of the enemy situation. The first indication of this reconsideration came on 29–30 October when it noted that "after early optimistic deductions, based on superficial sightings of 'nil activities,' it is more and more apparent that an echelon-ment [*sic*] in depth is in operation along the axis Kokoda-Buna . . . with a main defensive position, behind the Kumusi River, toward Buna."[28] This changing view was, not, however, widespread at this time, and intelligence continued to argue that Japanese reinforcement of the beachheads was "improbable."[29] On 31 October, the commander of the 32nd Division, General Harding, wrote to GHQ CoS Richard Sutherland that "all information we have to date indicates that the Japanese forces in the Buna-Popondetta-Gona triangle are relatively light. Unless he gets reinforcements, I believe we will be fighting him on at least a three to one basis. Imbued as I am with considerable confidence in the fighting qualities of the American soldier, I am not at all pessimistic about the outcome of the scrap."[30]

It was not until the day after the first action of US troops at Buna that the officers of GHQ's G-2 section revised their appreciation of Japanese forces. Here, they added the arrival of Japanese reinforcements in early November, although this was offset, they stated, by their losses at the battle for Oivi-Gorari. While estimations of Japanese strength remained way off (still at below four thousand), they now recognized both the enemy's intention to defend the beachheads and their ability to provide reinforcements from Lae-Salamaua and Rabaul, as well as the Allies' inability to interdict these moves.[31]

Allied appreciations of the Japanese would finally change in late November 1942. In the days leading up to the Americans going into combat at Buna, NGF sent to the 32nd Division a string of messages about the arrival of Japanese reinforcements.[32] However, it would take the disastrous first clashes between the 32nd Division and the Japanese at Buna before the feeling of impending triumph, evident in October and early November in Port Moresby and back at GHQ in Brisbane, vanished and was replaced with anxiety over both the size and intentions of the Japanese force at the beachheads.

By the end of the month, the atmosphere at GHQ had changed completely. On 27 November, MacArthur wrote to Admiral Halsey, C-in-C SOPAC, that "the enemy is making every effort to reinforce and supply the garrison [at Buna and Sanananda] by sea and despite losses from air attack has recently succeeded to an extent sufficient to prevent my destroying his beach head. He is evidently increasing his efforts and is in position to make a move of considerable magnitude against New Guinea."[33]

Japanese reinforcements now became a major concern for the Allies. This was a direct result of the Allies' lack of sea control and air superiority during October and November. It meant that, under the cover of darkness, the Japanese were able to send small convoys of ships to the Buna-Sanananda area. Allied interdiction of these convoys was poor, and early on intelligence constantly speculated as to whether they were withdrawing or reinforcing, with an emphasis on the former over the latter. By the time that Allied forces closed in on Gona, Sanananda, and Buna in November, there were in fact some nine thousand Japanese troops in these positions, many of them fresh troops. Reinforcements continued to arrive throughout the early stages of the operation, bringing the defenders' strength up to approximately twelve thousand troops. Japanese reinforcements continued to arrive right up until the end of December 1942.[34]

These reinforcements were a reflection of the desire of the Japanese Army to hold the beachheads indefinitely. It planned to secure the beachheads in a defensive battle and then use this area as its base from which to crush MacArthur, using the full weight of its forces in the South Pacific after it had defeated the Americans at Guadalcanal. In order to do so, on 16 November it activated the Eighth Area Army at Rabaul under Gen. Hitoshi Imamura, which included the Seventeenth Army fighting on Guadalcanal and the new Eighteenth Army (Lt. Gen. Hatazō Adachi) to command the operations in Papua and New Guinea. This represented a major increase in commitment from the IJA to operations in the South Pacific.[35]

Concerns over SOPAC's efforts at Guadalcanal and the failure of Allied intelligence at the beachheads over both the size and intentions of the Japanese had major ramifications for the way the operations would unfold in November and December. These two elements greatly affected the attitude and approach of the SWPA high command toward the speed in which these operations had to be carried out. The emphasis on speed is one of the most controversial aspects of the campaign, and both MacArthur and Blamey have been heavily criticized in a number of the accounts of these battles for pressuring tactical commanders to quickly eliminate the Japanese and for showing a lack of understanding of the conditions at the battlefront. The constant pushing for results was, according to these accounts, due to MacArthur's and Blamey's callous disregard for casualties and the welfare of their troops and a lack of knowledge of conditions at the front lines, exacerbated by the fact that MacArthur and Blamey did not visit the battlefront until after the Japanese had been defeated. The emphasis on speed, it has been argued, was about personal ambition, vanity, and the desire of these senior commanders to save their own jobs.[36]

However, such an analysis totally disregards the strategic circumstances in which these operations were undertaken. The realization among senior commanders that a quick and easy victory had vanished in the face of exceptionally heavy and unexpected Japanese resistance meant that the pressure was mounting not just to save their jobs but also to ensure the security of the Allied position in Papua. This was principally driven by the widely recognized fact that the Allied position in Papua depended heavily on success at Guadalcanal. While this campaign remained in the balance, MacArthur and Blamey were eager to eliminate the Japanese at the beachheads in order to prepare their own defensive positions on the northern coast of Papua. Eliminating the Japanese at the beachheads would dramatically increase the Allied strategic position in Papua and would mean that they could prepare for a deliberate defense of the Buna area and Milne Bay, meaning the Petersburg Plan might not have to be put into operation if Guadalcanal fell. Ultimately, they were fighting to secure all of the hard-won gains from July 1942 onward and to ensure that they would not have to be abandoned.[37]

Furthermore, virtually all assessments of these operations completely overlook the heightened concern that MacArthur and Blamey had over the actions of the Japanese Sixteenth Army in Java after its expansion into East Timor and the surrounding islands. The air raids on northern Australia plus those on Merauke in Dutch New Guinea in early January, in addition to troop and naval buildups in the Arafura Sea, convinced GHQ that an invasion of Merauke was a distinct possibility. The result was further reinforcements being sent to protect its airfield and a greater need to provide for the security of the Allied position in Papua.[38] These moves were supported by the commander of the First Australian Army, Lt. Gen. John Lavarack, who was responsible for the defense of northeastern Australia and the Torres Strait.[39]

Concerns over Guadalcanal and Japanese intentions from Timor meant that GHQ and NGF placed an emphasis on the speedy elimination of the Japanese at Buna, Sanananda, and Gona in November and December. When GHQ and the Australians realized that the Japanese were much stronger than expected and that they were attempting to reinforce their positions in November and early December, combined with the threat from East Timor it gave rise to fears of a major Japanese repositioning toward Papua and New Guinea, which led to an even greater emphasis on clearing the Japanese out of the beachheads quickly.[40] While in reflection this emphasis on speed from MacArthur downward does not seem as warranted as it did at the time, it remained a critical part of the considerations of the high command for the operations at the beachheads. As such, any analysis must be cognizant to judge the actions of these commanders on the intelligence available at the time, rather than reveling in the benefit of hindsight.

THE 7TH AUSTRALIAN DIVISION

At the end of October, General Blamey had a sizable force in Papua. NGF, soon to be designated as an army-level command, had the 7th Australian Division of two infantry brigades under General Vasey operating on the Kokoda Trail. The 6th Australian Division of two militia and one AIF brigade, plus a divisional cavalry regiment, one squadron of light tanks, and two field artillery regiments under General Allen, were in position to defend Port Moresby. Wau was being held by Kanga Force and at Milne Bay, General Clowes commanded another division-sized force of three brigades. Two regiments of the US 32nd Division were now also in Papua. The 128th Regiment, as well as the attached 2/6th Australian Independent Company, were closing in on Wanigela and Pongani, while the 126th Regiment had its 2nd Battalion on the Jaure Trail and the other two battalions located around Moresby.[41]

Of these forces, the principal strike weapon of the Australians, and NGF in general, was the 7th Australian Division. This division, first under the command of Allen, and now Vasey, had rotated the Australian brigades in Port Moresby through combat on the Kokoda Trail, with the 16th and 25th Brigades AIF and the 3rd Militia Battalion in contact with the enemy through October and November. Like all of the AIF brigades, the 16th and 25th were elite troops who had seen extensive action in the Middle East, and while still adapting to jungle warfare, they had performed exceptionally well against the Japanese. They were well led, highly experienced, and battle proven.

Throughout the course of the battle, the division would remain under the command of General Vasey. Vasey had been transferred from his posting as DCGS to command the 6th Australian Division, while his HQ was moved to Port Moresby in September. On 27 October, Vasey was ordered to relieve General Allen in command of the 7th Division at Myola on the Kokoda Trail. Under Vasey's command, the division took Kokoda on 2 November, although the plan and most of the credit belonged to Allen. His performance in outflanking and destroying large sections of the IJA's SSF at the battle of Oivi-Gorari (5–10 November) was a masterstroke, and this action broke the back of the Japanese forces that had advanced along the Kokoda Trail. His command at the beachheads, however, was to be described by one historian as the "low point in an otherwise distinguished career."[42]

The major problem for Vasey's division in November 1942 was that by the time it descended out of the mountains onto the beachhead battlefields, it was worn out, riddled with disease, and greatly reduced in numbers. The 25th Brigade could muster only 850 men at Gona in late November; likewise, the 16th Brigade, which had already fought at Templeton's Crossing, Eora Creek, and Oivi Heights, had taken 561 battle casualties and had 396 evacuated sick before it went into action at the beachheads. However, when it made contact with the Japanese at Sanananda, it still outnumbered the 25th Brigade, having 66 officers and 974 men, still the equivalent of only one full-strength battalion. In addition many of the men were already suffering from malaria and other diseases. The 2/1st Battalion, 16th Brigade, had been hardest hit and could muster only 197 soldiers fit for action.[43]

The 21st Brigade was in the same position. Having borne the brunt of the early defensive battles on the Kokoda Trail, it was recuperating at Port Moresby but would soon be called into action. Like its fellow AIF brigades, it too was low on numbers and would go into action at Gona with fewer than eight hundred men. At Milne Bay, the 17th and 18th Brigades AIF were in a much better state of readiness and fitness, although the health of these units was suffering in this malaria-prone region. In addition, they would be unavailable for operations at the beachheads until the Allies established sea control around the southeastern section of Papua and the outcome of the SOPAC operations around Guadalcanal was more certain. MacArthur informed Blamey in late October that "information from most secret sources" (most likely Ultra signals intelligence) indicated that the Japanese were planning to make another attack on Milne Bay in November; thus he required that the two AIF brigades remain for the defense of the port and the airstrip.[44]

NGF did, however, release the 2/12th Battalion from the 18th Brigade to conduct an amphibious raid on Goodenough Island to eliminate the Japanese naval infantry who had been marooned there after their failed assault on Milne Bay in August and to secure the area for possible establishment of an airfield. While ultimately successful, this operation revealed some major tactical limitations in the Allied operations, and most of the Japanese escaped when they were evacuated by the IJN, although not before giving the 2/12th Battalion a bloody nose.[45]

The other major element of the Australian ground forces in Papua that would fight with the 7th Division was the militia. A number of these units, most notably the 3rd, 39th, and 53rd Battalions, had already served on the Kokoda Trail. Largely made up of conscripts, as opposed to the volunteers of the AIF, and with little intensive training or adequate equipment, these units had put in mixed performances. The 39th Battalion had performed valiantly, and the 3rd was acquitting itself well, but a cloud hung over the 53rd. Of the two militia brigades available in Port Moresby, in which these battalions belonged, Blamey had grave reservations. He wrote to MacArthur at the start of the main offensive toward the beach-heads that "I am not satisfied that either of the militia brigades, the 14th and the 30th, are at present fit for offensive operations against the Japanese." While he held out some hope, noting that "we have got them down hard training and I will defer final opinion,"[46] setbacks at the beachheads at the end of November would mean that Blamey would be left with little choice but to cut short their training and thrust them into battle before they were ready.

In 1942, these units were far from well prepared for combat. With the best men and equipment having been allocated to the AIF units, the conscripts of the militia were initially provided with only ninety days of training. In order to bolster their effectiveness, in January 1942 training had been vastly extended. Formations had been put on full-time service after 7 December 1941, and AIF officers were now being posted to militia units. Older, unfit officers and commanders were replaced with combat veterans, although this move was not as effective as it should have been, as the remaining troops were largely untrained.[47]

Within the 30th Brigade, the 49th Battalion was seen as undisciplined and undertrained.[48] In 1941, the CGS had called it "quite the worst [battalion] in Australia."[49] The battalion's history noted of its dispatch to Port Moresby that "with hindsight, it is unbelievable that army commanders or a government could have allowed troops as inadequately prepared as the 49th to move to a war zone."[50] The same could be said for the rest of the 30th Brigade's units.

However, it seems that the decision to send the 30th Brigade to Papua in early 1942 may well have been a calculated strategic decision. At this time, the Allies were under severe pressure from the rapidly advancing Japanese. With the Australian continent the priority for defense, and as the SWPA lacked adequate naval and airpower to defend Papua, there was a very high risk that Port Moresby could fall to a Japanese am-phibious invasion. Thus, the only defense against a Japanese invasion force was the US Pacific Fleet under Admiral Nimitz. If it were unable to intervene or were defeated in battle, Port Moresby would fall just as Timor, New Britain, and most of the islands to Australia's north had in early 1942. It was on the basis of this strategic assessment that the 30th Brigade was dispatched to Port Moresby rather than one of the better-trained militia or AIF formations on the Australian mainland. Ultimately, the Australian troops in Papua in early 1942 were saved by the intervention of the USN at the battle of the Coral Sea and the hesitation of the IJN amphibious task force commander. It was only after the victory at Midway that Blamey looked to reinforce Papua with high-quality troops.

The main problem for the 30th Brigade was that its poor state upon arrival in Papua was not alleviated by its time in country. Instead of receiving adequate training and equipment, the poor infrastructure in the port and the need to construct defensive works meant the troops were largely used as labor gangs, leaving little time for unit-level training. Of the two other militia brigades in Papua, Blamey considered the 14th Brigade a "poor show," and while the 7th Brigade at Milne Bay was regarded as better trained, only five of its officers had seen active service before, and only one, the commander, had seen action in the war.[51] The army rated the 7th Brigade at Milne Bay as only "efficient in a static role." The 14th Brigade at Port Moresby was considered a level *E* unit, where "a considerable amount of training . . . is required," while the 30th Brigade was a level *F* formation—the lowest rating possible, meaning "unit training is not complete."[52]

At the start of the beachhead operation, the 7th Brigade had seen action at Milne Bay and performed credibly, given its level of training and lack of experience, but it had suffered badly from malaria. The 14th Brigade was required to man the defenses of Port Moresby, so in December the 30th Brigade, which now included a number of units from the 7th and 14th Brigades, went into action under the command of the AIF brigadier, Selwyn Porter. Despite this injection of a highly experienced commander, the brigades' performance was, unsurprisingly, less than impressive.

THE RED ARROW DIVISION

For the Americans, the 32nd "Red Arrow" Division was the first US Army formation to go into action in the SWPA, and as such it was under intense scrutiny. Despite evidence detailing shortcomings at all levels of command, the division's commander, his officers, and his troops expected that they would perform well and that the Japanese would be "easy pickings."[53] This confidence was highly misplaced and based more on a false belief in cultural superiority of the American fighting man rather than a realistic appraisal of the division's training and leadership. The majority of failings of the division observed by Major Parker at Buna can be traced back to its poor preparation for combat.

The 32nd Division was a National Guard formation from Wisconsin and Michigan. It had been called up in September 1940 along with three other divisions, but it was woefully short of personnel at the time of activation. It participated in the 1942 Louisiana Maneuvers and had been slated to go to the European theater but was rerouted in some haste to the SWPA on 22 April 1942. This move separated the division from its combat engineering unit, which had already departed for Northern Ireland. In addition to receiving a new engineering battalion, some three thousand new replacements joined the division as it left the country. However, this still left the division short some four thousand men.[54]

The 32nd Division's commanding general was Maj. Gen. Edwin Forrest Harding. Born in 1886, Harding entered the US Military Academy in 1905. Upon leaving West Point, he was commissioned in the infantry and served in the Philippines, China, and Hawaii, commanding a platoon, a company, a battalion, and a regiment. He graduated from the Infantry School at Fort Benning, Georgia, the Command and General Staff School at Fort Leavenworth, Kansas, and the US Army War College in Pennsylvania. His other positions included instructor at West Point, editor of the *Infantry Journal*, and instructor at the Infantry School, under the leadership of George C. Marshall. Other section heads at Fort Benning at the time included Joseph Stilwell and Omar Bradley.[55]

Just before the United States entered the war, Harding was the commander of the 9th Infantry Division at Fort Bragg, North Carolina.[56] On paper he had a model career progression, and he was regarded as an officer of great promise. However, he was solid rather than brilliant. As one GHQ officer noted, he "knew what he was doing . . . a good four-square artilleryman [*sic*]. He was not a brilliant person or a quick thinker, but he was steady."[57] Unfortunately for Harding, the situation in which the 32nd Division found itself at Buna required a commander who was brilliant and a quick thinker. "Steady" was to prove to be just not good enough for the circumstances.

The division arrived in Adelaide on 14 May and then moved to Brisbane from 28 July to 10 August 1942.[58] The training experience in Adelaide had been entirely unsuitable, and although conditions were better in Queensland, time was fast running out. In addition to its movement, the division had received some training in amphibious operations and had also been required to detach the 3/127th Regiment to act as a demonstration battalion at the Joint Overseas Operational Training School at Port Stephens in NSW.[59] While the movement and the splintering of the division had undoubtedly affected its ability to train, the opportunities that were forthcoming had not been adequately exploited.

When the division was reviewed in September 1942 by the newly appointed I US Corps commander Lt. Gen. Robert L. Eichelberger (a West
Point classmate of Harding's), he found the division in high spirits but
poor shape. He noted to Sutherland that "aggressive leadership seems
lacking and the resulting deficiencies in small unit training have been
observed." Simple things such as basic skills in areas such as "scouting
and patrolling" were lacking, and I Corps HQ was also critical of the
training program that the 32nd Division had put together, calling it both
unrealistic and inadequate. Eichelberger would also note that he did not
consider the troops to be mentally prepared for combat and that the chain
of command had not accepted responsibility for training the division.[60]
In the end, Eichelberger rated the division as "barely satisfactory" in
combat efficiency and, just like Blamey had assessed the Australian militia
in Papua, told MacArthur that the 32nd Division "was not sufficiently
trained to meet Japanese veterans on equal terms."[61]

Even accounting for the disrupted movements, Harding's dereliction in
the training of his division was considerable. He decentralized training
down to the units, and while the divisional training directive he set for
July–September 1942 included a requirement to practice company-level
motorized security missions, it made no mention of jungle warfare.[62] By
his own admission he had not used the US Army's jungle warfare doctrine
as the basis for training, as he considered it out of date. As the American
historian Jay Luvaas has noted, "had more careful attention been paid
to the manual's advice . . . many American lives might have been spared
at Buna."[63]

Like many National Guard divisions in 1942, the 32nd retained a
large number of its prewar Guard officers. When Harding took command of the 32nd on 9 February 1942, he believed it prudent to hold on
to as many of these officers as he could, even though some of them were
far from competent in their positions.[64] One of the major problems that
arose, as with a number of such US divisions, was the close relationship
between the officers and men that had carried over into wartime training
from their civilian lives before the war. This, as one senior division officer
noted, caused the National Guard officers to be hesitant in demanding
strict obedience to orders and created problems enforcing discipline.[65]

The National Guard officers were also not as tactically proficient as
their regular army colleagues. Instead of investing heavily in improving
their skills and knowledge, Harding chose to rely on his small clique of
regular officers at divisional headquarters. Thus, the bulk of the staff
officers spread throughout the division remained undertrained.[66] This
approach would backfire considerably at Buna when the pace of the

battlefield, casualties, and disease would add to the difficulty of the operations and when deficiencies in staff work only became more acute. This greatly hindered the operational planning and the logistics arrangements for the division, compounding an already desperate situation at Buna.

Despite the poor state of its training, especially compared to the other US division in Australia at that time, Eichelberger had selected the 32nd to move to Papua. The rationale was an administrative preference. The division's training ground outside of Brisbane had been deemed less than optimal, so I US Corps had started to progress the movement of the division to Rockhampton, where the training ground for the 41st Division had proven to be excellent. The process of movement made it expedient for I US Corps HQ to simply reroute it to Papua. Harding, however, had claimed that his division was ready and just as well prepared and trained as the 41st Division. In addition, there was speculation that Eichelberger and the 41st Division's commander, Maj. Gen. Horace Fuller, were not necessarily getting along and that this may also have influenced the decision to move his less well-trained division with a more trusted and affable commander into combat first.[67] Eichelberger's decision would prove to be his biggest mistake of the Papua campaign.

Once the division landed in Papua and began assembling, it immediately started to display another grave weakness—overconfidence. As noted, General Harding believed that his troops would face only a battalion of Japanese troops at Buna and that they would be "easy pickings." He went on to declare that, even if the enemy was in greater strength than he imagined, "I don't think it would be too much trouble to take Buna with the forces we can put against it,"[68] and he confidently predicted that he would capture Buna by 1 November.[69] This overconfidence seeped through the entire division, and Harding did nothing to stem the belief among his soldiers that they were superior to both the Australians and the Japanese. He even believed that Blamey had been holding his division back from combat because he thought they would embarrass the Australians.[70] This misplaced self-confidence would be shattered when the division came into contact with the Japanese defenses near Buna, where the effect on the morale of the 32nd Division's troops was devastating.

COMMAND

By this stage in the campaign, the command structure had started to evolve. MacArthur and Blamey were now both in Port Moresby. Herring had been in command of NGF since Sydney Rowell had been sacked, but as the 7th Division had started to descend from the mountains and the 32nd Division had begun to move over the Owen Stanley Range to close on Buna from the south, command arrangements in Papua and New Guinea were rearranged. Blamey decided to split NGF HQ. The original NGF HQ, which had been created out of Rowell's I Australian Corps, would move over the Owen Stanleys to Popendetta to command the 7th and 32nd Divisions as Advanced (Adv) NGF HQ—a corps-level formation. NGF HQ would be taken under direct command by Blamey and operate as an army-level HQ controlling all ground forces in Papua and New Guinea, including Adv NGF, Kanga Force at Wau, Milne Force, as well as directly commanding the forces defending Port Moresby.

With the order to split the HQ, Herring took command of Adv NGF and brought with him the original I Australian Corps staff. General Berryman, the DCGS, took over as the senior staff officer (MGGS) of NGF and would build up the staff in Port Moresby by bringing forward a number of officers from First Australian Army HQ and Adv LHQ back in Australia. This would mean that Blamey would be in command of the AMF, the ALF, and NGF. Berryman, meanwhile, would continue as DCGS and add the role of MGGS to his portfolio.

With the opening of Adv NGF HQ, Herring took direct command of the two frontline divisions and divided their area of operations at the Girua River. The 7th Division would be responsible for operations at Gona and Sanananda and would soon take the US 126th Regiment under command to reinforce the Australian brigade operating at Sanananda. Meanwhile, the 32nd Division's operational area was further divided, by terrain, into two key fronts: Urbana Force, operating in front of Buna Village, Buna Mission, and the Triangle, and Warren Force, covering the old and new airstrips and Cape Endaidere.

TERRAIN

The command arrangements were clear and straightforward, but the battlefield confronting the Allies was far from ideal. While the battlefront was only some seven and a half miles from Gona to Buna, the region was divided into three distinct operational areas by the rivers and swamps that inundated the area. This meant that although Adv NGF would fight one operation, it would control three very distinct and separated battlefronts with poor lateral communications, making it virtually impossible for the

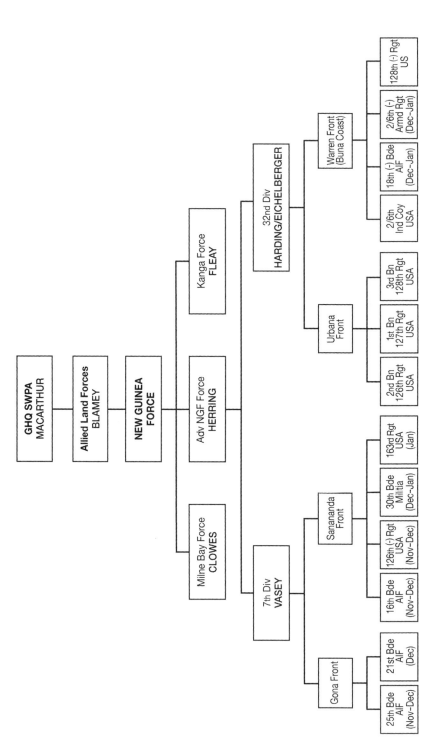

Figure 6.2 Command Diagram, Papua Campaign, November 1942–January 1943

troops at Gona, Sanananda, or Buna to support one another. Each area along the front consisted of coconut groves and razor-sharp kunai grass on a low-lying flat plain that was covered with jungles and swamps. In addition, the area was alive with mosquitos that caused major problems with malaria, while compounding this problem was an abundance of other tropical diseases. This made mere survival—let alone combat—for the troops exceptionally difficult. General Berryman noted that "the Jap is, in one sense only, our worst enemy, malaria and other tropical diseases claim far more victims."[71] Indicative of this is the fact that the "fresh" 32nd Division was to suffer a 66 percent sickness rate, while by the end of 1942 the Australians were to have some 15,575 cases of sickness due to the tropical conditions, including 9,249 cases of malaria.[72]

JAPANESE DEFENSES

The Japanese positions within this horrendous terrain consisted of heavily fortified bunkers, blockhouses, trenches, and weapon pits, situated on the only dry ground in the area. They had made excellent use of the landscape to maximize their defenses, which one US official report described as "perfect."[73] At Sanananda, the Japanese occupied forward positions along the Killerton Trail that allowed them to develop their defense in depth, while in the Buna area the terrain and the Japanese defenses effectively divided the region into four very restricted operational areas: Buna village, the Triangle, the narrow bridge across the airstrips, and the coconut plantation below Cape Endaiadere.

The 2/6th Australian Independent Company fighting as part of the 32nd Division noted of the Japanese defenses that

> all emplacements appeared to be made of cocoanut [sic] logs laid lengthwise with others placed on bearers forming the roof. The whole was then camouflaged according to the country in which it was situated. . . . In most cases the loopholes were hidden to view by a screen of bush or camouflage, although vision from the inside out was still possible, and in most cases the pillbox or emplacement was not discovered until you were right on to it.[74]

The Japanese used the "high ground"—that is, the small amount of terrain not in swamps and above the water table—to construct their defenses, using interlocking arcs of fire and mutually supporting positions consisting of machine guns, direct-fire antitank and antiaircraft artillery, mortars, rifleman, and snipers. Their positions were, as one US official publication described it, a defensive "masterpiece."[75]

LOGISTICS: THE LIFE BLOOD OF WAR

The major Allied operational difficulty of the beachheads was to be logistics. At the theater level there were not enough merchant ships in the SWPA to carry all of the necessary supplies around the area of operations, while in Papua both Port Moresby and Milne Bay's infrastructure was very underdeveloped. The supply line over the Kokoda Trail was severely limited due to the terrain and the small number of native carriers, while the lack of sea control in the waters around the northern coast of Papua made the sea line of communication precarious. As a result, in the initial stages of the advance, the Australian and US forces were heavily dependent on air supply. This limited the number of troops available for operations, but most significantly it limited the use of artillery and tanks. For instance, it took seventeen planeloads to move just one troop of two 25-pounder artillery pieces to the beachheads area from Port Moresby, including just 306 rounds of ammunition per gun. In Papua, air resupply was further hampered by the atrocious weather. During October and November, it effectively put a handbrake on the two divisions' abilities to conduct combined arms operations.[76]

This was evident to the senior commanders. Blamey noted in late October that the "advance along the North East coast still remains precarious. The main supply line will be continued to be developed by small boats . . . but the route passing Cape Tufi still remains very vulnerable in view of the fact that we do not have not surface control over the sea approach."[77] Blamey would remain highly critical of the Allied navy for what he saw as a lack of effort in this area, especially when the Japanese seemed to be able to operate destroyers and light cruisers in the waters off Buna from November 1942 to January 1943.[78] However, the ANF in the SWPA was still small, and "there was a grave shortage of suitable shipping and escorts, and the waters through which the convoys would have to sail were poorly charted" and highly contested.[79] MacArthur would note in early October that "the enemy has complete control of the sea lanes and we are not now, nor have any reasonable expectations to being, in a position to contest that control."[80]

The hazardous nature of this sea line of communication was driven home to the Allies on the afternoon of 16 November, when a small convoy of three luggers and a captured Japanese landing barge carrying the command element of the 32nd Division (as well as ammunition, equipment, 81 mm mortars, .50-caliber heavy machine guns, two 25-pounder artillery pieces, and their ammunition) came under Japanese air attack rounding Cape Sudest. Eighteen Zeros lashed the convoy, whose air cover had departed a short time earlier to make it back to its airfields before dark. Twenty-three Allied personnel were killed and many more wounded, but, most important, the barge, the luggers, and all of the supplies were sunk.[81]

Generals Harding and Waldron survived but had to swim for the shore. The cruel irony of this situation is that Harding had been specifically warned about such an outcome by the Advance Echelon Fifth Air Force commander, Maj. Gen. Ennis Whitehead, only three weeks earlier. Harding had passed on this warning to Brig. Gen. Hanford MacNider, then commander of the division's advance guard, noting that Whitehead had stated that "sure as hell the Nips would be over to strafe our water-borne troop movement one of these fine days. . . . Anything like that would cost us plenty." Harding had gone on to state that "I'd rather be slow than sorry in this particular instance." Three weeks later, he ignored his own advice. Compounding the error, Whitehead had specifically cautioned Harding against operating between 8:00 a.m. and 5:00 p.m.[82]

The next morning, the Japanese struck again, sinking another two luggers, one each at Embogo and Mendaropu. The loss of the boats was, as the US official history notes, "a catastrophe of the first magnitude."[83] The lost equipment could not be replaced for weeks, and there were no ready replacements for the small craft. This all occurred on the eve of the first attack by the 32nd Division. It meant that the whole supply plan for the division's advance on Buna was disrupted and severely degraded. Limited air resupply would have to be relied upon until the sea lines of communication could be restored. Hereafter, NGF prohibited the daylight movement of small ships and instructed the 32nd Division to "carefully select hiding places for lying up by day of replacement vessels."[84]

The lack of sea control and coastal craft for resupply was a constant thorn in MacArthur's and Blamey's plans and for the operations at the front lines. The situation was so dire that MacArthur wrote to Admiral Halsey, C-in-C of SOPAC, noting that "pending the establishment of seaborne line of communication the number of troops I can employ is definitely restricted by limited air transport. . . . The Chief of Staff of the Army, after discussing with the navy in Washington, has suggested that I take up with you the detailed naval requirements for the support of my immediate operations."[85] In this endeavor MacArthur was to have no joy. Under heavy Japanese pressure around Guadalcanal, Halsey replied that he would only move units to MacArthur's aid in the event of a major Japanese naval move against New Guinea or Australia. Short of that, he argued, "I believe that my greater contribution to our common effort would be to strengthen my position . . . while continuing to maintain a naval force in being on the flank on any possible Japanese large scale advance against Australia or [the] Southern New Guinea coast."[86]

Some help would be forthcoming from Halsey but only in the form of a small number of US PT boats to operate against the Japanese off Buna.[87] They were not to go into action until late December, and their first major success was a friendly fire incident in which they blew up an Australian resupply lugger off Haroki.[88] The coastal supply situation would slowly increase as Allied airpower was able to exert more control during the course of the battle and the first convoys of merchant ships, escorted by RAN corvettes, began shuttling equipment and supplies, most significantly tanks and bulk artillery ammunition, north from Port Moresby in early December.[89] However, this meant that during November and most of December, logistics for the beachheads was a major limitation on the conduct of operations. Probably the best overall assessment of the supply situation during these operations comes from Brig. Gen. Clarence A. Martin, commander of the 126th Regimental Combat Team, who noted that the troops at the beachheads "went in on a shoestring, and the shoestring was mildewy rotten."[90]

COMBINED ARMS OPERATIONS

The biggest restriction that the poor lines of communication to the beachheads had on Allied operations was on the ability of the divisions to practice combined arms operations. This was as critical to operations in Papua as it was in any other theater of war. The jungle terrain did not change the basic principles of war, although this was not initially recognized by a number of senior officers in Papua. As Peter Williams has demonstrated, while the Australian forces on the Kokoda Trail were not outnumbered by the Japanese in their retreat across the Owen Stanley Range, they were outgunned. Carrying little more than small arms, the Australians had struggled against the more heavily equipped Japanese, especially in indirect-fire weapons.[91] A reversal of this situation would have a major impact on the success of the Allies in Papua and New Guinea as the war progressed.

As a result of the precious supply line, both of the divisions went into action at the beachheads with little in the way of artillery. US doctrine called for a 1942 US infantry division like the 32nd to field thirty-six 105 mm howitzers and twelve 155 mm howitzers while the 7th Australian Division was supposed to have three field artillery regiments of three batteries each in action.[92] In reality, the 32nd would have fewer than fifteen artillery tubes in support at Buna, and most of these would not arrive until late in the operations. Moreover, only one would be a US 105 mm howitzer, while the remainder were the much less effective Australian 25-pounders.[93] To make matters worse, the loss of the supplies to Japanese air attack meant that the infantry battalions had little in the way of heavy machine guns or mortars. In addition, as Adv NGF was a corps-level formation under normal operational circumstances, it would have been supplied with a regiment, or more, of medium guns.

Further constraining the ability of the divisions to confront the heavy Japanese defenses using combined arms operations was the lack of armored support in the initial battles. Proposals had been put forward by NGF as early as 17 November to move tanks from the 2/6th Armoured Regiment at Milne Bay to Pongani to support the advance of the 32nd Division, but the loss of the barges and luggers on 16 and 17 November delayed this order.[94] This meant that these light tanks would not be available until December, when they were used in conjunction with the reinforcing 18th Brigade AIF at Buna. Their introduction, as a result of a vastly improved supply situation, along with additional artillery, meant that combined arms operations were finally able to be implemented. Tactical success followed as a result.

STALEMATE AT THE BEACHHEADS

While the Americans were receiving their baptism of fire at Buna on the northern edge of the battlefield, the veteran 25th Brigade AIF under Brig. Ken Eather struck the formidable Japanese defenses at Gona. Defended largely by Japanese naval infantry, this was the smallest of the three defensive localities at the beachheads, but it would be no less stubbornly defended. The first assault went in on the day after the 32nd Division's first contact at Buna, on 22 November, with small gains made against the exceptionally strong Japanese defenses at the cost of over one hundred casualties. The 25th Brigade tried again on the twenty-third, but little headway was made, and more casualties were taken. During this period the brigade lost seventeen officers and 187 men in battle. Reinforced by the 3rd Militia Battalion, the brigade tried again on 25 November, this time supported by an air bombardment of the Japanese positions, but the result was the same, although casualties were relatively light.[95]

The inability of the 25th Brigade to break through in the face of stiff resistance, combined with its declining numbers, meant that the 21st Brigade was brought forward to reinforce it. Veterans of the withdrawal across the Kokoda Trail and still desperately short of numbers themselves, the first elements of the brigade went into action at Gona on 28 November. The battle was a grinding affair of attrition as the Australians slowly whittled away at the Japanese defenses, with the 25th Brigade in a containing role and the 21st Brigade attacking the main defenses. On 2 December, Brigadier Porter's 30th Militia Brigade entered the battle, with the 39th Battalion attached to the 21st Brigade, allowing the 25th Brigade to be relieved.

The offensive resumed at Gona on 6 December, with the Japanese being squeezed into an ever-decreasing defensive perimeter under heavy fire from rifles, machine guns, mortars, artillery, and air strikes. Soon the Japanese were being killed trying to infiltrate their way out of the position, and another major attack two days later broke through the remaining Japanese defenses. That night, the Japanese troops attempted to break out but were shot to pieces. The following day, after bitter hand-to-hand fighting, the last Japanese positions were eliminated. It had cost the Australians some 750 casualties.[96] The Australians now pushed westward along the coast to Haddy's Village (which they captured on 18 December), in order to eliminate elements of the 3rd Battalion, 170th Japanese Infantry Regiment, which had landed there in early December to support the Gona garrison. The final Japanese resistance in this area was eliminated just prior to Christmas 1942.[97]

Farther south at Sanananda, the 16th Brigade AIF had emerged out of the mountains to close with the Japanese. Vasey was soon given permission to reinforce Brig. John Lloyd's brigade with elements of Col. Clarence Tomlinson's 126th US Infantry Regiment. The news was keenly received by the Australians, with the 2/3rd Battalion regarding it as "very welcome information."[98] On arrival at the front, the 2/1st Battalion thought the 126th "very well equipped and [they] appear keen to get to grips with the Japs."[99]

Somewhat optimistically, Lloyd had ordered this lead battalion, the

2/3rd, to march for the sea on 19 November. Some resistance was encountered from a small delaying position on the Soputa Trail in the late afternoon. On the following morning, the 2/1st Battalion took over the advance and ran into heavy opposition at the Japanese forward defensive positions, which included artillery and heavy machine guns. In a free-flowing battle over the next few days, attack and counterattack took place across the 16th Brigade's entire front, engaging all three of its battalions. By 21 November, the brigade had been fought to a standstill, eliminating the forward Japanese outpost but wearing itself out in the process. It lost one-third of its strength.[100]

The Japanese now withdrew to their main defensive position astride the junction of the Killerton and Sanananda Trails, midway between Girua and Soputa. In this position were some four thousand Japanese troops. US reinforcements, along with two 25-pounder Australian field guns, now entered the fray. The reinforcements included the 126th Regiment's force, consisting of HQ and HQ Company, two rifle companies (C and D) of the 1st Battalion under Maj. Richard D. Boerem, Maj. George Bond's 3rd Battalion, the regimental Cannon and Anti-Tank Companies, a detachment of the Service Company, and attached medical and engineering troops—a total of fourteen hundred men.[101] Tomlinson decided to use three companies to envelope the Soputa-Sanananda Trail, two to the left and one to the right, while another two companies pushed straight up the track. The frontal attack was stopped cold, but K and I Companies continued to make their wider envelopment of the position. The US infantry realized that the Japanese had a strong forward position, with flanking defensive positions in support and a depth position a mile to the north along the main track.

On 30 November, I and K Companies, followed by the Cannon and Anti-Tank Companies, broke through between the Japanese main and depth positions and established a roadblock along the track at 5:00 p.m. An hour later, D Company, 2/3rd Battalion, in support of the Americans, saw the Japanese moving into a bivouac area, "whereupon a bayonet attack was ordered by two platoons, one led by Capt Shirley US [Army], and one Lieu Daniels RAA [Royal Australian Artillery], the result being the killing of fourteen enemy and the capture of three trucks. Both Capt Shirley US and Lieu Daniel lost their lives."[102]

This force then came under the command of US Army captain Meredith Huggins, for which the position was named. Reinforced by another US company on 14 December, the force held out against determined Japanese efforts to eliminate it. Being behind the main Japanese defensive position meant that resupply parties had to fight their way into the roadblock. While this position was held, the other three 126th Regiment companies, L, C, and D under Major Boerem, continued to operate against the forward Japanese defensive positions and against their flank.[103] With both sides exhausted, stalemate soon set in on the Sanananda front. Vasey therefore decided to halt operations there to reinforce his position farther north and eliminate the Japanese at Gona.

Both the Australians and the Americans at the battle for the Killerton-Sanananda Trail had performed admirably. The 16th Brigade had fought tenaciously to eliminate the advanced Japanese defensive position, while the 126th Regiment had pulled off "notable achievement"[104] in its first battle by penetrating the main defensive position and establishing the "Huggins Roadblock." The 126th had "stumbled upon exactly the right spot to make the envelopment," and "ready to go, they had executed this envelopment successfully."[105] However, with the 16th Brigade now exhausted and the 126th Regiment much reduced, "all hope of a quick decision north of the [Girua] River had now vanished."[106]

As November drew to a close, farther south at Buna, Harding's situation had not improved. In order to bolster his attack, the 2/126th Regiment was removed from Tomlinson's command on the Sanananda Trail and moved across to support the 2/128th Regiment at Buna. The two "second" battalions, situated near the Triangle and Buna Village, became known as Urbana Force and were initially placed under the command of Lt. Col. Herbert Smith. Harding soon felt that Smith was making little progress, so he was replaced with Col. John Mott, the division CoS. Meanwhile, over on the right flank, facing the new strip and pushing out to the coast were the 3/128th Regiment, the 2/6th Independent Company, and the elements of the 1/126th Regiment not at Sanananda, including C Company, HQ and HQ Company, and the Anti-Tank and Cannon Companies. Collectively these units were known as Warren Force, which was placed under the command of Col. J. Tracy Hale. Warren Force had the advantage of receiving some adequate artillery support in the form of eight 23-pounders and two 3.7-inch mountain howitzers of the Royal Australian Artillery.

After its initial setback, the 32nd Division had tried again to eliminate the Japanese in these two positions with attacks on 26 November (which cost Colonel Smith his Urbana Force command), followed by a major effort on 30 November by both forces. These attacks went in with much better coordinated air and mortar support, but the gains proved to be minor. The attacks at Buna had stalled, with the 32nd Division suffering

492 battle casualties "without making a single penetration of the enemy's line."[107]

The "mopping up" of the "depleted" Japanese at the beachheads had ground to a halt in the face of murderous enemy fire from well-prepared positions in difficult country. But, as Peter Brune has noted,

> the Americans [at Buna] hadn't really stood a fair chance. These troops were National Guardsman from Wisconsin and Michigan whose lack of basic training . . . made them greener than the jungles and kunai grass in which they were deployed. They had not fought their first battles in the Middle East, as had the Australians. Therefore, they had not been tried and tested; and most importantly, their officers had predominately been elevated from the promotion list and not from the crucible of battle. And to add to their degree of difficulty, these unseasoned troops were facing their baptism of fire in a campaign that was proving a terribly exacting test for the tough, experienced Australians of the 7th Division.[108]

Supplies were lacking, the troops were sick and exhausted, the deficiencies in their training had been brutally revealed, and their overconfidence had quickly turned to pessimism. Morale was low. Something had to happen to change their fortunes, or the front lines at Buna would solidify. If the USMC and USN at Guadalcanal faltered, time and the tide of battle would move against them.

7

Decision at Buna and Sanananda

GEN. DOUGLAS MACARTHUR WAS IN AN AGITATED MOOD. He had arrived in Port Moresby to oversee operations on 6 November 1942, a mere
month since he had issued his directive for the offensive that was designed
to drive Maj. Gen. Tomitarō Horii's South Seas Force back across the
Kumusi River and force the remaining Japanese out of Papua.[1] But while
the elimination of Horii's main force had been swift, costing the Japanese
general his life, the battle for the beachheads at Sanananda and Buna had
ground to a halt. MacArthur's optimism of October was starting to shift
to pessimism in November.[2]

Even more disturbing for MacArthur were the reports filtering back
from the front lines of the poor performance of the troops of the US 32nd
Division, "stories of inaction and even cowardice . . . [with] cases of men
throwing away their rifles, abandoning their machine guns and running
in panic."[3] After months of calling into question the fighting abilities of
his Australian coalition partners, it was humiliating for MacArthur to be
on the receiving end of gibes from the Australians.

On 25 November, MacArthur called a conference of his senior commanders to address the problems at the beachheads. In the midst of one
of his infamous sermons on strategy and the Japanese, he stated that he
would be ordering the US 41st Division forward from Rockhampton in
far northern Queensland to fight at the beachheads. At this point, the
Australian C-in-C, Thomas Blamey, retorted that he would prefer to send
in a worn-out Australian AIF brigade instead of the fresh US troops,
because at least "he knew they would fight."[4] AAF commander George
Kenney, who was present at the meeting, recorded that "it was a bitter
pill for General MacArthur to swallow."[5]

Blamey was clearly recalling the exchanges he and MacArthur had
shared over the last few months on the fighting qualities of the Australian troops. In particular, he was still reeling from a note MacArthur had
sent him on 7 September stating that if a US general had been in command at Kokoda, he would have been relieved. MacArthur's secretary,
Warrant Officer Paul Rogers, recorded that "Blamey had already relieved

two generals and sat smiling smugly now that the shoe was on the other foot."[6]

MacArthur clearly had to do something about the lackluster performance of the 32nd Division. Kenney noted that its commander, Maj. Gen. Edwin Harding, "was getting the blame, as he had not weeded out incompetent subordinate commanders who didn't know what to do."[7] MacArthur sent GHQ CoS Richard Sutherland to the Buna front to investigate, and he reported that leadership in the division was lacking. A few days later, GHQ's G-2, Charles Willoughby, also visited the 32nd Division and returned with an endorsement of Sutherland's view.[8]

As a result, MacArthur sent for Lt. Gen. Robert Eichelberger, commander of I US Corps. On arrival in Port Moresby on 30 November, Eichelberger and his CoS, Brig. Gen. Clovis Byers, met with MacArthur, Kenney, and Sutherland at Advanced GHQ (Adv GHQ) in the afternoon. During the meeting, Harding was held responsible for the 32nd Division's problems, and MacArthur ordered Eichelberger to go the front, take command, and relieve Harding. Eichelberger recorded that MacArthur stated to him that "Harding has failed miserably. Send him back to America, Bob, or I'll do it for you."[9]

With the imminent threat of Japanese reinforcement of their beachhead positions and the continuing uncertainty of the outcome at Guadalcanal, MacArthur also pushed Eichelberger for a quick and decisive action at Buna. Eichelberger recorded that MacArthur specifically stated to him, "Time is of the essence, hurry Bob! Our dangers increase hour by hour."[10] MacArthur then drove home his concerns with his now infamous order for Eichelberger to take Buna "or not come back alive."[11]

THE RELIEF OF GENERAL HARDING

There is no denying that Harding had been handed a difficult and demanding task in November 1942. There is also no denying that even taking into account the difficulty of the task and the strength and resilience of the Japanese defenders, Harding was not up to his job. Harding had not dedicated his efforts to training his division properly, especially his HQ staff. Worst of all, he continually overassessed the capabilities of his division (including himself) and imbued it with a sense of self-confidence that was not warranted.

On arrival in Papua, Harding also showed an almost complete ignorance of the terrain at the beachheads. Despite having access to terrain

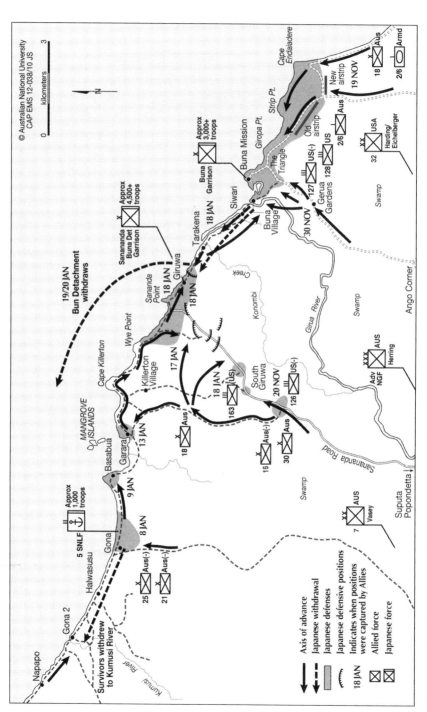

Figure 7.1 Beachheads Operations: Gona, Buna, and Sanananda, October 1942–January 1943

reports stating the contrary, he believed "there is considerable open country in the area over which we will operate,"[12] that the roads were well developed, and that the terrain would allow him to maneuver his force so as to "bring greater force to bear on the enemy than he can to oppose us."[13] Furthermore, his approach to planning the advance on Buna almost totally discounted any Japanese resistance. He noted to Sutherland on 20 October, "Tell General MacArthur that what promised to be a long, dull plodding campaign against inhospitable nature, is beginning to look more like Marengo than Hannibal Crossing the Alps."[14] To be fair, GHQ was constantly providing him with intelligence updates stating that he would meet little resistance.

Beyond the capabilities of his division, the terrain, and the Japanese, one of the other most critical elements to Harding's success or failure would be his relationship with his Australian coalition partners and especially his relationship with Lt. Gen. Edmund Herring, the Australian corps commander under whom he would serve. Initially Harding developed good relations with NGF and the Australians. He developed an early rapport with Blamey and Herring, and they established a position of mutual understanding and trust regarding the defense of Port Moresby, the training of the US troops, and the plans for the 32nd Division's movement over the Owen Stanley Range.[15] Harding noted to Sutherland on 31 October that "we are getting along very well with the Aussies. General Herring, with whom I do most of my business, is especially fine to work with."[16]

However, this positive relationship would not last long. Once the 32nd Division got into action and was stopped cold by the Japanese, Harding's relationship with Herring deteriorated rapidly. The first instance that kicked off some bad feeling was when Herring moved the 126th US Infantry Regiment to Sanananda to support Maj. Gen. George Vasey.[17] Thereafter, Harding started what was soon to become a barrage of complaints about "Herring [being] uncooperative."[18] Soon after the failure of the 32nd Division at Buna, Herring was to comment that Harding cut a "pathetic figure," that he was not using his troops properly, and that after the initial setback his division suffered at Buna "he had lost his nerve."[19]

By now Harding's time in command was on notice. Before Eichelberger left for the front, MacArthur had told him that at Buna he would find more of the 32nd Division's troops in the rear than in the front lines—an assessment that Eichelberger and his staff were soon to verify.[20] He noted, "I found conditions far worse than those responsible would have been willing to admit. There was no front line discipline of any kind . . . [and] there was never any idea of the men going forward."[21] Units were "like scrambled eggs . . . [and in many places] the men were intermingled. Men [had thrown] away their packs with food and ammunition."[22]

It was clear to Eichelberger and the members of the I Corps staff he had taken with him to the front that the supply situation within the division had broken down, with the men on short rations, with little or no shelter, their clothes in rags, and their shoes falling off their feet.[23] Even worse, they were short on gun oil, patches, and other cleaning aids to keep their weapons serviceable. There was also a lack of ammunition.[24] This was largely a result of the inadequate training of the 32nd Division's staff. Worse still, the poor handling of logistics by Harding's staff was hindering not only the 32nd Division but also the operations of Adv NGF.

Harding rejected this criticism, instead preferring to argue that he was not receiving a proper share of administrative support from Adv NGF HQ and that Herring had lost interest in the 32nd Division.[25] Harding's complaint was taken up by Sutherland with Blamey, but on investigation Blamey noted to MacArthur that the "complaint of discrimination against US troops . . . [was] . . . completely unfounded." He went on to break down supply allocations at the front lines, which revealed that the 32nd Division's area was actually receiving 55 percent of supplies allocated to Adv NGF, as well as considerably more of the "conforts [sic]"— supplies such as "tobacco, cigarettes, toothpaste, candy, handkerchiefs etc."[26] The problem was clearly Harding and his staff's logistics planning and organization.

Poor staff performance in the division, however, went much further than just logistics. Eichelberger also found a number of the officers "ineffective . . . for other than physical reasons."[27] There was a lack of reconnaissance patrols going out, and these and other patrols were "neither determined, aggressive nor resourceful. They were [also] consistent in their overestimat[ion] of enemy strength and prowess." Eichelberger found that the officers were "far too prone to sympathise with nervous and frightened soldiers" and that this led to a lack of determination.[28]

Despite these findings, Eichelberger originally gave Harding the benefit of the doubt. He listened to his problems, toured the front lines to get a feel of the situation, and then told Harding that they would leave him in command of the division if he was willing to remove a number of ineffective officers. Harding instead chose to support his officers to a man. After an altercation with Harding and the 32nd Division's CoS, Col. John Mott (commanding Urbana front), Eichelberger decided that Harding had to go.[29]

In his official report to MacArthur, Eichelberger noted upon Harding's relief that "General Harding seemed unable to galvanize his troops into sufficient aggressiveness to accomplish a successful attack. His desire to protect his officers caused him to excuse and explain failures rather than to acknowledge the presence of such ineffectiveness. Because of his unwillingness to take remedial action and in spite a lifelong friendship I was forced to request General Harding's relief."[30]

Harding has to be held largely accountable for the poor state of training of his troops, the division's staff officers, and the overconfidence of his men. In action, his command-and-control arrangements in his area of operations were overly complicated, with battalions from different regiments intermingled. This structure was so complex that Harding had companies and platoons from different battalions and regiments mixed together.[31]

Dudley McCarthy, the Australian official historian, notes that in late November, Harding addressed the divisional disorganization by "superimposing a rather curious readjustment in command on his already curious control system." At one point, Harding inserted two commanders between himself and one of his regiments, with one of these officers not actually being a part of his command at the time.[32] In addition, Harding had failed to maintain a positive relationship with Herring and the staff at Adv NGF HQ, and he had failed to manage his relationship with MacArthur and GHQ. Not only was the supply situation completely incompetent, but discipline in his formation had also broken down, and yet he was refusing to hold any of his division's officers to account. Even considering Harding's difficulties with the terrain, lack of supplies, little artillery, and no tank support, the evidence against him is a damning indictment of his command.

After leaving Buna, Harding met with MacArthur in Port Moresby, who duplicitously told him that he knew nothing of his relief. He then promised Harding another command, but after returning to Brisbane Harding soon found himself on his way to the United States. Later he was given command of the backwater Panama Canal Zone, then the Antilles Department in the Caribbean, and finally in 1945 the directorship of the Historical Division at the War Department for the JSC. He retired in 1946.[33]

ENTER EICHELBERGER

Eichelberger had made his gravest mistake of the campaign before even setting foot in Papua. For administrative expediency he had sent the 32nd

Division to Papua instead of the better-trained and -led 41st Division. It was his one and only major mistake of the campaign. However, his accomplishments at the beachheads that would follow must be viewed with this major blunder in mind.

Eichelberger arrived at the front with his chief of staff, six senior staff officers, and nine enlisted men from his I Corps HQ.[34] On arrival, he moved swiftly to ensure hot meals for the troops and sort out the command-and-control arrangements in the division. He also spent plenty of time in the front lines talking to his men. Eichelberger's efforts greatly improved morale and refocused the division's efforts. His commitment to inspiring the men was not without risk. Eichelberger's senior aide was shot and badly wounded while standing next to his commander on 3 December, as was Brig. Gen. Albert Waldron, whom Eichelberger had originally ordered to replace Harding.

Eichelberger then appointed his CoS, Brig. Gen. Clovis Byers, to take over the 32nd Division, but he lasted only two days in command before he, too, was wounded on the front lines. Eichelberger's direction that senior officers lead by example had taken its toll. From then on, Eichelberger took direct command of the division. He would also follow his own direction and on 5 December personally led an attack by "three companies against the barricades" at Buna Village.[35] Herring would note that Eichelberger "went everywhere, into every place that was regarded as dangerous, and everyone who knew him regards the fact that he was not either killed or wounded as, in the circumstances, almost miraculous."[36]

Eichelberger had also brought with him the bulk of his I Corps HQ staff, a "body of highly trained staff officers in whom he [Eichelberger] had the greatest confidence and from what transpired, justly so."[37] Eichelberger put his I Corps staff in charge of logistics in the division, and Col. J. Tracey Hale Jr. (commander of Warren Force) was replaced with Col. Clarence A. Martin, the G-3 on the I Corps staff. Colonel Mott, who had quarreled with Eichelberger, was also replaced, and Col. Melvin McCreary took command of Urbana Force. McCreary was soon moved over to command the artillery, and Col. John E. Grose, I Corps inspector general, was given command of Urbana Force.[38]

While it must be emphasized that Eichelberger was to eventually receive much of the support that had been denied to Harding, it is also critical to acknowledge that where Harding failed, Eichelberger was to succeed. The contrast in styles and effectiveness between the two men was vast. Where Harding struggled to get his voice heard and his difficulties acknowledged, Eichelberger was much more effective.[39] The 32nd

Division's new commander wrote to MacArthur often to outline his views and to update the C-in-C, and he also wrote daily to MacArthur's CoS, the powerful and highly critical Richard Sutherland, to ensure that GHQ was informed of every move and all of his issues. At the same time, he opened up an excellent line of communication with Herring so that his requests for support were taken up through the NGF chain of command, as well as directly by GHQ.[40]

Where Harding's relationship with Herring and Adv NGF could be best described as strained, Eichelberger's was nothing short of excellent. Herring thought that he was "a very pure breath of fresh air [that] blew away a great deal of the impurities that were stopping us from getting the job done."[41] Herring noted that once Eichelberger arrived with this "highly experienced staff [things changed and that] . . . one cannot speak too highly . . . of his performance. . . . He and the members of his staff set an example of courage which cannot have often been surpassed. . . . General Eichelberger kept the [32nd Division] going and he proved himself to be a most courageous officer, his efforts could not be surpassed."[42] It was the start of what would become a lifelong friendship between Eichelberger and Herring and would in the postwar period resemble a two-man mutual admiration society.[43]

ADVANCES ON THE BUNA FRONT

As November turned to December, Blamey summed up the problems that the Allies faced at the beachheads in a letter to Lt. Gen. John Northcott on the first anniversary of the attack on Pearl Harbor (7 December 1942):

> The Jap . . . is covered in on his front by the filthiest country imaginable and by extraordinarily strong defences. The country consists of mangrove areas intersected by tidal creeks and boggy, swampy ground. . . . Sickness takes a very heavy toll . . . [and] we are now suffering the very common lot of armies who have advanced beyond the region of capacity for supply. . . . The bulk of our supply has to be taken in by aeroplane and landed on landing grounds that are not very good and sometimes out of action on account of the weather. . . . [As a result] we are unable to develop superior firepower because of the difficulty in getting guns across and maintaining [them] . . . and while we have air superiority we are unable to utilise it to the full. . . . The consequences are that as soon as our protec-

tive umbrella returns, the news is flashed from Buna to Lae and the enemy comes out on strafing and bombing expeditions. . . . For these reasons the rapid clearing up of the Japanese has been delayed.[44]

Just after Eichelberger took command, in some respects the situation looked even more ominous. During the night of 1–2 December, the Japanese had managed to push through another reinforcement convoy that was estimated to have included an additional thousand Japanese troops.[45] The following day, Eichelberger observed an American ground attack scheduled before his arrival. Eichelberger was present on the Urbana front while two of his senior staff officers observed an "unenthusiastic feint in the New Strip area" of the Warren front.[46]

While the Japanese reinforced, Eichelberger reorganized. Dislocated platoons, companies, and battalions were sent back to their parent HQs while his staff worked prodigiously on improving the supply situation, including providing new clothing, additional supplies, and sufficient ammunition to the front.[47] Eichelberger also replaced ineffective commanders and shook up the command-and-control organization of his depleted and demoralized division. Colonel Martin now commanded the Warren front along the coast and in front of the airstrip, while Col. John E. Grose (I Corps inspector general) took command of the Urbana front outside of Buna Village until 7 December when Col. Clarence Tomlinson's 126th Regiment HQ was moved over from the Sanananda front.[48] With these measures in place, plus an open line of communication to both Herring at Adv NGF HQ and to Adv GHQ in Port Moresby, Eichelberger was able to make a fresh start to the capture of Buna and Cape Endaiadere.

In additional to resupplying, reorganizing, and refreshing the division, Eichelberger was also able get the first, albeit small, reinforcements for his front. On 3 December, a platoon of Australian Bren gun carriers arrived in the area and were allocated to Colonel Martin on the Warren front. These were open-topped, lightly armed, and lightly armored troop carriers, and as the 2/6th Independent (Commando) Company noted, they "have a tank task to do for which they are not suited."[49] It was a sign, however, of the desperation that was being felt by the entire chain of command. Three days later on 6 December, Blamey would also call for reinforcements for the 32nd Division from its largely inactive artillery battalions back in Australia to help fill the gaps caused by the rapid deterioration of the 32nd's infantry strength through combat losses and disease.[50]

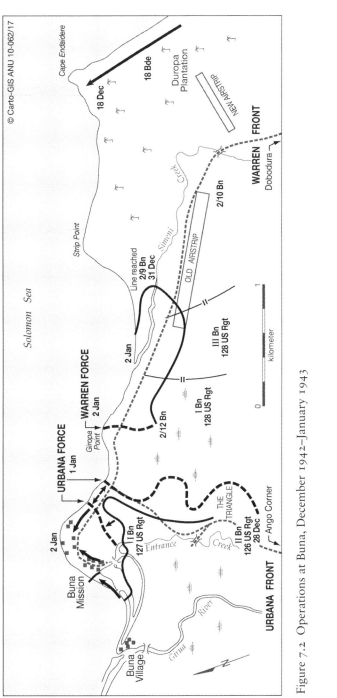

© Carto-GIS ANU 10-062/17

Solomon Sea

Cape Endaidere

18 Dec

18 Bde

Duropa
Plantation

NEW AIRSTRIP

WARREN FRONT

Dobodura

Strip Point

Line reached
2/9 Bn
31 Dec

Creek

2/10 Bn

2 Jan

WARREN FORCE
2 Jan

OLD AIRSTRIP

Simemi

III Bn
128 US Rgt

URBANA FORCE
1 Jan

Giropa
Point

II

2/12 Bn

I Bn
128 US Rgt

0   kilometer   1

2 Jan

Buna
Mission

I Bn
127 US Rgt

THE
TRIANGLE

Ango Corner

Entrance

Creek

II Bn
126 US Rgt
28 Dec

URBANA FRONT

Buna
Village

Girua River

N

Figure 7.2 Operations at Buna, December 1942–January 1943

Eichelberger's first big push came on 5 December. On both fronts a general advance was made after an air and artillery bombardment, and on both fronts heavy resistance was met. The five Bren gun carriers on the Warren front were all knocked out within thirty minutes after an exceptionally gallant attack.[51] However, on the Urbana front, progress was much more encouraging. Here a platoon from 126th Infantry under S. Sgt. Herman Bottcher "drove a wedge through to the sea between Buna Village and Buna mission."[52] It was during this assault that General Waldron was shot through the shoulder and Eichelberger took direct command.

This was a much-improved performance on the Urbana front, and the achievements of Bottcher, accomplished at great risk, had created a deep reentrant in the Japanese line that was open to counterattack. But it also presented a great opportunity to crumble the remaining Japanese positions.[53] The Japanese, realizing the gravity of the situation, vigorously counterattacked Bottcher's position, but his men held firm, and the 32nd Division struck back almost immediately with a two-company attack from the 2/126th Infantry on the morning of 7 December. Bottcher's drive to the sea led to a period of almost continuous action on the Urbana front that resulted in the capture of Buna Village on 14 December.

Despite the steady progress, it was still far too slow for MacArthur. The pressure he was feeling at the strategic level, due to the seesawing battle for Guadalcanal and the increasing pressure on his western flank from the Japanese in the NEI, was being driven down to his frontline commanders relentlessly. As Buna Village fell, MacArthur wrote to Eichelberger to remind him that "time is fleeting and our dangers increase with its passage. . . . Hasten your preparations. . . . Time is working desperately against us."[54]

DECISION AT BUNA

With the pressure still firmly on MacArthur and the whole Allied position in Papua, a key moment had been reached in early December. Vasey had been making steady progress at Gona, and Eichelberger had finally gotten the front lines moving at Buna, but the advances were not decisive. It was at this time that the decisive point came for the battle for Buna. On the same day that Gona fell, 8 December 1942, Blamey opted to take a significant operational risk. Despite intelligence from GHQ indicating that the Japanese still intended to move on Milne Bay, Blamey decided that the improving Allied position in the skies above Papua and the correspondingly slow but steadily improving seaborne line of supply to the beachheads along the northern coast of Papua meant that he could risk a significant shift of his combat power north. Blamey decided to take the 18th Brigade (AIF) from Milne Bay and move it to Buna and placed it under Eichelberger's command. In doing so, he was injecting a fresh brigade of elite troops into the fight.

Furthermore, this would be accomplished alongside a significant increase in artillery support for the Buna front and the introduction of adequate armored support in the form of light tanks from the 2/6th Armoured Regiment. Their transportation and landing "in and around Kariki, some few miles from the battle field was [seen as] an amazing achievement in view of the equipment available to the men charged with the task."[55] It was a decision that would not only weaken Milne Bay's defenses but also strain to the breaking point the exceptionally fragile logistics system at Buna. It was a high-risk, high-reward approach but one that would prove to be decisive.

While NGF HQ put in train the movement of the 18th Brigade, the tanks, and additional artillery, the battle progressed slowly at Buna. On 14 December, Eichelberger's men had finally occupied Buna Village, while, four days later on the Warren front, the 1st and 3rd Battalions of the 128th Regiment advanced near the airstrip making small gains that allowed the 18th Brigade and its tanks more space to deploy.[56] Meanwhile, the Japanese made several unsuccessful attempts to counterattack from around Buna Government Station (also known as the Buna Mission) against the 2/128th.[57] The Japanese attempts to counterattack, plus the capture of the first IJA officer of the operation and the arrival of the first IJA deserter in the Allied lines, all pointed toward a tipping point in the operations on the Buna front.[58] By now, the Urbana front had the better part of three battalions (2/126th, 2/128th, and 3/127th) around Buna Government Station, squeezing the Japanese into an ever-smaller pocket with their backs to the sea.

To the southeast, the Warren front had the equivalent of three battalions facing north, parallel to the new airstrip. On the western flank, elements of the 1/126th and 3/127th held the apex of the old and new airstrips, the 2/6th Independent Company was positioned in a screen across the southern edge of the new airstrip, and the 1/128th and 3/128th Battalions were between the end of the New Strip and the coast.[59] The men of the 32nd Division, however, were suffering. On 13 December, a Captain Rolwarth (3/128th) toured his front lines and reported back that the men are very tired, feverish, nervous and in poor moral, dysentery is prevalent, the men contend that they are able to get very little rest or sleep because of the rain, sniper [fire], enemy grenades and movement during the night. . . . None of the men seem to think it is possible to advance against the present fire. . . . Most of them are afraid of our bombing near the front. . . . [However,] during the past few days the spirits have livened up a bit.[60]

It was clear that on the Warren front, without an injection of fresh troops, better fire support, and some way of overcoming the Japanese bunkers, there was little chance of a rapid advance.

The most significant event of the Buna operation now unfolded. The 18th Brigade AIF, under command of Brig. George Wootten, arrived at the front with a small number of Stuart light tanks from the 2/6th Armoured Regiment. The brigade initially consisted of the 2/9th Battalion plus supporting arms, with the 2/10th Battalion to follow on and the 2/12th Battalion to arrive later after it returned from its mission to Goodenough Island. The brigade was a veteran of the Middle East, having served in Cyrenaica and Tobruk. In the SWPA, it had been at the forefront of the defense of Milne Bay under Cyril Clowes. They were elite troops, battle hardened, and exceptionally well led.

On arrival, 18th Brigade had been tasked by NGF HQ to "clear up the areas of the New Strip and Old Strip to Buna Mission held by the enemy."[61] Wootten arrived at Eichelberger's HQ on 12 December, and at this meeting the 32nd Division's commander placed Wootten in command of the Warren front, including taking under command the 128th Regiment (Colonel Martin), which consisted of the 1st and 3rd Battalions of the regiment and the 1st Battalion of the 126th Regiment. Eichelberger noted that "the [Australians] seem surprised at my generous attitude [of appointing Wootten to command Warren Force] but it looked to me like a perfectly feasible proposition. I realize it is up to me to get along with our allies."[62]

On December 13 and 14, the officers of the 18th Brigade made a reconnaissance of the Warren front while the troops of the 2/9th landed at Oro Bay and marched overland to their concentration points. Further reconnaissance was undertaken by the 18th Brigade's units on 16 December, and the following day Wotton took command.[63] He decided to put his brigade straight into the attack, using the 2/9th Battalion, all of the artillery, some engineers, and six tanks, supported by all of the US units in the area. The 3/128th was to move in behind the 2/9th Battalion to consolidate the ground won, while the 1/128th provided logistics support and the 1/126th was in immediate reserve.[64]

The assault kicked off at 7:00 a.m. on 18 December after a ten-minute bombardment by the three artillery troops and the mortars of the 128th Regiment. Surprise was complete, and the assault was "gallantly and brilliantly executed . . . although casualties were heavy." Within an hour, the coastline of Cape Endaiadere was reached, and the "backbone of the Japanese resistance in this area was broken."[65] The Japanese defense was ferocious, with one IJA soldier jumping onto a tank and firing through the view ports, wounding the tank commander and gunner before being killed.[66] Fighting continued throughout the day, with the mopping up of the positions being carried out by the 3/128th. This attack had created a large *L*-shaped position on the Warren front lines, with the vertical side formed by the assault, which had driven to the sea at the cape and cleared one and a quarter miles of terrain inland, and the horizontal line formed by the New Strip.[67] The attack cost two of the precious tanks and the two senior armored officers, including the CO of the 2/6th Armoured Regiment, Lt. Col. C. R. Hodgson, who was wounded in the early stages. For the infantry, the 2/9th Battalion lost 160 men on 18 December, including 5 officers killed and 6 wounded, 44 soldiers killed, and a further 105 soldiers wounded.[68]

The mopping-up continued the next day, and on 20 December another concerted push was made. By now, the 2/9th and 3/128th Battalions occupied the newly won ground, and the next drive was due west, clearing the area to the north and perpendicular to the New Strip. Once again, the 2/9th Battalion took the lead, supported by the 3/128th with the 1/126th operating along the New Strip to clear the area to the south. At the end of the day, despite more heavy casualties, the assault force had pushed up to the end of the Old Strip forming a line along the Simemi Creek.

The 1/126th tried to cross the creek under the cover of darkness, but the attempt failed. Wootten, however, was keen to get across as soon as possible, and the following day ordered up the 2/10th Battalion from reserve, which, along with the 2nd and 3rd Battalions of the 128th Regiment, pushed for a crossing point. An exploitation was made that afternoon, and by 23 December the creek had been crossed. Soon thereafter, the US engineers constructed a bridge crossing for the tanks under heavy Japanese fire.[69]

On 23 December, the 2/10th and 1/126th Battalions pushed across the southern end of the Old Strip, while the 2/9th and 3/128th pushed up against the Simemi Creek line. Momentum now moved to the southern end of the Warren line, and the tanks were allocated to the 2/10th. On Christmas Eve, they attacked along the Old Strip, only to run into heavy resistance from IJA antiaircraft guns being used in an antitank and antipersonnel role, which knocked out two tanks and pinned down the infantry. Attempts to continue the assault were made, but progress was slow and the fighting was intensely bitter. However, Christmas Eve was a turning point in the overall operation. On that day, GHQ was confident enough of the outcome at Buna after the previous days fighting to issue "Warning Instruction No. 1" for the establishment of two fighter-landing strips at Buna, one of which in time would be converted into a bomber strip. It also outlined the units to make up this force.[70]

There was to be no break on Christmas Day, with a general advance on both the Warren and Urbana fronts. The 2/9th advanced parallel to the coast in a northwesterly direction, while the 2/10th advanced another four hundred yards along the strip, albeit at the cost of four tanks put out of action. The 1/126th and 1/128th advanced over the southern end of the strip, three-quarters of which was now under Allied control. Meanwhile, the 127th Regiment advanced into the garden area at Buna Government Station, with all three battalions involved.[71] By 28 December, all of the Old Strip was under Allied control, and on the same day the 2/12th Battalion was landed at Oro Bay, bringing the 18th Brigade up to strength. As the advance continued beyond the Old Strip, the 2/10th Battalion was able to link up with the 127th at the Buna Gardens–Government Station area. Having looped around, this move created a pocket, with the 2/9th on the coast and the 1/128th, 1/126th, and 3/128th forming the bottom of the bowl and the 127th Regiment forming its other side. By the last day of 1942, the Japanese positions at Buna had become hopelessly untenable, and many Japanese soldiers were taking to the sea to try to extricate themselves from the pocket but with little reward.[72] By early in the New Year, the position had been cleared, with fifty Japanese prisoners taken. On 3 January, all organized resistance ceased. The 18th Brigade had taken 863 casualties, including 257 killed, while the 32nd Division's long haul at Buna had cost it 1,954 casualties, including 353 killed.[73]

THE US–AUSTRALIAN RELATIONSHIP AT BUNA

The relationship between the two armies was critical to the success of the operations in front of Buna. The first major change to the poor state of the relationship came with the arrival of Eichelberger and his staff. From the moment Eichelberger took command, not only did the performance of the 32nd Division improve but so too its relationship with Adv NGF. There was a high degree of respect between Herring and Eichelberger, which was extended to Wootten and his brigade when they arrived at Buna, and Eichelberger entrusted the Australian with the command of the Warren front.

Overall, the relationship that developed at the more senior command level on the Buna front from mid-December to early January was excellent. Col. Clarence A. Martin, commander of the 128th Regiment at Buna in mid-December, was placed under Wootten's command, and his battalions played key roles in supporting the attacks of the three 18th Brigade battalions. He noted that "there was ample fighting for all hands and a mutual respect and esteem between Australians and Americans developed. . . . The Aussies grew to respect the fighting abilities and spirit which the Americans displayed. . . . The Americans in turn admired the fighting qualities of the Australians. This mutual respect increased and grew stronger as the operation progressed, with the forces fighting side by side."[74] Lt. Col. Alexander J. MacNab, CO of the 3/128th Regiment from 10 December 1942, noted that "there was never better comradeship-in-arms than that I saw between them (Aussies) and my own troops. They were, and are, happy, courageous and self-sacrificing comrades. I would rather fight alongside an Australian outfit than any other I have ever seen."[75]

Eichelberger was consistently full of praise for the AIF troops from the 18th Brigade, as well as for their commander, Brigadier Wootten. Eichelberger noted the "wonderful fighting Australians did at Buna. No finer soldiers ever moved to the attack than those who so willingly went through the bunkers south of Cape Endaiadere."[76] In addition, he noted to Sutherland and MacArthur on 18 December that "Wootten put on a good show over on the right. . . . All our officers and the men of our right battalion are high in their praise of the valor of the Australians. Wootten has done a nice job and I am very proud of him."[77]

Eichelberger's letters to Sutherland and MacArthur throughout this period are full of praise for the Australians and Herring and Wootten in particular. This is despite the fact that praise of the Australians was not welcome at GHQ and did nothing to increase Eichelberger's reputation with MacArthur and especially Sutherland. Eichelberger's feeling toward the Australians was thoroughly reciprocated. In comparison to Harding, Herring would note that "one cannot speak too highly [of Eichelberger]. . . . He and the members of his staff set an example of courage which cannot have often been surpassed."[78]

The relationship between the troops was also very positive. Colonel MacNab noted how closely his battalion was integrated with the

Australian 2/9th Battalion in the final push at the Buna airstrips. The men shared their Christmas rations, clothing, and equipment and fought side by side. There was also a "comradely rivalry and friendly recrimination between our battalions," with companies in the battalions pushing forward to advance faster than one another. MacNab noted that "everybody's spirits were high as we were putting on the finishing touches to a most unpleasant job."[79]

From US veterans' perspective, their view of the Australians is overwhelmingly positive. Their oral histories held at the Michigan Military Institute and the Wisconsin Veterans Museum reveal that the common, "everyday soldiers did get along well with each other." These records highlight interactions between the two nations' armies on tactical insights, training, jungle warfare, and fighting the Japanese, and firsthand accounts show that they "were friendly and even helpful to one another, which is something that the written texts fail to document."[80]

While more critical of the US troops, Australian records also stand in opposition to many of the Australian popular histories of the battle. Troops of the 2/10th Battalion AIF had fought with US infantry companies side by side and at times under Australian command. The battalion history, written by a former officer present at Buna, notes that relations with the US troops were largely good and that they were "excellent types of manhood, generous, [and] friendly."[81]

Yet the Australians, who were highly trained and experienced soldiers by 1942, were also keenly aware that the US troops were also "completely untrained in jungle life, of which they had perforce to learn the hard way." Capt. Frank Allchin believed that these soldiers suffered "through no fault of their own," as they had been "improperly trained."[82] This sentiment was also shared by veterans of the 2/9th Battalion, who noted that in addition to these problems, the Americans did not have the benefit of an infusion of highly experienced AIF officers like the Australian militia units did.[83] These observations are reflective of many of the Australian veterans' oral histories.[84] While noting the very good personal relationships, many Australian veterans question the performance of the 32nd Division's units. The Australians noted the division's poor training and its "lack of leadership . . . [and] initiative,"[85] contrasting this to their own experience having "been through the Middle East."[86]

The 2/6th Independent Company, which fought as part of the 32nd Division at Buna throughout the operations, noted, "The U.S. Inf[antry] in this area suffered, as we did, from lack of battle experience" but that "the relationship between their units and us was most cordial."[87] But they also noted the change in the leadership of the 32nd Division in early December. The 2/6th's war diary notes on 2 December, "Col. Martin–US Army—takes over comd of Task Force and pushes more aggressive policy and more determined method to US Inf."[88] The 2/Sixth Independent Company's report of the campaign noted that the "drive put into these attacks [by the US units in December] was gradually improving as the Inf. gained in battle experience and their leaders acquired confidence."[89]

The experience of the 16th Brigade AIF at Sanananda working with 126th Regiment is similar. The 2/1st Battalion of the 16th Brigade, which fought alongside the 126th Regiment at Sanananda, noted that their troops "lost no time in making friends with the Americans."[90] While the 2/1st acknowledged that the "raw American conscripts had much to learn,"[91] their success on the Sanananda Trail and in establishing the Huggins Roadblock and advancing against the Japanese was in marked contrast to "all other fronts [where] American attack[s] were a dismal failure."[92] For the 2/1st Battalion, the US troops that were attached to them were seen as "great assets," and at Sanananda the battalion history records that the US troops alongside them "fought magnificently."[93]

THE HIGH COMMAND

After the relief of Harding and the arrival of Eichelberger, the tension in the US-Australian relationship was mainly centered on the HQs in Port Moresby. Herring and Eichelberger were under extreme pressure as MacArthur fretted over the progress of the battle for Guadalcanal and became alarmed by Japanese moves toward Papua from the NEI. Blamey was also worried, but his concerns were more isolated to the performance of his corps commander, Edmund Herring. Much of the tension in Port Moresby came to a head around Christmas 1942.

On Christmas Eve, Brig. John Broadbent, the assistant adjutant and quartermaster general at NGF, had visited Adv NGF HQ and reported back to Blamey that Herring looked "tired."[94] Blamey decided that it was best that he assess Herring's state for himself, so he recalled Herring to Port Moresby for Christmas Day. Berryman, who was present at the meetings and the dinner, noted that "Herring had a very worrying time and carried a big load" and that the "strain was starting to show."[95] Later that evening, Blamey called in Berryman and stated that he was worried about Herring's mental state and that Broadbent's analysis had not been overstated. Blamey was now in a tight spot. MacArthur was laying on the pressure, and he had already relieved a corps commander (Rowell) and a divisional commander (Allen). Relieving another senior commander, one handpicked by Blamey, would leave him vulnerable and would also be an admission of the problems that Adv NGF was experiencing. So, instead, Blamey took a different tack. He relieved Herring's BGS, Brig. Ronald Hopkins, who was also struggling in his role, and ordered Berryman to Adv NGF to take command of the staff and the operational planning.[96]

In many ways, Blamey's choice of Berryman was rather odd. Berryman was the DCGS and acting MGGS of NGF, and now Blamey was sending him over to also be BGS of a corps. However, Blamey did not have much choice, and sending his most capable staff officer and someone completely familiar with the tactical situational to support Herring and sort out his problematic HQ did manage to cauterize the situation and instill new life into the operations of Adv NGF. In the end, it was to prove to be an inspired choice.

While Blamey maneuvered to shore up Adv NGF HQ, Blamey sent Herring to pay his respects, and put his requests for reinforcements, to MacArthur. MacArthur conceded to Herring's request,[97] but he also gave him a stern lecture. Herring would later tell Eichelberger that MacArthur had, once again, placed a huge emphasis on speed and added for dramatic effect that "young man, if this Buna fight continues another week I am ruined, and that applies to you also, young man."[98]

Herring's request for reinforcements was to also touch off the second major issue in the US and Australian command relationship between MacArthur and Blamey. The relationship was tense between the two men, especially after Blamey had criticized the 32nd Division's performance. Blamey remained skeptical of the US soldiers' abilities, noting to Herring in December that "I would be very sorry to do anything that would impair the good relations you have established with the Americans, but I doubt very much whether Buna would be captured if we rely on them."[99] MacArthur, however, now decided to bring forward the 163rd Infantry Regiment from the 41st Division to reinforce Herring. On being allocated this additional force, Herring made plans to use it at Sanananda after the 126th Regiment from the 32nd Division was moved over to the Buna front. However, on arrival, MacArthur ordered the 163rd Regiment to Buna and placed it under the command of the 32nd Division.

Blamey wrote to MacArthur directly about the tactical allocation of this force in his command, noting that he "regret[s] this change of plan exceedingly" and that "I regret I cannot concur in the soundness of this plan." Blamey's objections were over the relative allocation of forces, the terrain, and the need to relieve the Australian brigade at Sanananda, which had been reduced to an effective strength of only 233 men. Blamey pushed this view vigorously and went on to explain that there should be no concern about the mixing of "American and Australian troops at this phase of the battle," noting that the 18th Brigade was currently serving under Eichelberger.[100]

Most significantly, however, Blamey ended his letter with a clear statement about MacArthur's approach to command, arguing very forcefully to the C-in-C SWPA, "I believe that nothing is more contrary to the sound principles of command than that the Commander-in-Chief or the Commander, Allied Land Forces, should take over the personal direction of [a] portion of the battle. This can only result in disturbing the confidence of the inferior commanders."[101] MacArthur responded to this admonishment with both a denial of his intent and a fig leaf of coverage about what he was doing. He noted to Blamey that "I do not for a moment agree with your view that I am unduly interfering with the local details of operations. I am in no way attempting to control the tactical execution on the front but am merely strategically advising as to where I believe it would be wise to exert the main effort of the ground forces."[102] It was a blatantly dishonest statement on MacArthur's behalf, as this is exactly what he was doing, had done earlier in the campaign, and would continue to do when it suited him in the SWPA.

This clash over the chain of command had been brewing since the battle on the Kokoda Trail a number of months earlier, and while MacArthur relented and the regiment did in fact go to Sanananda, it marked a key turning point in the MacArthur-Blamey relationship. MacArthur's natural instinct was for US forces to be under US command, as it was for him to want to command any land force directly. Now it was not just an issue of national command coherency but also of control. Blamey had won this battle, but it set in MacArthur's mind that it was much easier to control US Army officers than it was a defiant and forthright Australian ALF commander. Thus, after the Papua campaign, MacArthur would do everything in his power to remove US Army formations from Blamey's command and to limit his control as ALF commander.

THE END AT SANANANDA

While MacArthur was callous about the need for a speedy end to operations at Buna, his fears were not founded on personal vanity and vulnerability alone. As noted in chapter 6, omnipresent in the SWPA's strategic calculations was its vulnerability and how beholden it was to the success or failure of the SOPAC forces at Guadalcanal. But as December stretched on, MacArthur, GHQ, and the Australians all became worried about another potential vulnerability—their western flank. In mid-December, GHQ's intelligence section was becoming increasingly concerned about Japanese activities in the northwest, which included the occupation of the Tanimbar, Kai, and Aroe Islands and the building of an airfield in East Timor.

These moves, coupled with the continual Japanese air attacks on northern Australia, principally at Darwin, forced MacArthur to cancel plans to move the US troops based there to Papua. On 23 December, MacArthur wrote to Blamey of these concerns and the possibility of a Japanese strike in the region of the Torres Strait and the southern coast of New Guinea. As a result, Blamey ordered more garrison forces into Cape York Peninsula and reinforcements to Merauke in southwestern Papua,[103] while MacArthur kept pressing Blamey to speed up their movement.[104] Compounding these fears were a number of Japanese air raids on Merauke in early January, plus continued IJA and IJN buildups in the NEI, which convinced GHQ that an invasion of Merauke was a distinct possibility. As a result, desperately needed reinforcements for the beachheads were diverted to Merauke to protect its airfield.[105]

Meanwhile, at Sanananda, the situation was stalled. From 2 December to the sixth, the 16th Brigade had attempted several attacks to break through to the US positions at the Huggins Roadblock, but in the face of the extensive Japanese defensives it made little progress. With the 16th Brigade a totally spent force, it was now the turn of the Australian Militia to go into the meat grinder. Brig. Selwyn Porter's 30th [Militia] Brigade launched a series of attacks on 7 December and again December 10–15, but with little result. The only small success was made by the 2/7th Cavalry Regiment (AIF), which made it through to the roadblock, but in general the attacks were failures. Vasey made them push on until 22 December before he called a halt to the slaughter.

The performance of the 30th Brigade in these attacks was far from satisfactory. Its commander noted that "in the 39 and 49 Aust Inf Bns the bulk of the trained and resolute leaders have become casualties, and those that remain are not up to the standard of the units when they originally arrived here. Seven members of the 39th Aus Inf Bn are under arrest on charges of cowardice; this condition is not peculiar to 39 Aust Inf Bn as similar action could be taken in numerous cases in other units."[106]

The 2/7th Cavalry Regiment AIF also came in for its share of criticism, with General Vasey noting that "I am not yet convinced that [it is] up to the standard of the A.I.F. Inf Bns. . . . It failed to show that aggressiveness necessary for successful offensive action." Meanwhile, Brig. Selwyn Porter reported to 7th Division HQ on 22 December 1942 that the 55/53rd and 36th Militia Battalions "are NOT fit for war under the present conditions."[107]

The key position on this front remained the Huggins Roadblock just south of the Killerton Trail junction. Cut off from their own lines, with few supplies and under constant fire and enemy counterattack, elements of the 126th Regiment put up a valiant defense. As noted, the 16th and 30th Brigades had exhausted themselves against the extensive Japanese defenses in order to provide supplies for the road block and also to break down the Sanananda positions. On 2 January 1943, the 163rd Regiment took over the positions along the axis of the main Soputa-Sanananda Trail and was tasked with capturing the main Japanese roadblock.

Under the command of Col. Jens Doe, this regiment was much better prepared for combat than its counterparts in the 32nd Division, yet it still had nowhere near the experience or capability of the 18th Brigade. Most significantly, while artillery support had improved markedly on this front by the time that the 163rd Regiment arrived, it lacked tank support. In addition, by the time Doe and his men arrived, a virtual stalemate had existed on this front for some seven weeks, and there was no hope that the infantry, without large-scale artillery and tank support, would break through. Therefore, by this time, Adv NGF had already ordered the 18th Brigade and its tanks—along with all the artillery from the Buna front—to move to Sanananda to carry out the coup de grâce.[108]

For the first three days, Doe and the 163rd Regiment carried out patrols and used their mortars to reduce the number of Japanese tree snipers. On 8 January, they launched their first probing attack, with C Company launching an assault that was rebuffed with "slight losses." The regiment continued to carry out a number of small operations in preparation for the arrival of the 18th Brigade, whereupon the 163rd launched a frontal assault on the position, and the brigade, with its supporting tanks, undertook a wide outflanking movement to the east of the trail. These patrols and small, nibbling attacks continued until 11 January, which allowed the regiment to concentrate its full force and the 18th Brigade to move into position.

The main assault came on 12 January 1943, when the 2/9th and 2/12th Battalions, supported by mortars, tanks, and artillery, drove into the

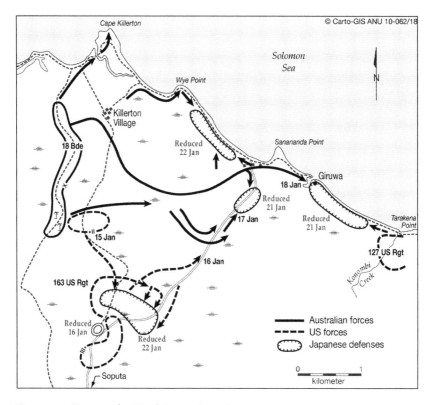

Figure 7.3 Sanananda, Final Operations, January 1943

Japanese positions. However, the Japanese had used the long interval between the secession of the attacks on 22 December and the 18th Brigade's
assault to strengthen their position. A well-sited antitank gun knocked
out two of the three supporting tanks, which meant that the infantry assault ground to a halt under intense fire, with the two assault battalions
suffering 140 casualties without securing any Japanese positions.[109]

   The failure of 12 January was a bitter pill for Herring, Eichelberger,
and Vasey to swallow, as they had high expectations of the 18th Brigade
after its success at Buna. The failure of this elite brigade, supported by
a heavy concentration (for this campaign) of field artillery and the last
remaining tanks, called into question the operations before and after the
18th Brigade's assault and thus the future of the situation thereafter at Sanananda. Vasey's pessimism, which had been growing steadily throughout
December, led him to argue that, after the loss of the tanks, to continue
the attack against deeply entrenched Japanese positions using only infantry was inviting a repetition of the "costly mistakes of 1915–1917"

and that such attacks were "unlikely to succeed."[110] It was an observation that could easily have been made regarding the assaults of the 16th Brigade, the 126th Regiment, the 30th Brigade, and the 163rd Regiment over the preceding two months.

Vasey made a number of suggestions to Herring, Berryman, and Eichelberger, including rejecting the resumption of the current line of attack and instead arguing for a flanking assault or the landing of additional troops from the sea in the Killerton area.[111] Berryman rejected an amphibious assault out of hand, citing the lack of trained troops and assault craft and the poor terrain. Instead, he reviewed the situation and noted that the entire northern coast (with the exception of Sanananda) was under Allied control. Thus, the airfields at Dobodura and Buna were now secure. The improving situation at Guadalcanal, as well as the now strong Allied air superiority over Papua and the introduction of US PT boats in the surrounding coastal region, meant that concerns over the possibility of Japanese reinforcements had all but disappeared. Therefore, he proposed a blockade of the remaining Japanese positions: "General Vasey, General Berryman and Brigadier Wootten are all agreed . . . [that] the best plan would seem to be to surround the area and cut off all supplies, accompanied by plenty of mortar fire and constant harassing."[112] Eichelberger, who by now was commander of Adv NGF after Herring returned to command NGF at Port Moresby, tentatively accepted Berryman's plan. However, it would never be put into action. On the same day that Berryman's plan was agreed upon, the Japanese decided to abandon Papua and withdraw their remaining troops.

On the morning of 14 January, patrol reports and a prisoner interrogation provided Adv NGF HQ with their first indication of the withdrawal. Vasey contacted Eichelberger to inform him that the "buggers [were] gone," and Berryman noted, "Vasey was a different man today now that things were going his way." Eichelberger noted, "Vasey from pessimism has changed 100%."[113] Vasey pushed both the 18th Brigade and the US 163rd Regiment forward, and they advanced steadily over the next few days against ever-diminishing resistance. The last Japanese resistance in Papua ceased on 21 January 1943, six months to the day after the campaign commenced.[114]

US–AUSTRALIAN RELATIONSHIP AT SANANANDA

As noted above, while the relationships between the soldiers and units at Sanananda mirrored the experience at Buna, on this part of the front the divisional command took a wholly different view. The performance of the 163rd Regiment and its predecessor, the 126th Regiment, did not please Vasey, who noted that the 126th Regiment had "maintained a masterful inactivity."[115] He went on to argue that the 163rd Regiment "lack[ed] offensive spirit" and that aggression in the formation was lacking "when it comes to close work as is necessary to finish the Japs."[116] After the discovery of the Japanese withdrawal, Vasey criticized the 163rd for inaction, noting in one situation report, "163 Regt, 41st Div, see Hebrews, Chap 13, Verse 8 [Jesus Christ the same yesterday, and today and forever]."[117]

Vasey's comments provoked the ire of Eichelberger. Eichelberger wrote to Sutherland on 30 December that "Vasey does not seem to like the commanders he draws but then maybe if we were to hear from them maybe it would be mutual. . . . Vasey is getting a grand officer and a good regiment when he gets the 163rd. I hope he stops yapping about the tools which have been given him with which to do his job."[118] Vasey was the only senior Australian officer with whom Eichelberger felt he could not work effectively, mainly due to Vasey's hostile attitude to the Americans and their units under his command.

Eichelberger decided to take the bull by the horns with Vasey. He arranged for Vasey to go with him to meet Colonel Doe to take a tour of the 163rd Regiment's front lines. The three officers then went within fifty yards of the Japanese positions and observed the 163rd's men at work. Eichelberger noted that there was heavy firing along the line and that Colonel Doe "impressed me very favourably and before I left, I felt that General Vasey had the same impression. At any rate, I made a report that night to General Herring and that was the last criticism I heard of Colonel Doe."[119]

Vasey's view was not widely held in his command. Certainly, as noted earlier, the 16th Brigade's soldiers understood the problems and issues that the 32nd Division's soldiers faced. The commander of 30th Brigade, Brigadier Porter, having fought alongside the 126th Regiment and the 163rd Regiment, wrote to Eichelberger to "express my appreciation of what the men of your division under my command have done to assist our efforts. . . . Your men are worthy comrades and stout hearts."[120] The performance of all of the troops at Sanananda must also be viewed through the prism of the failure of the 18th Brigade's assault, with its heavy artillery and tank support. If this elite unit could not break through with such support, what chance did the undertrained and inexperienced US National Guard and Australian Militia have with less than adequate artillery support and no tanks?

As Herring noted, "the task set them [the 126th Regiment] was one which seasoned veterans with the aid of tanks later found very stiff proposition, so it is not to be wondered that the Americans in their first endeavour found the Japanese defenses beyond them."[121] This also puts into perspective the success of the 126th Regiment in breaking into the Japanese defenses in November and establishing the Huggins Roadblock in the first place. This initial success was, as E. G. Keogh has pointed out, "a notable one."[122]

SANANANDA: MOPPING UP?

On 8 January 1943, with the fall of Buna, MacArthur took the opportunity to return to Australia and in doing so declared the campaign in Papua over. Sanananda was, according to MacArthur, merely "mopping up."[123] This was a neat trick. It gained MacArthur his victory and suitable publicity back in the United States, and according to Eichelberger, MacArthur did it deliberately; otherwise, the "Australians would not give the Americans any credit."[124] This was the first in what became a routine "cute little trick" of MacArthur's, to declare victory before a campaign was complete, which he also did in later campaigns such as the 1944 New Guinea campaign and at Leyte in 1944.[125] At the time MacArthur declared victory in Papua, the strategic situation was no longer in doubt, but it was horribly insensitive to the commanders and troops still fighting the Japanese at Sanananda. In all of these operations, tactically and operationally, there was still plenty of fighting to come.[126]

MacArthur's decision to announce a victory prematurely also clarifies the intent of his directive regarding the allocation of the 163rd Regiment to the Buna front. When Blamey clashed with MacArthur over his tactical interference in the handling of NGF's operations, what was really behind MacArthur's plan was to force Herring to clean up Buna as soon as possible so as to allow him to declare victory irrespective of the state of the Japanese positions at Sanananda. It also demonstrated MacArthur's lack of awareness of the terrain and the tactical situation at Buna. Blamey and Herring were correct in that the allocation of the 163rd to Buna would have done nothing to speed up the conclusion of this operation, when instead this regiment was desperately needed to relieve the worn-out 30th Brigade at Sanananda.

After MacArthur declared victory, he left Port Moresby to return to Brisbane to undertake his duties as C-in-C SWPA. This also gave Blamey the opportunity to return to Brisbane a few days later to undertake his roles as commander ALF and C-in-C AMF. Blamey's move led to Herring being brought back over to Port Moresby to command NGF and Eichelberger being elevated to the corps command at Adv NGF. As noted above, this meant that Eichelberger would oversee the final battle at Sanananda in early 1943.

BATTLE FOR THE BEACHHEADS: ASSESSMENT

After the success on the Kokoda Trial and at Milne Bay, eliminating the Japanese at the beachheads was supposed to be a relatively easy task, more akin to MacArthur's claims of "mopping up." Instead, what resulted was one of the most grueling operations in the history of the Pacific War. The battles of Gona, Buna, and Sanananda were to cost the Australian and US forces some fifty-five hundred battle casualties, with thousands more evacuated sick. They were battles that, for the most part, were typified by assaults against heavily fortified Japanese positions with little fire support; as such, they represented some of the darkest episodes in the history of arms in the SWPA. Col. Clarence A. Martin, commander of the 128th US Regimental Combat Team at Buna, noted, "All in all, I think Buna was the most severe action of the war. I cannot imagine troops going into action under more unfavorable conditions. From the highest commander to the lowest private there was not the slightest conception of what this operation was to turn out to be."[127] This is a powerful assessment, given that Martin was to go on to be the assistant divisional commander of the 32nd Division during the 1943–1944 campaigns and the commander of the 31st Division in the Philippines campaign.

One of the key reasons for the beachhead battles being such a slugging match was that they were conducted under many restrictions. During the early part of the operation, sea control and air superiority were hotly contested. It was not until mid to late December that the Allies were able to provide continuous air superiority over the battlefield in daylight and develop enough local sea control to run convoys to carry reinforcements, supplies, artillery, and tanks to the front lines and sustain them there. The seaborne logistics effort, code-named Operation Lilliput, was one of the most crucial aspects of the campaign.[128] Set up in October 1942, it was carried out by a mixed RAN-USN task group (70.5) directed by the RAN and made up of a paltry number of requisitioned small ships.[129] However, as noted, AAF and ANF operations on the northern coast of Papua did not stop the Japanese from providing reinforcements and supplies by sea into the beachheads up until January 1943, nor did they stop them from evacuating the remainder of their troops as the campaign came to a close.

As outlined earlier, the major consequences of these issues were difficulties of supply, which exacerbated the already difficult situation in which the troops found themselves. The general situation throughout November and much of December is summed up by the 2/6 Independent Company at Buna, which noted in its war diary that

> the supply line seems unnecessarily bad and slow or unorganized. Some stores come in by air but as the first strip . . . was considered unsuitable by the Air Corps another had to be made . . . and as the strip was not at first well drained the Air Corps could not use it to any great extent. Coastal luggers . . . did not appear to run to any tangible program as their movement was constantly ordered and counter ordered—they spent much time on moving tps [troops] for short distances which could easily have been marched and allowed the luggers to build up a decent supply dump in the fwd areas. We suffered from this deficiency for some time afterwards. Then, unfortunately, 4 luggers were sunk by enemy A/C [aircraft] while moving in daylight.[130]

As noted, the operation of naval vessels in these waters was complicated by oceanographic issues, particularly the poor charts and multitude of reefs in the area but also the lack of air and sea control in November and early December, the inadequate number of the small coastal supply vessels, and the lack of adequate disembarkation points for offloading bulk supplies.[131] All of these issues had a dramatic impact on force concentration, logistics, and the ability to maintain sufficient numbers of artillery and tanks in the forward areas. This meant that both the Americans and Australians lacked the ability to implement their basic tactical doctrine and retarded the development of combined arms operations. It was only the Allies' ability to exert air and sea control over the battle space, the injection of fresh, elite troops, and adequate logistics that led to the breakthrough at Buna.

Airpower was critical to the Allied success, but it also demonstrated its limitations during the Papua campaign. The greatest impact that the AAF had on the beachhead battles was at the operational level. The achievement of air superiority in November and December, the continued attacks on the main Japanese base at Rabaul, and the provision of transport aircraft for logistics, force concentration, and reinforcement were all vital to the success on the ground. However, close air support (CAS) of the ground troops was far from effective, and a substitute for artillery it was not, despite Kenney's claims. The major restrictions on effective CAS were a "complicated and clumsy" system to request air support, a limited ability to effectively coordinate aircraft onto targets from the ground and the poor training and lack of experience of the pilots and crews in the AAF.[132] As the 126th Regiment noted, while the "5th Air Force was more than cooperative," there were four main factors that affected the provision of CAS: inaccurate maps and the difficulties higher headquarters had knowing accurately where the Allied troops were, the difficulties in jungle terrain of marking the front lines, the inability to establish direct air-ground communications, and the inadequate briefings of pilots on direct-support missions. These problems affected the level and type of support and also led to a number of friendly-fire incidents.[133] As a result, CAS was "a negligible factor in the hard-won Allied victories at Buna."[134]

The other significant factor was the strength of the Japanese defenses and the high quality of the Japanese troops that occupied them. This was the first time that the Allies in the SWPA had come up against deeply fortified defenses with an enemy determined to hold at all costs. As the 2/9th Battalion noted at Buna during its attack on 18 December, in order to come to grips with the enemy the battalion had to advance into "terrific fire from lines of pill boxes constructed of coconut trunks interlaced, roofed in some instances with steel and covered with 6' [feet] of earth, very well camouflaged and built to resist arty fire."[135] The 2/9th Battalion found the defenses so tough that it was "impossible to move without tk [tank] assistance."[136] The battalion's experience is instructive given the fact that the 7th Australian Division at Gona and Sanananda and the 32nd Division at Buna had been required to battle against such defenses for over a month with no armored support and negligible artillery.

If operational factors and excellent Japanese defensive positions were not enough, the troops and their commanders also had to deal with exceptionally difficult terrain and a horrible operating environment. One of the greatest consequences of this was the prevalence of disease among the troops. Malaria was rampant, infecting some 85 to 90 percent of troops in the front lines. As such, it became commonplace for soldiers to remain on duty until their temperature went over 104 degrees.[137] With other diseases such as scrub typhus, skin ulcers, and dysentery commonplace, the ratio of disease to battle casualties was almost five to one.

With all of the strategic and operational factors in mind, how well did the Allied troops perform? In the first instance, it has to be remembered that the Allies won the campaign, although it revealed a number of limitations in the effectiveness of the troops and their commanders. One of the most significant factors was the level of training of the troops involved. As Eichelberger noted to the commanding general of the 41st Division, Maj. Gen. Horace Fuller, "when you arrive up in this jungle you will find rising up in front of you, to haunt you, the specter of all those things you have failed to teach your men."[138]

Eichelberger's observation was neither profound nor revolutionary, but it was a lesson that over millennia militaries have had to constantly relearn. The poor training and preparation of the US National Guard and the Australian Militia units was telling. After the poor performance of the 32nd Division following its initial actions at Buna, Blamey used the opportunity to tell MacArthur that the American soldiers would not fight. As E. G. Keogh points out, however, that "all this, of course, was sheer downright nonsense. . . . The U.S. 32nd Division failed initially at Buna basically for the same reason that the Australian militia units failed—lack of training."[139]

In the end there were really three Allied armies present at the beachheads: the Australian Militia, the US National Guard, and the AIF. In the first two, leadership, training, and experience were all lacking. Here, however, the militia had a considerable advantage, as Blamey was able to move highly competent senior and junior officers from the AIF to the militia units to bolster their performance.

The third Allied army on the battlefield—the AIF—was the standout. Its performance was generally exceptional, and this was based on firm foundations that the other two armies lacked. The AIF demonstrated all of the components of an elite formation: combat experience, high-level leadership at the officer and NCO levels, proper training, excellent staff work and coordination, and a strong sense of determination to get to grips with the enemy and win. When married with proper logistics and other support to allow effective combined-arms operations, as the 18th Brigade had been at Buna in late December, they proved devastatingly effective. But even for such elite troops the close and dense terrain and tenacious enemy with their backs to the sea meant that the casualties among the AIF troops were exceptionally high.

As for their senior commanders, the report card is mixed.[140] While MacArthur's concerns over the strategic situation in his theater, which caused him to push for quick results from his commanders at the beachheads, were justified, his ignorance of combat conditions at the front lines was reprehensible. He constantly lectured Blamey, Herring, and Eichelberger on tactics at the front lines, and these diatribes only reinforced his inability to grasp the logistics and terrain problems, as well as the strength and depth of the Japanese defenses evident at Buna, Gona, and Sanananda. While such admonishments could easily be rebuffed by field commanders, it led MacArthur to underestimate the impact of some of his decisions on tactical developments and to argue with his commanders over reinforcements and other issues.[141]

Compounding this problem was MacArthur's decision not to visit the battlefront to see conditions for himself. While he was right not to do this for the fighting on the Kokoda Trail, the ease of air access to the beachheads from Port Moresby left him with little excuse in this case. That said, Blamey's own inability to do this may well have hampered MacArthur's movement. However, tact and consideration for subordinate commanders were not skills that MacArthur had demonstrated in the past, nor did he develop them during the war. While MacArthur showed good strategic acumen, his lack of operational and especially tactical insight meant he was often more of a hindrance than a help. At these levels, his greatest impact was in the decision to relieve Harding and bring in Eichelberger and the staff of I US Corps HQ. However, his duplicitous nature meant that he lied to Harding about the circumstances of his relief on his return to Port Moresby.

Blamey's performance at the beachheads was mixed. His strategic insights were very sound, and at the operational and tactical levels he demonstrated thorough awareness of the requirements for operating in the jungle and the stress and difficulties it placed on his subordinate HQs and the troops. However, he never grasped a full knowledge of the terrain and the conditions at the beachheads. The most "inexplicable" element of his command was his "tardiness in visiting the front."[142]

However, most of the tactical developments came from Blamey (as opposed to Herring), including the disastrous decision to send the Bren gun carriers into action and the correct decision to send tanks and the 18th Brigade. The latter was a brave but calculated decision, and it was done with considerable operational risk as it ran counter to the intelligence from GHQ about Japanese intentions toward Milne Bay.[143] Blamey also had to deal with MacArthur, and here he stood firm in the face of the C-in-C's interference and made strong representations in support of his commanders. While this saw a series of short-term tactical "victories" for Blamey in the long run, this further damaged his relationship with MacArthur. This, however, says more about MacArthur's personality defects than it does Blamey's command performance.

Herring's job was not an easy one, and the battleground on which he had to fight did not allow him to demonstrate any great tactical or operational flair, although this was in some ways lucky, as he did not possess the capability for either. He seemed unable to fully grasp the situation he faced, he was largely devoid of tactical ideas, he managed his staff poorly, and he had a strained relationship with Vasey. Blamey noted to Herring in December how poor his tactics were and rebuked him for his inability to provide his C-in-C clear updates on Adv NGF's logistics and operational requirements.[144] His inability to get a firm grip on his command meant that he was almost replaced on Christmas Day. Blamey's shrewd decision to send his senior staff officer over to help Herring saved his command and radically improved the operations of his HQ.

Herring's greatest asset was that he was a "commander of cheerful temperament" who was "prepared to co-operate to the limit."[145] This he demonstrated in his relationships with Blamey and especially Eichelberger. He had been placed in command during the Kokoda campaign so that Blamey would have a corps commander who he knew would follow orders unquestionably and to the letter—no more, no less. In this, he was highly effective, but the best that could be said in this regard was that he could be described as "General Acquiescence."[146] He was not a bad corps commander, but he was not a good one either, and his shortcomings, especially in a more independent command, would become apparent in the 1943 campaign.

For the divisional commanders, it was a mixed bag. Vasey performed admirably on the Kokoda Trail, but by the time the beachheads operations started he was tired and worn out. Blamey had suggested to Herring that Tubby Allen be brought back to replace him, but Herring rejected this idea due to the personal animosity he had toward Allen. Vasey therefore had to soldier on. During the battle, he demonstrated his short temper, difficult personality, and lack of tactical foresight. He also had an unwarranted sense of cultural snobbery toward the Americans. He was very critical of the Americans' combat performance in general and those under his command in particular. This is despite the fact that in many cases these US troops were to perform no worse, and in some cases better, than the Australian Militia units he commanded. Of particular note is the fact that Vasey was the only commander with whom Eichelberger could not work constructively. Vasey was to go on to prove himself as arguably the most effective division commander in the Australian Army during World War II, but as Australian author Peter Brune notes, his performance at the beachheads was the "low point in an otherwise distinguished career."[147]

As for the Americans, Harding and Eichelberger were as different as night and day. Where Harding failed, Eichelberger succeeded. Harding was overconfident and then overawed. He failed to prepare his himself, his division, or his staff for combat, and he failed to take the necessary steps to rectify the situation. He ignored direct advice about the movement of his troops, which cost him his bulk supplies, jeopardized his lines of communication, and almost cost him his life. His command-and-control arrangements were overcomplicated, and he failed to deal with ineffective subordinates. Even taking into account Harding's difficulties with the terrain, lack of supplies, scant artillery, and no tank support, his period in command serves as a damning indictment of his performance.

Eichelberger, however, presented almost the exact opposite. He opened an effective line of communication with Herring, Sutherland, and Mac-Arthur, revitalized his command, replaced ineffective officers, unscrambled units, and led from the front at great personal risk. Brune, who is rather critical of the Americans' performance at Buna and Sanananda, notes that Eichelberger "turned a near fiasco into a serious fighting concern. . . . By his sheer leadership qualities, drive and personality, he was able to reinvigorate his untrained and dispirited charges to far greater performance."[148] In the end, Eichelberger was the only senior officer to walk away from Buna with his reputation enhanced. In many respects, it was the making of him as a soldier.

CONCLUSION

There were many failures at the beachheads: a failure of intelligence regarding Japanese strength, intentions, and dispositions; a failure of supply; a failure to apply the correct doctrine; a failure of the US and Australian divisions to initially cooperate effectively; and a failure to undertake combined-arms warfare. These factors, coupled with the lack of resources available in the SWPA and the strategic circumstances, forced MacArthur into fighting a large-scale land campaign in a maritime environment. The result was high casualties and slow progress.

Success, however, was forthcoming but at a terrible price. The casualties of the Australian and US troops at the beachheads were greater per capita than those of the USMC at Guadalcanal.[149] However, success in Papua was dependent on success at Guadalcanal, especially the success of the USN in tying down the bulk of the Japanese fleet based at Rabaul and its supporting airpower, and the USN's casualties in the waters of the South Pacific were considerable.

The eventual victory in January 1943 was built off of the back of the cooperation between the US and Australian forces in Papua and Australia. It was a difficult and bumpy road and one that came to a head once the 32nd Division failed in combat at Buna in November. Thereafter, the battlefield cooperation between the two Allies slowly improved. Without a common sense of doctrine and command, and in the face of a determined enemy, ad hoc organizations and arrangements had proven sufficient for the time and circumstances. However, it was clear that there was never going to be a full integration of these two very different countries' militaries.

What had worked most efficiently was putting in place effective commanders who looked to understand and cooperate with their Allies. This was best demonstrated in the relations between Herring, Eichelberger, Wootten, and their subordinate officers. The battle for the beachheads also revealed that relationships tended to be much better the farther one got from GHQ and the closer to the front lines one stood.

Much had been accomplished during 1942 in Papua in forging a unified team in the SWPA, but as the 1943 campaign in New Guinea would expose, many of the same mistakes in combined operations would be repeated. Moreover, while the relationship at the operational and tactical levels would improve dramatically, at the very top it was becoming more and more evident that it was already fractured beyond repair.

Part 3

The Southwest Pacific Area, 1943

8

Operation Cartwheel

Plans, Preparations, and the Battle of the Bismarck Sea

WHEN MACARTHUR AND BLAMEY returned to Brisbane in January 1943, they had much to be satisfied with, but the road to Rabaul, let alone Tokyo, was still long and daunting. MacArthur's forces had removed the Japanese from Papua, shoring up the main Allied base at Port Moresby. They had also secured strong defensive positions and forward operating bases at Milne Bay, the beachheads, and Goodenough Island, but the main Japanese positions in New Guinea centered on Lae and Salamaua remained completely intact.

While the Japanese had sustained their first major defeats in Papua and at Guadalcanal, their power and ability to strike back at the Allies was far from diminished. Furthermore, their positions in New Guinea provided a strong launching pad if they decided to go over to the offensive. As if to prove the point, the Japanese were quick to seize the initiative after the fall of the beachheads by pouring reinforcements into New Guinea and using these fresh troops to place the Allied position in Papua under pressure.

As the Japanese were able to maintain sea and air control over the Bismarck Sea, they were able to run a line of communication from Truk to Rabaul and then onto New Guinea. This supply line was critical for the Eighth Area Army in Rabaul to maintain the Eighteenth Army in New Guinea. With their main base located at Lae, the Japanese had to run supply convoys from Rabaul either along the southern coast of New Britain directly to Lae or along the northern coast of New Britain, around Cape Gloucester, and down through the Vitiaz Strait. From Lae the Eighteenth Army was able push troops to Salamaua and other forward outposts so as to conduct operations into the coastal and inland border regions between New Guinea and Papua.

In order to shore up the Japanese position in New Guinea, the commander of the Eighth Area Army, Gen. Hitoshi Imamura, reinforced the

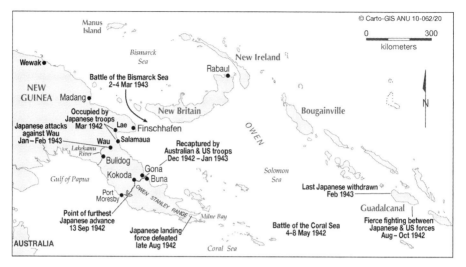

Figure 8.1 Major Operations in the Rabaul, New Guinea, and Solomon Islands Area, January 1942–March 1943

Eighteenth Army. Elements of the 5th Japanese Division were sent to Wewak and Madang to develop base facilities and airfields, while the 20th and 41st Japanese Divisions were sent forward from Formosa and China to reinforce New Guinea. Imamura was keen to seize the initiative and keep the Allies on the back foot. As soon as the decision had been made to withdraw from Guadalcanal and the beachheads, he organized to move the 51st Japanese Division from Rabaul to Lae. The 51st's commander, Lt. Gen. Hidemitsu Nakano, considered that the "whole fate of the Japanese Empire [now] depends upon the decision of the struggle for Lae-Salamaua."[1]

Imamura's plans were not based on a passive defense. He correctly assessed that the Allied position in the New Guinea highlands at Wau was a staging post that threatened his defenses at Salamaua and Lae. Thus, he planned to capture Wau as soon as possible.[2] Lt. Gen. Hatazō Adachi, the commander of the Eighteenth Army, planned to move one reinforced regimental combat team from Lae to undertake the Wau operation. In order to do this, the Japanese were required to run a major reinforcement convoy from Rabaul to Lae.

The convoy consisted of five transports and five IJN destroyers carrying the 102th Infantry Regiment plus attachments, together known as the Okabe Detachment, after the 102th's commander, Maj. Gen. Toru Okabe. Okabe departed Rabaul on 5 January 1942, and despite the ferocious air

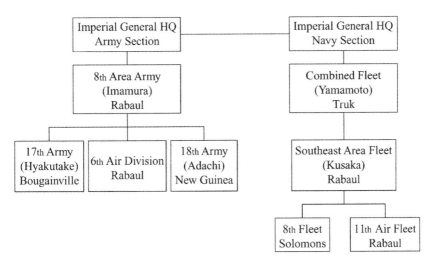

Figure 8.2 Japanese Command Organization in the South and Southwest Pacific, January 1943

battles above the convoy, it arrived at Lae on 7 January having lost only one transport. The 102nd Regiment was then transported to Salamaua on barges, bringing the number of troops in the area to over forty-five hundred. Okabe soon put these troops to work advancing on Wau.[3] The failure of the AAF to interdict this convoy did not go unnoticed by MacArthur and other senior Allied commanders, and it was a major point of embarrassment for the AAF and General Kenney.

Blamey had correctly assessed the threat to Wau in late December 1942.[4] With the town being occupied by only the 2/1st and 2/5th Independent Companies and a small number of New Guinea Volunteer Rifles troops, NGF HQ saw it as imperative that reinforcements were forthcoming. To provide the additional troops, Blamey released his only uncommitted AIF brigade, the Seventeenth, under the command of Brig. Murray Moten at Milne Bay. The brigade was ordered to move to Wau by air on 8 January 1943, with the first elements arriving on 14 January, having been delayed by bad weather. The brigade arrived in the "nick of time," with the Okabe Detachment approaching the outskirts of the town and its precious airfield in late January, making its bid to capture this vital terrain on 29 and 30 January.[5]

General Berryman, still on hand at NGF HQ to provide some continuity and to support the new GOC NGF, Lt. Gen. Iven Mackay, visited Moten at Wau on 29 January. On viewing the action firsthand, Berryman was convinced not only of the urgency of the operation but also of the pivotal role that the AAF's transport squadrons were playing in providing reinforcements, medical evacuations, and resupply. Berryman immediately liaised with the Fifth US Air Force to ensure that adequate aircraft for the arrival of Moten's remaining troops were available and that logistics flows were able to support the ground troops. In a piece of excellent Allied cooperation, USAAF transport planes delivered the remainder of Moten's brigade under fire directly onto the airfield, where it disembarked and went straight into action, sealing the outcome of the battle in the Allies' favor.[6]

The actions at Wau, and in particular the importance of airpower for the movement and concentration of force in Papua and New Guinea, were critical lessons for the Allies. This capability had proven itself in the movement of US reinforcements from Australia to Port Moresby, as well as in the effective use of transport aircraft to move troops into position around the beachheads and to maintain an air-resupply hub at Dobodura. But it was the actions at Wau, where the troops went into action straight off the runway, that captured the attention of the Allied planners. Blamey recognized the importance of airpower in the concentration, supply, and support of land forces in the SWPA, and he noted to MacArthur that the support provided by the air force in the operations against Wau was a "magnificent success."[7] This innovative use of airpower was to have a lasting effect on the commanders and staff officers at GHQ, Adv LHQ, and NGF HQ.

The operational effect achieved at Wau was only realized by the excellent working relationship that had developed between NGF and the Fifth Air Force in New Guinea, made all the easier by Brig. Gen. Ennis Whitehead (USAAF), the operational commander in New Guinea. Whitehead was an exceptionally capable officer who had established very positive relations with Berryman and other senior Australian officers at Port Moresby. Mackay noted that he found Whitehead "extremely cooperative . . . in fact there is no question of asking for help—he takes the initiative."[8]

STRATEGY, PLANS, AND TASK FORCES

With Wau secure and Moten's brigade slowly pushing the Japanese back, both adversaries in the South Pacific focused their attention on consolidating their positions and planning their next moves. For the Japanese, this meant further reinforcement of their positions in the Solomon Islands and New Guinea while preparing spoiling attacks to thwart any Allied moves in these areas. For the Allies in the SWPA, they now turned to the operational plans for the capture of New Guinea.

By January 1943, the Allies' positions in the SWPA had advanced no farther than six months earlier when MacArthur had been ordered to take Rabaul. The Papua campaign had been a slugging match to remove the Japanese after they forestalled MacArthur's attempt to take Buna. MacArthur's JCS Directive of July 1942 therefore still stood, and this drove the planning by MacArthur's and Blamey's HQs. Well before the fall of Sanananda, these concepts and plans for the capture of New Guinea and the march to Rabaul were under way.

As 1943 dawned, the global position of the Allies in the war was under consideration at the Casablanca Conference (14–24 January 1943). From this meeting emerged the doctrine of unconditional surrender and a reevaluation of the strategic priorities of the Allies. Unfortunately for the Pacific theater, the policy of "Europe first" did not change, and in the global order of priorities the Pacific was ranked fifth behind the Atlantic, the Soviet Union, the Mediterranean, and Britain. MacArthur was incensed, especially as the SWPA ranked behind Nimitz's POA. However, he had a kindred spirit in John Curtin. With interests aligned, Curtin and MacArthur lobbied incessantly for more resources—MacArthur to the JCS and Curtin to Roosevelt and Churchill.[9]

The Allied CCS report of 23 January at Casablanca had set the following priorities for the Pacific theater:

1. Continuation of Operation Watchtower (Guadalcanal) and
   the operations in New Guinea against Rabaul and to break the
   Bismarck Barrier,
2. To advance westward toward Truk and Guam,
3. To make the Aleutians secure,
4. To advance along the New Guinea-Mindanao axis as far as Timor,
5. To recapture Burma in order to help China.[10]

From here, the setting of the overall strategy for the SWPA was a prerogative of the JCS, and it directed that tasks 1 and 4 were to fall to MacArthur and the SWPA. This move reaffirmed its directive of July 1942, wherein the JCS had outlined the ultimate objective of seizing the New Britain–New Ireland–New Guinea region by three tasks:

Task I: Seizure and occupation of the Sanata Cruz Islands, Tulagi,
    and adjacent positions (Guadalcanal operation)
Task II: Seizure and occupation of the remainder of the Solomon
    Islands, Lae, Salamaua, and northeastern New Guinea
Task III: Seizure and occupation of Rabaul and adjacent positions in
    the New Guinea–New Ireland area.[11]

SOPAC had achieved task I with support from the SWPA, while tasks II
and III remained to be fulfilled under MacArthur's control.

   In order to achieve these objectives, MacArthur's staff developed the
Elkton series of plans, and Sutherland and Kenney put the SWPA's latest
version to the JCS in March 1943. Out of this conference came the JCS
directive of 28 March, which polished MacArthur's objectives. The JCS
allocated to the SWPA

(a) the establishment of airfields on Kiriwina and Woodlark Islands,
(b) the seizure of Lae-Salamaua-Finschhafen-Madang and occupation
    of western New Britain (Cape Gloucester), and
(c) the seizure of the Solomon Islands, including the southern portion
    of Bougainville.[12]

From here, GHQ SWPA developed Elkton III, which was released on 26
April 1943. This plan broke the JCS directive's first two objectives into a
three-phase operation under MacArthur's direct command in the SWPA,
while the third directive, under SOPAC's command but under Mac-
Arthur's strategic "direction," was also broken into three phases. The operations of both the SWPA and SOPAC, code-named "Cartwheel," would
be coordinated through MacArthur's GHQ and occur concurrently. The
overall aim was the reduction of the Japanese fortress at Rabaul.

   In order to prosecute the SWPA's portion of the Cartwheel plan, Mac-
Arthur, in line with his thoughts on centralized command and his belief
that he was the only joint commander in the theater, chose to break up
his command into a series of task forces.[13] The first two of these were
built around his air force and navy, while the third and fourth were built
around the division of his ground forces into two nationally based forces.
The first of these was Blamey's ALF, within which MacArthur kept all of
the Australian Army formations. The second was Alamo Force, which
consisted of virtually all of the US Army formations in the SWPA.[14]

   Restricted from taking command of the ground forces by the JCS directive establishing the SWPA and saddled with Blamey despite all his

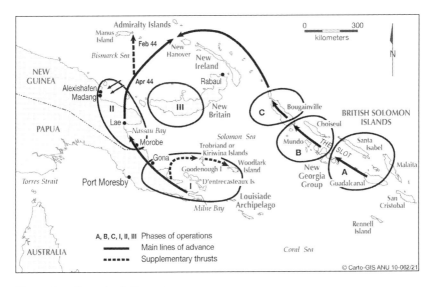

Figure 8.3 Cartwheel Operations, 1943

maneuvering, MacArthur had had to work cooperatively with the Australians in 1942, especially as they provided the vast bulk of his ground forces. But after the showdown with Blamey at the beachheads over the performance of the US troops, MacArthur was determined to find a way of sidelining Blamey. The creation of Task Force Alamo, reporting directly to GHQ, was MacArthur's solution.

By 1943, the idea of using task forces to achieve missions was well established in both the US and Australian armies in the SWPA.[15] Blamey had operated a series of task forces in ALF in 1942, the most significant being NGF, which included Advanced NGF, Milne Bay Force, and Kanga Force. The idea of allocating task forces had a tradition in the British Army dating back to World War I, and they were used extensively in the Middle East in 1940 and 1941, where Blamey had seen extensive service, the most well-known being Western Desert Force (later the Eighth Army).

This idea was also well established in GHQ. As early as April 1942, Brig. Gen. Stephen Chamberlin (GHQ's G-3) proposed a concept of operations for the SWPA based on a series of "task force[s] of combined arms with naval support."[16] The original plan to take the beachheads area in July 1942 before the Japanese arrived was based on the establishment of Buna Force, made up of US and Australian units task-allocated by GHQ to a hand-selected commander to achieve a specific mission set.[17] At the beachheads, Harding had divided his command at Buna into

Urbana Force and Warren Force. During this same period, NGF created Drake Force for the amphibious raid on Goodenough Island.

While the notion of task forces was well established, Blamey had, in part, also used NGF as a way of keeping control of operations and the selection of his subordinate commanders. During late 1942, NGF HQ had evolved from the command of a military district to an operational corps and then to an army-level HQ. In order to achieve the rapid increase of staff and responsibilities, Blamey had first ordered Rowell and the staff of the I Australian Corps HQ to Port Moresby to take over NGF. Later, when he arrived and split off Advanced NGF under Herring, Berryman brought forward a significant number of staff officers from the First Australian Army HQ and Adv LHQ to complete the "new" NGF HQ.

During this period, the commander of the First Army, Lt. Gen. John Lavarack, one of Blamey's archrivals, had agitated for his HQ to be sent to Papua to take command. He approached both Blamey and MacArthur directly, but Blamey resisted at every turn, claiming that New Guinea was a "task force" and not an army command. Lavarack saw it as a deliberate attempt to sideline him, an observation that seems to have been rather prescient.[18]

By mid-1942, NGF HQ's scope and responsibilities had grown considerably, and so, in August 1942, Rowell pressed Blamey to bring Lavarack and his HQ to Port Moresby. Rowell claimed that Blamey's response was that "to do that would be to bring in a commander I don't want. . . . He meant Lavarack."[19] Further evidence was provided by the fact that in 1944, after Lavarack was posted to Washington, Blamey replaced NGF with the First Australian Army HQ, now under the command of Lt. Gen. Vernon Sturdee. Sturdee's army was to run the operations in New Guinea and Bougainville for the rest of the war.

MacArthur was certainly aware of Blamey's moves in 1942, as Lavarack had brought his request to the personal attention of the C-in-C SWPA. It seems that Blamey's moves to exclude Lavarack from command during 1942 through his use of task forces may well have been one of the inspirations for MacArthur's maneuver to sideline Blamey from commanding large numbers of Americans troops.

MacArthur's moves to create Alamo Force had been helped by the decision by the JCS to provide MacArthur with two additional US Army divisions in 1943. They also conceded to MacArthur's request for a senior US Army officer for his theater. In relenting, Marshall allocated MacArthur the HQ of the Sixth US Army and its commander, Lt. Gen. Walter Krueger.

In appointing Krueger, MacArthur had deliberately overlooked Eichelberger, who had ruled himself out after his victory at Buna. As Kevin Holzimmer has argued, in seeking publicity for his exploits, Eichelberger had "committed the cardinal sin" in MacArthur's eyes.[20] MacArthur had turned on Eichelberger quickly: shortly after the Buna campaign he threatened Eichelberger with a reduction in rank to colonel and being sent home.[21] By bringing in Krueger, MacArthur was superseding Eichelberger in the command chain. To add insult to injury and to prove just how far his vindictive streak ran, MacArthur deliberately kept Eichelberger away from operational postings while also refusing a request from Marshall to release Eichelberger from the SWPA to take command of the First US Army.[22]

As a final insult, MacArthur denied Eichelberger awarding of the Medal of Honor, for which he had been recommended and which Marshall had been willing to approve. As Adm. Daniel E. Barbey, the commander of VII Phib, noted, "there was no place in the Southwest Pacific for two glamorous officers. For almost a year he [Eichelberger] fretted his time away in comparatively unimportant training roles in northeast Australia."[23] By way of contrast, in Krueger MacArthur got a no-nonsense general who eschewed publicity. Described as "unsmiling, hard-bitten, direct and stubborn,"[24] Krueger knew his place, and if he had any thoughts of stardom in the SWPA, Eichelberger's experience served as a clear warning as to what happened to any officer who dared claim some of MacArthur's credit.

The Sixth US Army initially consisted of the 32nd and 41st Divisions, the newly arrived 2nd Engineering Special (Amphibious) Brigade (2nd ESB), the 1st Marine Division (which was in Melbourne recovering from Guadalcanal), two antiaircraft batteries, a newly arrived paratrooper regiment, and a field artillery battalion.[25] Krueger arrived in Australia on 7 February 1943, and his "army" became operational nine days later. Soon after, almost the entire staff of the Sixth US Army became New Britain Force (in line with its objectives in the Cartwheel plan) and, from July, Alamo Force. The effect of this "not too subtle move by MacArthur withdrew US Army units from Blamey's control, made his position of ALF commander practically meaningless, and left him in charge of little more than a task force."[26]

Krueger certainly saw it as a way to remove his command from Blamey, and Willoughby noted after the war that the utility of Alamo Force was that "special task forces could undertake specific missions without complex inter-Allied command adjustment."[27] It was part of a

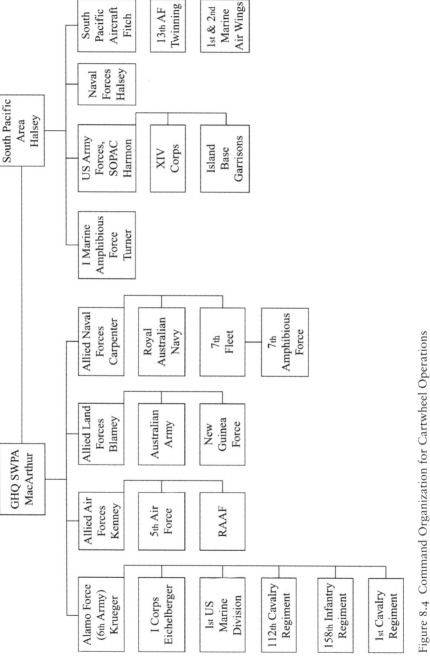

Figure 8.4 Command Organization for Cartwheel Operations

long-held desire by the Americans to command their own troops, which went back to the establishment of the SWPA in March 1942, through the Richardson Report, MacArthur's attempts to command Buna Force and then the 32nd Division directly, and Eichelberger's original assessment of operations in Papua in September 1942. As such, it came as no surprise to Blamey and the Australians.

Blamey's response to all this was typical of his temperament: he went fishing for a week. Others, however, have seen it differently. Gavin Long, in the final volume of the Australian Army's official history, noted that MacArthur "by stealth and by the employment of subterfuges that were undignified, and at times absurd," achieved this new command arrangement.[28] MacArthur's move was done without consultation with the JCS or discussion with the Australian government. In fact, Blamey made it clear that "at no stage" was he informed "as to the proposals" for the arrival of the Sixth Army.[29]

By going fishing, Blamey conceded that this was really about MacArthur acting as his own land forces commander, a desire the C-in-C SWPA had expressed to Marshall at the establishment of his command. Blamey knew, however, that he would eventually be confined to commanding only Australia's military forces.[30] As Blamey's biographer David Horner notes, MacArthur and Blamey also knew that given the eventual shift of the scale of forces throughout 1943 as a result of the overwhelming asymmetry of the coalition in the SWPA, this move "would have been . . . the only one . . . [that] was politically acceptable in Washington" over the longer term.[31]

Beyond nationalism and asymmetry were the practical realities of coalition warfare and the effect of the operational terrain in the SWPA on the organization of military forces. Blamey was sanguine on these points, raising no major objections to the change in circumstances even though he had the right to take it directly to the Australian prime minister. Instead, he wrote to MacArthur on 15 February 1943 that he was "in general agreement with" the notion of task forces and "their relationship to Headquarters and details of command" and that he would like to talk to MacArthur about their composition.[32] In the end, "there is no evidence that Blamey lost any sleep over MacArthur's machination or the implied threats to his positions" as commander, ALF—it was just the practical reality.[33] Instead, Blamey got on with reorganizing his own command to complete the most important part of Cartwheel, phase 2, which fell to the Australians and would mean that they would continue to provide the bulk of the ground forces for the operations scheduled in the SWPA during 1943.

ALLIED NAVAL AND AIR FORCES

Other major organizational changes were also under way in the SWPA. These were part of the changing character of Allied operations as part of the broader Pacific War, including the changing balance of forces as US mobilization swung into action. MacArthur's naval and air force commands also underwent expansion, reorganization, and reform. For the navy, two key changes occurred in early 1943. The first was the arrival of Barbey and VII Phib. This command was a major addition to MacArthur's arsenal and critical in the development of capabilities to implement his maritime strategy. A highly capable amphibious force was essential to the prosecution of the campaigns from 1943 until the end of the war. Further, as part of the slow but steady expansion of the US forces in the SWPA, MacArthur's naval command was redesignated the Seventh Fleet on 14 March 1943.[34] The Seventh Fleet (Vice Adm. Arthur S. Carpenter) would now consist of a number of naval task forces, including the following:

TF 70: Motor torpedo boats and the survey force
TF 71 and TF 72: US submarines based in Fremantle and Brisbane (but under the operational control of the US submarine commander in Pearl Harbor)
TF 74: Cruisers and destroyers under Rear Adm. Victor Crutchley (RN)
TF 76: VII Phib
TF 78: Minesweepers and escort vessels.[35]

Carpenter reorganized his internal command arrangements to ensure that he continued to provide for the maritime security of Australia's approaches and convoy protection for the movement of supplies and troops in and out of the theater, while gearing up the Seventh Fleet and VII Phib for offensive operations. Toward this end, the SWPSF was established on 4 March 1943. This new command would (a) provide for the protection of sea communications within the SWPA and (b) route shipping within that area.[36] The chief of the Australian Naval Staff (Vice Adm. Guy Royle [RN]) was designated as commander of the SWPSF and reported to the commander of the ANF, Admiral Carpenter.[37]

Prior to the establishment of the SWPSF, Carpenter had controlled convoys proceeding to New Guinea to support operations there. However, he had exercised his command through the RAN naval officers in charge (NOICs) of the various Australian ports.[38] Royle's new command would also exercise command through the NOICs. While this smoothed many operational elements of the ANF initially, the SWPSF had to overcome issues relating to the use of signal codes by the establishment of a special USN coding unit in the Australian Naval Board HQ in Melbourne. A more persistent problem, however, was the movement of escort vessels between task forces and the SWPSF, which resulted in a duplication of effort.[39]

The scope of the SWPSF's operations was significant. From 1941 to 1943 (covering Carpenter's and Royle's command periods), some 189,128 military personnel were transported safely to New Guinea. Furthermore, during Operation Lilliput (December 1942 to June 1943), some sixty thousand tons of supplies and 3,802 troops were moved via convoy along the northern coast of Papua to Oro Bay.[40] This was also done in the face of two major Japanese submarine campaigns in 1942 and 1943 and significant Japanese naval and air forces operating in New Guinea.

Overall, the SWPSF "would evolve to engage nearly 90 escort vessels from four countries in convoy duties as far north as Hollandia . . . [and represent] the most significant Australian naval command of the Second World War."[41] Given the relative balance of forces between the RAN and the USN, and how this dramatically changed over the period 1943–1944 with the massive expansion of USN elements of the Seventh Fleet, this presented the highest point of Australian naval command in the Pacific War (even if the admiral, Royle, was British). As David Stevens has noted, "the SWPSF was a subordinate command within the hierarchical structure of the SWPA . . . [and] the Australian Navy was [just] too small for MacArthur to have ever entertained the idea of a joint command arrangement or indeed of offering Royle the position of CANFSPWPA [Seventh Fleet]."[42]

While the logic of the ANF's reorganization in early 1943 was self-evident, the AAF's structure, command, and organization remained hidebound by the trials, tribulations, and dysfunction of the RAAF's command system. In early 1943, the dual command of the RAAF was still not resolved, and in early March, Curtin wrote to Blamey to seek his advice on whether the RAAF should be reorganized like the AMF, with a single "air officer commanding" (and consequently the abolition of the Air Board). Blamey strongly recommended such an approach, and Curtin undertook to talk to London about a suitable RAF officer for this post.[43]

In the meantime, Air Vice Marshal George Jones approached MacArthur

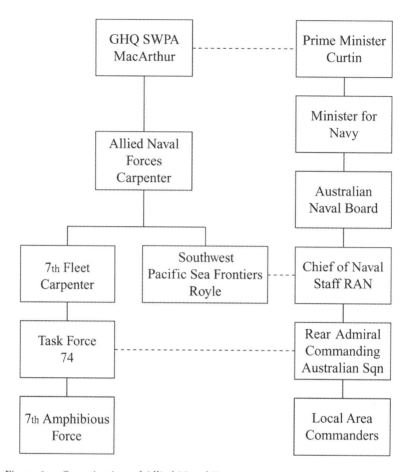

Figure 8.5 Organization of Allied Naval Forces, 1943–1944

with a series of proposals to reform the RAAF. These concentrated on the setting up of an RAAF expeditionary air force made up of the squadrons and associated units assigned to MacArthur as C-in-C SWPA. He proposed that the commander of this formation report to Kenney as C-in-C AAF SWPA, that this RAAF command be given all necessary administration powers from RAAF HQ, and that as the expeditionary formation moved beyond Australia, all RAAF forces left behind for the defense of Australia would come under his personal command. This would mean reorganizing the RAAF with most of the operational squadrons moving into the expeditionary force along the lines of No. 9 Operational Group of the RAAF, which was currently a part of Advance Echelon Fifth Air Force in New Guinea. Jones also wanted the RAAF expeditionary force kept together rather than its groups and squadrons being split up within the Fifth Air Force.[44]

Jones's plan would mean the continuation of the dual command system, which he argued was necessary as "whilst there are strong arguments in favour of unified command of the whole RAAF under one officer, it would be difficult for such a commander to discharge his operational responsibilities in the field and at the same time bear the full administrative responsibility to the Australian government, and to be available for advice."[45] Air Vice Marshal William Bostock wrote to MacArthur, arguing strongly against the dual command system, and instead supporting the idea of a single commanding officer such as that which Curtin was now exploring.[46] While this was unfolding, Bostock's relationship with the air minister (Arthur Drakeford) remained tense, so the Air Board took matters into its own hands and transferred Bostock from No. 9 Operational Group (where he was replaced by Air Commodore Hewitt) to the North-West Area Command, a subordinate formation.[47]

These issues were a matter for the Australian government, but they were also intricately linked to MacArthur through his position as C-in-C SWPA. As such, MacArthur shot down Jones's proposal, stating, "I do not believe that the suggested outline submitted by you is comprehensive enough to be used as a basis for further discussion. I hope, however, that ways and means may shortly be found to settle definitely the issues involved."[48] While MacArthur may well have been hinting as to Curtin's thinking on the subject, the idea of a single commander for the RAAF soon fell afoul as a result of MacArthur's obstinacy. Curtin was very concerned that arrangements for the command of the RAAF met with MacArthur's approval, especially as he was approaching Washington on behalf of Australia to secure an increased allotment of American aircraft for the RAAF to meet its expansion as part of a seventy-two-squadron plan.[49]

Curtin approached London and received the names of two viable RAF candidates, including Air Marshal Peter Drummond, deputy air officer C-in-C Middle East, an Australian. MacArthur, however, was having none of it. He argued that neither of the proposed candidates was suitable and so the current arrangement of dual command should continue. It is unclear why MacArthur persisted with this approach, but it may well have been because Kenney was happy with the arrangement as it was and he felt no need for a change.[50] It also may have been because a divided RAAF command was easier to manipulate, as compared to the AMF under Blamey's command.

By now it was June 1943, and the issue of the RAAF command was resolved under the notion of no change. The situation had been created in April 1942 and persisted through the reorganization of the AAF in September 1942, and the reorganization of the SWPA had occurred in the first half of 1943. The Air Board and Drakeford wanted Jones in command, MacArthur wanted the situation to remain the same, and Curtin wanted to placate MacArthur, so the prime minister dropped the idea of getting an RAF officer to command a unified RAAF. In the end, the troubled history of the organization of the air forces, and in particular the RAAF, continued on in 1943 as it would for the rest of the war. For the operations in 1942, the Fifth Air Force would continue to lead the way with No. 9 (later No. 10) Operational Group of the RAAF forming a major component of the Fifth Air Force's command, and eventually, by default, Jones's March 1943 proposal would be implemented.[51]

Despite its rather chaotic organization, the air forces in the SWPA were to form one of MacArthur's key strike weapons, and as a result of the Pacific War Conference in March 1943, Kenney's forces were to be increased by an additional heavy bomber group, 524 combat planes, and 336 noncombat planes. As part of this increased effort, Kenney received the 348th Fighter Group (P-47 Thunderbolts), the 380th Heavy Bomber Group (B-24 Liberators, to operate from Darwin in 1943), the 345th Medium Bombardment Group (B-25 Mitchells), and the 54th Troop Carrier Wing.[52]

This increased force of US aircraft would dramatically improve Mac-Arthur's principle strike weapon in the theater. As noted, land-based airpower in the SWPA was providing MacArthur with not only control of the skies but also sea control, and thus it formed a key plank in his maritime strategy. While the reduction of Rabaul through airpower was continuing unabated, the next big test for the AAF was to come with the Battle of the Bismarck Sea.

The events in the Bismarck Sea on 2–4 March 1943 were a watershed for Allied air operations in the SWPA. After the embarrassing performance of the AAF in its attempts to halt the Japanese convoy carrying the Okabe Detachment to Lae in January, Kenney and his commander in New Guinea, Ennis Whitehead, were determined to ensure that the next Japanese reinforcement convoy would meet its doom. This time, Kenney and Whitehead had time to plan their attacks and make major adjustments to their tactics and force composition.

More broadly, the AAF in New Guinea moved from high- to low-altitude attacks on shipping in early 1943 and started to place a greater emphasis on night tactics and the development of long-range fuel tanks

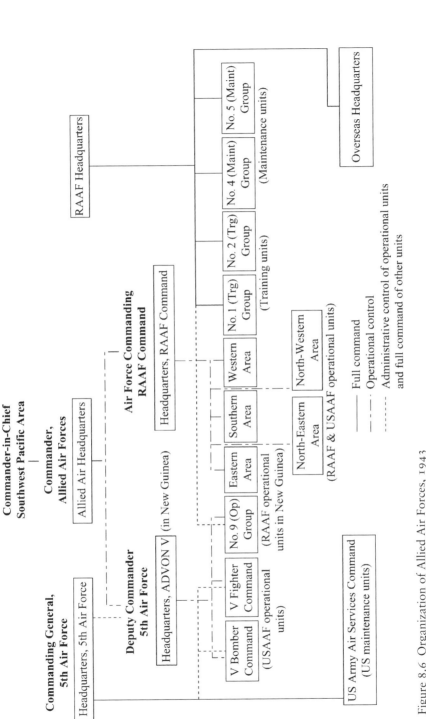

Figure 8.6 Organization of Allied Air Forces, 1943

in order to provide greater fighter cover. Kenney also converted a number of B-25 Mitchell bombers to commerce destroyers by adding four .50-caliber guns to the nose and one more to each side of forward fuselage. These were just some of a range of tactical innovations that Kenney and his staff were developing in the SWPA to improve the performance of the air force.[53]

In the lead-up to March, Kenney greatly benefited from excellent Allied intelligence from both aerial surveillance of Rabaul and decrypted Japanese signals. These intelligence sources revealed the rough size, composition, and support that the next convoy would receive, as well as the most likely departure date. This allowed Kenney and Whitehead to fully prepare and train their forces to ensure a maximum effort. The accurate intelligence even allowed the AAF to plan and conduct a full-scale rehearsal of the attack.[54]

The Japanese convoy, consisting of eight destroyers escorting eight transports carrying almost seven thousand men and supplies from the IJA's 51st Division, departed Rabaul on 28 February under the cover of a major storm. Flush from their previous success in January, the Japanese decided on a route that brought them within range of all the Allied aircraft in New Guinea. The convoy remained undetected until 1 March. At this point, Kenney's plan swung into action. As part of a coordinated Allied effort, all aircraft from Advance Echelon Fifth Air Force, including a full complement of strike aircraft from Air Commodore Hewitt's No. 9 Operational Group, were prepared for the assault.[55]

The first strike consisted of B-17 heavy bombers, which were unable to locate the convoy. Throughout the night, RAAF Catalina flying boats shadowed the convoy and undertook harassing attacks. Next, early on 2 March, RAAF Boston bombers struck the Japanese airfield at Lae to limit the fighter protection that the Japanese could provide to the convoy, while the long-range B-17s reached out to attack the convoy in two strike groups. They reported sinking one ship and damaging two more. The Catalinas once again tracked the convoy through the night and carried out harassing attacks.[56]

By 3 March, the convoy was now in range of the Allies 's medium attack aircraft, and now the real slaughter began. The first sortie was by No. 100 Squadron RAAF, whose Beaufort torpedo bombers attempted a night attack but were thwarted by the bad weather. However, as the day dawned clear, the full weight of the Allied airpower struck. RAAF Bostons once again hit the Lae airfield as the convoy steamed into Vitiaz Strait. Soon after, US P-38 Lightnings provided air cover and tackled the defending Japanese fighter aircraft, after which, at ten in the morning, the bombers went to work.

Coming in three waves only seconds apart, with the aircraft at three different altitudes, the attack was devastating. First, thirteen B-17 heavy bombers at medium altitude hit the convoy to disperse it and break up its antiaircraft formation. Second, the "whispering death," thirteen RAAF Beaufighters with four cannons in the nose and six machine guns in the wings, bored in. Fearing a torpedo attack, most Japanese ships turned nose on to the RAAF aircraft, but this only played into the Beaufighters' hands. Their role was actually suppression (and destruction) of enemy air defenses, or SEAD mission in the modern parlance, and lining up the ships end-to-end down their length provided a perfect target. They wrought havoc on the ships' antiaircraft guns and killed large numbers of the officers and crew exposed on deck.

Soon after, twelve US Mitchell bombers made a medium-altitude strike while another twelve modified "commerce destroyer" Mitchells struck from mast height. The commerce destroyers claimed seventeen direct hits and were soon followed up by US Boston bombers. From here on in, the RAAF and USAAF aircraft intermingled as they pulverized damaged ships and completed the rout. Later in the afternoon, more waves of Allied bombers, including RAAF Bostons, would return to the area to ensure the complete destruction of the convoy. Over twenty-eight hundred Japanese troops and sailors were killed, and all eight transports were sunk, along with three destroyers. A fourth destroyer was sunk the following day.[57] Only six Allied aircraft were lost and twenty-five crew.[58]

The success, a result of a truly combined effort between the USAAF and the RAAF, was overwhelming. Kenney had driven the technical developments, and RAAF Group Capt. William "Bull" Garing had convinced Whitehead and Kenney of the need to develop the mast-height, low-level massed attacks after the failure in January. In action, the RAAF and USAAF aircraft operated as one tactical team. It was an outstanding display of coalition cooperation.

The operational outcomes were profound. The Japanese never again tried to run a convoy from Rabaul to Lae in such a manner and instead fell back on the use of barges, submarines, and fast destroyers, greatly restricting their supply lines and creating massive problems for their force concentration in New Guinea. The Japanese now had to move bulk supplies and reinforcements much farther west to Wewak and Madang and then move them overland across jungle-covered mountain terrain (with no major road infrastructure) or by barge along the coast. This had a major impact on the outcome of the battles for Salamaua and Lae. Most significantly, it cemented the domination of the AAF over the Japanese army and naval air arms. While there were many brutal battles to come in the air over New Guinea and throughout the SWPA, the Japanese were never able to really effectively challenge the superiority of Allied air forces again.[59]

The success was overwhelming, but unsurprisingly Kenney and MacArthur pushed their claims well beyond reality. Kenney reported that eleven to fourteen transports were sunk, fifteen Japanese aircraft were destroyed, and fifteen thousand Japanese personnel lost their lives. MacArthur took these figures and piled on for good measure, publicly stating that the Japanese lost twenty-two ships, one hundred aircraft, and fifteen thousand personnel. It was a gross exaggeration. In typical MacArthur form, he also made no mention of the RAAF's efforts in the battle. Both nationalities were amalgamated under the notion of "MacArthur's air force." Kenney, in his memoirs, makes only one reference to five Australian light bombers in relation to the RAAF's efforts, downplaying their considerable role.[60]

The exaggerated Japanese losses also created a major controversy. After a formal investigation, Kenney was ordered by the USAAF Air Staff to tone down the losses recorded. MacArthur bellicosely refused and threatened to take action against those questioning his reports.[61] It was an undignified end to what, on its own terms, was a major triumph. The stage was now set for the Allies to move over to the offensive permanently and for the remaining Japanese in New Guinea to be destroyed.

9

Working Together for a Common Purpose

The Development of Amphibious Warfare in the SWPA, 1942–1945

ON THE AFTERNOON OF 22 OCTOBER 1942, two RAN destroyers, HMAS *Arunta* and HMAS *Stuart*, slipped their mooring lines and made their way out of Milne Bay. On board were members of Drake Force, consisting primarily of the officers and men of the 2/12th Battalion AIF. Their mission, in the modern parlance, was to conduct an "amphibious raid" on Goodenough Island, situated in the D'Entrecasteaux Islands, fifteen miles north of Papua and eighty miles from Milne Bay. Drake Force, therefore, was about to undertake the first amphibious operation by the Australian military since Gallipoli in 1915 and the first of dozens of similar operations undertaken by the Allies in the SWPA.[1]

At Goodenough Island, Drake Force was to destroy the three hundred Japanese naval infantry who had been marooned there after their landing craft has been destroyed by the RAAF during the failed assault on Milne Bay in August. Drake Force's mission would deny the Japanese the use of the island for any further assaults on Milne Bay. This would also enable the Allies to conduct a reconnaissance for the possible establishment of airfields on the island.[2]

Drake Force's mission was to prove to be an inglorious start to amphibious warfare in the SWPA. Intelligence incorrectly stated that the Japanese were hungry and demoralized and possessed limited equipment and weapons.[3] Poor preparation meant that the 2/12th Battalion had neither time for a proper reconnaissance nor rehearsals for their mission.[4] Compounding these factors was the systemic neglect of amphibious warfare in the Australian military in the interwar period, which meant that no one in the AMF or the RAN in 1942 had much of an understanding of the complexity of such operations. The final thing working against Drake Force was that with local maritime and air superiority being highly contested, the threat of intervention by Japanese naval and airpower remained high.

In keeping with British amphibious doctrine of the time, Drake Force arrived off Goodenough Island in darkness. The RAN destroyers disembarked their passengers at two locations well away from the last known position of the Japanese troops. From there they were to establish a firm base and then advance on and destroy the enemy. In fitting with the poor preparations and lack of experience, the landings proved to be cumbersome and rather noisy affairs.[5] Furthermore, neither the troops ashore at the two landing sites nor the two destroyers at sea had radio communications with each other. For the RAN, this nearly led to a friendly fire incident between the destroyers. After they received a radio message from Milne Bay warning about the possible presence of an IJN light cruiser in the area, they remained unable to communicate effectively and therefore almost opened fire on each other during their postlanding rendezvous.[6]

Adding to the problems, the heavens soon opened up, and rain fell intensely. As the troops marched toward the enemy, it soon became clear that the four-hour patrol to the objective was totally unrealistic for heavily laden soldiers on a dark, stormy night along a dangerous jungle track without prior reconnaissance. Arriving two and half hours late, the main body of the battalion finally made contact with the Japanese. Exhausted and with no contact with the second, company-sized landing party, the first landing party postponed its assault until the following day. Meanwhile, the second landing party had met with considerable resistance soon after landing. Under counterattack from the Japanese and with no contact with the rest of the battalion, the company commander, Maj. Keith Gatehead, was forced to withdraw his troops to their landing site. Soon afterward, he pulled his company out and moved via small boat around the island to the battalion's main landing site, arriving the following morning.[7]

By the morning of 24 October, the main body of the 2/12th Battalion had launched its attack. It met very heavy resistance, and with no heavy weapons immediately available or the means to coordinate naval gunfire support or close air support, the battalion commander, Lt. Col. Arthur Arnold, called off his attack. Clearly the intelligence was wrong: the Japanese were heavily dug in, well supplied, and in good spirits. This development was rather unexpected, as this was one of the first times that Allied troops had come across such well-prepared and heavily dug-in enemy positions in the SWPA.[8] The Adv LHQ report on the operation noted that the "Jap commander selected the best terrain features for a defensive position. . . . It was located on commanding ground with an obstacle of a stream with steep precipitous banks to the front and thick jungle on the flanks. All automatic weapons were carefully sited and their fire coordinated."[9] Colonel Arnold later noted that the Japanese "post would have done justice to a Field Works Course."[10] A few weeks later at Buna, Gona, and Sanananda, overcoming Japanese dug-in defensive positions would cause the Allies such difficulties that General Vasey would call for an amphibious landing in January 1943 at Sanananda to resolve the deadlock.

Arnold resolved to break his own deadlock by bringing forward mortars from his firm base at the main landing site and arranging for air support on the morning of 25 October. The air support never arrived, yet when the advance continued the 2/12th Battalion found that the enemy had gone. The Japanese, having had the Australians under close observation from the time of landing, had decided to withdraw to neighboring Fergusson Island and thereafter were evacuated by an IJN cruiser. The operation cost the Australians thirteen killed and eighteen wounded and the Japanese twenty killed and fifteen wounded.[11] Tactically it had not been very successful, but operationally there was a positive outcome for the Allies: Goodenough Island was denied to the Japanese, and eventually the Allies developed airfields on the island for use by the USAAF and the RAAF.

The difficulties at Goodenough Island and Vasey's unfulfilled request for an amphibious landing at Sanananda in early January 1943 reflected the major operational limitations that the Allies faced precisely because they did not have an effective amphibious capability. The postoperational report on Drake Force, prepared by Blamey's headquarters, noted the problems in reconnaissance and communications, the lack of heavy weapons, and the physical condition of the troops. Interestingly, however, nothing was said about the maritime elements of the operation, the lack of air support, the neglect of naval gunfire support, and the haphazard and rushed manner in which it was undertaken.[12] The problems of Drake Force and the evaluation of its operation were a derivative of the Allies' approach to operations in 1942, which emphasized land operations in what was fundamentally a maritime environment. To break this deadlock, the Allies had to overcome their major deficiencies in amphibious operations or they would have to reconcile themselves to never getting off the island of New Guinea.

On the Japanese side, they had tried to use maritime maneuver twice in Papua in 1942. The first time was the amphibious assault on Port

Moresby that was defeated by the strategic setback they suffered at the battle of the Coral Sea. The second was the failed amphibious assault on Milne Bay in August 1942, which was defeated by their lack of air and maritime superiority in daylight around the eastern end of Papua and the numerically superior Australian forces in place at Milne Bay. However, what the long campaign for Papua was revealing was the slow but steady shift in air, and thus maritime, superiority from the Japanese to the Allies, an outcome that would condemn the Japanese to fighting highly restricted campaigns in the SWPA from 1943 to 1945 while freeing up the Allies to undertake maritime maneuver.

1942 AND AMPHIBIOUS DEVELOPMENT IN THE SWPA

The development of an amphibious capability in the SWPA was easier ordered than done. The SWPA suffered from serious handicaps from the very beginning. From the Australian perspective, the prevailing military culture saw amphibious warfare as a virtual anathema. This is despite the fact that Australia is the sixth largest country in the world and the only one of the top six to be completely surrounded by water. Australia's aversion to this type of warfare was driven by its strategic culture being dominated by its relationship with the British Empire, which derived a "way of warfare" focused on the provision of single-service forces that were designed to be integrated into their corresponding British service counterparts under the protection of Britain's longstanding global maritime dominance.[13] Joint expeditionary operations in the Southwest Pacific were therefore not perceived as part of Australian military strategy.

This meant that although the landing at Gallipoli in 1915 plays a central place in the ANZAC legend and Australian national consciousness, the ANZAC spirit emanates not from the amphibious aspects of this operation but rather the battles that occurred once the troops were ashore. As Jeffrey Grey has pointed out, Australia's approach to warfighting has always been distinguished by the quality of its expeditionary infantry, who are usually sent overseas as part of a wider coalition and depend on a larger ally for logistics and other support.[14] Such an approach to warfare, as well as the interwar Singapore Strategy, meant that Australia's military forces had little experience or interest in amphibious warfare in the lead-up to the Pacific War.

From the US perspective, the dominant force in the SWPA was General MacArthur and the US Army. Unlike the POA, neither had the benefits of the experience or knowledge of the interwar USMC, and what USN presence MacArthur did have was exceptionally small. The maritime nature of the theater in the SWPA was further hampered by MacArthur and GHQ's intense dislike of the USN, something historian Richard Frank describes as MacArthur's "great bête noire."[15] MacArthur's vitriol was matched by the head of the USN, Adm. Ernest King, who "waged an unrelenting campaign of personal vilification" against MacArthur.[16] This meant that not only did the Seventh Fleet in the SWPA largely go without capital ships (aircraft carriers and battleships) until the invasion of the Philippines in 1944, but it was also denied anything but the smallest numbers of the most critical platform in the development of an amphibious capability: the large amphibious attack transports (APAs). This relegated MacArthur's amphibious capability in 1943 and 1944 to a shore-to-shore rather than oceangoing amphibious force. On top of this, MacArthur's US ground forces were largely made up of National Guard formations, and they, like most of his staff at GHQ, were ignorant of amphibious doctrine and devoid of such experience.[17]

On top of these challenges was logistics. Virtually everything that was needed in the SWPA had to come from the United States. Logistics were the main burden on MacArthur's command. A system of reverse lend-lease provided MacArthur's US forces with raw materials, food, lodging, clothing, and a myriad of other supplies to the point where Australia was the only Allied country to which the United States was indebted through lend-lease at the end of the war.[18] However, major equipment such as shipping and landing craft, military supplies, and troops all had to come from the United States. Critically, "the same amount of shipping that would move two men in the Southwest Pacific would serve to shuttle five to Europe," and this extended to maintaining them there on operations.[19]

The other key operational restriction was shipping, one of the most important requirements in a maritime environment. However, like with all other logistics, the SWPA was so low on Allied global strategic priorities that merchant and amphibious ships were exceptionally difficult to come by in 1942 and 1943. This meant that MacArthur was originally going to rely on the provision of ten Dutch merchant ships to act as troop transports, but these ships never materialized.[20] The situation was so dire that throughout 1942 it proved virtually impossible for the provision of a single ship to support the running of the main amphibious training school in the SWPA. Stephen Chamberlin, the G-3 at GHQ, noted that merchant and amphibious shipping in 1942 "seem to be about as precious as gold, or more so."[21] As a result, for most of 1942–1944, MacArthur had to make do with only the APA USS *Henry T. Allen* and three RAN equivalent vessels (landing ships, infantry [LSIs]), which in late 1942 and early 1943 were only just being created by converting the armed merchant cruisers HMAS *Manoora*, *Kanimbla*, and *Westralia*.[22]

The new, smaller, specialized landing craft now coming into service were therefore to be critically important to the amphibious forces of the SWPA, but in 1942 they were even more difficult to come by than APAs. It was soon realized that local production would not be sufficient, so MacArthur requested large numbers of the 36-foot landing craft vehicle, personnel (LCVP), the 50-foot landing craft, mechanized (LCM), and the 120-foot landing craft, tank (LCT) types from the United States. Given global strategic priorities and shortages of landing craft, MacArthur was informed that these would not be forthcoming. A lifeline arrived only with the cancellation of amphibious operations in Europe in 1942, which freed up some 456 landing craft for the SWPA. However, shipping them to the theater would prove so difficult that by January 1943 only seventy-nine had arrived.[23]

This force was supplemented by the decision in late 1942 to allocate one of the three US Army engineering special brigades (ESBs) to the SWPA. The allocation of the 2nd ESB to MacArthur was a considerable windfall, as it included some 360 officers, seven thousand men, and six hundred landing craft. In order to expedite their move, the craft were shipped disassembled to Australia and reassembled at a plant built at Cairns in far northern Queensland.[24]

Given the lack of APAs in the SWPA, the major impact for the type and style of amphibious operations in the SWPA was the introduction into service of the oceangoing 1,490-ton landing ship, tank (LST) and the 390-ton landing craft, infantry (LCI). Again, the cancellation of operations in Europe led to the SWPA receiving seventy-two LSTs and thirty-six LCIs, which along with the smaller landing craft would form the backbone of SWPA amphibious operations in 1943 and 1944.[25]

AMPHIBIOUS TRAINING SCHOOLS: 1942

Despite the Australians' lack of an amphibious culture, the need to develop a capability was recognized early the Pacific War.[26] In March 1942, the deputy chief of the General Staff in Australia, Maj. Gen. Sydney Rowell, recommended the acquisition of specialist equipment and the establishment of a school of combined (amphibious) operations. Rowell had, however, recognized that the raising of such a force would be a long-term endeavor. It was also realized that this would eventually be a cooperative undertaking between the US and Australian forces in the theater.[27] Thus, the story of the development of amphibious warfare capability in the SWPA, especially in the period of 1942–1944, is really an Allied story built around US-Australian cooperation. It remains the one area in which neither nation could claim expertise in the SWPA in 1942 and one where both countries had to cooperate effectively.

Following on from Rowell's March 1942 long-range planning document, the First Australian Army, based in Toowoomba, Queensland, started in April to press for the training of the troops under its command in amphibious operations. It entered into discussions with Blamey's LHQ, and in May 1942 this preliminary planning was significantly aided with the arrival of Lt. Col. M. W. Hope (Royal Artillery), previously the senior instructor at the British amphibious warfare school in Egypt, and Cdr. Fredrick Norton Cook (RAN), who had returned home after commanding HMS *Tormentor*, one of the Royal Navy's combined training centers focused on landing craft operations.[28] Cook had been mentioned in dispatches during the Norway campaign in 1940, and as the senior naval officer in charge of the Bruneval commando raid on France in 1942, he received the Distinguished Service Cross for his "daring, skill and seamanship . . . against the enemy."[29] Colonel Hope and Commander Cook, along with Maj. Alfred Rose from First Australian Army HQ, undertook reconnaissance down the length of the eastern seaboard in search of appropriate sites for training facilities. The subsequent Hope-Cook Report recommended a center for the training of staff at Port Stephens on the NSW mid-northern coast and a training school for units at Bribie Island (Toorbul Point, now Sandstone Point) in Queensland near Brisbane.

In the following month, June 1942, MacArthur issued an instruction for the establishment of the first of a number of amphibious warfare training establishments in the form of a Joint Overseas Operational Training School (JOOTS). The JOOTS was set up at the Port Stephens site and designed as a US-Australian training center for army, naval, and air forces. MacArthur described its mission as

> training of Land Forces in overseas operations in conjunction and cooperation with Naval Forces and Air Forces, both land and carrier based. . . . The task will involve the combat loading of ships, the disembarkation of troops and supplies in small boats in the face of an enemy, the landing on hostile shores, a rapid and strong thrust

inland, and the occupation of hostile coast lines with continued operations into the interior, all tasks in coordination with Naval and
Air support.[30]

The original plan called for a force of one corps to be trained in amphibious operations, made up of two US divisions and one Australian
division.[31] This two-thirds/one-third split was carried through the provision of staff, equipment, logistics, and the costs in setting up the training
schools. To meet demand, in addition to JOOTS the Australians also
set up the First Australian Army Combined Training School (CTS) in
Queensland at Toorbul Point, which utilized the beaches on nearby Bribie
Island to conduct landing exercises.

As these training establishments were initially army-run facilities, they
were approved by GHQ and Blamey's Allied LHQ in June 1942. Interestingly, the staff officers at GHQ were rather slow to act on MacArthur's
orders, and although GHQ held a number of conferences in June and July,
its final approval for JOOTS was not given until 9 August 1942. It was
also made clear by MacArthur that while LHQ would run the facilities,
GHQ controlled the decisions around doctrine and landing technique.[32]

By the time GHQ issued its final orders, the Australians had already
had the First Australian Army CTS at Toorbul Point up and running for
four days, while the JOOTS at Port Stephens began operations only six
days after the final GHQ approval, on 15 August 1942.[33] Cognizant that
amphibious operations could not be undertaken by the army alone, the
RAN developed its own plans for a training establishment. Commander
Cook was given command, and he wisely chose to locate the aptly
named HMAS *Assault* alongside JOOTS at Port Stephens. HMAS *Assault* was commissioned into service by the RAN on 1 September 1942.[34]
In Queensland, Major Rose, who had formed part of the Hope-Cook
Report team, was promoted to lieutenant colonel and given command
of the First Army's CTS. The naval component of this command was
commanded by Lt. John Morrell Band, who ran the RAN's small-boat
training facility from October 1942.[35]

These decisions highlighted one of the major problems for the development of an amphibious capability in 1942: MacArthur's preference for
cooperative rather than joint command. From the very beginning, GHQ
noted that the army and naval staffs would "be responsible for their own
instruction. . . . The two staffs will then cooperate and work as they see
fit."[36] This would result, throughout 1942, in interservice arguments over
roles, staffing, coordination, and the allocation of resources, and these
issues seriously hampered the development of the training schools.

The focus of JOOTS was initially heavy on the theoretical and doctrinal elements of amphibious operations and was designed to run courses to train officers of formations and units, who would then go on to train their troops. The program was split into two courses, one a senior officer's course run over twenty days and the second a much larger, unit officer's course of fifteen days, normally attended by approximately fifty officers from the rank of captain to lieutenant colonel.[37] The DCGS, Maj. Gen. Frank Berryman, noted to First Australian Army HQ that JOOTS's courses would "standardise the training of the Allied forces in Combined [amphibious] Operations and train selected representatives from each of the services in order that they in turn may form a nucleus of trained instructors for further training of their formations."[38] The first instructors graduated from the school on 25 September 1942.

While the Australians had been the leading elements in setting up these training establishments, no one was in doubt that they would have to be developed as "Allied" facilities. As such, the original staff establishment of JOOTS consisted of twenty-one staff officers made up of ten US Army officers (including two from the USAAF), seven Australian Army officers, two instructors from the RAAF, and one RAN officer. The first commanding officer at JOOTS was a US Army Cavalry colonel, Byron Q. Jones, who was seconded from his staff position at GHQ. Among the seven Australian Army personnel were two British officers, Colonel Hope (coauthor of the Hope-Cook Report) and Lt. Col. Thomas K. Walker (Royal Marines).

From the start, this mixed staff group mirrored most of the difficulties evident in the wider coalition in the SWPA in 1942. As a result, from mid to late 1942, the staff at JOOTS were unhappy and in conflict with one another. This is a result of the fact that, like most areas involving joint or combined cooperation in the SWPA in 1942, JOOTS suffered from its own version of poor intercultural communication set on a foundation of strong cultural imperialism. Colonel Jones arrived at JOOTS enamored of the prevailing GHQ attitude at the time, which looked down upon the Australian military and placed a high premium on US superiority of methods, experience, and approach.[39]

Furthermore, Jones was also in a rather difficult position. He was a regular army officer but had spent the majority of his career as one of the pioneers of aviation in the US military. However, Jones had had a major falling out with the US Army Air Corps command over doctrine and approaches to military aviation. As a result, Jones transferred back to the ground forces in 1938 and served in various mechanized cavalry staff positions before arriving in the SWPA in July 1942.[40] It is unknown whether

Jones attended any specialist amphibious warfare courses in the United States before being posted to the SWPA, but it seems that GHQ had appointed an officer to command JOOTS who in all likelihood had little in the way of practical knowledge or experience in amphibious warfare. However, in his defense, few if any senior officers in the SWPA possessed such qualifications at the time.

This was not the case, however, for some of Jones's staff and for his two British officers in particular. Colonel Hope had considerable experience and had been working on the development of the capability in Australia for a number of months, and he was already at Nelson Bay when Jones arrived to take command. According to one US officer who was present at the very first meeting between Jones and Hope, Hope "made a stab for running the school," but Jones left him in no doubt about the role of GHQ and "where Hope stood."[41]

A few days later, the second British officer arrived for duty at JOOTS. Lt. Col. Thomas K. Walker (Royal Marines) was a particularly valuable addition to the team. A highly experienced officer, Walker had previously been the deputy assistant adjutant general for the Royal Marines and in 1940 had prepared a detailed report, *Preparation for Combined Operations on a Major Scale*. This document outlined the requirements for successful amphibious operations, including the organization of a staff, formations, equipment, training establishments, and naval and air support. As the historian Donald Bittner has noted, Walker's report "proposed the correct solution, but its implementation [in the British military] would be over a long period of time and on a scale hardly envisioned in 1940."[42]

Jones seemed to get off on a much better foot with Walker, and he delegated to him the responsibility of setting the program for the staff course, yet Walker apparently also let Jones know that "he was an expert" and that he had been "brought over at the request of Gen. Blamey to run the show."[43] Walker also noted of his time at JOOTS that the Americans were "too rigid theoretically" and that their training methods were based on "rather out of date theory from American Army textbooks."[44]

What transpired from here seems to be a generally unhappy staff with a lot of "gripping" from both US and Australian officers and a collision of views between the two British officers, who were generally backed by the Australians on staff, and Jones, who was supported by the senior supply officer on staff, another US Army colonel, Bird S. Dubois. Soon criticism of Jones's style of command and his approach to the school made its way back to GHQ. After Jones had been in command six weeks, Chamberlin wrote to him and warned that he had "heard from three different sources that some individuals are complaining at the school about your methods." He went on to say that "I know nothing of the justification of these complains, but I do know that sooner or later, if they continue, they will reach the ears of the Commander-in-Chief [MacArthur] and if the same action is adopted as is usual in such cases it will probably not be favourable for you."[45]

Despite the warning, little changed, and it seems that a lot of the tension emanated as a result of the unsuitability of Jones to his command. He had come from GHQ and was firmly entrenched in the view that American methods were superior and that the Australians and British needed to buckle down. News of the discord at JOOTS soon made its way back to Blamey's headquarters, and at Adv LHQ it was decided that Jones was the problem. By now, the relationships at JOOTS had deteriorated to the point where Colonel Hope, who felt that he had been assigned a junior role at the school well below his rank and level of expertise, requested that he be sent back to the Middle East. For Berryman, Jones was "not all together suitable. . . . He has been trained as a staff officer, but appears to be academic and unable to handle his staff. . . . It is inevitable that there should be difficulties when a school is first established, but making allowances for this, I feel that under his [Jones's] direction the place will never be a success."[46]

Three days after Berryman made this observation to Blamey, Jones was replaced at JOOTS by Brig. Gen. Robert H. Van Volkenburgh (US Army).[47] In addition, Colonel Hope was transferred to the First Australian Army's amphibious training school at Toorbul Point. Interestingly, a few months later, Van Volkenburgh was requesting Hope's return to a senior position at the school, a proposition made difficult after GHQ had requested "his relief." However, by January 1943, GHQ seemed not to have held Hope at fault, and he was cleared to return on approval by Blamey. Meanwhile, Jones was returned to the United States and was retired from the US Army in 1944.[48]

With the arrival of Van Volkenburgh, relations at the school improved markedly. Van Volkenburgh had been selected to command the mixed US-Australian task force to occupy Buna in Operational Providence until the Japanese spoiled MacArthur's plans. An artillery officer by trade, Van Volkenburgh had been in the SWPA since March 1942 and was given command of the Allied antiaircraft artillery on arrival. This meant that he had considerable experience by mid-1942 working with the Australians. He noted that the Americans and Australians in his command "mixed pretty well" and that he made "very good . . . friends" among the Australians with whom he worked.[49]

Van Volkenburgh was, therefore, a much more suitable commander of a combined training school than Jones. In addition, he proved himself to be a much more proficient officer who was able to work constructively with the Australian and British officers. From this point onward, the focus became developing the curriculum and solving the mountain of problems in front the Allied amphibious forces in the SWPA. Soon after Van Volkenburgh took command, agreed methods were reached, and training was able to move forward. This in turn was particularly important, as the first formation to undergo training was the 41st US Infantry Division, then under the command of the First Australian Army, which would be responsible for the establishment of their "combined training program" utilizing the graduates of JOOTS at the First Australian Army CTS.

There were, however, still major problems at the beginning of 1943. The shortage of landing craft was acute, the desperate nature of which is underscored by the fact that JOOTS had only six small landing boats on hand until March 1943. Another key problem was that despite the fact that GHQ resolved to control amphibious doctrine and technique, the differences in US and British doctrine resulted in the schools altering training based on the nationality of each unit. When the Australians were in camp, they used the British *Combined Operations Doctrine 1942*. When the US units were under instruction, they used *FM 31: Landing Operations on a Hostile Shore 1941* (identical to USN FTP-167); *FM 31-5: Landing Operations on a Hostile Shore (Air Operations) 1941*; *Joint Action of the Army and Navy 1935* (USN FTP-155); and *Landing Operations Doctrine 1938* (USN FTP-167). This, of course, caused confusion and created friction, especially as the instruction at JOOTS on the staff courses was not purely based on one country's doctrine.

In addition, due to the shortages in equipment, specialized troops, and trained instructors, most of the training in 1942 was also substandard. Improvisation was thus the major feature, with ships' cargo nets hung over cliffs, the construction of simulated ramps and ships, and a heavy emphasis on dry-shod training. At every level, stopgap measures were being put in place. For example, to help JOOTS fulfill its mission, GHQ allocated a demonstration battalion that was originally sourced from the 32nd US Infantry Division. This unit had no specialized amphibious training, and as it was a combat unit, it was always going to be withdrawn from JOOTS after a short period of service to go to Papua. It was not until 15 November that the 19th Militia Battalion AMF took on the demonstration role and was dedicated to the task full time.[50] Moreover, initially much of the troop training was restricted in 1942 to training in small rubber or folding boats. Despite these difficulties, the high demand for amphibious training in the SWPA meant that the operations of JOOTS were expanded in November 1942 to included unit-level instruction in basic amphibious operations.[51]

Despite these difficulties, there were a number of achievements. The forward-looking and early approach to amphibious training, and the decision to establish the two schools despite the lack of equipment, meant that considerable time, effort, and energy was put into the development of the capability. This meant that the cycle of learning and adaption started early, and so both of the coalition partners were well placed when landing ships and craft started to arrive in sufficient numbers. In addition, a considerable number of officers and units had been exposed to at least preliminary training. While the number of officers and units trained and specialist courses run at JOOTS is unknown, at the Toorbul Point training center from August 1942 to March 1943 all the infantry battalions of the 41st US Infantry Division, three from the 32nd Division, and its divisional HQ troops were trained, as well as five Australian infantry battalions, two independent companies, the 2/7th Cavalry Regiment, two Australian field regiments, the 2/4th Armoured Regiment (AIF), along with divisional troops from the 3rd Australian Division. This amounted to some twenty thousand troops.[52]

Most of the training included liberal use of smoke, live ammunition, air support, and at times extended field exercises. At JOOTS, troops rotating through the amphibious school from November combined basic amphibious training with field craft and infantry tactics to extend their training programs. In addition, the training schools themselves developed into highly effective organizations. The training sections welded together as an effective team of US and Australian personnel from all three services that included the demonstration troops, staff and landing craft from HMAS *Assault*, RAAF meteorologists, an RAAF photography team, and RAAF air liaison officers, as well as personnel and aircraft from the Australian 5th Army Cooperation Squadron from RAAF Base Williamtown. JOOTS also included an experimental section under a Major Gilmore (Royal Australian Engineers) that worked on the development of beach matting, modified sleighs, and temporary piers. Meanwhile, HMAS *Assault* trained the crews of the landing craft for all three Australian LSIs as well as Toorbul Point.[53]

However, at the beginning of 1943, three major problems remained:

command and leadership, doctrine and landing technique, and the tyranny of distance. First, command and leadership problems were epitomized by the lack of joint command and centralized authority in amphibious warfare driven by GHQ's attempt to retain control of everything in the theater and MacArthur's cooperative approach to command. In amphibious warfare, this was causing major problems in terms of responsibility, authority, and the allocation of tasks between the army and navy. To give just one example, it was not until 19 November 1942, some four months after JOOTS started operations and three and a half months since HMAS *Assault* was established, that a liaison officer was put in place to coordinate the operations of both establishments.[54]

The second major problem, the development of a common doctrine and defined landing technique, was exacerbated by the lack of a unified command. In 1942, doctrine was divided by nationality, and no one had the authority to take the lead in the development of a landing technique related to the strategic and geographic circumstances of the theater, the operational intentions of the C-in-C, and the equipment available. The third major problem was the tyranny of distance in SWPA. Port Stephens had been selected as the major training establishment "because of the excellent natural features available at that location," but by October 1942, "eight of the eleven Infantry Regiments (or Australian Brigades) which had been designated for training in overseas operations were in New Guinea. The other three regiments are now in Rockhampton." Thus, the location of JOOTS was "far removed from the location of the troops which are to be trained."[55]

SEVENTH AMPHIBIOUS FORCE

The first of these problems, command and control, was solved with the arrival of Rear Adm. Daniel E. Barbey and VII Phib in late December 1942.[56] Barbey was an outstanding choice for his command. He had considerable experience in amphibious warfare, having worked on the issue with the USMC in the interwar period. Most recently, he had been on Admiral King's staff in the amphibious warfare section testing and developing the new landing ships and craft. US naval historian Samuel Eliot Morison described his appointment as a "Christmas gift for MacArthur."[57] While experienced and hardworking, at first Barbey was not universally respected. Col. Arthur G. Trudeau, an engineering officer in the US Army, noted "that he lacks drive and I would never classify him as an advanced thinker. That the entire picture of amphibious operations is still in a muddle mess is no tribute to Barbey."[58] Trudeau's assessment may well have been influenced by the competition between the USN and the US Army over the latter's amphibious engineers. However, Barbey soon established himself as one of the true aficionados of amphibious warfare in World War II. Most significantly Barbey, like Kenney, developed a close rapport with MacArthur, and through his progressive thinking, adaptability, and impressive control of his command, he became, along with Adm. Bull Halsey, was one of the very few USN officers MacArthur ever esteemed.[59]

While Barbey's arrival started with a fight for control with GHQ, eventually MacArthur relented. GHQ then set up VII Phib to report directly to GHQ for operational control (rather than through the Seventh Fleet), and Barbey was given command of all amphibious training and forces allocated to the SWPA.[60] However, not everyone was happy with Barbey assuming control. While the move caused resentment among some of the staff at GHQ and upset Van Volkenburgh, as it meant that he would be superseded as CO of JOOTS, it was outright opposed by the Australians.[61]

With the arrival of VII Phib, the Australians felt they were being pushed out and that their ability to influence the development of amphibious warfare in the theater would be severely limited. Therefore, Blamey made a play to separate the Australians out of this new command arrangement and established their own combined operations command that would liaise with VII Phib when required but remain outside of Barbey's command.[62] This was obviously an intuitive response to the problems at JOOTS, with amphibious training in 1942, and the US-Australian relationship more generally, but it spelled disaster for the future of a unified command structure.

Fortunately, Barbey responded vigorously, and GHQ backed its new amphibious commander, whereby Blamey had no option but to relent.[63] As a concession, Barbey realized that it would be critical to include Australians on this staff and for a close bond to develop with the Australians at both the training and operational levels. A number of Australian officers were attached to Barbey's HQ, the most import of them being Brig. Ronald Hopkins, formerly BGS of Adv NGF. Hopkins would play a central role in Barbey's HQ, commanding one of his two planning cells in 1943 and 1944 and earning himself the US Legion of Merit award for exceptionally meritorious conduct, "judgment, industry, and high professional military skill" with VII Phib.[64] In the end, Barbey's insistence with both GHQ and the Australians for a centralized command structure was absolutely essential in professionalizing the training and conduct of amphibious operations.

DOCTRINE AND LANDING TECHNIQUE

Once the issue of command and control was sorted out, Barbey faced the fundamental problem of bringing together two separate nations into one system of amphibious warfare. While he was never able to create a seamless approach to amphibious warfare by the US and Australian militaries, Barbey was able to weld together a highly successful team built around the principles of innovation and adaptation that made the best possible use of the people, tools, and doctrine available to VII Phib.

The first thing Barbey did was move to take over amphibious warfare training.[65] JOOTS and Toorbul Point were brought under a single Amphibious Training Group (ATG) under a USN officer, Capt. J. W. "Red" Jamison, "who had had considerable experience in amphibious training in the Atlantic and who had served as beachmaster during the North African Landings."[66] This ATG was to establish amphibious training centers (ATCs) at both Port Stephens and Toorbul Point to take over from the existing schools. Almost immediately, Barbey and Jamison also brought in additional instructors from the USN, the USMC, and the US Army. In addition, they also received the welcome boost of a cadre of officers from the 9th Australian Division (AIF) who had returned from the Middle East having been trained at the British Combined Operations School in Egypt.[67] Almost all of these US and Australian officers were combat veterans, many with experience of amphibious operations in the Mediterranean or at Guadalcanal.[68]

Barbey initially moved to standardize doctrine on USN FTP 167 as he was insistent that if Australian troops were to be aboard American vessels, then "they must follow the entire American technique."[69] This he saw as a relatively smooth transition related by the fact that, in his view, there was "little difference in the two techniques [British and American] and they were readily integrated into the training program."[70] The only problems he noted were "a few differences in communication procedures [that] cropped up and caused minor problems."[71] He did, however, provide some concessions, such as allowing the Australians to use British doctrine where it did not impede on the US landing techniques.

Barbey's assessment in relation to the two countries' doctrine was based on the type of landings that the USN had undertaken in the Mediterranean and at Guadalcanal. Here there is little to argue with Barbey's assessment. However, the direction of USN landing doctrine in the interwar period, and especially as it was developing in the Central Pacific, meant that it was on a highly divergent path from the SWPA in 1943 and 1944. The two key factors in this divergence were geography and equipment. In the Central Pacific, the USN, the USMC, and the US Army faced a terrain dominated by small atolls. To successfully assault these features, the USN needed to provide for deep-strike operations enabled by their large fleet aircraft carriers. The carriers would enable the approach and the ability to seal off an operational area to allow for a direct frontal assault against the heavily defended atolls.[72]

Thus, in the Central Pacific, the USMC-USN amphibious approach focused on direct frontal assaults emphasizing massive firepower and daylight landings, due to the heavy dependence on naval gunfire and air support. This was all enabled by the exceptionally large size of the USN fleet in the Central Pacific and the use of a large number of aircraft carriers, battleships, cruisers, and large amphibious ships.[73] In the USMC-USN amphibious approach, operational surprise was an objective, but tactical surprise was not a necessity, and night landings were rejected, except for reconnaissance.[74]

In the SWPA, however, geography was dominated not by island atolls but rather by New Guinea—the second largest island in the world—which Samuel Eliot Morison described as that "half bird and half reptile . . . prehistoric monster"[75] of an island to Australia's north. This meant that the fighting in the SWPA during 1942–1944 was "characterized by fewer naval engagements but much larger land operations than that in the Solomons" or in the Central Pacific.[76] Airpower was mainly land-based, as the USN did not trust MacArthur with its fleet carriers, and the geography meant there was considerably less sea room for large aircraft carriers, battleships, and fleets to operate.

This restricted the ability of the SWPA to project its force and meant that MacArthur would focus on an indirect approach to amphibious landings, in particular landings where there was no enemy opposition. MacArthur's preeminent weapon, therefore, was his USAAF and RAAF land-based airpower. He needed to exploit this powerful weapon to the full so that it would enable his amphibious troops to assault key geographical features, hopefully bypassing key Japanese bases and forces in the process. His air force operations against Japanese airpower and bases in the region would be the catalyst for his naval power to land his army to seize advanced bases and airfields. For MacArthur, "command of the air gave command of the sea which gave initiative and control of the ground," providing both a clear edge to the Allied forces in logistics, as well as "unrivalled strategic mobility."[77]

In addition, as the SWPA was very low in the priority allocation of resources, Barbey had to modify standing USN doctrine to account for a force based mainly around smaller landing ships and craft (LSTs, LCTs, LCIs, LCMs, and LVCPs), with little support from APAs. Thus, FTP 167 was not a suitable solution, and a new, hybrid doctrine suited to the conditions of the SWPA was required. Barbey therefore charged Captain Jamison and his coalition staff at the newly created ATC at Port Stephens (the old JOOTS) with "developing this new and untried technique."[78] This approach combined the best and most relevant features of British and USN doctrine and was developed and formalized through the establishment of standard operating procedures (SOPs) for VII Phib—for example, the adoption on 31 August 1943 of the SOP for boat teams in small boats developed by the ATC.[79] This new doctrinal approach was an unqualified coalition success story.

In addition to developing new doctrine and landing techniques, the Port Stephens ATC was expanded to run specialist programs on communications, navigation, reconnaissance, logistics, and shore parties. The major instructors of each of these courses and their various components were a combination of Australian and US personnel who worked together in a cooperative, interservice coalition environment. Alterations were also made to unit-level training, and now during the rehearsal and exercise phases of instruction, regimental officers and NCOs from the combat units were paired with naval officers and NCOs down through the ranks. After the rehearsals and training exercises, a debriefing and critique was provided by both army and navy officers, which was deemed "very effective."[80]

MOBILE TRAINING SCHOOLS

The third major problem was the tyranny of distance. The problem of suitable training grounds in Australia and the movement and location of combat troops was a topic of discussion at all senior headquarters shortly after the decision to establish the amphibious warfare schools at Port Stephens and Toorbul Point. After numerous reports and inquiries into alterative locations, in December 1942 MacArthur resolved that

JOOTS and HMAS *Assault* and Toorbul Point would all remain in place. However, the soon-to-arrive 2nd ESB would be located in far northern Queensland at Rockhampton and Cairns (much closer to the Australian training grounds and the operational areas of the theater), and JOOTS would raise three mobile training teams with the necessary boats, ships, and landing craft to be attached to forward divisional headquarters to train formations in situ.[81]

Once VII Phib took over amphibious training, the development of the mobile training teams became the responsibility of the new ATG. In addition, VII Phib also took on the task of reviewing the findings of the Hope-Cook Report. Like GHQ before it, VII Phib found that Port Stephens and Toorbul Point were the only suitable locations along the whole of the Australian eastern seaboard. In all of these reports, it was noted that Toorbul Point was far from ideal. In particular, while it

> provided a sheltered anchorage for landing craft, the area was narrow and ocean-going assault ships could not approach the site; there were sand bars between the site and Bribie island; and there was no sheltered beach close to the camp that was usable at all stages of the tide for training (although there were such beaches on Bribie Island). . . . [In addition] . . . the only hinterland terrain type was dead flat and covered in thick scrub. As a result . . . Toorbul Point [was] unsuitable for actually embarking troops for an expedition or carrying out final rehearsals in comparative secrecy.[82]

Barbey eventually decided that Port Stephens was just too far away, and in June 1943 the decision was made to move the school and staff there forward to Toorbul Point in October. In addition to these reforms, a new ATC was established in June 1943 at Cairns where the 2nd ESB was located and put under the command of Capt. P. A. Stevens (USN).[83] Distance continued to be an issue as the battlefront moved forward rapidly in 1943 and 1944, and the main ATC was moved from Toorbul Point to Milne Bay on 26 January 1944 and from there to Luzon in the Philippines in June 1945. By 1945, VII Phib's ATG Group had expanded in size so much that Rear Adm. J. L. Hall Jr. (USN), commander of Amphibious Group 12, reported for duty to Barbey as the new commander of the ATG, which was in full swing training Allied units and formations for the planned invasion of Japan.

The major development in overcoming the tyranny of distance in the SWPA was the decision in late 1942 to establish the mobile training teams. Based along the original two-thirds/one-third split of resources for amphibious training, JOOTS had proposed the development of three mobile training units, two under the command of US Army officers and one under the command of an Australian Army officer. This plan was eventually followed through by VII Phib's ATG based on the new SWPA hybrid doctrine. Most significantly, the training teams were allocated to SWPA units and formations based on availability and need rather than nationality. As such, the Third Mobile Trailing Team under Maj. C. L. Woodcliff (US Army) trained the 6th, 7th and 9th Australian Divisions in Cairns during 1944, while the 1st Mobile Trailing Team, under Lt. Col. C. T. Barton (AIF), trained the 33rd, 40th, and 43rd Infantry US Divisions, as well as the 112th US Cavalry Regiment and 6th Ranger battalion in New Guinea and New Britain in 1943 and 1944.[84]

VII PHIB AND US–AUSTRALIAN RELATIONS

One of the key factors in the development of amphibious warfare capability in the SWPA was the high level of cooperation between US and Australian personnel, especially after the arrival of VII Phib. Both Barbey and the CO of the ATG in 1943, Captain Jamison, were particularly complimentary about working with their Australian counterparts. Capt. J. Louis Landenbeger (USN), one of Barbey's key staff officers at his VII Phib HQ, who was "very closely associated with the training operations at Port Stephens, Toorbul Bay and other places," noted that the "comradeship between the Australians and the 7th Amphibious Force was most cordial at all times." He also noted that "I am convinced that this period of training was well worth while."[85] Another of Barbey's staff officers, Royce N. Flippin, was also attached to JOOTS. In his view,

> Capt Jamison was ideally fitted for CO of the base. He was very popular with Australian officers as well as our own, with the result that we had an unusually harmonious relationship with each other. With Army, Navy and Air Corps officers from the two countries working together, frictions understandably might have developed; but, as a result of Capt Jamison's tact, good nature and excellent leadership, we had a very happy ship. Our relationship with the battalion of Aussie Army troops stationed at Nelson's Bay was equally pleasant. The officers and men of the small boat Maintenance group [HMAS *Assault*] stationed at Nelson's were of inestimable value. . . . Here

again the finest spirit of co-operation existed. . . . [They] proved themselves worthy of the highest traditions of the naval service.[86]

Soon after the arrival of VII Phib, another US officer, Lt. Cdr. Walter Wemyss, was made CO of the landing craft unit and officer in charge of all US forces at Toorbul Point (they soon came under the command of Jamison at Port Stephens in early 1944). At Toorbul, he worked closely with his RAN counterpart, Lt. Jack Bank (RANR), the navy base commander. Wemyss noted that "Jack and I became fast friends and he did everything in the world to help [the USN]." Lt. Col. Alfred Rose (AIF) ran the training school at Toorbul, with the USN personnel under Wemyss operating the Higgins boats (LVCP), a number of which were crewed by RAN personnel.[87] Bank ran the communications and administration of the base. Wemyss noted that Toorbul started with only forty staff when he arrived but soon had over a thousand personnel, further noting that they labored "day and night under the direction of the Australian General Army staff" to prepare troops of the US 32nd and 41st Infantry Divisions and the 6th, 7th and 9th Australian Divisions for amphibious warfare.[88]

Lt. Cdr. William Swan (RAN) served at JOOTS in Port Stephens while he was the training officer aboard HMAS *Westralia*. Early on, *Westralia* acted as the accommodation and depot ship for HMAS *Assault*, and Swan played a critical role in the training of the landing craft crews as well as supporting the staff and training at JOOTS/ATC. He remembered his training time at Port Stephens and his vast operational experience in amphibious landings as services that were "a great privilege to have rendered . . . to the United States, to the SWPA command and to the Allies."[89] He was so impressed by his time with VII Phib that as a regular navy officer after the war, he "encouraged the closest co-operation with the USN."[90]

Swan's views were widespread among the RAN's amphibious warfare specialists. Sub-Lt. Ronald Penglase, also of HMAS *Westralia*, noted that "we had no trouble with [the American naval personnel], they were good. They were very thoughtful people, they knew what was going on."[91] Arthur Le Page, a midshipman on *Westralia*'s sister ship HMAS *Manoora*, trained with both US Marines in Melbourne and US Army troops at the ATC and thought they troops "were an extremely great bunch of soldiers."[92]

Of course, intercultural communication was not always smooth. Able Seaman Bryan Wearne (RAN), who was also serving on *Westralia* at Port Stephens at this time, noted that during the training he

never made a friendship with any of them [US soldiers or sail-
ors]. . . . We only used them for the purpose to see what we could
get out of them, cigarettes mainly. . . . When you had a barge load
of Americans you know you were more concerned about what you
were doing than fraternising with them to that extent. No, pretty
impersonal I think our relationship would be. . . . They were camped
away from us anyway.[93]

This, of course, did not mean that Able Seaman Wearne did not find
time to fraternize outside of training, noting that "we used to get into
a few brawls with the Yanks, yeah quite a few brawls with the Yanks."
When asked "what would instigate those brawls?" he noted that it was
"the fact that they were Yanks." He went on to qualify his interest in
trans-Pacific boxing at local hotels around the Newcastle area in 1943
with the following statement: "As I've said to my young grandchildren,
'Take no notice of what your grandpa says, [but] just remember this, if
it hadn't been for the Americans, you'd be speaking Japanese. Don't ever
forget it. . . . No matter how much we knock them, just remember that
you'd be speaking Japanese if it wasn't for the Americans. And that's a
fact.'"[94]

By 1943, VII Phib and the ATG were a fine example of Allied cooperation undertaken in the most stressful of circumstances. Despite some
strains, all of the amphibious warfare activities were enormously successful and were undertaken with the minimum of equipment during the
development of a new doctrine with army, navy, and air force personnel
from two systems and three countries. Moreover, it was done—at least,
almost—in the spirit of total cooperation, according to Able Seaman
Wearne. Despite the tensions that were to develop in 1944–1945 in the
US-led coalition in the SWPA, in the area of amphibious warfare the command structure and systems put in place by the VII Phib led to high levels
of coalition cooperation. This occurred from 1943 all the way through
to the end of the war and included the full integration of RAN ships and
Australian sailors and soldiers into the VII Phib in both training and
operations. In addition, there was outstanding cooperation between the
Americans and Australians in terms of the conduct of joint amphibious
operations in New Guinea in 1943 and in Borneo in 1945.

Part 4

The New Guinea Campaign,
1943

IO

Victory and Discord

The Battle for Salamaua

THE DNA OF THE SALAMAUA OPERATION lies in the victory that the Australians secured at Wau in February 1943 and the plan for the capture of the main Japanese base in New Guinea at Lae (Operation Postern). With the defeat of the offensive against Wau, by 1 March 1943 the Japanese had largely withdrawn from the Mubo Valley. During April and May, the 17th Brigade AIF had been protecting the approaches to the Bulolo Valley and preparing for an offensive to drive the Japanese back on Salamaua.

This was easier said than done. The Bitoi River to the south and the Francisco River to the north dominated the terrain between Mubo and Salamaua. To the south, the Bitoi River created precipitous gorges that ran to within a mile of the coast and were surrounded by a series of exceptionally steep ridgelines and features. To the west, the main geographical features were Observation Hill, Bobdubi Ridge, Old Vickers, and Kunai Spur. To the south, there was Lababia Ridge, Green Hill, Bitoi Ridge, Mount Tambu, Davidson Ridge, Roosevelt Ridge, and Scout Ridge. Between them, they covered the western and southern approaches to Salamaua, and thus the battle for the town was to be dominated by the fights to secure these vital pieces of terrain.[1]

In order to ensure the defense of Wau and to provide adequate forces for the conduct of offensive operations, Lt. Gen. Iven Mackay (GOC NGF) wrote to Blamey and argued that a two-brigade division was required for the task. Blamey concurred and alerted HQ 3rd Australian Division for a move to the area to command the Wau sector. Maj. Gen. Stanley Savige arrived in Port Moresby with his staff on 24 March 1943 to get his orders before moving to Wau to take command. In his division, Savige would have the 17th Brigade AIF (2/5th, 2/6th, 2/7th Battalions), the 2/3rd and 2/7th Independent Companies, and the 24th Militia Battalion (15th Brigade). The 15th Brigade HQ and the 58/59th Militia Battalion and supporting units would be added to the division in late May. By this time, NGF consisted of Savige's 3rd Australian Division, the 11th

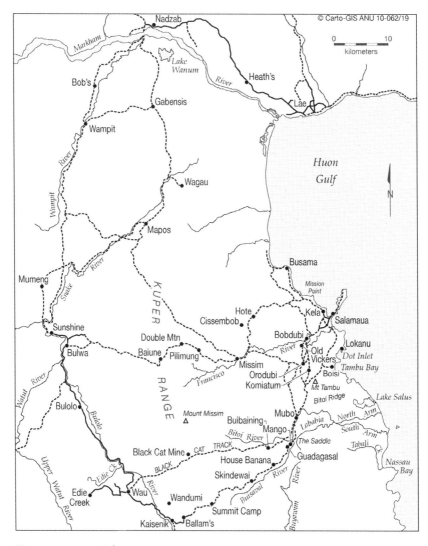

Figure 10.1 Lae-Salamaua Front, 1943

Australian Division securing Port Moresby, 5th Australian Division defending Milne Bay, the 41st US Infantry Division securing and developing
the Buna-Oro Bay area, and the 2/7th Independent Company operating in
the central highlands.[2] Merauke Force (11th Brigade), defending the vital
airstrip on the southern coast of New Guinea, was under the command
of the First Australian Army.[3]

In order to prepare for offensive operations toward Salamaua and to
protect the Bulolo Valley, the 3rd Australian Division undertook an active

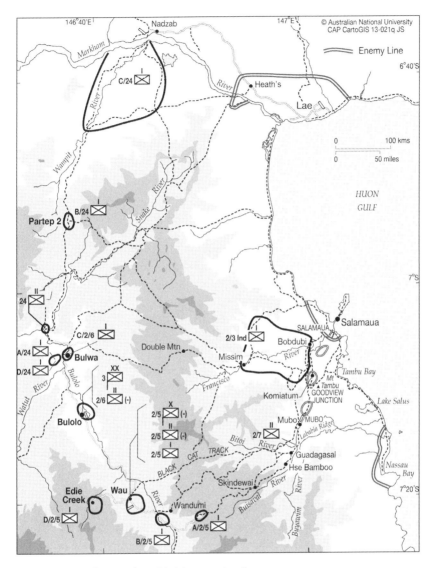

Figure 10.2 3rd Australian Division, 30 April 1943

defense and a small number of limited offensive operations, the most significant being the 2/7th Battalion's costly assaults on a key feature known as the Pimple. These attacks were largely a failure and highlighted the futility of frontal assaults with limited fire support against entrenched Japanese positions on the ridgelines. By June, the planning for a large-scale offensive had begun. This was based around the 17th Brigade, located around Lababia Ridge in the southeast, and the 15th Brigade, in the west near Bobdubi Ridge. One of the keys to the success of this offensive was an amphibious landing at Nassau Bay to provide a base for future operations and a sea line of communication to supply the 3rd Division, which up to this time was still dependent on supplies being flow into Wau and then moved forward over the rugged mountain tracks by a limited number of native carriers.[4]

THE SALAMAUA DECEPTION

The concept of operations for the assault on New Guinea from Papua had been months in development. Blamey and Berryman had been discussing the operation to take Salamaua and Lae since October and November 1942.[5] In the end, while it would take some eleven months from the point of conception to completion and involve thousands of hours of planning and preparation, Blamey's concept for Salamaua was relatively simple. As the town was situated to the south of the main Japanese base Lae and had been used as a forward base by the Japanese, they would be compelled to defend it. Blamey therefore proposed that the 3rd Division would close in on Salamaua, drawing as many Japanese forces down from Lae as possible. This operation would serve as a mask for his real objective, the double envelopment of Lae from the air and sea. NGF and Savige's operations in front of Salamaua were, therefore, one big deception operation—a magnet to draw in the Japanese. NGF was advised that although it was to start a steady advance against this objective using Savige's 3rd Division, the town was not to be captured until after the landing at Lae.

Blamey had tasked his senior operations officer, General Berryman, with the planning and organization of the assault on Lae and the Huon Peninsula. On 17 May 1943, Berryman outlined the concept to Herring, who would soon take over NGF from Mackay. In particular, Berryman noted to Herring that NGF's role would be concentrated on the Salamaua operation and the preparation of the base areas in Papua and New Guinea for the coming offensives. A special staff under Berryman's control would handle the operational planning of the assault on Lae, while tactical planning was to be devolved to the two Australian division commanders who would conduct the double envelopment of the town.[6]

During Berryman's early planning for the assault on Lae, and after consulting with the assistant CoS at GHQ, it became apparent that the US Army's 2nd ESB did not have the range to transport the 9th Division from the current bases in Papua to their landing beaches outside Lae.[7]

Berryman thus proposed that an "an area about" Nassau Bay was required, and Blamey took this to MacArthur. Such an operation would not
only serve as a forward operating base for the 9th Division but also have
the benefit of opening up a sea line of communication to the 3rd Division,
greatly relieving its supply situation. In addition, Berryman believed that
"the capture of Nassau Bay at such a time . . . will cause the enemy to
send troops south just before the attack [on Lae] is launched."[8]

MacArthur agreed to the proposal for an amphibious operation at
Nassau Bay and granted Blamey permission to use a regiment from the
US 41st Division as the assault force. MacArthur was particularly happy,
as this operation would help to relieve the pressure he was feeling from
the JCS and Admiral King (CNO) over the apparent lack of progress in
the SWPA. The planned landing date of 30 June would coincide with
phase 1 of Cartwheel, the landing of Alamo Force elements on Woodlark
and Kiriwina Islands by Barbey's VII Phib.[9]

The landing at Nassau Bay would also be a combat landing, as opposed to the Woodlark and Kiriwina landings. The latter were more of
an amphibious exercise, given that both islands were undefended. Alamo
Force would "storm ashore" to be met by a small number of Australian
units who had been on the islands for many months, as well as by their
own advance party that had been in place since 23 June. Blamey had
vigorously opposed the landings at Woodlark and Kiriwina and called
the operation "one of the jokes of the war."[10] As Admiral Barbey noted,
the landings provided "no experience . . . in defending against bomber
attack or in landing troops against opposition ashore."[11] As Blamey predicted, the plan to establish airfields on these two islands never provided
the type of return on investment that such a major amphibious landing warranted.[12] The chief outcome of the landing was a chance for VII
Phib and the SWPA to undertake their first-ever major amphibious operations, to draw lessons from the experience, and to begin refining their
techniques.[13]

Like its umbrella operation, the plan for the landing at Nassau Bay was
relatively simple in conception but difficult in execution. Col. Archibald
MacKechnie was to form a task force, in his own name, consisting of
the 1st Battalion, 162nd Infantry Regiment (1/162nd), the 218th Field
Artillery Battalion (FAB), and a series of attachments of engineers, signalers, logistics, and antiaircraft units, as well as two companies of the
532nd Boat and Shore Regiment (2nd ESB) and A Company, Papuan
Infantry Battalion (PIB). MacKechnie Force was tasked with the mission to "proceed by water from its present assembly areas (Morobe) on

night D–1 and land on the Nassau Bay beach . . . secure the beach . . . destroy enemy forces in the Nassau Bay–Duali area and prepare to push inland."[14]

To support MacKechnie Force, a beach party was to be provided by the 2/6th battalion AIF while D Company from the same battalion would also launch a diversion on the track leading inland from Duali. Upon landing, MacKechnie Force would come under command of the 17th Australian Infantry Brigade (Brig. Murray Moten), while the beach party of the 2/6th Battalion would temporarily come under MacKechnie's command.[15] Moten made clear his requirements for MacKechnie Force, and it seems that the substance of the concept for, and planning of, the landing had mainly emanated from him.[16] On 15 June, at a conference at the Summit near Wau, attended by Berryman, Herring, Savige, Lt. Col. John Wilton (the senior staff officer of the 3rd Division), MacKechnie, and Col. K. S. Sweeny (CoS, 41st Division), it had been Moten who outlined the details of the plan, as opposed to Savige and his staff, who had overall command of the operation and by rights should have chaired the conference and detailed the plan.[17]

Moten detailed that MacKechnie move inland to Napier no later than D+3 and that they commence their move onto Bitoi Ridge on D+5 as part of the 3rd Division's offensive against the approaches to Salamaua. At this time, the 2/6th Battalion would assault Observation Hill, and from here the enemy in Mubo would be "encircled and destroyed." Thereafter, a second Australian battalion (2/5th) would advance and secure the area around Goodview Junction and Mount Tambu.[18]

41ST DIVISION AND 162ND INFANTRY REGIMENT

The key US unit to take part in this operation was the 41st Infantry Division. Originally named the "Sunset Division," after its red and orange shoulder patch, the men of the formation would rename themselves the "Jungleers" after their experiences in Papua and New Guinea. By the end of the war they were to claim more months of jungle combat than any other US Army division.[19] The division had been activated for World War I in 1917 and later reactivated as part of the National Guard in 1921. Originally consisting of the 161st through 164th Infantry Regiments, in 1925 the 164th was swapped for the 186th Regiment, making the division recruitment area based in the northwestern states of Idaho, Montana, Orgeon, Washington, and Wyoming. It was one of the first divisions federalized in 1940, after which it was turned into a triangular division when the 161st became a separate regimental combat team. It was the first complete US division to arrive in Australia in April and May 1942. As detailed in chapter 7, the 163rd Regiment saw service at Sanananda.[20]

For the Salamaua operations, MacKechnie Force—and later, Coane Force—was built around the 162nd Infantry Regiment, as well as the division's artillery, engineer, and logistics units. The 162nd had relieved the 163rd at Buna-Sanananda before starting to leapfrog its way up the coast to Morobe in late February and March 1943.[21] During this period, the regiment had the opportunity to work with members of the PIB and to conduct patrols in their operational areas and acclimatize. It also meant, however, exposure to disease and operational conditions that would reduce some of the regiment's units by up to two-thirds before they saw major action.[22]

Unlike the 32nd Division, which entered combat with no jungle warfare training, the 41st Division's troops had time to conduct extensive training and absorb the lessons from Papua. However, each campaign was different, and Colonel MacKechnie noted that his regiment's training was largely based on lessons from the Malaya campaign, where the Japanese were on the offensive, and from Buna and Sanananda, where the Japanese were in their final defensive positions in low, flat swampy terrain with their backs to the sea.[23] By contrast, the operations in front of Salamaua would involve extensive patrolling, long marches, and fighting mostly undertaken on steep ridges and against positions dug into hillsides in exceptionally rugged terrain.[24] In the forthcoming campaign, the key personnel and commanders involved would be the 162nd's commander, MacKechnie; the commanding general of the 41st Division, Maj. Gen. Horace Fuller; Brig. Gen. Ralph Coane, who would be given command of a second task force; and Maj. Archibald B. Roosevelt, CO of the 3rd Battalion, 162nd Regiment (3/162nd).

SALAMAUA: THE COMMAND CONTEXT

The key factors shaping the coalition of the United States and Australia in the SWPA in this campaign were the same as those that had been in place before the beachheads operation. Given that the relationship was one created in the haste of wartime and that there was a lack of common doctrine and planning for long-term integration, the level of "interoperability" (to use a modern term) remained relatively low. Given the command culture and organizational structures that continued in 1943, the key factors remained: training, combat experience, competency of units and commanders, and the capabilities and personalities of senior officers and their staff.

Like at the beachheads, MacArthur's insistence on cooperative command meant a reliance on individual commanders' abilities to collaborate, and once again this was to have a major impact on the conduct of operations. At the tactical level this was to be compounded by a lack of continuity in units and their commanders. As noted, Eichelberger was in a MacArthur-imposed exile and thus removed from the command chain. Herring provided some continuity in terms of his continued command of the main operational corps (NGF), but his limitations as a commander had been laid bare at the beachheads. He had learned some complex lessons from that operation, especially in terms of his relationship with senior US commanders. Into the fragile mix came two new divisions, the Australian 3rd and the US 41st Infantry, two new divisional commanders, Fuller and Savige, and a whole range of new regimental/brigade and battalion commanders and their staffs.

For the Americans, the commander of the 41st Division was General Fuller. He has been described as "efficient, stubborn, chain-smoking and respected,"[25] and it seems that he developed a strong rapport with Herring, who called Fuller "a charming fellow, most cooperative in every way."[26] The feeling was mutual, with Fuller noting that Herring appreciated "the problems that faced my troops . . . and has been responsible in great part for the reasons for the success of our activity."[27]

However, to a number of other Australian officers, Fuller was not regarded as either overly cooperative or an overly competent commander, and Savige described him at an early planning meeting as a "dour looking fellow without humor."[28] His role in the Salamaua operation was limited but influential, particularly in command issues and in the attitude of the officers in his division who were called upon to cooperate closely with the Australians. The remainder of Fuller's career is also somewhat controversial. MacArthur had promised to promote him to corps command when Eichelberger was given an army command after the Hollandia operation in 1944, but he soon went out of favor, and after his failure at Biak, Fuller was relieved of his command of the 41st Division.[29]

Col. Jens Doe's 163rd Infantry Regiment (41st Division) had been depleted in the final battles for Sanananda and in the mopping-up and occupation of the beachheads area and thus was not involved at Salamaua.

Nor was Maj. Gen. George Vasey, who was back in Queensland with his 7th Division, training and preparing plans for the landing at Nadzab as part of Operation Postern. Blamey and Berryman were also in Brisbane, as was the staff of Adv GHQ. This meant that the only continuity at the tactical level in this operation from the last campaign was Herring and the commander of Advance Echelon Fifth Air Force, Maj. Gen. Ennis Whitehead.

As the 41st Division was to provide one regimental combat team and its artillery units, the two key US officers were Col. Archibald MacKechnie (162nd Regiment) and Brig. Gen. Ralph Coane. MacKechnie was initially viewed by the Australians as too old for jungle warfare and the rigors of modern campaigning. However, his reputation was to grow throughout the operation, and by its conclusion the Australian commanders viewed him as a trusted and respected commander.[30]

General Coane was much more controversial and would be relieved of his command by General Savige. Coane had joined the US Army in 1918 for World War I and was discharged into the National Guard at the end of the war. Serving throughout the interwar period as an artillery officer, he was made a brigadier general in March 1942 and made artillery commander of the 41st Division. He would serve in the unit until 1944, when he was wounded in action and returned to the United States.[31]

On the Australian side, the two key tactical officers were Maj. Gen. Stanley Savige and Brig. Murray Moten. Savige, a Gallipoli and Western Front veteran of World War I, had served in the militia throughout the interwar period and been given command of the 17th Brigade AIF in 1939. He commanded the brigade at Bardia and Tobruk amid controversy. Questions were raised as to his performance at Bardia, and he came in for heavy criticism from Vasey, Berryman, and Brig. Horace Robertson in the Middle East. These were all senior regular army officers, a factor that helped to drive the antipathy that was often felt between some regular and militia officers in the Australian Army.[32]

As a result, Savige became rather defensive in his command style, but he performed well in the abortive Greek campaign, while again courting controversy over his command performance in Syria. At the start of the Pacific War, it was argued that Savige, one of Blamey's close confidants, was overpromoted and that his command of the 3rd Division was as a result of his personal relationship with Blamey.[33] Personally brave but "a bit old womanly,"[34] he was known to look after the welfare of his troops, although his tactical acumen was often questioned. His tenure in command throughout the war was controversial, with many claiming he was overly reliant on his regular army staff officers and that the majority of his successes were a consequence of his subordinate commanders' abilities.[35]

The most significant senior officer dispute in this operation was, however, an all-Australian one: between Herring as GOC NGF and Savige as GOC 3rd Division. Herring and Savige had served together in the 6th Division in North Africa, where they developed an acrimonious relationship. This meant that relations when Herring returned to New Guinea in May 1943 were strained, and by August they had broken down completely. The difficulties in this connection were mirrored in Herring's dealings with Arthur "Tubby" Allen during the Papua campaign. Herring had effectively ended Allen's career at Kokoda, and now his attention had turned to Savige.[36] During the campaign, the relationship between 3rd Division HQ and NGF got so bad that Savige regarded 3rd Division's enemies as "1—NGF, 2—terrain, 3—weather, 4—supplies, 5—Japs."[37] The poor rapport was also not just between the two commanders, with Herring's staff also coming in for considerable criticism from the 3rd Division. Herring's DA&QMG, Lt. Col. Rudolf Bierworth, was particularly contentious.[38] To make matters worse, the poor relationship between the two HQs was well known throughout New Guinea, and many Australian officers in subordinate units were actively taking positions in support of, or in opposition to, the two commanders.[39]

The result of these tensions was that the Australian Army's internal divisions fueled many of the command issues that would flair up to an intense state and dysfunctional level. This meant that just as GHQ was beset with personality issues and divisions that affected the relationship with the Australians during the Papua campaign, during the battle for Salamaua the internal divisions between the senior Australian officers, in particular Herring and Savige, were to affect the relationship between the US and Australian commanders. As Brigadier Moten, commander of the 17th Brigade, noted of his high command, "Herring, Berryman and Savige didn't like one another and I was the cat's paw."[40] Added to this volatile command relationship was MacArthur's continual insistence on interfering in operations down to the lowest tactical level and the merry-go-round of cultural, doctrinal, and personality clashes that continued to dominate the upper echelons of the SWPA command, especially between GHQ and Adv LHQ. These factors supercharged many of the same friction points that had developed in the early part of the battles at Sanananda and Buna.

MACKECHNIE FORCE: THE INITIAL LANDING

After only one incomplete rehearsal with the 2nd ESB, MacKechnie Force was landed at Nassau Bay in the early hours of 30 June 1943. The approach to the landing site had been difficult, with rough seas, poor visibility, and heavy, driving rain.[41] Navigation issues meant that the assault force, consisting of 29 LCVPs and three LCMs escorted by three USN patrol boats, overshot the landing site and had to turn around, creating chaos in their landing formation. On approach to the beach, they encountered rough conditions with waves of up to ten to twelve feet. During the landing, the second wave cut across the first, causing a number of near collisions. The heavy seas meant that only eighteen landing craft made it ashore (eleven turned back), all bar one were wrecked, and the remainder were stranded on the beach.[42] Luckily, there were no losses of personnel, but three different types of radios were submerged and rendered useless, and only one radio set was in operation. Only one LCM made it ashore, and much of the equipment from the other two was lost.

Despite the problems at the landing, some 740 personnel, including A and B Companies from Lt. Col. Harold Taylor's 1st Battalion, 162nd Regiment (1/162nd), were put ashore. Both of these companies quickly fanned out to the north and south to cover the landing site after linking up with the Australian platoon covering the landing.[43] Despite the chaotic arrival, it was acknowledged that, given the conditions, "it was a great effort on the part of the troops and the inexperienced navigators in the landing craft, that they ever managed to reach the beach in one piece."[44]

Tactically, things did not go as expected. The Australian diversion operation failed to contact the enemy, and the covering platoon had arrived at the beachhead late, forgotten to put out one set of landing lights, and according to the 162nd, "they knew nothing of the enemy situation and were unable to furnish guides who knew anything about the beach area."[45] However, Japanese resistance was only sporadic. Although they probed the perimeter to the beachhead at 4:30 a.m., no serious counterattack was made. During the day, the 1/162nd had its A Company patrol to the north of the beach and C Company to the south, while D Company (2/6th Battalion) patrolled to the west. A number of small contacts were made with the Japanese during the day across the front but nothing that risked the landing site.[46] By the end of the day, the landing site was a muddle, but the troops were safely and successfully ashore.

While MacKechnie Force was ashore, its first few days were not overly successful. Operations were delayed by the bad weather and the disorganized beachhead—largely a result of the chaotic nature of the landing. Over these days, more troops and guns arrived, but this only seemed to add to the confusion of the landing area. These factors created a poor first impression on the Australian troops in the area. A major incident during the first night after the US troops landed generated particular concerns for the 2/6th Battalion. As noted, during the day there had been multiple contacts with the Japanese, and they continued as the US and Australian troops settled into their night routine. The events of the night, however, remain somewhat confused and contradictory. Many in the 41st Division claim that a major Japanese assault was made on the beachhead, while the Australians believe that, at best, there was a very small number of Japanese probes of the position.[47] It seems that the heavy fighting that night was among US troops who mistook their comrades for the enemy or spent their time firing at shadows in the dark. The Australians dubbed it "Guy Fawkes night."[48] Colonel MacKechnie later noted that "our men were 'trigger happy' during the first few nights and there was much promiscuous fire and MG fire."[49] The unfortunate result of this fratricide was twenty-three US troops killed and another twenty-seven wounded.

The green US troops were also sluggish, and MacKechnie struggled to organize his force and inject it with the sense of urgency that the 3rd Division demanded. The Australians were unimpressed, and both Moten and Savige became increasingly frustrated by the lack of progress. The troops of the 2/6th Battalion and the liaison officers from 17th Brigade complained of MacKechnie's placement "of a bloody great tent, a marquee, on the beach itself," the hesitancy of the US troops, and their clustering, which invited air attack.[50] On 2 July, Savige noted that "the show on the beach appeared to be sticky. I instructed Moten to act firmly, but courteously, to get things moving."[51] Savige also contacted Fuller, urging him to send the rest of the US engineers and artillery to Nassau Bay as soon as possible and "to instruct MacKechnie that his forward elements must begin to move from the beach-head to the assembly area."[52]

These problems were exacerbated by the lack of communication between MacKechnie, Moten, and Savige due to the loss of the radios and the inexperience of the US signalers.[53] However, Savige's and Moten's urging seemed to have had little effect, and on 6 July two Australian liaison officers reported that conditions on the beach were "generally chaotic."[54] The problematic landing, the friendly fire incidents, and the difficulties of adjusting to combat conditions were showing just how inexperienced the American troops were. An Australian company commander, Maj.

W. R. Dexter, called the beachhead the "rummest show I have seen in all my life."[55] Maj. R. L. Hughes, the NGF liaison officer, tried to provide MacKechnie some advice about organization and operations, but MacKechnie simply responded by requesting that Hughes carry out his own suggestions. Capt. C. B. N. Rolfe, the liaison officer from 3rd Division HQ, visited the beachhead at this time and reported back to Savige that "no appearance of organisation was apparent." He went on to state that Capt. I. H. McBride, staff captain to Brigadier Moten, reported that MacKechnie had stated that "his tps [troops] have had a physical and mental shock." Rolfe went on to record that "there appears to be no drive at all displayed by the Comd, and he [MacKechnie] also appears to be indecisive, in what orders or decisions he may have to give. A younger man and more active would perhaps be better in the place at the moment."[56] By 4 July, the situation had improved. The Japanese had launched two air attacks on the beachhead with little effect, while the Japanese at Cape Dinga to the south had abandoned their positions. Colonel Taylor's battalion had moved inland, but MacKechnie was worried over his lack of supplies and the need to concentrate on developing the artillery positions on the coast; he reminded Moten that Fuller had ordered him not to take the offensive until proper supplies, fire support, and concentration of force could be achieved. These delays were frustrating Savige and Moten, and Moten reassured MacKechnie that Australian patrols were covering Bitoi Ridge and awaiting the Americans' arrival. He also arranged with MacKechnie to communicate directly with Taylor's battalion as it moved inland. The Australians, however, remained frustrated at the slow progress in the linkup between the 17th Brigade and the Americans on Bitoi Ridge and the delay in developing the beachhead.[57]

Things were not all rosy for the Australians either. On 30 June, to coincide with the landings at Nassau Bay and Woodlark and Kiriwina Islands, Savige had launched the first part of his assault with the 58/59th Militia Battalion and the 2/3rd Independent Company (15th Brigade), attacking Bobdubi Ridge on the northwestern end of the battlefield. On the same day that Savige was looking to replace MacKechnie, the 15th Brigade was writing to the 3rd Division to note the poor performance of the 58/59th Battalion, which had let large numbers of Japanese pass through its lines.[58]

Morale in the untested 58/59th Battalion was low, and it was given an exceptionally difficult task with little support against strong Japanese defenses. The battalion commander called the lack of fire support for his assault "criminal." After these failed attacks, morale plummeted, and in the middle of July the battalion had thirteen cases of self-inflicted wounds. The brigade medical officer noted that the 58/59th "had no idea how to live along the track. . . . The officers were hopeless, morale non-existent." The brigade commander, Brig. H. H. "Tack" Hammer, called them "as poor as piss."[59] The battalion was led by Lt. Col. P. D. S. Starr, whom Moten had sacked as CO of the 2/5th Battalion "when he let the Japs through after Wau." Instead of sending him back to Australia, however, Savige had given him command of the 58/59th Battalion. Starr's new brigade commander, Brigadier Hammer, would soon have him removed from command.[60]

The efforts of MacKechnie Force and the 58/59th Battalion in late June and early July highlight that the impact of green troops, tough conditions, and poor leadership do not vary on the basis of nationality. There were no natural soldiers within either force and the performance of both the US National Guard and the Australian Militia units paled in comparison to the tough, highly experienced, and exceptionally well-led AIF troops in the 17th Brigade under Moten. This meant that operations were developing more slowly than Moten and Savige had hoped.

However, steady progress was being made. MacKechnie Force had opened up a coastal supply line, and artillery had been brought in to help reduce the major Japanese defenses on the ridgelines. Furthermore, the Allies had proven the advantages of maneuver from the sea, and the 17th Brigade was now in position to launch an offensive on Mubo, Observation Hill, and the Pimple. The main assault kicked off on 7 July, with the Americans taking control of Bitoi Ridge on 8 July. The 17th Brigade had surrounded the Japanese in Mubo, and in a series of superbly executed company attacks, supported from 8 July by US artillery landed at Nassau Bay and Taylor's battalion from the 162nd Regiment, the 2/5th and 2/6th Battalions routed the enemy.

The 15th Brigade, however, was unsuccessful in its assault on Bobdubi Ridge. Savige ordered it to continue with the attacks while he ordered Moten to exploit his victory by advancing north to Komiatum and northeast to Lokanu. In Moten's way stood the formidable defenses of Goodview Junction and Mount Tambu. With progress now being made, MacArthur was also willing to provide NGF with further troops and artillery from the 41st Division to make another landing on the coast to support the advancing operations against Salamaua.

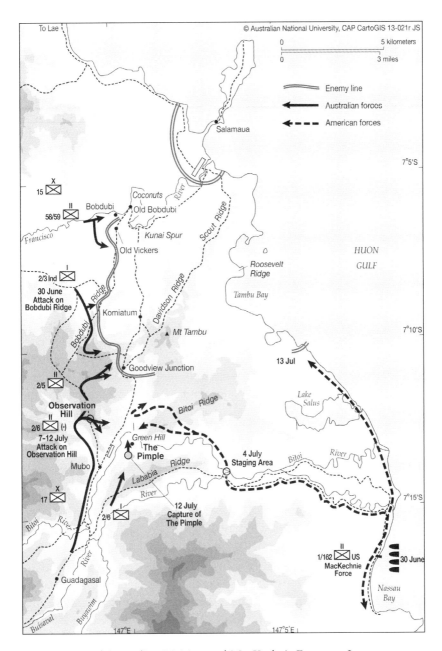

Figure 10.3 3rd Australian Division and MacKechnie Force, 30 June–
12 July 1943

COMMAND PROBLEMS

Clarity of command was shaping up to be one of the major features of the Salamaua operation. However, unlike during the Papua campaign, the difficulties were not just the command setup imposed by MacArthur or MacArthur's interference in tactical deployments. Rather, the Australian lieutenant general, Herring, was proving to be the initiator of the majority of the problems in New Guinea that were developing between the two armies.

The first issue was over the command chain between MacKechnie, Moten, Savige, and Fuller. Savige was under the firm impression, based on written orders and the coordination conferences in May, that MacKechnie would come under his command, and thus he placed the American under Moten. However, Herring had been more ambiguous in his discussions with Fuller, who continued to communicate with MacKechnie and issue him orders while Savige and Moten did the same. Both divisions were also involved in requests for air support, to the confusion of everyone.[61] MacKechnie thus felt himself to be in the insidious position of serving two masters (Fuller and Savige). On 5 July, Herring had to hold a conference to clarify arrangements and place MacKechnie Force firmly under Savige's sole command. Herring claimed that the reason he had not put it under Savige initially was that his HQ was so far from the coast and he worried it "might protest to MacArthur."[62] Herring had developed a good rapport with Fuller, and this relationship and his concern about keeping the Americans onside were clearly interfering with his judgment on the development of the operations against Salamaua, the command chain in the forward areas, and his orders to 3rd Division.

While command-chain issues were clarified on 5 July, Savige still remained concerned, and he suggested to General Fuller that he send a senior 41st Division officer forward to relieve MacKechnie of his command of the beachhead and the supply area to allow him to concentrate on forward operations. The following day, Savige wrote to Moten and stated, "I have suggested to Gen Herring that MacKechnie be replaced."[63]

Into this mix now came a further addition to help exploit the advance on Salamaua, but unfortunately it also led to more confusion in the command chain. NGF received permission from MacArthur to use Coane Force (the 2nd and 3rd Battalions, 162nd Regiment, the 205th and 218th Field Artillery Battalions, and supporting troops) from the 41st Division for another amphibious landing.[64] Coane Force was to be inserted farther up the coast at Tambu Bay, which was nestled in the shadows of the last major obstacles to Salamaua from the direct south: Roosevelt and Scout Ridges. This location was ideal to land artillery to support the next phase of operations, as the front lines were leaving the position at Nassau Bay behind. Additionally, this new landing would further ease the supply situation for the 3rd Division, which, once again, was becoming very strained.

Herring's decision to land at Tambu Bay was, tactically, exceptionally sound. By utilizing maneuver from the sea, NGF was exploiting one of the key emerging strengths of the Allies in the SWPA. However, Herring repeated the critical command-chain issues that had dogged the landing and initial operations at Nassau Bay. With Savige's HQ still some way inland and the majority of the troops in this new force being American, Herring put Fuller in command, while leaving the impression in Savige's mind that these troops would, like MacKechnie Force, fall under his command.

The buildup of Coane Force was slow, but by 12 July the initial landing force of the 3/162nd Regiment, under Major Roosevelt (youngest son of former president Theodore Roosevelt), was in position at Tambu Bay. On 11 July, Fuller ordered Coane to take command of all US forces in the Nassua Bay–Mageri Point–Morobe area, with the exception of MacKechnie Force. His mission was to operate the supply base and to develop operations to the north under Fuller's HQ.[65]

For MacKechnie, this meant that two-thirds of his regiment was now reassigned to Coane, leaving him little more than Taylor's battalion under his command. At the same time, Savige signaled Herring, indicating that MacKechnie had informed him that the 2/162nd was now directly under Fuller's command and that he thought this situation absurd. This situation was compounded by the fact that Herring had not bothered to inform the 3rd Division about the formation of Coane Force.[66] Savige believed he had command of all MacKechnie's troops, being the whole of the 162nd Regiment; Herring, however, only gave him command of the much-reduced MacKechnie Force (1/162nd).

Savige, confident in his command of all troops in the area, gave orders that put Roosevelt's 3/162nd at Tambu Bay under Moten. However, on 14 July, Roosevelt, a difficult and combative officer, sent an especially curt signal direct to Savige's HQ that pointed out 3rd Division's inadequacies and provided advice on how to run the operations, all the while making it clear that he did not take orders from the 3rd Division but only from his own chain of command, which he identified as Fuller and the 41st Division HQ.[67] Savige signaled Herring, demanding "single control of tps allocated to this area" and noting that "any guarantee for success under any other arrangements can NOT be given."[68] On 15 July 1943, Herring was forced to clarify command arrangements in the forward area for the second time in ten days. MacKechnie Force was to remain under Moten's 17th Brigade, while the forces landed at Tambu Bay were to come under Savige's HQ. Coane Force's role was reaffirmed as to secure the landing site at Tambu Bay, land the remaining combat teams of artillery to support the 3rd Division, and drive on Scout Ridge.[69]

The confusion, however, did not end there. With the arrival of a significant amount of artillery in the 3rd Division's area, it was imperative that a divisional artillery commander (commander, Royal Artillery [CRA]) be appointed. Given that the majority of the guns were American, the most obvious appointment was Coane, the 41st Division's artillery commander. However, Coane had command of all US troops at Nassau and Tambu Bay, and so his deputy artillery commander in the 41st Division, Col. William D. Jackson, was appointed as CRA instead.[70]

With some clarity provided as to command between Coane Force and the 3rd Australian Division, the unresolved issue was Colonel MacKechnie. As a result of his dual command chain, whereby his frontline units reported to Moten and his beachhead now came under Coane's command, MacKechnie asked on 22 July to be relieved. It was clear to MacKechnie that the downgrading of his responsibilities was a result of Fuller's perceptions of his performance. Fuller held MacKechnie to account for all of the command confusion that had come about so far. He cited MacKechnie's inability to hold his command together and that he had not referred orders from Savige and Moten to the 41st Division for approval, and he questioned MacKechnie's performance at Nassau Bay, in particular moving his troops inland without apparently clearing up the enemy near the landing site.[71]

A close analysis of MacKechnie's performance makes Fuller's claims seem rather spurious. The notion that MacKechnie had to refer orders from Savige to Fuller, who was not in the chain of command, was nothing more than a case of nationalism, self-interest, and egotism trumping unity of command. The movement of Taylor's battalion inland was tactically sound, especially as the Japanese were withdrawing from Cape Dinga, which was covered by the PIB and Australian patrols. As for not keeping his units together, MacKechnie wisely allowed terrain and tactical circumstances to dictate his deployments rather than national unity. His sins in Fuller's eyes seem to mainly stem from his close cooperation with the Australians, and while the Australians did question MacKechnie's age, health, and drive, they never faulted his cooperation and focus on the operation.[72]

Herring's clarifying signal of 15 July could not, however, change the attitude of some commanders. Major Roosevelt continued to begrudge Coane Force's command by the 3rd Division and remained resentful of the need for cooperation with the Australians. This attitude was reflected in the approach to command by Coane, who like Roosevelt was a difficult subordinate for Savige. Both of these officers seemed driven by their basic belief in the superiority of US approaches and methods over the Australians', and they showed little regard for the Australians' experience in jungle warfare; they also lacked the humility to recognize their own inexperience. Meanwhile, the war dragged on. The victory at Mubo had allowed the 15th and 17th Brigades to unite and a (somewhat) continuous front to be formed all the way to the Americans on the coast, creating a semicircle around the approaches to Salamaua from the south to the north. The landing at Tambu Bay was, however, isolated, and the key to the linking up of this force to the 17th Brigade was the Japanese positions at Mount Tambu and Komiatum.

The 2/5th Battalion secured the forward slopes of Mount Tambu on 16 July and then fought off a series of major counterattacks, but its attack on 24 July was repulsed. Moten now planned a major assault with Taylor's battalion (1/162nd) on Mount Tambu and the 2/5th Battalion on Goodview Junction. The 1/162nd went into action on 30 July and ran into major resistance. The battle swung back and forth, with the Americans taking the forward Japanese pits before being repulsed in a counterattack. By noon, the Americans were pinned down, and by the time they withdrew, one-third of the attacking force was dead or wounded.[73] Both the 2/5th and the 1/162nd's efforts were valiant, but just like at the Pimple frontal assaults were proving to be futile.

For Coane Force, the key piece of terrain was the ridgeline that overlooked Tambu Bay to its immediate north, quickly named Roosevelt Ridge after the 3rd Battalion's commander. Roosevelt Ridge was a razor-sharp ridge jutting in from the coast, and the Japanese considered it one the best pieces of terrain in the area to stop the Allied advance.[74] This ridgeline dominated the area, was heavily defended by the Japanese, and was the gateway to Scout Ridge, the last major feature before Salamaua.

Operations against Roosevelt Ridge, supported by guns of the 2/6th Field Regiment AIF (having landed at Tambu Bay), started on 20 July. Boisi Village was quickly taken, but soon afterward heavy machine-gun and mortar fire from the Japanese on the ridge stopped the advance.

The Japanese also shelled the landing beaches as more reinforcements and supplies arrived. The 3/162nd made another unsuccessful attack on the ridge on 22 July. On 24 July, I Company, 3/162nd, patrolling to the west, moved onto Scout Ridge, confirming that a gap existed between this feature and Roosevelt Ridge. The 3rd Battalion now consolidated its position in front of Roosevelt Ridge before making another effort on 30 July, but again it was unsuccessful, as were a number of smaller follow-on operations.[75] The Japanese, sensing the danger to their positions, launched a series of counterattacks on the Americans, all of which were repulsed. At the same time, more US and Australian artillery units arrived in the area to support operations across the Allied front. The stalemate at Roosevelt Ridge persisted, and by 4 August the Australians were becoming increasingly frustrated by Coane and Roosevelt's inability to secure this objective.

The delay in capturing this position inevitably led to questions about the performance of the 3/162nd and its CO. Roosevelt was, at fifty, the oldest battalion commander in the US Army—having been the youngest company commander in the US Army in World War I. Exempt from service in World War II, he had lobbied his cousin, President Franklin Roosevelt, for permission to go on active duty.[76] It was noted that he was struggling with the rigorous nature of combat and the formidable terrain of New Guinea, and he was later to acknowledge that he was "too old physically speaking and mentally . . . [and that my tactics are] rusty and old fashioned."[77] Maj. Mike Trapman, the acting CoS of the 41st Division, noted that by 7 August Roosevelt "had lost 38 pounds, is very much run down, [and] extremely nervous."[78] Compounding Roosevelt's physical and tactical issues was his poor attitude toward his chain of command, especially the Australians, who despite his own failures he constantly criticized. Brigadier Moten bluntly stated that "Roosevelt was a bastard."[79]

Roosevelt, using the political advantages of his heritage, also took the extraordinary step of writing to MacArthur directly. In his letter, he went to lengths to complain about the Australians and the chain of command, noting that the "intermingling of the two armies—Australian and American—. . . will steadily become worse to the detriment of the U.S. Army."[80] Roosevelt's attitude and inactivity, however, meant that he lacked widespread support within the 41st Division. Lt. Col. C. A. Fertig, who assumed command of the 162nd Regiment after MacKechnie, noted to Roosevelt that he was "more concerned about the attitude of the men in

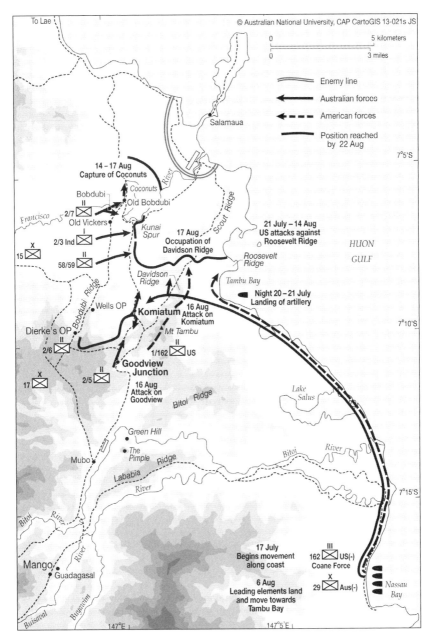

Figure 10.4 3rd Australian Division, including MacKechnie Force and Coane
Force, 14 July–17 August 1943

your battalion at the moment than I am about any attempt of the Aussies to throw a block on us."[81]

Savige, perturbed by Roosevelt's inactivity at Tambu Bay, rapidly lost confidence in him. He was no more impressed by his CO, General Coane, whom he regarded as spending all his time in his tent, "most of it lying on his bed."[82] Savige continued to have concerns over the abilities and performance of these officers, especially in regard to their ability to follow orders from his division and its commanders and to cooperate effectively. Savige would later comment:

> I agree with the necessity to obtain mutual trust and co-operation between allied forces, which we obtained in abundance from Taylor and Mason, commanding U.S. battalions, from Jackson, my (U.S.) CRA, and, later, from MacKechnie when he was again posted to command 162 Regt. On the other hand, despite attempts to do so, it was not forthcoming from Coane or Roosevelt—all of whom were under the direct influence of Fuller and his Chief of Staff [Col. Kenneth Sweany].[83]

As a result, Savige decided to relieve both officers. In this he got Herring's support, although Herring's signal to MacArthur asking for Coane's relief is insightful. He noted that with Jackson in place as CRA, there was no need for Coane as CRA in the 3rd Division and that with the 162nd not being at full strength, Coane "merely sits as an extra link between Savige and Mason [162nd Regiment]. This set up is most unsatisfactory and I believe endangering success." Furthermore, Herring, at Savige's behest, noted concerns for Coane's mental state for command, arguing that he had been "taking counsel of his fears" and that Savige would not accept him as CRA. Herring went on to state that the best solution was to reinstall MacKechnie, who also had Jackson's full support, noting that Fertig had not taken command of the 162nd but rather served as Coane's chief of staff.

Herring also outlined Savige's views on Roosevelt and suggested that MacKechnie make the decision regarding his future once he arrived and reassumed command. Most significantly, Herring hit home on the reality of the problem—how MacKechnie and Coane Forces had been set up—arguing that the best way to solve the command issues was for the new commanders of US troops in the forward areas near Salamaua to be "free from all control [from] 41 US Div in operational matters."[84] The great irony here was that Herring was writing to MacArthur to support

Savige with sacking two US officers to solve command problems that he had created.

This request was, of course, highly charged politically—especially given that Roosevelt was the president's cousin. It was a request that could not be taken lightly by the C-in-C SWPA. Yet Herring would note after the war just how supportive MacArthur was of the decision to relieve Coane and Roosevelt. Noting that "all requests I made [to MacArthur] for changes in command in his American units to eliminate frustration were given effect immediately, though some of these changes, I should imagine, may have given him some embarrassment."[85] It is interesting to speculate why MacArthur was so amenable. It may well have been that he was cognizant of his demands that Australian senior officers be relieved during the Papua campaign or that, once Harding had been removed, MacArthur was more comfortable with the removal of ineffective US officers. In Roosevelt's case, the request coming from the Australians may well have provided him the type of political cover that would not have existed if the request had gone through the American chain of command.

With the reappointment of MacKechnie to command his regiment and all US troops in front of Salamaua, the tactical command problems at the front lines were finally solved. In addition, major tactical progress was now forthcoming. The key to unlocking these positions was the discovery by Taylor's battalion (1/162) of an undefended ridgeline paralleling the Komiatum Trail. The Australians soon occupied this position in force, which allowed them to interdict the Japanese supply lines and force them off Mount Tambu and out of Goodview Junction. With this success, Taylor's battalion returned to the control of the rest of its regiment, uniting the 162nd on the coastal flank in front of Salamaua.[86]

Meanwhile, on Roosevelt Ridge, a similar operation transpired. After reassuming command in mid-August, MacKechnie pushed out US patrols into the area between Roosevelt and Scout Ridges. By 27 August, a patrol from K Company, 3/162nd, pushed over Scout Ridge and occupied a position on C Ridge (behind Roosevelt Ridge), interdicting the Japanese supply line. Realizing the gravity of this move, the Japanese reacted violently, and after nine failed attacks on K Company involving desperate hand-to-hand fighting, the Japanese gave up. But out of ammunition, desperately short of supplies, and with heavy casualties, the Americans withdrew. However, this small battle and the rigorous patrolling of the Americans proved to be the catalyst for the collapse of the Japanese position, and on 29 August they withdrew from their positions on both Roosevelt and Scout Ridges.[87]

FIGHTING OVER SALAMAUA: THE HIGH COMMAND

In parallel to the battles at the front lines ran a major operational command issue of the battle for Salamaua: the debate over the town's role in Operation Postern. This problem was the cause of a number of issues between the 3rd Division and NGF HQ. The principal issue was that Herring did not keep Savige informed as to his actual role (a mask to draw off the Japanese from Lae) due to a combination of issues, mainly operational security, their poor personal relationship, and Herring's vacillation, despite clear orders from Blamey regarding when the town was to be taken.

One of the reasons for Herring's vagueness with Savige, which led to such strong disagreements, was the susceptibility of Herring to the influence of senior US commanders and staff officers who had constant contact with him at NGF HQ in Port Moresby. It became apparent during June and July 1943 that the Fifth US Air Force and GHQ were happy to abandon Blamey's plan to use Salamaua as a magnet to draw off Japanese forces from Lae, and instead they wanted Herring to directly assault the town and take it as soon as possible. These tensions eventually led to a showdown between MacArthur and Blamey and subsequently between Blamey and Berryman against Herring and Savige.

Herring had developed a very good relationship with Whitehead, and they worked closely every day. Under MacArthur's cooperative command model, both of these officers had responsibility for the conduct of operations in the air and on the ground in New Guinea. Therefore, it was exceptionally important that they work closely together. Herring was also to work closely with Admiral Barbey once his command team arrived in the lead-up to the assault on Lae. While these engagements were very positive, relations between the different staffs were, at times, still rather fragile, and Herring noted that he often had to correct his own staff for assessing issues based on nationality, as opposed to operational and tactical requirements.[88]

While tactical-level cooperation at NGF HQ was excellent, it became apparent that Herring was starting to be influenced about the broader development of operations in New Guinea by Whitehead and the more senior US commanders, namely Kenney and MacArthur. It quickly became obvious that Herring was working both sides of the street—his own command chain and the senior US commanders—assuring Berryman and Blamey that he was adhering to their plan while discussing with US commanders proposals to take Salamaua as soon as possible. A major reason for this position was Herring's deference to and concern for senior US officers' views, especially those of Kenney and MacArthur. This was a product of Herring's experience of MacArthur's interference in operations on the Kokoda Trail and at the beachheads. However, unlike at the beachheads, Herring's deference to these officers, rather than his own chain of command, was threatening the success of operations.

After his visit to New Guinea in June, Blamey's DCGS, General Berryman, became very concerned about both the Herring-Savige relationship and the way that Herring was approaching the operations as a result of the pressure he was getting from Whitehead, Kenney, and MacArthur. After discussions with Herring on the plans for Salamaua, and after reviewing NGF's orders, Berryman wrote to the C-in-C to express major reservations about Herring's commitment to the use of Salamaua as a mask for Lae. Blamey wrote to Herring on 15 June, making absolutely clear his intentions and his concerns over Herring's control of operations:

I note one divergence from the plan I had approved for future operations. You will remember that it had been decided that Salamaua should not be seized; it should be by-passed. The reasons for this are:

A. The seizure of Salamaua would be a definite signal for the assembly of additional enemy strength at Lae
B. That Salamaua would not affect preparations for the operations against Lae provided Komiatum Ridge was held by us
C. After the capture of Lae, the capture of Salamaua would follow with little difficulty

In the communication from General Berryman dealing with his discussions with you, this has been ignored and the outline of [the plan] indicates that Salamaua would be first seized.[89]

Herring assured Blamey that this was not the case, arguing rather unconvincingly that he was "afraid we have been referring to the preliminary operation for the seizure of the Komiatum Ridge as the Salamaua operation" and insisting that he was conforming to Blamey's original plan.[90] Berryman, however, did not buy it and had noticed the ambiguity in the orders that Herring was providing to the 3rd Division. If Berryman believed that Herring was planning to take Salamaua, then this would account for the mixed signals being sent to Savige.

Despite the clarity Blamey provided on 15 June, this was not the end of the matter. Whitehead continued to press "for [the] capture of Salamaua so a fighter strip could be developed,"[91] as did Kenney, MacArthur, and

GHQ.[92] To MacArthur, the offer of Coane Force to NGF was predicated on a quick and decisive move against Salamaua.[93] Herring noted to Savige that his job was to drive the Japanese north of the Francisco River but directed, in the same signal, that he prepare plans for the capture of Salamaua. After a conference with Herring on 25 July, Berryman noted in his diary that Blamey was "worried about 3 Div ops and report[ed] it is difficult to get a clear picture of what Savige is trying to do." Six weeks on from Blamey's clarifying signal, Herring was still sending mixed messages about the role of the 3rd Division and his intentions over Salamaua.

By now, Blamey's concerns about the plan for Postern and the role of Salamaua drove him to seek a meeting with the C-in-C. On 28 July, he met with MacArthur and got a commitment from GHQ that Salamaua would not be taken until after the landing at Lae.[94] Blamey had his assurance, but he remained concerned about the handling of the operation in front of Salamaua. On 4 August, Berryman noted, "The ops of Doublet [Salamaua] do not seem to be taking the course GOC NGF desired." A few days later, Berryman noted Herring's criticisms of Savige's disposition of his forces and his lack of force concentration.[95]

On 15 August, Blamey met with Berryman, Herring, and Maj. Gen. Allan Boase, who had just returned from a visit to the 3rd Division's front. Two sets of concerns were played out at this meeting. Herring, as he had a number of times before, raised questions about Savige's competence and urged his replacement. Blamey and Berryman, meanwhile, were worried about Herring's performance. Blamey decided to break the impasse by utilizing Berryman and proposing that the DCGS should go forward and assess operations as he had done in New Guinea around Christmas 1942 during the beachhead operations.[96]

Berryman recorded in his diary that "C-in-C . . . suggested that I should visit 3 Div and give firm directions about the conduct of operations and get an eye full of the country." The following day, Blamey decided that, in line with his policy to rotate headquarters in the trying tropical conditions, Maj. Gen. Edward "Teddy" Milford's 5th Division would relieve the 3rd Division HQ.[97] Berryman's role was therefore not only to pass judgment on Savige and Herring but also to inform Savige of his relief. Berryman was an interesting choice. On the outside it looked as if the decision had already been made, as it was well known throughout the army that Berryman had been highly critical of Savige in the Middle East and that he did not rate him highly as a commander. To Herring, the choice of Berryman must have seemed like a vindication of his position. However, things were to turn out rather differently.

Blamey was well aware of Berryman's "very low opinion of Savige's military competence,"[98] but by now Blamey was also well aware that Berryman also had major concerns about Herring's handling of the operation, and unlike Herring's view of Savige, Berryman's was not based on personal differences but rather on his view of his professional competence. Blamey was thus very confident that Berryman would pass judgment on the basis of the details of the operation itself, not on his opinion of Savige's character. So, as Brigadier Moten noted, Berryman "came up to [3rd Division HQ] to give a bowler hat either to Savige or me if unsuccessful or to Herring for not knowing what was going on."[99]

Berryman left Port Moresby on 17 August and arrived at Moten's HQ a full day before his planned meeting with Savige. There he grilled Moten, who was one of Berryman's protégés and thus an officer in whose judgment he placed great trust. Moten briefed Berryman on his operations, and together they conducted a tour of the front lines. Moten noted that "Berryman asked [me] what was going on as nobody in Moresby seemed to know."[100] Afterward, Berryman concluded that Moten's brigade had made a "*perfect plan*" and noted that "2/6 Bn [was] in great form and tomorrow promises great results."[101]

The next day, Berryman spent the morning out on the front lines watching Moten's battalions push forward. This time he noted that the 2/6th Battalion's approach march to Komiatum "was the greatest piece of tactical surprise I've seen in the campaign and [it] will crumble the Nip in front of Goodview Junction–Mount Tambu."[102] A few days later, writing to his wife, he noted that "the campaign from Wau to Salamaua [went] through country as difficult as the Owen Stanleys [and] is in my opinion our most successful to date. . . . The tactical work was as good as if not better than anything to date. . . . History will give it pride of place as a military achievement."[103]

Berryman then met with Savige and Wilton and challenged Savige's conduct of the campaign. Savige had a sound response for every one of Berryman's questions, and he also produced a signal from Herring urging his division on toward Salamaua and rebuking him for his handling of the campaign. Berryman reviewed Herring's signals, which Wilton, another of Berryman's protégés, described as "stupid," and concluded that they were "most unjustified . . . especially as no senior officer from NGF except me had visited [the] front line."[104] Savige, who "had no idea the plot was on,"[105] then rounded on Berryman, asking him what he was doing there. By now convinced that Savige and his division had the most troublesome time at the hands of Herring, Berryman informed Savige that in a fortnight's time he was to move his headquarters over to Tambu Bay for a relief by Milford.[106] Savige replied, "Frank, I have had a rather difficult and trying time but as you see we have got away with it."[107]

Before he left, Berryman briefed Savige on the full plan for Postern, and it was only then that he understood Salamaua was not to fall until the Lae operation was started. Upon his return to Port Moresby, Berryman's report to Blamey fully supported Savige's actions. He noted that the 3rd Division's plan was "excellently conceived and admirably carried out."[108] Berryman also singled out Wilton and Moten for the highest praise.[109] In Savige's mind, Berryman's report had fully vindicated his actions and prevented him from being sacked.[110] His replacement in command, General Milford, believed that Savige was later promoted to a corps command on the basis of Berryman's vindication of his actions at Salamaua.[111] On leaving Port Moresby on 20 August, Wilton noted that Berryman had "never thought [that he would] have to admit that Savige was right."[112]

While vindicating Savige, the outcome seriously damaged Herring's credibility and called into question his handling of NGF. It was apparent to both Blamey and Berryman that Herring had allowed personal differences to influence his relations with Savige.[113] This personal animosity, and his "flirting" with taking Salamaua at the behest of senior US officers, had led Herring to avoid giving clear directions to the 3rd Division.[114] By rights, Blamey should have sacked Herring for his handling of the operations and for jeopardizing Operation Postern. However, with only a few days to go before the operation kicked off, Herring was saved from being replaced as GOC I Australian Corps. However, his continued questioning of Blamey's operational plans at the behest of senior US officers and his ongoing poor judgment would soon lead to his demise.

COOPERATION AT THE FRONT LINES: THE TACTICAL VIEW

While command confusion dominated the level of brigade/regiment and above, at the front lines the soldiers got on with the job at hand. As noted, the situation for each of the units involved was different depending on experience, capabilities, and mission, but overall the relations between the different armies at the front lines were positive. As the Australian official history has noted, there existed a "genuine friendship between the Australian and Americans troops in the frontline."[115]

While relations were generally positive, there were a number of differences evident during the campaign, mainly as a result of the lack of combat experience or combat-experienced leaders in the US units. This issue stood in contrast to the veteran Australian AIF units and the militia units—now led by experienced AIF officers—that made up the majority of the Australian components of the 3rd Australian Division. This meant that the US units initially made basic errors common to all inexperienced troops, such as "cluster[ing] in a close perimeter at night instead of holding the ground gained."[116] Like most troops new to combat, they hesitated in some tactical situations, lacked fire discipline at night, had to develop their offensive and defensive skills, "were not used to hard jungle marches and carried too much gear."[117]

The majority of Australian units that served alongside the 41st Division troops noted how "green" and "inexperienced" the US soldiers were, although it was also noted that they were "a nice bunch of blokes, and appeared keen enough."[118] As Brigadier Moten, commander of the 17th Brigade, noted, the "Yanks [were] not bad. . . . [They were] very raw but eager to learn."[119] Moten also noted that some of the US junior officers were good leaders and good tacticians, and he singled out Capt. Del Newman, one of the 1/162nd's company commanders, for high praise.[120]

Not all of the 162nd's officers were of the caliber of Newman. One of the ways the 17th Brigade was able to help in the development of the US units under their command was by providing cadres of experienced junior officers and NCOs to support their units and subunits. For instance, D Company, 2/5th Battalion, supported Colonel Taylor's battalion (1/162nd, MacKechnie Force) by providing experienced NCOs to lead US patrols.[121] The Australian official history noted that the close cooperation between the veteran Australian units and the inexperienced Americans meant that the former "help[ed] the Americans to reorganize and proceed with their task[s]."[122]

Patrolling and the establishment of smaller, more distributed defensive positions was one of the key deficiencies of the US units in the initial phases of combat. Brigadier Moten complained that the US troops used "huddling tactics" (bunching up), and he demanded that they disperse their units more and that company positions be rearranged.[123] Colonel MacKechnie agreed, noting that his troops were "initially hesitant about moving in small patrols or to maintain small outposts at any distance from the main positions. This permitted the Jap to move freely and without our knowledge." However, with support from the Australians and increasing confidence of his own troops and their commanders, within in a short time MacKechnie Force "quickly assumed a feeling of superiority to the Jap and moved out with a reasonable sense of security."[124] As the 162nd Regiment's men learned and adapted to the conditions, they changed their patrolling and defensive tactics, they moved from frontal assaults to encircling the enemy like the Australian units did, and they reorganized their subunits' defensive layouts.[125]

While in many respects the two forces started to adopt similar tactics, fundamental differences in training and doctrine remained. General Milford noted after taking over from Savige that "the Americans methods are different to ours and they look for a tremendous amount of fire support and do a great deal of patrolling but the patrols are more in the nature of recce patrols than fighting patrols. Companies are[, however,] at last remaining out at night on any ground gained during the day."[126] The 162nd Regiment was also conscious of these differences, noting that "differences in operational methods, expressions and customs sometimes caused misunderstanding between American and Australian forces."[127] Added to this were the issues of natural difficulties of communications, terrain and tactical situation, which caused "no little confusion at times,"[128] although "these were quickly adjusted."[129]

Differences, however, remained. One of the key issues here was disparity in training and doctrine. The US Army, as illustrated by Fuller's orders to both MacKechnie and Coane, continued to focus on battalion-level operations based on concentration of force with liberal amounts of artillery and air support. The Australians, however, relied more on company-level operations and aggressive fighting patrols and focused on infantry minor tactics. Each doctrinal approach had its benefits and drawbacks, and both would prove successful in the SWPA in defeating the Japanese. However, at Salamaua, the rawness of the Americans units and their faith in their firepower-based doctrine meant that US perceptions of the performance of MacKechnie Force and Coane Force differed considerably from those of the Australians.

The Australians often complained about the slowness of US troops to get into action, their reluctance to close with and destroy the enemy using infantry minor tactics, and their emphasis on massed attacks. As Phillip Bradley points out, the Americans were slow to realize that in the New Guinea terrain, with its precarious mountains and noncontinuous front lines, more often than not a "small well-led force acting quickly and decisively could achieve more than an entire battalion with artillery and air support. . . . [However,] the majority of American commanders were

unable to come to grips with the nature of the fighting in New Guinea."[130]
Even late in the operation, General Berryman remained critical of the lack
of aggressive patrolling by some US units, describing Colonel Taylor's
(1/162nd) patrol plan at Mount Tambu as "stupidity."[131] However, as
the Australian official history notes, the Americans adapted quickly, and
by 27 July the "Americans were learning that it was futile to batter well
prepared positions and best to encircle them."[132]

Over time, Australian confidence in US units greatly improved. By 28
July, Brigadier Moten noted that "I have complete faith in these comds
and the ability of [the] AIF troops. Taylor's men [1/162nd] should succeed
also."[133] By the time the US units were fighting for Roosevelt and Scout
Ridges in mid- to late August, many small units had developed a high
level of tactical acumen along the lines of the AIF battalions. As Bradley
notes, the performances of some US companies and platoons in offensive
patrolling and defensive battles were "outstanding."[134] More broadly,
the Australians continued to understand the level of capability of the
US units and the difficult conditions and missions that they often faced.
As the 2/5th Battalion history noted of the failure of the assaults by the
162nd Regiment on 30 July 1943, "it would be unfair to point a finger at
them [the Americans] as it was an extremely formidable task given to a
Company of inexperienced, untried troops and even with battle-hardened
troops, courage alone was not going to crack this fortress."[135] It was not
lost on these elite Australian soldiers that, only six days beforehand, the
same task had also been beyond their own abilities.

One area where there was mutual agreement over the high performance
of US units was with their artillery. With the exception of General Coane,
the Australians held the US artillery units and their commanders in high
regard. At the end of the campaign, the Australian divisional commander,
General Milford, noted to the commander of the US artillery units, Col.
William Jackson, who also served as the division's CRA, that this was the
"first jungle campaign in which adequate artillery has been able to support our forces and to exercise its tremendous power. I am certain that
our success has in no small measure been due to the devastation and de-
moralization caused by the artillery." Milford went on to thank Jackson
personally, as well as his units, for their service. He noted that Jackson's
"willing cooperation and constant personal contact has been a source of
much pleasure to me."[136] US commanders also noted their artillery's high
performance.[137]

Again, though, differences in operational approach were noted. The
Australians noted that "U.S. methods are slower and more expensive in

amn. . . . Fire discipline is not as exacting as that practiced in Aust Arty units." The Australians also felt that senior US artillery officers should have left their HQ much more often to make personal reconnaissance. There was also a considerable difference in observed fire techniques:

> As far as possible an American and an Australian OPO occupied each OP, and each observed the fire of such of the American or Aust guns respectively which were suitable to the task at hand. Occasionally it was necessary for Australians to observe the fire of American guns, and vice versa, but this was not satisfactory as OPOs had difficulty in adjusting their different operational methods. . . . Generally the practice of manning the OPs by a representative of each Arty national group proved very satisfactory and helped materially in the liaison between Aust and American Arty units.[138]

While the Australians complained about Coane's lackluster performance, GHQ was, at least initially, satisfied with the performance of the US troops. Col. Bernard Peyton, the GHQ liaison officer attached to NGF HQ, toured Coane Force's front lines in early August and reported back high praise for the units involved "under very adverse conditions and marvels that there are any men left doing the fighting. Very favorably impressed with the work that the artillery as a whole is doing."[139]

Overall at Salamaua, just as at the beachheads, the farther one got from senior headquarters and the closer to the battlefront, the greater cooperation increased, especially once command issues involving Mac-Kechnie, Roosevelt, and Coane were solved. For the Australians, the relationship between the two forces in the front lines was exceptionally close and respectful, and to the 162nd Infantry Regiment, the "Australian and American troops who fought alongside each other were equally high in their praise of the other and parted with mutual respect and admiration for the fighting qualities of their brothers in arms."[140]

VICTORY AT SALAMAUA

Given all of the difficulties evident at Salamaua, the development of this operation was one that hung on the notion of "harmony," which as David Horner has argued, "ultimately rested on the personalities of the commanders involved."[141] Thus, any evaluation of the US-Australian coalition in the battle for Salamaua must rest on an evaluation of the performance of the senior commanders involved in these operations.

MacArthur continued to provide the framework for operations in the theater, and once again he interfered in operations, pushing Herring to take Salamaua. He continued to have a troubled relationship with Blamey, and his interference in operations in New Guinea eventually led Blamey to call a conference with MacArthur to reaffirm his commitment to Blamey's plan. MacArthur's insistence on taking Salamaua threatened to unpick the campaign plan and demonstrated his impatience. MacArthur, of course, recorded none of this in his reminiscences and instead claimed full credit for Blamey's ideas and work while hardly even mentioning the Australians.[142] On the positive side, MacArthur did support Savige and Herring in the removal of Coane and Roosevelt from command; in fact, Berryman recorded in his diary that when Blamey raised this issue with him on 12 August, MacArthur noted he had already dealt with this issue. In December 1942, the removal of Harding had caused major strains in the relationship, but on this occasion Berryman noted that MacArthur was "particular bright and friendly—there is no doubt about his charm of manner and personality."[143]

Overall, Herring's performance was poor. He allowed his personal dislike of Savige to color his approach to their relationship. He lacked clarity in his orders to Savige, and he deliberately kept Savige in the dark about the operation against Lae. At first, this decision was justified by operational security, but soon thereafter the continual withholding of information from Savige was negligent. There is no doubt that Savige was a difficult subordinate and that he should shoulder a share of the blame for the poor relationship with NGF, but Herring did nothing but perpetuate the already strained relationship. He only went forward to visit Savige at his HQ once, and he did nothing proactive to improve NGF's relationship with the 3rd Division. Much of Herring's trouble with Savige seems to have emanated out of the NGF's commanders' relationship with senior US officers.

Herein lays the paradox in Herring's command of NGF. Herring's close relationship with the Americans was, on the one hand, his greatest asset. With MacArthur's cooperative command setup and the brittleness of the US-Australian coalition, Herring noted that "my job is largely getting everyone to play together, Americans & ourselves, and I think they are doing it well."[144] He maintained his friendly relations and thought the senior US officers were "grand people. . . . Their generosity no's [*sic*] no bounds."[145] However, this close relationship also worked against the operations at hand. It seems that Herring's lack of clarity in orders to Savige was fueled by the fact that, during the operation against Salamaua, he was susceptible to undue influence from US senior commanders.

Herring was thus hedging his bets between his own C-in-C and MacArthur. This led him to deliberately leave Savige's orders and mission ambiguous, so as to placate Blamey or seize the opportunity to take Salamaua if ordered to do so. His close relationship with senior US officers also led him to be overly sympathetic to them and to establish a confusing and contradictory chain of command between Savige and MacKechnie Force and Coane Force. To his credit, he saw the errors of his way and supported Savige's request to remove Coane and Roosevelt, although he made sure that GHQ knew that it was at Savige's insistence. In terms of the lack of clarity of orders, the major risk to the operations, Berryman's visit at Blamey's behest and his vindication of Savige's actions put the blame squarely on Herring. By all rights, Blamey should have removed Herring from command.

Savige had a mixed campaign. In most senses, he was vindicated by Berryman's report and by the conduct of his division under exceptionally trying circumstances against a determined, resourceful, and highly experienced enemy. However, Savige was a difficult subordinate, and there were questions to be asked about how far he kept his HQ from the front lines and about his dependence on his senior staff officer, Wilton, and his key commanders, Moten and Hammer. Milford believed that Wilton really ran the show, that Savige was too old, and that this was why he never visited his frontline units and instead spent most of this time at his HQ.[146] While these criticisms may be valid, overall Savige's performance was more than satisfactory. He handled his troops well, knew his limitations, and exploited the talents of his subordinates. Moreover, while impatient with his US commanders, he worked well with those who were cooperative and insisted on MacKechnie being given back his command. Blamey would reward his performance with a promotion and corps command in the operations in Bougainville in 1944 and 1945.

Moten's performance at Salamaua was nothing short of outstanding. He handled his brigade brilliantly and he managed the difficult command issues between Savige and Herring with a deft touch. He got on well with the Americans, provided them support where necessary, and understood their limitations. His only failings were his underestimation of the enemy at the Pimple and Mount Tambu. Coane and Roosevelt revealed their limitations as commanders, and their removal from command was fully justified. MacKechnie had been sacked, was recalled, and ended the operation with an enhanced reputation, but the difficulties of the campaign, his age, his health, and the politics of the US Army caught up with him: he was sent before a medical board, reclassified, and sent home to a training position for the rest of the war. It was a bitter end to the career of an officer who had fought hard for his troops and for the Allied coalition.

Overall, the major problems of the Allied coalition in the SWPA at Salamaua were not too dissimilar to those in Papua in 1942. The major difference was that internal Australian command relationships, rather than US frictions, added a layer of complexity and difficulties in operations that could well have been avoided. However, like the beachheads, Salamaua was a great success. While the performance of some Australian and American units and commanders was mixed, the outcome could not be faulted, and cooperation at most levels was particularly smooth given the nature of the coalition.

By now, the stage was set for the largest set-piece assault of the SWPA so far in the war—an operation that would far and away dwarf the efforts of 1942. With VII Phib in place and amphibious training and doctrine development firmly under way, the first of the major cadres from these training schools would soon be plying their trade in operations. Despite the internal Australian Army friction and the continued tension at the edges of the US-Australian relationship, Salamaua was an unqualified success in terms of drawing off Japanese forces from Lae and fixing their gaze on the notion of an overland advance from Salamaua to Lae. This meant that the back door to Lae was wide open for the Allies to exploit.

I I

Operation Postern

Planning and Airpower

AS THE PREPARATIONS FOR OPERATION CARTWHEEL PROGRESSED, the depth of the coalition in the SWPA was evident. In 1943, Australia relied heavily on the United States for military support, especially air and naval capabilities, while MacArthur was heavily dependent upon Australia for bases, logistics support, and the majority of his ground force. Hard lessons had been learned in 1942, and as MacArthur and Blamey had both looked down the barrel of dismissal, commanders had been replaced, new communication means had been established, and a greater depth of understanding had developed between the two military forces.

The year 1943 was to see the foundational work in the SWPA come together in a series of devastating offensives that were to break the back of Japanese power in the theater. As chapter 10 demonstrated, the friction of war in 1943 continued unabated, but by now the Allies had demonstrated their superiority over the Japanese strategically, tactically, and logistically, at sea, in the air, and on land. These frictions would continue, but the planning and later the conduct of Operation Postern (phase 2 of Cartwheel) would demonstrate how effectively the US-Australian coalition could work and how devastating this coalition was to the enemy.

Operation Postern was a deliberate attack utilizing a coordinated effort across all domains of military power. Exploiting a maritime strategy supported by Allied dominance in air and at sea, the Allies in the SWPA were able to use maneuver warfare to completely shatter the Japanese positions in eastern New Guinea. Postern was the platform for the follow-on attack on New Britain (phase 3 of Cartwheel) that, together with the capture of Lae and the Huon Peninsula, would secure the Vitiaz Strait and allow the Allies to project naval and land power into the Bismarck Sea.

The campaigns of 1943 were to prove the high point of the operational success of the US-Australian coalition in the Pacific War. In a combined effort against the main enemy in the key Pacific theater, these two countries were to plan and execute a series of operations that were to totally defeat the Japanese.[1] Postern was a key link in the chain of operations for the completion of Cartwheel, which would form the foundation from which MacArthur would launch his march to the Philippines in 1944.

COALITION RELATIONS IN 1943

At the start of 1943, two key things drove the US-Australian military relationship in the SWPA. First, the relationship between MacArthur and Blamey, which had never been close, had by the middle of the year largely fractured. At this point, the two generals were still able to work together cooperatively at the operational and tactical levels; however, strategically the relationship was very tense. In early January 1943, MacArthur met with the Australian secretary of defense, Frederick Shedden, where he criticized Blamey and other Australian generals, placing the blame for the drawn-out campaign in Papua on their doorstep. MacArthur argued that Blamey had had an "easy time in New Guinea" and that he was "not a very sound tactician." MacArthur went on to argue that Blamey's subordinates did most of the work, and he lambasted him for not showing them due recognition in Blamey's public broadcast on 17 January. MacArthur obviously missed the irony of his statement, given his almost total lack of recognition of the Australian efforts in Papua and his ostracizing of Eichelberger due to the publicity he received after the victory at Buna.

MacArthur then warned Shedden that Blamey had political ambitions (a baseless claim) and argued that he should be removed as commander of the ALF and be made C-in-C of the Home Forces and that Lt. Gen. Leslie Morshead should command Australia's expeditionary forces.[2] It was an extraordinary attack, although typical of MacArthur in regard to officers whom he saw as lacking in unremitting loyalty. It was also advocating a command system that would have replicated all the problems that the RAAF was suffering under, a position that MacArthur saw as satisfactory to his and GHQ's requirements. Divide and conquer seemed to be part of MacArthur's plan for his coalition. Most significantly, MacArthur's suggested changes to command would have sidelined Blamey, removed Adv LHQ from the command chain, and reduced the Australians' abilities to influence GHQ's military strategy and the conduct of operations in the SWPA.

The second key issue was the relationships that had developed within the senior command of the SWPA. While there continued to be clashes over strategy, doctrine, and command culture that would affect the

relationship for the rest of the war, by early 1943 the cooperation between GHQ and Adv LHQ was at the best point it had been during
the war. While Sutherland and Willoughby continued to be difficult, a
cooperative and professional working relationship had been developed
between Chamberlin and Berryman, the two key operations officers, between Marshall and Chapman, the two key logistics officers, and among
the task force commanders.

Furthermore, the relationship between senior commanders had developed exceptionally well, and this dramatically reduced the impact of the
infamous Bataan Gang inside GHQ. The two constants in 1943 were
GHQ's internal division and MacArthur's continued feud with the USN.
Throughout 1943, the relationship of Vice Adm. Arthur S. Carpenter
(commander ANF) with MacArthur and GHQ remained tense, and Vice
Adm. Thomas Kinkaid would replace him late in the year. Meanwhile,
Carpenter maintained an excellent working relationship with the RAN,
and Barbey's arrival cemented an already close relationship between the
two navies. Kenney had squared off with Sutherland early on, and he
developed a very close rapport with MacArthur, as did his operational
commander, Ennis Whitehead. During 1943, he strengthened his already
excellent working relationship with the RAAF, NGF, and Adv LHQ.

Kenney was also a colorful personality who was prone to outlandish
comments. Berryman would note that later in the war Kenney stated that
he "bluffed the senior generals and admirals at GHQ conferences. . . . He
said he [Kenney] could make almost any statement and get away with it
because by the time it was checked it was stale and of not much importance."[3] There was, however, never a question as to his commitment to
forging an excellent working relationship with the Australians in order
to defeat the Japanese. Between the air forces, the relationship remained
very positive, but in 1943, like in 1942, the internal command crisis in the
RAAF would continue to dog the coalition. Between the navies, cooperation only increased with the arrival of VII Phib, and once the Australian
Army and the RAAF had largely been sidelined from the main theater
of operations in 1944, the RAN would continue to be at the front lines,
forging ever-closer relationships between the two naval services. Thus,
the paradox of the coalition in the SWPA during 1943 was that while the
two most senior commanders were at loggerheads and their relationship
continued to decline, at the operational and tactical levels their key staff
officers and commanders were forging an excellent working relationship
that was a key feature of the success of the 1943 campaign.

THE REORGANIZATION AND EXPANSION OF THE ALF

The establishment of the Sixth US Army and the arrival of Lt. Gen. Walter Krueger, as well as the considerable injection of American aircraft and VII Phib, had radically changed the balance of forces in the Allied coalition in the SWPA. However, while Krueger had an army HQ, at the beginning of 1943 he lacked substantial US ground formations to send into combat. Through 1942 while US airpower came to dominate the coalition, the Australian Army continued to provide the vast bulk of MacArthur's ground forces in the SWPA and the RAN the lion's share of naval power. As 1943 dawned, the USN's modest increase in strength in the region thoroughly outweighed the RAN's and consigned it to a junior role. For Krueger, however, the slow pace of the arrival of US ground forces would mean his army would remain the junior partner until the close of 1943.

The rise of US Army power in the SWPA was slow but steady during 1943. At the start of the year, MacArthur could still only muster I US Corps, consisting of the 32nd and 41st Divisions. Of these the 32nd Division was wrecked and in need of rest, major reinforcements, and retraining. In the 41st Division, the 163rd Regiment had suffered badly from disease during the Papua campaign and had taken modest battle causalities, while the remainder of the division was garrisoning the Gona-Sanananda-Buna Area. Beyond these divisions throughout 1943, a number of formations and units would be added to Krueger's army, including the 24th Infantry Division, the 1st Cavalry Division, the 1st Marine Division, and three separate infantry regimental combat teams (equivalent of another division): the 158th Infantry, the 112th Cavalry (Texas National Guard), and the 503rd Parachute Infantry Regiment (PIR).[4]

The most significant of these formations were the cavalry and Marines. The US National Guard formations sent to the SWPA in 1942 and 1943 lacked training, equipment, and personnel and were generally ranked the lowest in terms of combat readiness and capability by the leaders of the US Army ground forces.[5] The 1st Cavalry Division, however, was a regular army formation and one of the elite units of the US Army. It retired its horses in February 1943 and converted to an "augmented leg infantry division," based on two cavalry brigades of four cavalry regiments and three field artillery battalions, before shipping out to Australia in May.[6] It would train in northern Queensland before moving to New Guinea late in the year to stage for the Admiralty Islands operations. Its first combat, however, was not until February 1944.[7]

Alongside the 1st Cavalry, the 1st Marine Division was also an elite formation. These veterans of Guadalcanal, who adopted "Waltzing Matilda" as their divisional song after their furlough in Melbourne, constituted the most experienced and best US division in the Pacific at the time. They had been sent to Australia to recuperate from their epic performance in the South Pacific and in response to MacArthur's demands for a trained amphibious assault division. The Marines would take many months to recuperate and to reform their division; however, they would be available for the assault on New Britain late in 1943.[8]

In the 503rd PIR MacArthur also received another elite unit. Airborne units were made up of volunteers and, like the US Army Rangers, they took the cream of the crop from the arms corps. The 503rd PIR was formed on 2 March 1942 at Fort Benning, Georgia. From there it moved to California in October 1942 before shipping out to Australia and the SWPA in December. Designated a separate regiment (i.e., not part of any division), it would play a key role with the Australians in Operation Postern.[9]

As noted, the 1st Marine Division would undertake phase 3 of Cartwheel when it assaulted Cape Gloucester in New Britain, while the 112th Cavalry Regiment landed at Woodlark Island in June 1942 (phase 1 of Cartwheel) and would form the landing force for the assault on Arawe in New Britain on 15 December 1943. The 1st Cavalry Division landed at Los Negros on 29 February 1944, thus completing the isolation of Rabaul. The 24th Infantry Division had been on duty at Schofield Barracks during the attack on Pearl Harbor, and in May 1943 the division was altered for movement to Australia. The division was not complete in Australia until September 1943, after Postern was launched, and it would not see combat until April 1944, when it landed at Tanahmerah Bay in Hollandia.[10]

On the Australian side, the rapid expansion of the Australian Army in 1942 would pay dividends to Blamey and the Allies in 1943. In many ways Operation Postern was to be the pinnacle of its operational success, since thereafter manpower issues and major changes to the coalition in the SWPA would mean that the Australian Army would miss the major campaigns of 1944 and be consigned to minor roles in the coalition in 1945. The major addition to Blamey's order of battle in 1943 was the veteran 9th Division. The famous "Rats of Tobruk" had won enduring fame in the Middle East, finishing their tour there with a major role in the Battle of El Alamein. Having cleaned out the AIF reinforcement depot in the Middle East before its return, on arrival in Australia the division was overstrength, and this allowed Blamey to redistribute its troops to bring the 7th Division and other AIF units close to full strength for Operation Postern.[11]

Furthermore, the 9th Division brought to the SWPA another very senior and experienced commander, its GOC, General Morshead. One of the outstanding Australian commanders of World War II, on arrival Morshead would hand over the division to Maj. Gen. George Wootten (18th Brigade commander at the beachheads) and take over II Australian Corps. On news of his dispatch home, Blamey gave Morshead and his division clear, simple, and prophetic training instructions given the task ahead: first "combined (amphibious) training and opposed landings" and second "jungle warfare."[12]

In addition to the arrival of the 9th Division, Blamey undertook a number of reforms to the Australian Army for the operations in New Guinea in 1943. The most significant of these was the establishment of the "jungle division." The AIF infantry divisions, along with the 3rd, 5th, and 11th Militia Divisions, were modified to this new structure, which removed the divisional cavalry regiment along with HQ Royal Artillery, two field regiments, the antitank regiment, and the survey battery. Supply, transport, and medical services were also reduced. The brigade's battalions were similarly affected, and overall a jungle division had approximately four thousand fewer soldiers than a standard British infantry division.[13] These moves, coupled with the return of the last elements of the AIF from the Middle East, meant that by September 1943 Blamey would have a war establishment that would be able to put into the field six infantry divisions, an armored brigade, and a number of independent (commando) companies, plus corps, army, and base troops—some 155,500 men. An additional 106,300 men were operating in defense of the mainland and New Guinea as garrison troops, and a further 108,500 were in logistics and support units. Thus, the Australian Army committed some 370,300 men to the 1943 campaign in the SWPA.[14]

As Blamey had decided on his concept of operations for Postern well in advance of the GHQ warning instruction, the major roles for the AIF divisions in the plan had already been decided upon, and training had commenced on the basis of Blamey's concept of operations. The 7th Division was allocated to the land operation for the Wau–Markham–Nadzab–Lae region and the 9th Division to the amphibious assault on Lae and the Huon Peninsula. The 5th and 11th Divisions, plus the 4th Armoured Brigade (AIF), were slated as follow-on forces, while the 6th Division was in reserve. Berryman's planning staff confirmed the allocation of units and tables of organization on 12 May,[15] and after a long meeting between Blamey, Berryman, and Herring on 17 May, Adv LHQ was able to issue orders to NGF for the planning of the offensive.[16] Thereafter, each of the brigades in the 7th and 9th Divisions were allocated five to seven weeks of specialized and focused training before they were required to be ready for movement to New Guinea.[17]

Overall this meant that between the Australian AIF divisions, the US 1st Cavalry and 1st Marine Divisions, the Australian independent (commando) companies, and the US 503rd PIR, the SWPA had a strong cadre of highly trained and elite infantry formations. In support were the 3rd, 5th and 11th Australian Divisions (largely made up of militia units), the 41st and 32nd US (National Guard) Divisions, and the 112th Cavalry Regiment (Texas National Guard). From early 1944, the regular army 24th Infantry Division would become available for operations, and in May the 33rd US (National Guard) Division would arrive in New Guinea direct from Hawaii. All of these units/formations provided were more than capable of taking on and defeating the IJA's and IJN's ground forces in the SWPA.

PLANNING OPERATION POSTERN

GHQ's warning instruction of 30 April directed NGF to seize the Markham Valley, Lae, and Salamaua and secure the Huon Peninsula–Markham Valley area with the eventual outcome of seizing the northern coast of New Guinea as far as Madang.[18] The key was the Japanese base at Lae; however, Lae was not an end unto itself. As part of the broad-ranging strategy in the SWPA, the key pieces of terrain were airfields and ports (or locations where they can be developed). Lae would provide airfields for bomber and fighter squadrons and a major port to support the subsequent operations into the Huon Peninsula and the Markham Valley, as well as to support operations against New Britain and farther along the New Guinea coast toward the Philippines.[19]

As soon as the GHQ warning instruction was released, Berryman stepped up planning at Adv LHQ. He had set up a special planning team from within the staff at Adv LHQ, and he had a detailed scale model of the Huon Peninsula and Markham Valley constructed in a room at Adv LHQ. He ordered that this model be exact in every detail, down to swamps, bends in rivers, and areas of kunai grass. In order to ensure security, Berryman had the windows boarded up, a special lock fitted, and the room guarded twenty-four hours a day.[20] Initially access was restricted to himself, Blamey, Herring, and the immediate planning staff—a total of only eight officers.[21]

Berryman and Blamey responded to GHQ's warning instruction of 30 April 1943 with a note on 5 May 1943. With a target date of 1 August, Adv LHQ argued that the key determining factors would be logistics. Given the inhospitable terrain of New Guinea, the primitive infrastructure, the prevalence of disease, and the area's geographical isolation, Operation Postern was to be undertaken on a logistics shoestring. First, the shoestring had to be put in place, and second, Blamey and GHQ had to be certain that the shoestring would not unravel or break at the first sign of stress or strain.

To begin with, the Bulldog-Wau Road had to be complete to ensure an overland supply line from Wau to Nadzab. Second, DUKW amphibious vehicles needed to be available for the 7th Division to cross the Markham River. Third, the logistics base at Oro Bay had to be complete. Oro Bay was designed to support Alamo Force's operations in New Britain, as the current bases in Papua could not support both the Australian and US operations concurrently.[22] Significantly, it would take until June 1943 before Liberty cargo ships were able to enter Oro Bay and July before the first deepwater wharf was in operation.[23]

By 17 May 1943, Adv LHQ was able to issue orders. Phase 1 consisted of the "seizure of the Binocular [Lae]—Exchequer [Nadzab] area," while phase 2 consisted of subsequent operations in the Markham Valley and along the coast of the Huon Peninsula to secure Madang. Initially the focus of planning and preparations would evolve almost entirely around phase 1. With limited fire support available from the ANF and no carrier-based aircraft to support phase 1 operations, Adv LHQ directed that the 9th Division with the 2nd ESB would conduct a "shore to shore operation" in an area that will provide for an "unopposed landing . . . outside the range of field artillery in Binocular [Lae]." This division was to concentrate at Milne Bay but with the final assault being undertaken "as close to the landing as possible, but NOT more than 60 miles" from the objective—the range of the 2nd ESB's landing craft.[24] The latter requirement led to the operation at Nassau and Tambu Bays in June and July 1943. However, as noted, it was soon realized that the 2nd ESB would not be enough to transport the 9th Division, and instead the whole of VII Phib would be required to assault Lae.

For the 7th Division, the overland assault plan was based on the "seizure and development of an airfield at Nadzab." The airfield was to be

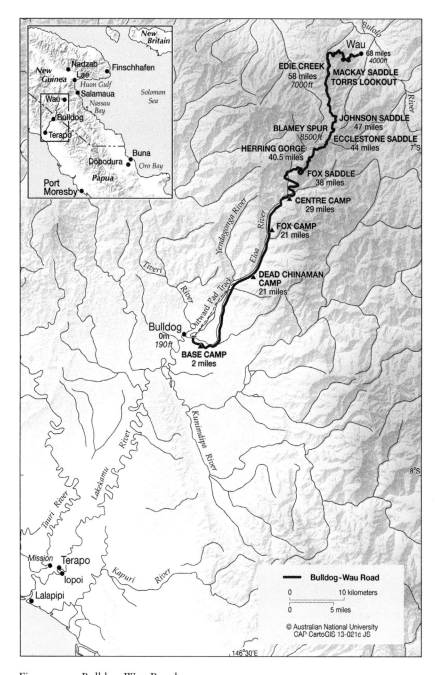

Figure 11.1 Bulldog-Wau Road, 1943

taken in order to make a pincer movement on Lae. However, the main role of 7th Division was to stop the overland reinforcement of Lae from the Markham Valley and form an anvil upon which the hammer of the 9th Division struck. This assault was originally to be achieved by moving the 7th Division overland and maintaining it via the Bulldog-Wau Road. Adv LHQ did, however, note that "initially maintenance [of the 7th Division] may be by air."[25] This was predicated on the fact that a second USAAF transport group (an additional fifty-two C-47 Dakota aircraft) had arrived in the SWPA, and six RAAF transport squadrons were available to support the USAAF's two groups. The Australians had also organized two air maintenance companies in New Guinea to work with the transport groups. A further two US C-47 transport groups would arrive in the second half of 1943.[26]

Kenney was highly critical of the resources expended on the Bulldog-Wau Road, and it would soon prove that he was right. The Australian overcautiousness was, however, driven by the management of risk. After the Wau airstrip almost fell to the Japanese in early 1943, staff officers at NGF feared that if Nadzab were retaken by the Japanese or they were able to interdict its operation with artillery and heavy weapons, the assault of the 7th Division on the airfield and its maintenance in the Markham Valley might fail. This concern was also predicated on the operational assessment that the Australians would face extensive Japanese defenses at Lae, along the lines of those seen at the beachheads. The unknown factor to NGF in early 1943 was just how powerful the Fifth Air Force would become, especially in transport aircraft. In the end, the additional support that GHQ and the Fifth Air Force were able to provide was to ensure the success of the operation and make the Bulldog-Wau Road largely superfluous.[27]

THE JAPANESE PLAN FOR 1943

The Allied plans were not being developed in isolation—the enemy got a vote on how Operation Postern would play out. IGHQ's position was insidious, although not desperate. As the Japanese had lost air superiority over New Guinea and its surrounds, they had also lost sea control. This greatly hampered their ability to supply, reinforce, and maneuver their troops. Their advantage in New Guinea was largely one of position. They could operate on interior lines to develop a response to the Allies.

However, the virtual absence of modern infrastructure in New Guinea, especially in terms of roads, severely curtailed their positional advantage.

The Allies' air superiority conferred a logistics superiority, and given the vast distances and inhospitable terrain, the Allied advantage was magnified. It also allowed the Allies "unrivaled strategic mobility," which gave them the ability to concentrate in time. Lacking this option, the Japanese had to push their forces forward and defend all possible lines of attack, leaving themselves vulnerable to being cut off and defeated in detail, or to hold key positions while holding centralized reserves to counterattack and defeat Allied attacks. Both of these options had major drawbacks. In the end, they decided to hold the key locations of Salamaua and Lae in force, while building up an air counterattack force and developing infrastructure to support the overland movement of their reserve forces.[28]

In order to undertake this plan, the 51st Japanese Division was ordered to continue operations in front of Salamaua, and Lae was reinforced to six thousand defenders. In January and February 1943, the 20th and 41st Divisions were landed at Wewak, out of the range of Allied aircraft, and thereafter the 20th made its way overland to Madang and then along the coast to Lae, while the 41st secured Wewak. To support these operations, in May the IJA decided to try to construct a road from Madang to Lae. Supply problems and a focus on combat over support units meant that the Japanese in New Guinea had to build this road largely by hand, as they lacked basic engineering equipment. The road was scheduled to be complete by June, but by September it was only one fifth of the way to Madang.[29]

INITIAL PLANNING: GHQ AND ADV LHQ

In outlining his initial plan, Blamey made it clear that he would return to NGF to take command of Postern just before the offensive got under way. Herring would command the initial operations against Salamaua, and once the target date approached, Blamey would resume command of NGF, again raising it to an army-level HQ, while Herring would assume command of the 7th and 9th Divisions for the assault on Lae via I Australian Corps HQ. This would replicate the command relationship used during the beachhead battles. To complement these moves, Berryman would move forward with Blamey to again take on the role of MGGS NGF, while also continuing as DCGS. This organization also reflected the command relationship that MacArthur had put in place, whereby Blamey no longer functioned as commander of the ALF but rather as a task force commander. MacArthur's orders had placed Blamey in command of New Guinea and the Australian ground task force, and so commanding Postern was part of Blamey's command responsibilities.

MacArthur also took time during the planning of Cartwheel to reiterate his role and that of his task force commanders. GHQ would once again send an advance element to Port Moresby for the offensive with the four task forces—NGF, New Britain (Alamo) Force, AAF, and ANF—under direct command.[30] For the Australians, MacArthur's position as the sole joint commander was well understood. LHQ's "Operational Instruction No. 46, Co-ordination of planning and operations between Navy, Army and Air Force," released on 6 May 1943, details MacArthur's centralist and directive control of operations:

> With the institution of Allied Command the South-West Pacific Area and the *application to certain areas* of the principle of unified command, it has become necessary to revise previous instructions. . . . The principal effect of this revision is to eliminate all Combined Defence Headquarters and Combined Operational Intelligence Centres with the exception of the C.O.I.C. located with GHQ, S.W.P.A.
>
> The appointment of a Commander-in-Chief, South-West Pacific Area provides the means for controlling and directing the operation of the Navy, Army and Air Force on the highest military plane. The recent operations in New Guinea [1942 Campaign], where the C-in-C, S.W.P.A. personally directed activities of the three Services, shows how this procedure *may* be used in actual operations.[31]

There was, however, no "may" about it. MacArthur's two warning instructions for Cartwheel clearly outlined his commitment to this approach to command. At times MacArthur would direct that certain forces, such as the 2nd ESB, come under NGF's "control" for limited periods of time or specific tasks but never its "command."[32] Centralized, top-down command from GHQ would remain, as would MacArthur's role as the sole joint commander and the need for cooperative, rather than unified, command between the services.

Coordination for Operation Postern, especially air and naval support for NGF, would thus have to be undertaken by Blamey's HQ and GHQ. Blamey and Berryman put their planning system in place based on their training and doctrine. Adv LHQ was to control high-level issues such as logistics, force concentration, and command relationships requiring coordination with GHQ. In addition, Blamey directed Berryman and his staff to take over most of the initial corps-level planning, especially that pertaining to the establishment of supply dumps and logistics bases and coordination of operational plans with the divisions. This was done to allow Herring and his staff to concentrate on the Salamaua deception operation, but it was also a case of Blamey selectively applying British command doctrine.

By this stage of the war, Blamey was well aware of Herring's limitations as a commander, especially in planning and staff work. In addition, he was also conscious of the general lack of training and high-level planning experience among Herring's staff. Blamey therefore centralized army and corps planning in the hands of Berryman, who was widely recognized as the army's most experienced and expert planner.[33] From here, following the British decentralized approach, Blamey and Berryman delegated tactical planning down to the two very experienced divisional commanders, George Vasey and George Wootten, both of whom were highly trained staff officers, with well-trained and proficient staffs. In order to coordinate efforts, Berryman held a planning conference every Wednesday at Adv LHQ at 10:30 a.m. to "co-ordinate the administrative planning for POSTERN with the operational planning."[34] Early on, the Australians thought that the target date of 1 August was too ambitious and focused on 1 September instead. This was reaffirmed when Blamey got a commitment from MacArthur that the operation would not commence until the Bulldog-Wau Road and the training of I Australian Corps were complete.[35]

The first major issue between GHQ and Adv LHQ was over the scheme of maneuver. Where Blamey envisaged the main effort being the 9th Division's amphibious landing, supported by the 7th Division in the Markham Valley, GHQ saw the operation unfolding in reverse. GHQ's concerns were over its ability to support a two-brigade assault with the 2nd ESB, a view that was mainly driven by the availability of VII Phib after phase 1. On meeting with Chamberlin's staff on 16 May on this issue, Berryman and one of his senior staff officers, Barham, as well as the senior Australian staff officer on Barbey's staff, Brig. Ronald Hopkins, lobbied hard. Given the most likely date for operations was September, rather than August, VII Phib should be available, and the use of the whole of the 9th Division as the main effort would provide a much higher chance of Lae falling quickly.

Chamberlin and Berryman meet again on 21 May, and Blamey also discussed the plan and the role of the 9th Division with MacArthur on the same day.[36] Chamberlin saw the merits in the plan and the allocation of

Barbey's amphibious force to the operation, and he wrote to Sutherland a few days later, arguing that "to all who have studied this problem it appears extremely risky to believe that the Engineer Brigade can accomplish this mission assigned without assistance. It is unanimously believed that substantial elements of the Amphibious Force must be employed."[37]

When Chamberlin and Berryman met again at the end of the month, the use of Barbey's force had become self-evident.[38] In addition, II Australian Corps HQ staff, along with the GOCs of the 6th, 7th, and 9th Divisions, Brig. Gen. W. F. Heavy (CO 2nd ESB), and Capt. Roy Husdon (USN liaison officer at GHQ), conducted a staff exercise in Brisbane on the landing. At this conference it was realized that the nature of the operation was far beyond the capabilities of the 2nd ESB. In order to complete the mission, VII Phib would have to be used to land the troops, and the 2nd ESB would be needed to maintain the force ashore. This meant that Barbey would assume command of the 2nd ESB and conduct the planning with the 9th Australian Division. For Barbey this was a major problem, as he still lacked a proper planning staff, and what staff officers he did have were absorbed with the planning for phase 1 of Cartwheel. In response, MacArthur contacted the JCS with a specific request for additional support for Barbey. However, VII Phib's planners would only become available to the Australians from 27 June 1943.[39]

Berryman and his staff then traveled to Queensland and Port Moresby to confer with the divisional commanders and their staffs and NGF HQ.[40] During these meetings both Herring and Vasey raised concerns about moving and maintaining the 7th Division via a land-based line of communication in the Markham Valley. Vasey was especially concerned about operational security and the physical effects on his troops of marching overland and then making a major river crossing. Instead he proposed that a US paratroop battalion be used to take the abandoned airfield at Nadzab so that his entire division could then be flow in and resupplied by air.[41] It was a high-risk, high-reward proposal but one that could potentially be decisive. Blamey, Berryman, and Herring all studied the idea and gave it their full support. Blamey took it to MacArthur, who denied the request for a US paratroop battalion, instead offering the whole of the 503rd PIR. As the plan evolved, the 503rd PIR would be supported by an Australian pioneer battalion and an engineering field company, which would take the 7th Division's original overland route to marry up with the US paratroopers and then prepare the airstrip to allow two brigades of the 7th Division to be flown in using the Fifth Air Force's transport fleet.[42]

Throughout May and June 1943, Adv LHQ had worked with GHQ on major changes to the plans for Operation Postern. At every turn GHQ had been supportive and forthcoming in its support. MacArthur had conceded to Blamey's request for addition time to allow for planning and training and for the use of VII Phib to land two brigades of the 9th Division, with the third as a follow-on force, and he had provided a whole regiment of paratroopers in response to Blamey's request for a battalion. The planning and liaison conferences went smoothly, and the coalition operated in harmony. However, as May and June turned to July and August, two major issues confronted the Allies: first, the need to provide air support over the Huon Peninsula, and second, logistics, force concentration, and tactical planning issues for Postern. The first of these problems would highlight the flexibility of the coalition and the outstanding tacticians who commanded the task forces in the SWPA. The second would lay bare the fundamental differences in doctrine and planning between the two nations.

KENNEY AND THE CRITICAL ROLE OF AIRPOWER

Airpower was to play a major role in the success of Operation Postern. The decision to air-land the 7th Division at Nadzab and use an entire paratroop regiment, as well as cover the amphibious landing of the 9th Division, was all predicated on the increase of airpower in the SWPA in the lead-up to the assault on Lae. As noted earlier, large-scale air reinforcements from the United States made this possible, and the delay in D-day from August to September helped to ensure that these reinforcements were in place. By September, the 380th Heavy Bombardment Group had started operating out of Darwin, and the US Troop Carrier Wing could field fourteen squadrons.[43]

The major operational problem that now faced the Allies for the assault on Lae was the buildup of Japanese airpower at Wewak. On 27 July, IGHQ had ordered Lt. Gen. Kumaichi Teramoto's Fourth Air Army from the NEI to the Southwest Pacific. Teramoto's command included the 6th and 7th Air Divisions and the 14th Air Brigade. By basing his planes at Wewak, Teramoto would be able to support operations over Lae and the Huon Peninsula while being located outside of the range of Allied fighter aircraft, making any bombing mission against the Japanese air bases highly vulnerable. To the Japanese, the air fighting over New Guinea in early 1943 had been indecisive, and they felt that with these substantial reinforcements momentum in the air war might well shift in their direction.[44]

Kenney and Whitehead solved this issue in their typical aggressive style. They aimed to destroy Japanese airpower in New Guinea before the offensive got under way by drawing the Japanese into a series of battles before September 1943. To do this, Kenney decided to build a secret air base deep behind Japanese lines in New Guinea that would provide him the range to launch his bombers with heavy fighter support against the Japanese bases. The location selected was the area around Tsili Tsili near the Watut River, some forty miles (by air) northwest of Wau, and west of Lae. The irony of the name was not lost on Kenney or on the staff at GHQ, who thought the plan as ridiculous as the name. Kenney decreed the new airfield would be known as Marilinan, after the town four miles to the south. This airfield would also prove vital in supporting the operations of I Australian Corps around Lae and in particular the landing of the 503rd PIR at Nadzab.[45]

Kenney needed grounds troops to support his plan, and despite opposition at GHQ he secured support for the scheme from Blamey and Berryman. NGF provided the 57th/60th Militia Battalion, while the Fifth Air Force provided the US 871st Airborne Engineers to develop the airstrip into an airfield capable of handling fighter and transport aircraft.[46] The danger of Allied airfields in this area was not lost on the Japanese, and in June they had been observing the movement of PIB and some small Allied patrols around the airfield at Bena Bena (fifty miles by air northwest of Marilinan) with concern and added it to their list of targets.

Aware of the Japanese interest in Bena Bena, Kenney decided to put a deception plan in place to protect his project at Marilinan. He arranged for NGF to use the Allied troops and sympathetic local population at Bena Bena to start constructing a dummy airstrip in a manner that would attract the attention of the Japanese. Meanwhile, the troops arrived at Marilinan on 16 June, by 1 July transport aircraft were able to land on the strip, and by 26 July the first fighter aircraft arrived.[47] At Bena Bena the Japanese were making almost daily attacks to stop construction, and by 10 August the Fourth Japanese Air Army had amassed over 250 aircraft at Wewak for an air counteroffensive. So far the deception was playing perfectly, but Kenney noted that his "fingers by this time were getting calluses from being crossed so hard, but the Japs still showed no signs of knowing that we were building an [air]field right in their back yard."[48]

On 14 August, Kenney moved two fighter squadrons from the 35th Fighter Group into Marilinan. They arrived on the same day as the first Japanese reconnaissance aircraft. A heavy US fighter screen met the first Japanese strike the next day. Three days later Kenney went on the offensive, striking at the Japanese air bases at Wewak with heavy and medium bombers escorted by the 35th Fighter Group and other fighters who had staged through Marilinan. The assault became known as the "the black day of August 17" for the Japanese Army Air Force, costing it over one hundred aircraft destroyed and hundreds of air and ground crew members killed. Kenney pounded these airfields relentlessly in the days and weeks that followed, effectively destroying the vast majority of Japanese airpower in New Guinea by the end of the month.[49]

PLANNING TENSIONS: JULY–AUGUST 1943

In July, the discussions between Adv LHQ and GHQ mainly centered on logistics and force concentration, and here the tensions started to show in the different approaches to planning. Force-concentration planning was especially difficult given the worldwide shortage of shipping. On 2 July, Adv LHQ lodged its shipping requirements with GHQ, and it became clear that the Australians' needs outstripped the current transport arrangements. This shortage posed a risk to Adv LHQ's ability to move the troops to their staging areas in New Guinea on time.

For GHQ and Adv LHQ, the issue over logistics started to cause major divisions based on their yin-and-yang approach to planning. Chamberlin wanted to know the full details of the Australians plans in order to assess logistics requirements, while the Australians wanted to know the shipping and support assets available so as to do their planning. The addition of VII Phib to the landing of the 9th Division further complicated force-concentration issues and affected planning for training as well as operations. However, neither Adv LHQ nor NGF could inform VII Phib as to their tonnage requirements for the operation, as GHQ had not provided the shipping or transportation details for the movement of the 9th Division to New Guinea. Thus, tactical planning for the 9th Division was being delayed, as it could not predict issues such as ammunition, rations, stores, and fuel allocations until the shipping tonnage allocations to move the division to New Guinea were solved.[50]

An initial compromise was reached to reduce demand, when Chamberlin agreed that the motor transport of the 41st Division could be left in the Buna area and be taken over by Australian forces.[51] Soon afterward, Blamey, Berryman, Chapman, and Lt. Gen. John Northcott (Australian CGS) met with MacArthur, Chamberlin, Sutherland, Marshall and Kenney on 15 July to review the progress of operations. Force concentration and logistics were the major topics. At this conference, MacArthur came to realize the extent of the problem, and on 29 July he ordered GHQ to provide Operation Postern with first-order logistics priority.[52]

MacArthur's order was unable to solve the shortage of shipping or recover the delays caused by weeks of debate and argument. Eventually the 9th Division scaled back its logistics requirements to the bare minimum, and GHQ was able to procure some additional shipping. This, combined with the swapping of the motor transport with the 41st Division and the rearrangement of other convoy and transport arrangements, meant that the 9th Division was able to make it to Papua on time and with just enough equipment and supplies to fulfill its mission. However, the delays and ambiguity over tonnage limits and supplies complicated the 9th Division's and VII Phib's planning, and it meant that loading arrangements were not settled early enough to allow for effective testing and rehearsals.[53]

To Chamberlin these problems were being caused by the inadequacies of the Australian planning. On 10 July, Chamberlin got a letter from Barbey with an attached plan for his discussions with Herring on the 9th Division's operations. Chamberlin's reply included his desire that Barbey push "the matter of detailed planning" as the "Australian staff were undoubtedly new to the game."[54] Chamberlin was starting to become concerned by the lack of detail GHQ had on the tactical planning for the 9th and 7th Divisions. Berryman kept reassuring GHQ that planning was progressing well, but GHQ's inquiries to the Fifth Air Force and VII Phib were raising concerns. Furthermore, GHQ was particularly displeased that Adv LHQ and NGF HQ seemed to have not done any planning for phase 2 of Postern.

Chamberlin decided to bring the matter to a head with Berryman on 4 August 1943. At this meeting Chamberlin directly questioned Berryman on the details of the tactical plans for the two Australian divisions. Berryman batted away the questions, but when Chamberlin persisted, Berryman noted that he had nothing further to add to Blamey's comments to MacArthur at their meeting a few days earlier. He went on to say that he only expected detailed tactical plans to be finished "about ten days before D-Day when Gen Blamey would be in New Guinea." To Chamberlin this was completely abhorrent. Berryman retorted by arguing that detailed planning had been given to the corps and divisional HQ "in accordance with the general outline plan as submitted," per Australian Army doctrine.[55] Chamberlin replied that if Adv LHQ's plan had been submitted to the US Army Command and General Staff School, it would have gotten a mark of "no more than 20 per cent."[56] The direct cause of this disagreement was, as Berryman noted in his diary after the meeting, that "we [Australians] work on a decentralised [planning] basis where GHQ have a highly centralised one."[57]

The next day, Chamberlin wrote to Sutherland that Adv LHQ was not planning on submitting any further details, and he noted that Berryman seemed to know nothing of this planning other than "he was confident it was progressing well." Chamberlin also noted that he was "given the impression that there was little conception on the part of the Chief of Staff, Allied Land Forces [Berryman] of the logistic problem" and that Berryman apparently had no details of the operations of the 7th Division and its coordination with the Fifth Air Force because Adv LHQ had not been "informed of the plans prepared" by NGF. Both of these suggestions were rather insidious given Adv LHQ had been arguing with Chamberlin and Marshall (G-4 GHQ) over logistics since early June and that on 25 July a major conference had taken place at NGF HQ between the 7th Division and the Fifth Air Force to fix the planning for Nadzab and they had been meeting almost daily ever since. Chamberlin, however, seemed to be motivated by a desire to paint the whole Australian planning process as inadequate, and he ended by suggesting that GHQ therefore directly bypass Adv LHQ and coordinate directly with Herring's HQ.[58]

Such interference was as much anathema to the Australians as the lack of planning details were to GHQ. In fact, Berryman was being rather duplicitous with Chamberlin. He knew full well the details, having been put in charge of all planning by Blamey and having just completed a round of visits to all HQs. However, Berryman and Blamey were determined to plan their way and make sure that MacArthur and GHQ did not interfere in the planning and operations as they had done in Papua in 1942 and were currently doing in the operation against Salamaua.

Sutherland took up Chamberlin's suggestion of direct intervention. On 14 August, he wrote directly to Herring, demanding that he provide all detailed plans to GHQ by 1 September. Given that this was the deadline for the commencement of operations, it is unclear what Sutherland hoped to achieve. Chamberlin also complained to MacArthur that "the missions omitted [in the Australian plans] are more numerous than those covered. . . . Judged from our standard of the preparation of combat orders, it is elementary and incomplete."[59]

As a result, MacArthur wrote to Blamey on this issue, and he responded with two separate notes on 31 August 1943. This seems to have satisfied MacArthur, as there is no evidence of him ever responding to

Blamey's clarifications or of any meetings being held to discuss these issues. By then it was only a few days before the start of the offensive, and it seems Berryman's stalling tactics had bought Adv LHQ and NGF all the time they needed to complete the detailed tactical plans without GHQ interference.[60]

The final major problem that dogged preparations for Postern involved the support and landing time for the amphibious assault. However, this was largely a result of interservice, as opposed to inter-Allied, coordination and planning. The 9th Division wanted to land as early as possible to achieve surprise and to allow time to unload the ships. The navy also favored an early landing time due to concerns over air attack, but it, much to Wootten's displeasure, planned to reduce its exposure on the beaches by reducing the logistics loads in the landing ships to decrease unloading times. The Fifth Air Force wanted a later time to provide close air support to the landing. A further rift developed when the army and navy requested direct air cover over the landing, which was rejected by the Fifth Air Force, which proposed to provide air cover through offensive operations against the Japanese air force.[61]

This resulted in Blamey, Berryman, Wootten, Barbey, Carpenter, Whitehead, and Kenney all arguing in various forums about the timing of the landing at Lae and the layout of the air cover. The planning had thus reached an impasse. As MacArthur was the sole joint commander, it fell to him to arbitrate. As he dealt with most such issues, MacArthur decided on a compromise solution that satisfied no one. The final timing for the landing was set at 6:30 a.m., and MacArthur sided with Barbey over the issue of providing a combat air patrol over the landing site, much to Kenney and Whitehead's displeasure. The major cause of this problem was that joint planning had not been affected properly. In particular, the AAF had sent only junior officers to the planning meetings with VII Phib and the 9th Division. Barbey's postoperational report was firm on the need for this to change in the future.[62]

CONCLUSION

The planning for Postern had been long and exhausting for all involved, but by the end of August it was complete. On 20 August, Blamey and key staff officers arrived at Port Moresby to take command of NGF.[63] On 23 August, Australian jeeps finally passed on Bulldog-Wau Road,[64] and on 27 August, Herring opened I Australian Corps headquarters at

Dobodura, while the 7th and 9th Divisions were able to issue their final operational orders.[65] With MacArthur's final consent, Berryman issued Blamey's order to start the offensive on 4 September with the landing of Wootten's division, followed a day later with the paratroop assault on Nadzab. In the end, all of the major problems and difficulties around planning for the offensive had been worked out. In the face of two different command and staff systems, the key to working out an effective plan and coordinating all the elements of military power in the SWPA had been the senior officers at GHQ and Adv LHQ. From there, tactical-level planning had been undertaken in an exceptionally cooperative manner, other than some interservice difficulties.

This process was not without its difficulties. The issues over force concentration and logistics highlighted the problems with MacArthur's cooperative command system. The plan was fused together, but the logistics elements remained fragile and far from ideal. As Blamey would note, Postern was launched before the logistics system was functioning properly, simply because to delay any longer would have allowed the Japanese more time to prepare their defenses and concentrate their troops. His major concern was that while he believed that the supply system could support phase 1 of the operation, the capabilities to support phase 2 (Postern) and phase 3 of Cartwheel (the US landings on New Britain) were completely dependent on the rapid collapse of the Japanese position at Lae and a swift expansion of logistics support once its port was captured. This level of risk was deemed acceptable. The key to pulling off phases 2 and 3 of Cartwheel would now completely depend on the swift capture of Lae.[66]

12

The Liberation of New Guinea

THE YEAR 1943 WAS THE TURNING POINT in the Western Allies' war against the Japanese. The assault on Lae was the first-ever major, deliberate assault of a joint and combined nature in the SWPA, and as such it was one of the key events that heralded a new era of operations against the Japanese. However, it is a period that is more often than not overlooked in the history of the Pacific War. Operations such as those in New Guinea in 1943 lack the tension and drama of the battles of 1942, such as the Coral Sea, Midway, Guadalcanal, Milne Bay, and Kokoda. Furthermore, they were of a smaller scale than many of the battles fought in 1944 and 1945, and thus they lack the climactic feel of the actions at Leyte Gulf, the Philippines Sea, Luzon, Okinawa, and Iwo Jima.[1] Despite being often sidelined in both the US and Australian historiography and memory of the war, the liberation of New Guinea was one of the key platforms for victory in the SWPA, and it helped to lay the foundations for the assault on the Philippine Islands in 1944.

A number of key features of these operations stand out. Operation Postern was the first major joint sea, air, and land assault in the SWPA. It saw the first use of paratroopers by the Allies in the Pacific War and the first use of paratroopers and air-landing troops combined with an amphibious assault. These were all major achievements that demonstrate just how far the coalition in the SWPA had come from the dark days of December 1942 at Buna and Sanananda.

THE TIGER AND THE WOLF

At the beginning of September, the Japanese maintained a considerable force at Lae. Some six thousand troops were dug in around the town, including parts of the 80th, 41st, and 21st Infantry Regiments, artillery from the 21st Independent Mixed Brigade and the 14th Field Regiment, 5th Sasebo Naval Infantry, and an assortment of engineers and logistics troops. Furthermore, Lt. Gen. Hidemitsu Nakano's 51st Division had thousands of more troops in contact with the 3rd Australian Division outside of Salamaua.[2]

Nakano had positioned his troops to stop an overland advance on Lae from Salamaua, but on 3 September, all of his planning came to nothing. Sixteen miles east of his position, a huge Allied armada had assembled offshore. Because it landed outside the range of the guns of his 14th Field Regiment, Nakano had no choice but to plead for air support and desperately try to rearrange his defenses. Sending out an advance force to make contact with the Allies, he hoped it would buy enough time for the bulk of his force to dig in (again) and hold the town.

Facing Nakano on that morning was an overwhelming task force. VII Phib had arrived in the predawn light and commenced unloading two brigades of the 9th Division under the cover of a barrage from the Seventh Fleet's destroyers. The first echelon of Wootten's troops, some 560 men, came ashore from Barbey's fast destroyer transports, while the second echelon splashed ashore from eighteen LCIs. These two waves consisted of 4,240 men, behind which came the large LSTs that started to dispense guns, vehicles, ammunition, food, and support troops.

The soldiers and sailors worked desperately to unload the ships. With MacArthur's compromise on the landing arrangements, Wootten's men had lost four hours of unloading time, so they worked at breakneck speed to get as much out of the ships as possible. Meanwhile, Barbey and his sailors constantly scanned the skies for Japanese aircraft. Not long after the landing of the LCIs, three Japanese bombers, escorted by six fighters, broke through Kenney's fighter screen and streaked toward the beachhead. The troops ashore scattered, and the ships pumped out as much antiaircraft fire as they could as the fighters strafed the beach and the bombers spewed forth their loads. The first bomb hit *LCI-339*, driving through its thin decking and exploding deep inside. It blew steel plating and men from the 2/33rd Battalion high into the sky. The next bomber's load split a row of LCIs before blowing a large hole in *LCI-341*. Among those killed was Lt. Col. Reg Wall, the 2/23rd's commanding officer. Eight of his soldiers died alongside him, while another forty-five were wounded. A second raid would soon claim the lives of thirty-four Australians and seven US sailors, while crippling two LSTs. However, this was to be the only major resistance the Japanese were able to put up against the amphibious assault.[3]

Nakano's new plans were soon in further disarray. While his division had been quick to reorient itself and make contact with the Australian amphibious troops, the following day revealed the drone of Allied aircraft

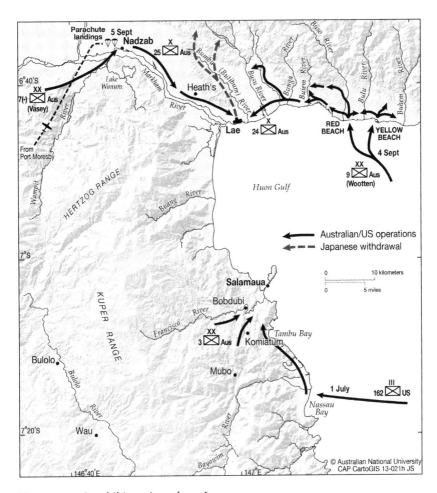

Figure 12.1 Amphibious Assault on Lae

to the northwest of his position. As the sun rose in the early morning, dozens of Allied fighter and bomber squadrons filled the skies above New Guinea. They targeted Nakano's fixed defenses and paralyzed movement across his front. Then, just before 10:30 a.m., a slow and steady drone of approaching aircraft could be heard. At 10:35, hundreds of parachutes blossomed over Nadzab airfield. Within minutes, Col. Kenneth H. Kinsler's 503rd PIR "blotted out the sky" and descended through the protective smokescreen right onto the airstrip.[4] Soon afterward, an "all-volunteer" detachment of Australian gunners from the 2/4th Field Regiment made their maiden parachute jump onto the strip along with two

25-pounder field guns. At the same time, Australian sappers and pioneers started to bridge the Markham River to the west, while later that afternoon the combined force under Kinsler's command secured the area and started to prepare the airstrip. At 11:00 a.m. on 6 September, the first C-47s started to land the advance troops of the 7th Division. Over the next two days, an additional 171 C-47s landed the HQ and the better part of two battalions of the 25th Australian Infantry Brigade.[5]

By now, Nakano's defensive plan had collapsed, and the Japanese position in eastern New Guinea had been completely unhinged. Lt. Gen. Kane Yoshihara, the Eighteenth Army's chief of staff, noted that "while the Lae units were keeping at bay the tiger at the front gate, the wolf had appeared at the back gate."[6] The fall of Lae was now inevitable.

THE RACE TO LAE

The key question for MacArthur, Blamey, and Herring was, how long would it take to secure Lae and its critically important harbor? If the Japanese resisted like they had at the beachheads, Salamaua, and on New Georgia, then it could well be months before this critical logistics node was in Allied hands. As phase 3 of Cartwheel depended on the opening of an advanced base at Lae in order to support the advance of both the Australian and American armies, its speedy capture was essential. When the advance got under way, Berryman prudently prepared orders for the 4th Armoured Brigade and troops from the 11th Division to reinforce Herring's corps.[7] In the meantime, Vasey and Wootten were racing to surround Lae and be the first into the town.

Neither route to Lae was easy. Wootten had plenty of troops ashore, but the Australians had totally underestimated the requirements to keep the beachhead open.[8] One well-placed Japanese air force bomb could have brought his whole division to a halt, and he was forced to pull more and more troops out of the front lines to unload ships and reorganize his base area. At the front, the 9th Division's troops struggled along the jungle shore and were forced to deploy against increasing Japanese resistance while making a full-scale assault across the Busu River.[9]

For Vasey, the main problem was the concentration of his division in order to have enough troops to exploit his tactical advantages. He got permission to use Kinsler's paratroopers in more offensive patrols but knew full well that these men were one of MacArthur's key strategic reserves and that they could be taken off him at any time; their longevity on

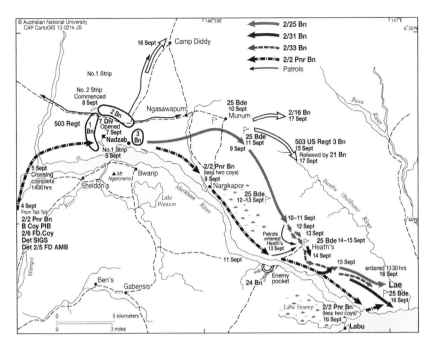

Figure 12.2 Airborne and Air-Landing Assault on Lae

the front lines was always going to be limited.[10] Bad weather had delayed the buildup for three days, but in the meantime 7th Division had pushed as hard as it could to fly in troops and supplies. The only major setback so far had been a catastrophic accident on the first morning of the operation. A fully laden US B-24 Liberator had failed its takeoff and plowed into trucks packed with infantry from the 2/33rd Battalion. The aircraft exploded in a ball of fire, killing the entire crew and fifty-nine soldiers while leaving another ninety-two wounded. This accident was the greatest single loss of life in the battle for Lae.[11]

With his position hopeless and both Australian divisions rapidly closing in on Lae, Nakano decided to withdrawal his troops rather than face annihilation. On 8 September, he ordered a breakout northward over the Finnisterre Range, along the line of the Busu River via Musom and Boana. Forming a strong rear guard, Nakano hoped to keep the Australians at bay while the bulk of his force escaped. However, on 14 September, the 2/25th Battalion (7th Division) routed an enemy-delaying position and captured a range of documents including the withdrawal order. It quickly made its way up the chain of command, and Blamey ordered that I Australian Corps move troops to interdict and wipe out the Japanese.

Instead of moving rapidly to secure a decisive victory, Herring sat on his hands. He prioritized arguing with NGF HQ over orders and protocol after objecting to a cable from Berryman, sent on Blamey's behest, that directed the movement of specific units into blocking positions. To Herring, he should have been given a mission order and been allowed to plan accordingly. While he engaged in a vigorous exchange of signals with Berryman over procedure, he did nothing to intercept the Japanese. Wootten followed Herring's lead, while Vasey had already taken matters into his own hands, redeploying the battalions of the 503rd PIR to cut off the Japanese in his area of operations.[12]

The period of 13–15 September proved to be the heaviest fighting at the front, as the Japanese sought to hold off the Australians and the US paratroopers and make good their escape. Herring continued to dither. After finally feeling that he had vented his frustration to Blamey, he gave orders to redeploy his units. The 9th Division did not move to intercept the Japanese until the morning of 16 September and deployed only half the force that NGF HQ had ordered. Wootten remained focused on beating Vasey to Lae. On the same day, the first elements of Vasey's division entered the town, only to be halted by the 9th Division's artillery. The confusion was compounded when the Fifth Air Force bombed both divisions.[13]

The rapid victory at Lae was a remarkable feat of arms. To Berryman and Blamey, it was a complete vindication of their resistance to MacArthur, Kenney, and Herring's push to take Salamaua as soon as possible.[14] The comparison to the operations in Papua in 1942 could not be more different. From fighting a land campaign in a maritime environment, the Allies were now conducting genuine combined-arms and joint operations utilizing maneuver warfare aimed at shattering the enemy's physical and moral cohesion. It was a major evolution from the grinding battles of attrition that preceded it. Cooperation between the 503rd PIR and the 7th Division had been outstanding, as was the relationship between the 9th Division and VII Phib.[15] The AAF continued to show its devastating effectiveness and ability to operate together with, as well as in support of, MacArthur's land and maritime forces.

It had taken only twelve days since the 9th Division's amphibious assault for Lae to fall. It cost I Australian Corps only 115 killed, 501 wounded, and 73 missing.[16] By way of contrast, the battles for Buna, Gona, and Sanananda had lasted sixty-four days and cost 6,900 casualties,[17] while Halsey's seizure of New Georgia in 1943 had cost the US Army 1,195 dead and 4,000 wounded in an operation that had lasted sixty-seven days.[18] As a result of the swift victory, Blamey was able to cancel the arrival of the armored brigade and follow-on troops, while instead support and logistics troops were quickly moved into the town and port to develop it as a base of operations. The break-in had been a spectacular success. GHQ and NGF HQ now needed to ensure that they exploited their advantages and moved quickly to keep the Japanese off balance.

POSTERN PHASE II: PLANNING AND THE ASSAULT ON FINSCHHAFEN

The issues around planning for phase 2 of Postern had long been a bone of contention between GHQ and Adv LHQ. Chamberlin, Sutherland, and MacArthur had all raised concerns about the lack of detail for operations after the fall of Lae. The Australians, however, had deferred planning until phase 1 was set and then looked at a number of contingencies depending on the time it took to capture Lae. Blamey had eventually released to GHQ an appreciation, prepared by Berryman and his staff on 3 1 August, for further operations in phase 2. In this document, Blamey outlined the importance of seizing both sides of the Vitiaz Strait, which would thereafter allow the Allies to advance either northwest or northeast depending on the strategic circumstances. In order to gain access to the strait, the most important immediate objective after Lae was identified as the area around Finschhafen. Finschhafen was a critical Japanese logistics node and a key part of their coastal line of supply. On its own, this made the area a significant target of the Allies, but its location opposite New Britain meant that it was also flagged as a staging point for the US forces to assault Cape Gloucester. Finschhafen also provided an ideal location for the development of a major base, port, and airfield.[19]

In order to capture the area quickly, Blamey warned I Australian Corps of the need to execute a landing at Finschhafen very shortly after the fall of Lae. Thereafter, I Australian Corps would clear the Huon Peninsula via a coastal advance. A second supporting advance was to be concurrently launched up the Markham Valley to seize key terrain for the construction of airfields and to protect the base area at Lae. The plan called for these two thrusts to eventually join hands at Madang. The greatest restrictions in executing this plan were logistics support and mobility (air transportation and VII Phib). Thus, it was critical for Blamey to convince MacArthur to continue to provide the Australians access to the bulk of the support from the SWPA's navy and air force.[20]

However, Blamey's plan was not the only one on offer. Kenney favored a bold advance up the Markham Valley, bypassing Madang and leaping directly to Hansa Bay in Dutch New Guinea. It was audacious but beyond the capabilities of the SWPA at the time. Kenney, however, had secured Herring's support, once again putting the Australian corps commander at odds with his C-in-C and the plans of Adv LHQ.

To decide on the next series of objectives, MacArthur called his senior staff—Blamey, Carpenter, Kenney, Sutherland, Chamberlin, Whitehead, and Berryman—to a conference on 3 September. The conference started with Blamey outlining his concept of operations, knowing full well that he already had two votes in his pocket: Berryman, who had written the appreciation, and Carpenter, with whom Blamey had met on 1 September in order to secure his support.[21] Kenney soon jumped on board and proposed that Dumpu be seized in the Markham Valley as the first of the sites for a major new series of airfields. Such a base, he argued, would allow the AAF to support the operations against both New Britain and along the Huon Peninsula. With three task force commanders throwing their weight behind the plan and with no major objections from his GHQ staff officers, MacArthur endorsed the concept of operations.[22]

Having secured unanimous support for his plan, Blamey then got adventurous with MacArthur. He proposed using his reserve division, the 6th Australian, to secure Cape Gloucester, thus taking over phase 3 of Cartwheel for the Australians. It was a radical suggestion, as it would mean replacing a US division, in this case the 1st Marine Division, with an Australian one. MacArthur was not at all pleased, and Chamberlin quickly countered the proposal by arguing that the two divisions of I Australian Corps might not provide enough combat power to secure all of the objectives just agreed upon. Blamey retorted that he had three militia brigades immediately on hand as follow-on forces. Chamberlin and Sutherland then responded that this would reduce the garrisons at Port Moresby, Milne Bay, and Oro Bay, leaving these critical base areas vulnerable. MacArthur then interjected, ending the debate. He had no intention of allowing the Australians to dominate all of Cartwheel's objectives and reiterated that there would be no change in plan—Alamo Force was to take Cape Gloucester.[23]

While a seemingly small incident in a long campaign, the meeting on 3 September is critical to the development of the US-Australian coalition in the SWPA. As David Horner has argued, this was the last time that "Blamey attempted to exert his authority as Allied Land Commander."[24] MacArthur's rejection of Blamey's proposal cemented his position as the actual land-component commander in the SWPA. It also meant that once the landings on New Britain commenced, the Australians would lose the bulk of the naval and air force support in the theater. From then on, they would work primarily in support of Alamo Force. The meeting was, therefore, one of the pivotal moments in the transfer of power away from Blamey and the Australian Army.

THE MARKHAM VALLEY OPERATION

The quick victory at Lae accelerated Blamey's plans for the second phase of Postern. GHQ ordered Finschhafen to be seized as soon as possible, and on 14 September GHQ affirmed its priorities:

1. The development of the Lae-Nadzab area as air and logistics base to support further operations;
2. The development of air and support facilities at Finschhafen; and
3. The establishment of airdrome installations and establishment of air forces in the lower Markham Valley.[25]

Over the following two days, Blamey's staff held a number of planning meetings with I Australian Corps HQ, Whitehead, and Barbey. Herring had ordered the 9th Division to prepare for the assault on Finschhafen, and the 7th Division was tasked to secure the Markham Valley. The corps's two divisions would thus reprise their roles during the capture of Lae, allowing for continuity in planning, units, and commanders.[26]

Vasey, in close consultation with Whitehead, planned to secure the Markham Valley in three phases. Phase 1 was the capture of the Japanese airstrip at Kaiapit, phase 2 the airstrip at Dumpu, and phase 3 the capture of Kankiryo Saddle in the Finisterre Range.[27] As the supporting thrust, Vasey had less air and logistics support than Wootten. He knew that seizing the initiative and maintaining momentum would be key, especially as significant parts of his division were still concentrating in theater. Even though his division lacked combat power, Vasey kicked off his assault utilizing the 2/6th Commando Squadron. This lightly equipped elite unit made a swift overland advance to Kaiapit to seize the airstrip. These troops arrived under the noses of the 78th Japanese Infantry Regiment, which, in advancing toward Lae, had chosen the airstrip at Kaiapit as its forward operating base.[28]

This success not only pushed back the major Japanese force in the area, but it also allowed Vasey to fly in the 21st Brigade from Nazab and

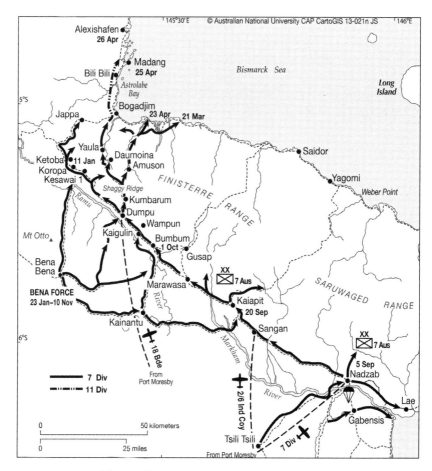

Figure 12.3 Markham Valley Operations

Port Moresby, thus avoiding a protracted overland advance. The 21st Brigade was soon advancing and seized Dumpu on 5–6 October against weak Japanese resistance. These swift advances had allowed the Fifth Air Force to develop significant airfields in the Markham Valley to support operations in the Huon Peninsula and surrounding areas much earlier than originally planned. The 7th Division now faced the daunting task of crossing the Finisterre Range to advance on Madang against increasing Japanese resistance. In the mountains, the 7th Division's operations were to slow down in the face of fanatical opposition set among some of the worst terrain in New Guinea.[29]

FINSCHHAFEN AND THE PROBLEMS OF
COOPERATIVE COMMAND

The amphibious assault on Finschhafen was put together at breakneck speed. The 9th Division was tasked to prepare one brigade for the assault landing, with a second brigade and divisional HQ planned to arrive over the subsequent days. Herring had briefed the 9th Division and 20th Brigade staffs on the morning of 18 September, and by 8:00 that night he had approved their plan. Two days later, the 20th Brigade sailed in Barbey's ships for its assault landing the following morning. Thus, the 9th Division and VII Phib had planned, organized, and set sail a brigade-sized amphibious assault against a defended shore in only three days.[30] While it had been a relatively smooth process, given the limited time available many shortcuts had been taken. The major sticking point was, like with the landing at Lae, over the timing of the landings. VII Phib remained concerned about the air threat, while the Australians were worried about their supply line and thus demanded that the ships be loaded properly and fully unloaded before they left. The end result was yet another compromise, with the timing set at halfway between the two initial proposals.[31]

As Task Force 76 sailed, a critical rift had also developed between NGF HQ and GHQ over their assessments of the enemy forces at Finschhafen and how the operations were expected to unfold once the 20th Brigade was ashore. The 9th Division had developed its plan based on Berryman's appreciation and Adv LHQ orders for phase 2-B for Postern. In these assessments, Berryman had judged that as Finschhafen was such a vital piece of terrain, the Japanese would react very strongly to the landing of the 20th Brigade and pour reinforcements into the area. Berryman's appreciation put Japanese troop numbers in the area at around one thousand, but he inserted a significant caveat—mainly that the Japanese could easily reinforce the area to five thousand troops inside seven days and that up to two enemy divisions could be expected to arrive by late October.[32] Thus, during the planning meetings with GHQ on 17 September, Blamey had emphasized the need for a second brigade and left the meeting believing that he had an agreement from MacArthur and GHQ to that effect. Accordingly, I Australian Corps planned to land the 20th Brigade on D-day, 22 September, with the 9th Division's HQ and a second brigade to follow a few days later.[33]

The problem was that Willoughby and his GHQ intelligence section completely disagreed with Berryman's assessment. They initially argued that there were in fact only 500–800 Japanese troops in the area, a number that they soon revised down to 350. In addition, they claimed that the Japanese troops that were in the area were noncombat troops.[34] Willoughby's estimation was that, with Lae captured, the value of Finschhafen to the Japanese would decline. He dismissed the idea that the Japanese would use the area as a potential staging base for an attack on Lae and rejected the view that the Japanese might well have assessed its location adjacent to the Vitiaz Strait as critical. GHQ argued that no "serious attempt will be made to defend this former staging area."[35]

The consequence of this GHQ assessment was that MacArthur ordered Barbey to withdraw his support for the Australians once the 20th Brigade was ashore and to concentrate on planning and preparing an accelerated timetable for the assault on Cape Gloucester.[36] At this junction, MacArthur left Port Moresby to return to Australia. Shortly thereafter, Blamey ordered Herring to send the 9th Division HQ and the second brigade to Finschhafen before he handed over NGF to Lt. Gen. Iven Mackay, as Blamey was to return to Australia and his duties as C-in-C AMF. Once again, he left Berryman behind to ensure continuity in operations and to be his eyes and ears at the battlefront.[37]

Herring and Mackay subsequently contacted Barbey to organize the movement of the additional brigade but were told in no uncertain terms that GHQ had specifically ordered them not to undertake such an operation. After some quick inquiries, the reason for the withdrawal of Barbey's support became apparent. Berryman noted that "our American friends seem to have the impression that we have thoroughly defeated the Japs and that the army requires but little further assistance. [A] GHQ staff officer told Barbey to stick it out against moving a second brigade gp [group] to Finsch."[38] The following day, Mackay, Berryman, and Herring met with Admiral Carpenter, who, after a detailed discussion, agreed to take the additional brigade to Finschhafen. However, later that night, Carpenter informed Berryman and Mackay that this would not occur until 3 October.[39] To the Australians this was unacceptable, given the risk to the 20th Brigade. On the same day, the brigade's commander, Brig. Victor Windeyer, had called a halt to his advance after his intelligence revealed a rapid buildup of Japanese forces in the area. This was confirmed the following day (26 September) when troops from the 20th Brigade captured a set of Japanese orders detailing counterattacks against the Australians to be launched by the 80th and 237th Infantry Regiments.[40]

Berryman had tried to smooth over the issues on 26 September with the GHQ Naval liaison officer, Cap. Roy C. Hudson (USN), yet NGF deemed the outcome of this meeting as "not satisfactory." Mackay then resolved to send a signal to both Blamey and GHQ, pointing out the urgency of the situation.[41] In response, MacArthur sent a brusque signal to NGF stating that to land reinforcements at Finschhafen would risk losses to his amphibious force, complicate supply issues, divert both air and naval assists from other operations, and put at risk the timetable for phase 3 of Cartwheel. He was emphatic that there was no need for additional troops at Finschhafen. Meanwhile, Willoughby was refusing to alter his intelligence assessment, despite the clear evidence to the contrary that the Australians were providing. It was clear that GHQ had "lost touch with reality"[42] and was putting future operations ahead of the current tactical reality.

Back at the battlefront, the 20th Brigade was suffering an acute shortage of supplies. It also had over two hundred casualties awaiting evacuation and had been forced over to the defensive in the face of increased Japanese opposition.[43] The following day, Mackay and Berryman again met with Carpenter, who agreed to move the troops in three to five days' time. At this juncture, Herring was starting to unravel after the stress of three long campaigns. He was becoming increasingly nervous over the situation, and he demanded that he be allowed to write to Blamey directly and to go to see MacArthur at GHQ. Yet another conference occurred the following day with Carpenter, at which NGF pushed for an immediate movement of the second brigade, but Carpenter stood firm. MacArthur again insisted that the GHQ estimate of 350 Japanese troops at Finschhafen remained accurate, stating that the Japanese "intend [to] or have started to evacuate the area" and that the only "reinforcements allowed were those to keep the current troops up to strength until an airfield was built."[44] This position was completely at odds with the situation at the battlefront, but it was not a result of a lack of information, as NGF HQ was keeping GHQ completely up-to-date on the 20th Brigade's action.[45]

By now, MacArthur was totally blind to the reality of the situation. His solution was to insist on building an airfield for supply and reinforcement, but this was pure fantasy. Such an option had been explored three days earlier and had been specifically ruled out by Kenney due to a lack of aircraft and the fact that it would take weeks to construct an airfield.[46] Over the preceding two days, the 20th Brigade had been under increasing enemy attacks, and Windeyer was now advising that he was at risk of losing the whole position. Blamey now interceded with a direct appeal to MacArthur, reminding him of his commitment of 17 September and outlining the urgency of the situation.[47]

MacArthur finally relented, albeit begrudgingly.[48] An Australian battalion was swiftly moved to the beachhead, and the rest of the brigade
soon followed, but it arrived piecemeal in the small landing craft of the
2nd ESB, not in the ships of VII Phib. MacArthur would later rewrite
the history of this event, claiming that "Finschhafen was one of the main
bastions in the enemy defense structure." He claimed full credit for the
assault, including noting a cable from Gen. George Marshall that stated,
"Congratulations, personal and official, on campaign just completed with
capture of Finschhafen. The combination of forces, tactics, and speed and
celerity with which the successive operations have followed are a splendid
promise for the future."[49] No mention is made of the reinforcement issues
or the threat that MacArthur's action posed on the outcome, either in his
account or in the US official history, which misrepresents Australian troop
levels at Finschhafen and completely ignores the reinforcement debate.[50]

The debate over the reinforcement of the 20th Brigade had been a tense
and trying episode. The resolution had taken five days, and as Herring
noted, "we damn nearly lost Finschhafen."[51] Recriminations abounded.
On the Australian side, Herring blamed Mackay and Berryman. He believed they failed to ensure Blamey's orders were carried out and did not
act with enough haste. Berryman, however, blamed Herring. He noted
that that the I Corps commander had made disparaging remarks about
the 2nd ESB and VII Phib to Barbey on 18 September. These arguments
had persisted on 19 and 20 September, with Berryman noting that Barbey
was being "accommodating and conciliatory" toward Herring but was
having a difficult time with the Australian. Nevertheless, Herring's bitterness continued, and Berryman noted that Barbey needed "an accredited
ref[eree] [to deal] with Herring."[52] When Herring again blew up over the
Finschhafen reinforcement issue, Barbey had had enough and sailed his
HQ ship back to Milne Bay. Berryman believed that Herring's behavior
jeopardized NGF's relationship with VII Phib and that this had led to the
loss of Barbey and Carpenter's support, causing the issue to bog down
and GHQ to refuse their requests.[53]

Blame in this incident, however, was shared. Blamey had obviously not
received the firm guarantee in the 17 September meeting that he thought
he had. Barbey and Carpenter had persistently exaggerated the risks to
their ships, while Willoughby was negligent in the extreme by persist-
ing with his intelligence assessments in the face of overwhelming contradictory evidence. MacArthur's persistence in not wanting to upset his
timetable for the New Britain operation in the face of a mounting crisis
at Finschhafen was delusional, justified only by the intelligence he and

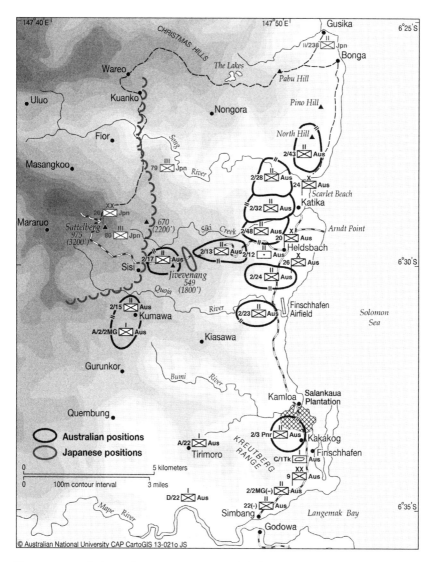

Figure 12.4 9th Australian Division at Finschhafen, October 1943

Willoughby believed in that did not accord with the evidence they were provided.

Overall the key question is, why was this situation allowed to develop? It is clear that the commander ultimately responsible for this calamity was MacArthur. It was his faulty command system in the SWPA that had created the vacuum for this situation to develop. If a proper joint commander had been appointed with the authority to make timely decisions, this situation would never have occurred. Instead, MacArthur insisted on remaining as the sole joint commander and refused to delegate this responsibility. He soon left the battlefront to run his theater and turned his attention back to strategic issues, abandoning his operational commanders and leaving them with contradictory orders and no local authority to resolve them. It was his insistence on the top-down, centralized control of all operations and cooperative command that was the major culprit. It was not the first time this had happened in the SWPA, and it would not be the last.

The near disaster at Finschhafen resulted in a number of changes within the Australian command structure. It was clear that Herring's nerves were fraying, and his limitations as a commander had become apparent for all to see. The evidence was now overwhelming, and Blamey could no longer ignore major issues such as poor planning and organization of his corps at the beachheads, the command problems at Salamaua, his willingness to compromise the operational plan for Postern, his reaction to the Japanese withdrawal order at Lae, his disputes with the USN, and his overreaction over Finschhafen.

Compounding this situation on 28 September, Herring's BGS, Brigadier Sutherland, had been killed in a plane crash. Herring had been on board and escaped uninjured, but the loss of his close colleague and friend shook him badly. The shock, stress, and strain meant that Herring now took to openly criticizing Mackay. It was clear he needed to be replaced, and Berryman wrote to Blamey noting that he had lost all confidence in him. Blamey concurred, and Morshead and his II Corps HQ were brought in to replace Herring. Three weeks later, the Australian government ordered Mackay to India as the Australian high commissioner, Morshead took over NGF, and Berryman was given II Australian Corps to command the operations to clear the Huon Peninsula. Upon returning to Australia, Herring realized that his time as a commander had come to an end, and he resigned from the army to become the chief justice of Victoria.[54]

US OPERATIONS: NEW BRITAIN AND SAIDOR

While the Australians were locked in combat against the Japanese at both ends of the Finisterre Range, Alamo Force had absorbed the lessons from the practice landings at Woodlark Island and the Kiriwina Islands and was preparing for its next major objective—New Britain. Code-named

"Dexterity," the assault on New Britain was planned around a series of landings against the western and southwestern corners of the island. The main effort was to be the landing at Cape Gloucester by the 1st Marine Division. Prior to the main assault, the 112th Cavalry Regiment (Director Task Force) was landed at Arawe on the southwestern corner of the island on 15 December. This landing was a success, with the only opposition being from some Japanese aircraft. Reinforced by a Marine tank company, Brig. Gen. Julian Cunningham's men fought off the inevitable Japanese counterattack early in the New Year before moving over to the offensive.[55]

In the meantime, the Marines got down to planning their assault. Like the Australians, they were unhappy about the centralized, top-down control exerted by GHQ and Alamo Force. The division's commander, Maj. Gen. William H. Rupertus, took exception to the plan of MacArthur and Alamo Force commander Lt. Gen. Walter Krueger, believing that it endangered the mission and his division. Like at Finschhafen, GHQ's intelligence analysis of the Japanese strength at Cape Gloucester varied widely from that of the troops who had been assigned to carry out the mission. The Marines rejected the use of the 503rd PIR to land on the airfield as far too dangerous and argued that the two Marine regiments to be landed on both sides of the peninsula to take the Japanese airfield would not have enough combat power. At a conference with the 1st Marine Division, MacArthur, Krueger, and the planning teams from Alamo Force and GHQ conceded to Rupertus's changes to the plan. The 503rd PIR was removed, and the two landings would go ahead, but the western landing would be much smaller and would be used as a blocking force to isolate the Japanese on the peninsula. The 1st Marine Division's landings got under way on 26 December 1943 and faced stiffening resistance as they closed in on the airfield. Reinforced by two additional Marine battalions on 28 December, Rupertus pushed on and secured his objectives by 29 December.[56]

The landing of the Marines on New Britain represented a major shift in the correlation of land forces in the SWPA, a situation not lost on the Australians. A few days prior to the landings, Blamey had released a "most secret" policy direction to his senior staff and commanders. In this document, he outlined that the US Army would now take over the main effort in Cartwheel and that the support that had been available to the Australians in terms of logistics, airpower, and naval forces would move over to Alamo Force. He outlined a plan for a return of the bulk of the AIF to northern Australia for rest and retraining.[57] In the meantime, the 5th and 11th Militia Divisions would take over the final assault on Madang.

MacArthur and Krueger also sensed the shift, and they moved quickly to cement their control. Another major landing was added to Dexterity, with the 32nd Division moving against Saidor (Operation Michaelmas) in northern New Guinea on 2 January 1944 in order to block the Japanese withdrawing in front of Berryman's corps on the Huon Peninsula. This move effectively ended Blamey's control as the task force commander for the ALF in New Guinea.

Coordination was undertaken on 28 December when Krueger met with Berryman to discuss their plans. However, Berryman noted in his diary that not a lot of coordination was carried out. Rather, Krueger spent most of the meeting lecturing him on strategy and tactics and complaining that the Marines on New Britain were having a tough time. Berryman left exasperated, especially as at this stage the Marines were yet to meet any serious resistance. Most significantly, Berryman was worried about Krueger's plan to dig in at both Cape Gloucester and Saidor behind barbed wire and pillboxes as soon as his troops got ashore. To the Australians, this tactical approach demonstrated quite "the wrong attitude."[58]

Berryman need not have been concerned about the Marines at Cape Gloucester, whose performance was once again excellent. For the lackluster 32nd Division, however, it proved to be prophetic. The 32nd had struggled in Papua and while its rest and retraining had led to some improvements, the combat effectiveness of the division was still under a cloud. In the lead-up to the operation, the Australian official historian, Gavin Long, would note in his diary, after interviewing a number of senior US officers, that there remained an "anxiety" about the "future of these divs (32nd and 41st)" given "their bad starts."[59]

These assessments were not far from the truth. The landing was spearheaded by a regiment under the command of Col. Clarence Martin and was unopposed.[60] By the end of the first day, Martin had 7,500 troops of the division ashore. However, instead of pushing rapidly inland to cut off and destroy the retreating Japanese, he ordered his troops to dig in and called for urgent reinforcements. Martin's actions were partly a result of the inadequacies of his troops and partly a result of a total overestimation of the Japanese forces in the area. From its analysis at Finschhafen and Cape Gloucester, GHQ had now swung full circle in its assessments. Suddenly there were Japanese troops everywhere, and it was believed they were going to try to destroy the 32nd Division at Saidor.

Alamo Force estimated that there were fourteen thousand Japanese between Sio and Saidor and that they were going to break through to the west. While this estimate was close in terms of numbers, the Americans had completely overestimated both the Japanese intentions and capabilities. By now, the Australians had eviscerated General Imamura's troops as an effective fighting force. The Japanese were desperately short of supplies, thousands of their men were sick and wounded, and many had resorted to cannibalism of their fellow soldiers to survive. With so little combat capability, virtually all organized resistance west of Saidor had ceased before the 32nd Division landed.[61] The remaining Japanese troops were fleeing desperately in front of the Australians in small, uncoordinated groups without any central command or control. The greatest problems for the Australians were not the Japanese but rather the difficult terrain and a lack of supplies.[62] To Krueger, however, the Japanese were "advancing westward" straight at the 32nd, and so he ordered them to dig in deeper and brought in the rest of the division.[63]

The Australians were increasingly frustrated by Alamo Force's attitude. Berryman met with Krueger twice more to urge action from the 32nd Division. As he pointed out, the Japanese were simply walking around their position.[64] The 32nd's posture, however, remained unchanged. Its lack of aggressive patrolling or offensive operations led one Australian liaison officer with the division to request to return to II Corps HQ, as he had "little opportunity to report on American tactics."[65] Krueger timidly let some thirteen thousand Japanese troops escape, many of whom recovered to fight the Australians around Wewak in 1945. As one of MacArthur's biographers, D. Clayton James, has noted, "the Americans had bungled a grand opportunity to trap" and destroy the remainder of the Japanese forces in New Guinea.[66]

INTELLIGENCE BREAKTHROUGH

Despite the bungling of the operations around Saidor, this phase of the war was to be one of the most significant in the SWPA. As the Australians troops neared Sio, the Japanese 20th Division was in total disarray, having been destroyed by the 9th Australian Division around Finschhafen. In their haste to retreat, the signalers of the Japanese division had chosen to bury their cryptography library in a series of metal trunks at the bottom of a riverbed. As the Australians advanced, a unit of the 9th Division serendipitously discovered the trunks. Inside were all the 20th Division's codebooks minus their covers, which had been taken as proof of their

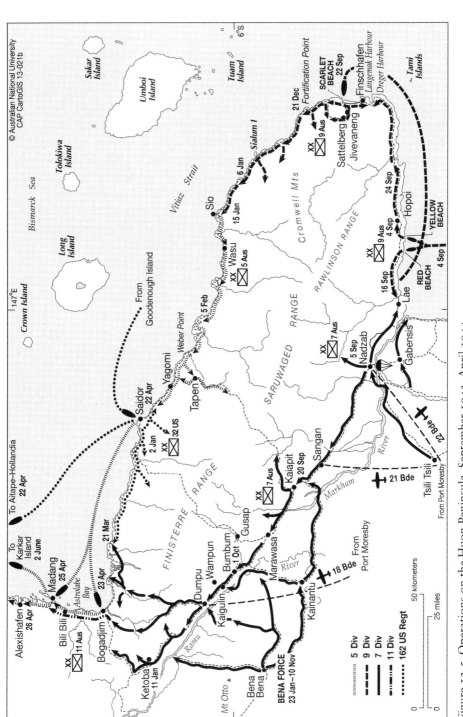

Figure 12.5 Operations on the Huon Peninsula, September 1943–April 1944

"destruction." The codebooks were dried out by the Allied intelligence services, and for the following two months they were able to read all of the IJA's messages in the theater. Thereafter, the codes were changed but not enough to fool the Allied intelligence experts, who were quickly able to continue to decipher the messages.[67] This intelligence was to prove to be an indispensable resource to MacArthur, who was able to plan his series of bold landings in 1944 with almost full access to the IJA's order of battle and operational plans for the region.[68]

THE FALL OF MADANG

The Australians and Americans linked up outside of Saidor on 22 March 1944, effectively cutting off the line of communications between Imamura in Rabaul and the Eighteenth Army. IJHQ was now forced to rearrange its defenses, and the remainder of the Eighteenth Army was transferred to the Second Area Army. Two subsequent American landings on the Admiralty Islands (29 February 1944, 1st Cavalry Division) and Emirau Island (20 March 1944, 4th Marine Regiment) were crucial in deciding the outcome of the campaign.[69] Their success meant that Rabaul was now isolated and Cartwheel's objectives were complete.[70]

The New Guinea campaign drew to a close on 24 April 1944 with the capture of Madang. The final victory was an anticlimax. The Japanese had largely been destroyed, and the town was taken after they offered only one burst of machine-gun fire in opposition. Other than signaling the end of the campaign, the most significant aspect of the town's liberation was the manner in which it was achieved. A relatively small force took Madang, but it signified all the positive elements of Allied operations in 1943 and 1944.

Two forces had set out to liberate the town—one from the coastal advance, led by the 5th Australian Division, which had relieved the 9th Division after Sio, and the other from the 11th Division, which had relieved the 7th Division after its victory in the Finisterre Ranges. The 57th/60th Battalion had put one of its patrols afloat in two USN PT boats to outflank the Golo River, the last obstacle between the 11th Division and Madang. While at sea, it met up with four LCMs carrying the HQ and one company of the 30th Battalion from the 5th Division. The two forces decided to combine their efforts and seized the town later that afternoon. An hour later, two RAN warships escorted Brig. Claude Cameron's 8th Brigade into the town. Madang fell with no fanfare and no victory parade.

It seems only fitting, however, that the ground forces from both thrusts, supported by the USN and the RAN under the cover of the AAF, worked together to take the final objective. It epitomizes what was achieved when the Allies operated as a truly joint and combined force.[71]

CONCLUSION

Overall, the campaign in New Guinea from March 1943 to April 1944 was one of the most successful coalition operations in the Pacific. It was the "first tactical employment of parachute troops . . . by Allied forces in the Pacific . . . [and the first] combination of airlifted troops [and] parachute troops in co-ordination with an amphibious assault had also been not used hitherto by the Allies in the Pacific."[72]

The operation was an outstanding success, with the only major problem being the difficulties experienced in the planning. This tension was most evident in late August as a result of the differences in doctrine between the two main coalition partners. This had caused some wringing of hands at GHQ, but ultimately all of the issues were smoothed over. The key to unlocking these problems were the relationships that had been formed between the major HQs and their commanders and staff. As Berryman later noted, "at Moresby senior members of my staff complained about the visits of Chamberlin's staff officers who wanted details of our plans and were not slow to criticize; however, by courteous patience we remained friends."[73] By September the tensions had been overcome, and Chamberlin would note to Berryman that GHQ watched the operations in New Guinea "with a great deal of interest and admiration. I believe that this will be a model for soldiers to study in their text books in the future."[74]

Despite the work of these staff officers, only so much could be done in the face of MacArthur's cooperative command structure and his insistence on centralized planning. This is obvious in the completely mixed-up timelines that occurred during Postern, with GHQ predicting up to six weeks for the capture of Lae (it took less than two) while insisting that Finschhafen be wrapped up within two weeks. In the end, the defeat of the Japanese took "more than two months of bitter fighting before [Finschhafen] was secure."[75]

Cooperative command had proven problematic, especially in regard to issues such as the timing of amphibious landings and the allocation of resources to different operations. MacArthur's demand to remain the only joint commander in the theater complicated operational decisions and proved to be a near disaster for the Australians at Finschhafen. Unfortunately, GHQ would not learn from this experience, and Krueger and Eichelberger were forced to deal with similar operational situations in 1944 and 1945 as a result of this practice. Finally, it seems that in many ways, MacArthur and his staff still did not understand how the Australian Army operated. As Gavin Long has noted, these

> misunderstandings underlined the weakness whereby since April 1942 an American general headquarters on which there was quite inadequate Australian representation reigned from afar over a field army that was, for present purposes, almost entirely Australian, and whose doctrine and methods differed from those of G.H.Q. It was evidence of the detachment of G.H.Q. that after 16 months, its senior general staff officers had little knowledge of the doctrines and methods of its principle army in the field.[76]

The approach of GHQ, however, stands in stark contrast to the level of understanding and cooperation at the battlefront. Cooperation between the US and Australians forces in New Guinea had been excellent. The 503rd PIR had worked seamlessly with the 7th Australian Division, and the air and naval cooperation had been outstanding. For the navy, these operations were to prove to be the swan song of Admiral Carpenter. Plagued by poor relations with GHQ, he was replaced by Vice Adm. Thomas C. Kinkaid on 26 November 1943. He was, however, fulsome in his praise of the Australians. After leaving the theater, he wrote to Berryman that "in all my work which I had as Commander of the Allied Naval Forces of the Southwest Pacific area there will stand out the friendship, loyalty, and cooperation of your countryman, not only in the land, sea, and air forces, but in civil life as well."[77] Barbey and VII Phib also continued to have excellent relations with the Australians, and the feeling was nothing if not mutual.[78] The feelings also extended to the USAAF, with Brig. Gen. Fred Smith, commanding general of the First Air Task Force, noting that "it has been an inspiration to have served with Australian units in our struggle against the common enemy."[79]

The importance of the role of the ANF to NGF's operations, even after the bulk of its effort moved over to support Alamo Force, cannot be underestimated. The use of naval power was the heart of the SWPA's operational approach from mid-1943 onward. The operations of I Australian Corps and later II Australian Corps were completely dependent on naval support provided by the 2nd ESB, as well as on air support from the Fifth Air Force.[80] Throughout the period of operations in the Huon Peninsula, a number of units of the 2nd ESB remained in support of the Australian corps to provide resupply, tactical maneuver, and offshore firepower via rocket-equipped LCVPs. Overall, the operations against Salamaua, Lae, and Finschhafen cost the 2nd ESB twenty-one killed, ninety-four wounded, with a further sixty evacuated with disease. In the coastal advance to Sio, a further four LCVPs were lost in action and another four for operational reasons.[81] In addition, the navy's small craft were crucial in interdicting the Japanese attempts to land reinforcements and supplies during darkness along the Huon Peninsula, while the efforts of the USN's PT boats drew particular praise from NGF.[82]

Airpower was essential to both the Markham Valley and Huon Peninsula operations. Kenney's operations in advance of the landing at Lae eviscerated Japanese airpower over New Guinea. Airpower was the key element of the operations against Nadzab, and NGF noted that "valuable cooperation was obtained from the Commander and Staff of the Fifth US Air Force who worked in close harmony with the staff of New Guinea Force and 7 Aust Div." The AAF provided protection for the movement of shipping and Task Force 76, as well as close air support for the troops and interdiction of Japanese supplies and reinforcements, "thus simplifying the task of the infantry." Air reconnaissance and army cooperation, especially from No. 4 Squadron RAAF, "proved of immense value."[83] Overall, as the I Australian Corps report on operations attests, "co-operation of Navy and Air Force was magnificent."[84]

This close and enduring cooperation on the battlefield meant that, ultimately, Operation Postern was "a masterpiece of planning"[85] and an "outstanding orchestration of the sea, land and air forces of two countries."[86] By the time of the fall of Madang, the Eighteenth Japanese Area Army had been virtually destroyed, losing some thirty-five thousand men.[87] The differences in the type and scale of operations between 1942 and 1943 were stark. As the US historian Edward Drea has noted, the campaigns in 1942 and 1943 in New Guinea were "really the story of two Allied armies fighting two kinds of war—one of grinding attrition [1942] and one of classic maneuver [1943]."[88] Even more impressive was the fact that such a decisive victory in this campaign was secured without the strategic advantage of Ultra intelligence gained from decrypted Japanese military signals (a fact that was all too evident at Finschhafen), which would prove so decisive for MacArthur's operations in 1944 and 1945.[89]

The fall of Madang also signified a major change in the coalition in the SWPA. As the campaign ended, the preponderance of US power in the Pacific had finally to come to pass, and the overwhelming asymmetry of the US-Australian relationship was plain for everyone to see. Operation Postern had been the apogee of the Australian Army's influence on operations in the SWPA. Thereafter, the eclipse of the Australian war effort was to occur in tandem with the overwhelming surge of US power.

By April 1944, Australia had been at war for four and a half years. The country had fully mobilized in the period of 1942–1943, and now it was facing an acute manpower crisis while strategically and operationally being consigned to junior-partner status in the SWPA. MacArthur was now looking to Australia as a base of operations and logistics support, rather than as a source of combat power. Nowhere was this starker than in the transfer of power to the US land forces that had occurred in late 1943. Starting with the operations against New Britain in November, the US Army rapidly furnished large-scale formations for the advance to the Philippines that were well beyond Australia's capabilities. As a result, the coalition in the SWPA would transform in 1944. MacArthur became ever more focused on accumulating US combat power to "fulfill his destiny" to liberate the Philippines. Increasingly he was able to put in place his long-held ambition to directly command the ground forces in his theater, focused almost exclusively on the US Army. The Australians, who laid the foundations for MacArthur's victories, would increasingly become marginalized.

Part 5

The Southwest Pacific Area,
1944–1945

13

Australia, MacArthur, and the Divergence of Interests

THE SHIFT OF POWER AND RESOURCES from the commander of the ALF to the US ground forces was at the forefront of GHQ's thinking in late 1943. Brig. Gen. Stephen Chamberlin, the GHQ G-3, had developed a close rapport with the Australians and had helped to smooth over most of the planning problems with Adv LHQ in 1943, despite a few hiccups. Irrespective of his close relationship with a number of Australian senior officers, he was also well aware of the C-in-C's view regarding Blamey and the Australians. He also realized the ease that a more separated command structure between the Americans and Australians would have, especially for his planning work. Therefore, while preparing the briefing documents for MacArthur for his forthcoming meeting with Admiral Halsey (C-in-C SOPAC), Chamberlin laid out a bold plan for the reorganization of the SWPA.

Chamberlin knew that SOPAC would soon reach its culminating point with the isolation of Rabaul. A key part of Chamberlin's role was the drafting of the Reno plans, MacArthur's concept for the advance to, and conquest of, the Philippines. For the advance to be a success, MacArthur would need a further injection of US forces, and Chamberlin thought that the absorption of SOPAC into the SWPA would go a long way to achieving this.[1] Moreover, the size of this force could easily grow if the American units that were garrisoning the ports and bases conquered in 1942 and 1943—but soon to be left far in the rear—could be handed over to "local" forces. To the senior staff officers of GHQ, there was a strong logic to this thinking, and it seemed axiomatic that the effect would be a reorganization of the command arrangements for the SWPA. Furthermore, as MacArthur approached the Philippines, the strategic situation for the United States would change. MacArthur and many Americans viewed the Philippines as their "territory," and every step closer to this goal was one that took them farther away from Australia, Papua, New Guinea, New Britain, and Bougainville. The logic stood, therefore, that each country had largely separate national geographic priorities. The big problem was that one was a strategic backwater and the other sat at the forefront of the defeat of the Japanese.

To Chamberlin the outcome of this was clear. The combined US forces from the SWPA and SOPAC would form an "exclusively" American force designed to undertake offensive operations in the Philippines. As a consequence, the SWPA could be split into geographically defined areas, which would allow for the separation of "elements of other nationalities from this force and allot them the static defensive role."[2] Sutherland agreed to raise the matter with the C-in-C, but MacArthur refused to enact Chamberlin's ideas. However, this was not because he disagreed with Chamberlin's assessment. Rather, to the C-in-C, such a clear-cut delineation, while organizationally efficient, would be strategically complicated. A more fluid and less defined structure, based on Chamberlin's thinking, was much more in the way of MacArthur's Machiavellian command principles. Either way, the Australians were to be excluded, not just operationally but now strategically and organizationally. Chamberlin's October memo encapsulated the thinking inside GHQ on the coalition in the SWPA in late 1943, and the majority of his views would become practice if not policy from here on.

As 1943 drew to an end and 1944 dawned, MacArthur's decision to land the 32nd US Infantry Division at Saidor and maintain it under Krueger's command made it clear that the landing at Lae was the last time that a US regiment, division, or corps would be placed under Australian command. The benefits of separation of the US and Australian armies were self-evident to GHQ. In addition, as the Australian official history notes, from an inter-Allied and strategic perspective "it was probably the only one that, in the circumstances that had developed, would have been politically acceptable in Washington."[3] MacArthur had unfailingly persisted in his attempts to establish himself in command of his own ground forces since March 1942, and now he had succeeded in this endeavor. This position was not to be challenged again, and Blamey knew that in reality from mid-1943 his command remit included only the AMF. MacArthur would cement this relationship soon thereafter by reestablishing the US Army Forces in the Far East with himself in command.[4]

The separation of the armies greatly eased logistics planning, smoothed over planning difficulties, and provided clarity to GHQ as it approached the Philippines. Dealing with its own forces meant there were no misunderstandings regarding organizational structures, commanders, and capabilities. Throughout the remainder of the war, mixed land task forces would not make another appearance. Under this new command

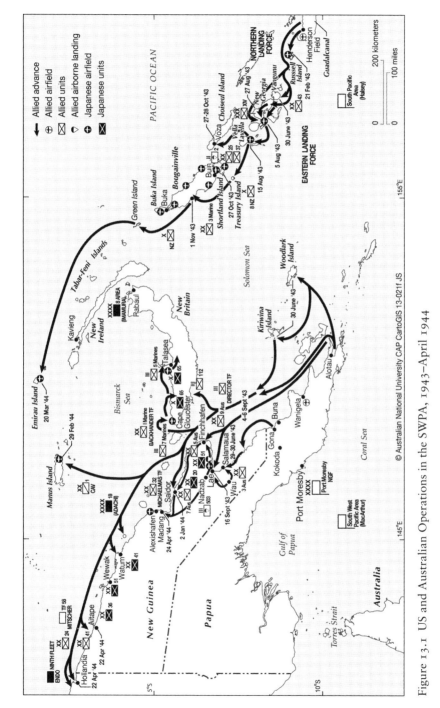

Figure 13.1 US and Australian Operations in the SWPA, 1943–April 1944

relationship, Blamey's forces would form a task force that reported directly to GHQ. This meant that, for the most part, the differences experienced over coordination, command, doctrine, and equipment in Papua and New Guinea in 1942 and 1943 were largely avoided.[5] It also reaffirmed that strategically the SWPA was a coalition of convenience. Neither side was willing to redress issues of interoperability by absorbing the other's doctrine or approaches to command, and if any part of the coalition was going to do so, given the lopsided nature of the two countries' military forces, it would have been the Australians.

As noted in chapter 9, the only area where this did happen in the period 1942–1944 was amphibious warfare. However, during the latter half of 1944, the massive increase in US support for MacArthur meant that the hybrid SWPA amphibious doctrine was slowly pushed aside for the adoption of the amphibious warfare tactics, techniques, and procedures being used in the CPA. This could be achieved due to the large increase in the SWPA from late 1944 of amphibious attack transports, armored landing craft, and carrier air support, as well as battleships and heavy cruisers for naval gunfire support. In terms of the US-Australian coalition, this change was to be on display in I Australian Corps's assault on Borneo in 1945 when the preponderance of Allied, in particular US, resources would mean that the Australians would largely adopt US amphibious techniques.[6]

The domination of GHQ by the US Army and the lack of a joint staff, despite MacArthur being ordered to create one in 1942, did cause problems. Inevitably the Australians got the short stick in this relationship. As the geographic distance between the two armies grew in 1944 and 1945, MacArthur continued to manipulate logistics and joint force resources, starving the Australian Army in New Guinea, Bougainville, and the islands of the South Pacific of supporting assets. In a more unified command setup, this would not have occurred.[7] In addition, the problems of a lack of a joint staff have been dealt with in detail, and while GHQ dramatically improved its understanding, coordination, and application of air and sea power, the lack of a truly integrated staff system in the SWPA continued to hamper coordination until the very end.

SOLVING THE COALITION "PROBLEM"

The major issue that arose in the US-Australian coalition in 1944 and 1945 was in determining a role for the AMF. Five key factors played into these debates: the dominance of the American military forces in the SWPA after November 1943, MacArthur's personal desires, the Australian manpower shortage, the restrictions on the use of Australian militia formations in the Australian mandated territories, and Blamey's attempts to find a role for the Australian Army.

Even before the conclusion of the isolation of Rabaul, MacArthur's gaze was firmly fixed on the approach to the Philippines. Chamberlin's planning staff had been busy on the Reno plans, and on 5 March, with the landings at Los Negros under way, Reno IV was presented to the JCS. In this iteration of the plan, GHQ had scrapped the plan for a landing at Hansa Bay and, armed with its new intelligence insights into the Japanese order of battle, proposed a series of extended jumps along the northern coast of New Guinea to Hollandia and Aitape. Once these were secure, MacArthur proposed to assault the Vogelkop Peninsula and then Halmahera, before launching into the Philippines. In support of these operations, MacArthur also proposed capturing the islands in the Arafura Sea to guard his southwestern flank. Despite not having approval for an assault on the Philippines, the JCS approved MacArthur's plans.[8]

Blamey had seen the various iterations of Reno and knew full well that the Australian Army did not figure in GHQ's planning. However, the Arafura Sea plan (Operation Auburn) would require an assault launched from Darwin, and here the Americans soon saw a supporting role for the Australians. Blamey had Adv LHQ prepare a full appreciation of the operation in line with GHQ's conceptual thinking. With a target date set for 1 June 1944, the strike force was built around two AIF divisions, spearheaded by the 6th Division (which had not played a role as a divisional HQ in New Guinea in 1943), one US paratroop regiment, a US antiaircraft group, and a US 155 mm field battery.[9]

The three key objectives were the Aroe, Kai, and Tanimbar Islands, each with between two thousand and three thousand Japanese defenders. These assaults would require a considerable naval covering force and amphibious assault force as well as two air force groups, one each based in northern Australia and the Humboldt Bay–Aitape area. Even with these bases, the distances for land-based aviation were great, restricting fighter coverage to P-38 and P-47 aircraft with only limited duration over the targets and enemy airfields in the surrounding area. It was deemed that carrier aviation for the assaults would considerably improve the outcome. Alternatively, Adv LHQ proposed preliminary landings to take airfields closer to the objectives to provide for land-based air support.[10]

The major problem with this version of the Reno plans was that it proposed "an advance on two roughly parallel axes approximately one thousand miles apart." The geography also dictated two separate base areas. The planning was further complicated by the fact that the two main operations (Arafura Sea and northern coast of New Guinea) would be undertaken concurrently to provide for mutual support. This would require each force to be "self contained and completely independent of each other in regard to support forces, naval and air." Blamey believed that the lack of sufficient air assets meant that this would not be possible but that any reduction in the proposed support by the AAF to Operation Auburn would be "fatal to success." The distances would also require a high degree of decentralization—not a GHQ strongpoint—and this would limit GHQ's ability to "co-ordinate action [and] maintain strategic control," something anathema to MacArthur's philosophy of command.[11]

Despite these difficulties, Adv LHQ did see a way forward for the operations, and detailed plans were developed, with the base area in Darwin receiving priority for development.[12] However, Operation Auburn would flounder in the face of the rapid advances being undertaken in both the SWPA and the CPA. When the operations were conceived in November and December 1943, no one had any idea of how quickly they would develop in 1944. In addition, the development of the base area and the reconstitution of the AMF for offensive operations on such a scale had meant that by early 1944 the plan had to push back the landing dates until August 1944.[13]

By late February, GHQ had told Blamey that MacArthur was having second thoughts about Auburn, given the need to concentrate his forces and the limitations in amphibious craft, although he requested the development of the Darwin base area to continue just in case.[14] As a consequence, the potential start date for Auburn was pushed back to October 1944! This was clearly unfeasible, and as a result "the three AIF divisions would not be employed for some time."[15]

A short while later this development was confirmed by Blamey, and he wrote to Morshead noting that, with the Admiralty operations "bringing matters to a very definite climax" in the South Pacific, he expected the Australian Army to be asked to "garrison the Mandated Islands."[16] A few weeks later, Blamey would note to Morshead that the prime minister had requested that he accompany him on a trip to London and Washington to discuss Australia's future role in the war. Thus, the attempt to continue the SWPA coalition on somewhat mutual terms had failed. However, the development of the planning for Operation Auburn would shape Blamey's thinking on the future role of the AMF, while the five key factors affecting the coalition in the SWPA would play out for the rest of the war.

A COMMONWEALTH ARMY TO RETAKE SINGAPORE

By March 1944, Blamey realized that MacArthur planned to give the Australian Army a minor role for at least the next year. As David Horner has noted,

> with the virtual conclusion of Australian Army operations, Blamey was playing a difficult game as he tried to determine appropriate employment for his forces in the next year. While MacArthur had promised Curtin to use the Australians in the Philippines, Blamey knew that . . . [MacArthur's] SWPA plans—RENO III and RENO IV—did not mention Australian formations. Furthermore, MacArthur's commitment to the use of task forces would edge him out of a role as Commander Allied Land Forces. The best hope was to see what he could achieve in London by encouraging the introduction of British forces into the SWPA.[17]

The other major factor that would influence the future role of Australia in the SWPA was the pace of operations in the theater, as well as the major operations farther north in Nimitz's CPA. Soon after the completion of Cartwheel, MacArthur's forces had made their sequence of amphibious assaults along the northern coast of New Guinea. Using a leapfrogging technique to land forces beyond the range of Allied fighter support, made possible through the extensive use of Ultra intelligence, MacArthur was able to implement a strategy of bypassing the main centers of Japanese resistance and extending the length of his assaults, making considerable progress. In only a little more than a month, MacArthur's forces had advanced to Biak Island via Aitape and Hollandia, a distance of some 750 miles. This advance into Dutch New Guinea in early to mid 1944 was, as American historian Edward Drea has pointed out, based on "the fruits of the Australians' gallant efforts in eastern New Guinea" and was enabled by the advances in signals intelligence that had allowed for the reading of the Japanese Army's codes.[18] These rapid advances made many plans, such as those for Operation Auburn, obsolete and complicated future planning as the pace and scope of operations expanded.

A further factor driving the evolution of the coalition in the SWPA was the state of the Australian war effort and the balance it had to strike between military and economic power. The rapid expansion of US forces in the SWPA in 1944 was matched by the exhaustion of the Australians. Having been at war since September 1939 and having initiated full mobilization in 1942, Australia had been operating beyond the full capacity of its manpower for quite some time.[19]

Manpower had been an issue for the Australian government and its military services since mid-1943. This was further complicated by the fact that the Australian war effort was not totally focused on the Pacific, but rather the government had decided to continue to support the war against Germany through the provision of aircrew for the Empire Air Training Scheme (EATS). Gradually, Australia's contribution to the scheme was wound back during 1944, but this was largely at Britain's instigation. The EATS effectively ended in October 1944, but it would take some time to wind down, and it was not formally suspended until 31 March 1945. In total, some thirty-seven thousand Australian airmen had taken part in this program, representing some 9 percent of the RAF's aircrew in the European and Mediterranean theaters.[20] This meant that, effectively, the RAAF had provided two air forces, one for operations in the SWPA and another in support of RAF Bomber Command. The EATS significantly affected the military preparedness of the RAAF in the Pacific in the lead-up to the war there and was a major brake on the development of the RAAF in the SWPA. In 1944 and 1945, it was also a major drain on Australian manpower.

The problem, however, was much broader than the EATS. The Australian government simply did not have enough manpower to maintain all three services at their current levels while supporting the economy. In July 1943, the government committed to an expeditionary force of three AIF divisions with enough militia troops to provide for the defense of Australia and its territories. The problem was, as Blamey pointed out, that the allotment of four thousand male and one thousand female recruits per month was not enough to sustain this force. As a result, with the threat of invasion passed, the army at home was reduced, with the 1st, 2nd, and 3rd Armoured Divisions removed from the order of battle.[21] The troops from these formations were used to reinforce the depleted AIF and militia units that had been on operations.[22]

By 1944, the government had decided to reduce the army further and direct more workers to industry. This approach was reaffirmed in early 1944, and later in the year the government directed that an additional thirty thousand men from the army and fifteen thousand from the RAAF be diverted to industry. This meant that the army would only be able to maintain six infantry divisions and two armored brigades. This, Blamey argued, would leave a shortage of some twenty-six thousand personnel by mid-1945. It would also lead to the reduction of the army by at least one militia division in mid-1945 and the disbandment of one of the two armored brigades. By September 1944, the army was receiving only 420 men and 500 women per month. The government saw this as part of a broader national policy: this was about balancing Australia's limited resources in a total war effort to best effect. Despite Blamey's concerns, the reductions in Australia's military forces and the boosting of the war economy would continue. Even in the face of these changes, in 1944 and 1945 Australia was maintaining a higher level of mobilization per capita than Britain and the United States.[23]

In addition, MacArthur had less need for Australian combat power now as his US military capability had increased so greatly. He did, however, have an escalating need for Australian resources and industry. This meant that by war's end, as one US administrator pointed out, "Australia was one country that actually returned more in Lend Lease goods than we gave them."[24] On the military side, the fact remained that Australia's combat power in two of its three services (army and air force) was diminishing. Both Blamey and MacArthur had to account for this in their military strategy and operational planning, and it was an especially important factor in the way Blamey tried to calibrate the Australian Army's efforts in the South Pacific in 1944 and 1945 and his plans for the army's role in the invasion of Japan in 1946 and 1947.

With all of this on his mind, on 5 April 1944 Blamey traveled to Washington (23 April) and London (29 April) with Curtin to ascertain a clear role for the nation's military forces in the Pacific. In the lead-up to the trip, Blamey had made it clear to the chief of the Imperial General Staff, Field Marshal Sir Alan Brooke, that there should be close cooperation on a British return to the Pacific and that Australia's involvement in the coalition with MacArthur had not weakened Australia's links to the empire. On arrival in London, it became clear to Blamey that the British chiefs of staff were also looking for a way to increase their role in the Pacific War.[25]

From the British perspective, Churchill wanted to launch an offensive to retake the former British possessions of Singapore, Borneo, and Malaya.[26] As the Australian official history has noted, as a result of the discussions at the Allied War Council meeting in Cairo in November 1943 (the Sextant Conference), the British chiefs decided that as soon as possible after the defeat of Germany (then assumed for planning purposes to take place by 1 October 1944), "the British Fleet should be sent to the Pacific . . . and that they should [also] aim at providing . . . four British divisions based on Australia for service in the Pacific zone."[27]

Soon after arriving in London, Curtin and Blamey attended the British Prime Minister's War Conference on 3 May. Here Curtin warmly welcomed the idea of basing British forces in Australia. While there were

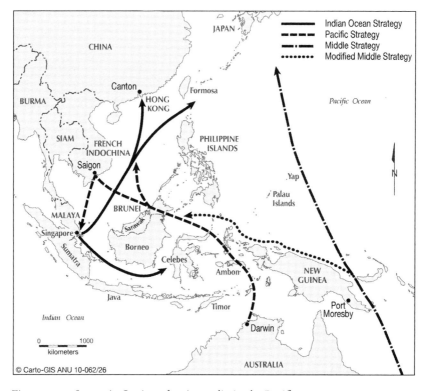

Figure 13.2 Strategic Options for Australia in the Pacific, 1944–1945

some good discussions toward brokering an outline suitable to both countries, it was not a respectable first effort from Blamey. Brooke described him as "not an impressive specimen. He looks entirely drink sodden and somewhat repulsive."[28]

In meetings over the next few days, it became apparent that MacArthur's US forces in the SWPA were advancing much faster than expected and that British forces would not arrive before the invasion of the Philippines. During these discussions, Blamey proposed that a Commonwealth Army, formed around British, Australian, and New Zealand troops supported by an integrated Commonwealth air force and fleet, retake Singapore. Based at Darwin, the army component would undoubtedly fall under Blamey's command. This idea formed the basis of much of the discussions between Blamey and the British chiefs of staff. Eventually they were able to agree on an estimation of forces and availability dates for the creation of this force, although there was no confirmation of a strategy.

On 26–28 May, a number of meetings were held between Blamey, Curtin, Churchill, and the British chiefs. Churchill was now proving to be a thorn in the side of the proposed Commonwealth Force for Australia. The British prime minster remained fixated on an amphibious landing on the tip of Sumatra, believing such a lodging would "force a withdrawal of Japanese forces in northern Burma and would liquidate our commitment in this area."[29] At this time Curtin now added more consternation for Blamey and the British chiefs. Brooke noted in his diary after the 26 May meeting that "Curtin who is entirely in MacArthur's pocket was afraid we were trying to oust MacArthur! He consequently showed very little desire for British forces to operate from Australia. On the other hand I know this outlook was not shared by the rest of Australia."[30]

On this issue, Brooke was both right and wrong—Curtin was in MacArthur's pocket but not in regard to the use of British forces in Australia. Curtin strongly supported the basing of UK forces in Australia, but MacArthur had convinced him that any British move in the SWPA would have to be on MacArthur's terms and, most significantly, under MacArthur's command. MacArthur would simply not abide a rival command in his region or the carving out of part of the SWPA for separate operations under a British-Australian command. Curtin was clearly struggling to reconcile his close personal relationship with MacArthur, the success of the SWPA so far, and the clear changes that were occurring in the theater and the Pacific War more broadly. Despite these setbacks, Brooke noted that as the meeting went on "it took a far better turn and in the end we obtained what we wanted for the present. Namely Darwin and Fremantle to be developed for future operations by us and representatives of our staff with the Australian General Staff."[31]

These discussions led Blamey to conclude that he had reached an agreement for his proposed Commonwealth Army to operate on MacArthur's western flank to retake Singapore. However, Blamey had misread both the strategy and the British chiefs. Furthermore, MacArthur was to use these plans to justify a further reduction in the role of the Australians in the Philippines and the formal removal of Blamey from his already defunct role as commander of the ALF in the SWPA.

THE FAILURE OF BLAMEY'S STRATEGIC PLANS

On returning to Australia, Blamey got on with the plan of basing the Commonwealth Army in Darwin. The outline for the proposal was based on an army of some 675,000 troops that would include five British divisions and two British tank brigades, as well as British commandos and lines-of-communication troops. Royal Navy battleships, aircraft carriers, cruisers, and destroyers and seventy-eight RAF squadrons would support this force. It would link up with an AIF expeditionary corps of three divisions, supported by Australian Militia formations and the majority of the RAAF and the RAN, as well as a New Zealand contingent.[32]

Unsurprisingly, MacArthur was horrified at the idea. If put in place, it would remove the Australians from his command, threaten his reliance on the Australian war economy, and greatly reduce his power in the war against Japan. Furthermore, it would allow the British into the Pacific War. He therefore strongly opposed any change to the current command arrangements. Back in England, disagreements among the British chiefs and between Brooke and Churchill over the prime minister's commitment to operations in the NEI went on for the next four months, causing Brooke to state on 8 August 1944 that he was at his "wit's end" over the lack of an agreement on Britain's Pacific strategy.[33] These delays greatly aided MacArthur, who made sure that the Australian prime minister and the US JCS were well aware of his fervent opposition.

Meanwhile, Blamey was back in Australia and running full tilt with the proposal that be believed had been agreed to with the British in May. He moved his most trusted staff officer, General Berryman, out of his corps command to set up a new HQ in Melbourne and began the development of Darwin as a base (greatly aided by the preparations for the now abandoned Operation Auburn). On 3 July 1944, Blamey gave Berryman the full outline of the plan, of which, according to Berryman biographer John Hetherington, "Berryman saw the great implications. . . . It would mean that a new Pacific theatre would be opened, and that Australia would be a partner with Britain and New Zealand in the reconquest of the Pacific. It would mean an enlargement of Australia's prestige, such as Australia could not hope for as the junior, very junior member of an American-Australian Relationship."[34] All the way through July, Berryman continued to work away on what he described in his diary as the "UK plot." However, toward the end of the month, obfuscation from the British became more apparent, and Blamey advised Berryman that he did not expect a decision on its outcome for "some time."[35] But time was not on Blamey's side. Every step that MacArthur's US forces took closer to the Philippines complicated his Commonwealth Army scheme, and his plan started to unravel in the face of MacArthur's opposition, the political situation in the SWPA, and direct negotiations between the British and the US JCS over Britain's role in the Pacific.[36]

When Blamey returned to Australia, he had assumed that MacArthur was well aware of his discussions in London. He formally broached the idea of the new Commonwealth Army with MacArthur in June, yet MacArthur feigned ignorance and told Blamey that he was "very disturbed" by the idea and that Blamey "had revealed an attitude which [was] . . . most unsatisfactory." According to MacArthur, Blamey then cast doubts on the ability of Australian forces to participate in the Philippines as a result of the Commonwealth Army plan. MacArthur noted to Frederick Shedden, the Australian secretary of defense, that Blamey had "instructed Lieut-Gen Berryman to take over the command of the British Forces which might be sent to Australia" and that from this discussion "MacArthur assumed that Blamey was taking the adoption of the new proposal for granted."[37]

The most significant consequence of these June discussions was the perception by MacArthur that Blamey was being disloyal. It was a self-indulgent and narcissistic approach from MacArthur, especially given his treatment of his coalition partner. It was, however, entirely predictable given his character. Returning to the diplomatic offensive, MacArthur countered this conversation by actively encouraging the Australian government to consider replacing Blamey as the C-in-C of the AMF.[38]

Blamey's major problem was that he did not have the standing with the Australian government that he needed to pull off the new command arrangements without MacArthur's support. Blamey's inability to influence Curtin and Shedden on these matters was further complicated by his low standing within the Australian government.[39] Ben Chifley, the treasurer, had a firm "dislike of Blamey," as did other senior Labor Party figures and ministers such as Frank Forde and John Dedman.[40] Neither Curtin nor the government trusted Blamey, and instead both took their counsel from MacArthur. However, this was 1944—not 1942—and the Australian government was confusing its personal affection for MacArthur with the reality of the divergence of interests between Australian strategy and MacArthur's personal ambitions and interests. Frank Forde, minister for the army, naively thought that "if MacArthur had been a native born Australian he could not have assisted or co-operated more magnificently with the government of Australia."[41] In fact, despite his rhetoric, MacArthur no longer had (if indeed he ever did) Australia's best interests at heart.

MacArthur was worried about his position being "undermined."[42] He wrote to Curtin that "such reinforcements [British fleet or troops] should be brought in without changing this battle-proven and integrated command set-up of veterans, which has been organized and molded into the finest of Pacific fighting teams."[43] The odds were clearly stacked against Blamey, but in spite of these obstacles he put his faith in the agreement that he thought he had reached with the British chiefs, relying on Brook to get agreement among the CCS for the plan. In the interim he pushed ahead with his idea, but Berryman's planning work was doomed even before it began.

Despite a number of setbacks in the planning stage, including opposition from senior British officers in Australia despite having orders from the British chiefs to fully cooperate, Berryman's initial report was finished by 23 August. The two-hundred-page study detailed the requirements for basing, training, and supply of the combined force of 675,000-plus; it noted that it would be a massive undertaking.[44] However, it soon became clear that Blamey "had taken too much for granted"[45] and that Blamey's visit to "London and Washington had failed to find a mission for the Australian Army."[46]

Soon after completing his report, Berryman was back at MacArthur's HQ as the senior Australian liaison officer, where he "began to have serious doubts about the establishment of the new theatre." Shortly after his arrival at GHQ in Hollandia, he raised the matter with MacArthur, hoping to sound him out in regard to his attitude toward the project. MacArthur retorted that "it will never come off."[47] The deathblow for Blamey's Commonwealth Army proposal came at the Quebec Conference, where the CCS negotiated a British role in the Pacific via an invasion of Burma and a British fleet for attachment to the CPA under Adm. Chester Nimitz.[48] George Marshall had cabled MacArthur, before his conversation with Berryman, that the British had withdrawn "their alternative proposal to form a British Empire Taskforce in the South West Pacific" and that there would not be "any change in your command set-up."[49] Without the backing of MacArthur or his own government, Blamey's concept had been ill-fated.

The failure of Blamey and Curtin's mission to ascertain a new direction in Australia's war effort meant that MacArthur would continue to be in charge of Australia's military forces. As John Wilton noted to Berryman in March 1944, from his new role on the Australian military mission to the United States, "our representative [in Washington] has no part whatsoever in planning the war. . . . MacArthur has a directive from the CCS, so that the planning as regards the employment of the AMF is a matter for direct settlement between MacArthur and LHQ. . . . I merely make this point that our representative . . . is apparently primarily one of prestige and he has great difficulty in occupying his time."[50] MacArthur used Blamey's machinations with the British chiefs as proof of his disloyalty, thereby reaffirming his decision to sideline the Australians from the Philippines campaign unless operational circumstances dictated otherwise.

THE PHILIPPINES CAMPAIGN AND THE SIDELINING OF AUSTRALIA

In mid to late 1944, two major events occurred that helped to cement the new direction for the coalition in the SWPA. The first was Blamey's long-anticipated request from MacArthur and GHQ for Australian troops to relieve US formations in the South Pacific, while the second was the movement of GHQ out of Australia from its long-standing base at the AMP Building in Brisbane—first to Hollandia in September 1944, then to Leyte in October, and finally to Manila in May 1945.

By now MacArthur had received permission from the JCS for his assault on the Philippines, and he desperately needed the US troops holding the Australian mandated territories. MacArthur wanted these troops released so as to form the Eighth US Army, under the command of the "rehabilitated" Lt. Gen. Robert Eichelberger. Six of Eichelberger's divisions were tied up garrisoning Torokina, Aitape, and New Britain.[51] These were set to become Australian responsibilities, and Berryman, reinstalled at Adv LHQ as its newly designated chief of staff, oversaw the arrangement for the transfer of forces with GHQ on 29 September 1944.[52]

While administratively smooth, the relief effort created some consternation between MacArthur and Blamey. Blamey looked to replace the US forces with the minimum number of troops possible, especially given his manpower restrictions from the government and the need to maintain his expeditionary force, so he proposed to replace the six US divisions with seven Australian brigades. MacArthur responded that this was totally inadequate, a reaction that it seems was based more on pride and appearance than military necessity.[53] MacArthur demanded that no fewer than twelve brigades be used, allocating four to Bougainville, one to Green, Treasury, and New Georgia Islands, three to New Britain, and four to mainland New Guinea. This was yet another case of top-down, centralized control from GHQ. Furthermore, it would have major repercussions for the AMF, as Blamey was now forced to use the 6th Australian Division AIF at Aitape. This reduced the AIF expeditionary force (I Australian Corps) by one-third, thus "making it even less likely that the AIF could be used in the Philippines."[54]

The Australian forces were to move into place from October 1944 to January 1945 and would come under the newly created First Australian Army, subsuming the role of NGF HQ and expanded to include the new territories in the South Pacific. By October 1944, MacArthur had secured the Vogelkop Peninsula, and he was planning to assault Leyte. He informed the JCS he could make the leap from Leyte to Luzon by 20 December. In the CPA, Nimitz forces had been making excellent progress, taking the Marshall Islands, assaulting the Marianas in June, and securing Peleliu by November 1944. In the same month, USAAF B-29 Superfortresses struck the Japanese homelands. By the time MacArthur's forces reached Vogelkop, they had bypassed and isolated one hundred thousand Japanese troops.[55]

The movement into the Philippines was a massive undertaking. During the New Guinea offensives, the SWPA had mainly operated at the regimental, divisional, and corps levels. Now, MacArthur would have to seize Leyte using virtually all of Krueger's army, made up of two corps with four divisions between them, with Eichelberger's army in support. While the RAN would continue to be on hand to support MacArthur, the RAAF and the army continued to play distant supporting roles. The question, however, remained as to the use of the AIF in the archipelago or in the landing on Luzon.

COMMAND ARRANGEMENTS

As the roles changed in the SWPA in 1944, the command setup in the theater evolved. With GHQ relocating to Hollandia, Blamey had to adjust his own HQ arrangements. As he continued to remain in command of both the AMF and the Australian Army in the field, he put in place a system of three HQs. LHQ remained in Melbourne to command the AMF administration, and Adv LHQ would initially remain in Brisbane to command all Australian Army operations, while a new HQ was created, Forward Echelon Adv LHQ, otherwise known as Forland. Forland would be colocated with GHQ, whereby its role was "primarily planning and liaison work with GHQ."[56] Berryman, whom Blamey had installed as chief of staff of Adv LHQ, would also take command of Forland and

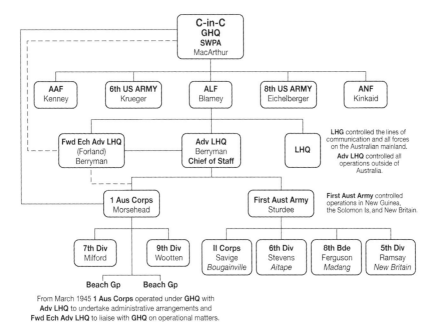

Figure 13.3 Command Structure, August 1944–1945

its staff. He saw his role as to "establish an Australian headquarters with [GHQ] so that I would know their plans, thoughts and secrets."[57] Blamey put it more bluntly: Berryman was there to "safe guard Australia's interests."[58] Forland opened at Hollandia on 7 September 1944.

Forland quickly evolved into the key Australian operational HQ in the SWPA. Its role was centered on the preparation of feasibility studies and the coordination of all planning and operations between GHQ and the Australians. Planning was done directly with GHQ up to the point where operational instructions were issued. Thereafter, Forland acted in a liaison capacity for Adv LHQ, I Australian Corps, and the First Australian Army. After October 1944, Forland was expanded to enable it to command AMF operations (subsuming much of Adv LHQ's work) and also to split into forward and rear sections. Berryman was also empowered by Blamey to bring forward the planning elements of I Australian Corps to his headquarters so that he could oversee the development of its plans with GHQ.[59] With Blamey largely absent from the forward area, he delegated command responsibilities to Berryman, effectively making him the day-to-day commander of the Australian Army Group in the field. Supporting the efforts of Forland were some eighty-five officers from the

Australian Army, the RAAF, and the RAN who were attached to GHQ across all areas of its operations.[60]

When Berryman took over Forland and arrived at GHQ, the role for the I Australian Corps remained in doubt. The pace of the advance across the SWPA and the CPA meant that planning staffs worked at a frantic pace to try to keep up with the various plans and opportunities that presented themselves. The first major scheme for Forland to assess was a proposed landing of the Australians at Aparri in northern Luzon. This was a supporting role but nonetheless an important operation in Mac-Arthur's overall scheme of maneuver. Forland did an immense amount of work on the planning for this operation, involving high-level engagement with GHQ, and initially it looked like a difficult yet achievable mission for the Australians.[61]

Berryman and Chamberlin once again clashed, just as at Lae, over the force requirements and shipping, while the two intelligence sections debated enemy strengths and intentions with the usual flavor—Willoughby and GHQ lowballing figures, and the operation commanders pushing back.[62] Genuine and mutual supportive planning was undertaken, but like many plans at this stage of the war events overtook it. With the JCS fully supportive of MacArthur's plans, by the end of September it was decided that the USN would now furnish large-scale aircraft-carrier support and additional light naval forces, obviating the need for the airfield and port at Aparri.[63]

At the time of the cancellation of the Aparri operation, MacArthur met with Curtin for the last time during the war. In this meeting, he proposed that "the Australian divisions would take part in the capture of Mindanao[, then] they would . . . be employed in the capture of British Borneo, and later again in the attack on Java."[64] Thereafter, the role of I Australia Corps took on a rather rapid series of twists and turns with numerous missions being proposed and scrapped. This included an assault on Sarangani (an island that GHQ had decided to bypass two days earlier), Aparri (again), Mindanao, and Davao Island.[65]

Berryman was soon despondent and worried about the vacillations of GHQ.[66] Both Berryman and Blamey knew that the firm commitment MacArthur had given to Curtin to use the Australians in the Philippines was disingenuous. In early October, Sutherland had told Berryman that it would not be expedient to use Australian forces in the Philippines for "political reasons."[67] Brig. Lindley Barham, the BGS at Adv LHQ, noted that GHQ's "conclusion was that we would be a damned nuisance. Add this to the political considerations!"[68]

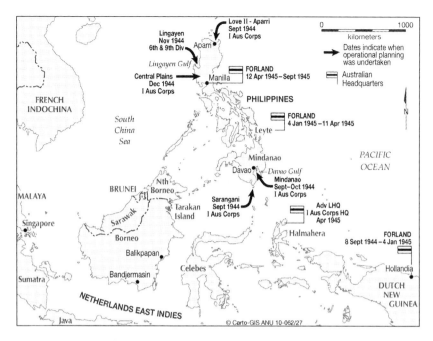

Figure 13.4 Australian HQ Locations and Proposed Operations in 1944

In early December, MacArthur told Blamey and Berryman that he intended to use the Australian corps to "clear up Luzon." However, as D-day for the assault on Luzon approached, there remained no clarity as to the Australians' role. By this time, the bulk of the AIF had been out of operations for more than ten months. With such a lapse in time and a lack of clarity as to their future, Lord Louis Mountbatten, C-in-C of Southeast Asia Command, made a play for I Australian Corps. MacArthur, of course, rejected it out of hand, but still no operational clarity was forthcoming. In assessing GHQ plans, what became clear was that MacArthur was employing I Australian Corps as his theater reserve. The landing at Luzon commenced on 9 January, and by early March MacArthur would have committed all of his US divisions in theater. Unsure as to the level of resistance he would face in Luzon, MacArthur was wisely keeping a corps of elite troops in reserve.[69]

This meant that MacArthur's plans for the use of the AIF were not completely disingenuous. Rather, they were based on firm military reasoning, guided by national interest and self-interest. MacArthur could well have chosen to commit the AIF to Luzon and kept a US corps as his reserve, but that was never going to happen. MacArthur finally wrote to

Curtin in March 1945 to confirm that the Australians would not be used in the Philippines. In doing so, he absolved himself of any responsibility, noting that Blamey was in fact to blame, as he had insisted that the AIF corps fight together as a national command, thereby ruining GHQ's plans to use the two AIF divisions in separate operations under direct American command. Berryman, ever the pragmatist, would note that "it was disappointing . . . not to have played a more prominent part . . . but if operations had not been successful beyond the original estimates we [I Australian Corps] would have been fully employed."[70]

The lack of the use of the AIF in the Philippines drove a further deterioration in the military relations between the two main coalition partners in the SWPA. MacArthur's hubris had gotten the better of him, and the Australians were starting to feel it acutely. This was unequivocal when he did not bother to invite a single Australian officer to his victory parade through Manila. Berryman would note in his diary that "one would think the AMF are not part of the SWPA." Berryman refused to mention the matter to GHQ, as he saw "our dignity and pride proof against inclusion in a flamboyant Hollywood spectacle." He noted that MacArthur's "ego allows him to forget his former dependence on the AMF and [this] is in keeping with GHQ policy to minimize the efforts of Australia in the SWPA."[71]

The disregard shown to the Australians in Manila was symptomatic of GHQ's entrenched neglect of the Australians since October 1944. More significant than victory parades was the fact that Forland was cut out of the information loop and was being left behind. The Australians had only learned of the landing at Leyte in October on the radio, having not received one situation report from GHQ. When GHQ moved to Leyte in November, Forland was left behind in Hollandia until January 1945. When Berryman and his staff had been allowed forward to GHQ during this time, arguments had broken out over accommodations. Senior US officers regarded the mess as exclusively for the US Army and that foreigners should not be there.[72]

The neglect of Forland and the Australians was so rampant that when Berryman was informed in February that the AIF was to be used to assault Borneo, he was also informed that they had decided to rearrange the command structure in the theater and that I Australian Corps would be attached to the Eighth US Army. Forland and Adv LHQ would thus have no role to play in the operation. Blamey noted to Shedden, "It is obvious to me that the intention of GHQ SWPA is to treat my Headquarters as a purely liaison element."[73]

Thus, GHQ refused to provide the shipping to move Adv LHQ forward to Morotai and insisted on dealing with Morshead and I Australian Corps HQ directly. Berryman protested vigorously, and Blamey moved forward to take up the matter with MacArthur directly. Blamey arrived in Manila on 13 March, whereupon he and Berryman were subjected to one of MacArthur's infamous sermons on strategy for over ninety minutes. At the very end, MacArthur announced that the SWPA would be split, with the Philippines remaining under his command as a base to invade Japan and the rest being handed over to the Australians and the Dutch. Blamey then demanded that his HQ be treated with respect. After some debate, MacArthur conceded that I Australian Corps would report directly to GHQ as a task force, with Forland and Adv LHQ responsible for planning and administration. Forland would be colocated with GHQ and Adv LHQ moved forward to Morotai and colocated with Morshead's corps HQ. With MacArthur consenting to a return of a degree of the sovereignty due the Australians, the stage was now set for the Australian invasion of Borneo.[74]

THE RAN AND RAAF IN 1944 AND 1945

While the spotlight was focused on the future role of the Australian Army, the RAN and RAAF were getting on with the job at hand, based largely on the command structure and system of cooperation established with their US counterparts in 1942. For the RAN, it was essentially business as usual in 1944 and 1945. Given the critical importance of maritime power in the SWPA, the RAN was not affected by the Australian government's manpower restrictions. The only major change was the increased tempo and its greatly reduced capability relative to the massive USN presence in the theater.

Unlike for the army, the RAN's central role (in the Seventh Fleet) continued throughout 1944.[75] In particular, the three RAN LSIs, *Manoora*, *Kanimbla*, and *Westralia*, were central to the assaults of Alamo Force in this period. With an almost complete lack of USN large amphibious assault ships, the three RAN LSIs were at the very core of Barbey's assault force in 1944. *Westralia* played an important role at Aware, Cape Gloucester, and Saidor. All three LSIs took part in the assaults on Tanahmerah Bay–Humboldt Bay–Aitape in April 1944 and Leyte in October 1944. *Manoora* was a part of the task force for Toem-Wakde in May 1944 and was present for the assault on Morotai in September along with *Kanimbla*. The RAN also played an important role in the covering forces, including naval gunfire support. The RAN heavy cruisers *Australia* and *Shropshire* and the destroyers *Arunta* and *Warramunga* became especially proficient at shore bombardment, with the two heavy cruisers present for the vast majority of MacArthur's amphibious assaults during 1944. In addition, during the same year, Rear Adm. Victor Crutchley (RN) handed over command of Task Force 74 to Cmdr. John Collins (RAN).[76]

The landings at Leyte Gulf in October 1944 are the largest single action in the history of the RAN. The RAN provided thirty-seven ships for the operation, including two heavy cruisers, two large destroyers, three LSIs, a frigate (*Gascoyne*), survey ships, minesweepers, and logistics ships. In this action, HMAS *Australia* was the first Allied ship hit by a kamikaze attack during the war, with a loss of thirty killed and sixty-four wounded. Among the dead was the ship's captain, while Commodore Collins was severely wounded.[77] *Australia* was damaged again by kamikaze attacks at Lingayen Gulf in January 1945, suffering a further forty-one killed and many more wounded. *Arunta* was also hit by a kamikaze but was able to stay on station. Soon afterward, *Shropshire* and *Arunta* took part in the last major fleet surface action of the war. At the battle of Surigao Strait, the Seventh Fleet clashed with the IJN's battleships, and *Shropshire* fired thirty-two 8-inch broadsides at the battleship *Yamashiro*, scoring a number of hits and helping to sink it. Later in the year, the light cruiser HMAS *Hobart* joined the ships of the Australian Squadron, which participated in most of the SWPA operations for the rest of the war. The RAN provided a maximum effort in support of the Australian landings in Borneo.[78]

Upon the arrival of the British Pacific Fleet in Australian waters, the RAN contributed eighteen corvettes as part of the 21st and 22nd Minesweeper Flotillas. However, the Australian Squadron remained part of the US Seventh Fleet until the end of the war, and Commodore Collins, recovered from his wounds, was in Tokyo Bay for the surrender. At its height, the RAN had expanded fivefold and consisted of 337 ships. The RAN's war had been one of smooth cooperation with the USN. Based on its long experience with the Royal Navy, the RAN was quickly integrated with the USN and played a major role in the SWPA's naval forces from 1942 to late 1944. In the final months of the war, the RAN's effort in the theater was dwarfed by the injection of USN assets into the Seventh Fleet that included aircraft carriers and battleships, but it continued to perform extraordinarily important roles, especially in convoy duty, mine-sweeping,[79] naval gunfire support, and amphibious operations.[80] While the army and the RAAF struggled to find a role during 1944–1945, the RAN remained in demand until war's end and as a result was at the forefront of all of MacArthur's major operations.

For the RAAF, its war in 1944 and 1945 was an extrapolation of both its difficulties and successes earlier in the war. Like for the Australian Army, the massive expansion of the US forces in the SWPA greatly affected its role. In addition, the RAAF was unable to procure the latest aircraft coming off the US manufacturing lines, especially fighter planes, which also greatly affected its utility. Furthermore, the continuation of the RAAF's divided command further undermined its performance.[81]

Early in 1944, No. 10 Operational Group remained in the forward area of New Guinea and racked up an impressive number of operational hours for its squadrons. However, by March it was clear that like the Australian Army, No. 10 Group was going to be left behind as the US forces made their rapid advance toward the Philippines. The one major addition to the RAAF at this time was the establishment of a number of squadrons of B-24 Liberator heavy bombers. At Aitape, the RAAF contributed two airfield construction squadrons, and a few weeks later fighters from No. 78 Wing were flying from these strips in support of operations over New Guinea. Meanwhile, the RAAF Catalina squadrons continued to provide sterling service.[82]

In June 1944, the RAAF claimed its last air-to-air victory in the Pacific, even though the war still had another year to run. While the RAAF provided solid support to the US operations in Dutch New Guinea during 1944, as the Americans advanced farther north the RAAF was left farther and farther behind. For the invasion of Leyte, the RAAF provided support to rear areas only, and the only RAAF unit in the Philippines campaign was No. 3 Airfield Construction Squadron. In October 1944, No. 10 Operational Group was renamed the First Tactical Air Force (First TAF).[83] Operational control moved from the Fifth US Air Force to the Thirteenth, and the First TAF's role was focused on the support of the Australian Army in New Guinea.[84] It relocated to Morotai in November, but as Mark Johnston has stated, the "results were rarely fruitful."[85] Frustration grew, and in April 1945 a number of senior officers in the First TAF tried to resign their commissions over what they saw as the wastefulness of their operations. Kenney intervened and empathized with their situation, telling Air Vice Marshal George Jones not to punish them. The RAAF's operational commander, Air Vice Marshal William Bostock, responded by relieving three other senior officers who seemed to be responsible for much of the poor conditions and morale in the First TAF.

For the operations in Borneo, the First TAF provided twenty squadrons and provided for a large part of the air plan, including control of a significant number of US aircraft. As impressive in size and scope as these operations were, the RAAF's First TAF had only nine contacts with enemy aircraft in the final nine months of the war. In addition, its efforts were totally dwarfed by the Americans'. In July 1945, the First TAF flew an impressive 877 sorties, while by comparison the USAAF in the SWPA flew 10,000 in just one week of the same month.

The RAAF's final eighteen months of the war had seen the experiences of a superb group of men and squadrons dominated by a "lack of enemies to fight, its dependence on its allies . . . its inadequate aircraft . . . and [its] continuing conflict at the top of the command structure . . . while [they] fulfilled a thankless task." For the RAAF, it was a bitter end to an often bitter war in the SWPA.[86]

THE ROAD TO NOWHERE: THE INVASION OF BORNEO

The Allied invasion of Borneo was to consist of three major amphibious landings that represent one of the tactical exemplars of the SWPA in World War II. The major problem is that they were strategically and operationally irrelevant. The decision by MacArthur and GHQ to insist on the invasion was a classic case of an operation looking for a justification. Originally planned around six operations, the purpose of these assaults was to liberate Borneo and Java in the NEI. Changes to planning, force structure, and capabilities meant that it was eventually whittled down to just three: Oboe 1 (Tarakan Island), Oboe 2 (Brunei Bay), and Oboe 6 (Balikpapan).

To MacArthur, these operations were justified on the basis of his moral obligation to liberate the peoples of the SWPA and his commitment to the NEI. He also added to the JCS a commitment to use the AIF troops under his command, as they had been without a mission and were becoming restless. Claims were also made by GHQ as to the usefulness of Borneo as a base for the British Pacific Fleet and the importance of the oil supplies that were critical for the Japanese war effort and could be captured for use by the Allies. GHQ informed Forland that the 9th Division would be used in Brunei Bay and Tarakan and the 7th Division at Balikpapan.[87]

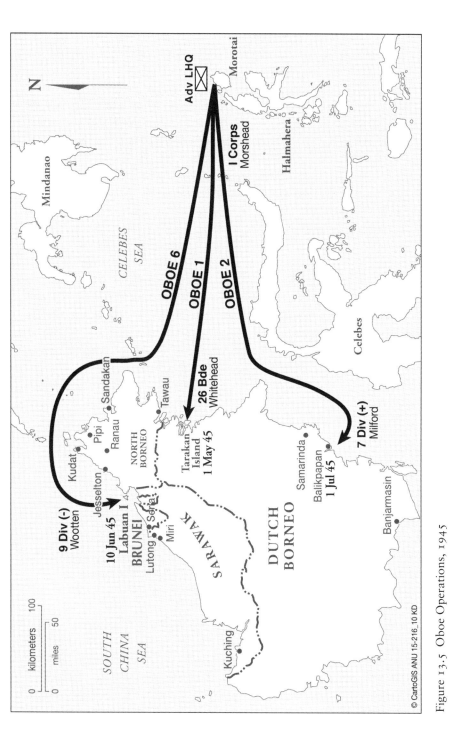

Figure 13.5 Oboe Operations, 1945

MacArthur's strategic justification for the Oboe landing was nothing but fantasy. The British had rejected the area as a base for their Pacific Fleet. As the Philippines were occupied and Nimitz's forces were driving north, the oil fields of Borneo were cut off from the Japanese. If successfully taken by the Allies, it would take months, if not years, for them to be put back in service, and as such this was not a priority for the Allied war effort. The operations lacked a strategic justification to everyone but MacArthur.[88]

The Australians were fully aware of the lack of a strategic rationale for the Oboe operations. Berryman wrote to Blamey on 10 February 1945, noting that "the operations in BORNEO would have little immediate impact on the war against Japan," adding that this was also the opinion of Gen. George C. Marshall.[89] What was just as troubling to Forland was that GHQ's plans also lacked an operational rationale. Tarakan was only to be assaulted to provide an air base to support the follow-on operations, but there were questions as to whether this forward base was needed and if it would be ready in time given the tight schedule. Balikpapan was only ever envisaged as a staging point to launch the final assault on Java, a mission that by June 1945 had been scrubbed. Operationally and strategically they represented a road to nowhere.

MacArthur, however, was insistent that they go ahead, and as he was the theater C-in-C, the allocation of forces was his prerogative. Nevertheless, the Oboe landings' lack of a rationale raised questions from both the JCS and the Australian government. Blamey and Berryman had kept the Australian government fully informed of these operations, and both officers were particularly skeptical of Balikpapan, which would require a full divisional assault. In order to push through the operations, MacArthur revealed himself as a master manipulator. He played one end against the other, telling the JCS that the operations had to go ahead because the Australian government was demanding them, while telling Curtin that they had to go ahead because the JCS required them. Lacking its own line of contact with the JCS, the Australian government reluctantly agreed.[90] Hundreds of Australian servicemen were to be killed or wounded on a mission that had no strategic value.

Planning of these operations by GHQ and Forland took on their usual feel, with Chamberlin and Berryman fighting over the order of battle and shipping. The G-2 staff at GHQ also revised down their estimation of the Japanese forces at Tarakan and Brunei Bay in order to justify Chamberlin's arguments. Beyond this, GHQ, Forland, I Australian Corps, and RAAF Command (which was colocated with Adv LHQ in

Morotai to improve coordination[91]) all worked closely on the plans, and with years of cooperation under their belts the planning went exceptionally smoothly. This is not to underestimate the highly complex nature of these operations. Their planning involved the Seventh Fleet, the Fifth and Thirteenth Air Forces, and the RAAF. In addition, amphibious assaults onto a hostile shore and the coordination of this massive amount of air and maritime power in a joint and combined environment represent some of the most complex operations that any military can undertake.

However, these operations were substantially different from those of 1942 and 1943, principally as no major US Army formations were involved. At this stage of the war, GHQ was able to lavish these operations with US air and naval support, but the land task force was a self-contained Australian operation. Given the nature of sea and air supremacy that the Allies possessed at Borneo, the air and naval elements were the supporting forces, their role being to help the ground force achieve all of its objectives. The only US Army addition to the AIF order of battle was some LVT armored amphibious assault craft (landing vehicles, tracked).[92]

With the weight of effort and the focus of I Australian Corps and Forland on these operations, the support efforts from all services were overwhelming. The first operation, Tarakan, was allocated to the 26th Brigade from the 9th Division. While it was nominally a brigade landing, by the time Brig. Ennis Whitehead's men were ready to go into action, the brigade had swelled to eleven thousand men—the size of a small division. This left Maj. Gen. George Wootten with only two brigades on hand for the Brunei Bay operations, but again with an avalanche of support elements his two-brigade division went into action with twenty-nine thousand troops.[93] This was largely a result of I Australian Corps attaching numerous units from its order of battle to support the individual landings, including the two Australian beach groups that had been created in 1943–1944.

For the assault on Balikpapan, the GOC 7th Australian Division (Maj. Gen. Teddy Milford) was provided with a supersized formation consisting of thirty-three thousand men, making it larger than many corps-level formations. GHQ's insistence on the airfield and oil refinery at Balikpapan being taken quickly, plus 7th Division's assessment of the operation, led to a rejection of a landing away from the objective followed by an overland assault, as at Lae. Instead, Milford planned to land directly onto the objective in a full-frontal assault.[94] This was only made possible by the size of the division, the overwhelming firepower available, and the LVTs, which meant that the 7th Division assessed that a frontal assault using the CPA's storm-landing doctrine was the best way to *minimize* casualties.[95]

Tactically, all three landings were a complete success. While the friction of war and chance were ever present, advances in training, doctrine, support measures, and operational planning had reaching their zenith for the US and Australian forces involved. Tarakan was assaulted on 1 May 1945, and within four days the Japanese defenses had been shattered and the airfield captured. With nowhere to withdraw to, the Japanese forces had fought bitterly and gave up their lives and positions at a heavy cost. Two hundred and twenty-five Australians were killed and another 669 wounded to secure the island and its airstrip—casualties that would mirror the much larger divisional assault at Balikpapan. As predicted, the airfield was not ready on time to support the landing at Balikpapan. However, as Tony Hastings and Peter Stanley have noted, the airfield did play a role in the wider Borneo operations, and if the war had continued on into 1946 as was expected, it would have continued to play a role in the war against Japan.[96] On balance, though, the cost in lives and resources meant that while tactically proficient, Tarakan was operationally unnecessary and strategically irrelevant.

At Brunei Bay the landings also went well. Given the size and scope of the effort, the outcome was never in doubt. Of the three Oboe operations, this was the least costly, as resistance was light. Still, the 9th Division suffered 114 killed to take a port area that was neither wanted nor needed. The final operation of Oboe, Balikpapan, was also to be the last amphibious assault of the Allies in World War II. The largest of the three landings, it had even less of a strategic and operational purpose than its predecessors. Blamey had asked the government to cancel the operation, but as Berryman noted, with all the forces ready to go and MacArthur's obstinacy the government had no choice but to acquiesce.[97]

The landings at Balikpapan look place on 1 July 1945. The 7th Division would go into action with some 33,446 troops under command, including more than 2,000 US and NEI troops. This included a full complement of artillery support, three complete infantry brigades, a commando regiment, a tank regiment, a pioneer battalion, a machine-gun battalion, and a US amphibious tractor battalion. In addition, both Australian beach groups were in support to ensure the landing went smoothly and that the problems in beach organization and logistics issues seen at Lae were not repeated. Backing up the division was the First TAF, which included the four B-24 heavy bomber squadrons, as well as all the heavy bombers in the Thirteenth Air Force and a wing from the Fifth Air Force. Additional fighter cover for the landing was provided by a division of USN escort carriers. The six thousand Japanese defenders were hit with "3,000 tons of bombs, 7,361 rockets, 38,052 shells from three to eight inches, and 114,000 rounds from automatic weapons."[98] During the first ten days of the operation, the division fired 41,800 rounds of 25-pounder artillery fire. As one brigade commander noted, the operation was a "lesson on the use of firepower."[99] Both airfields were in Australian hands by 9 July, but the Japanese defense, as usual, had been fierce and unrelenting. By the time the war finished, 229 Australians had been killed at Balikpapan and a further 634 wounded. Berryman noted that "never were our troops so well equipped, so well supported by Air and Navy, nor so well maintained."[100]

1944–1945: CONTROVERSY AND THE MANDATED TERRITORIES

While the AIF had turned its full attention to the operations in Borneo, the First Australian Army continued operations in support of Australian national interests in New Guinea and Bougainville. These were controversial campaigns, both at the time and in later years. To many, fighting the Japanese in areas that had been bypassed and were well behind the front lines meant that these were the "unnecessary campaigns."[101] However, they were fought with the support of the Australian government and GHQ, and unlike the campaign in Borneo they had a clear strategic rationale.

The nature of this campaign was driven by a number of political and strategic factors. Chief among them was that these were Australian sovereign territories that were occupied by the enemy, who had posed a direct threat to the nation's security and were suppressing the local population. Blamey's operational plans were guided by MacArthur's orders in 1944 that additional Australian troops garrison these areas and by the government's directive that the AIF be available to take part in the invasion of Japan in 1946 and 1947 while releasing men to support the war economy. From a military point of view, Blamey's objectives were well considered, given the nation's manpower crisis. Blamey gave the First Australian Army a clear role to "destroy the enemy where this can be done with relatively light casualties so as to free our territory and liberate the native population and thereby progressively reduce our commitment and free personnel from the army."[102]

Blamey's key objective was to reduce the garrison responsibilities in the mandated territories. This plan would allow for the release of troops, notably the 6th Australian Division AIF, for operations farther north while allowing the army to be reduced.[103] Ultimately Blamey was focused on the reduction of manpower in the army while being able to provide a three-division expeditionary corps from the AIF for the invasion of Japan. This was in line with the Australian government's priority of preserving a significant military presence in the forward battle area in order to maintain the country's "status at the peace table."[104]

Blamey's and Berryman's work in setting the army's strategy for 1945–1947 was based on a sound military assessment. While somewhat delayed, it would receive strong support from the secretary of defense, Frederick Shedden, who noted that "Blamey had made a very sound case in justification of the operations."[105] Thereafter, Blamey's plan was tabled at the Advisory War Council on 6 June, which wrote to Blamey giving its approval.[106] The only major complication was the length of time it took for the government to agree to this strategy and the very poor manner in which Blamey and his staff communicated this outside of their own senior command. Thus, while the tag "unnecessary campaigns" is still periodically used in the debate over Australia's war effort in the South Pacific in 1944 and 1945, no serious scholar of these operations questions their validity.[107]

In achieving these objectives, the First Australian Army was highly successful. They were achieved with only minimal air and, especially, naval support, which meant the First Australian Army "suffered such a poverty of ships and landing craft that, as a rule, the best that they could do was to put ashore a company or two on a hostile shore."[108] Both MacArthur and Blamey share some responsibility for this failure. MacArthur and GHQ starved the First Australian Army of support, as these operations did not meet specific US strategic objectives. Blamey and Berryman, meanwhile, focused their attention on I Australian Corps to such an extent that the GOC First Army, Lt. Gen. Vernon Sturdee, raised a series of complaints with Adv LHQ in 1945, which meant that Blamey and Berryman skipped the landings at Brunei Bay in order to tour the First Army's area of operations and resolve these issues.[109]

Despite the lack of attention, Sturdee's troops were highly effective in their role. By June 1945, Adv LHQ were able to plan with confidence for the transfer of the 6th Australian Division to the AIF expeditionary force for the invasion of Japan while also reducing the size of the militia by thirty thousand men in line with the government's directive. The garrison

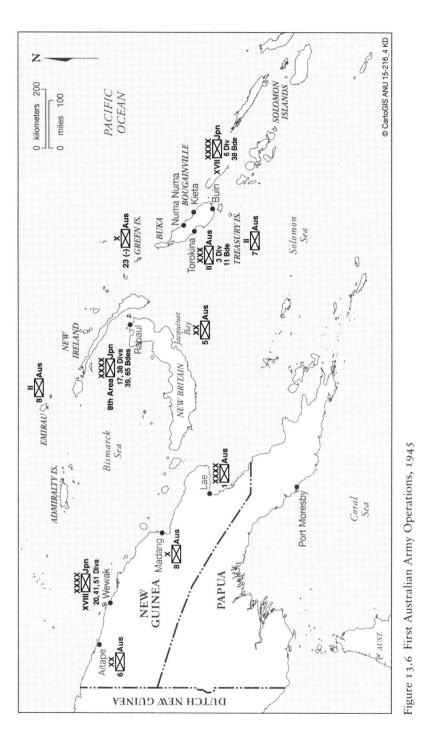

Figure 13.6 First Australian Army Operations, 1945

force in the First Australian Army's area was expected to be as little as three brigades.[110]

These moves were entirely in line with Blamey's plans for the continuation of the war against Japan into 1946 and 1947. With this in mind, he had achieved the government's strategic objectives and had prepared the army to provide the necessary strike force for the invasion of Japan, despite dwindling numbers in the AIF and militia. Australia was prepared for her part in the invasion, but this was a campaign that would never get under way. On 6 August 1945, the United States dropped the first of two atomic bombs on Japan, which surrendered on 15 August. In Australia, the military leadership and government were as surprised as anyone at the end of the war, having been kept in the dark about the development of the United States' nuclear capability.

Controversy about Australia's role in the Pacific during 1944 and 1945 does end with the Borneo landings and the operations in the mandated territories. The idea that Australia was no longer serving at the forefront of the war against Japan in this period invoked international controversy in 2007 when the English historian Max Hastings released his book *Nemesis: The Battle for Japan, 1944–45*. Hastings provocatively titled a chapter "Australians: 'Bludging' and 'Mopping Up.'" Hastings's account, which assesses morale in the military, performance on the home front, and the nature of Australia's military campaigns in 1944 and 1945, is overstated, but it raises some important points about how Australia's performance in this period of war is understood and assessed.[111]

Despite Hastings's finding plenty of fault with MacArthur over the Philippines campaign, *Nemesis* does not appreciate MacArthur's Machiavellian approach to his junior coalition partner in the last two years of the war, nor does it demonstrate an understanding of his iron grip over the Australian government, which continued to believe in MacArthur's fidelity toward their partnership forged in the dark days of 1942, despite growing evidence to the contrary. Significantly, it was this relationship that would decide the fate of Australia's armed forces and their relationship with MacArthur and the US war effort in the concluding battles of the Pacific War.

Hastings is entirely correct to state that "having won so much honour far away in the Mediterranean, Australia's share of the Pacific War ended in rancour and anti-climax." Nonetheless, it was not a case of "bludging"—an Australian word for avoiding work or responsibility—nor was it a "refusal [of Australia] to adapt to participation in a war of national survival," as he has claimed.[112] Three key points easily refute Hastings's claims. First, on 1 July 1945, the Australian Army had more troops in combat with the enemy than at any point in World War II. In addition, the RAN had been maintained at full strength since 1942, and its ships and units were on active duty with the US Seventh Fleet and the British Pacific Fleet. The RAAF was maintaining a full tactical air force on operations and was continuing to provide aircrew to the RAF. Second, the Australian war economy was playing an incredibly important role in sustaining both the Australian war effort and MacArthur's forces. As noted earlier, Australia ended the war with a positive lend-lease ledger with the United States and kindly erased the debt with its larger ally at war's end. Finally, as noted, Australia maintained a higher level of mobilization per capita than both the United States and Britain.

Ultimately the height of battlefield cooperation in the SWPA corresponded with a radical shift in the correlation of forces and the focus of US strategy. MacArthur's strategic interests diverged from Australia's, which meant that, excluding the RAN, the nation's army and air force struggled to find a mission in the final campaigns to defeat the Japanese. In 1943, MacArthur achieved his desire to command the land forces in his theater, and his increase in US combat power meant that thereafter Australia and its army and air force became an afterthought, relegated to the sidelines of the Pacific War. To the bitter end, the SWPA remained "MacArthur's coalition."

Conclusion

As David Horner and Peter Edwards have noted, Australia had no choice other than to surrender a certain amount of sovereignty to the United States in the crisis of 1942.[1] In return, the US JCS set up a curious system of command to run the Pacific War, which placed Douglas MacArthur, a brilliant but vain and unscrupulous commander, as the SWPA's key protagonist. This meant, according to American historians Williamson Murray and Allan R. Millett, that in 1942 MacArthur would go on to set himself up as the "de facto field marshal of the Australian armed forces" and that Australia became one of America's two new "wartime client" states, the other being Nationalist China.[2]

At the military-to-military level, on which this book has focused, the settings for the relationship were driven by the temporary nature of the coalition between the United States and Australia from 1942 to 1945 and the critically important role of MacArthur in setting the conditions for the character of this relationship. Most of the problems that were encountered early in the relationship emanated from differences in culture, doctrine, and experience and the pressures felt in the face of the enemy as the forces in the SWPA battled for survival and then fought to gain the upper hand over the Japanese.

The early experiences in the theater in managing and running a coalition military effort underscored the value of a basis of cooperation built on foundations such as common doctrine, continuous exchanges of military personal, the importance of liaison officers, high levels of interoperability, and combined training and exercises. These platforms form a basis for a sound coalition military effort, and all of them were absent in the SWPA in 1942.

In their absence, the dominating factor was MacArthur's personality and ambitions, his philosophy of command, the organizational structure of the SWPA, and the differences in doctrine between the United States and Australia. These factors caused a high level of tension between GHQ and the Australian high command throughout the war, especially between MacArthur and Blamey. Complicating this relationship was MacArthur's refusal to set up a truly joint and combined headquarters. Instead, GHQ was dominated by US Army officers and in particular the Bataan Gang. Too often, though, what is overlooked is the factions that existed within GHQ and that a number key officers in this HQ, notably

Stephen Chamberlin (G-3) and Richard Marshall (G-4), were either not a part of this clique or kept themselves removed from the factionalism that dominated the HQ.

In addition, the key commanders in the SWPA, such as Blamey, Herring, and Eichelberger from the land forces, Brett, Kenney, Whitehead, Bostock, and Hewitt in the air forces, and Carpenter, Crutchley, Crace, Barbey, and Collins in the naval forces, formed close working relationships that crossed national lines. This was replicated by key staff officers at all headquarters but in particular by Chamberlin and Berryman. Given the character of the coalition in the SWPA, it fell upon senior commanders and staff officers to solve issues and smooth the wheels of cooperation.

As this work has demonstrated, most of the tensions that existed at the highest command levels were not as evident lower down the chain of command, especially when the Allies were in contact with the enemy. Being open-minded, collaborative, competent, and professional were the key factors that drove cooperation in the face of organizational, structural, and doctrinal differences. These factors and the basic requirement to avoid attitudes of cultural imperialism reveal the importance of the human element of war, highlighting how personalities have a major impact—both positive and negative—on the conduct of operations.

Early on, MacArthur was able to admit that there were "some difficulties down the line and some severe antagonisms were present in the beginning" but said that he was "given full support from the Australians from the beginning," support that was provided even when the Australians thought that he was wrong.[3] Chamberlin probably summed up the situation best for both countries in September 1942 when he noted in a letter to the US commander at JOOTS that the heart of the problem was the fact that "we constantly have to deal with our allies. Their systems, their methods and their line of thought are different from ours. . . . Great patience is necessary. It behooved all of us [Americans and Australians] to know when to give in and when to be firm."[4]

Chamberlin's view represents the basic framework for cooperation that existed between the two militaries. In the end, over time, close cooperation did develop at virtually all levels. Both militaries recognized that proper joint training and planning, combat experience, adequate logistics, and cooperation was the formula for success, although it had not been without a few hiccups along the way. These were hard lessons to absorb for both militaries in 1942, and many mistakes were to be repeated in 1943. As outlined, the New Guinea campaigns of 1943 represent the high point of Allied cooperation on the battlefield in the SWPA. In many ways it is a shame that at the highest echelons MacArthur and Blamey were unable to come to an agreement for the continued use of Australian troops in the front lines in 1944 and 1945, namely, the invasion of the Philippines—a period that coincided with the peak of cooperation at the operational and tactical levels.

Despite the difficulties in working together at the military level in 1942 and 1943, the strategic partnership at this time was exceptionally strong. This was the period when MacArthur's interests and Australia's interests ran in parallel. For the military forces in the field, cooperation peaked in the latter part of 1943, coinciding with the fundamental change in the coalition as the asymmetrical nature of the relationship finally took hold. At this point, as strategic interests diverged, the operational and tactical levels of cooperation became less important, in particular for land power and air forces.

The events of 1944 and 1945 reveal the difficulties for a minor power such as Australia to carve out a strategy for itself in the face of the deliberations of major powers. In the end, Britain and the United States came to a mutually agreeable strategic solution to British involvement in the Pacific War that suited their strategic interests, and the needs and requirements of Australia were not taken into consideration other than in basing options, logistics, and support services. This left the AIF on the sidelines of the war for much of 1944, and once launched into battle in 1945 it took part in a campaign that was strategically and operationally irrelevant. For Australia, this was a bitter experience. In the period prior to the Pacific War, it had placed its faith, almost unreservedly, in British Empire loyalty. This had counted for little in the face of Churchill's global strategy for national survival. After the fall of Singapore, Australia had found itself reliant on a new major power for support, one with a close alignment of values but not always a close alignment of interests.

For MacArthur, the platform for his relationship with Australia had been laid out in mid-1942 when he outlined to Curtin that the United States' relationship with Australia was a coalition of convenience. MacArthur proved to be remarkably consistent in his approach, even though his rhetoric to Curtin, Shedden, and many others served to cloak these interests in grandiose and insincere platitudes. Many of Australia's leaders choose to accept MacArthur's oratory in 1943 and 1945, as opposed to judging him on his actions. In the end, MacArthur deliberately sought to exclude the Australians from major operations in the SWPA in 1944 and 1945, and he played an unscrupulous hand in terms of his relationship with Blamey and in his assessment of the need for the operations in

Borneo. Despite this, the Australian government could not bring itself to see that the strong bond it had forged with the SWPA's C-in-C in 1942 and 1943 had always been on predicated on MacArthur's self-interest, rather than the interests of Australia or a mutually beneficial "alliance."

Thus, the differences in the SWPA's coalition after November 1943 were profound. As Gavin Long, the Australian official historian, has noted,

> in effect Blamey controlled the Australian military operations in New Guinea throughout, and, in 1942 and most of 1943, the operations of all Allied land forces in the field. After late 1943 and until May 1945 MacArthur's headquarters was somewhat out of touch with the Australian Army (which still compromised about one-third of its strength) and the greater part of that army, consigned mostly to a rearward role, was starved of equipment.[5]

This was entirely predictable. MacArthur had given every indication that this was how he would operate his theater since his first weeks in Australia, and it came as no surprise to Blamey and senior members of the Australian high command. The greatest failure on Australia's part was the government's delusion in believing that MacArthur still had Australia's best interest at heart in 1944 and 1945 after MacArthur had outlined to Curtin in June 1942 just how temporary and transactional he saw the relationship.

In September 1944, MacArthur left Australia's shores and was never to return. As the geographic distance between himself and the continent grew, he became less and less interested in Australia or its military forces, except when it directly impacted on his ability to operate his theater as he saw fit or where it threatened his insatiable thirst for additional military power and control. After the war, MacArthur became completely focused on his role in leading the rehabilitation of Japan and then as supreme commander of the allied forces in the Korean War. His mental focus on Australia had resided only in the period coinciding with his physical presence in the country and the strategic alignment that had helped him secure a pathway for his return to the Philippines.

As the war drew to a close, the coalition of convenience in the SWPA started to fracture. In the absence of a formal alliance relationship when victory came in August 1945, there was no immediate thought of a mutual security pact between the two countries. By then the Australian military had already been looking to Britain for well over a year to reestablish defense ties. For Australia, however, it was not to be a return to the old days of Imperial Defence. As early as October 1944, the Defence Committee in Australia recognized that it could not rely solely on a future system of collective security and that after its experiences with the failures of Imperial Defence and the difficulties of the US coalition, Australia "should not accept the risk of relying primarily for its defence upon the assistance of a foreign power."[6] Standing forces, it argued, should provide for the initial defense of Australia until allies could arrive or the nation could be mobilized for war.

The "ally" Australia looked to at the end of 1945 was primarily Britain, reaffirming Australia's role in Commonwealth defense in the postwar period. The Chiefs of Staff Committee's 1946 *Appreciation of the Strategical Position of Australia* assessed that the nation was protected by its geographic situation and the collective-security system of the United Nations. However, because Australia was unable to defend itself unaided against a major power, its security was, therefore, again intrinsically linked to the British Empire. Although it also saw US assistance as essential, it placed no reliance on it being forthcoming, given the experience of relations with the United States in the two world wars.[7]

Disagreements between Australia and the United States would also occur over the nature of the peace treaty with Japan, a major stumbling block that would only be resolved when an Australian and New Zealand proposal for a three-way security treaty was accepted by the United States in 1951 and the ANZUS Treaty was born. Debate still rages as to whether the treaty was exhorted out of the United States in 1951 by Australia and New Zealand, which would not sign the peace treaty with Japan without a security guarantee, or if ANZUS was a mutually supportive agreement that the United States looked to sign as part of its global network of alliances designed to contain communism at the start of the Cold War.[8]

What the experience of the SWPA provided was a firm basis of military-to-military cooperation and many lessons at the strategic, operational, and tactical levels of what worked and what did not. It affirmed the notion that one had to know when to be firm with one's allies and when to compromise to get the best possible outcome on operations in the face of a determined and resourceful enemy. It also reinforced the importance of basing a true "alliance" relationship on more than transactional needs during wartime and that such relationships cannot be based on specific personalities. Rather, a broad alignment of strategic interests and objectives are critical, and these should form the basis of deep engagement at the strategic, operational, and tactical levels. However, despite all of the problems, it should not be overlooked that while often dysfunctional, MacArthur's coalition was ultimately successful in providing for the security of Australia, its development as major Allied base for operations, and the total defeat of the Japanese in the theater of operations.

NOTES

INTRODUCTION

1. John Curtin, "The Task Ahead," first published in the *Herald* (Melbourne), 27 December 1941, http://john.curtin.edu.au/pmportal/text/00468.html.

2. See, for example, William Jefferson Clinton, "Address by the President of the United States of America, House of Representatives," Official Hansard, 20 November 1996, http://www.aph.gov.au/binaries/hansard/reps/dailys/dr201196.pdf; George W. Bush, "Address by the President of the United States of America, House of Representatives," Official Hansard, 23 October 2003, http://parlinfo.aph.gov.au/parlInfo/download/chamber/hansards/2003–10–23/toc_pdf/2965–7.pdf;fileType=application%2Fpdf#search=%22chamber/hansards/2003–10–23/0003%22; Barack Obama, "Address by the President of the United States of America, House of Representatives," White House, November 17, 2011, https://obamawhitehouse.archives.gov/blog/2011/11/17/president-obama-addresses-australian-parliament; John Howard, "Address to the Joint Meeting of the United States Congress," Washington, DC, 12 June 2002, http://australianpolitics.com/2002/06/12/howard-addresses-us-congress.html; and transcript of Julia Gillard's speech to Congress, SBS, http://www.sbs.com.au/news/article/2011/03/10/transcript-julia-gillards-speech-congress. At the time of his address, Australian prime minister Howard was in the United States due to the events of 11 September 2001, and he invoked the ANZUS Treaty condition for the first time.

3. Roger Bell, *Unequal Allies: Australian-American Relations and the Pacific War* (Clayton: Melbourne University Press, 1977); A. J. Barker and L. Jackson, *Fleeting Attraction: A Social History of American Servicemen in Western Australia during the Second World War* (Nedlands: University of Western Australia Press, 1996); Joy Damousi and Marilyn Lake, eds., *Gender and War: Australians at War in the Twentieth Century* (Melbourne: Cambridge University Press, 1995); Kate Darian-Smith, *On the Home Front: Melbourne in Wartime 1939–45* (Melbourne: Melbourne University Press, 2009).

4. To name but a few: D. Clayton James, *The Years of MacArthur* (Boston: Houghton Mifflin, 1970); Geoffrey Perret, *Old Soldiers Never Die: The Life of Douglas MacArthur*, 1st ed. (New York: Random House, 1996); William Manchester, *American Caesar: Douglas MacArthur, 1880–1964* (New York: Dell, 1978); David Day, *John Curtin: A Life* (Sydney: HarperCollins, 2015); and Lloyd Ross, *John Curtin: A Biography* (South Melbourne: Macmillan, 1977).

5. David Horner, *High Command: Australia's Struggle for an Independent War Strategy 1939–1945* (St. Leonards: Allen & Unwin, 1992); David Horner, *Blamey: The Commander-in-Chief* (St. Leonards: Allen & Unwin, 1998); David Horner, *Inside the War Cabinet: Directing Australia's War Effort, 1939–1945* (St. Leonards: Allen & Unwin, 1996); David Horner, *Defence Supremo: Sir Frederick Shedden and the Making of Australian Defence Policy* (St. Leonards: Allen & Unwin, 2000).

6. To name but a few: Peter Williams, *The Kokoda Campaign 1942: Myth And Reality* (Port Melbourne: Cambridge University Press, 2012); Stephen R. Taaffe, *MacArthur's Jungle War: The 1944 New Guinea Campaign* (Lawrence: University Press of Kansas, 1998); Harry A. Gailey, *MacArthur's Victory: The War in New Guinea, 1943–1944*, 1st ed. (New York: Presidio, 2004); and John Coates, *Bravery above Blunder: The 9th Australian Division at Finschhafen, Sattelberg, and Sio* (South Melbourne: Oxford University Press, 1999).

7. See Thomas Stow Wilkins, "Analyzing Coalition Warfare from an Intra-Alliance Politics Perspective: The Normandy Campaign 1944," *Journal of Strategic Studies* 29, no. 6 (2006): 1121–1124.

8. See Stephan Frühling, *A History of Australian Strategic Policy since 1945* (Canberra: Defence Publishing Service, 2009).

9. For a similar approach at the grand strategic level, see Michael J. Green, *By More than Providence: Grand Strategy and American Power in the Asia Pacific Since 1783* (New York: Columbia University Press, 2017).

10. For instance, see Edward J. Drea, *MacArthur's ULTRA: Codebreaking and the War Against Japan, 1942–1945* (Lawrence: University Press of Kansas, 1992); Des Ball and David Horner, *Breaking the Codes: Australia's KGB Network, 1944–1950* (St. Leonards: Allen & Unwin, NSW, 1998); Horner, *High Command*; Jean Bou, *MacArthur's Secret Bureau: The Story of the Central Bureau, General MacArthur's Signals Intelligence Organisation* (Loftus, NSW: Australian Military History Publications, 2015); and Alan Powell, *War by Stealth: Australians and the Allied Intelligence Bureau, 1942–1945* (Carlton: Melbourne University Press, 1996).

11. The author currently has a PhD student working on this topic.

12. See Peter Edwards, *Permanent Friends? Historical Reflections on the Australian-American Alliance*, Lowy Institute Paper 08 (Sydney: Lowy Institute), 11–12.

13. Coral Bell, *Dependent Ally: A Study in Australian Foreign Policy* (Canberra: Allen & Unwin, 1988), 1.

CHAPTER 1. WAR PLANS AND PREPARATIONS: US-AUSTRALIAN RELATIONS IN THE INTERWAR PERIOD

1. The 1st through 5th Infantry Divisions and five brigades of Light Horse. A sixth infantry division was raised and then disbanded without seeing combat, while five brigades of Light Horse were raised and served in the

Australia and New Zealand Mounted Division, the Imperial Mounted Division, and the Australian Mounted Division. See Jean Bou, *Light Horse: A History of Australia's Mounted Arm* (Melbourne: Cambridge University Press, 2010).

2. David Day, *The Politics of War* (Sydney: HarperCollins, 2003), 1.

3. John McCarthy, *Australia and Imperial Defence 1918–39: A Study in Air and Sea Power* (St. Lucia: University of Queensland Press, 1976), 7.

4. Craig Wilcox, *For Hearths and Homes: Citizen Soldiering in Australia* (St. Leonards, NSW: Allen & Unwin, 1998), 83.

5. Ibid., 7–8. For details on Australia's foreign and defense policy during this period, see Neville Meaney, *The Search for Security in the Pacific 1901–1914: A History of Australian Defence and Foreign Policy 1901–1923*, vol. 1 (Sydney: Sydney University Press, 2009), and Neville Meaney, *The Search for Security in the Pacific 1914–1923: A History of Australian Defence and Foreign Policy 1901–1923*, vol. 2 (Sydney: Sydney University Press, 2009).

6. Timothy D. Saxon, "Anglo-Japanese Naval Cooperation, 1914–1918," *Naval War College Review* 53, no. 1 (2000): 88–92. Saxon notes that neither side, the British nor the US, was willing to continue close cooperation with the Japanese after World War I. For a discussion of the Anglo-Japanese Naval Agreement, the British government's changing policy toward Japan, and its misinformation to the Australian government during this time, see D. K. Dignan, "Australia and British Relations with Japan, 1914–1921," *Australian Outlook* 21, no. 2 (August 1967): 135–149.

7. Jeffrey Grey, *Australian Brass: The Career of Lieutenant General Sir Horace Robertson* (Cambridge: Cambridge University Press, 1992), 119.

8. Horner, *High Command*, 2.

9. Jeffrey Grey, *A Military History of Australia* (Melbourne: Cambridge University Press, 2008), 122.

10. Paul Hasluck, *The Government and the People, 1939–1941*, series 4, vol. 1, *Australia in the War of 1939–1945* (Canberra: Australian War Memorial [hereafter AWM], 1952), 16.

11. Horner, *High Command*, 2. Australian defense policy had actually been based around Singapore since 1921. The 1923 Imperial Conference merely formalized these previous arrangements. See David Day, "A Great and Impotent Friend: The Singapore Strategy," in *The Great Mistakes of Australian History*, ed. Martin Crotty and David Roberts (Sydney: UNSW Press, 2006), 125–126, and Ian Hamill, *The Strategic Illusion: The Singapore Strategy and the Defence of Australia and New Zealand, 1919–1942* (Singapore: NUS Press, 1981), 3.

12. McCarthy, *Australia and Imperial Defence*, 1–2.

13. Peter Dennis, "Australia and the Singapore Strategy," in *A Great Betrayal: The Fall of Singapore Revisited*, ed. Brian Farrell and Sandy Hunter (Singapore: Marshall Cavendish Editions, 2010), 20.

14. Malcolm Murfett, "The Singapore Strategy," in *Between Empire and Nation: Australia's External Relations from Federation to the Second World*

War, ed. Carl Bridge and Bernard Attard (Victoria: Australian Scholarly Publishing, 2000), 188–204. See also John J. Dedman, "Defence Policy Decisions before Pearl Harbour," *Australian Journal of Politics and History* 13, no. 3 (December 1967): 331.

15. "Review of Imperial Defence by the Chiefs of Staff Sub-Committee of the Committee of Imperial Defence, 22 February 1937," as quoted in John McCarthy, "Singapore and Australian Defence 1921–1942," *Australian Outlook* 25, no. 2 (1971): 165.

16. Horner, *High Command*, 2. See also John Gooch, "The Politics of Strategy: Great Britain, Australia and the War against Japan 1939–1945," *War in History* 10, no. 4 (October 2003): 425–426.

17. For the most recent discussion of the Singapore Strategy and Australian Defence Policy, see Augustine Meaher IV, *The Road to Singapore: The Myth of British Betrayal* (Victoria: Australian Scholarly Publishing, 2010). See also David Stevens, ed., *In Search of a Maritime Strategy: The Maritime Element in Australian Defence Planning since 1901* (Canberra: Strategic and Defence Studies Centre, 1997), especially the chapter by David Horner on the Australian Army as part of a maritime force.

18. Jeffrey Grey, *The Australian Army: A History* (Melbourne: Oxford University Press, 2006), 82.

19. Stanley Bruce as quoted in *Sixty Years On: The Fall of Singapore Revisited*, ed. Brian Farrell and Sandy Hunter (Singapore: Eastern Universities Press, 2002), 21.

20. Horner, *Defence Supremo*, 46. See also Murfett, "Singapore Strategy": "Most of the advice tendered to the Australian governments in the interwar period was wholly supportive of the Singapore strategy," 18.

21. Eric Andrews, *The Department of Defence* (Melbourne: Oxford University Press, 2001), 81.

22. Brett Lodge, *Lavarack: Rival General* (St. Leonards, NSW: Allen & Unwin, 1998), 51–55.

23. "Lavarack, Lieutenant-General John Dudley," in *The Oxford Companion to Australian Military History*, 2nd ed., ed. Peter Dennis et al. (Melbourne: Oxford University Press, 2008), 339–340. See also Lodge, *Lavarack*.

24. Andrews, *Department of Defence*, 84. According to Gavin Long, Wynter, who had devoted himself to "examining and re-examining" the "fallacy" of the Singapore Strategy, was "perhaps the clearest and most profound thinker the Australian Army of his generation had produced." See Gavin Long, *To Benghazi*, series 1, vol. 1, *Australia in the War of 1939–1945* (Canberra: AWM, 1952), 8.

25. Horner, *Defence Supremo*, 48. Wynter had used the same terms in his lecture on defense policy to the Royal United Services Institute in August 1935. The final straw for Parkhill, however, was the revelation that Wynter's son, a journalist, had published an article on defense policy in Sydney's *Daily Telegraph* on 3 April 1936 that again used material similar to Wynter's lecture.

26. Ibid.

27. "Parkhill, (Robert) Archdale," in Dennis et al., *Oxford Companion to Australian Military History*, 456.

28. Andrews, *Department of Defence*, 84; Horner, *Defence Supremo*, 49.

29. Andrews, *Department of Defence*, 84.

30. See Meaher, *Road to Singapore*.

31. Albert Palazzo, "The Overlooked Mission: Australia and Home Defence," in *Australia 1942: In the Shadow of War*, ed. Peter J. Dean (Melbourne: Cambridge University Press, 2013), 57.

32. See Hasluck, *Government and the People*, chap. 2, "Between the Two Wars, 1918–38."

33. For details of Australia's history and relationship with Britain after the World War I, see Gavin Souter, *Lion and Kangaroo: The Initiation of Australia* (Melbourne: Text Publishing, 2001).

34. The White Australia Policy "is the unofficial term that has gained wide currency to portray public attitudes to, and government policies for, Australia's past policies of racially restrictive immigration." This was personified by the Immigration Restriction Act 1901—the first act of the new Commonwealth Parliament. The basic premises of the policy were built on racial discrimination and the belief in the superiority of a white settler society and dates back to the early nineteenth century. See "White Australia Policy," Brian Galligan and Winsome Roberts, *The Oxford Companion to Australian Politics* (Melbourne: Oxford University Press, 2007).

35. Palazzo, "Overlooked Mission," 56.

36. Edward S. Miller, *War Plan Orange* (Annapolis: Naval Institute Press, 1991), xix.

37. "Annexation of Hawaii, 1898," US Department of State Archive, https://2001–2009.state.gov/r/pa/ho/time/gp/17661.htm.

38. From 1910 to 1922, Guam had dominated US strategic thought. See Miller, *War Plan Orange*, 250.

39. Russell Parkin and David Lee, *The Great White Fleet to Coral Sea* (Canberra: DFAT, 2008), 82.

40. Ibid.

41. Stephan Frühling, "Managing Strategic Risk: Four Ideal Defence Planning Concepts in Theory and Practice" (PhD diss., Australian National University, 2007), 149.

42. Henry G. Cole, *The Road to Rainbow: Army Planning for Global War, 1934–1940* (Annapolis, MD: Naval Institute Press), xviii. For War Plan Orange's place in the Naval War College curriculum, see Michael Vlahos, *The Blue Sword: The Naval War College and the American Mission, 1919–1941* (Newport, RI: Naval War College Press, 1980).

43. Parkin and Lee, *Great White Fleet to Coral Sea*, 82.

44. David F. Winkler, "Thrusters, Cautionaries, and War Games," *Seapower* 45, no. 10 (October 2002): 31.

45. Ibid.

46. Frühling, "Managing Strategic Risk," 150.

47. Kenneth J. Clifford, *Amphibious Warfare Development in Britain and America from 1920–1940* (New York: Edgewood, 1983), 85–125.

48. Earl H. Ellis, *Advanced Base Operations in Micronesia, Fleet Marine Force Reference Publication* (FMFRP) *12–46* (Washington, DC: Headquarters United States Marine Corps, 1992), http://www.ibiblio.org/hyperwar/USMC/ref/AdvBaseOps/index.html.

49. Merrill L. Bartlett, "Ben Hebard Fuller and the Genesis of the Modern United States Marine Corps, 1891–1934," *Journal of Military History* 69, no. 1 (January 2005): 82.

50. Frank O. Hough, Verle E. Ludwig, and Henry I. Shaw, *Pearl Harbor to Guadalcanal: History of U.S. Marine Corps Operations in World War II*, vol. 1 (Washington, DC: Government Printing Office, 1989), 14.

51. See Brian M. Linn, *The Echo of Battle: The Army's Way of War* (Cambridge, MA: Harvard University Press, 2009), 116–151; Terry C. Pierce, *Warfighting and Disruptive Technologies: Disguising Innovation* (London: Frank Cass, 2004), 51–69.

52. Praise and acceptance of War Plan Orange is far from universal. The most strident opponent of Miller's interpretation is Louis Morton, who argued that the planners failed to choose between their desires and the strategic reality. It was, rather, a compromise between an offensive and a defensive strategy that failed to deter Japan and exposed the Philippines to the Japanese in 1941 and 1942. See Louis Morton, "War Plan Orange: Evolution of a Strategy," *World Politics* 11, no. 2 (January 1959): 221–250.

53. Miller, *War Plan Orange*, 256–261.

54. Ibid., 250.

55. Ibid., 247–248.

56. Lloyd G. Churchward, *Australia and America, 1788–1972: An Alternative History* (Sydney: Alternative Publishing Cooperative, 1979), 125.

57. Parkin and Lee, *Great White Fleet to Coral Sea*, 7.

58. Root, as quoted ibid., 9.

59. Edwards, *Permanent Friends?*, 6.

60. More USN ships did visit Australia during the 1930s but nothing on the scale of these two visits. A cruiser visited in 1934. In 1938, four cruisers visited to help commemorate 150 years of European settlement in Australia, and two cruisers and five destroyers visited Sydney and Brisbane in March 1942.

61. Tom Frame, *Pacific Partners: A History of Australian-American Naval Relations* (Sydney: Hodder & Stoughton, 1992), 18.

62. Parkin and Lee, *Great White Fleet to Coral Sea*, 27–28.

63. Philip Bell and Roger Bell, *Implicated: The United States in Australia* (Melbourne: Oxford University Press, 1993), 59.

64. See C. E. W. Bean, *The A.I.F. in France 1918, Official History of Australia in the War of 1914–1918*, vol. 6 (Sydney: Angus & Robertson, 1942).

65. Parkin and Lee, *Great White Fleet to Coral Sea*, 50.

66. Edwards, *Permanent Friends?*, 8.

67. Churchward, *Australia and America*, 134. These measures were ended in 1938.

68. Edwards, *Permanent Friends?*, 8.

69. David Goldsworthy, ed., *Facing North: A Century of Australian Engagement with Asia* (Carlton: Melbourne University Press, 2003), 92–93.

70. Day, *Politics of War*, 93. Casey was particularly pro-British, and it was believed that he would be representing both Australian and British interests. See Carl Bridge, "Casey and the Americans: Australian War Propaganda in the United States, 1940–42" (working paper no. 30 Australian Studies Centre, University of London, 1988).

71. Norman Harper, *A Great and Powerful Friend: A Study of Australian Americans Relations between 1900 and 1975* (St. Lucia: University of Queensland Press, 1987), 86–87.

72. Bell, *Unequal Allies*, 11.

73. Horner, *High Command*, 51–53.

74. Ibid.

75. Ibid., 56, 63–64.

76. Ibid., 133–134.

77. Cablegram, "Australian Minister in Washington to Department of External Affairs, 20 August 1941, United States and British Empire Landing Grounds in the Pacific, Air Defence in the Far East—United States Proposals," War Cabinet Agendum No. 334/1941, National Archive of Australia, Canberra (hereafter NAA), A5954 555/7.

78. "Notes on Conferences at Victoria Barracks, Melbourne 21–23 November 1941, to discuss US projects, 'United States and British Empire Landing Grounds in the Pacific,'" A9695, 1123, NAA.

79. Harper, *Great and Powerful Friend*, 98.

80. David Stevens, "The Royal Australian Navy and the Strategy for Australia's Defence, 1921–42," in Stevens, *In Search of a Maritime Strategy*, 81.

81. Bell, *Unequal Allies*, 10. Roosevelt did give assurances to Churchill about US support in the Pacific against Japan six days before the bombing of Pearl Harbor.

82. Frame, *Pacific Partners*, 34.

CHAPTER 2. MACARTHUR'S RETREAT AND RESURRECTION:
THE ESTABLISHMENT AND HIGH COMMAND OF THE
SOUTHWEST PACIFIC AREA

1. Douglas MacArthur, *Reminiscences* (Annapolis, MD: Naval Institute Press, 1964), 158.

2. D. Clayton James, *The Years of MacArthur*, vol. 2, *Triumph and Disaster 1945–1964* (Boston: Houghton Mifflin, 1985), 109.

3. Perret, *Old Soldiers Never Die*, 283.

4. D. Clayton James, "American and Japanese Strategies in the Pacific War," in *Makers of Modern Strategy: From Machiavelli to the Nuclear Age*, ed. Peter Paret (Princeton, NJ: Princeton University Press, 1986), 707.

5. Louis Morton, *Strategy and Command: The First Two Years, United States Army in World War II* (Washington, DC: Office of the Chief of Military History, US Army, 1962), 156–157.

6. "Constitution of the ABDA Command, 2 January 1942," in SWPA and ABDA Organisation, B6121, 3, NAA (emphasis added).

7. Ibid., 2. For full details, see SWPA and ABDA Organisation, B6121, annex 1, "Boundaries of the ABDA Area," NAA.

8. Steven B. Shepard, "American, British, Dutch and Australian Coalition: Unsuccessful Band of Brothers" (master's thesis, US Army Command and General Staff College, Fort Leavenworth, KS, 2003), 1.

9. "Wavell's Fighting Family," *News* (Adelaide), 5 January 1942.

10. "Despatch by the Supreme Commander of the ABDA Area to the Combined Chiefs of Staff on the Operations in the South-West Pacific, 15 January to 25 February 1942," AWM67 6/52, AWM.

11. "Commander V. E. Kennedy to Director of Naval Intelligence, Melbourne, Australia, 26 January 1942," in SWPA—ABDA organization, MP1049/5, NAA.

12. "Wavell's Fighting Family."

13. Lionel Wigmore, *The Japanese Thrust*, series 1, vol. 4, *Australia in the War of 1939–1945* (Canberra: AWM, 1952), 205–206.

14. "Despatch by Supreme Commander of ABDA Area."

15. A British BGS was roughly equivalent to the chief of a US general's command staff.

16. Lodge, *Lavarack*, 200–202.

17. Lavarack Diary (in author's possession); Berryman Diary, 27 January 1942, PR84/370, Papers of Lt. Gen. Sir Frank Horton Berryman (hereafter Berryman Papers), series 1, AWM.

18. Horner, *High Command*, 155.

19. "Notes on Situation in South West Pacific–2 Feb 1942," AWM52, item 1/4/4, I Australian Corps Air Party Java, appendix C, AWM (emphasis in original).

20. John Coates, *An Atlas of Australia's Wars* (Oxford: Oxford University Press, 2001), 223–224.

21. "Berryman to Lieutenant-General Sir Thomas Daly, CGS, 29 April 1971," Berryman Papers, item 16, AWM.

22. Wigmore, *Japanese Thrust*, 446.

23. Berryman Diary, 17 February 1942 (emphasis in original).

24. Lavarack to Long, 7 October 1953, AWM67, 3/209, part 1, AWM.

25. Lloyd as quoted in Horner, *High Command*, 166.

26. "Wavell to British Joint Staff Mission, Washington, 25 February 1942," in "ABDA Strategic Area-Directive issued to General Wavell Australian representations Anzac Naval Area; Proposed Far Eastern Council Australian Representation in Allied War Organisation," 2937, 1, NAA.

27. Samuel E. Morison, *The Rising Sun in the Pacific, 1931–April 1942*, vol. 3, *History of United States Naval Operations in World War II* (Annapolis, MD: Naval Institute Press, 2010), 380.

28. Chris Coulthard-Clarke, *The Encyclopaedia of Australia's Battles* (St. Leonards, NSW: Allen & Unwin, 2001), 201–202, 207–208.

29. John Coates, "Timor," in Dennis et al., *Oxford Companion to Australian Military History*, 529–530.

30. See "Cablegrams from Australian Minister, Washington (Casey) to the War Cabinet, 24 September 1940, 6 February 1941," in PAC 3 War Records—Pacific Australia—United States Joint Defence Board, A981, NAA.

31. Mark Johnston, *Whispering Death: Australian Airmen in the Pacific War* (St. Leonards, NSW: Allen & Unwin, 2011), 105.

32. Wigmore, *Japanese Thrust*, 403–410. See appendix 4, 653–674, for details of the fate of the POWs captured on New Britain and the evacuation of the four hundred survivors.

33. Morton, *Strategy and Command*, 201.

34. Chief of the Imperial General Staff Gen. Sir Alan Brooke noted in his diary on 12 January that "the area allotted to Wavell's Supreme command (i.e. ABDA area . . .) is continually giving trouble owing to the original mistake of including Burma and not including Australia and NZ." Alex Danchev and Daniel Todman, eds., *War Diaries 1939–1945: Field Marshall Lord Alanbrooke* (Berkeley: University of California Press, 2001), 219.

35. Morton, *Strategy and Command*, 201.

36. This area encompassing the oceans around eastern Australia and New Zealand was named after the Australian and New Zealand Army Corps (ANZAC) of World War I fame. The term "ANZAC" had become synonymous with the two nations' combined military efforts, and thus the use of this title in this instance linked both geography and military history. In modern parlance, "ANZAC" refers to the military formation and "Anzac" to Australian soldiers, a place (Gallipoli Peninsula in Turkey), a national day, and the myth and legend about the prowess of Australia's military forces, as well as their attitudes and belief and their role in Australian national memory.

37. G. Hermon Gill, *Royal Australian Navy, 1939–1942*, series 2, vol. 1, *Australia in the War of 1939–1945* (Canberra: AWM, 1952), 519–520. Crace was an Australian serving with the RN.

38. Ibid., 521. Leary, however, was not to command the carrier task force directly. Control over aircraft carrier forces remained with Admirals King and Nimitz.

39. "Mr. R. G. Casey, Minister to the United States, to Department of External Affairs, Cablegram 404 WASHINGTON, 6 March 1942, 12.41 A.M., September 11, 2013," http://dfat.gov.au/about-us/publications/historical-doc uments/Pages/volume-05/392-mr-r-g-casey-minister-to-the-united-states-to -department-of-external-affairs.aspx.

40. "Mr. R. G. Casey, Minister to the United States, to Department of External

Affairs, Cablegram 1162, Washington, 17 December 1941, 7.12pm, September 11, 2013," http://dfat.gov.au/about-us/publications/historical-doc
uments/Pages/volume-05/203-mr-r-g-casey-minister-to-the-united-states
-to-department-of-external-affairs.aspx.

41. Ian W. Toll, *Pacific Crucible: War at Sea in the Pacific, 1941–1942* (New
York: W. W. Norton, 2011), 185.

42. Maurice Matloff and Edwin Snell, *Strategic Planning for Coalition Warfare
1941–1942* (Washington, DC: Office of the Chief of Military History, US
Army, 1959), 88.

43. "Mr John Curtin, Prime Minister, to Mr R. G. Casey, Minister to the United
States, Cablegram 1103 CANBERRA, 23 December 1941," http://dfat.gov.au
/about-us/publications/historical-documents/Pages/volume-05/214-mr-john
-curtin-prime-minister-to-mr-r-g-casey-minister-to-the-united-states.aspx.

44. Morton, *Strategy and Command*, 149–150.

45. "Operations in ABDA Area: Review by Lt. Gen. Sir John Lavarack and
Statement by General G. H. Brett," A2684, 799, NAA.

46. Dudley McCarthy, *South-West Pacific Area—First Year: Kokoda to Wau*,
series 1, vol. 5, *Australia in the War of 1939–1945* (Canberra: AWM,
1959), 16.

47. "War Cabinet minutes, Sydney 18 February 1942, Appreciations on the
Defence of Australia and the ANZAC Area," A2684, 905, 68, NAA.

48. Horner, *High Command*, 180.

49. "Telegram—Australia to Dominion Office, Draft of the Proposed Directive
to the Supreme Commander, 7 March 1942," Defence of Australia and
ANZAC Area, Jan.–April 1942, A5954, 563/1, NAA.

50. Morton, *Strategy and Command*, 208–213.

51. Matloff and Snell, *Strategic Planning for Coalition Warfare*, 114–115.

52. For a detailed discussion on the fate of I Australian Corps, see Horner, *High
Command*, 155–162.

53. For details on the bombing of Darwin and its impact on Australia, see Alan
Powell, "The Air Raids on Darwin, 19 February: Image and reality," in
Australia 1942: In the Shadow of War, ed. Peter J. Dean (Melbourne: Cambridge University Press, 2013), 140–156. For further details on the debate
over the destination of I Australian Corps, see Horner, *Inside the War Cabinet*, 103–104.

54. Stephen R. Taaffe, *Marshall and His Generals: U.S. Army Commanders in
World War II* (Lawrence: University Press of Kansas, 2011), 15.

55. Morton, *Strategy and Command*, 244.

56. On arrival in Australia on 17 March 1942, MacArthur became commander
of the US Army forces in the country. On the very same day, the previous
commander, General Brett, wrote to the Australian prime minister on advice
from the US government that "should it be in accord with your wishes and
those of the Australian people, the President suggests that it would be highly
acceptable to him and pleasing to the American people for the Australian
Government to nominate General MacArthur as the Supreme Commander

of all Allied Forces the South-West Pacific." See "Brett to Curtin, 17 March 1942," RG 3, *Official Correspondence 1942–1944*, DMMA.

57. See Peter J. Dean, "MacArthur's War: Strategy, Command and Plans for the 1943 Offensives," in *Australia 1943: The Liberation of New Guinea* (Port Melbourne: Cambridge University Press, 2014), 45–50, for more details.

58. Taaffe, *Marshall and His Generals*, 17.

59. Jason B. Barlow, "Interservice Rivalry in the Pacific," *Joint Forces Quarterly* (Spring 1994): 79.

60. Williamson Murray, *Military Adaption in War: With Fear of Change* (New York: Cambridge University Press, 2011), 7.

61. Ronald Spector, *Eagle against the Rising Sun* (New York: Vintage, 2004), 145.

62. "Mr John Curtin, Prime Minister, to Mr R. G. Casey, Minister to the United States, Cablegram SW16 CANBERRA, 17 March 1942, 7.25pm," http://dfat .gov.au/about-us/publications/historical-documents/Pages/volume-05/416 -mr-john-curtin-prime-minister-to-mr-r-g-casey-minister-to-the-united-states .aspx.

63. Perret, *Old Soldiers Never Die*, 84.

64. "'Napoleon of Luzon': Man Who Stopped the Japanese," *Mercury* (Hobart), 5 March 1942.

65. "General MacArthur's Arrival in Australia," *Herald* (Cootamundra), 18 March 1942.

66. "MacArthur Favors Offensives," *News* (Adelaide), 18 March 1942.

67. "General MacArthur's Arrival."

68. "Appointment Creates Enthusiasm," *Argues* (Melbourne), 19 March 1942.

69. "U.S. Reaction to MacArthur News," *Sun* (Sydney), 19 March 1942.

70. "Dickover to Johnson, 27 April 1942," RG 3, Records of Headquarters, SWPA, 1942–1945, DMMA.

71. MacArthur, *Reminiscences*, 161–163.

72. Wilkinson as quoted in Michael Schaller, *Douglas MacArthur: The Far Eastern General* (New York: Oxford University Press, 1989), 74.

73. George H. Brett, "The MacArthur I Knew," *True*, October 1947.

74. The original Purple Heart Medal had been created by George Washington but had fallen into disuse. MacArthur's iteration saw it awarded under two criteria: meritorious service (as under pervious use) and physical wounds in battle. During World War II, the medal was extended to the USN and USMC, and the meritorious service criterion was removed when other awards were created for this area of service.

75. David Horner, "MacArthur, Douglas (1880–1964)," in *Australian Dictionary of Biography*, vol. 15 (Carlton: Melbourne University Press, 2000).

76. Matthew R. Pettinger, "Held to a Higher Standard: The Downfall of Admiral Kimmel" (master's thesis, US Army Command and General Staff College, Fort Leavenworth, KS, 2003), 57.

77. Paul P. Rogers, *The Good Years: MacArthur and Sutherland* (New York: Praeger, 1990), 165.

78. James, *Years of MacArthur*, vol. 2, 129.

79. Ibid., 131–133.

80. Ibid. The best biography of Curtin remains David Day's *John Curtin*. This work is particularly strong on the Labor narrative of Curtin as one of Australia's greatest leaders ever.

81. Clem Lloyd and Richard Hall, *Backroom Briefings: John Curtin's War* (Canberra: National Library of Australia, 1997), 14–15.

82. For detailed accounts of the Curtin-MacArthur relationship, see Horner, *High Command*; Paul Hasluck, *The Government and the People, 1942–1945*, series 4, vol. 2, *Australia in the War of 1939–1945* (Canberra: AWM, 1970); Gavin Long, *The Six Years War: A Concise History of Australia in the 1939–45 War* (Canberra: AWM, 1973); and Bell, *Unequal Allies*.

83. Peter Edwards, "Curtin, MacArthur and the 'Surrender of Sovereignty,'" *Australian Journal of International Affairs* 55, no. 2 (July 2001): 175–185.

84. David Horner, *The Evolution of Australian Higher Command Arrangements, Command Paper no. 2* (Canberra: Australian Defence College, 2002), 13.

85. Horner, *High Command*, 191.

86. "MacArthur, Douglas (1880–1964)," 150–152.

87. Geoffrey Serle, "Curtin, John (1885–1945)," in *Australian Dictionary of Biography*, vol. 13 (Carlton: Melbourne University Press, 1993), 550–558.

88. See Edwards, "Curtin, MacArthur," 175–186.

89. See "War Cabinet Minute No 1734—Machinery for higher direction—Pacific Council 1942," A2676 1734, NAA.

90. Churchill's position was also supported by the chief of the Imperial General Staff, Field Marshal Alan Brooke. The British could not fathom that Australia would want to be independently represented rather than as one element of the empire. He wrote in his diary on 22 January 1942, "COS this morning at which we examined most recent development of the situation caused by Australia insisting on being represented on a Defence council in Washington instead of London!" Danchev and Todman, *War Diaries 1939–1945*, 223.

91. "Advisory War Council Minutes Volume 5, 1 Apr 1942," A5954 814/1, 513, NAA.

92. Horner, *Defence Supremo*, 144–145.

93. Christopher Thorne, *Allies of a Kind: The United States, Britain, and the War against Japan, 1941–1945* (Oxford: Oxford University Press, 1978), 265.

94. Horner, *Defence Supremo*, 143, 145.

95. MacArthur, *Reminiscences*, 158.

96. "Prime Minister's War Conference, 8 April 1942," A5954 1/1, NAA.

97. Williamson Murray and Allan Millett, *A War to Be Won: Fighting the Second World War, 1937–1945* (Cambridge, MA: Harvard University Press, 2000), 199.

98. Ibid.

99. "Prime Minister's War Conference."

100. Horner, *Defence Supremo*, 145.

101. "Shedden to MacArthur, 23 August 1963, Personal Correspondence with General MacArthur," A5954 75/6, NAA.

102. Arthur Calwell, *Be Just and Fear Not* (Victoria: Lloyd O'Neill in association with Rigby, 1972), 106. I wish to thank Kim Beazley for drawing this quote to my attention.

103. James Curran, *Curtin's Empire: Australian Encounters* (Melbourne: Cambridge University Press, 2011), 1–25.

104. Lloyd and Hall, *Backroom Briefings*, 32.

105. Curran, *Curtin's Empire*, 12.

106. "Minutes of the Prime Minister's War Conference," 1 June 1942, A5954 1/1, NAA.

CHAPTER 3. COMMAND AND ORGANIZATION IN THE
SOUTHWEST PACIFIC AREA, 1942

1. "General Order, no. 1, GHQ SWPA, 18 April 1942," RG 407, 98-GHQ1-3.2, G-3 Journals and Files, box 566, April–May 1942, National Archives and Records Administration (US) (hereafter NARA).

2. Morton, Strategy and Command, appendix C, 614–616.

3. Ibid.

4. "American Secret: U.S. Men Have Settled Down Under in Australia," *News* (Adelaide), 18 March 1942.

5. Samuel Milner, *Victory in Papua* (Washington, DC: Office of the Chief of Military History, US Army, 1957), 22.

6. James, *Years of MacArthur*, vol. 2, 122.

7. Morton, *Strategy and Command*, 615 (emphasis added).

8. Morton, *Strategy and Command*, 253; Milner, *Victory in Papua*, 22.

9. Horner, *Evolution of Australian Higher Command*, 13.

10. Alastair Cooper, "The Effect of World War II on RAN-RN Relations," in *The Royal Australian Navy in World War II*, ed. David Stevens (St. Leonards, NSW: Allen & Unwin, 1996), 50–51.

11. David Stevens, "South-West Sea Frontiers: Seapower in the Australian Context," in Stevens, *Royal Australian Navy*, 89–90.

12. Ian Pfennigwerth, "A Novel Experience: The RAN in 1942, Defending Australian Waters," in *Australia 1942: In the Shadow of War*, ed. Peter J. Dean (Melbourne: Cambridge University Press, 2013), 179.

13. Gill, *Royal Australian Navy*, 1939–1942, 34.

14. Ian Pfennigwerth, *The Royal Australian Navy and MacArthur* (Dural, NSW: Rosenberg Publishing, 2009), 18.

15. Pfennigwerth, "Novel Experience," 182–184. For more detail on the intelligence services in the SWPA, see Ian Pfennigwerth, *A Man of Intelligence: The Life of Captain Eric Nave, Australian Codebreaker Extraordinary* (Dural, NSW: Rosenberg Publishing, 2006).

16. Pfennigwerth, "Novel Experience," 182.

17. Chris Coulthard-Clark, *Action Stations Coral Sea: The Australian Commander's Story* (St. Leonards, NSW: Allen & Unwin, 1991), 22.

18. Samuel E. Morison, *Coral Sea, Midway and Submarine Actions, May 1942–August 1942*, vol. 4, *History of United States Naval Operations in World War II* (Boston: Little, Brown, 1949), 39.

19. Stevens, "South-West Sea Frontiers," 98.

20. James Goldrick, "1941–1945: World War II; The War against Japan," in *The Royal Australian Navy*, ed. David Stevens (Melbourne: Oxford University Press, 2001), 134.

21. Horner, *High Command*, 363.

22. Manchester, *American Caesar*, 265.

23. James, *Years of MacArthur*, vol. 2, 171.

24. Ibid., 189.

25. Ibid., 226.

26. Pfennigwerth, *Royal Australian Navy and MacArthur*, 18.

27. James, *Years of MacArthur*, vol. 2, 359.

28. Pfennigwerth, "Novel Experience," 187–188. Fletcher has come in for significant criticism for his tactical handling of the operation. For a defense of Fletcher and an overview of his career, see John B. Lundstrom, *Black Shoe Carrier Admiral: Frank Jack Fletcher at Coral Sea, Midway and Guadalcanal* (Annapolis, MD: Naval Institute Press, 2006).

29. Goldrick, "1941–1945: World War II," 136.

30. Morison, *Coral Sea, Midway and Submarine Actions*, 39.

31. For details, see David Jenkins, *Battle Surface! Japan's Submarine War against Australia 1942–44* (Sydney: Random House, 1992), and David Stevens, *A Critical Vulnerability: The Impact of the Submarine Threat on Australia's Maritime Defence 1915–1954* (Canberra: Commonwealth of Australia, 2005), chaps. 7, 8, and 11.

32. Goldrick, "1941–1945: World War II," 136.

33. Pfennigwerth, "Novel Experience," 190–191.

34. Goldrick, "1941–1945: World War II," 130.

35. See "Reports from General Brett on Air Operations in Australia 1942," RG 18, box 897, NARA.

36. "RAAF Command Headquarters—Organisation—Allied Air Forces," A11093, 320/5C1, NAA.

37. Peter Helson, *The Private Air Marshal: A Biography of Air Marshal Sir George Jones, KBE, CB, DFC* (Canberra: Air Power Development Centre, 2010), 151.

38. "Air Force Organisation—Letters to General Brett," A816, 31/301/216, NAA.

39. Richard L. Watson, "The Defense of Australia," in *The Army Air Forces in World War II: Plans and Early Operations January 1939 to August 1942*, ed. Wesley Craven and James Cate (Chicago: University of Chicago Press, 1948), 420.

40. "Organization of the AAF HQ May 1942," *Allied Air Forces Historical Studies*, no. 9, The Allied Air Forces in Australia to the Summer of 1942, AWM54 85/3/51, part 1, AWM.

41. Douglas Gillison, *Royal Australian Air Force 1939–1942*, series 3, vol. 1, *Australia in the War of 1939–1945* (Canberra: AWM, 1962), 478.

42. "Organization of the AAF HQ May 1942," 73.

43. Gillison, *Royal Australian Air Force*, 478.

44. "Organization of the AAF HQ May 1942," 72.

45. Joe Hewitt, *Adversity in Success: Extracts from Air Vice-Marshal Hewitt's Diaries 1939–1948* (Melbourne: Langate Publishing, 1980), 30.

46. Anthony Cooper, *Kokoda Air Strikes: Allied Air Forces in New Guinea, 1942* (Sydney: NewSouth, 2014), 94, 190–193.

47. "Organization of the AAF HQ May 1942," 71–75.

48. "Richardson to MacArthur, 4 July 1942," Richard J. Marshall Papers, box 1, folder 1, US Army Heritage and Education Center (hereafter USAHEC).

49. Cooper, *Kokoda Air Strikes*, 206–207.

50. Jones as quoted in Helson, *Private Air Marshal*, 193.

51. Douglas A. Cox, *Airpower Leadership on the Frontline: Lt. Gen. Georgie H. Brett and Combat Command* (Maxwell Air Force Base, AL: Air University Press, 2006), 55–60.

52. Kenney Diaries, 12 July 1942, RG 54, DMMA.

53. Kenney Diaries, 28 July 1942, ibid.

54. Beryl Daley interview, 2 February 2004, Australians at War Film Archive, archive no. 1419.

55. Thomas E. Griffith Jr., *MacArthur's Airman: General George C. Kenney and the War in the Southwest Pacific* (Lawrence: University Press of Kansas, 1998), 66–70.

56. See "Oral Reminiscences of General George C. Kenney, 16 July 1971," D. Clayton James Collection, DMMA.

57. Ibid.

58. Jones as quoted in Helson, *Private Air Marshal*, 193.

59. George Kenney, *General Kenney Reports: A Personal History of the Pacific War* (New York: Duell, Sloan & Pearce, 1949), 39.

60. Ibid., 41.

61. Kenney Diaries, 29–30 July 1942, RG 54, DMMA.

62. Griffith, *MacArthur's Airman*, 60.

63. Hewitt, *Adversity in Success*, 30.

64. "MacArthur to Curtin, 4 September 1942, Organization of the RAAF—File No 1 to 30 September 1944," A816 31/301/196A, NAA.

65. Donald Goldstein, "Ennis C. Whitehead: Aerospace Commander and Pioneer" (PhD thesis, University of Denver 1971), 104.

66. Jones, *From Private to Air Marshal*, 89.

67. Hewitt, *Adversity in Success*, 30.

68. Griffith, *MacArthur's Airman*, 60–65.

69. Richard Williams, *These Are Facts: The Autobiography of Air Marshal Sir*

Richard Williams, KBE, CB, DSO (Canberra: AWM and Australian Government Publishing Service, 1977), 299.

70. Griffith, *MacArthur's Airman*, 62.

71. Gillison, *Royal Australian Air Force*, 475–478.

72. "Minutes of the Prime Minister's War Conference, 30 April 1942," A5954 1/1, NAA.

73. "Curtin to Brett, 30 April 1942, Air Force Organisation: Letters to General Brett etc.," A816 31/301/216, NAA.

74. Alan Stephens, *The Royal Australian Air Force, Australian Centenary History of Defence*, vol. 2 (Melbourne: Oxford University Press, 2001), 118.

75. George Jones, *From Private to Air Marshal: The Autobiography of Air Marshal Sir George Jones KBE, CB, DFC* (Victoria: Greenhouse Publications, 1988), 83.

76. Stephens, *Royal Australian Air Force*, 121.

77. Norman Ashworth, *How Not to Run an Air Force*, vol. 1 (Canberra: Air Power Development Centre, 1999); Norman Ashworth, *How Not to Run an Air Force*, vol. 2 (Canberra: Air Power Development Centre, 1999).

78. Stephens, *Royal Australian Air Force*, 110.

79. Mark Lax, "MacArthur and the Rise of Australian Air Power" (paper presented at the conference "General Douglas MacArthur: Agent of Change," Victoria Barracks, Brisbane, 21 July 2012).

80. Milner, *Victory in Papua*, 19.

81. Marshall to MacArthur, as quoted in Milner, *Victory in Papua*, 19.

82. David Horner, "Blamey, Sir Thomas Albert (1884–1951)," *Australian Dictionary of Biography*, vol. 13, 1993, http://adb.anu.edu.au/biography/blamey-sir-thomas-albert-9523. For the best biography of Blamey, see Horner, *Blamey*.

83. The 1st AIF had been raised for overseas service in 1914 and consisted of the 1st through 5th Australian Infantry Divisions and the 1st Light Horse Division. This was because under the Commonwealth Militia Law, CMF (Militia) units and formations could not serve outside of Australia. At the outbreak of World War II, the 2nd AIF was raised, and its major formations/units were the First Australian Army; the I, II, and III Australian Corps; the 6th, 7th, 8th, and 9th Australian Divisions; and the 1st and 2nd Armoured Divisions. Brigades were also raised to follow on from World War I, thus the first new brigade in the 6th Division was the 16th Brigade. Battalions and regiments were named after their World War I forbearers, with the prefix "2/" added to distinguish the new units. For example, the 16th Brigade, 6th Australian Division, in 1939 consisted of the 2/1st, 2/2nd, and 2/3rd Battalions. During the Pacific War, the CMF was able to operate in the Australian territories, including Papua and New Guinea.

84. Ibid.

85. See Kenney, General Kenney Reports, and "Oral Reminiscences of General George C. Kenney," D. Clayton James Collection, DMMA.

86. "Charles Willoughby Interview, 30 July 1971," D. Clayton James Oral History Collection, DMMA.

87. "Faubion Bowers Interview, 18 July 1971," ibid.

88. "Robert H. Van Volkenburgh Interview, 26 August 1971," ibid.

89. "Mr John Curtin, Prime Minister, to General Sir Thomas Blamey, Allied Deputy Commander-in-Chief in the Middle East, Cablegram 8 CANBERRA, 20 February 1942," DFAT Historical Documents, http://www.dfat.gov.au /publications/historical/volume-05/historical-document-05-349.html.

90. David Horner, *Crisis of Command: Australian Generalship and the Japanese Threat, 1941–43* (Canberra: ANU Press, 1978), 57–58.

91. Ibid., 184.

92. Lodge, *Lavarack*, 232.

93. Peter J. Dean, *The Architect of Victory: The Military Career of Lieutenant General Sir Frank Horton Berryman* (Victoria: Cambridge University Press, 2011), 165.

94. Horner, *Evolution of Australian Higher Command*, 14.

95. "John Curtin to General George Brett, 27 March 1942," AWM SP 1116, extracts from AG GHQ file no. 323-36, "Higher Direction of the War," AWM.

96. "Operations Report for the Australian Army, 19 July 1942," in Horner, *Crisis of Command*, appendix 10, 302–304.

97. Phillip Bradley, *Wau 1942–1943* (Canberra: Army History Unit [hereafter AHU], 2010), 5–32.

98. Horner, *Crisis of Command*, 96–97.

99. Ibid., 104–105.

CHAPTER 4. THE US–AUSTRALIAN MILITARY
RELATIONSHIP IN 1942

1. MacArthur, *Reminiscences*, 161–163. This claim is also made in Douglas MacArthur, *Reports of General MacArthur: The Campaigns of MacArthur in the Pacific*, vol. 1, *Center of Military History* reprint (Washington, DC: Government Printing Office, 1994), 34–35. (The reports were originally produced by MacArthur's Tokyo headquarters in 1950.)

2. Horner, *High Command*, 178–197.

3. "Probable immediate Japanese moves in the proposed new ANZAC area, War Cabinet Agendum—No 143/1942, 5 March 1942–11 March 1942," A2670 143/1942, NAA; "Mr John Curtin, Prime Minister, to Dr H. V. Evatt, Minister for External Affairs (in Washington), Cablegram PM50 CANBERRA, 20 April 1942," http://dfat.gov.au/about-us/publications/his torical-documents/Pages/volume-05/471-mr-john-curtin-prime-minister-to -dr-h-v-evatt-minister-for-external-affairs-in-washington.aspx.

4. "Mr John Curtin, Prime Minister, to Dr H. V. Evatt, Minister for External Affairs (in Washington), Cablegram SW34 CANBERRA, 28 April 1942," http://dfat.gov.au/about-us/publications/historical-documents/Pages/vol ume-05/475-mr-john-curtin-prime-minister-to-dr-h-v-evatt-minister-for -external-affairs-in-washington.aspx.

5. "Hugh Casey to Major General Eugene Reybold, Chief of Engineers US Army, 1 December 1942," Casey Papers, Office of US Army Corps of Engineers, folder 26.

6. Ibid.

7. As Harold R. Winton argues, the US Army approach to doctrine and officer development in the interwar period ascribes seven key attributes for what it defined as an "ideal commander": the assumption of all responsibilities in command, strength of will (moral courage), the mental abilities to size up problems quickly and accurately and act on them, the appreciation of differences in terrain, care for subordinates, rapidity of action, and the ability to suffer in the face of the stress of command. See Harold R. Winton, "Corps Commanders of the Bulge: Six American Generals and Victory in the Ardennes," presentation to the US Army War College, 17 March 2010, http://www.youtube.com/watch?v=zd6LrT7Zrjo. See also *FM 100-5: Field Service Regulations, Operations, 1941* (Washington, DC: War Department, 1941), 24–26.

8. Harold R. Winton, *Corps Commanders of the Bulge: Six American Generals and Victory in the Ardennes* (Lawrence: University Press of Kansas, 2007), 24.

9. *FM 100-5: Tentative Field Service Regulations, Operations, 1939* (Washington, DC: War Department, 1939), 34.

10. Coates, "War in New Guinea," 45.

11. Harold R. Winton, "Toward an American Philosophy of Command," *Journal of Military History* 64, no. 4 (October 2000): 1058.

12. *FM 100-5: Field Service Regulations, Operations, 1944* (Washington, DC: War Department, 1944), 34 (emphasis added).

13. Patrick Rose, "Allies at War: British and US Army Command Culture in the Italian Campaign, 1943–1944," *Journal of Strategic Studies* 36, no. 1 (2013): 3.

14. *FM 100-5, 1941,* 24–25.

15. *British Army General Staff, Field Service Regulations, Volume III: Operations; Higher Formations, 1935* (London: His Majesty's Stationery Office, 1936), 9.

16. David French, *Raising Churchill's Army: The British Army and the War against Germany 1919–1945* (Oxford: Oxford University Press, 2000), 13.

17. Ibid., 19.

18. David French, "Doctrine and Organisation in the British Army, 1919–1932," *Historical Journal* 44, no. 2 (June 2001): 515.

19. For an example, see the planning approach used by GHQ for Operation Postern in 1943 (chap. 11 of this volume), which involved a more centralized operational planning at Adv LHQ, leaving less responsibility at the corps level but then delegating tactical plans to the division and brigade levels. In contrast, Adv LHQ took a much more hands-off approach to the Oboe operations when the I Australian Corps HQ had a much more

prominent role (see chap. 13). Overall, delegation and decentralization was, however, much more prominent than in the US system. See also Peter J. Dean, *The Architect of Victory: The Military Career of Lieutenant General Sir Frank Horton Berryman* (Victoria: Cambridge University Press, 2011), chaps. 9–11.

20. The fundamental differences in command approaches and doctrine between the British and the Americans is explored in detail in Eitan Shamir, *Transforming Command: The Pursuit of Mission Command in the U.S., British and Israeli Armies* (Stanford, CA: Stanford University Press, 2011). In this work Shamir notes that the US Army is "Inspired by Corporate Practices" (the title of his chap. 4) and the British Army is "Caught between Extremes" (chap. 5).

21. Rose, "Allies at War," 3; Martin van Creveld, *Fighting Power: German and U.S. Army Performance, 1939–1945* (Westport, CT: Greenwood Press, 1982), 51.

22. Eitan Shamir, "The Long and Winding Road: The US Army Managerial Approach to Command and the Adoption of Mission Command (Aufragstaktik)," *Journal of Strategic Studies* 33, no. 5 (2010): 649; van Creveld, *Fighting Power*, 37.

23. John A. English, *The Canadian Army and the Normandy Campaign: A Study of Failure in High Command* (Westport, CT: Praeger, 1991), 89.

24. Van Creveld, *Fighting Power*, 48.

25. "Planning History and Instructions," Berryman Papers, PR84/370, item 48, AWM.

26. See Coates, *Bravery above Blunder*, 285–286, for a discussion on this point, see van Creveld, *Fighting Power*, 156.

27. For an example of this system in practice at the divisional level in the Australian Army in North Africa, see Dean, *Architect of Victory*, chap. 5.

28. *FM 101-5: Staff Officers' Field Manual; The Staff and Combat Orders, August 1940* (Washington, DC: War Department, 1940), 1, 7. This document states, "All orders from a higher to a subordinate unit are issued by the commander of the higher unit to the commander of the subordinate unit."

29. Coates, "War in New Guinea," 56.

30. Shamir, "Long and Winding Road," 649.

31. Van Creveld, *Fighting Power*, 35.

32. *FM 100-15: Field Service Regulations; Larger Units, 1942* (Washington, DC: War Department, 1942), 5.

33. Ibid., 6.

34. MacArthur as quoted in Rogers, *Good Years*, 82–83.

35. Kevin C. Holzimmer, "Joint Operations in the Southwest Pacific, 1943–1945," *Joint Force Quarterly*, no. 38 (2005): 102–103.

36. Ibid.

37. Barbey, *MacArthur's Amphibious Navy: Seventh Amphibious Force Operations, 1943–1945* (Annapolis, MD: United States Naval Institute, 1969), 24.

38. "Brett to Kenney, 2 August 1942," Kenney Diaries, vol. 1, RG 54, DMMA.

39. Morris Janowitz, *The Professional Soldier: A Social and Political Portrait* (Glencoe, IL: Free Press, 1960), 21.

40. John Miller, *Cartwheel: The Reduction of Rabaul* (Washington, DC: Office of the Chief of Military History, US Army, 1959), 189.

41. "Report on Australia for Commander in Chief Allied Forces," RG 496, Record of GHQ SWPA, box 1908, NARA.

42. Ibid.

43. Marshall interview, 27 July 1971, D. Clayton James Collection, DMMA.

44. Horner, *High Command*, 206.

45. Taaffe, *Marshall and His Generals*, 22.

46. Kenney interview, 16 July 1971, D. Clayton James Collection, DMMA.

47. Kenney, *General Kenney Reports*, 26.

48. Taaffe, *Marshall and His Generals*, 22.

49. "Frank Berryman to Muriel Berryman, 15 December 1942," Berryman Family Papers (hereafter BFP); Berryman Diary, 11 December 1942, Berryman Papers, AWM.

50. Krueger as quoted in Drea, *MacArthur's ULTRA*, 16.

51. "Brett to Kenney, 3 August 1942," Kenney Diaries, DMMA.

52. Maj. Gen. Frank H. Britton interview, 28 July 1971, D. Clayton James Collection, DMMA.

53. Drea, *MacArthur's ULTRA*, 17.

54. Manchester, *American Caesar*, 184.

55. Perret, *Old Soldiers Never Die*, 229.

56. James, *Years of MacArthur*, vol. 2, 79.

57. Robert H. Van Volkenburgh interview, 26 August 1971, D. Clayton James Oral History Collection, DMMA.

58. Virtually all officers interviewed by D. Clayton James for his biography of MacArthur made highly positive comments about Chamberlin.

59. MacArthur, *Reminiscences*, 168.

60. "Brett to Kenney, 3 August 1942," Kenney Diaries, DMMA.

61. Drea, *MacArthur's ULTRA*, 18.

62. Ibid.

63. D. Clayton James, *Years of MacArthur*, vol. 2, 182.

64. Horner, *High Command*, 295.

65. Barbey, *MacArthur's Amphibious Navy*, 24.

66. Thomas E. Griffith Jr., *MacArthur's Airman: General George C. Kenney and the War in the Southwest Pacific* (Lawrence: University Press of Kansas, 1998), 57.

67. Jay Luvaas, ed., *Dear Miss Em: General Eichelberger's War in the Pacific, 1942–1945* (Westport, CT: Greenwood Press, 1972), 30.

68. "Brett to Kenney, 3 August 1942," Kenney Diaries, DMMA.

69. Kenney, *General Kenney Reports*, 28, 124.

70. Horner, *High Command*, 252.

71. Maj. Gen. Robert C. Richardson Jr., "Memorandum for the Chief of Staff

United States Army: Subject—Australia, 9 July 1942, New Caledonia," 3–4, Sutherland Papers, RG 30, box 25, folder 8, DMMA (emphasis added).

72. Ibid.

73. Horner, *High Command*, 208–209.

74. Marshall as quoted in James, *Years of MacArthur*, vol. 2, 184.

75. See the records of interviews of senior officers from GHQ in D. Clayton James Oral Interview Collection, DMMA.

76. The Australian Militia can be seen as an equivalent of the US National Guard.

77. David Horner argues that there is some evidence to suggest that MacArthur was much more willing to tolerate a combined HQ but that Sutherland was bitterly opposed to it and convinced MacArthur to adopt his point of view. See Horner, *High Command*, 206.

78. MacArthur to Shedden, 19 February 1945, quoted in "Correspondence about book: Paper of Gavin Long on the command Problem in the SWPA 1942–1945—Request to Secretary for comments," A5954 119/1, NAA.

79. MacArthur to War Department, 8 April 1942, as quoted in Horner, *High Command*, 206–207.

80. Vasey interview, 21 April 1944, Records of Gavin Long, AWM67, notebook 44, AWM.

81. Maj. D. McCarthy interview, Records of Gavin Long, AWM67, notebook 39, AWM (emphasis in original).

CHAPTER 5. THE BATTLES FOR KOKODA AND MILNE BAY

1. Morton, *Strategy and Command*, 198.

2. Morison, *Rising Sun in the Pacific*, 220.

3. Toll, *Pacific Crucible*, 182.

4. "Prime Minister's War Conference Minutes, 11 June 1942," No. 1 of 8/4/42 to No. 69 of 14/1/43 (and Nos. 78 and 79 of 17/3/43), NAA.

5. Samuel E. Morison, *The Two-Ocean War: A Short History of the United States Navy in the Second World War* (New York: Galahad Books, 1963), 165.

6. Henry P. Frei, *Japan's Southward Advance and Australia: From the Sixteenth Century to World War II* (Honolulu: University of Hawaii Press, 1991), 160.

7. Steven Bullard, "Japanese Strategy and Intentions towards Australia," in Dean, *Australia 1942*, 126–127.

8. Ibid., 128.

9. Hiroyuki Shindo, "The Japanese Army's 'Unplanned' South Pacific Campaign," in Dean, *Australia 1942*, 113.

10. See Williams, *Kokoda Campaign 1942*, chap. 3.

11. Steven Bullard, trans., *Japanese Army Operations in the South Pacific Area: New Britain and Papua Campaigns, 1942–43* (Canberra: AWM, 2007), 58.

12. Shindo, "'Unplanned' South Pacific Campaign," 110–111.

13. Ibid., 112.

14. Bullard, "Japanese Strategy and Intentions," 133.

15. Ibid., 136.

16. Murray and Millett, *War to Be Won*, 191–192.

17. Richard B. Frank, *Guadalcanal: The Definitive Account of the Landmark Battle* (London: Penguin, 1992), 21, 25.

18. Powell, "Air Raids on Darwin," 140–141.

19. Mark Johnston, "Vanquished but Defiant, Victorious but Divided: The RAAF in the Pacific, 1942," in Dean, *Australia 1942*, 165.

20. *History of the 49th Fighter Group, January to December 1942*, Air Force Historical Research Agency GP-49-HI, Maxwell AFB.

21. Johnston, *Whispering Death*, 137.

22. Brian Weston, *Coming of Age for Australia and Its Air Force* (Canberra: Air Power Development Centre, 2014), 6.

23. Wesley Craven and James Cate, eds., *The Army Air Forces in World War II*, vol. 1 (Washington, DC: Office of Air Force History, 1983 [reprint]), 424; Weston, *Coming of Age*, 6.

24. Joseph E. Hewitt, *Adversity in Success* (Victoria: Langate, 1980), 36.

25. Ibid.

26. Bruce Gamble, *Fortress Rabaul: The Battle for the Southwest Pacific, January 1942–April 1943* (Minneapolis: Zenith Press, 2010), 63–67.

27. James, *Years of MacArthur*, vol. 2, 188.

28. "Operation Providence, 12 July 1942," D767.95.76.1942A, USAHEC.

29. James, *Years of MacArthur*, vol. 2, 191.

30. "Operation Providence," D767.95.76.1942A, USAHEC.

31. "Daily Summary of Enemy Intelligence, no. 112, GHQ SWPA, 13 July 1942," RG 407, 98-GHQ1-3.2, G-3 Journals, box 567, July 1942, NARA.

32. "Order RE Occupation and Construction of Airdrome in the Vicinity of Buna Bay, Southeast Peninsula of New Guinea, 24 July 1942," RG 407, 98-GHQ1-3.2, G-3 Journals, box 568 July 1942, NARA.

33. "Memo: Movement of Reinforcements to Port Moresby 13 May 1942," RG 407, 98-GHQ1-3.2, G-3 Journals, box 566, April–May 1942, NARA.

34. See "Preliminary Plan to Defeat a further Japanese Effort to Capture Port Moresby; Reinforcement of Combat Means in Northeast Australia, 25 May 1942," RG 407, 98-GHQ1-3.2, G-3 Journals, box 566, April–May 1942, NARA.

35. "Location and Construction of New Airfield Southeast Tip New Guinea, 12 June 1942," RG 407, 98-GHQ1-3.2, G-3 Journals, box 567, June 1942, NARA; "War Diary LHQ, Melbourne, 1 July 1942," AWM52 1/1/1/11, AWM.

36. "Allied Land Forces Operational Report 11 July 1942," RG 407, 98-GHQ1-3.2, G-3 Journals, box 567, June 1942, NARA; "War Diary 7th Infantry Brigade July 1942," AWM52 8/2/7, AWM.

37. "Memo GHQ 22 June 1942," RG 407, 98-GHQ1-3.2, G-3 Journals, box 567, June 1942, NARA.

38. "War Diary, Advance Land HQ G Branch, August 1942," AWM52 1/2/1, AWM.

39. Dudley McCarthy, *South-West Pacific Area: First Year; Kokoda to Wau*, Australia in the War of 1939–1945, series 1, vol. 5 (Canberra: AWM, 1959), 122.

40. "Terrain Study in the Vicinity of Buna-Preliminary, G-2 GHQ, 17 June 1942," RG 407, 98-GHQ1-3.2, G-3 Journals, box 567, June 1942, NARA.

41. Norris as quoted in Karl James, "On Australia's Doorstep: Kokoda and Milne Bay," in Dean, *Australia 1942*, 202.

42. See Osmar White, *Green Armour* (Sydney: Angus & Robertson, 1945).

43. Williams, *Kokoda Campaign 1942*, 202.

44. Horner, *Blamey*, 319.

45. McCarthy, *South-West Pacific Area*, 110.

46. Ibid.

47. Kenney, *General Kenney Reports*, 89.

48. David Horner, *Crisis of Command: Australian Generalship and the Japanese Threat, 1941–43* (Canberra: ANU Press, 1978), 104–105; Berryman Diary, 31 July 1942.

49. James, *Years of MacArthur*, vol. 2, 202.

50. "G2 Daily Summary of Enemy Intelligence, 24–27 July 1942," RG 407, 98-GHQ1-3.2, G-3 Journals, box 568, July 1942, NARA. G-2 did concede on 25–26 July that it was within Japanese capabilities that they could undertake an advance on "Kokoda and the Gap," although this assessment was largely rejected over the following days.

51. "Prime Minister's War Conference Minutes, 17 August 1942," A5954 1/1, 36, NAA.

52. "Prime Minister's War Conference Minutes, 18 August 1942," A5954 1/1, 39, NAA.

53. Horner, *Blamey*, 318–320.

54. See Williams, *Kokoda Campaign 1942*, 35–46, on the Nankai Shitai.

55. Ibid., 240.

56. "Prime Minister's War Conference Minutes, 17 August 1942," A5954 1/1, NAA.

57. Horner, *Blamey*, 321.

58. Ibid.

59. Kenney, *General Kenney Reports*, 48–49.

60. See David Horner, *General Vasey's War* (Melbourne: Melbourne University Press, 1991), 1–35.

61. Kenney, *General Kenney Reports*, 49.

62. Grey, *Australian Brass*, 53–54.

63. Long, *To Benghazi*, 50.

64. Berryman interview, n.d., AWM93 50/2/23/331, 2, AWM.

65. Horner, *General Vasey's War*, 183.

66. "Vasey to Rowell, 28 August 1942," Papers of Field Marshal Sir Thomas Albert Blamey [hereafter Blamey Papers], 3DRL 664 2/138, AWM.

67. "Vasey to Rowell, 28 August 1942," in Horner, *General Vasey's War*, 184.

68. "Vasey to Rowell," Blamey Papers, 3DRL 664 2/138, AWM.

69. "Rowell to Vasey, 30 August 1942," in Horner, *General Vasey's War*, 185–186.

70. James, *Years of MacArthur*, vol. 2, 209.

71. "Blamey to Rowell, 1 September 1942," Blamey Papers, 3DRL 6643 2/138, AWM.

72. Horner, *Crisis of Command*, 143.

73. Horner, *Blamey*, 322.

74. Kenney Diaries, 3 and 11 September 1942, RG 54, box 1, DMMA; James, *Years of MacArthur*, vol. 2, 209.

75. Horner, *Crisis of Command*, 150.

76. James, "On Australia's Doorstep," 207.

77. Lavarack Diary, 20 August 1942.

78. "Rowell to Blamey, 17 September 1942," Blamey Papers, 3DRL 6643 3/4, AWM.

79. Berryman Diary, 22 September 1942.

80. Berryman was DCGS from September 1942 until October 1943, when he took command of I Corps and then later II Corps at the end of the Huon Peninsula campaign. He returned as Blamey's senior staff officer, DCGS, and CoS in May 1944 until the end of the war.

81. John Hetherington, *Blamey: Controversial Soldier; A Biography of Field Marshal Sir Thomas Blamey* (Canberra: ANU Press), 343.

82. Berryman interview, n.d., AWM93 50/2/23/331, 2, AWM.

83. "Berryman to Long, comments on draft of official history," chap. 10, "Before Lae," AWM93 50/2/23/331, AWM.

84. See "Frank Berryman to Muriel Berryman, 15 December 1942," BFP. Berryman had met Eather when he was brigade major of 14th Brigade in Sydney during the 1930s.

85. "War Diary, 25th Brigade, 16 September 1942," AWM52 8/2/25, AWM.

86. Horner, *Crisis of Command*, 160.

87. "G-2 Daily Summary of Enemy Intelligence, 16–17 September 1942," RG 407, 98-GHQ1-3.2, G-3 Journals, box 571, September 1942, NARA.

88. "Berryman to Long, comments on draft of official history," AWM67 3/30, AWM.

89. Horner, *Blamey*, 327.

90. Ibid.

91. Berryman interview, n.d., AWM93 50/2/23/331, AWM.

92. Berryman Diary, 27 September 1942.

93. Horner, *Blamey*, 335.

94. "MacArthur to Blamey, 17 October 1942," Sutherland Papers, RG 200, box 14, NARA.

95. James, "On Australia's Doorstep," 212.

96. "MacArthur to Blamey, 20 October 1942," Sutherland Papers, RG 200, box 14, NARA.

97. "Prime Minister's War Conference Minutes, 7 September 1942," A5954 1/1, 47, NAA.

98. "Blamey to MacArthur, 29 September 1942," RG 407, 98-GHQ1-3.2, G-3 Journals, box 571, September 1942, NARA.

99. "Blamey to MacArthur, 13 October 1942," RG 407, 98-GHQ1-3.2, G-3 Journals, box 573, October 1942, NARA.

100. "Blamey to MacArthur, 16 and 18 October 1942," RG 407, 98-GHQ1-3.2, G-3 Journals, box 573, October 1942, NARA.

101. Bill Edgar, *Warrior of Kokoda: A Biography of Brigadier Arnold Potts* (St. Leonards, NSW: Allen & Unwin, 1999), 196.

102. Berryman interview, n.d., AWM93 50/2/23/331, 3, AWM.

103. Ibid. See also Stuart Braga, *Kokoda Commander: A Life of Major-General "Tubby" Allen* (South Melbourne: Oxford University Press, 2004), for details of the Herring-Allen relationship and Herring's role in Allen's sacking.

104. Berryman Diary, 3 November 1942.

105. "Berryman, telegram," as quoted in Braga, *Kokoda Commander*, 258.

106. Braga, *Kokoda Commander*, 262–263.

107. Planning for the beachheads was set down at a conference at GHQ on 11 October 1942. See "G3 Journal, Plan of Commander Allied Land forces in New Guinea, as arranged in conference, Objective Capture of Buna-Gona Area," AWM54 581/7/24, AWM.

108. "Eichelberger to Anders, 17 October 1953," Leslie Anders Collection, USAHEC.

109. "Eichelberger to MacArthur, 29 October 1942," RG 407, 98-GHQ1-3.2, G-3 Journals, box 571, October 1942, NARA.

110. "Disturbances between Australian and Americans Troops, 5 December 1942," Adv LHQ, 3DRL 6643 2/7, Blamey Papers, AWM.

111. "Donaldson to Marshall, 7 November 1942," Marshall Papers, RG 29c, box 1, folder 2, DMMA.

112. Peter Thompson and Robert Macklin, *The Battle of Brisbane: Australia and America at War* (Canberra: BWM Books, 2000).

113. "Donaldson to Marshall, 28 November 1942," Marshall Papers, RG 29c, box 1, folder 2, DMMA.

114. "Disturbances between Australian and Americans Troops, 2–3, Adv LHQ," 3DRL 6643 2/7, Blamey Papers, AWM.

115. Darryl McIntyre, "American Military Forces in Australia 1942: Australian Attitudes and Responses," Paper of Brigadier Maurice Austin, PR86/062, AWM; Chris Clark, *The Encyclopaedia of Australia's Battles* (Sydney: Allen & Unwin, 2010), 233–234.

116. "Brisbane, battle of," in Dennis et al., *Oxford Companion to Australian Military History*, 107.

117. Disturbances between Australian and Americans Troops, Adv LHQ, 3DRL 6643 2/7, Blamey Papers, AWM.

118. McIntyre, "American Military Forces."

119. "Blamey to Berryman, 3 December 1942," 3DRL 6643 2/7, Blamey Papers, AWM.

120. See "Donaldson to Marshall, 28 November 1942," Marshall Papers, RG-29c, box 1, folder 2, DMMA.

121. Horner, *General Vasey's War*, 190.

122. MacArthur quoted in the *Sydney Morning Herald*, 6 March 1945, as quoted in James, "On Australia's Doorstep," 213.

CHAPTER 6. THE BATTLE FOR THE BEACHHEADS, NOVEMBER 1942: STRATEGY AND STALEMATE

1. Samuel Milner, *Victory in Papua* (Washington, DC: Office of the Chief of Military History, US Army, 1957), 106. The other units that arrived at Wanigela by air included the 2/6th Australian Independent Company (IC) and the 2nd Battalion, 128th Regiment. Miller's battalion was the first to land at the airstrip. While the 2/6th IC, advancing first, managed to cross the river, rising water stopped Miller's battalion.
2. Miller as quoted in Papers of James Kincaid, unpublished memoir, MSS 17, folder 21, Wisconsin Veterans Museum (hereafter WVM).
3. "Lieutenant-Colonel Miller to the US Official Historian," in Milner, *Victory in Papua*, 107n17.
4. Miller as quoted in Kincaid Papers, WVM.
5. Kincaid Papers, WVN.
6. Milner, *Victory in Papua*, 175–177.
7. Kincaid Papers, WVM.
8. "1/128th Inf Regt, Journal, Buna, 20 November 1942," RG 407, 32nd Infantry Division, 332-INF (128)-3.7, box 8058, NARA; Milner, *Victory in Papua*, 177–178.
9. W. B. Parker, "Notes on Operations near Buna, New Guinea, US Army Liaison officer 1942," AWM54 417/1/4, 5–8, 12–19, AWM.
10. ANZAC in this context being part of a national mythology that encompasses the fight prowess of Australian and New Zealand soldiers.
11. The most provocative histories on the topic are Peter FitzSimons, *Kokoda* (Sydney: Hodder, 2004); Jack Galloway, *The Odd Couple: Blamey and MacArthur at War* (Brisbane: University of Queensland Press, 2000); Paul Ham, *Kokoda* (Sydney: ABC Books, 2004); Roland Perry, *Pacific 360: Australia's Battle for Survival in World War II* (Sydney: Hachette, 2012); and Peter Thompson, *Pacific Fury: How Australia and Her Allies Defeated the Japanese Scourge* (Sydney: William Heinemann, 2008). All of these works are popular histories written by popular historians who focus on what Robert Stevenson has called "diggerography," delivered on the back of the notion that a good story is more important than good history. Such works are often large in size and heavily reliant on oral histories of aging veterans. They also tend to be short on archival evidence and analysis. One of their other key features is a focus on the supposed incompetence of the high command, especially if these officers were provided by Australia's "great and powerful friends" Britain or the United States.
12. The Battle of the Beachheads refers collectively to the three operational areas of Adv New Guinea Force at Gona, Sanananda, and Buna from November 1942 to January 1943.

13. Blamey's plan for the advance on the beachheads was finalized on 10 October 1942 after a conference with GHQ. See "G-3 Journal 19 October 1942, Plan of Commander ALF in New Guinea, as arranged in conference, Objective capture of Buna-Gona Area," AWM54 581/7/24, AWM.

14. For details of this crossing, see James Campbell, *The Ghost Mountain Boys: Their Epic March and the Terrifying Battle for New Guinea; The Forgotten War in the South Pacific* (New York: Crown, 2007).

15. "NGF War Diary, October 1942," AWM52 1/5/51/19, AWM. See "Operational Instruction No 35," which defines the role of the 32nd Division for attacking Buna from the south and the southeast. The first units to arrive at Wanigela were a US antiaircraft battery and the 2/10th Battalion AIF, named Hatforce. The 128th Regiment started to move by air on 14 October, and Blamey visited Hatforce on 15 October. Harding and Herring visited on 18 October.

16. See "Chamberlin to Sutherland, 'GHQ Plan of Action,' 30 October 1942," RG 407, 98-GHQ1-3.2, G-3 Journals and Files, box 574, October–November 1942, NARA.

17. "Blamey to MacArthur, 27 October 1942," RG 407, 98-GHQ1-3.2, G-3 Journals and Files, box 574, October–November 1942, NARA.

18. This fact was well understood at GHQ. See "Weekly Summary of Naval Intelligence, 17 and 25 October 1942," RG 407, 98-GHQ1-3.2, G-3 Journals and Files, box 573, NARA.

19. Up until 16–17 January 1943, Allied intelligence believed that IJN activity around Guadalcanal was offensive in nature. Thus, only from mid to late January did it become apparent that they were withdrawing their troops. See "GHQ G-2 Daily Intelligence Summary 16–30 January 1943," RG 407, 98-GHQ1-3.2, G-3 Journals and Files, box 578, NARA.

20. "Petersburg Plan, Copy No. 1 on Redistribution of Allied Forces SWPA in the event of a Japanese Success in the Solomon Islands, 31 October 1942," USAHEC.

21. See "GHQ G-2 Daily Intelligence Summaries for November 1942–January 1943," RG 407, 98-GHQ1-3.2, G-3 Journals and Files, boxes 574–579, NARA. These intelligence summaries show increasing evidence of concern over the activities of the Sixth Japanese Army, which occupied Java and its surrounding islands.

22. "MacArthur to Blamey, 23 December 1942," RG 407, 98-GHQ1-3.2, G-3 Journals and Files, box 576, December 1942, NARA.

23. "MacArthur to Eichelberger, 25 December 1942," RG 319, Center for Military History, Victory in Papua, Eichelberger Letters, NARA.

24. "GHQ Operations Instructions No. 23, 10 November 1942," RG 407, 98-GHQ1-3.2, G-3 Journals and Files, box 574, NARA. This instruction set out NGF's role to destroy the Japanese defending the beachheads area.

25. "Blamey to MacArthur, 7 October 1942," RG 407, 98-GHQ1-3.2, G-3 Journals and Files, box 572, NARA.

26. "GHQ G-2 Daily Intelligence Summary 6–7 October 1942," RG 407, 98-GHQ1-3.2, G-3 Journals and Files, box 572, NARA.

27. "GHQ G-2 Daily Intelligence Summary 10–11 October 1942," RG 407, 98-GHQ1-3.2, G-3 Journals and Files, box 572, NARA.

28. "GHQ G-2 Daily Intelligence Summary 29–30 October 1942," RG 407, 98-GHQ1-3.2, G-3 Journals and Files, box 573, NARA.

29. "GHQ G-2 Daily Intelligence Summary 14–15 November October 1942," RG 407, 98-GHQ1-3.2, G-3 Journals and Files, box 574, NARA.

30. "Harding to Sutherland, 31 October 1942," RG 407, 98-GHQ1-3.2, G-3 Journals and Files, box 573, NARA.

31. "GHQ G-2 Daily Intelligence Summary 20–21 November October 1942," RG 407, 98-GHQ1-3.2, G-3 Journals and Files, box 574, NARA.

32. See message traffic "NGF to 32nd Division 15–21 November," RG 407, WWII Operations Reports, G-2 and G- Reports Buna Operations, 32nd Division, 332-07, box 7796, NARA.

33. "CINC SWPA (MacArthur) to COMSOPAC (Halsey) 27 November 1942," RG 4, box 10, folder 2 "Correspondence—Navy," DMMA.

34. Lt. Gen. Kane Yoshihara, *Southern Cross: An Account of the Eastern New Guinea Campaign* (Tokyo: US Army Office of Military History, 1955).

35. Shindo, "Japanese Army's 'Unplanned' South Pacific Campaign," 114. A Japanese "area army" consisted of two or more armies, which were the size of an Australian or American corps. An area army was therefore equivalent in size to an Australian or American "army."

36. Peter Brune, *A Bastard of a Place: The Australians in Papua* (Crows Nest, NSW: Allen & Unwin, 2003), 492.

37. The final defensive layout of the area was set down in "NGF instruction 59, 13 January 1943," War Diary, NGF HQ, AWM52 1/5/51/24, January 1943, part 2, appendixes, AWM. However, it had been discussed by GHQ and NGF HQ throughout November and December 1942. In January 1943, a Japanese landing was considered unlikely, although it was assessed in the defensive scheme and was the focus of earlier defensive plans. See "Suitability of Beaches for Landing Oro Bay-Amboga River Mouth," appendix 3, NGF Operational Instruction No. 59, RG 407, 98-GHQ1-3.2, G-3 Journals and Files, box 578, NARA.

38. "GHQ G-2 Daily Intelligence Summary 4–5 January 1953" and "Mac-Arthur to Rear Admiral F.W. Coster, Senior Naval Officer Royal Netherlands Forces in Australia, 5 January 1943," RG 407, 98-GHQ1-3.2, G-3 Journals and Files, box 578, January 1943, NARA.

39. Lavarack Diary, 2 January 1943.

40. This argument is also outlined in Peter J. Dean, "Anzacs and Yanks: US and Australian Operations at the Beachhead Battles," in Dean, *Australia 1942*, 217–239.

41. See outline of disposition and plans in Blamey to MacArthur, 27 October 1942, RG 407, 98-GHQ1-3.2, G-3 Journals and Files, box 574, NARA.

42. Brune, *Bastard of a Place*, 611.

43. "16 Brigade War Diary, 22 November 1942," AWM54 8/2/16, AWM.

44. "MacArthur to Blamey, 20 October 1942," RG 200, Personal Papers of General Sutherland, box 14, NARA.

45. See "Operations Goodenough Island, 22–26 October 1942, Lessons from Operations No. 4, Adv LHQ," RG 407, 98-GHQ1-3.2, G-3 Journals and Files, box 573, NARA. For a detailed appraisal of the operation, see Peter J. Dean, "Raid on Goodenough Island: Australia's First Amphibious Operation in the Second World War," *Australian Naval Review* 1, vol.1 (2016): 53–73.

46. "Blamey to MacArthur, 27 October 1942," RG 407, 98-GHQ1-3.2, G-3 Journals and Files, box 573, NARA.

47. A. B. Lodge, "Geese and Swans: The Australian Militia in Papua, 1942–1943," Papers of Brig. M. Austin, PR86/62, AWM.

48. McCarthy, *South-West Pacific Area*, 44.

49. Horner, *Crisis of Command*, 81.

50. Frederick Cranston, *Always Faithful: A History of the 49th Australian Infantry Battalion 1916–1982* (Brisbane: Boolarong Publications, 1983), 168.

51. Lodge, "Geese and Swans," 9–16.

52. Horner, *Crisis of Command*, 87.

53. Horner, *High Command*, 288.

54. "32nd Infantry Division Factsheet, 32nd Division History," RG 407, 332–332.03, 32nd Infantry Division box 7793, NARA; "The 32D Infantry Division in World War II: The 'Red Arrow,'" http://www.32nd-division.org/history/ww2/32ww2-1.html#Mobilization.

55. "Notes on Activities of the Fourth Section, The Infantry School, 1930–1933, Headed by Major Edwin Forest Harding by Brigadier Richard G. Tindall, 5 July 1973," Leslie Anders Collection, box 1, USAHEC.

56. "Harding—biographical details," Leslie Anders Collection, box 1, USAHEC.

57. Brig. Gen. Robert H. Van Volkenburgh interview, 26 August 1971, D. Clayton James Oral History Collection, DMMA.

58. "32nd Division History," RG 470, WWI Operational Reports, 32nd Infantry Division 333–332-0.3, box 7793, NARA.

59. Barbey, *MacArthur's Amphibious Navy*, 35; "32nd Division Fact Sheet," RG 470, WWII Operational Reports, 32nd Infantry Division, 333–332-0.3, entry 427, box 7793, NARA; "A Summary of Combined Operations Training in Australia (amphibious) 1942–1945," AWM54 943/16/1, AWM.

60. "Memo, Eichelberger to Sutherland, 6 September 1942," G-3 Information 20 September 1942, RG 496, Records of General Headquarters SWPA, "Training: May 7 1942 to Nov 1 1943," box 667, NARA.

61. Robert Eichelberger, *Our Jungle Road to Tokyo* (New York: Viking, 1950), 11.

62. "HQ 32nd Division Training Directive, 15 July 1942–16 September 1942," RG 338, Record of US Army Operational, Tactical and Support Organizations, 32nd Infantry Division, box 3913, NARA.

63. Jay Luvaas, "Buna, 19 November 1942–2 January 1943: A 'Leavenworth Nightmare,'" in *America's First Battles: 1776–1965*, ed. Charles E. Heller and William A. Stofft (Lawrence: University Press of Kansas, 1986), 188, 192.

64. Luvaas, "Buna: 'Leavenworth Nightmare,'" 191–192.

65. "Major-General Clarence A. Martin to Samuel Milner, 6 March 1951," RG 319, Records the Army Staff, Centre of Military History, "Victory in

Papua," boxes 1–3, NARA. The same situation occurred in the Central Pacific with the 27th Infantry Division, also a National Guard formation. See Sharon T. Lacy, *Pacific Blitzkrieg: World War II in the Central Pacific* (Denton: University of North Texas Press, 2013), 136.

66. Lt. Gen. Clovis E. Byers interview, 24 June 1971, D. Clayton James Oral History Collection, DMMA.

67. Luvaas, "Buna: 'Leavenworth Nightmare,'" 192.

68. "Harding to Sutherland, 14 October 1942," AWM54 581/3/5, AWM.

69. "Harding to Sutherland, 20 October 1942," RG 407, 98-GHQ1-3.2, G-3 Journals and Files, box 573, NARA.

70. Milner, *Victory in Papua*, 138.

71. Berryman to Irving, 7 January 1943, Berryman Papers, PR 84/370, item 11, AWM.

72. Milner, *Victory in Papua*, 372.

73. "History of the Buna Campaign," 1 December 1942–25 January 1943, G-3 History Division, GHQ, AFPAC, 5 October 1945, AWM 54 581/6/8, 8, AWM.

74. "War diary, 2/6th Independent Company, 30 November 1942," AWM52 25/3/6/4, AWM.

75. Milner, *Victory in Papua*, 143.

76. For logistics details on the campaign, see John Moreman, "A Triumph of Improvisation: Australian Army Operational Logistics and the Campaign in Papua, July 1942 to January 1943" (PhD thesis, UNSW, Sydney, 2000).

77. "Blamey to MacArthur, 27 October 1942," RG 407, 98-GHQ1-3.2, G-3 Journals and Files, box 573, NARA.

78. "Blamey to MacArthur, 7 November 1942," RG 407, 98-GHQ 1–3.2, G-3 Journals and Files, box 574, October–November 1942, NARA.

79. Pfennigwerth, "Novel Experience," 192.

80. "MacArthur to Blamey, 20 October 1942," RG 200, Personal Papers of General Sutherland, box 14, NARA.

81. "G-2 Journal, 32nd Division 16 November," RG 407, WWII Operations Reports, G-2 and G-3 Reports Buna Operations, 32nd Division, 332-07, box 7796, NARA.

82. "Harding to MacNider, 21 October 1942," RG 407, WWII Operations Reports, G-2 and G-3 Reports Buna Operations, 32nd Division, 332-07, box 7796, NARA.

83. Milner, *Victory in Papua*, 170–171. See also Kenneth J. Babcock, "Mac-Arthur's Small Ships: Improvising Water Transport in the Southwest Pacific," *Army History* 90 (Winter 2014), 26–42.

84. "Message NGF to 32nd Div HQ 18 November 1942," RG 407, WWII Operations Reports, G-2 and G-3 Reports Buna Operations, 32nd Division, 332-07, box 7796, NARA.

85. "CINC SWPA (MacArthur) to COMSOPAC (Halsey), 27 November 1942," RG 4, box 10, folder 2, Correspondence–Navy, DMMA.

86. "COMSOPAC (Halsey) to CINC SWPA (MacArthur) 28 November 1942," RG 4, box 10, folder 2, Correspondence—Navy, DMMA. MacArthur also

wrote to the Navy requesting submarine support to interdict the flow of supplies to Buna. See "COMINCH to COMSOPAC 22 November 1942," Record of the War Department's Operations Division, 1942–1945, part 1, series B, reel 22.

87. "COMSOWESPACFOR to MacArthur 28 November 1942," RG 4, box 10, folder 2, Correspondence–Navy, DMMA.

88. "Berryman to Irving, 24 December 1942," Berryman Papers, item 11, AWM.

89. Gill, *Royal Australian Navy*, 45–47.

90. "Clarence A. Martin to Samuel Milner, 6 March 1951, New Guinea Operations, 1942–1943," RG 319, Records of Army Staff, Center of Military History, NARA.

91. Williams, *Kokoda Campaign*.

92. Kent Roberts Greenfield, Robert R. Palmer, and Bell I. Wiley, *The Organization of Ground Combat Troops* (Washington, DC: Office of the Chief of Military History, 1947), 274–275. The Army Ground Forces did not organize a "light" or "jungle" division until March 1943, and MacArthur and his staff remained opposed to the structure that the Army Ground Forces proposed. Only one division (the 10th Mountain Division) was establishing under this program, and it served in Italy during World War II.

93. Charles R. Anderson, *Papua*, vol. 72, no. 7, *US Army Campaigns of World War II* (Washington, DC: US Army Center of Military History, 1992), 20.

94. "Message NGF to Milne Force repeated 32nd Division, 13 November 1942," RG 407, WWII Operations Reports, G-2 and G-3 Reports Buna Operations, 32nd Division, 332-07, box 7796, NARA.

95. "War Diary, 25th Brigade AIF, 23–25 November 1942," AWM52 8/2/25/15, AWM; McCarthy, *South-West Pacific Area*, 421.

96. Eustace G. Keogh, *South-West Pacific 1941–1945* (Melbourne: Greyflower Productions, 1965), 257–258.

97. McCarthy, *South-West Pacific Area*, 422–448.

98. "War diary, 2/3rd Battalion, 20 November 1942," AWM52 8/3/316, AWM. The battalion incorrectly identified the troops as belonging to the 128th Regiment.

99. "War diary, 2/1st Battalion, November–December, 22 November 1942," AWM52 8/3/1, AWM.

100. McCarthy, *South-West Pacific Area*, 385–394.

101. Milner, *Victory in Papua*, 154.

102. "War diary, 2/3rd Battalion, 30 November 1942," AWM52 8/3/316, AWM.

103. "History-Buna (Papuan Campaign), 126th Infantry Regiment," RG 407, 332-HQ-0.1 to 332-INF (126)-0.3, WWII Operations Reports 1940–48, 32nd Infantry Division, box 7998, NARA.

104. Keogh, *South-West Pacific 1941–45*, 225.

105. Milner, *Victory in Papua*, 162.

106. Keogh, *South-West Pacific 1941–45*, 225.

107. Milner, *Victory in Papua*, 195.

108. Brune, *Bastard of a Place*, 491.

CHAPTER 7. DECISION AT BUNA AND SANANANDA

1. A number of the arguments presented in this chapter were first published in Dean, *Australia 1942*, and Peter J. Dean, "Grinding Out a Victory: Australian and American Commanders during the Beachhead Battles," in *Kokoda: Beyond the Legend*, ed. Karl James (Melbourne: Cambridge University Press, 2017), 164–187.
2. Horner, *Blamey*, 360.
3. Kenney, *General Kenney Reports*, 154, 157.
4. Horner, *Blamey*, 361.
5. Kenney, *General Kenney Reports*, 151.
6. Rogers, *Good Years*, 336.
7. Kenney, *General Kenney Reports*, 150.
8. For details of the visits of GHQ staff to the front, see Milner, *Victory in Papua*, 202–203.
9. "Eichelberger to Lauer, 17 October 1953," Leslie Anders Collection, box 1, USAHEC.
10. Ibid. Eichelberger noted that "the question of the nature of my orders [from MacArthur] is very important because it explains the necessity for haste."
11. Robert Eichelberger, *Our Jungle Road to Tokyo* (New York: Viking, 1950), 45; "Eichelberger to Lauer, undated," Leslie Anders Collection, box 1, USAHEC. Eichelberger noted after the war that MacArthur said, "Bob, get Buna! Don't come back alive without it!" Paul Chwialkowski, *In Caesar's Shadow: The Life of General Robert Eichelberger* (Westport, CT: Greenwood Press), 52–53. See also McCarthy, *South-West Pacific Area*, 372. McCarthy's account comes from Lt. Col. W. T. Robertson, who was a senior staff officer officer at NGF.
12. "Harding to Sutherland, 21 October 1942," RG 407, 98-GHQ1-3.2, G-3 Journals and Files, box 573, NARA.
13. "Harding to Sutherland, 20 October 1942," ibid.
14. Ibid.
15. "Harding to Sutherland, 13 October 1942," RG 407, 98-GHQ1-3.2, G-3 Journals and Files, box 572, NARA.
16. "Harding to Sutherland, 31 October 1942," RG 407, 98-GHQ1-3.2, G-3 Journals and Files, box 573, NARA.
17. McCarthy, *South-West Pacific Area*, 358.
18. Clayton James, *Years of MacArthur*, vol. 2, 241.
19. Horner, *High Command*, 289.
20. "Robert Eichelberger to Emma Eichelberger, 4 December 1942," in Luvaas, *Dear Miss Em*, 39.
21. Ibid., 38–39.
22. "Eichelberger to Fuller, 14 December 1942," RG 41, Eichelberger Papers, box 1, folder 2, DMMA.
23. See "Eichelberger to Fuller, December 1942," Eichelberger Papers, fol. 1, DMMA, for a full description of the poor state of the troops.

24. The supply situation in the 32nd Division was also criticized by the corps commander. See Edmund Herring, "The Battle of the Beachheads," AWM54 581/6/10, 5, AWM, and Milner, *Victory in Papua*, 196.

25. "Harding Diary, 30 November 1942," RG 319, Records of the Army Staff Center for Military History, Victory in Papua, 270/19/7/1, box 1–3, NARA.

26. "Blamey to MacArthur, 20 December 1942," RG 200, Papers of General Sutherland, box 14, NARA.

27. Notebooks 4 and 5, Papers of Gavin Long, AWM67, AWM.

28. Ibid.

29. "Eichelberger to Sutherland, 3 December 1942," RG 319, Victory in Papua, Eichelberger Letters, box 1–3, NARA; "Eichelberger to Lauer, 17 October 1953," Leslie Anders Collection, box 1, USAHEC.

30. "Eichelberger to MacArthur, Report on Relief of Major-General E. R. Harding, 19 February 1943," RG 30, Papers of Lt. Gen. Richard Sutherland, box 1, folder 6, NARA.

31. "An account of the participation of the American troops in the Buna Campaign," 32nd Division HQ, AWM54 581/6/8, 15, AWM.

32. McCarthy, *South-West Pacific Area*, 361–362.

33. See Leslie Anders, *Gentle Knight: The Life and Times of Major General Edwin Forrest Harding* (Ohio: Kent State University Press, 1985).

34. "History of the Buna Campaign, 1 December 1942–25 January 1943," 32nd Division HQ, AWM54 581/6/8, AWM.

35. "Colonel Gordon B. Rogers to Major-General Orlando P. Ward, 5 July 1950," RG 319, 270/19/7/1, box 5, NARA.

36. Herring, "Battle of the Beachheads," 5.

37. Ibid., 4.

38. Milner, *Victory in Papua*, 196.

39. James, *Years of MacArthur*, vol. 2, 263–264.

40. See "Correspondence between Eichelberger and Sutherland" in RG 30, Papers of Lt. Gen. Richard Sutherland, box 1, folder 6, and RG 41, Eichelberger Papers, box 1, folder 3, both at the DMMA.

41. Herring as quoted in Horner, *High Command*, 289.

42. Herring, "Battle of the Beachheads," 4.

43. See the postwar correspondence between Eichelberger and Herring in the Herring Papers, State Library of Victoria (hereafter SLV). Eichelberger was to also host Herring and his wife in their postwar visit to the United States.

44. "Blamey to Northcott, 7 December 1942," Berryman Papers, PR83, item 11, AWM.

45. "An account of the participation of the American troops in the Buna Campaign," 32nd Division HQ, AWM54 581/6/8, 16, AWM; "Weekly Summary of Enemy Naval Intelligence, 6 December 1942," RG 407, 98 GHQI-3.2, G-3 Journals and Files, box 576, NARA.

46. "History of the Buna Campaign, 1 December 1942–25 January 1943."

47. Milner, *Victory in Papua*, 234–235.

48. "History of the Buna Campaign, 1 December 1942–25 January 1943."

49. "War diary, 2/6th Independent Company, 4 December 1942," AWM52 25/3/6/4, AWM.

50. "Blamey to MacArthur, 6 December 1942," RG 407, 98 GHQ1-3.2, G-3 Journals and Files, box 576, NARA.

51. McCarthy, *South-West Pacific Area*, 376–378.

52. "History of the Buna Campaign, 1 December 1942–25 January 1943."

53. Milner, *Victory in Papua*, 243.

54. "MacArthur to Eichelberger, 13 December 1942," Eichelberger Papers, folder 1, DMMA.

55. Herring, "Battle of the Beachheads."

56. "Daily Operational Report Allied Land Forces, 15, 18 December 1942," RG 407, 98 GHQ1-3.2, G-3 Journals and Files, box 576, NARA.

57. "2/128th Battalion Journal 17 December, 1942," RG 407, 32nd Division, 332-INF(128)7-0.7, box 8026, NARA.

58. "GHQ Daily Intelligence summary, 14–15 December 1942," RG 407, 98 GHQ1-3.2, G-3 Journals and Files, box 576, NARA.

59. "GHQ Daily Intelligence summary, 18 December 1942," RG 407, 98 GHQ1-3.2, G-3 Journals and Files, box 576, NARA.

60. "3/128th Inf Regt, Unit Journal, 13 December 1942," RG 407, 32nd Infantry Division, 332-INF(128)7-1.13, box 8065, NARA.

61. "Report on Operations 18th Brigade Group at Cape Endaiadere, Giropa Point and Sanananda Areas, 14 December 1942–14 January 1943," War Diary, 18th Brigade, December 1942, AWM52 8/2/18/32, AWM.

62. "Eichelberger to Sutherland, 13 December 1942," Papers of Robert Eichelberger, RG 41, box 1, DMMA.

63. Ibid.

64. "18th Brigade Operational Instruction No. 1, 17 December 1942," War Diary, 18th Brigade AIF, December 1942, appendixes, AWM52 8/2/18, AWM.

65. "Report on Operations 18th Brigade Group at Cape Endaiadere, Giropa Point and Sanananda Areas."

66. "Armoured Training Vehicle Training Memo, No. 2, March 1943," MP385 52/101/145, NAA.

67. "G-3 Situation Map, Buna Drome Area, 1700hrs, 18 December, GHQ Daily Intelligence summary," 1, RG 407, 98 GHQ1-3.2, G-3 Journals and Files, box 576, NARA.

68. "Report on Operations 18th Brigade Group."

69. Ibid.

70. "Warning Instruction No. 1, 24 December 1942," RG 407, 98 GHQ1-3.2, G-3 Journals and Files, box 577, NARA.

71. "Operations Report, ALF HQ, 25th December 1942," RG 407, 98 GHQ1-3.2, G-3 Journals and Files, box 577, NARA.

72. "Eichelberger to Sutherland, 1 January 1943," Papers of Robert Eichelberger, RG 41, Box 1, DMMA.

73. Milner, *Victory in Papua*, 323.

74. "Martin to Milner, 6 March 1951, Papuan Campaign: The Buna-Sanananda

Operations," RG 319, Records of the Army Staff, Office of the Chief of Military History, box 1–3, NARA.

75. "MacNab to Milner, 19 November 1949, Papuan Campaign: The Buna-Sanananda Operations," RG 319, Records of the Army Staff, Office of the Chief of Military History, box 1–3, NARA.

76. "Eichelberger to Herring, 17 December 1943," Herring Papers, box 37, SLV.

77. "Eichelberger to Sutherland, 18 December, 1942," Papers of Robert Eichelberger, RG 41, box 1, DMMA.

78. Herring, "Battle of the Beachheads," 4.

79. "MacNab to Milner, 19 November 1949."

80. Kelli Brockschmidt, "The New Guinea Campaign: A New Perspective through the Use of Oral Histories," *McNair Scholars Journal* 9, no. 1 (2005).

81. Frank Allchin, *Purple and Blue: The History of the 2/10th Battalion, A.I.F.* (Adelaide: Griffin Press, 1958), 273.

82. Ibid.

83. Bill Spencer, *In the Footsteps of Ghosts: With the 2/9th Battalion in the African Desert and the Jungles of the Pacific* (St. Leonards: Allen & Unwin), 118, 122.

84. These observations are drawn from an analysis of 168 Australian Papua campaign veterans' interviews, available at the Australians at War Film Archive, http://www.australiansatwarfilmarchive.unsw.edu.au.

85. Raymond Coombes, 2/2nd Battalion AIF, record no. 1124, Australians at War Film Archive.

86. Leonard Bennetts, 2/10th Battalion AIF, record no. 1868, Australians at War Film Archive.

87. "War Diary, 2/6th Independent Company, General Report, November 1942," AWM52 25/3/6/4, AWM.

88. "War Diary, 2/6th Independent Company, 2 December 1942," AWM52 25/3/6/4, AWM.

89. "War Diary, 2/6th Independent Company, General Report, December 1942," AWM52 25/3/6/4, AWM.

90. "War Diary, 2/1st Battalion, November–December, 22 November 1942," AWM52 8/3/1, AWM.

91. Ibid.

92. Ibid.

93. E. C. Givney, *The First at War: The Story of the 2/1st Australian Infantry Battalion, 1939–45, the City of Sydney Regiment* (Earlwood, NSW: Association of First Infantry Battalions, 1987), 296, 309.

94. Horner, *Blamey*, 375.

95. "Frank Berryman to Muriel Berryman, 28 December 1942," BFP.

96. Dean, *Architect of Victory*, 188.

97. "Herring to D. Clayton James, 22 May 1972," Herring Papers, box 37, SLV.

98. "Eichelberger to Lauer," Leslie Anders Collection, USAHEC.

99. "Blamey to Herring 11 December 1942," Blamey Papers, 3DRL/6643, series 2, wallet 135.

100. "Blamey to MacArthur, 27 December 1942," RG 200, Papers of General Sutherland, box 14, NARA.

101. Ibid.

102. "MacArthur to Blamey, 28 December 1942," RG 200, Papers of General Sutherland, box 14, NARA.

103. "MacArthur to Blamey, 23 December 1942," RG 407, 98-GHQ1-3.2, G-3 Journals and Files, box 576, December 1942, NARA.

104. "Chamberlin to MacArthur, 29 December 1942," RG 407, 98-GHQ1-3.2, G-3 Journals and Files, box 578, January 1943, NARA.

105. "GHQ G-2 Daily Intelligence Summary 4–5 January 1943" and "MacArthur to Rear Admiral F. W. Coster, Senior Naval Officer Royal Netherlands Forces in Australia, 5 January 1943," RG 407, 98-GHQ1-3.2, G-3 Journals and Files, box 578, January 1943, NARA.

106. "Report by Brigadier Porter and Major Sublet on condition of troops under command of 7th Australian Division and Strength State, Sanananda, 1942," AWM54 581/7/16, AWM.

107. Ibid.

108. "163rd Combat Team, New Guinea Campaigns," AWM54 581/7/36, AWM.

109. "Report on Operations 18th Brigade Group."

110. "Notes on Situation—Sanananda Area 13 Jan 43," War Diary, Adv NGF HQ, AWM52 1/5/51, AWM.

111. Ibid.

112. "Eichelberger to Herring, 13 January 1943," RG 41, Eichelberger Papers, box 1, DMMA.

113. See Dean, *Architect of Victory*, 198–199.

114. Keogh, *South-West Pacific*, 276.

115. "Vasey to Blamey, 25 November 1942," Blamey Papers, 3DRL6643 2/171.2, AWM.

116. "Eichelberger to MacArthur, 18 January 1943," RG 41, Papers of Robert Eichelberger, box 1, DMMA; "Vasey to Hopkins, 16 January 1943," Vasey Papers 2/9, National Library of Australia (hereafter NLA).

117. Horner, *General Vasey's War*, 140.

118. "Eichelberger to Sutherland, 30 December 1942," RG 41, Eichelberger Papers, box 1, DMMA.

119. "Eichelberger to H. J. Manning, 13 March 1961," Herring Papers, box 37, SLV.

120. "Porter to Eichelberger, January 1943," RG 41, Eichelberger Papers, box 1, DMMA.

121. Herring, "Battle of the Beachheads," AWM54 581/6/10, 4, AWM.

122. Keogh, *South-West Pacific*, 255.

123. "Eichelberger to Lauer, 17 October 1953," Leslie Anders Collection, USHEC.

124. "Eichelberger to Milner, 6 January 1955," RG 319, Records of the Army

Staff Center for Military History, Victory in Papua, 270/19/7/1, boxes 1–3, NARA.

125. Ibid.

126. For MacArthur's record for declaring campaigns over early in the SWPA, see Taaffe, *MacArthur's Jungle War.*

127. "Clarence A. Martin to Samuel Milner, 6 March 1951," interviews, New Guinea Operations, 1942–43, RG 319, Records of the Army Staff Center for Military History, Victory in Papua, 270/19/7/1, boxes 1–3, NARA.

128. "Task Forces–Military–SWPA–Composition," B6121/3 297, NAA.

129. James Goldrick, "1941–1945: World War II; The War against Japan," in *The Royal Australian Navy*, ed. David Stevens (Melbourne: Oxford University Press, 2001), 136.

130. "General Report to Vol V War Diary, November, 1942, O.C 2/6 Australian Independent Company," AWM52 25/3/6/4—November 1942, 2, AWM.

131. The debate between GHQ, Adv LHQ, and the ANF over the use of destroyers and other vessels in support of the beachheads operations was long and protracted. For details of most of this major correspondence and discussions, see RG 200, Personal Papers of General Sutherland, box 14, "Correspondence with Allied forces 1942–45," NARA.

132. Jo Gray Taylor, "American Experience in the Southwest Pacific," in *Case Studies in the Development of Close Air Support*, ed. Ben Cooling (Washington, DC: Office of Air Force History, 1990), 302–304.

133. "126th Infantry Regiment, History—Buna (Papuan Campaign)," RG 407, 332-HQ-0.1 to 332-INF (126)-0.3, "WWII Operations Reports 1940–48," 32nd Infantry Division, box 7998, NARA, 15.

134. Taylor, "American Experience in Southwest Pacific," 304.

135. War Diary, 2/9th Battalion, 18 December 1942, AWM52, AWM.

136. Ibid.

137. Allen S. Walker, *The Island Campaigns* (Canberra: AWM, 1957), 86.

138. "Eichelberger to Fuller, December 1942," Eichelberger Papers, folder 1, DMMA.

139. Keogh, *South-West Pacific*, 279.

140. For a more detailed assessment of the performance of each of these commanders at the beachheads, see Dean, "Grinding Out a Victory." Much of the analysis from this section can be found in here.

141. MacArthur's lack of understanding of combat conditions is most vivid in his correspondence with Blamey on 13 December 1942. See "MacArthur to Blamey, 13 December 1942," RG 200, Papers of General Sutherland, box 14, NARA.

142. Horner, *Blamey*, 384.

143. Ibid.

144. "Blamey to Herring, December 1942," Herring Papers, box 10, SLV.

145. Geoff Brown, "Herring, Sir Edmund Francis (Ned) (1892–1982)," *Australian Dictionary of Biography*, http://adb.anu.edu.au/biography/herring-sir-edmund-francis-ned-12626, accessed 13 January 2014.

146. See Dean, "Grinding Out a Victory," 164–187.
147. Brune, *Bastard of a Place*, 611.
148. Ibid., 606.
149. "Eichelberger to Lauer, 17 October 1953," Leslie Anders Collection, USAHEC.

CHAPTER 8. OPERATION CARTWHEEL: PLANS, PREPARATIONS, AND
THE BATTLE OF THE BISMARCK SEA

1. Hidemitsu Nakano as quoted in Barbey, *MacArthur's Amphibious Navy*, 70.
2. Morton, *Strategy and Command*, 364–370.
3. Phillip Bradley, *Wau 1942–1943* (Canberra: AHU, 2010), 74–90.
4. See Dean, *Architect of Victory*, 200–202; and David Horner, *Blamey*, 382–384.
5. For details, see "17th Brigade, War Diary, January 1943," AWM52 8/2/17/72, AWM.
6. "War Diary, New Guinea Force Headquarters and General (Air), January–February 1943," AWM52 1/5/51/23 and AWM52 1/5/51/25, AWM.
7. "Blamey to MacArthur, 9 March," RG 407, GHQ SWPA 98-GHQ1-3.2, G-3 Journals and Files, box 582, March 1943, NARA.
8. McCarthy, *South-West Pacific Area*, 564.
9. David Horner, "MacArthur and Curtin: Deciding Australian War Strategy in 1943," in *Australia 1943: The Liberation of New Guinea*, ed. Peter J. Dean (Melbourne: Cambridge University Press, 2013), 27.
10. Samuel E. Morison, *Breaking the Bismarcks Barrier: 22 July 1942–1 May 1944*, vol. 6, History of United States Naval Operations in World War II (Boston: Little, Brown, 1950), 6.
11. Morton, *Strategy and Command*, appendix E, 619.
12. "JCS to GHQ SWPA, NR: 2407," RG 407, 98-GHQ1-3.2, G-3 Journals and Files, box 582, March 1943, NARA. This is the signal from the JCS to MacArthur that cancels JCS Directive 0221000 of 19 July 1942 and replaces it with the new JCS directives outlining the task for the SWPA, for what would become the Cartwheel series of operations.
13. MacArthur constantly reiterated the point that he was the sole joint commander. See "GHQ Warning Instruction No. 2, 6 May 1943," RG 407, 98-GHQ1-3.2, G-3 Journals and Files, box 586, May 1943, NARA; "MacArthur to Blamey 30 August 1943," and "Blamey to MacArthur 31 August 1943," RG 407, 98-GHQ1-3.2, G-3 Journals and Files, box 597, August 1943, NARA.
14. "GHQ Warning Instruction No. 2, 6 May 1943," RG 407, 98-GHQ1-3.2, G-3 Journals and Files, box 586, May 1943, NARA.
15. In the SWPA, eighteen task forces were created for operations in the period January 1942–Feburary 1944. See "Task Forces-Military-SWPA-Composition," B6121/3 297, NAA.

16. "Offensive and Defensive Possibilities, SWPA," RG 407, 98-GHQ1-3.2, Journals and Files, box 556, 5–15 April 1942, NARA.

17. "Operation Providence, GHQ SWPA, 15 July 1942," D767.95.P76 1942a, USAHEC.

18. See Lavarack Diary, August–November 1942, and Lodge, *Lavarack*, 232–234.

19. Sydney F. Rowell, *Full Circle* (Melbourne: Melbourne University Press, 1974), 127–131.

20. Kevin C. Holzimmer, "On the Offensive: US Operations in the Southwest Pacific Area and South Pacific Area in 1943," in Dean, *Australia 1943*, 100.

21. See Dean, "Grinding Out a Victory," 164–187.

22. Taaffe, *Marshall and His Generals*, 31–33.

23. Barbey, *MacArthur's Amphibious Navy*, 27.

24. Taaffe, *Marshall and His Generals*, 34.

25. The 2nd ESB would become part of Barbey's VII Phib in the first half of 1943, bringing all of the amphibious force assets together.

26. James, *Years of MacArthur*, vol. 2, 312–313; see also Morton, *Strategy and Command*, 407.

27. Walter Krueger, *From Down Under to Nippon: The Story of Sixth Army in World War II* (Washington, DC: Combat Forces Press, 1953), 10; Charles A. Willoughby, *MacArthur, 1941–51* (New York: McGraw-Hill, 1954), 124.

28. Gavin Long, *The Final Campaigns*, vol. 7, *Australia in the War of 1939–1945* (Canberra: AWM, 1963), 599.

29. David Dexter, *The New Guinea Offensives* (Canberra: AWM, 1961), 221.

30. Ibid.

31. Horner, *Blamey*, 390.

32. Ibid.

33. Ibid., 391.

34. Morison, *Breaking the Bismarcks Barrier*, 89.

35. "Operational Plan No. 2–43, HQ Allied Naval Forces, 7 April 1943," RG 407, 98-GHQ1-3.2, G-3 Journals and Files, box 583, April 1943, NARA; Ian Pfennigwerth, "The Naval Perspective: The RAN in 1943," in Dean, *Australia 1943*, 144.

36. "South West Pacific Sea Frontiers: Establishment, Organization and Administration," B6121 296B, NAA. It was originally called the Southwest Sea Frontiers Command on 4 March 1943 but soon was changed to Southwest Pacific Sea Frontiers (SWPSF).

37. "Establishment of South West Pacific Sea Frontiers Command, Signal Order Serial 0353, CANF SWPA, 16 March 1943," RG 407, 98-GHQ1-3.2, G-3 Journals and Files, box 582, 4–17 March 1943, NARA.

38. For details of the NOIC areas of responsibility and command reporting, see "Australian Naval Administration and Operational Commands throughout the war," AWM69 23/46, "Official History, 1939–45 War: Records of G Hermon Gill," March 1949, AWM.

39. David Stevens, "South-West Sea Frontiers: Seapower in the Australian Context," in Stevens, *Royal Australian Navy in World War II*, 95.

40. David Stevens, "The Naval Campaigns for New Guinea," *Journal of the Australian War Memorial* 34, no. 1 (2001), https://www.awm.gov.au/journal/j34/stevens.asp.

41. Pfennigwerth, "Naval Perspective," 144.

42. Stevens, "South-West Sea Frontiers," 98.

43. George Odgers, *Air War against Japan 1943–1945*, series 3, vol. 2, *Australia in the War of 1939–1945* (Canberra: AWM, 1957), 16.

44. "Chief of Air Staff RAAF to C-in-C SWPA, Organisation of the RAAF, GHQ SWPA," RG 407, 98-GHQ1-3.2 G-3 Journals and Files, box 582, March 1943, NARA.

45. Ibid.

46. "Bostock to MacArthur, 25 March 1943, GHQ SWPA," RG 407, 98-GHQ1-3.2, G-3 Journals and Files, box 582, March 1943, NARA.

47. Odgers, *Air War against Japan*, 16.

48. "MacArthur to Jones, 25 March 1943, GHQ SWPA," RG 407, 98-GHQ1-3.2, G-3 Journals and Files, box 582, March 1943, NARA.

49. Alan Stephens, *The Royal Australian Air Force: A History* (Melbourne: Oxford University Press, 2006), 152.

50. Kenney, *General Kenney Reports*, 80; Griffith, *MacArthur's Airman*, 61–62.

51. No. 9 Operational Group would take over the air defense of the New Guinea area, with No. 10 Operational Group fulfilling the expeditionary role with the Fifth Air Force. No. 10 would evolve into the First Tactical Air Force, RAAF.

52. Miller, *Cartwheel*, 195.

53. Griffith, *MacArthur's Airman*, 98–99.

54. Drea, *MacArthur's UTLRA*, 68; Griffith, *MacArthur's Airman*, 105.

55. Advance Echelon Fifth Air Force was based on New Guinea under Whitehead's command. This included No. 9 Operational Group, RAAF. Other elements of the Fifth Air Force remained based in northern Australia throughout this time.

56. Mark Johnston, "Perspiration, Inspiration, Frustration: The RAAF in New Guinea in 1943," in Dean, *Australia 1943*, 125.

57. Stephens, *Royal Australian Air Force*, 163–164.

58. Griffith, *MacArthur's Airman*, 107.

59. Johnston, "Perspiration, Inspiration, Frustration," 128.

60. Kenney, *General Kenney Reports*, 205–206.

61. Griffith, *MacArthur's Airman*, 109–110.

CHAPTER 9. WORKING TOGETHER FOR A COMMON PURPOSE: THE DEVELOPMENT OF AMPHIBIOUS WARFARE IN THE SWPA, 1942–1945

1. Peter J. Dean, "The Raid on Goodenough Island: Australia's First Amphibious Operation in the Second World War," *Australian Naval Review* 1, no. 1 (2016).

2. "Operational Order (OO) No. 1, 21 October 1942, 2/12th Infantry Battalion," War Diary, 2/12th Battalion, AWM52 8/3/12/9, October–December 1942, AWM. According to the war diary, the task of the battalion was to "destroy all the Japs on Goodenough Island." This order is similar to that issued by Milne Bay Force, but it leaves out two important roles for Drake Force ordered by NGF—namely, "to determine the practicability of channels and approaches to Goodenough Island for supply purposes" and "to determine the practicability of the terrain for the constn [construction] of air fields." See "NG Force Op Instn No. 39, 17 October 1942," War Diary, New Guinea Force, AWM52 1/5/51/19, October 1942, AWM.

3. "Operations Goodenough Island 22–26 October 1942: Lessons from Operations—No. 4," RG 407, 98 GHQ1-3.2, G-3 Journals and Files, November 1942, box 604, NARA.

4. "War Diary, 2/12th Battalion, October–December 1942," AWM52 8/3/12, AWM. The battalion was notified of the mission on 19 October, an air reconnaissance by the CO and Maj. K. A. I. Gategood was undertaken on 20 October, planning was undertaken on 21 October, and the mission was launched on 22 October.

5. McCarthy, *South-West Pacific Area*, 347.

6. Gill, *Royal Australian Navy*, 182.

7. "Report on New Guinea Operations: Milne Bay and Goodenough Island 22 October–26 October 1942," AWM54 581/7/35, AWM.

8. The Australian troops on the Kokoda Trail had faced a heavily dug-in Japanese position at Templeton's Crossing just before the landing on Goodenough Island.

9. "Operations Goodenough Island 22–26 October 1942."

10. Ibid.

11. McCarthy, *South-West Pacific Area*, 349.

12. "Operations Goodenough Island 22–26 October 1942."

13. See Peter J. Dean, "The Alliance, Australia's Strategic Culture and Way of War," in *Australia's American Alliance: Towards a New Era?*, ed. Peter J. Dean, Stephan Frühling, and Brendan Taylor (Melbourne: Melbourne University Press, 2016), 224–250.

14. Grey, *Military History of Australia*, 5.

15. Richard Frank, *MacArthur: A Biography*, Great Generals Series (New York: Palgrave Macmillan, 2007), 72.

16. Ibid.

17. Barbey, *MacArthur's Amphibious Navy*, chaps. 1 and 2.

18. There is a lack of clarity on this issue, with some reports stating that at the end of the war the balance sheet was slightly in the US favor. One of the key issues in 1945 was the US use of Australian war matériel and complaints from Blamey that the US forces were being favored over his own and that MacArthur's forces were not making full use of their Australian supplies. See S. J. Butlin and C. B. Schedvin, *War Economy 1942–1945*, *Australia in the War of 1939–1945*, series 4, vol. 4 (Canberra: AWM) 469–471.

19. Frank, *MacArthur*, 71, 66.

20. "Combined Training for Amphibious Operations," GHQ Memo, June 1942, "Combined Training for Offensive Operations, MacArthur to Blamey, 4 June 1942," RG 496, G-3 General Correspondence 1942–45, box 667, JOOTS folder, NARA.

21. "Stephen Chamberlin to Colonel B. Q. Jones, 6 September 1942," RG 496, G-3 General Correspondence 1942–1945, box 667, JOOTS folder, NARA.

22. Admiral Barbey would note on arrival in the SWPA that *Henry T. Allen* was in such poor shape and in need of a major overhaul that it could not be used on operations.

23. Ross Mallett, "Together Again for the First Time: The Army, the RAN and Amphibious Warfare," in *Sea Power Ashore and in the Air*, ed. David Stephens and John Reeve (Ultimo, NSW: Halstead Press, 2007), 119.

24. "Memo on Engineer Amphibious Units, Office of Chief Engineer SWPA to C-in-C SWPA, 17 November 1942, Military Theaters of Operations," SWPA E-117 to E-134, X-90, US Army Corps of Engineers Historical Division.

25. Mallett, "Together Again for the First Time," 120–122.

26. The author has published numerous articles on amphibious operations in the SWPA. For greater detail, see Peter J. Dean, "Amphibious Warfare: Lessons from the Past for the ADF's Future," *Security Challenges* 8, no. 1 (Autumn 2012): 57–76; Peter J. Dean, "Divergence and Convergence: Army vs Navy; Allied Conduct of the Pacific War," in *Armies and Maritime Strategy*, ed. Peter Dennis (Newport, NSW: Big Sky Publishing, 2014), 167–201; Peter J. Dean and Rhys Crawley, "Amphibious Warfare: Training and Logistics 1942–1945," in *Australia 1944–45: Victory in the Pacific*, ed. Peter J. Dean (Melbourne: Cambridge University Press, 2016), 257–277; and Peter J. Dean, "To the Jungle Shore: Australia and Amphibious Warfare in the SWPA 1942–1945," *Global War Studies* 11, no. 2 (2014): 64–94.

27. "Long Range Planning for offensive Action—Landing operations, 13 March 1942," B6121 289, NAA. See also Mallett, "Together Again for the First Time." In the British, and thus Australian, military, amphibious landings were referred to as "combined" operations, as opposed to the US terminology of "joint" operations.

28. Frederick Norton Cook, RAN Personal Record, A3978, Cook FN, NAA.

29. Ibid. and "A Summary of Combined operations Training in Australia (Amphibious) 1942–1945," AWM54 943/16/1, AWM; "Record of Commander Fredrick Norton Cook," PR00631, Papers of HMAS *Assault*, AWM.

30. "Combined Training for Offensive Operations, MacArthur to Blamey, 4 June 1942," RG 496, G-3 General Correspondence 1942–45, box 667, JOOTS folder, NARA.

31. "Amphibious Training, GHQ, 19 November 1942," RG 496, Records of GHQ SWPA, G-3 General Correspondence 1942–45, box 667, NARA.

32. "Joint Overseas Operational Training School, 9 August 1942," RG 496, Records of GHQ SWPA, G-3 General Correspondence 1942–45, box 667, NARA.

33. "A Summary of Combined Operations Training in Australia (Amphibious) 1942–1945," AWM54 943/16/1, 2, AWM.

34. "Australian Naval Administration and Operational Command Throughout the War," AWM69 23/46, AWM; "Landenberger to Barbey, 26 April 1962," Barbey Papers, correspondence box 2.

35. "Combined Operations Training," First Australian Army HQ, 1 July 1942, Training Equipment—Combined Operations Training Toorbol Bribie Island, MP729/6 39/401/281, NAA.

36. "Conference Notes, Report of recce, of Port Stephens Area, GHQ, 17 July 1942," RG 496, G-3 General Correspondence 1942–45, box 667, JOOTS folder, NARA.

37. GHQ Directive, "Joint Overseas Operational Training School, 9 August 1942," RG 496, G-3 General Correspondence 1942–45, box 667, JOOTS folder, NARA.

38. "Training in Combined Ops, DCGS [Major General F. H. Berryman] to First Australian Army, 26 September 1942," MP508/1, 323/701/804, NAA.

39. "Colonel Bird S. Dubois to Colonel Stephen Chamberlin, 30 September 1942," Chamberlin Papers, box 1, folder 1942, USAHEC.

40. See Byron Q. Jones, https://en.wikipedia.org/wiki/Byron_Q._Jones, accessed 23 March 2016.

41. "Colonel Bird S. Dubois to Colonel Stephen Chamberlin, 30 September 1942," Chamberlin Papers, box 1, folder 1942, USAHEC. Dubois is not a completely independent source, having worked at JOOTS as an instructor and being equal rank to Jones and also close to him. Dubois was relieved of his post on 30 September and returned to the United States for reassignment.

42. Donald F. Bittner, "Britannia's Sheathed Sword: The Royal Marines and Amphibious Warfare in the Interwar Years—A Passive Response," *Journal of Military History* 55, no. 3 (July 1991): 359.

43. "Colonel Bird S. Dubois to Colonel Stephen Chamberlin, 30 September 1942," Chamberlin Papers, box 1, folder 1942, USAHEC.

44. Walker as quoted in Russell Parkin, *A Capability of First Resort: Amphibious Operations and Australian Defence Policy 1901–2001* (Canberra: Land Warfare Studies Centre, 2002), 20.

45. "Colonel Stephen Chamberlin to Colonel B. Q. Jones, 17 September 1942," Chamberlin Papers, box 1, folder 1942, USAHEC.

46. "Berryman to Blamey, 'Amphibian Training,' 22 September 1942," PR84/370, Berryman Papers, item 11, AWM.

47. "Special Orders No. 146, GHQ SWPA, 25 September 1942," RG 496, Records of GHQ, G-3 General Correspondence 1942–1945, box 662, NARA; Berryman Diary, 26 September 2942, PR84/370, AWM.

48. "Chamberlin to Sutherland, 3 January 1943," RG 496, Records of GHQ, Amphibious Training 1942–1943, 290/46/12/6, box 667, NARA.

49. Van Volkenburgh interview, 26 August 1972, D. Clayton James collection, DMMA.

50. "War diary 19th battalion, September–December 1942," AMF, AWM52 8/3/58/3, AWM.

51. Barbey, *MacArthur's Amphibious Navy*, 35.

52. "A Summary of Combined Operations Training in Australia 1942–45," AWM52 943/16/1, 5–7, AWM.

53. "Jamison to Barbey, 4 March 1960 and 31 August 1962," Barbey Papers, correspondence box 2.

54. "Memo No. 12, Commandant JOOTS, 18 November 1942," War Diary, 19th Battalion AMF, AWM52 8/3/58/3, September–December 1942, AWM. The officer in question was Lt. Cdr. J. N. Lancaster (RAN).

55. "Joint Overseas Operational Training School, Memo Sutherland to Blamey, 15 October 1942," RG 200, Papers of General Sutherland, GHQ SWPA, Correspondence with Allied Forces 1942–45, NARA.

56. Naval Forces SWPA were renamed the Seventh Fleet on 15 March 1943, although as Samuel Eliot Morison notes, the fleet was rather "impoverished" and "numbered in the tens rather than thousands." Morison, *Breaking the Bismarcks Barrier*, 130.

57. Ibid., 131.

58. "Colonel Arthur G. Trudeau to Major-General H. J. Casey, Chief engineer, SWPA, 21 December 1942," Personal Papers of H. J. Casey, folders 22–28, SWPA, Personnel File 1942, US Army Corps of Engineers Historical Division.

59. Frank, *MacArthur: A Biography*, 72.

60. The 2nd ESB would eventually be brought under Barbey's command in late May 1943.

61. Van Volkenburgh interview, 26 August 1972.

62. "Training of Australian Amphibious Force, Chief of the General Staff, 11 January 1943," RG 496, box 667, "Amphibious Training Oct 1942–Oct 31 1943," NARA.

63. "MacArthur to Admiral Guy Royal, Chief of Naval Staff RAN, 9 February 1943"; "Amphibious training, C-in-C SWPA 8 February 1943"; "Chamberlin to Sutherland, 13 February 1943"; and "MacArthur to Blamey, 20 February 1943," RG 496, box 667, "Amphibious Training Oct 1942–Oct 31 1943," NARA.

64. "Hopkins, Ronald Nicholas Lamond (1897–1990)," ADB Online, http://adb.anu.edu.au/biography/hopkins-ronald-nicholas-lamond-12655.

65. "Notes from Conference, GHQ, 18 January 1943," RG 496, box 667, "Amphibious Training Oct 1942–Oct 31 1943," NARA; Combined Operations: RAN Beach Commandos, B6121,194B, 2, NAA.

66. "Command History: 7th Amphibious Force," http://www.ibiblio.org/hyperwar/USN/Admin-Hist/OA/419-7thAmphib/7thAmphibs-2.html, ii-11.

67. "Landenberger to Barbey, 26 April 1962," Barbey Papers, correspondence box 2.

68. Ibid.

69. "Notes from Conference, GHQ, 18 January 1943," RG 496, box 667, "Amphibious Training Oct 1942–Oct 31 1943," NARA.

70. Barbey, *MacArthur's Amphibious Navy*, 34–42.

71. Ibid.

72. CNO Adm. H. R. Stark (USN), foreword to USN FTP 167, *Landing Operations Doctrine*, http://www.ibiblio.org/hyperwar/USN/ref/Amphibious/index.html.

73. See Joseph H. Alexander, "Across the Reef: Amphibious Warfare in the Pacific," in *The Pacific War Companion: From Pearl Harbor to Hiroshima*, ed. Daniel Marston (Oxford: Osprey, 2005), 203.

74. See Edward J. Drea, "Collision Course: American and Japanese Amphibious/Counter-Amphibious Doctrine, Tactics and Preparation for the Decisive Battle of the Homeland," in *1945: War and Peace in the Pacific; Selected Essays*, ed. Peter Dennis (Canberra: AWM, 1999), 22–37; Alexander, "Across the Reef."

75. Morison, *Breaking the Bismarcks Barrier*, 27.

76. David Horner, "General MacArthur's War: The South and Southwest Pacific Campaigns 1942–1945," in Marston, *Pacific War Companion*, 128.

77. Archer Jones, *Elements of Military Strategy: An Historical Approach* (Westport, CT: Praeger, 1996), 121.

78. Barbey, *MacArthur's Amphibious Navy*, 48–49.

79. "Commander Seventh Amphibious Force to C-in-C SWPA, 31 August 1943," RG 496, box 667, "Amphibious Training Oct 1942-Oct 31 1943," NARA. GHQ issued the order for its adoption on 4 September 1943, and it was put into circulation after amendments on 14 October 1943.

80. "Jamison to Barbey, December 1960," Barbey Papers, correspondence box 2.

81. "Amphibian Training, C-in-C SWPA, 4 December 1942," RG 496, box 667, NARA.

82. "Combined (Operations) Training Centre, Toorbul Point: 7th Amphibious Training Centre and 1st Water Transport Training Centre," Queensland Historic World War II Places, Queensland Government, http://www.ww2places.qld.gov.au/places/?id=1373, accessed 26 March 2016. For an assessment of the facility at the time, see "Training Equipment: Combined Operations Training Toorbol Bribie Island."

83. Command history, 7th Amphibious Force, http://www.ibiblio.org/hyperwar/USN/Admin-Hist/OA/419–7thAmphib/7thAmphibs-2.html, accessed 26 March 2016.

84. "Jamison to Barbey, 14 November 1961," Barbey Papers, correspondence box 2.

85. "Landenberger to Barbey, 24 January 1961," Barbey Papers, correspondence box 3.

86. "Royce N. Flippin to Daniel Barbey," n.d., Barbey Papers, correspondence box 1.

87. "Wemyss to Barbey, 23 March 1961," Barbey Papers, correspondence box 4.

88. "Wemyss to Barbey, 12 January 1962," ibid.

89. "Swan to Barbey, 26 April 1961," ibid.

90. "Swan to Barbey, 25 July 1962," ibid.

91. Ronald Penglase interview, no. 1727, Australians at War Film Archive.

92. Arthur Le Page interview, no. 1672, ibid.
93. Bryan Wearne interview, no. 2148, ibid.
94. Ibid.

CHAPTER 10. VICTORY AND DISCORD: THE BATTLE FOR SALAMAUA

1. "Report on Wau-Salamaua Operation, 17th Brigade AIF, 3rd Australian Division," AWM54 587/7/34, AWM.
2. Horner, *Blamey*, 409.
3. "War Diary, First Australian Army, March 1943," AWM52 1/3/2, AWM.
4. Gavin Keating, *The Right Man for the Right Job: Lieutenant General Sir Stanley Savige as a Military Commander* (Melbourne: Oxford University Press, 2005), 93–96.
5. "Interview with General Herring, 6 April 1951," AWM67 1/5, item 13, AWM.
6. "Berryman to Herring, Future Operations—New Guinea, 17 May 1943," in "Planning 'Postern' Reference Advanced LHQ, letter to GOC New Guinea Force, Initial inquiries 'G' factors influencing replies and sequence planning," AWM54 589/3/7, AWM.
7. See "Berryman Notes on I Aust Corps Report on Operations in New Guinea, 22 March 1944, 1st Australian Corps Report on Operation, New Guinea," AWM54 589/7/1, AWM.
8. "Elkton Plan—Deception and Cover Plans, DCGS [Berryman] Adv LHQ, 11 May 1943," Operation Cartwheel – Correspondence – Messages and Plan, AWM54 389/3/10, AWM. At this stage, the assault on Lae was being planned for July and August but was eventually delayed until the beginning of September.
9. "Future Operations—New Guinea 1943, Operational Instruction, Adv LHQ, 17 May 1943," AWM 54 589/4/8, AWM.
10. Horner, *Blamey*, 413.
11. Barbey, *MacArthur's Amphibious Navy*, 68.
12. Morison, *Breaking the Bismarcks Barrier*, 134.
13. Barbey, *MacArthur's Amphibious Navy*, 67–69; Morison, *Breaking the Bismarcks Barrier*, 134–135.
14. "Field Order No. 2, 162nd Regiment, 26 June 1943, Operational Reports Morobe-Salamaua 162nd Regiment," RG 407, 41st Infantry Division, 341-INF (162)—0.3, NARA (hereafter "162nd Infantry Regiment: Report on Operations–Salamaua").
15. Issue of command would soon become very important. This command arrangement is confirmed in Field Order No.2 "162nd Infantry Regiment: Report on Operations–Salamaua" and "War Diary 17th Infantry Brigade, 15 June 1943," AWM52 8/2/17, June 1943 AWM. The date 15 June was when Moten outlined his plan at the conference at the Summit.
16. See "Interview with Brig Moten, 11 April 1952," AWM67 1/5, item 13, AWM, and Keating, *Right Man for the Job*, 107–108.

17. "Berryman to Dexter, 2 February 1954," Berryman Papers, PR84/370, item 3, AWM.
18. "Report on Wau-Salamaua Operations, 1943, 17th Australian Infantry Brigade," AWM54 587/7/34, AWM.
19. "Information Requested in Radiogram CX 17495," RG 407, WWII Operational Reports, 41st Infantry Division, 341–0 41st Division History, NARA.
20. "Unit History, HQ 41st Infantry Division," RG 407, 41st Infantry Division, 341–0.1, 41st Division History, July 17–17 June 1945, NARA.
21. David Dexter, *The New Guinea Offensives* (Canberra: AWM, 1961), 84.
22. See "Staff Journal Morobe—Salamaua Campaign, 162nd Regiment," RG 407, 41st Infantry Division, 341-INF (162)—0.7, and "162nd Infantry Regiment: Report on Operations–Salamaua."
23. "Memo to General Handy: Notes on Campaign 162d Infantry," 41st Division in New Guinea, RG 407, 41st Infantry Division, 341-INF (162)—0.3 Operational Reports Morobe-Salamaua, NARA.
24. "Notes on Campaign 162d Infantry in New Guinea by Colonel A. R. Mac-Kechnie," Savige Papers, 3 DRL 2529, item 36, AWM.
25. Taaffe, *MacArthur's Jungle War*, 82.
26. "Edmund Herring to Mary Herring, 19 July 1943," Herring Papers, box 46, SLV.
27. "Fuller to Herring, 27 July 1943," Herring Papers, box 11, SLV.
28. "Lieutenant-General Stanley Savige, Comments on Official History," AWM67 3/349, part 4, AWM.
29. Taaffe, *Marshall and His Generals*, 135–137.
30. For example, see Berryman Diary, 17 August 1943.
31. 41st Infantry Division Commanders, 41st Infantry Division website, http://jungleer.com/sunset-division/19-sunset-division/24–41st-infantry-division-commanders, accessed 20 December 2016.
32. See David Horner, "Staff Corps versus Militia: The Australian Experience in World War II," *Defence Force Journal*, no. 26 (January/February 1981), and Dean, *Architect of Victory*, especially chaps. 3–7.
33. "Berryman, Notes on the Official History," n.d., BFP.
34. "Interview with Major-General Alan Ramsay, 17 December 1952," AWM172, item 13, AWM.
35. Gavin Keating, "Savige, Sir Stanley George (1890–1954)," *Australian Dictionary of Biography*, http://adb.anu.edu.au/biography/savige-sir-stanley-george-11617, accessed 20 December 2016.
36. See Braga, *Kokoda Commander*, 262.
37. Savige interview by David Dexter, AWM172, item 13, AWM.
38. Official war historian working notes, source material, "Volume VI Army" (interviews with commanding officers), AWM67 1/5, item 13, AWM.
39. "Berryman to Dexter, 2 February 1954," AWM93, 50/2/23/331, AWM.
40. "Interview with Brig Moten, 11 April 1952," AWM67, 1/5, item 13, AWM.
41. William F. Heavey, *Down Ramp! The Story of the Army Amphibian Engineers* (Washington, DC: Infantry Journal Press, 1947), 84–86.

42. "Report on Operations—New Guinea: Wau-Salamaua, by 17th Australian Infantry Brigade," AWM54, 587/7/34, AWM.

43. "162nd Infantry Regiment: Report on Operations–Salamaua."

44. Dexter, *New Guinea Offensives*, 96.

45. "162nd Infantry Regiment: Report on Operations–Salamaua."

46. "Report on Operations—New Guinea: Wau-Salamaua."

47. William F. McCartney, *The Jungleers: A History of the 41st Infantry Division* (Nashville, TN: Battery Press, 1988), 55; "162nd Infantry Regiment: Report on Operations–Salamaua."

48. Dexter, *New Guinea Offensives*, 96.

49. "Notes on Campaign 162d Infantry in New Guinea by Colonel A. R. MacKechnie," Savige Papers, 3 DRL 2529, item 36, AWM.

50. Phillip Bradley, *To Salamaua* (Melbourne: Cambridge University Press, 2010), 172.

51. "War Diary, 3rd Australian Division, July 1943," AWM52 1/5/4/055, AWM.

52. Dexter, *New Guinea Offensives*, 102.

53. For details on the communications issues, see "Report on Operations of 17th Brigade, Mubo—Salamaua Area," appendix 11, 5, AWM52 8/2/17/89, AWM. The report notes that "complaints of this nature did however become less noticeable later and the co-operation rendered by the Signal Officer 1 Bn 162 US Regt is worthy of high praise."

54. Bradley, *To Salamaua*, 173.

55. David Hay, *Nothing over Us: The Story of the 2/6th Australian Infantry Battalion* (Canberra: AWM, 1984), 324.

56. "Report on Visit to MacForce by Captain CBN Rolfe," Savige Papers, 3DRL/2529, item 52, AWM.

57. Dexter, *New Guinea Offensives*, 98–104.

58. "15th Brigade to 3rd Division, 6 July," Savige Papers, 3DRL/2529, item 52, AWM.

59. Garth Pratten, *Australian Battalion Commanders in the Second World War* (Cambridge: Cambridge University Press, 2009), 222–223.

60. Keating, *Right Man*, 107.

61. Dexter, *New Guinea Offensives*, 104.

62. "Notes of Interview with General Herring, 6 April 1952," AWM67 1/5, item 13, AWM.

63. "Message Savige to Moten, 6 July," Savige Papers, 3DRL/2529, item 52, AWM.

64. McCartney, *Jungleers*, 61.

65. "Letter of Instruction to Brigadier-General Ralph Coane, 41st Division HQ, 11 July 1943," Savige Papers, 3 DRL 2529, item 51, AWM.

66. Dexter, *New Guinea Offensives*, 139.

67. "Roosevelt to 3rd Division, 14 July 1943," Savige Papers, 3 DRL 2529, item 51, AWM.

68. "Savige to Herring, 15 July 1943," Savige Papers, 3 DRL 2529, item 51, AWM.

69. "3rd Division to Brig Coane, 17 Bde, Mackforce, 41st Div, 15 July 1943," Savige Papers, 3 DRL 2529, item 51, AWM.

70. Horner, *High Command*, 293.

71. "MacKechnie to Moten, 24 July 1943," Savige Papers, 3 DRL 2529, item 51, AWM.

72. "Moten interview with Dexter," n.d., AWM67, 1/5, item 13, AWM.

73. "162nd Infantry Regiment: Report on Operations–Salamaua," 16–17; McCartney, *Jungleers*, 61.

74. Bradley, *To Salamaua*, 234.

75. "162nd Infantry Regiment: Report on Operations–Salamaua," chap. 6.

76. Bradley, *To Salamaua*, 231.

77. Roosevelt, as quoted in Horner, *High Command*, 293.

78. "Major Mike A. Trapman to Horace Fuller, 7 August 1943, Informal Report, Historical 10 June 1943–13 September 1943," RG 407, 41st Infantry Division—Miscellaneous Historical Info, 341–0.20, box 9003, NARA.

79. "Moten interview with David Dexter," n.d., AWM 67, 1/5, item 13, AWM.

80. Roosevelt to MacArthur, quoted in Horner, *High Command*, 294.

81. Fertig to Roosevelt, ibid., 294.

82. "Interview with Savige, 3 February 1945," Records of Gavin Long, AWM69, AWM.

83. "Savige, Comments on Official History," AWM67, 3/348, part 4, AWM.

84. "NGF to GHQ Cable No. B106 10," Herring Papers, box 11, SLV.

85. "Herring to D. Clayton James, 22 May 1972," Herring Papers, box 37, SLV.

86. McCartney, *Jungleers*, 57.

87. "162nd Infantry Regiment: Report on Operations–Salamaua," chap. 6; Bradley, *To Salamaua*, 246–248.

88. "Notes of Interview with General Herring, 6 April 1952," AWM67, 1/5, item 13, AWM.

89. "Blamey to Herring, 15 June 1943," Blamey Papers, 3DRL/6643, series 2, wallet 135, AWM.

90. "Herring to Blamey, 18 June 1943," ibid.

91. "Conference Notes—Cartwheel, Postern planning, May–July 1943, 22 July 1943," AWM54 213/3/20, AWM; Berryman Diary, 22 July 1943.

92. See "Herring to Blamey, 6 July 1943," 3DRL/6643, series 2, wallet 135, AWM; "Conference Notes, NGF HQ, 22 August 1942," AWM54 589/3/7, AWM; and Kenney, *General Kenney Reports*, 257.

93. "Herring to Blamey, 6 July 1943," 3DRL/6643, series 2, wallet 135, AWM. Herring notes in this letter MacArthur's visit and his insistence that the 162nd Regiment was provided to take Salamaua as quickly as possible but also notes that he reminded MacArthur of Blamey's original plan.

94. "Blamey to Herring, 30 July 1943," ibid.

95. Berryman Diary, 4 August 1943.

96. Berryman Diary, July–August 1943.

97. Berryman Diary, 15–16 August 1943.

98. Daley as quoted in Keating, *Right Man*, 123.

99. Moten, interview with David Dexter, 11 April 1951, in "Notes on Strategy, Volume VI," AWM172, item 13, AWM.

100. Ibid.

101. Berryman Diary, 18 August 1943 (emphasis in original).

102. Berryman Diary, 19 August 1943.

103. "Frank to Muriel Berryman, 25 August 1943," BFP.

104. Berryman Diary, 19 August 1943.

105. Moten, interview with David Dexter, 11 April 1951.

106. Ibid.

107. Savige as quoted in Horner, *Strategic Command*, 111.

108. "Blamey, signal to MacArthur, 22 August 1943," Berryman Papers, item 11.

109. Berryman to Drake-Brockman, 9 April 1945, Berryman Papers; Moten, interview with David Dexter, 11 April 1951.

110. Keating, *Right Man*, 94.

111. Dexter, Milford interview, "Notes on Strategy, Volume VI," AWM172, item 13, AWM.

112. Wilton, interview with David Dexter, 25 May 1951, ibid.

113. Keating, *Right Man*, 132.

114. Berryman Diary, 4 September 1943.

115. Dexter, *New Guinea Offensives*, 105.

116. "Report of Captain Sturrock, Australian Liaison Officer, Coane Force," Savige Papers, 3DRL/2529, item 51, AWM. Berryman complained that even in mid-August, the 1/162nd tended to bunch together and remain too far in the rear. See Berryman Diary, 17 August 1943.

117. Dexter, *New Guinea Offensives*, 102.

118. Hay, *Nothing over Us*, 323. Syd Trigellis-Smith, *All the King's Enemies: A History of the 2/5 Australian Infantry Battalion* (Loftus, NSW: Australian Military History Publications, 2010), 236.

119. Moten interview, AWM67, 1/5, item 13, AWM.

120. Ibid.

121. Ibid.

122. Dexter, *New Guinea Offensives*, 102.

123. "Précis of telephone conversation GOC [3rd Division] with Brigadier Moten, 23 July 1943, War Diary 3rd Australian Division," part 2, miscellaneous appendixes, AWM52, 1/5/4/12, AWM.

124. "Notes on Campaign 162d Infantry in New Guinea by Colonel A. R. MacKechnie," Savige Papers, 3DRL 2529, item 36, AWM.

125. Dexter, *New Guinea Offensives*, 159.

126. "Letter from Adv HQ 5th Australian Division, 30 August 1943," Blamey Papers, 3DRL/6643, series 2, wallet 135, AWM.

127. "162nd Infantry Regiment: Report on Operations—Salamaua."

128. McCartney, *Jungleers*, 51.

129. "162nd Infantry Regiment: Report on Operations–Salamaua."

130. Bradley, *To Salamaua*, 248.

131. Berryman Diary, 17 August 1943.

132. Dexter, *New Guinea Offensives*, 159.

133. "Précis of telephone conversation GOC [3rd Division] with Brigadier Moten, 28 July 1943."

134. Bradley, *To Salamaua*, 248.

135. Trigellis-Smith, *All the King's Enemies*, 136.

136. "Milford to Jackson, 18 September 1943, Unit History, HQ & HQ Bty, 41st Division Artillery, 23 April to 4 October 1943," RG 407, WWII Operation Reports, 41st Infantry Division, 341-ART-0.3, box 9044, NARA. See also notes in this file on Savige's praise of the US artillery.

137. "Major Mike A. Trapman to Horace Fuller, 11 August 1943, Informal Report, Historical 10 June 1943–13 September 1943," RG 407, 41st Infantry Division—Miscellaneous Historical Info, 341-0.20, NARA.

138. "Artillery Notes on Salamaua Campaign, October 1943, HQ RAA, 11th Australian Division, War Diary, 3rd Australian Division," part 4, appendixes, AWM52, 1/5/4/19, AWM.

139. "Major Mike A. Trapman to Horace Fuller, 11 August 1943, Informal Report, Historical 10 June 1943–13 September 1943," RG 407, 41st Infantry Division—Miscellaneous Historical Info, 341-0.20, NARA.

140. "162nd Infantry Regiment: Report on Operations–Salamaua."

141. Horner, *High Command*, 294.

142. MacArthur, *Reminiscences* , 193–193.

143. Berryman Diary, 12 August 1943.

144. "Edmund Herring to Mary Herring, 19 July 1943," Herring Papers, box 46.

145. "Edmund Herring to Mary Herring, 4 July 1943," ibid.

146. "Interview with General Milford, 25 May 1951," AWM172, item 13, AWM.

CHAPTER 11. OPERATION POSTERN: PLANNING AND AIRPOWER

1. Many would argue that the key theater was actually the CPA. However, it must be noted that the first of the large-scale offensive operations in this operational area, the assault on Tarawa, did not commence until 20 November 1943. The follow-on operation in the Marshall Islands did not commence until the end of January 1944, with the main operations against the Eniwetok Islands not occurring until 17 February 1944. Thus, throughout 1943, the major operations against the Japanese in the Pacific were undertaken in the SOPAC and the SWPA.

2. Horner, *Blamey*, 389–391.

3. "Berryman to Dexter, 17 September 1956," AWM93 50/2/23/331, AWM.

4. Frank, *MacArthur*, 68. For details on the development of the US Army in World War II and the problems it had with the selection and procurement of combat troops for infantry units, see Robert R. Palmer, *The Procurement and Training of Ground Combat Troops* (Washington, DC: Center for Military History, 1948).

5. See Eric Bergerud, *Touched with Fire: The Land War in the South Pacific* (New York: Viking, 1996), 200–225, and Frank, *MacArthur*, 68.

6. Kent Roberts Greenfield, Robert R. Palmer, and Bell I. Wiley, *The Organization of the Army Ground Forces* (Washington, DC: US Army Center of Military History, 1987), 336–337. See also table of organization, *History of the 1st Cavalry Division*, chap. 2, http://www.first-team.us/tableaux/chapt_02/.

7. Taaffe, *MacArthur's Jungle War*, 61.

8. Bergerud, *Touched with Fire*, 148–176.

9. "History of the 503rd Parachute Regiment," n.d., RG 407, 503rd PIR, INGR-503–01, box 17061, NARA.

10. For details, see US Army official history volumes Miller, *Cartwheel*, and Robert Ross Smith, *The Approach to the Philippines* (Washington, DC: Office of the Chief of Military History).

11. Mark Johnston, *That Magnificent 9th: An Illustrated History of the 9th Australian Division* (St. Leonard's, NSW: Allen & Unwin), 2002.

12. Blamey to Morshead, as quoted in Coates, *Bravery above Blunder*, 44–45.

13. Albert Palazzo, "Organising for Jungle Warfare," in *The Foundations of Victory: The Pacific War 1943–44*, ed. Peter Dennis and Jeffrey Grey (Canberra, AHU, Department of Defence, 2004), 183–186.

14. Albert Palazzo, *The Australian Army: A History of Its Organisation 1901–2001* (Melbourne: Oxford University Press, 2001), 175.

15. "Operation Cartwheel, BGS operations Adv LHQ 12 May 1943," "Operation Cartwheel—Correspondence—Messages and Plans," AWM54 389/3/10, AWM.

16. Berryman Diary, 16 May 1943.

17. "Operations:—6-7-9 Aust Divs, 7 May 1943," AWM54 389/3/10, AWM; "Points for submission to the C-in-C RE Cartwheel, 8 May 1943," AWM54 389/3/10, AWM.

18. "GHQ Warning Instruction 2, GHQ SWPA, 30 April 1943," Sutherland Papers, DMMA.

19. "Operations Cartwheel—Long Range Supply Plan," AWM54 389/3/10, AWM.

20. Horner, *Blamey*, 407.

21. A second model was constructed and eventually sent to Port Moresby for use by NGF and I Australian Corps in planning.

22. "Adv LHQ to GHQ, RE: Warning Instructions No. 2, 30 April 1943," AWM54 589/3/11, part 1, AWM.

23. Ross A. Mallett, "Logistics and the Cartwheel Operations," in Dean, *Australia 1943*, 168.

24. "Future Operations—New Guinea, 17 May 1943," AWM54 589/4/8, AWM.

25. Ibid.

26. Mallett, "Logistics and the Cartwheel Operations," 178.

27. "Berryman to Dexter, 17 September 1956," AWM93 50/2/23/331, AWM.

28. Jones, *Elements of Military Strategy*, 120–122.

29. Hiroyuki Shindo, "The Japanese Army's Search for a New South Pacific Strategy, 1943," in Dean, *Australia 1943*, 72–74.

30. "GHQ Warning Instruction 2 update, GHQ SWPA, 6 May 1943," RG 407, 98-GHQ1-3.2, G-3 Journals, box 586 May 1942, NARA.

31. "LHQ Operational Instruction, No. 46 Co-ordination of planning and operations between Navy, Army and Air Force, GHQ SWPA, 6 May 1943," RG 407, 98-GHQ1-3.2, G-3 Journals, box 586, May 1942, NARA (emphasis added).

32. "GHQ to Blamey, RE 2d Engineer Brigade, GHQ SWPA, 15 May 1943," ibid. (emphasis added).

33. See "Future operations—New Guinea—Report by DCGS, 11 June 1943," Memos and Orders—Cartwheel—April–September 1943, AWM54 589/3/11, AWM. See also Berryman Diary, May–August 1943.

34. "Agenda—Conference to co-ordinate CS and AQ Planning for Postern, 26 May 1943," Conference Notes, Cartwheel—Postern—Planning May–July 1943, AWM54 213/3/20, AWM.

35. "Conference between C-in-C ALF and Gen MacArthur, 21 May 1943," Conference Notes, Cartwheel—Postern—Planning May–July 1943, AWM54 213/3/20, AWM.

36. Berryman Diary, 21 May 1943.

37. "Chamberlin to Sutherland, RE Control of Operations of 2d Engineer Brigade, GHQ SWPA, 25 May 1943," RG 407, 98-GHQ1-3.2, G-3 Journals, box 586 May 1942, NARA.

38. "Discussion between DCGS and Gen Chamberlin G3 GHQ, 31 May 1943," Conference Notes, Cartwheel—Postern—Planning May–July 1943, AWM54 213/3/20, AWM; Berryman Diary, 31 May 1943.

39. "Cartwheel—Conference GHQ, 2 June 1943," Conference Notes, Cartwheel—Postern—Planning May–July 1943, AWM54 213/3/20, AWM.

40. Berryman Diary, 19–24 June 1943.

41. Berryman Diary, 23 June 1943; Horner, *General Vasey's War*, 257–259.

42. "Conference, Postern, HQ NGF, 25 July 1943," AWM54 589/3/7, AWM.

43. Miller, *Cartwheel*, 195.

44. Shindo, "Japanese Army's Search," 74.

45. See Kenney, *General Kenney Reports*, 253.

46. "Future operations—New Guinea—Report by DCGS, 11 June 1943," Memos and Orders—Cartwheel—April–September 1943, AWM54 589/3/11, AWM. See also Berryman Diary, 27 May 1943 and 12 June 1943.

47. Kenney, *General Kenney Reports*, 253–254.

48. Ibid., 271.

49. Griffith, *MacArthur's Airman*, 128–129.

50. "Seventh Amphibious Force Notes on Amphibious Operations No. 3 SWPA, Report on Postern Operation, 30 September 1943," AWM54 589/3/9, AWM.

51. The formal request for this to happen had occurred on 28 June 1943. See "DCGS to GHQ SWPA, Transfer of Equipment 41 US Div, 28 June 1943," AWM54 389/3/10, AWM.

52. Ross Mallett, "Australian Army Logistics 1943–45," PhD thesis, University of New South Wales (ADFA), 2007, 152.

53. "Notes on Amphibious Operations No. 3 SWPA, Report on Lae Operation, 30 September 1943," Action Reports, Seventh Amphibious Force—Lae, Salamaua, United States Naval History and Heritage Command.

54. "Chamberlin to Barbey, 13 July 1943," American Australian Amphibious Planning, Postern, July–August 1943, AWM54 589/3/9, AWM.
55. Berryman Diary, August 4, 1943, PR84/370, AWM.
56. Chamberlin as quoted in Horner, *High Command*, 295.
57. Berryman Diary, 4 August, 1943.
58. "Chamberlin, letter to Sutherland, RE Status of plans for Postern, August 5, 1943," AWM54 589/4/9, AWM.
59. Chamberlin to MacArthur, as quoted in Dexter, *New Guinea Offensives*, 281.
60. Blamey to MacArthur, 31 August 1943, Berryman Papers, item 11.
61. See Peter J. Dean, "From the Air, Sea and Land: The Capture of Lae," in Dean, *Australia 1943*.
62. "Notes on Amphibious Operations No. 3 SWPA, Report on Lae Operation, 30 September 1943."
63. "Commander Allied Land Forces, Report on New Guinea Operations 4 September 1943–26 April 1944," AWM54 519/6/58, AWM.
64. Berryman Diary, 23–24 August 1943.
65. "War Diary, I Australian Corps, 27 August 1943," AWM54 1/4/1/40, AWM.
66. Dexter, *New Guinea Offensives*, 230.

CHAPTER 12. THE LIBERATION OF NEW GUINEA

1. See Vincent O'Hara's introduction to Morison, *Breaking the Bismarcks Barrier*, 3.
2. "Intelligence Annex, Field Order No. 1, 503rd PIR, 3 September 1943," RG 407, INGR-503–3.9, NARA.
3. Dean, "From the Air, Sea and Land," in Dean, *Australia 1943*, 217.
4. Yoshihara, *Southern Cross*, 34
5. "War Diary, 7th Australian Division, September 1943," AWM52 1/5/14/49, AWM.
6. Ibid.
7. "War Diary, New Guinea Force HQ, September 1943," AWM52 1/5/51, AWM.
8. "Report on the Naval Aspects of the Lae Operation," AWM54 589/7/27, AWM; Dean, "To the Jungle Shore," 64–94; Mallett, "Together Again," 119.
9. "9th Australian Division, War Diary, September 1943," AWM52 1/5/20/37, AWM.
10. "Report on 503rd PIR in the Markham Valley 1943," RG 407, 503rd PIR, INGR-503–3.5m box 17075, NARA.
11. "2/33rd Battalion AIF, War Diary July—September 1943," AWM52 8/3/33/11, AWM.
12. Dean, *Architect of Victory*, 246–248.
13. Dean, "From the Air, Sea and Land," 229.

14. Berryman Diary, 4–5 September 1943.

15. "Admiral Carpenter Interview," B6121 3 R, NAA; Barbey, *MacArthur's Amphibious Navy*, 69–87.

16. Dexter, *New Guinea Offensives*, 392.

17. Milner, *Victory in Papua*, 367–368.

18. Brian Altobello, *Into the Shadows Furious: The Brutal Battle for New Georgia* (Novato, CA: Presidio, 2000), 354.

19. The town would become the major staging base for the Sixth US Army and an important USAAF airfield. See "Morshead to Blamey, 29 February 1944," Blamey Papers, 2/137; Miller, *Cartwheel*, 311.

20. "Blamey to MacArthur, 31 August 1943," Berryman Papers, item 37; Berryman Diary, 31 August 1943.

21. Berryman Diary, 1 September 1943.

22. "Conference for 'Dayton,' 3 September," Berryman Papers, item 37.

23. Ibid.

24. Horner, *Blamey*, 420.

25. "Operations Markham-Ramu and Vitiaz Strait Areas, GHQ G-3 conference, 14 September," RG 407, GHQ1–3.2, G-3 Journals, box 598 September 1943, NARA.

26. "I Australian Corps Report on Operations in New Guinea, 22 January–8 October 1943," AWM54 519/6/32, AWM.

27. "War Dairy, 7th Australian Division, August–December 1943, Combined Operations," AWM52 1/5/14/50, AWM.

28. Dexter, *New Guinea Offensives*, 417–419.

29. Lachlan Grant, "Operations in the Markham and Ramu Valleys," in Dean, *Australia 1943*, 233–254.

30. "Seventh Amphibious Force, United States Fleet, Report on operations, Finschhafen, 1943, AWM54 591/7/7 PART 1," and "War Diary, 9th Australian Division, September 1943," AWM52 1/5/20/37, AWM; Barbey, *MacArthur's Amphibious Navy*, 88–92.

31. "Finschhafen Operations—Report On, Commander Seventh Amphibious Force, 23 October 1942," RG 407, GHQ1–3.2, G-3 Journals, box 599 October 1943, NARA.

32. "Operations for the Capture of Madang," Berryman Papers, item 37.

33. "Commander Allied Land forces, Report on New Guinea operations 4 September 1943–26 April 1944," AWM54 519/6/59, part 6, 35, AWM.

34. "GHQ, G-2 Daily Summary of Enemy Intelligence, 18–26 September 1943," RG 407, GHQ1–3.2, G-3 Journals, box 599 September 1943, NARA.

35. "GHQ, G-2 Daily Summary of Enemy Intelligence, No. 549, GHQ SWPA, 22–23 September 1943," RG 407, 98-GHQ1–3.2, G-3 Journals, box 599, NARA.

36. Miller, *Cartwheel*, 272–273.

37. "Herring, interview with Hetherington, 22 June 1970," 3DRL 6224, AWM.

38. Berryman Diary, 24 September 1943.

39. Ibid., 25 September 1943.

40. "War Diary, 20th Brigade, 26 September 1943," AWM52 8/2/20/65, AWM. The brigade describes the captured orders as the first piece of reliable information on the Japanese in the area.

41. Berryman Diary, 26 September 1943.

42. Garth Pratten, "Applying the Principles of War: Securing the Huon Peninsula," in Dean, *Australia 1943*, 266.

43. Ibid., 266–267.

44. "NGF to I Australian Corps, 28 September 1943," replies in quote of GHQ signal, AWM54 591/7/21, AWM.

45. See "Daily Operations Reports, GHQ G-3 Journals and Files, September 1943," RG 407, 98-GHQ1–3.2, G-3 Journal, box 599, NARA.

46. "Conference at Adv 5th AF, notes, 25 September 1943," AWM54 589/3/7, AWM.

47. Horner, *Blamey*, 424.

48. Berryman Diary, 28–29 September 1943.

49. MacArthur, *Reminiscences*, 180.

50. Miller, *Cartwheel*, 218–221. Miller makes no mention of the reinforcement arguments and states that the 9th Division had two brigades on hand to repulse the initial counterattack and that a third brigade was transported by Barbey on request.

51. Horner, *Blamey*, 424.

52. Berryman Diary, 18–20 September 1943.

53. "Berryman to Blamey, 8 October 1943," Blamey Papers, 2/138.

54. Dean, *Architect of Victory*, 255–257.

55. Miller, *Cartwheel*, 282–289.

56. Ibid., 289–295.

57. "C-in-C, Australian Military Forces, Policy Directive 1943–44, 23 December 1943," Blamey Papers, 2/23 item 11.

58. Berryman Diary, 28 December 1943.

59. Long Diary, 30 October 1943, AWM67 1/3, AWM.

60. "Report of the Saidor Operation, VII Amphibious Force, 3 February 1944," AWM54 597/7/3, AWM.

61. "II Australian Corps Report on Operations, October 1943–March 1944," AWM52 1/4/8/18, 53, AWM.

62. See "Morshead to Blamey, 31 January 1944," and "Morshead to Blamey, 17 February 1944," Blamey Papers, 2/137.

63. Miller, *Cartwheel*, 303.

64. Berryman Diary, 5 January 1944.

65. "Report by Infantry Observer," AWM54 597/7/3, 4, AWM.

66. James, *Years of MacArthur*, vol. 2, 347.

67. John Blaxland, "Intelligence and Special Operations in the Southwest Pacific, 1942–45," in Dean, *Australia 1944–45*, 160–161.

68. Drea, *MacArthur's UTLRA*, 92–93.

69. "Blamey to Morshead, 3 March 1944," Blamey Papers, 2/137.

70. Morison, *Breaking the Bismarcks Barrier*, 448.

71. See Dean, *Australia 1943*, 286–287.

72. Miller, *Cartwheel*, 191.

73. "Berryman to Dexter, 17 September 1956," AWM93 50/2/23/331, AWM.

74. "Chamberlin to Berryman, 13 October 1943," Berryman Papers.

75. Coates, "War in New Guinea," 56 (emphasis in original).

76. Dexter, *New Guinea Offensives*, 283.

77. "Barbey to Berryman, 21 February 1944," AWM54 225/1/6, AWM.

78. "Barbey to Berryman, 18 December 1943," ibid.

79. "Smith to Berryman, 2 December 1943," ibid.

80. "Commander of Allied Land Forces, Report on Operations 4 September 1943–22 April 1944," AWM54 519/6/58, AWM; "Berryman to Morshead, 5 February 1944."

81. Miller, *Cartwheel*, 221.

82. "Commander of Allied Land Forces, Report on Operations 4 September 1943–22 April 1944," AWM54 519/6/58, AWM.

83. Ibid.

84. "1st Australian Corps Report on Operations, New Guinea, Situation following the capture of Sanananda, Operation 'Postern' up to the Capture of Lae," AWM54 589/7/1, AWM.

85. Peter Leahy, "Introduction," in Dennis and Grey, *Foundations of Victory*, xv.

86. Horner, *Blamey*, 425.

87. Peter Stanley, "The Green Hole Reconsidered," in Dennis and Grey, *Foundations of Victory*, 202–211.

88. Edward J. Drea, *New Guinea: The U.S. Campaigns of World War II* (Washington, DC: Office of the Chief of Military History, 1993), 29–30.

89. Drea, *MacArthur's ULTRA*, 88.

CHAPTER 13. AUSTRALIA, MACARTHUR, AND THE DIVERGENCE OF INTERESTS

1. "Chamberlin to Sutherland, 7 October 1943," RG 407, GHQ1-3.2, G-3 Journals and Files, box 601, NARA. In the end, SOPAC's forces would be split between the SWPA and the CPA. However, MacArthur would get the Thirteenth Air Force and the majority of the land forces from SOPAC, representing a major injection of US military assets into his theater. See Frank, *MacArthur*, 70–71.

2. "Chamberlin to Sutherland, 7 October 1943."

3. Dexter, *New Guinea Offensives*, 222.

4. Long, *Final Campaigns*, 594.

5. Dexter, *New Guinea Offensives*, 222.

6. Dean, "Divergence and Convergence," 167–201.

7. Long, *Final Campaigns*, 594.

8. Peter J. Dean and Kevin Holzimmer, "The Southwest Pacific Area: Military Strategy and Operations 1944–45," in Dean, *Australia 1944–45*, 33.

9. "Appreciation of the Situation on 30 December 1943 [Arafura Sea Operations]," Blamey Papers, 2/45.

10. Ibid.

11. "Blamey to GHQ, 18 December 1943," Blamey Papers, 2/45.

12. "Comment on Outline Plan—Auburn, Adv LHQ, 13 February 1944," Blamey Papers, 2/45; "Conference on Auburn, 18 February 1944, GHQ-Adv LHQ," Blamey Papers, 2/45.

13. "Comment on Outline Plan—Auburn."

14. "Memo RE: Auburn, Brigadier Barham to Blamey, 7 March 1944," Blamey Papers, 2/45.

15. "Conversation Major-General Chamberlin- Brigadier White AIF, 25 February 1944, RE Reno Op Plan," Blamey Papers, 2/45.

16. "Blamey to Morshead, 3 March 1944," Blamey Papers, 2/137.

17. Horner, *Blamey*, 445–446.

18. Drea, *New Guinea*, 29–30.

19. See Horner, *Inside the War Cabinet*, chaps. 9 and 14.

20. For details, see Stephens, *Royal Australian Air Force*, 59–73; John Herington, *Air War against Germany and Italy, 1939–1943* (Canberra: AWM, 1954), and *Air Power over Europe, 1944–1945* (Canberra: AWM, 1963).

21. The 2nd Armoured Division was disbanded in February 1943, the 1st Armoured Division in September 1943, and the 3rd Armoured Division in November 1943. The army also disbanded the 3rd Australian Army Tank Brigade in 1943. In early 1944, the Australian Armoured Corps had been reduced to two brigades, but by September only the 4th Armoured Brigade was left. See Palazzo, *Australian Army*, 182–183.

22. Dexter, *New Guinea Offensives*, 222–223.

23. Long, *Final Campaigns*, 31–37. See also Horner, *Defence Supremo*, 122–123, 167–168, 180–182, and 210–211.

24. Frank, *MacArthur*, 71.

25. Long, *Final Campaigns*, 9.

26. Nicholas Evan Sarantakes, "One Last Crusade: The British Pacific Fleet and Its Impact on the Anglo-American Alliance," *English Historical Review* 121, no. 491 (April 2006): 432.

27. Long, *Final Campaigns*, 5. For the best account of this trip from an Australian point of view, see Horner, *Defence Supremo*, chap. 9.

28. Danchev and Todman, *War Diaries 1939–1945*, 544.

29. Ibid., 8 August 1944, 579.

30. Ibid., 26 May 1944, 550.

31. Ibid., 550–551.

32. "The basing of UK forces in Australia," Berryman Papers, item 29.

33. Churchill remained interested in the Sumatra operation through a significant part of 1944, much to the dismay and frustration of the British chiefs of staff. See Danchev and Todman, *War Dairies*, 8 August 1944, 579.

34. Hetherington, *Blamey*, 213.

35. Berryman Diary, 19, 20, and 28 July 1944.

36. Christopher Baxter, "In Pursuit of a Pacific Strategy: British Planning for the Defeat of Japan 1943–45," *Diplomacy and Statecraft* 15, no. 2 (2010): 253–256.
37. "Shedden, note of discussions with MacArthur, 27 June 1944," DFAT Historical Documents online, www.dfat.gov.au/historical/index.html.
38. Horner, *Blamey*, 462–465.
39. Horner, *Defence Supremo*, 193, 206–210.
40. "Hetherington to Rowell, 12 October 1970" and "Dedman, interview with Hetherington, 4 August 1970," 3 DRL 6224, AWM.
41. "F. M. Forde to Hetherington," 3 DRL 6224, AWM.
42. Baxter, "In Pursuit of a Pacific Strategy," 256.
43. "MacArthur to Curtin, 6 September 1943," RG 3, Official Correspondence, GHQ SWPA, DMMA.
44. "The basing of UK forces in Australia," part 1, Berryman Papers, item 29, 3.
45. "Hetherington, 'Blamey' manuscript," 3 DRL 6224, 643, AWM.
46. Horner, *Blamey*, 460.
47. Hetherington, *Blamey*, 214–215.
48. Baxter, "In Pursuit of a Pacific Strategy," 256.
49. "Marshall to MacArthur, 12, 14 September 1944," RG 3, Papers of R. K. Sutherland, DMMA.
50. "Wilton to Berryman, 2 March 1944," BFP.
51. "Operations of the First Australian Army in Mandated Territory of New Guinea, August 1944," Blamey Papers, 2/45.
52. "Conference on Relief of US Forces by Australian Forces in New Guinea, New Britain and Northern Solomons, 29 October 1944," RG 3, Papers of R. K. Sutherland, DMMA.
53. Long, *Final Campaigns*, 23.
54. Horner, *Blamey*, 470.
55. Dean and Holzimmer, "Southwest Pacific Area," 37.
56. "Activities of Fwd Ech LHQ, 27 June 1945," Berryman Papers, item 48.
57. "Berryman to Mackay, 17 September 1945," Berryman Papers, item 13.
58. Blamey to Forde, 26 October 1944, as quoted in Long, *Final Campaigns*, 24.
59. "Matters Discussed with C-in-C by Chief of Staff and Directions Given, October 1944," Blamey Papers, 2/44.
60. See "GHQ SWPA Officers Roster, Part II: Allied Officers," RG 3, DMMA.
61. "Appreciation of the Situation by GSO I (Ops) Plans, 28 August 1944," Blamey Papers, 2/45.
62. Dean, *Architect of Victory*, 283.
63. Horner, *Blamey*, 481.
64. "Note of Discussion between Curtin, MacArthur and Wilson, Canberra, 30 September 1944," DFAT Historical Document no. 303.
65. See "Berryman to Blamey, 15, 16, 17 September 1944," Blamey Papers, 2/139, and Berryman Diary, 17–23 September 1944.
66. See Berryman Diary, September–December 1944.

67. Berryman Diary, 7 October 1944.
68. Barham as quoted in Horner, *Blamey*, 469.
69. Long, *Final Campaigns*, 29.
70. "Berryman to Major-General F. Derham, 8 April 1945," Berryman Papers, item 12a.
71. Berryman Diary, 11 February 1945.
72. Berryman Diary, 28 January and 3 February 1945.
73. "Blamey to Shedden, 19 February 1945," DFAT Historical Documents on-line, www.dfat.gov.au/historical/index.html.
74. Berryman Diary, 12–14 March 1945.
75. "Australian Squadron (ANZAC Squadron, TF 44 & 74)—Composition and Operational History," B6121, 152G, NAA.
76. See Gill, *Royal Australian Navy*, chaps. 14, 17, and 21.
77. Ian Pfennigwerth, "The RAN at War, 1944–45," in Dean, *Australia 1944–45*, 184.
78. Goldrick, "1941–1945: War against Japan," 145.
79. "Minesweeping Operations by Australian Minesweepers—Enemy and Allied Minefields," B6121, 283F, NAA.
80. "South West Pacific Sea Frontiers—Establishment, Organisation & Administration 1943–49," B6121, 296B, NAA.
81. See "Note on War Cabinet Agendum 399/1944, Appointment of a Chief of Air Staff," Organization of the RAAF—File No. 1 to 30 September 1944, A816, 31/301/196A, NAA.
82. Mark Johnston, "'On the Scrap Heap of the Yanks': The RAAF in the Southwest Pacific Area, 1944–45," in Dean, *Australia 1944–45*, 192–193.
83. "RAAF Organisation, 31 May 1944," Organization of the RAAF—File No. 1 to 30 September 1944, A816, 31/301/196A, NAA.
84. "RAAF Command Headquarters—Formation of Fifth Air Force—Policy," A11093, 320/5C4, NAA.
85. Ibid., 197.
86. Ibid., 204–205.
87. Horner, *Blamey*, 518–519.
88. Dean, *Architect of Victory*, 295.
89. "Berryman to Blamey, 10 February 1945," Blamey Papers, 2/139.
90. Horner, *Inside the War Cabinet*, 183.
91. Dean, *Architect of Victory*, 290–294. For the Oboe operations, the First Australian Tactical Air Force was moved from the Thirteenth Air Force to RAAF Command, which now controlled all operations south of the Philippines. See Odgers, *Air War against Japan*, 435.
92. At Balikpapan, the 7th Division had the 727th Amphibious Tractor Battalion (less one company), one company of the 672nd Tractor Battalion, and one boat and shore battalion from the 2nd ESB. Direct USN support consisted of twenty-one units or detachments. See Long, *Final Campaigns*, appendix 6, 625–632.
93. Coulthard-Clarke, *Encyclopaedia of Australia's Battles*, 253–254.

94. "Staff Study, Operation Oboe Two, GHQ, 21 March 1945," RG 3, Records of Headquarters, Southwest Pacific Area (SWPA), 1942–1945, box 158, G-3 Operations, Oboe II, DMMA.

95. "War Diary, 7th Australian Division, June 1945, Operation Orders, Oboe Two," AWM52 1/5/14/74, AWM (emphasis added).

96. Tony Hastings and Peter Stanley, "To Capture Tarakan: Was Operation Oboe 1 Unnecessary?" in Dean, *Australia 1944–45*, 293–294.

97. Hetherington, *Blamey*, 365.

98. Long, *Final Campaigns*, 511.

99. Ibid., 531.

100. "Berryman to Kingsley Norris, 19 July 1945," Berryman Papers, item 12a.

101. Peter Charlton, *The Unnecessary War: Island Campaigns of the South-West Pacific 1944–45* (Melbourne: Macmillan, 1983).

102. "Appreciation on Operations of the AMF in New Guinea, New Britain and the Solomon Islands, 18 May 1945," Blamey Paper, 2/17.

103. "Berryman to Lumsden, 24 December 1944," Berryman Papers, item 12.

104. Horner, *Inside the War Cabinet*, 160.

105. Horner, *Blamey*, 535.

106. Long, *Final Campaigns*, 69.

107. See Horner, *Blamey*; Horner, *Defence Supremo*; Horner, *High Command*; Dean, *Architect of Victory*; Karl James, *The Hard Slog: Australians in the Bougainville Campaign, 1944–45* (Melbourne: Cambridge University Press, 2012); and Dean, *Australia 1944–45*.

108. Long, *Final Campaigns*, 547.

109. Dean, *Architect of Victory*, 298–299.

110. "Daily Journal, Forland, May–June 1945," AWM52 1/2/3/16, AWM.

111. Max Hastings, *Nemesis: The Battle for Japan, 1944–45* (London: Harper-Collins, 2007).

112. Ibid., 364.

CONCLUSION

1. Edwards, "Curtin, MacArthur," 175–186; David Horner, "Australia 1942: A Pivotal Year" in Dean, *Australia 1942*, 27.

2. Murray and Millett, *War to Be Won*, 188, 199.

3. MacArthur, quoted in "Memorandum for General George C. Marshall on SWPA by Lieutenant General Brehon Sumervell, 3 October 1943," RG 44, Papers of Bonner F. Fellers, box 1, DMMA.

4. "Chamberlin to Colonel B. Q. Jones, Commandant, Joint Operational Training School, 17 September 1942," RG 30, Sutherland Papers, box 25, folder 8, DMMA.

5. Long, *Final Campaigns*, 597–598.

6. "Defence Committee, Minute No. 335/1944, 18 October 1944," A5799, 206, NAA.

7. "An Appreciation of the Strategical Position of Australia, February 1946,"

in Stephan Frühling, ed., *A History of Australian Strategic Policy since 1945* (Canberra: Australian Department of Defence, 2009), 58.

8. See W. David McIntyre, *Background to the Anzus Pact: Policy-Making, Strategy and Diplomacy, 1945–55* (Christchurch, NZ: Canterbury University Press; New York: St. Martin's, 1995).

SELECTED BIBLIOGRAPHY

PRIMARY SOURCES

Australians at War Film Archive

No. 1124: Coombes, Raymond
No. 1419: Daley, Beryl
No. 1672: Le Page, Arthur
No. 1727: Penglase, Ronald
No. 1868: Bennetts, Leonard
No. 2148: Wearne, Bryan

Australian War Memorial (AWM)

AWM52: 2nd AIF and CMF unit war diaries, 1939–1945 War
AWM54: Written records, 1939–1945 War
AWM55: ATIS (Allied Translator and Interpreter Section) publications
AWM64: RAAF formation and unit records
AWM67: Official History, 1939–1945 War: Records of Gavin Long, General Editor
AWM69: Official History, 1939–1945 War, series 2 (Navy): Records of G. Hermon Gill
AWM76: Official History, 1939–1945 War, biographical files
AWM78: Reports of Proceedings, HMA Ships and Establishments
AWM93: Australian War Memorial registry files, first series
AWM172: Official History, 1939–1945 War, series 1 (Army), volume VI: Records of David Dexter

Australian War Memorial, Private Records

PR00631: HMAS Assault Association
PR84/370: Papers of Lt. Gen. Sir Frank Horton Berryman
PR86/062: Papers of Brig. Maurice "Bunny" Austin DSO, OBE
3DRL 2529: Papers of Lt. Gen. Sir Stanley Savige
3DRL 2632: Papers of Lt. Gen. L Morshead
3DRL 4143: Papers of Maj. Gen. C. A. Clowes
3DRL 6224: Papers of John Hetherington
3DRL 6643: Papers of Field Marshal Sir Thomas Albert Blamey

Berryman Family Papers (BFP)
Correspondence, various, 1918–1954

Douglas MacArthur Memorial Archives, Norfolk, VA (DMMA)
RG 3: Records of Headquarters, Southwest Pacific Area (SWPA), 1942–1945
RG 4: Records of Headquarters, US Army Forces Pacific (USAFPAC), 1942–1947
RG 10: Gen. Douglas MacArthur's Private Correspondence, 1848–1964
RG 23: Papers of Maj. Gen. Charles A. Willoughby, US Army, 1947–1973
RG 23a: Facsimiles of Papers of Maj. Gen. Charles A. Willoughby, US Army, from the National Archives, 1942–1945
RG 29c: Papers of Maj. Gen. Richard J. Marshall, US Army Deputy Chief of Staff, SWPA
RG 30: Papers of Lt. Gen. Richard K. Sutherland, US Army Chief of Staff, SWPA, 1941–1945
RG 41: Selected Papers of Lt. Gen. Robert L. Eichelberger, US Army Commanding General, Eighth Army, SWPA/USAFPAC/FECOM
RG 49: D. Clayton James Collection
RG 54: Diaries of Gen. George C. Kenney

National Archives of Australia, Canberra (NAA)
A816: Correspondence files, multiple-number series (classified 301)
A981: Correspondence files, alphabetical series
A2670: Reference set of War Cabinet agenda with minutes, annual single-number series
A2676: War Cabinet minutes without agenda files
A2684: Advisory War Council minutes files
A2937: Correspondence files, alphabetical series
A5954: Shedden Collection, two-number series
A11093: Correspondence files, multiple-number system with activity suffixes
B6121: Naval historical files, single-number series with alphabetical suffixes
MP508/1: General correspondence files, multiple-number series
MP729/6: Secret correspondence files, multiple-number series with "401" infix
MP1049/5: Correspondence files (general)

National Archives of the United States, Washington, DC (NARA)
RG 18: Records of the Army Air Forces (AAF)
RG 200: Papers of General Sutherland, GHQ, SWPA
RG 319: Records of the Army Staff
RG 338: Records of US Army Operational, Tactical, and Support Organizations (World War II and thereafter)
RG 407: Records of the Adjutant General's Office, 1917
RG 496: Records of General Headquarters, SWPA and US Army Forces, Pacific (World War II)

National Library of Australia, Canberra (NLA)
MS3782: Papers of the Vasey Family

State Library of Victoria, Melbourne (SLV)
Papers of Sir Edmund (Ned) Francis Herring

United States Army Heritage and Education Center, Carlisle, PA (USAHEC)
Leslie Anders Collection
Papers of Richard J. Marshall
Papers of Stephen J. Chamberlin

United States Naval History and Heritage Command, Washington, DC (NHHC)
Papers of Vice Adm. Daniel E. Barbey

Wisconsin Veterans Museum (WVM)
Papers of James Kincaid

UNPUBLISHED DIARIES

Diaries of Lt. Gen. Sir John Lavarack

NEWSPAPERS

Argus (Melbourne)
Cootamundra Herald
Mercury (Hobart)
News (Adelaide)

OFFICIAL HISTORIES

Australia: World War II
Dexter, David. *The New Guinea Offensives.* Canberra: Australian War Memorial, 1961.
Gill, G. Hermon. *Royal Australian Navy, 1939–1942.* Series 2, vol. 1, *Australia in the War of 1939–1945.* Canberra: Australian War Memorial, 1952.
———. *Royal Australian Navy, 1942–1945.* Series 2, vol. 2, *Australia in the War of 1939–1945.* Canberra: Australian War Memorial, 1969.
Gillison, Douglas. *Royal Australian Air Force 1939–1942.* Series 3, vol. 1, *Australia in the War of 1939–1945.* Canberra: Australian War Memorial, 1962.
Hasluck, Paul. *The Government and the People, 1939–1941.* Series 4, vol. 1, *Australia in the War of 1939–1945.* Canberra: Australian War Memorial, 1952.
———. *The Government and the People, 1942–1945.* Series 4, vol. 2, *Australia in the War of 1939–1945.* Canberra: Australian War Memorial, 1970.
Herington, John. *Air Power over Europe, 1944–1945.* Canberra: Australian War Memorial, 1963.

———. *Air War against Germany and Italy, 1939–1943*. Canberra: Australian War Memorial, 1954.

Long, Gavin. *The Final Campaigns*. Vol. 7, *Australia in the War of 1939–1945*. Canberra: Australian War Memorial, 1963.

———. *The Six Years War: A Concise History of Australia in the 1939–45 War*. Canberra: Australian War Memorial, 1973.

———. *To Benghazi*. Series 1, vol. 1, *Australia in the War of 1939–1945*. Canberra: Australian War Memorial, 1952.

McCarthy, Dudley. *South-West Pacific Area: First Year; Kokoda to Wau*. Series 1, vol. 5, *Australia in the War of 1939–1945*. Canberra: Australian War Memorial, 1959.

Odgers, George. *Air War against Japan 1943–1945*. Series 3, vol. 2, *Australia in the War of 1939–1945*. Canberra: Australian War Memorial, 1957.

Walker, Allen S. *The Island Campaigns*. Canberra: Australian War Memorial, 1957.

Wigmore, Lionel. *The Japanese Thrust*. Series 1, vol. 4, *Australia in the War of 1939–1945*. Canberra: Australian War Memorial, 1952.

Japan: World War II

Bullard, Steven, trans. *Japanese Army Operations in the South Pacific Area: New Britain and Papua Campaigns, 1942–43*. Canberra: Australian War Memorial, 2007.

United States: World War II

Anderson, Charles R. *Papua*. Vol. 72, no. 7, *US Army Campaigns of World War II*. Washington, DC: US Army Center of Military History, 1992.

Craven, Wesley, and James Cate, eds. *The Army Air Forces in World War II*. Vol. 1. Washington, DC: Office of Air Force History, 1948.

Greenfield, Kent Roberts, Palmer, Robert R., and Wiley, Bell I. *The Organization of the Army Ground Forces*. Washington, DC: US Army Center of Military History, 1987.

Hough, Frank O., Verle E. Ludwig, and Henry I. Shaw. *Pearl Harbor to Guadalcanal: History of U.S. Marine Corps Operations in World War II*. Vol. 1. Washington, DC: Government Printing Office, 1989.

MacArthur, Douglas. *Reports of General MacArthur: The Campaigns of MacArthur in the Pacific*. Vol. 1. Center of Military History. Washington, DC: Government Printing Office, 1994 (reprint).

Matloff, Maurice, and Edwin Snell. *Strategic Planning for Coalition Warfare 1941–1942*. Washington, DC: Office of the Chief of Military History, US Army, 1959.

Miller, John. *Cartwheel: The Reduction of Rabaul*. Washington, DC: Office of the Chief of Military History, US Army, 1959.

Milner, Samuel. *Victory in Papua*. Washington, DC: Office of the Chief of Military History, US Army, 1957.

Morison, Samuel E. *Breaking the Bismarcks Barrier: 22 July 1942–1 May 1944*.

Vol. 6. History of United States Naval Operations in World War II. Boston: Little, Brown, 1950.

———. *The Rising Sun in the Pacific, 1931–April 1942*. Vol. 3. History of United States Naval Operations in World War II. Annapolis, MD: Naval Institute Press, 2010.

Morton, Louis. *Strategy and Command: The First Two Years*. United States Army in World War II. Washington, DC: Office of the Chief of Military History, US Army, 1962.

Palmer, Robert R. *The Procurement and Training of Ground Combat Troops*. Washington, DC: Center for Military History, 1948.

Smith, Robert Ross. *The Approach to the Philippines*. Washington, DC: Office of the Chief of Military History, 1953.

BOOKS AND OTHER PUBLISHED WORKS

Allchin, Frank. *Purple and Blue: The History of the 2/10th Battalion, A.I.F.* Adelaide: Griffin Press, 1958.

Altobello, Brian. *Into the Shadows Furious: The Brutal Battle for New Georgia*. Novato, CA: Presidio, 2000.

Anders, Leslie. *Gentle Knight: The Life and Times of Major General Edwin Forrest Harding*. Kent, OH: Kent State University Press, 1985.

Andrews, Eric. *The Department of Defence*. Melbourne: Oxford University Press, 2001.

Barbey, Daniel. *MacArthur's Amphibious Navy: Seventh Amphibious Force Operations, 1943–1945*. Annapolis, MD: United States Naval Institute, 1969.

Bean, C. E.W. *The A.I.F. in France 1918*. Official History of Australia in the War of 1914–1918. Vol. 6. Sydney: Angus & Robertson, 1942.

Bell, Coral. *Dependent Ally: A Study in Australian Foreign Policy*. Canberra: Allen & Unwin, 1988.

Bell, Philip, and Roger Bell. *Implicated: The United States in Australia*. Melbourne: Oxford University Press, 1993.

Bell, Roger. *Unequal Allies: Australian-American Relations and the Pacific War*. Victoria: Melbourne University Press, 1977.

Bergerud, Eric. *Touched with Fire: The Land War in the South Pacific*. New York: Viking, 1996.

Bou, Jean. *Light Horse: A History of Australia's Mounted Arm*. Melbourne: Cambridge University Press, 2010.

Bradley, Phillip. *To Salamaua*. Melbourne: Cambridge University Press, 2010.

———. *Wau 1942–1943*. Canberra: Army History Unit, 2010.

Braga, Stuart. *Kokoda Commander: A Life of Major-General "Tubby" Allen*. South Melbourne: Oxford University Press, 2004.

Brune, Peter. *A Bastard of a Place: The Australians in Papua*. Crows Nest, NSW: Allen & Unwin, 2003.

Calwell, Arthur. *Be Just and Fear Not*. Victoria: Lloyd O'Neill in association with Rigby, 1972.

Campbell, James. *The Ghost Mountain Boys: Their Epic March and the Terrifying Battle for New Guinea; The Forgotten War in the South Pacific.* New York: Crown, 2007.

Churchward, Lloyd G. *Australia and America, 1788–1972: An Alternative History.* Sydney: Alternative Publishing Cooperative, 1979.

Chwialkowski, Paul. *In Caesar's Shadow: The Life of General Robert Eichelberger.* Westport, CT: Greenwood Press.

Clark, Chris. *The Encyclopaedia of Australia's Battles.* Sydney: Allen & Unwin, 2010.

Clifford, Kenneth J. *Amphibious Warfare Development in Britain and America from 1920–1940.* New York: Edgewood, 1983.

Coates, John. *An Atlas of Australia's Wars.* Oxford: Oxford University Press, 2001.

———. *Bravery above Blunder: The 9th Australian Division at Finschhafen, Sattelberg and Sio.* Melbourne: Oxford University Press, 1999.

Cole, Henry G. *The Road to Rainbow: Army Planning for Global War, 1934–1940.* Annapolis, MD: Naval Institute Press, 2003.

Cooper, Anthony. *Kokoda Air Strikes: Allied Air Forces in New Guinea, 1942.* Sydney: NewSouth, 2014.

Coulthard-Clark, Chris. *Action Stations Coral Sea: The Australian Commander's Story.* St. Leonards, NSW: Allen & Unwin, 1991.

———. *The Encyclopaedia of Australia's Battles.* St. Leonards, NSW: Allen & Unwin, 2001.

Cox, Douglas A. *Airpower Leadership on the Frontline: Lt. Gen. Georgie H. Brett and Combat Command.* Maxwell Air Force Base, AL: Air University Press, 2006.

Cranston, Frederick. *Always Faithful: A History of the 49th Australian Infantry Battalion 1916–1982.* Brisbane: Boolarong Publications, 1983.

Curran, James. *Curtin's Empire: Australian Encounters.* Melbourne: Cambridge University Press, 2011.

Danchev, Alex, and Daniel Todman, eds. *War Diaries 1939–1945: Field Marshall Lord Alanbrooke.* Berkeley: University of California Press, 2001.

Day, David. *John Curtin: A Life.* Sydney: HarperCollins, 1999.

———. *The Politics of War.* Sydney: HarperCollins, 2003.

Dean, Peter J. *The Architect of Victory: The Military Career of Lieutenant General Sir Frank Horton Berryman.* Victoria: Cambridge University Press, 2011.

———, ed. *Australia 1942: In the Shadow of War.* Melbourne: Cambridge University Press, 2013.

———, ed. *Australia 1943: The Liberation of New Guinea.* Melbourne: Cambridge University Press, 2014.

———, ed. *Australia 1944–45: Victory in the Pacific.* Melbourne: Cambridge University Press, 2016.

Dennis, Peter, and Jeffrey Grey, ed. *The Foundations of Victory: The Pacific War 1943–1944.* Canberra: Army History Unit, Department of Defence, 2004.

Dennis, Peter, Jeffrey Grey, Ewan Morris, and Robin Prior, with Jean Bou. *The*

Oxford Companion to Australian Military History. 2nd ed. Melbourne: Oxford University Press, 2008.

Drea, Edward J. *MacArthur's UTLRA: Codebreaking and the War against Japan, 1942–1945*. Lawrence: University Press of Kansas, 1992.

———. *New Guinea: The U.S. Campaigns of World War II*. Washington, DC: Office of the Chief of Military History, 1993.

Edgar, Bill. *Warrior of Kokoda: A Biography of Brigadier Arnold Potts*. St. Leonards, NSW: Allen & Unwin, 1999.

Eichelberger, Robert. *Our Jungle Road to Tokyo*. New York: Viking, 1950.

English, John A. *The Canadian Army and the Normandy Campaign: A Study of Failure in High Command*. Westport, CT: Praeger, 1991.

Farrell, Brian, and Sandy Hunter, eds. *Sixty Years On: The Fall of Singapore Revisited*. Singapore: Eastern Universities Press, 2002.

FitzSimons, Peter. *Kokoda*. Sydney: Hodder, 2004.

Frame, Tom. *Pacific Partners: A History of Australian-American Naval Relations*. Sydney: Hodder & Stoughton, 1992.

Frank, Richard B. *Guadalcanal: The Definitive Account of the Landmark Battle*. London: Penguin, 1992.

———. *MacArthur: A Biography*. Great Generals Series. New York: Palgrave Macmillan, 2007.

Frei, Henry P. *Japan's Southward Advance and Australia: From the Sixteenth Century to World War II*. Honolulu: University of Hawaii Press, 1991.

French, David. *Raising Churchill's Army: The British Army and the War against Germany 1919–1945*. Oxford: Oxford University Press, 2000.

Galloway, Jack. *The Odd Couple: Blamey and MacArthur at War*. Brisbane: University of Queensland Press, 2000.

Gamble, Bruce. *Fortress Rabaul: The Battle for the Southwest Pacific, January 1942–April 1943*. Minneapolis: Zenith Press, 2010.

Givney. E. C. *The First at War: The Story of the 2/1st Australian Infantry Battalion, 1939–45, the City of Sydney Regiment*. Earlwood, NSW: Association of First Infantry Battalions, 1987.

Goldsworthy, David, ed. *Facing North: A Century of Australian Engagement with Asia*. Carlton: Melbourne University Press, 2003.

Grey, Jeffrey. *The Australian Army: A History*. Melbourne: Oxford University Press, 2006.

———. *Australian Brass: The Career of Lieutenant General Sir Horace Robertson*. Cambridge: Cambridge University Press, 1992.

———. *A Military History of Australia*. Melbourne: Cambridge University Press, 2008.

Griffith, Thomas E., Jr. *MacArthur's Airman: General George C. Kenney and the War in the Southwest Pacific*. Lawrence: University Press of Kansas, 1998.

Ham, Paul. *Kokoda*. Sydney: ABC Books, 2004.

Hamill, Ian. *The Strategic Illusion: The Singapore Strategy and the Defence of Australia and New Zealand, 1919–1942*. Singapore: NUS Press, 1981.

Harper, Norman. *A Great and Powerful Friend: A Study of Australian American*

Relations between 1900 and 1975. St. Lucia: University of Queensland Press, 1987.

Hastings, Max. *Nemesis: The Battle for Japan, 1944–45*. London: HarperCollins, 2007.

Hay, David. *Nothing over Us: The Story of the 2/6th Australian Infantry Battalion*. Canberra: Australian War Memorial, 1984.

Heavey, William F. *Down Ramp! The Story of the Army Amphibian Engineers*. Washington, DC: Infantry Journal Press, 1947.

Hetherington, John. *Blamey: Controversial Soldier; A Biography of Field Marshal Sir Thomas Blamey*. Canberra: Australian War Memorial, 1973.

Hewitt, Joseph E. *Adversity in Success: Extracts from Air Vice-Marshal Hewitt's Diaries 1939–1948*. Victoria: Langate Publishing, 1980.

Horner, David. *Blamey: The Commander-in-Chief*. Sydney: Allen & Unwin, 1998.

———. *Crisis of Command: Australian Generalship and the Japanese Threat, 1941–43*. Canberra: ANU Press, 1978.

———. *Defence Supremo: Sir Frederick Shedden and the Making of Australian Defence Policy*. St. Leonards, NSW: Allen & Unwin, 2000.

———. *The Evolution of Australian Higher Command Arrangements*. Canberra: Australian Defence College, 2002.

———. *General Vasey's War*. Melbourne: Melbourne University Press, 1991.

———. *High Command: Australia's Struggle for an Independent War Strategy, 1939–1945*. St Leonards, NSW: Allen & Unwin, 1982.

———. *Inside the War Cabinet: Directing Australia's War Effort, 1939–1945*. Crows Nest, NSW: Allen & Unwin, 1996.

———. *Strategic Command: General Sir John Wilton and Australia's Asian Wars*. Melbourne: Oxford University Press, 2005.

James, D. Clayton. *The Years of MacArthur: 1941–1945*, vol. 2, *The Years of MacArthur*. Boston: Houghton Mifflin, 1975.

———. *The Years of MacArthur: Triumph and Disaster 1945–1964*, vol. 3, *The Years of MacArthur*. Boston: Houghton Mifflin, 1985.

James, Karl. *The Hard Slog: Australians in the Bougainville Campaign, 1944–45*. Melbourne: Cambridge University Press, 2012.

Janowitz, Morris. *The Professional Soldier: A Social and Political Portrait*. Glencoe, IL: Free Press, 1960.

Jenkins, David. *Battle Surface! Japan's Submarine War Against Australia 1942–44*. Sydney: Random House, 1992.

Johnston, Mark. *That Magnificent 9th: An Illustrated History of the 9th Australian Division*. St Leonards, NSW: Allen & Unwin, 2002.

———. *Whispering Death: Australian Airmen in the Pacific War*. St Leonards, NSW: Allen & Unwin, 2011.

Jones, Archer. *Elements of Military Strategy: An Historical Approach*. Westport, CT: Praeger, 1996.

Jones, George. *From Private to Air Marshal: The Autobiography of Air Marshal Sir George Jones KBE, CB, DFC*. Victoria: Greenhouse Publications, 1988.

Keating, Gavin. *The Right Man for the Right Job: Lieutenant General Sir Stanley Savige as a Military Commander*. Melbourne: Oxford University Press, 2005.

Kenney, George C. *General Kenney Reports: A Personal History of the Pacific War*. New York: Duell, Sloan & Pearce, 1949.

Keogh, Eustace G. *South-West Pacific 1941–1945*. Melbourne: Grayflower Productions, 1965.

Krueger, Walter. *From Down Under to Nippon: The Story of Sixth Army in World War II*. Washington, DC: Combat Forces Press, 1953.

Lacy, Sharon T. *Pacific Blitzkrieg: World War II in the Central Pacific*. Denton: University of North Texas Press, 2013.

Leary, William, ed., *We Shall Return! MacArthur's Commanders and the Defeat of Japan*. Lexington: University Press of Kentucky, 1988.

Linn, Brian M. *The Echo of Battle: The Army's Way of War*. Cambridge, MA: Harvard University Press, 2009.

Lloyd, Clem, and Richard Hall. *Backroom Briefings: John Curtin's War*. Canberra: National Library of Australia, 1997.

Lodge, Brett. *Lavarack: Rival General*. St. Leonards, NSW: Allen & Unwin, 1998.

Lundstrom, John B. *Black Shoe Carrier Admiral: Frank Jack Fletcher at Coral Sea, Midway and Guadalcanal*. Annapolis, MD: Naval Institute Press, 2006.

Luvaas, Jay, ed. *Dear Miss Em: General Eichelberger's War in the Pacific, 1942–1945*. Westport, CT: Greenwood Press, 1972.

MacArthur, Douglas. *Reminiscences*. Annapolis, MD: Naval Institute Press, 1964.

Manchester, William. *American Caesar: Douglas MacArthur 1880–1964*. Boston: Little, Brown, 1978.

Marston, Daniel, ed. *The Pacific War Companion: From Pearl Harbor to Hiroshima*. Oxford: Osprey, 2005.

McCarthy, John. *Australia and Imperial Defence 1918–39: A Study in Air and Sea Power*. St. Lucia: University of Queensland Press, 1976.

McCartney, William F. *The Jungleers: A History of the 41st Infantry Division*. Nashville, TN: Battery Press, 1988.

Meaher, Augustine, IV. *The Road to Singapore: The Myth of British Betrayal*. Victoria: Australian Scholarly Publishing, 2010.

Meaney, Neville. *The Search for Security in the Pacific 1901–1914: A History of Australian Defence and Foreign Policy 1901–1923*, vol. 1. Sydney: Sydney University Press, 2009.

———. *The Search for Security in the Pacific 1914–1923: A History of Australian Defence and Foreign Policy 1901–1923*, vol. 2. Sydney: Sydney University Press, 2009.

Miller, Edward S. *War Plan Orange*. Annapolis, MD: Naval Institute Press, 1991.

Morison, Samuel E. *The Two-Ocean War: A Short History of the United States Navy in the Second World War*. New York: Galahad Books, 1963.

Murray, Williamson. *Military Adaption in War: With Fear of Change*. New York: Cambridge University Press, 2011.

Murray, Williamson, and Allan R. Millett. *A War to Be Won: Fighting the Second World War, 1937–1945*. Cambridge, MA: Harvard University Press, 2000.

Palazzo, Albert. *The Australian Army: A History of Its Organisation 1901–2001.* Melbourne: Oxford University Press, 2001.

Parkin, Russell. *A Capability of First Resort: Amphibious Operations and Australian Defence Policy 1901–2001.* Canberra: Land Warfare Studies Centre, 2002.

Parkin, Russell, and David Lee. *The Great White Fleet to Coral Sea.* Canberra: DFAT, 2008.

Perret, Geoffrey. *Old Soldiers Never Die: The Life of Douglas MacArthur.* New York: Random House, 1996.

Perry, Roland. *Pacific 360: Australia's Battle for Survival in World War II.* Sydney: Hachette, 2012.

Pfennigwerth, Ian. *A Man of Intelligence: The Life of Captain Eric Nave, Australian Codebreaker Extraordinary.* Dural, NSW: Rosenberg Publishing, 2006.

———. *The Royal Australian Navy and MacArthur.* Dural, NSW: Rosenberg Publishing, 2009.

Pierce, Terry C. *Warfighting and Disruptive Technologies: Disguising Innovation.* London: Frank Cass, 2004.

Pratten, Garth. *Australian Battalion Commanders in the Second World War.* Cambridge: Cambridge University Press, 2009.

Rogers, Paul P. *The Good Years: MacArthur and Sutherland.* New York: Praeger, 1990.

Rowell, Sydney F. *Full Circle.* Melbourne: Melbourne University Press, 1974.

Schaller, Michael. *Douglas MacArthur: The Far Eastern General.* New York: Oxford University Press, 1989.

Shamir, Eitan. *Transforming Command: The Pursuit of Mission Command in the U.S., British and Israeli Armies.* Stanford, CA: Stanford University Press, 2011.

Souter, Gavin. *Lion and Kangaroo: The Initiation of Australia.* Melbourne: Text Publishing, 2001.

Spector, Ronald. *Eagle against the Rising Sun.* New York: Vintage, 2004.

Spencer, Bill. *In the Footsteps of Ghosts: With the 2/9th Battalion in the African Desert and the Jungles of the Pacific.* St. Leonards, NSW: Allen & Unwin.

Stephens, Alan. *The Royal Australian Air Force: A History.* Melbourne: Oxford University Press, 2006.

Stevens, David. *A Critical Vulnerability: The Impact of the Submarine Threat on Australia's Maritime Defence 1915–1954.* Canberra: Commonwealth of Australia, 2005.

———, ed. *In Search of a Maritime Strategy: The Maritime Element in Australian Defence Planning since 1901.* Canberra: Strategic and Defence Studies Centre, 1997.

———. *The Royal Australian Navy in World War II.* St. Leonards, NSW: Allen & Unwin, 1996.

Taaffe, Stephen R. *MacArthur's Jungle War: The 1944 New Guinea Campaign.* Lawrence: University Press of Kansas, 1998.

———. *Marshall and His Generals: U.S. Army Commanders in World War II.* Lawrence: University Press of Kansas, 2011.

Thompson, Peter. *Pacific Fury: How Australia and Her Allies Defeated the Japanese Scourge*. Sydney: William Heinemann, 2008.

Thompson, Peter, and Robert Macklin. *The Battle of Brisbane: Australia and America at War*. Canberra: BWM Books, 2000.

Thorne, Christopher. *Allies of a Kind: The United States, Britain, and the War against Japan, 1941–1945*. Oxford: Oxford University Press, 1978.

Toll, Ian W. *Pacific Crucible: War at Sea in the Pacific, 1941–1942*. New York: W. W. Norton, 2011.

Trigellis-Smith, Syd. *All the King's Enemies: A History of the 2/5 Australian Infantry Battalion*. Loftus, NSW: Australian Military History Publications, 2010.

van Creveld, Martin. *Fighting Power: German and U.S. Army Performance, 1939–1945*. Westport, CT: Greenwood Press, 1982.

Vlahos, Michael. *The Blue Sword: The Naval War College and the American Mission, 1919–1941*. Newport, RI: Naval War College Press, 1980.

Weston, Brian. *Coming of Age for Australia and Its Air Force*. Canberra: Air Power Development Centre, 2014.

White, Osmar. *Green Armour*. Sydney: Angus & Robertson, 1945.

Wilcox, Craig. *For Hearths and Homes: Citizen Soldiering in Australia*. St. Leonards, NSW: Allen & Unwin, 1998.

Williams, Peter. *The Kokoda Campaign 1942: Myth and Reality*. Melbourne: Cambridge University Press, 2012.

Willoughby, Charles A. *MacArthur, 1941–51*. New York: McGraw-Hill, 1954.

Winton, Harold R. *Corps Commanders of the Bulge: Six American Generals and Victory in the Ardennes*. Lawrence: University Press of Kansas, 2007.

Yoshihara, Lt. Gen. Kane. *Southern Cross: An Account of the Eastern New Guinea Campaign*. Tokyo: US Army Office of Military History, 1955.

ARTICLES AND CHAPTERS

Alexander, Joseph H. "Across the Reef: Amphibious Warfare in the Pacific." In Marston, *Pacific War Companion*, 192–207.

Babcock, Kenneth J. "MacArthur's Small Ships: Improvising Water Transport in the Southwest Pacific." *Army History* 90 (Winter 2014): 26–42.

Barlow, Jason B. "Interservice Rivalry in the Pacific." *Joint Forces Quarterly* (Spring 1994): 76–81.

Bartlett, Merrill L. "Ben Hebard Fuller and the Genesis of the Modern United States Marine Corps, 1891–1934." *Journal of Military History* 69, no. 1 (January 2005): 73–91.

Baxter, Christopher. "In Pursuit of a Pacific Strategy: British Planning for the Defeat of Japan 1943–45." *Diplomacy and Statecraft* 15, no. 2 (2010): 253–277.

Blaxland, John. "Intelligence and Special Operations in the Southwest Pacific, 1942–45." In Dean, *Australia 1944–45*, 145–168.

Bridge, Carl. "Casey and the Americans: Australian War Propaganda in the United States, 1940–42." Working paper no. 30. Australian Studies Centre, University of London, 1988.

Brockschmidt, Kelli. "The New Guinea Campaign: A New Perspective through the Use of Oral Histories." *McNair Scholars Journal* 9, no. 1 (2005): 25–34.

Bullard, Steven. "Japanese Strategy and Intentions towards Australia." In Dean, *Australia 1942*, 124–139.

Coates, John. "Timor." In Dennis, *Oxford Companion to Australian Military History*, 529–530.

———. "The War in New Guinea 1943–1944: Operations and Tactics." In Dennis and Grey, *Foundations of Victory*, 44–75.

Cooper, Alastair. "The Effect of World War II on RAN-RN Relations." In Stephens, *Royal Australian Navy in World War II*, 44–52.

Day, David. "A Great and Impotent Friend: The Singapore Strategy." In *The Great Mistakes of Australian History*, edited by Martin Crotty and David Roberts, 123–138. Sydney: UNSW Press, 2006.

Dean, Peter J. "Amphibious Warfare: Lessons from the Past for the ADF's Future." *Security Challenges* 8, no. 1 (Autumn 2012): 57–76.

———. "Anzacs and Yanks: US and Australian Operations at the Beachhead Battles." In Dean, *Australia 1942*, 217–239.

———. "Divergence and Convergence: Army vs Navy; Allied Conduct of the Pacific War." In *Armies and Maritime Strategy*, edited by Peter Dennis, 167–201. Newport, NSW: Big Sky Publishing, 2014.

———. "From the Air, Sea and Land: The Capture of Lae." In Dean, *Australia 1943*, 210–232.

———. "Grinding Out a Victory: Australian and American Commanders during the Beachhead Battles." In *Kokoda: Beyond the Legend*, edited by Karl James, 164–187. Melbourne: Cambridge University Press, 2017.

———. "MacArthur's War: Strategy, Command and Plans for the 1943 Offensives." In Dean, *Australia 1943*, 45–67.

———. "To the Jungle Shore: Australia and Amphibious Warfare in the SWPA 1942–1945." *Global War Studies* 11, no. 2 (2014): 64–94.

Dean, Peter J., and Rhys Crawley. "Amphibious Warfare: Training and Logistics 1942–1945." In Dean, *Australia 1944–45*, 257–277.

Dean, Peter J., and Kevin Holzimmer. "The Southwest Pacific Area: Military Strategy and Operations 1944–45." In Dean, *Australia 1944–45*, 28–50.

Dedman, John J. "Defence Policy Decisions before Pearl Harbour." *Australian Journal of Politics and History* 13, no. 3 (December 1967): 331–345.

Dennis, Peter. "Australia and the Singapore Strategy." In *A Great Betrayal: The Fall of Singapore Revisited*, edited by Brian Farrell and Sandy Hunter, 20–33. Singapore: Marshall Cavendish Editions, 2010.

Dignan, D. K. "Australia and British Relations with Japan, 1914–1921." *Australian Outlook* 21, no. 2 (August 1967): 135–149.

Drea, Edward J. "Collision Course: American and Japanese Amphibious/Counter-Amphibious Doctrine, Tactics and Preparation for the Decisive Battle of the Homeland." In *1945: War and Peace in the Pacific; Selected Essays*, edited by Peter Dennis, 22–37. Canberra: Australian War Memorial, 1999.

Edwards, Peter. "Curtin, MacArthur and the 'Surrender of Sovereignty.'" *Australian Journal of International Affairs* 55, no. 2 (July 2001): 175–185.

———. *Permanent Friends? Historical Reflections on the Australian-American Alliance.* Lowy Institute Paper 08. Sydney: Lowy Institute for International Policy, 2005.

French, David. "Doctrine and Organisation in the British Army, 1919–1932." *Historical Journal* 44, no. 2 (June 2001): 497–515.

Goldrick, James. "1941–1945: World War II; The War against Japan." In *The Royal Australian Navy,* edited by David Stevens, 127–154. Melbourne: Oxford University Press, 2001.

Gooch, John. "The Politics of Strategy: Great Britain, Australia and the War against Japan 1939–1945." *War in History* 10, no. 4 (October 2003): 424–447.

Grant, Lachlan. "Operations in the Markham and Ramu Valleys." In Dean, *Australia 1943,* 233–254.

Hastings, Tony, and Peter Stanley. "To Capture Tarakan: Was Operation Oboe 1 Unnecessary?" In Dean, *Australia 1944–45,* 278–297.

Holzimmer, Kevin C. "Joint Operations in the Southwest Pacific, 1943–1945." *Joint Force Quarterly* 38 (2005): 100–108.

———. "On the Offensive: US Operations in the Southwest Pacific Area and South Pacific Area in 1943." In Dean, *Australia 1943,* 93–116.

Horner, David. "General MacArthur's War: The South and Southwest Pacific Campaigns 1942–1945." In Marston, *Pacific War Companion,* 123–139.

———. "MacArthur and Curtin: Deciding Australian War Strategy in 1943." In Dean, *Australia 1943,* 25–42.

———. "MacArthur, Douglas (1880–1964)." In *Australian Dictionary of Biography.* Vol. 15. Carlton: Melbourne University Press, 2000. http://adb.anu.edu .au/biography/MacArthur-douglas-10890.

———. "Staff Corps versus Militia: The Australian Experience in World War II." *Defence Force Journal* 26 (January/February 1981).

James, D. Clayton. "American and Japanese Strategies in the Pacific War." In *Makers of Modern Strategy: From Machiavelli to the Nuclear Age,* edited by Peter Paret, 703–734. Princeton, NJ: Princeton University Press, 1986.

James, Karl. "On Australia's Doorstep: Kokoda and Milne Bay." In Dean, *Australia 1942,* 199–216.

Johnston, Mark. "'On the Scrap Heap of the Yanks': The RAAF in the Southwest Pacific Area, 1944–45." In Dean, *Australia 1944–45,* 190–208.

———. "Perspiration, Inspiration, Frustration: The RAAF in New Guinea in 1943." In Dean, *Australia 1943,* 123–141.

———. "Vanquished but Defiant, Victorious but Divided: The RAAF in the Pacific, 1942." In Dean, *Australia 1942,* 161–178.

Leahy, Peter. "Introduction." In Dennis and Grey, *Foundations of Victory,* xiv–xvii.

Mallett, Ross A. "Logistics and the Cartwheel Operations." In Dean, *Australia 1943,* 167–185.

———. "Together Again for the First Time: The Army, the RAN and Amphibious Warfare." In *Sea Power Ashore and in the Air,* edited by David Stephens and John Reeve, 118–132. Ultimo, NSW: Halstead Press, 2007.

McCarthy, John. "Singapore and Australian Defence 1921–1942." *Australian Outlook* 25, no. 2 (1971): 165–180.

Morton, Louis. "War Plan Orange: Evolution of a Strategy." *World Politics* 11, no. 2 (January 1959): 221–250.

Murfett, Malcolm. "The Singapore Strategy." In *Between Empire and Nation: Australia's External Relations from Federation to the Second World War*, edited by Carl Bridge and Bernard Attard, 188–204. Victoria: Australian Scholarly Publishing, 2000.

Palazzo, Albert. "Organising for Jungle Warfare." In Dennis and Grey, *Foundations of Victory*, 86–101.

———. "The Overlooked Mission: Australia and Home Defence." In Dean, *Australia 1942*, 53–69.

Pfennigwerth, Ian. "A Novel Experience: The RAN in 1942, Defending Australian Waters." In Dean, *Australia 1942*, 179–198.

———. "The RAN at War, 1944–45." In Dean, *Australia 1944–45*, 171–189.

Powell, Alan. "The Air Raids on Darwin, 19 February 1942: Image and Reality." In Dean, *Australia 1942*, 140–156.

Pratten, Garth. "Applying the Principles of War: Securing the Huon Peninsula." In Dean, *Australia 1943*, 255–284.

"Robert Eichelberger to Emma Eichelberger, 4 December 1942." In Luvaas, *Dear Miss Em*, 39.

Rose, Patrick. "Allies at War: British and US Army Command Culture in the Italian Campaign, 1943–1944." *Journal of Strategic Studies* 36, no. 1 (2013): 42–75.

Sarantakes, Nicholas Evan. "One Last Crusade: The British Pacific Fleet and Its Impact on the Anglo-American Alliance." *English Historical Review* 121, no. 491 (April 2006): 429–466.

Saxon, Timothy D. "Anglo-Japanese Naval Cooperation, 1914–1918." *Naval War College Review* 53, no. 1 (2000): 62–92.

Serle, Geoffrey. "Curtin, John (1885–1945)." In *Australian Dictionary of Biography*. Vol. 13. Carlton: Melbourne University Press, 1993.

Shamir, Eitan. "The Long and Winding Road: The US Army Managerial Approach to Command and the Adoption of Mission Command (*Aufragstaktik*)." *Journal of Strategic Studies* 33, no. 5 (2010): 645–672.

Shindo, Hiroyuki. "The Japanese Army's Search for a New South Pacific Strategy, 1943." In Dean, *Australia 1943*, 68–88.

———. "The Japanese Army's 'Unplanned' South Pacific Campaign." In Dean, *Australia 1942*, 106–123.

Stanley, Peter. "The Green Hole Reconsidered." In Dennis and Grey, *Foundations of Victory*, 202–211.

Stevens, David. "The Naval Campaigns for New Guinea." *Journal of the Australian War Memorial* 34, no. 1 (2001). https://www.awm.gov.au/journal/j34/stevens.asp.

———. "The Royal Australian Navy and the Strategy for Australia's Defence, 1921–42." In Stevens, *In Search of a Maritime Strategy*, 67–86.

———. "South-West Sea Frontiers: Seapower in the Australian Context." In Stephens, *Royal Australian Navy in World War II*, 87–99.

Watson, Richard L. "The Defense of Australia." In *The Army Air Forces in World War II: Plans and Early Operations January 1939 to August 1942*, edited by Wesley Craven and James Cate, 403–426. Chicago: University of Chicago Press, 1948.

Winkler, David F. "Thrusters, Cautionaries, and War Game." *Seapower* 45, no. 10 (October 2002): 31.

Winton, Harold R. "Toward an American Philosophy of Command." *Journal of Military History* 64, no. 4 (October 2000): 1035–1060.

THESES, DISSERTATIONS, AND OTHER WORKS

Frühling, Stephan. "Managing Strategic Risk: Four Ideal Defence Planning Concepts in Theory and Practice." PhD diss., Australian National University, 2007.

Goldstein, Donald. "Ennis C. Whitehead: Aerospace Commander and Pioneer." PhD diss., University of Denver, Colorado, 1971.

Mallett, Ross A. "Australian Army Logistics 1943–45." PhD thesis, University of New South Wales (ADFA), 2007.

Moreman, John. "A Triumph of Improvisation: Australian Army Operational Logistics and the Campaign in Papua, July 1942 to January 1943." PhD thesis, University of New South Wales, Sydney, 2000.

Pettinger, Matthew R. "Held to a Higher Standard: The Downfall of Admiral Kimmel." Master's thesis, US Army Command and General Staff College, Fort Leavenworth, KS, 2003.

Shepard, Steven B. "American, British, Dutch and Australian Coalition: Unsuccessful Band of Brothers." Master's thesis, US Army Command and General Staff College, Fort Leavenworth, KS, 2003.

Winton, Harold R. "Corps Commanders of the Bulge: Six American Generals and Victory in the Ardennes." Presentation to the US Army War College, 17 March 2010. http://www.youtube.com/watch?v=zd6LrT7Zrjo.

MILITARY REFERENCE PUBLICATIONS

British Army General Staff. *Field Service Regulations, Volume III: Operations; Higher Formations, 1935*. London: His Majesty's Stationery Office, 1936.

Ellis, Earl H. *Advanced Base Operations in Micronesia*. Fleet Marine Force Reference Publication (FMFRP) 12–46. Washington, DC, Headquarters United States Marine Corps, 1992. http://www.ibiblio.org/hyperwar/USMC/ref/AdvBaseOps/index.html.

FM 100-5: Field Service Regulations; Operations, 1941. Washington, DC: War Department, 1941.

FM 100-5: Field Service Regulations; Operations, 1944. Washington, DC: War Department, 1944.

FM 100-5: Tentative Field Service Regulations; Operations, 1939. Washington, DC: War Department, 1939.

FM 100-15: Field Service Regulations; Larger Units, 1942. Washington, DC: War Department, 1942.

FM 101-5: Staff Officers' Field Manual; The Staff and Combat Orders, August 1940. Washington, DC: War Department, 1940.

INTERNET RESOURCES

Australian Dictionary of Biography. http://adb.anu.edu.au.

Australians at War Film Archive. http://www.australiansatwarfilmarchive.unsw
.edu.au.

Combined (Operations) Training Centre, Toorbul Point: 7th Amphibious Training Centre and 1st Water Transport Training Centre. Queensland Historic
World War II Places, Queensland Government. http://www.ww2places.qld.gov
.au/places/?id=1373.

Command History: 7th Amphibious Force. http://www.ibiblio.org/hyperwar
/USN/Admin-Hist/OA/419-7thAmphib/7thAmphibs-2.html.

Department of Foreign Affairs and Trade historical documents. http://dfat.gov.au
/about-us/publications/historical- documents/Pages/historical-documents.aspx.

41st Infantry Division website. http://jungleer.com/sunset-division.

H. R. Stark, Admiral, US Navy, Chief of Naval Operations. Foreword to USN
FTP 167, *Landing Operations Doctrine*. http://www.ibiblio.org/hyperwar/USN
/ref/Amphibious/index.html.

The 32D Infantry Division in World War II: The "Red Arrow." http://www.32nd
-division.org/history/ww2/32ww2-1.html#Mobilization.

INDEX